INDIVIDUAL DIFFERENCES IN INFANCY:

Reliability, Stability, Prediction

Edited by

JOHN COLOMBO
University of Kansas
JEFFREY FAGEN
St. John's University

LAWRENCE ERLBAUM ASSOCIATES, PUBLISHERS
1990   Hillsdale, New Jersey   Hove and London

Lawrence Erlbaum Associates, Inc., Publishers
365 Broadway
Hillsdale, New Jersey 07642

Library of Congress Cataloging-in-Publication Data

Individual differences in infancy   : reliability, stability, prediction
/ edited by John Colombo, Jeffrey Fagen.
     p. cm.
Based on a symposium organized at the April 1987 Meeting of the
Society for Research in Child Development held in Baltimore, Md.
   Includes bibliographical references.
   Includes index.
   ISBN 0-8058-0369-6
   1. Individual differences in infants.   I. Colombo, John.
II. Fagan, Jeffrey.   III. Society for Research in Child Development.
Meeting (1987 : Baltimore, Md.)
   [DNLM: 1. Child Behavior--congresses. 2. Child Psychology-
-congresses.   3. Individuality--in infancy & childhood. BF 720.I55
I39 1987]
BF720.I55I53   1990
155.42'2822--dc20
DNLM/DLC
for Library of Congress   90-3390
                                                       CIP

Printed in the United States of America
10 9 8 7 6 5 4 3 2 1

Contents

Preface

The study of infancy has always been a topic common to a number of sub-disciplines of medical and behavioral science, but the systematic study of early human development has its historical roots in the early part of the 20th century. As a response to the perceived deficiencies of draftees for the first World War, a motivation to promote an understanding and improvement in human intellectual and emotional development through scientific investigation emerged. This in turn led to the establishment of centers during the 1920s and '30s to study child development throughout the United States at major universities (e.g., Iowa, Minnesota, Yale, and California) and private foundations in Detroit (The Merrill-Palmer Institute), and Yellow Springs, Ohio (The Fels Research Institute). In many cases, these centers established long-term longitudinal studies that began with measurements during infancy and then followed individuals through the life span.

Following the second World War, students who received graduate degrees from these institutions began to conduct research programs in child development and infancy; these programs were furthered by advances in technology developed in the late 1950s and early 1960s for studying infants' attention and learning, social development, and temperament. These new techniques in turn spurred a proliferation of experimental work on human infants that began in the 1960s and has continued virtually unabated since. This research has come to yield a conceptualization of the human infant as a sophisticated, complex, and "competent" individual, and has suggested the importance of infancy in the course of the individual through the lifespan. In the 1980s, many researchers began to apply the general principles gleaned from the experimental and normative research on infancy to the individual infant in an effort to demonstrate and to account for some of the previously unexplained variance typical of experimental work.

As part of this wave of individual difference research, a symposium was organized at the April 1987 meeting of the Society for Research in Child Development that included the two of us. The symposium was entitled "Individual Differences in Infancy: Reliability, Stability, and Prediction," and featured papers by both of us, Susan Rose, and a discussion by Frances Horowitz. The symposium was well attended and discussions of both the data and the issues raised about such research went on long after the allotted time. This enthusiasm made it evident that the topic of the symposium might make a good topic for an edited book. We talked with some senior researchers after the convention who agreed that a compilation of readings on the topic of individual differences in infancy might indeed be timely; at that time, there were no good source volumes of this recent research on early individual differences, and the topic of individual differences had received little attention within particular chapters in recently released editions of Mussen's *Handbook of Child Psychology* (1983) or Osofsky's *Handbook of Infant Development* (1986). It is our hope that this book fills this gap as a companion to these larger works.

This volume includes chapters by researchers and theorists who are active in the field of individual differences, or active in research on a particular domain that has potential for individual difference analyses. We have asked the authors to provide the reader with some sense of the current state of affairs in each domain, with a special emphasis on their own research programs. In several cases, the chapters include new data or reanalyses of previously reported data with an eye toward individual differences.

The book begins with four general overviews. Horowitz provides a chapter on conceptual models for individual differences during infancy, Thelen discusses individual differences from the point of view of dynamical systems theory, Thompson outlines the logic of behavioral genetic designs and how they can be used to delineate genetic contributions to individual differences, and Green covers some of the basic statistical treatments for individual difference data with a special focus on cluster analysis.

Two chapters deal with neurobehavioral development. Thoman and Whitney detail the potential power of neonatal state profiles for individual differences, and Worobey reviews methods for assessing individual differences in neonates.

The third section, on individual differences in infant information processing and output, is the longest one. It features reviews on individual differences in conditioning and memory (Fagen and Ohr) and on visual habituation and attention (Colombo and Mitchell). Rose and Feldman review recent advances from their laboratory on the predictive value of novelty preferences, and Ruff reviews her recent work on the development of sustained attention. Chapters on early audition (Morrongiello) and spatial cognition (Acredolo) that follow offer directions for future research in areas that hold promise for individual difference analysis. This third section also includes two chapters on early communication and language; Fogel reviews research on preverbal communication from the dynamical systems viewpoint, and Thal and Bates provide an overview of individual differences in language development.

The last section of the volume covers aspects of early socioemotional development. Gunnar reviews the psychobiological bases of temperament, and Rothbart and Alansky-Mauro provide detailed analyses of questionnaire assessments of temperament. Finally, Plomin et al. feature recent data from a McArthur Foundation project on socioemotional style during later infancy.

The editors have many people to thank with regard to this volume. Our authors have been extraordinarily prompt in the preparation of their contributions, and we thank them for their cooperation. We received editorial and clerical assistance from several dedicated and cheerful individuals, including Marjorie Hagerty, Michelle Knoll, Laura Maag, and Deborah Silverman. When faced with topical areas in which we had little expertise, we sought advice and external reviews from other scientists. In particular, we wish to thank Jay Atwater, Bernard Gorman, Lorraine McCune, and Mabel Rice for their assistance in this regard. A special note of thanks goes to Frances Degen Horowitz for her helpful advice at the start of this project. Finally, we are grateful for the advice and input from several people associated with Lawrence Erlbaum Associates during the production of this book: Judi Amsel, Carole Lachman, and Sondra Guideman.

It is our hope that this volume will help to focus attention on, and raise enthusiasm for the investigation of the development of individual differences. We further hope that such attention and enthusiasm will not be channelled into the simple development or refinement of standardized evaluative assessments of such differences; that activity more closely characterizes the normative tradition of the study of child development, which we feel has yielded little toward either a true explanation of behavioral development, or individual differences in behavioral development. Rather, we believe that an approach involving rigorous and thoughtful investigation of those processes that yield individual differences during infancy will better serve both the understanding of human individuality and developmental psychology as a whole.

John Colombo
Jeffrey Fagen

INDIVIDUAL DIFFERENCES IN INFANCY: OVERVIEWS

1 Developmental Models of Individual Differences[1]

Frances Degen Horowitz
The University of Kansas

The story of development, as Wohlwill (1973), McCall (1977), and others have noted, is the story of change. Whether the search for the laws that tell that story is made in the context of an organismic or behaviorist model, it is a search dominated by the desire to discover the generic laws that account for the phenomena of development and those that tell us the rules by which change occurs. Developmentalists, by the very definition of their enterprise, focus on what changes and how the changes occur. By contrast, the study of individual differences involves looking for stabilities across time, stabilities that persist in the face of change, characteristics that endure as constants even as the rules governing change may vary over time. Perhaps that is why the traditional study of individual differences has been a largely "adevelopmental" field, even though some attention has been given to interindividual variation and individual differences (e.g., Baltes & Nesselroade, 1973).

In opening this volume, devoted to a discussion of individual differences in infancy, it is useful to describe some of the traditional adevelopmental approaches to individual differences, to discuss the possible distinctions that can be made if individual differences are considered in a developmental context, and then to suggest how one might incorporate individual differences into a comprehensive model of development.

---

[1]Some portions of this chapter were originally presented as an invited address at the First International Conference on Individual Differences: Psychological, Educational and Neurological Implications, in Ramat Gan, Israel, in July 1988.

TRADITIONAL VIEWS OF INDIVIDUAL DIFFERENCES

The topic of individual differences has a long history and several grand traditions. The one that is probably the most familiar to psychologists who have had significant statistical training is to regard individual differences as a source of error. The second most familiar approach to individual differences is in the context of tests and measurements. Another approach involves an interest in individual differences as typologies. The recent emphasis and interest in behavior genetics also proceeds from an individual-difference strategy. Brief discussions of these four "traditional" views of individual differences follow.

Individual Differences as Error

According to Anastasi (1965), the first record of systematic interest on individual differences was reported by astronomers in the late 18th and early 19th centuries. As early as 1796 it was noted that two astronomers, making the same observations, would differ by as much as seven-tenths of a second. When it was clear that this was the result of "individual differences" in reaction time, a method to correct for these "errors" was developed in order to make the observations of different observers comparable. Thus, one of the earliest approaches to individual differences was to try to compensate for them. This was done by developing strategies that eliminate individual differences to better approximate the general laws that govern the phenomena.

A similar strategy has been adopted for much of general experimental psychology where the interest is in establishing general laws of behavior. Whether the experimental methodology involves group or single-subject designs, the assumption is made that individual differences in response to the stimulus conditions are basically error variance (Horowitz, 1969). In the group design approach one deals with error variance by statistical methods; in the single-subject design approach one deals with individual differences as error variance by ignoring subject to subject variation. The general form of the stimulus–response relationship is sought in replications using different subjects.

Individual differences are also ignored, or diminished in importance, in the normative tradition. Normative research involves describing the "average" course of development, be it in terms of an ages and stages description or in terms of the typical sequence of events. Indeed, individual-difference questions have been deemed orthogonal to developmental questions (Wohlwill, 1973).

A waggish characterization of these strategies might be one of "see no individual differences." The "see no individual differences" efforts have been productive. They have yielded considerable information about general laws of behavior and also about general topographies of development. We made good use of the results whether it be in knowing average age when walking begins, the average age when the first word is spoken, or the general laws of reinforcement. Unquestionably, regarding individual differences as error or noise in the system is a strategy that has advanced our knowledge about the laws of behavior.

Individual Differences as Tests and Measures

Individual differences is a topic with its own tradition of investigation in the context of tests and measurements. Anastasi noted that James McKeen Catell was the one who first introduced the term *mental test* to the English psychological literature in his 1890 article entitled ''Mental tests and measurements'' (Anastasi, 1965; Catell, 1890). Although tests designed to measure individual differences evaluate many different kinds of behaviors, the testing world has been heavily dominated by the construction of tests of intelligence and associated behaviors.

The study of individual differences in relation to testing has become highly sophisticated. It has been very dependent for some of its progress on collateral developments in psychometrics. A large body of accepted standards and procedures and of data analysis now exists for application to the study of individual differences. This approach to the study of individual differences can be thought of as a ''product'' approach. The test is used to sort individuals on a particular dimension. The test measure is the product of their performance in the area of intelligence, personality, creativity, etc.

The central theme in the study of individual differences as tests and measurements has been the search for stability. The stability is adevelopmental. It can be defined by test–retest criteria, in terms of test–test relationships, or in terms of test measures to other kinds of measures. The interest here is the degree to which stability is observed over time. However, because of the particular nature of the psychometrics applied, the approach to stability has been more in terms of stability of an individual's performance in relation to the performance of other individuals. This is reflected in the use of correlations to answer the question of how well performance on one test relates to performance on another test or task. The magnitude of the correlation provides an index of the extent of the relationship. As all students of elementary statistics know, this underdescribes the degree to which an individual stayed or changed places in a rank order of the scores on one measure compared to where that same individual was in the rank order of the scores on the second measure.

The industry of investigation into the reliability and validity of tests and measurements has produced considerable knowledge and many useful tools for the study of human behavior. Much of this knowledge is descriptive in nature and not developmentally oriented. Indeed, as in the search for the earliest infant test that would predict later intelligence, the quest has been to identify unchanging rather than changing characteristics—at least in terms of the individuals' relative positions within a group.

Individual Differences as Typology

A subsidiary enterprise in the study of individual differences and one somewhat related to tests and measurements is the study of individual differences as typology. Although there have been typological interests in the area of intelligence (e.g., cognitive styles or verbal as compared with spatial intelligence), the most fully typological efforts have occurred in the areas of personality and psychopathology. Frequently this work is done using standard tests and measurement strategies. But as Tyler (1978) noted, the typological investigations could lie as well outside of the tests and measurements traditions. She cited Kelly's "personal construct" theory as generating a different kind of measuring instrument—a sorting approach as opposed to looking for the rank order of individuals in relation to one another.

The typology approach is typified by Q-sort strategies and checklist observations that ultimately sort individuals into groups. There are tasks that can be used to differentiate individuals as field dependent/field independent, as extroverted or introverted, as reflective or impulsive. Interestingly, these strategies are typically most informative only when the extremes of the dimension are extracted and further studied. Subjects in the top and bottom quartiles of a particular scale (e.g., extroversion/introversion) are selected for study, leaving the equally large middle group unstudied. Traditionally, typological research has not been strongly developmental though there are a few exceptions (e.g., the work of Block & Block, 1980).

Individual Differences and Behavioral Genetics

The source of individual differences is a topic of considerable debate. In 1869 Francis Galton's publication on "hereditary genius" used familial relationships to study the role of heredity with respect to particular traits and abilities in individuals. Galton's claims, and those made subsequently by others, as well as the counterclaims, have continually fueled the nature–nurture controversy even into the present. The basic question: To what degree can individual differences be attributed to hereditary influences and to what degree can they be accounted for by environmental experience.

This debate has waxed and waned. It became clear that hereditary and environmental influences were difficult to separate given the relatively unsophisticated techniques of inquiry available until the late 1950s (Anastasi, 1958; Anastasi & Foley, 1948). With the development of more sophisticated statistical techniques and the use of stronger comparative strategies, the questions have taken on new life in the field labeled behavioral genetics. Particularly popular are studies of twins reared together and apart, and children reared by adoptive and biological parents (Plomin, 1986, 1989; and see Thompson, this volume).

Questions of individual differences in the context of the study of behavioral genetics are really subordinated to the larger issue of parceling out the percentage of influence attributable to the influence of heredity and environment with respect to behavior. The typical estimate of "heritability" in which a certain percentage of the variance is assigned to genetic factors is an estimate for a group of individuals and not for the individuals themselves. Thus, in the strictest sense, behavioral genetics is more the study of group differences than of individual differences, even though the groups are constituted by individuals who differ in comparison to one another on an individual-difference dimension.

The importance of behavioral genetics in a discussion of individual differences has a historical basis. Galton's work and that of others, trumpeting the hereditarian position, was displaced by environmentalists from the 1930s to the early 1960s. Biological and genetic factors were all but dismissed as having any relevance to behavior and behavioral development. As current evidence has accumulated, showing genetic contributions to behavior, a more balanced view has developed. Plomin (1989), recognizing this, had commented: "As the pendulum swings from environmentalism, it is important that the pendulum be caught mid-swing before its momentum carries it to biological determinism." (p. 110).

Genetic influences obviously account for a portion of the variance in human behavior. But so do environmental influences. This is abundantly the case in experimental explorations of the role of environment on the anatomy of the brain in rats (Diamond, 1988). In the instance of most of the human behavioral repertoire it would appear that, even as genetic determinants are demonstrable and significant, they are often accounting for less than half of the variance. In other words, genetic contributions are significant and substantial but the same is true of environmental contributions. As Thompson (this volume) notes, recent behavior genetic studies are increasingly studies of both environmental and genetic influences.

INDIVIDUAL DIFFERENCES AND
DEVELOPMENTAL THEORIES

Even though the direct study of individual differences typically occurs in an adevelopmental context, it is a fact that all models and theories of development take note of individual differences. Gesell (1954) regarded them as hereditary factors that controlled the rate of development. As such, they were unlikely to be impacted by environmental experience. He believed personality and temperament as well as different rates of development in motor, language, and learning behavior were due primarily to hereditary influences. His own data longitudinal studies convinced him that by and large children remained in essentially the same place within a group over a period of time, and that individual developmental trajectories were basically stable individual-difference characteristics.

Most "organismic" theorists make similar assumptions. Gruber and Voneche's (1977) referential compendium on Piaget does not even contain the term *individual differences* in the subject index. Piaget's work is the quintessential example of the developmentalist's interest in the orderly changes that constitute development. Like Gesell, Piaget and his followers consider individual differences in rate of development a reflection of hereditary influences. When asked about whether intervention programs could speed up the rate of intellectual development, Piaget is reported to have said that he regarded such preoccupation with rate of development as an "American" problem.

Behaviorists have focused on development more in the context of the laws that account for changes in the behavioral repertoire while generally ignoring the more traditional developmental phenomena that make up the stuff of most child development textbooks. Interestingly however, Clark Hull, in his elaborate hypothetico—deductive equational strategies, included individual differences ("i") as a parameter in the theoretical formula that was to account for response acquisition (Hull, 1945). Little research on the role and function of this parameter appears to have been done. As noted earlier, the quest for these general laws tends to relegate individual differences to error variance. In the Skinnerian single-subject design strategy, individual differences are essentially ignored in favor of finding a replicated functional relationship across subjects.

The strong emphasis on environmental controls puts most behaviorists in the position of rejecting individual differences as reflecting hereditary influences. Rather, if pressed, behaviorists typically attribute individual differences to the different cumulative histories of individuals. Individual differences thus become more important in accounting for response acquisition because the cumulative history will affect the processes involved. Thus, the study of individual differences becomes one of building experiential histories and seeing how these histories affect subsequent behavior. Development tends to be viewed as the net result of a relatively linear cumulative history, so in this sense individual differences become explanatory of how an organism interfaces with the environment at any given moment in developmental time.

Those who rely on an essentially Freudian model of development are probably among those who take individual differences more seriously as a variable affecting the interplay of the organism and the environment. Like behaviorists, they tend to give great credit to individual histories as critical elements in development. Additionally, research on the period of early development from the psychoanalytic point of view has focused on the influence of initial individual differences as affecting early development. Heider (1960) discussed these differences in terms of "vulnerability." Escalona (1968) has studied how differences affect normal developmental patterns in infancy. Since these early studies there has been a continuing stream of publications and research directed at trying to understand how initial individual differences play out across the dynamics of the developmental processes posited within the Freudian framework. These include the now extensive New York Longitudinal Study begun by Thomas and Chess (Thomas et al., 1963; Thomas & Chess, 1977, 1984), studies of coping (Murphy & Moriarty, 1976), and increasing attention to the issues of risk, vulnerability, and resilience (Anthony & Cohler, 1987).

Consideration of the various "truths" of different developmental theories and a deep interest in trying to factor in individual differences into a theoretical framework that would account for developmental outcome contributed to this author's proposal and refinement of a Structural/Behavioral Model of development (Horowitz, 1969, 1978, 1982, 1984, 1987). This model is based on an acceptance of some of the basic premises of both organismic/systems theories and behavioral theories. Namely, that a full account of behavioral development will have to include assumptions about species-typical developmental sequences, periodic systemic reorganizations, as well as learning as a critical and central mechanism for the acquisition of responses.

One of the aspects of the Structural/Behavioral Model is the parsing of behaviors into Universal and non-Universal categories. The Universal behaviors are those that are acquired by all normal organisms in a variety of environmental contexts. They include the species-typical behaviors in the motor, social, language, and cognitive domains. They are the behaviors that come into the repertoire without many obvious opportunities for formal instruction. In this model, however, the incidental opportunities for learning Universal behaviors matched with organismic capacity are considered critical to their acquisition. For example, language is acquired by all normal children under a wide variety of incidental teaching environments as long as some minimum threshold for receipt of auditory stimulation is present and as long as some minimum level of environmental input occurs. The rough aspects of sequence are quite similar from child to child, suggesting the influence of species-typical variables in genetic characteristics. The normal human organism learns to talk, not whistle, as its major communicative mode; the normal human organism learns to walk and not crawl as its major mode of mobility, etc. Additionally, some modes of communicating (e.g., chirping) or moving (e.g., flying) are not even possible given the nature of the human species.

These Universal behaviors can be thought of as providing the defining template of the basic human behavioral repertoire. Whereas learning plays a role in their acquisition, the basic topography of the behaviors is highly canalized and therefore ultimately highly probable. The different rates of acquisition of these behaviors likely reflect some inherent individual-difference characteristics as well as the differentially facilitative nature of the environmental inputs necessary to their acquisition. As noted elsewhere, these are the behaviors unlikely to be deflected by the presence of strong environmental factors typically considered to put children at social risk, although the acquisition of the behaviors may be slowed (Horowitz, in press.) These are the behaviors that may be distributed by risk factors that work more directly on biological or genetic structures, although for full disturbance the risk factors need to be quite massive.

Although Universal behaviors define the basic "human" nature of the behavioral repertoire, the majority of the behaviors that are acquired in the course of a lifetime are of the non-Universal kind. Spoken language is a Universal behavior for all normal individuals, but the particular language acquired differs as a function of environment. Similarly, whereas the basic cognitive processes that permit one to read, calculate, and write are Universal, the particular behaviors are not and must be specifically learned. The base emotions of the human organism may be Universal, but how they are elaborated and influence behavior are not. Attitudes, values, and the relative importance of such things as veracity, compassion, empathy, and fidelity are environmentally determined and based on culturally mediated opportunities to learn. The basic laws that govern learning may be Universal in nature, but much of what the human organism learns is not inherently Universal.

In this Structural/Behavioral Model the quality and rate of the acquisition of behaviors is the result of a complex interplay of organismic and environmental variables. Individual differences are entered into this model as part of the organismic dimension that affects the processes of acquisition—as one of the major controls of the parameters of change in development. To understand this approach to individual differences, it is necessary to draw some distinctions about process and product in development.

INDIVIDUAL DIFFERENCE AND PROCESS IN DEVELOPMENT

The Product–Process Distinction

The product–process distinction is best illustrated by the efforts that have been made and that continue to be made with respect to understanding the development of intelligence. Much of the investigation of the continuity of intelligence, the fixedness of intelligence, and the relation of intelligence measures over time is "product" oriented—we search for a measure of intelligence at a point in time and try to determine its stability over time. Infant tests of intelligence devised in the late 1920s and 1930s were designed to obtain an early measure of this "fixed" characteristic of an individual.

As anyone knows, such stability in intelligence measures from infancy to later childhood was not found. Explanations have ranged from the proposition that intelligence is not a stable individual difference detectable in infancy, to the suggestion that the behaviors that ultimately define intelligence are just not available for measurement during infancy. McCall commented that, after 50 years of research seeking continuity between infant and later intelligence, perhaps it was time to accept the null hypothesis and conclude that the stability of individual differences in this realm was not to be found (McCall, 1981, 1989).

Recent research efforts suggest otherwise. Instead of correlating an IQ test to an IQ test, Fagan and his colleagues (Fagan, 1975, 1984; Fagan & McGrath, 1981; Fagan & Singer, 1983) have shown that a recognition memory task administered to infants between 4 and 7 months of age yields correlations with later IQ scores at 4 and 7 years of age, ranging in magnitude from the .30s to .60s. Rose and his colleagues have replicated these results in England, using a visual habituation task. Infants tested in an habituation/dishabituation paradigm ranging in ages from 3 months to 1 year and tested again at 1, 2, 4, and 7 years show correlations ranging from .37 to .57 (Rose, Slater, & Perry, 1986). Others report similar results.

Four observations can be made about this body of recent work. First, there has been sufficient replication to convince one that a relationship between the task performance and IQ test performance exists. Second, the correlations are typically significant and many would consider them impressive. However, they generally do not account for more than half the variance. Third, as McCall (1989) has pointed out, whereas the magnitude of the correlations between the infant recognition memory test are higher than has been found for correlations between infant and childhood IQ tests, one can generally obtain a comparable prediction of later childhood IQ from just knowing the level of education of the parents. Hence, these infant tasks are not necessarily more predictive than parental education. Fourth, most importantly, these predictions reflect an essentially product–product relationship. They do not (nor do they claim to) illuminate the processes that are responsible for the stabilities and the instabilities in the early to later relationships in intelligence.

The predictive studies of novelty recognition and later IQ exemplify a product orientation to individual-differences research. A quite different strategy of individual-difference research, one that focuses on a process–product relationship, offers a promising alternative (Mitchell, 1988). In this approach, the goal in the case of predicting later intelligence is to understand the nature of the processes that contribute to higher IQ scores. For example, in the Kansas infant research laboratories, studies of visual attention relative to the individual differences have been focused on the question of how infants appear to "encode" stimulus information. One of the most stable individual-difference characteristics in infant visual attention behavior (see Colombo & Mitchell in this volume) is the duration of the peak fixation during a session. Further, the shorter the peak fixation the more "efficient" the infant is in the task (Colombo, Mitchell, & Horowitz, 1988; Colombo, Mitchell, O'Brien, & Horowitz, 1987). Measures of peak fixation and their relation to efficiency begin to open a window on the possible processes involved in cognitive behavior. As Mitchell (1988) has noted, a cognitive science that does not focus on the processes involved in cognition will never be able to be relevant to understanding individual differences in cognitive behavior.

Process and Developmental Function

Although one finds a predominance of product–product correlational strategies to study individual differences in intelligence, such is not the case in other domains of development. There has been much more of a process–product orientation to explain individual differences in the areas of language develop-ment, affective and emotional development, and some areas of social develop-ment. Perhaps this is a function of the fact that the study of language, affective and emotional development, have a less dense historical involvement with the nature–nurture issue and the question of fixedness of individual-differences char-acteristics than is the case with intelligence. For example, in a recent review of the literature on infant language and communication, the discussion of individual differences was immediately coupled with the ''mechanisms'' that may be re-sponsible for the strands of variation observed between the ages of 10 and 28 months (Bates, O'Connell, & Shore, 1987; see also Thal & Bates, this volume).

Some of the emphasis on individual differences as process has been influ-enced by the study of newborn infants. The development of the Neonatal Behav-ioral Assessment Scale (NBAS) (Brazelton Als, Tronick, & Lester, 1979; Bra-zelton, Nugent, & Lester, 1987) was fueled by an interest in documenting the range and variability of individual differences in the normal newborn infant. One of the major issues surrounding the NBAS has been the stability of individual differences and the meaning of instability (Horowitz, Sullivan, & Linn, 1978; Horowitz, Linn, & Buddin, 1983). Interestingly, those most schooled in the product-predictive approach to testing are most uncomfortable with the lack of stability in the NBAS. Alternatively, one might view instability as an index of dynamic change-over time with the initial individual differences detected by the NBAS seen as a key to how these individual differences serve as control param-eters of infant/environmental interaction.

Recent interest in individual differences in affective responsiveness in infants has focused on the stability and variability in the behavior that defines person-ality and the genetic contributions to these individual differences. Many candi-dates are being nominated for evidence of genetic influence: Shyness (Kagan, Reznick, & Snidman, 1988) is one. The larger area of temperament is another, with a particular focus on emotionality, activity level, and sociability (Buss & Plomin, 1984; Plomin et al., 1988). In all these discussions considerable atten-tion has been given to the effect of environment on the disposition to be shy, active, sociable, etc. Such focus begins to move away from product measure to questions of process. Perhaps because the areas of language, affective behavior, and temperament have been less subject to psychometric test strategies than, for example, intelligence, the interest in individual differences has not been as heavily weighted toward the product perspective. By moving toward process questions, we also move toward the question of how individual differences enter in developmental processes.

The role of individual differences in how they enter into processes may be different for the Universal as compared to the non-Universal behaviors. With Universal behaviors, where the basic topography is species fixed, individual differences may largely affect rate of acquisition. The source of these individual differences is likely biological in nature initially, although with time and the cumulative effect of experience, environmental factors will also be contributing factors. The biological/organismic elements may be more heavily weighted initially for Universal behaviors than environmental variables. Conversely, with non-Universal behaviors, the cumulative learning history of the organism may be more heavily weighted than the biological factors, although the latter also play a role. A fuller discussion of this requires consideration of how we might conceptualize the sources of individual differences if we are interested in individual differences largely in terms of their contributions to the processes involved in development.

Sources of Individual Differences

The basic premise here is that the study of individual differences ao the equation that determines developmental outcome.

The Structural/Behavioral Model of development shown in Fig. 1.1 (Horowitz, 1980, 1982, 1984, 1987) can be used to illustrate how one enters individual differences as elements of the organismic dimension that interact with the environment in accounting for development outcome.

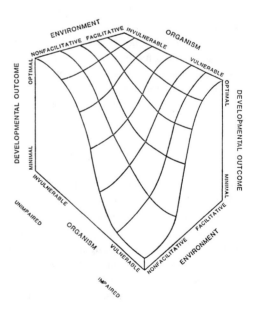

FIG. 1.1. The structural/ behavioral model of development (From Horowitz, 1987).

In this model the organismic dimension includes those biological characteristics that constitute natural constraints on the organism (we learn to walk and
we cannot learn to fly), the biologically governed developmental functions that
map the general topography of Universal behaviors, genetic influences, and
"constitutional influences." These latter are not synonymous with genetic factors though they may include genetic elements. They reflect the sum total of
environmental experiences that leave a constitutional or biological residue (e.g.,
the history of infection, illness, accidents, exposure to hazardous substances,
etc.).

One assumption in the Structural/Behavioral Model is that there are periodic
constitutional reorganizations where the weight and nature of the variables in the
equation determining developmental outcome change. Thus, individual differences and the role they play in the developmental outcome equation will not
necessarily remain constant from one period of development to the next—though
for some individuals they might. For example, extreme values on the individual-
difference continuum may be more likely to remain stable than values of individual differences in the middle of the continuum. The strength of the genetic
influences on developmental function of particular behaviors may be stronger
during one period of development than during other periods. The influence of
organismic variables at any given period of time may be different for different
domains of behavior. Genetic and constitutional variables may take one set of
values in, for example, language development in infancy, whereas they may take
another set of values in social development during this same period of time.

The basic thesis here, that individual differences viewed as elements in process—whether at the relatively microprocess level of cognitive acts or the more
macroprocess level of respect to the form and function of the developmental
equation determining developmental outcome in different domains of behavior—
is likely to be a more fruitful approach to the understanding of human behavior
and development than the focus on individual differences strictly in the context
of product relationships epitomized most strongly by the focus on task and
testing correlations as the definition of the study of individual differences.

IMPLICATIONS FOR INFANT RESEARCH

As already noted, one of the major efforts in infant individual-difference research
was to find the earliest measure of intelligence that would predict later intelligence. Assuming intelligence to be a fixed characteristic, infants became the
subjects of choice for this search. Initially, the results were disappointing. Recently, with the work of Fagan and others, new "hope" has been contributed to
a revived quest. Ultimately, however, such a quest has its limitations. We will
likely find a portion of the variance accounted for in the stabilities; most of the
variance will remain unaccounted for in the instabilities.

An alternative (or companion) strategy is to focus on documenting the range and stability and variability of individual differences in young infants and to study how these individual differences interact with environmental conditions. We should not expect that early identification of individual differences will predict strongly to later measures if we believe that individual differences contribute to the processes involved in behavioral development as variables in a complex equation that includes environmental events that cannot be foreseen. In the Structural/Behavioral Model the environment ranges from facilitative to nonfacilitative. Excellent developmental progress may be made in one period of development under conditions of a mildly facilitative environment where, for example, an infant is relatively invulnerable or resilient. This infant may exhibit highly efficient information-processing behavior so that even under minimally stimulating and reinforcing conditions good progress is made in the cognitive area.

Good developmental progress will continue if the equation stays the same or if changes in the equation occur that balance off to maintain the same essential functional relationship. This will produce "continuity." However, noncontinuity will occur if changes in the equation occur that do not balance off to maintain the same essential functional relationship. For example, illness or accident may change the organism to reduce information-processing efficiency; the environment may become less facilitative of development and thus become unable to meet the needs of the organism to maintain the same rate of growth; or point of systemic biobehavioral reorganization may occur that will result in a change in the infant's position on the organismic continuum of vulnerability–invulnerability.

One maintains a status of being vitamin sufficient across the life-span only if the equation determining such sufficiency retains the essential balance of organismic utilization and environmental input. This analogy is especially apt for the issue of prediction of developmental outcome or status when the measures of developmental outcome involve evaluation of those aspects of the behavioral repertoire that are heavily non-Universal in their characteristics. This has special importance for thinking about the kinds of questions we ought to pose concerning individual differences in infancy.

Because many of the most salient behaviors developing during infancy are Universal behaviors, focusing on these behaviors as key individual differences that will predict later development may not be particularly fruitful; for example, age of onset of walking, indicators of level of language development, etc. Substituting the probability of novelty recognition at a particular age may also not be the most fruitful strategy. However, the process behaviors involved in novelty recognition such as characteristics of visual fixations may be quite useful variables in the organism/environment interactional equation. Highly efficient visual information-processing behavior may presage the relatively "invulnerable" infant who, even under minimally environmentally facilitative circumstances, will show good developmental progress and will display the kinds of learning strategies that contribute to more optimal developmental outcome.

Information-processing behaviors, state organization and stability, and other process indices of relative invulnerability or resiliency are likely candidates for the kinds of individual-difference variables that can be entered into the organism/environment equation to account for developmental outcome. State variables may have particular promise for understanding individual differences. It has been suggested that state may serve as a lead process variable during the neonatal period (Colombo & Horowitz, 1987). Early state characteristics may influence behavioral organization in such a manner as to affect the development of information-processing abilities (Moss, Colombo, Mitchell, & Horowitz, 1988). Early state characteristics are also implicated in the subsequent occurrence of developmental problems (Thomas et al. 1963; see also Thoman and Whitney, this volume).

The use of early variables as functional elements in the processes of development is a promising approach to understanding the role of individual differences in developmental outcome. It is very important, however, to keep in mind that, if one takes a model such as the Structural/Behavioral Model seriously, continuities from early to later development/behavior *are neither necessarily expected nor predicted*. The interest in individual differences in young infants ought not to be driven by this search for continuity. Rather, the interest should be maintained by an understanding that individual differences are a key to the process behaviors necessary to the equations that determine whether continuities or discontinuities will be observed. The goal is to understand the continuities and discontinuities in process, not in phenomena or product.

REFERENCES

Anastasi, A. (1958). Heredity, environment and the question "How?." *Psychological Review, 65,* 197–208.

Anastasi, A. (1965). *Individual differences,* New York: Wiley.

Anastasi, A., & Foley, J. P. (1948). A proposed re-orientation in the heredity–environment controversy. *Psychological Review, 55,* 239–249.

Anthony, E. J., & Cohler, B. J. (1987). *The invulnerable child.* New York: Guilford Press.

Baltes, P., & Nesselroade, J. (1973). In J. Nesselroade & H. Reese (Eds.), *Life-span developmental psychology: Methodological issues* (pp. 219–251). New York: Academic Press.

Bates, E., O'Connell, B., & Shore, C. (1987). Language and communication in infancy. In J. D. Osofsky (Ed.), *Handbook of infant development* (2d ed., pp. 149–203). New York: Wiley.

Block, J. H., & Block, J. (1980). The role of ego control resiliency in the organization of behavior. In W. A. Collins (Ed.), *Minnesota Symposia on Child Psychology, 13,* 39–101. Hillsdale, NJ: Lawrence Erlbaum Associates.

Brazelton, T. B., Als, H., Tronick, E., & Lester, B. (1979). Specific neonatal measures: The Brazelton Neonatal Behavioral Assessment Scale. In J. D. Osofsky (Ed.), *Handbook of infant development* (pp. 185–215). New York: Wiley.

Brazelton, T. B., Nugent, J. K., & Lester, B. M. (1987). Neonatal Behavioral Assessment Scale. In J. D. Osofsky (Ed.), *Handbook of infant development* (pp. 780–817). New York: Wiley.

Buss, A., & Plomin, R. (1984). *Temperament: Early developing personality traits.* Hillsdale, NJ: Lawrence Erlbaum Associates.

Catell, J. McK. (1890). Mental tests and measurements. *Mind, 15,* 373–380.

Colombo, J., & Horowitz, F. D. (1987). Behavioral state as a lead variable in neonatal research. *Merrill-Palmer Quarterly, 33,* 320–330.

Colombo, J., Mitchell, D. W., & Horowitz, F. D. (1988). Infant visual attention in the paved—comparison paradigm: Test–retest and attention–performance relationships. *Child Development, 59,* 1198–1210.

Colombo, J., Mitchell, D. W., O'Brien, M., & Horowitz, F. D. (1987). Stability of infant visual habituation across the first year. *Child Development, 58,* 474–487.

Diamond, M. D. (1988). *Enriching heredity.* New York: The Free Press.

Escalona, S. (1968). *The roots of individuality.* Chicago: Aldine.

Fagan, J. F. (1975). Infant recognition memory as a present and future index of cognitive abilities. In N. R. Ellis (Ed.), *Aberrant development in infancy* (pp. 187–202). Hillsdale, NJ: Lawrence Erlbaum Associates.

Fagan, J. (1984). The relationship of novelty preferences during infancy to later intelligence and later recognition memory. *Intelligence, 8,* 339–346.

Fagan, J. F. III, & McGrath, S. K. (1981). Infant recognition memory and later intelligence, *Intelligence, 5,* 121–130.

Fagan, J. F., & Singer, L. T. (1983). Infant recognition memory as a measure of intelligence. In L. P. Lipsitt & C. K. Rovee-Collier (Eds.), *Advances in infancy research* (pp. 31–78). Norwood, NJ: Ablex.

Gesell, A. (1954). The ontogenesis of infant behavior. In L. Carmichael (Ed.) *Manual of child psychology* (2nd Ed.) New York: Wiley.

Gruber, H. E., & Vonèche, J. J. (1977). (Eds.) *The essential Piaget.* New York: Basic Books.

Heider, G. (1960). Vulnerability in infants. *Bulletin of the Menninger Clinic, 24,* 104–114.

Horowitz, F. D. (1969). Learning, developmental research, and individual differences. In L. P. Lipsitt & H. W. Reese (Eds.), *Advances in child development and behavior* (Vol. 4, pp. 84–126). New York: Academic Press.

Horowitz, F. D. (1978). Toward a functional analysis of individual differences. *Presidential address to the Division of Developmental Psychology,* American Psychological Association meetings, Toronto, Canada.

Horowitz, F. D. (1980). Intervention and its effects on early development: What model of development is appropriate? In R. R. Turner & H. W. Reese (Eds.), *Life-span development psychology: Intervention* (pp. 235–248). New York: Academic Press.

Horowitz, F. D. (1982). Child development for the pediatrician. *Pediatric Clinics of North America,* (April), *29,* 359–375.

Horowitz, F. D. (1984). The psychobiology of parent–offspring relations in high-risk situations. In L. P. Lipsitt (Ed.), *Advances in infancy research* (pp. 1–22). New York: Ablex.

Horowitz, F. D. (1987). *Exploring developmental theories: Toward a structural/behavioral model of development.* Hillsdale, NJ: Lawrence Erlbaum Associates.

Horowitz, F. D. (1989). Using developmental theory to guide the search for the effects of biological risk factors on the development of children. *Journal of Clinical Nutrition, 50,* 589–597.

Horowitz, F. D., Linn, P. L., & Buddin, B. J. (1983). Neonatal assessment: Evaluating the potential for plasticity. In T. B. Brazelton & B. Lester (Eds.), *New approaches to developmental screening of infants* (pp. 27–50). New York: Elsevier.

Horowitz, F. D., Sullivan, J. W., & Linn, P. (1978). Stability and instability in the newborn infant: The quest for elusive threads. In A. Sameroff (Ed.), Organization and stability of newborn behavior: A commentary on the Brazelton Neonatal Behavioral Assessment Scale. *Monographs of the Society for Research in Child Development, 43,* 29–45.

Hull, C. L. (1945). The place of innate individual and species differences in a natural science theory of behavior. *Psychological Review, 52,* 55–60.

Kagan, J., Reznick, J. S., & Snidman, N. (1988). Biological bases of childhood shyness. *Science, 240,* 167–171.

McCall, R. B. (1977). Challenges to a science of developmental psychology. *Child Psychology, 48,* 333–344.

McCall, R. B. (1981). Nature–nurture and the two realms of development: A proposed integration with respect to mental development. *Child Development, 52,* 1–12.

McCall, R. B. (1989). Infancy research: Individual differences. *Merrill–Palmer Quarterly.* Special Issue.

Mitchell, D. W. (1988). *Process and product: The assessment of individual differences in the psychometric and cognitive traditions.* Unpublished paper, Department of Human Development and Family Life, The University of Kansas, Lawrence.

Moss, M., Colombo, J., Mitchell, D. W., & Horowitz, F. D. (1988). Neonatal behavioral organization and visual processing at three months. *Child Development, 59,* 1211–1220.

Murphy, L. B., & Moriarty, A. E. (1976). *Vulnerability, coping and growth.* New Haven, CT: Yale University Press.

Plomin, R. (1986). *Development, genetics and psychology.* Hillsdale, NJ: Lawrence Erlbaum Associates.

Plomin, R. (1989). Environment and genes: Determinants of behavior. *American Psychologist, 44,* 105–111.

Plomin, R., Pedersen, N. L., McClearn, G. E., Nesselbroade, J. R., & Bergeman, C. S. (1988). EAS temperaments during the last half of the life span: Twins reared apart and twins reared together. *Psychology and Aging, 3,* 43–50.

Rose, D. H., Slater, A., & Perry, H. (1986). Prediction of childhood intelligence from habituation in early infancy. *Intelligence, 10,* 251–263.

Thomas, A., Birch, H. G., Chess, S., Hertzig, M. E., & Korn, S. (1963). *Behavioral individuality in early childhood.* New York: New York University Press.

Thomas, A., & Chess, S. (1977). *Temperament and development.* New York: Bruner/Mazel.

Thomas, A., & Chess, S. (1984). Genesis and evolution of behavioral disorders from infancy to early adult life. *American Journal of Psychiatry, 141,* 1–9.

Tyler, L. E. (1978). *Individuality.* San Francisco: Jossey-Bass.

Wohlwill, J. (1973). *The study of behavioral development.* New York: Academic Press.

2 Dynamical Systems and the Generation of Individual Differences

Esther Thelen
Department of Psychology, Indiana University

In 1987, Plomin and Daniels published a paper with the captivating title, "Why are children in the same family so different from one another?" From their review of behavior genetic research using twins and adopted children, these authors reached a conclusion probably less surprising to parents than to the researchers: Two children in the same family are no more alike than any pair of children selected randomly in the population. How can two individuals whose coefficient of genetic relatedness is 50% *and* who grow up in the same family diverge so dramatically on measures of cognition, personality, and psychopathology?

Individual differences—illustrated by the stubborn refusal of siblings to conform to our commonsense expectations that they should be more alike than not—have both plagued and fascinated developmental researchers. For those studying developmental universals in cognition, perception, action, and emotion, individual differences mean large and unwelcome standard deviations, infants who cannot or will not complete the experiment, and the general sense of optimistic unease whenever a new subject enters the baby lab. For those concerned with populations at medical or social risk, individual differences are the source of hope for the most hopeless cases, and of puzzlement when a favorable course turns for the worse. For the developmental theorist, individual differences pose an enormous challenge. A successful theory must account for *both* the large sweep of developmental change, where all normal infants look more or less alike, *and* the bewildering range of differences within those broad outlines of change.

Developmental theory has not met this challenge with much success. Siblings are a case in point. Plomin and Daniels (1987) assign the source of sibling individual differences not accounted for by either shared heredity or environment to what they call *nonshared environment,* or environmental differences acting on children in the same family. These authors are exclusively concerned with *systematic* nonshared influences, which might include family composition, gender differences, birth order, peers, and differential treatment. If, for example, parents systematically treat their children differently, this should contribute measurably and reliably to the children's personal traits. In fact, however, parents' treatment of siblings is less a reflection of differing parental styles than of the ages of the children. Parents treat siblings of the same age quite similarly, according to parents, observers, and the siblings themselves. Research confirming other systematic influences of nonshared environment is equally weak or nonexistent. Little is known, for instance, about the effects of peers and of siblings on each other. Although preliminary evidence has suggested that children in the same family may perceive these interactions differently, it is questionable whether these interactions are sufficiently powerful to account for the already striking differences between siblings noted even in infants. Birth order, another systematic factor, exerts a modest influence on IQ and sociability, but these differences are generally measured across, not within, families. Indeed, overall family size is a much more powerful predictor than birth order per se (Falbo & Polit, 1986). It is not yet clear if and how family macroenvironments differ sufficiently to produce two children who may as well be strangers.

Plomin and Daniels (1987) talk about systematic effects of the environment because these fit the models used by quantitative behavioral genetics, that is, that all variance should be accounted for by a combination of heritable and environmental factors in a linear fashion. They dismiss as a "gloomy prospect" (p. 8) the second possibility—that *nonsystematic* events such as accidents, illness, or other chance events may contribute to individual differences. Although they acknowledge that it is possible that "stochastic events . . . when compounded over time, make children in the same family different in unpredictable ways," they conclude that this prospect is "a dead end for research" (p. 8).

When development is viewed from the linear models of quantitative behavioral genetics, the spectre of a process dominated by unknowable events is indeed a chilling one, and one that may stop the enterprise entirely. Thus, it is prudent to move on to tractable problems. However, Plomin and Daniels may have dismissed their nonsystematic influences too hastily. Indeed, I argue here that it is precisely the unsystematic events throughout development that give rise to families with both poets and engineers and actresses and accountants. In its behavior genetic formulation, the concept of nonshared environment is entirely a post hoc explanation for variance not explained by the two shared sources of similarity in siblings: genetics and environment. It is theoretically unsatisfactory because it offers no principled account of the dimensions of the nonshared environment, or of the processes by which such environments lead to disparate outcomes. Such a principled basis for development is possible when linear models are abandoned and the role of chance is admitted as a central feature of development. In turn, the research endeavor will not be a dead end, but it may require different assumptions and strategies.

The theme of this chapter, then, is that both individual differences and species similarities are constructed in ontogeny by the very same nonlinear processes. Richness and variability are both the sources of global similarities and local differences in new structures and functions. Contemporary studies in embryology and developmental neurobiology and the growing new science of complex systems provide a theoretical and empirical basis for my claim, and I rely on these disciplines to suggest principles for the origins of developmental outcome.

Applying these new insights to human development requires, however, that we reexamine two long-held assumptions and begin to ask new and different questions. The first assumption questioned is that the sources of human variability can be neatly partitioned into those influences that are inherited and come in the genetic material and those that arise from the environment (Oyama, 1985). Postulating any simple interaction between genes and environment is equally untenable. (An interactionist position states that the environment impacts differently on different children because of their genetic differences.) Following Oyama (1985), I reject the notion that any pre-established code or source of information either within or outside the organism directs development. Rather, developmental information (and individual differences) are *created* during the process. The second cherished assumption is that we can detect continuity in development by conventional linear predictions of beginning and end states. I substitute instead a stochastic view where certain outcomes have high probability and others are virtually nonpredictable. Stable outcomes result from strong organic or contextual constraints; probabilistic outcomes are a product of more relaxed constraints.

In the next section, I describe general principles of nonlinear, complex systems that apply to developing systems at all levels of analysis. I then show how the *neuronal group selection* theory of Edelman (1987) provides, within a dynamic framework, the anatomical and behavioral evidence for the origins of individual differences. In the third section, I illustrate how these principles may be used to explain both commonalities and variability in early motor development. Finally, I conclude with some suggestions how a dynamical approach may redirect the empirical study of development.

DEVELOPMENT AS A DYNAMICAL PROCESS

Individual differences are indeed puzzling when viewed from the mechanistic model of (genes + environment = behavior), that is that all the information about the outcome is specified from the start. Their origins are more understandable when developing organisms are viewed as one category of complex, dynamical systems, that is, systems composed of many heterogeneous subelements that change over time. When energy flows through these systems in a particular fashion, they behave according to general principles that have wide application regardless of their material substrate, level of organization, and scale. Most relevant for the current discussion is that such systems show spontaneous pattern generation, openly exchange energy with the surrounds, exhibit quasi-random fluctuations, and are essentially nonlinear, reflected in qualitative phase shifts and an exquisite sensitivity to initial conditions (a small initial difference can result in dramatically divergent outcomes).

This new science, variously called *synergetics* (Haken, 1983), or the study of *self-organizing systems* (Prigogine & Stengers, 1984; Madore & Freedman, 1987; Yates, 1987), *nonlinear dynamical systems* (Schoner & Kelso, 1988), or *chaos* (Gleick, 1987), shares many principles with *general systems theory* (von Bertalanffy, 1968), which has been warmly embraced by many developmental theorists (e.g., Brent, 1978; Horowitz, 1987; Kitchener, 1982; Lerner, 1978; Overton, 1975; Sameroff, 1983; Wolff, 1987). Readers will also recognize a strong affiliation with what is known as the *organismic* approach to development (Lerner, 1978). Contemporary dynamical systems theory has proved to be remarkably general and robust in its application to a very wide variety of physical, chemical, and biological systems, including aspects of physiological, neural, and cognitive functioning (see, for example, Degn, Holden, & Olsen, 1987; Kelso, Mandell, & Shlesinger, 1988; Kugler & Turvey, 1987, among others).

What, then, are common characteristics of systems as diverse as laser lights, clouds, crystals, fluid flows, and behaving and developing organisms? These are all systems made up of very many, often diverse, and "noisy" constituent elements, which are potentially free to act either as individual particles or to combine in a nearly infinite number of ways. But under certain thermodynamic conditions (see Prigogine & Stengers, 1984), these systems show coherence: The elements cooperate to produce form and flow that has pattern and complexity. It is clear from the simple physical and chemical examples that the patterns that emerge from the system's cooperativeness are not coded anywhere beforehand. Order emerges from the interaction of the elements. A similar but much less intuitive claim is made for biological systems: Within a set of initial conditions and constraints, complexity arises that is nowhere contained in the initial elements alone.

Such self-organizing systems have properties that provide a principled basis for the origins of both species similarities and of individual differences (Fogel, this volume; Fogel & Thelen, 1987; Thelen, 1989; Thelen, Kelso, & Fogel, 1987). First, I discuss these properties, and in a subsequent section I show how such principles may be instantiated in known processes of embryological and neurobiological development.

Open Exchange of Energy with the Surrounds

The essential thermodynamic condition for emergent pattern formation is that the system be *far-from-equilibrium*. All living systems are in thermodynamic nonequilibrium: They are open to the continual flow of energy and matter, and they indeed must continually extract energy from their environment and store it to maintain their order. Because biological systems must be in a continual energy dialogue with their surrounds, there can be no logical distinction between the organism and the environment in creating emergent order. Organisms are never decontextualized. All pattern comes from the intimate relations between the pulses of energy the organism extracts from energy sources outside of it and from the energy it, in turn, dissipates (Kugler & Turvey, 1987; Yates, 1987).

This openness means that agents of change may lie equally inside or outside the organism. In dynamical systems, new forms may be engendered by rather nonspecific but essential elements that configure the pattern, such as ambient temperature, chemical gradients, pressure, or gravity. For example, in early embryogenesis the developmental fate of a particular cell or group of cells may be determined by their relative orientation to the gravitational field. These parameters contain no specific prescriptions for, or information about, the outcome configurations. Thus, there is a subtle but crucial distinction between a conventional interactionist position, which proposes that the genes plus the environment together provide all the logically sufficient and necessary information for the final form, and a dynamic view (Oyama, 1985). In the former, information not attributed to directly measured heritable or environmental components was assumed to be "out there," but improperly measured, as in the concept of nonshared environment. In the present view, the unexplained variances—the individual differences—are created in the developmental process as a direct result of systems open to and assembled by their context. The information is not configured somewhere else; it arises in ontogeny (Oyama, 1985).

Self-assembly into Preferred Configurations

Systems that have many components and use energy from their environment can produce patterned behavior that is collectively much simpler than the behavior of the individual elements. Imagine a fluid in a pipe. When the fluid pressure is low, the behavior of the molecules are random in respect to one another, and there is no way to describe the macroscopic behavior of the fluid. When the pressure is increased (requiring the addition of energy), the molecules begin to act collectively; they organize into laminar and turbulent flow patterns that *can* be described by mathematical functions. The enormous potential number of degrees of freedom of individual molecules are lost, and the molecules act as if they are communicating with one another. The flow patterns may indeed be complex, but they can be described much more simply than the behavior of each of the participating molecules. Likewise, whereas, at any level, the behavior of biological systems is complex, there are potentially very many more descriptors needed to characterize the component structures and processes.

The point for explaining the origins of differences is that the compressed configuration, the form into which the components assemble, can be thought of as a *preferred* state of the system under very specific constraints. Preferred means that the system contains no prescriptions ahead of time for that form, the system settles into that form autonomously and returns to it when perturbed, known in dynamic terminology as the preferred *attractor*. Under other conditions, the system components may reassemble into other stable configurations. Under low pressure, the fluid in the pipe is random; under increased pressure the water assumes a set configuration without "knowing" ahead of time the dimensions of that configuration. What determines the system topology is the precise interaction of the components in a given context. This is the sense that a developing system does not know its endstate at its inception. That the precise endpoint is not knoweable is due to the essential *nonlinearity* of complex dynamic systems. This is explained next.

Nonlinearity: Phase Shifts and Sensitivity to Initial Conditions

Complex systems in thermodynamic nonequilibrium that produced patterned behavior exhibit a fundamental nonlinearity that is the key to emergent order. Nonlinearity means that there is no one-to-one correspondence between changes on the microscopic level and changes on the macroscopic level. Sometimes small changes in the constituents of the system have no effect on the collective behavior of the system; under other conditions, even very tiny changes can have drastic consequences, qualitatively reorganizing the system behavior, causing a *phase shift* (see Gleick, 1987). Thus, although the system may have quite stable behavior within a range of values of its constituent parts or external parameters, at critical points, even slight perturbations may shift the whole system into a qualitatively new mode. The collective behavior of a system is the compression of very many individual "noisy" elements. When these internal fluctuations disrupt the dynamic stability of the system, it seeks a new, more stable configuration.

In dynamical systems, this nonlinearity is also reflected in what is called *sensitivity to initial conditions*. This concept is difficult to grasp. First, initial conditions can be defined anywhere along a dynamic trajectory and refers to the fact that, from any starting point, the fate of two very close points on a state space cannot be predicted after *n* iterations. If a system's parameters were to be completely identical and free any random elements, it would trace an identical trajectory through time at each iteration. However, the fact that the individual elements of the system are noisy (variability is inherent in complex systems) means that the starting parameters *can never be identical*. Even small differences in these initial conditions (which can be defined anywhere along the trajectory) can cause the system to assume widely diverging paths. Here we begin to see the principled basis for individual divergences. First, an example from a physical system.

In many ways, the generation of individual differences in human development can be likened to the classic nonlinear dynamical system, global weather. When viewed over a long span of time and space, the weather is generally patterned: Seasons follow each other with reassuring regularity and countries on the equator do not have blizzards. The mass of the earth, its distance and trajectory around the sun, its tilt, the composition of the atmosphere, and so on act as strong constraints on the assembly of the weather system. Only a limited range of stable solutions are possible under these constraints and despite local perturbations—a few mild days—winter is never converted into summer. However, weather changes, although following some very general patterns, are essentially unpredictable beyond the scale of a day or two. Weather patterns never quite repeat themselves, and to the frustration of meteorologists, even their most complete information is not enough to specify the subsequent behavior of the weather system. In his book *Chaos,* Gleick (1987) talks about the computer simulations of global weather by the meteorologist Lorenz, where the tiniest rounding-off difference in numbers simulating the initial conditions led the whole system to diverge dramatically into a new weather pattern. Lorenz called this the ''butterfly effect,'' because the smallest perturbation—metaphorically, the beating of the wings of a single butterfly—can be amplified into dramatic differences in global weather, rendering it virtually unpredictable beyond a few days. Although the components of the weather system—winds, temperatures, pressure systems—are many and complex, the weather of the entire globe is influenced by even the smallest element.

So it is with developing organisms. Over the life-span, the ontogenetic pathway of all members of a species are globally similar (all intact humans learn to walk, speak a language, reach reproductive maturity, and so on). The nature of the nuclear and cytoplasmic chemical composition of humans, their growing anatomical structures, their prenatal milieu, and the nature of their physical and social worlds after birth strongly define the state space in which the developing system can assemble. Yet the local pathways and niches may be highly variant. Just as small changes are amplified in the weather, the growing and changing structures and processes are a cooperative whole, potentially sensitive to the minute deviations of each of the participating elements. This means that at any point in the ontogenetic process, small pushes and nudges from within or without can direct the subsequent trajectory *in essentially indeterminate and unpredictable ways at this local level*. The indeterminancy of the developmental process is such that neither shared genes nor shared environment contain any deterministic blueprints for the ontogenetic pathway. Successive new forms arise as the current stable attractors dissolve in the face of these pushes and nudges.

Thus, the lesson from dynamical systems is that intrinsic "noisiness" of any complex system is both the wellspring of its stability and global pattern and of its variability in endpoint status. Because the system is exquisitely sensitive to its own internal milieu and open to the context in which it lives, it responds in a generally similar manner to these universal features, and, within those constraints, stays within a preferred attractor regime. It is this same noisiness and openness that gives rise to individual variability. Developing human organisms share universal internal and external boundary conditions that produce normal, functioning adults. Within these boundaries are a nearly infinite and indeterminate number of permissible endstates. How this indeterminancy is actually manifest is the subject of the next section.

DYNAMIC SOURCES OF INDETERMINANCY IN ONTOGENY

By their intrinsic complexity and openness, ontogenetic processes generate potential variability and outcomes that are, a priori, essentially unknowable. Because we are interested in behavioral diversity, we especially focus on the development of the nervous system, but the epigenetic events that lead to neural growth and differentiation follow the same principles as those underlying embryonic development in general.

Context-specificity and Self-organization in Early Morphogenesis

All living things begin as a single cell. The central question of morphogenesis— the development of form—is how a one-dimensional genetic code, that is, chemicals strung out along a string, can specify a three-dimensional, multicellar organism. The genome alone cannot contain the specific information about the morphological characteristics and exact functional position in time and space of every cell in the body (Waddington, 1972). Although the egg itself may have some internal structure, it is far less complex than the complete animal. Where does structure come from?

Contemporary embryologists explain spatial order and specificity in developing organisms as emergent through the same self-organizing, dynamical processes as those creating pattern in strictly physical systems. Mathematical models of such pattern formation show that very simple gradients of chemical substances, rather unspecific and gradual cues depicting a directional orientation, are all that are needed to initiate a cascade of effects leading to emergent and irreversible fixations of much more complex patterns (Gierer, 1981; Madore & Freedman, 1987). These emergent properties are not mysterious, but the results of the complex, kinetic interactions of biological molecules, the mechanical changes in cell structures arising from these interactions, and the inherent non-linearity of the processes. This means that only slight local fluctuations or deviations from uniform conditions can be amplified (autocatalysis). This local activation occurs at the expense of deactivation elsewhere (lateral inhibition). When such processes are sequenced over time (Satoh, 1985), one epigenetic event providing the field for subsequent gradients and nonlinearities, extremely complex patterns can emerge including stripes and layers, localized crystalizations, invaginations and spheres, multiple peaks, and other periodic or gradient patterns (Gierer, 1981).

The molecular basis of morphogenesis is just beginning to be understood. One elegant example of the influence of chemical and mechanical factors in morphogenesis is the regeneration of the tip of hairs in the marine alga *Acetabularia*. First, it is known that the viscosity and elasticity of the cell cytoplasm changes as a function of calcium concentration. Second, it is also true that calcium concentration itself is affected by the mechanical state of the cytoplasm, that is, the ratio of free and bound calcium changes when the system is compressed, such as by changes in the algal cytoskeleton. Using these simple initial conditions and assuming a change in the mechanical state of the algal tip from the cut, Goodwin and Trainor (1985) used dynamical field equations to show the emergence of the characteristic whirl pattern as bifurcations from the initial calcium gradients. The perturbed algal cell—through a mechanical change—thus sets up the conditions for its own repair through very basic properties of the interaction of calcium and the cytoskeleton.

Edelman (1987) offers a general theory of the molecular basis of morphogenesis using dynamical principles. In brief, Edelman has identified a group of cell-surface molecules that mechanicochemically regulate cell divisions and movements that lead to emergent structures. These are a relatively small class of glycoproteins called cell-adhesion molecules, or CAMs. CAMs are genetically activated and deactivated at critical junctures in the epigenetic cycle. However, once activated, the precise configuration of CAMs is a local event; they are altered specifically in response to local cell surface modulation. In other words, the CAMs themselves are not very specific; their specificity is determined locally and not by genetic blueprint. In response to local conditions, CAMs change in concentration, position, or chemical nature. These locally modulated CAMs function to alter the binding properties of cells, making some cells differentially "sticky," and changing the rate at which they move, and thus enabling cells to aggregate into collectives with defined borders. The formation of a cell collective, modulates, in turn, the subsequent CAM expression on local and bordering cell collectives and acts as an inductive event for further cell migration, including a likely feedback mechanism on the genome itself (Fig. 2.1). Thus, a cycle of

FIG. 2.1.   A CAM regulatory cycle in an epigenetic sequence.
Early induction signals (heavy
arrow at left) lead to CAM gene
expression. Surface modulation
alters the binding rates of cells.
This regulates morphogenetic
movements, which in turn affect embryonic induction or mil-
ieu-dependent differentiation.
The inductive agents can again
affect CAM gene expression as
well as the expression of other
genes for specific tissues. The

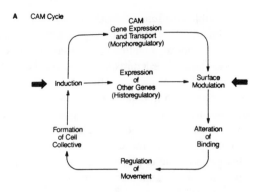

heavy arrows left and right refer to candidate signals for initiation of induction that are
still unknown. These signals could result from global surface modulation as a result of
CAM binding or from release of morphogens affecting induction or both; in any case, a
mechanicochemical link between gene expression and morphogenesis is provided by
the cycle (From *Neural Darwinism: The Theory of Neuronal Group Selection*, by Gerald M.
Edelman. Copyright © 1987 by Basic Books, Inc. Reprinted by permission of Basic
Books, Inc., Publishers.

interactive events can proceed from extremely simple initial conditions: simple
field gradients in chemical concentration known to exist in the initial aggregation
of cells inducing CAM expression, which is, in turn, sensitive to local topographies and cell contacts. Modulation of local CAMs thus induces differential
morphology, which in turn may alter CAM expression and/or set up cascading
new morphologies, which again function to alter gene expression. Such differential cycles of CAM expression and morphogenetic events have indeed been
identified (Edelman, 1987).

Why are these processes occurring at the very onset of embryological development important to those studying human behavioral differences? Most importantly, these new insights show how variability may arise from the intricacies of
ontogeny alone that can never be accounted for in any deterministic gene-en-
vironment model. Note that cells, in a continual dialogue with the genetic material, are the sources of emergent form. In other words, it is only the genome in
interaction with the chemical and physical properties of the cell that allows
morphogenesis to proceed. This allows for a modal similarity of form, but the
potential for considerable local variability because the interactions at the local
level are entirely dynamic: gradients, local changes in cell stickiness, etc. The
conditions molding developmental change are mundanely nonspecific, often
simple mechanical or chemical fields or gradients (e.g., Cooke, 1986; French,
Bryant, & Bryant, 1976; Mittenthal, 1981). Neither the genetic information nor
the cellular fields contains any a priori information as to the succeeding patterns.
These agents merely set the stage for the emergent properties that naturally
organize under particular thermodynamic conditions.

There is compelling evidence that these epigenetic events lead to considerable local variability in the structure of the nervous system, as I explain further in the next section. How much individual variability is accounted for by these processes in the earliest embryogenesis is not known. All biological processes are "noisy," to some degree, and this inherent variability is essential for species survival. On the other hand, variability must have limits. It seems likely that strong phylogenetic constraints have made not only individuals but also species diverge more as they progress further "downstream" in ontogeny. Because later developmental processes depend on earlier ones, early processes should be more general purpose and more constrained. A change in early structure or function can be magnified and disrupt all consequent developmental events, whereas variability in later events may have much less profound ramifications. This would exert strong selective pressure on maintaining more uniformity in earliest ontogeny, both through the necessary specific genes and gene products and in the unfolding organic context (Rasmussen, 1987). Modal structures and processes must be preserved where they are vital to the integrity of the organism. The same processes that conserve modal features also generate considerable morphological variability. The importance of this variability, especially as reflected in the central nervous system, is the topic of the next section.

The Generation of Variability-Within-Constancy in the Central Nervous System

The discovery that a relatively small number of CAMs modulate, but do not specify, the spatiotemporal organization of the embryo means that neural patterns, in their fine anatomical details, are a product of local dynamics rather than predetermined instructions. The processes of neural development insure that the central nervous system is both topographically ordered and locally variant. In his review, Cowan (1978) identifies seven major phases of neurogenesis: cell proliferation, cell migration, selective cell aggregation, neuronal cytodifferentiation, cell death during development, formation of connections, and center–periphery adjustment and interrelations. As Edelman (1987) points out, whereas neuronal differentiation—the overall shape of the neuron—is invariant, the other processes building the fundamental structure of the nervous system are highly dynamic, stochastic, selective, and although constrained by the neuronal type, causally independent of it. Thus, cell proliferation appears to be specific to certain spatial and temporal sequences, much like general cell division, rather than to a particular afferent or efferent connectivity. Cell migration, the movement of neural cells, appears to be guided by glial pathways mediated by CAM expression and other dynamic changes in cell matrices. The final branching pattern in differentiating neural processes, although not the characteristic morphology, is highly locally variant and probably determined by the variability induced by particular input connections. The strongest evidence for stochastic rather than predetermined neural patterning is the phenomenon of neuronal cell death. In some areas, up to 70% of cells die during development, and sometimes within a very short time. Cell death is largely stochastic and depends on contingent events such as the timing and nature of the connectivity of that area. Likewise, both the establishment of central connections and maps and their subsequent adjustments to the periphery appear to be the result of complex local events where competition and selection occur under the influence of CAMS and differential cell adhesions without precise chemical specificity. Each developmental event itself sets the context for the succeeding events. Like the global weather pattern, such a system can produce maps and tracts with great similarity among individual members of the species, but because of the inherent fluctuations in the local events, essential unpredictability in the finer details. The local branching and connectivity is not genetically specified. The multifarous sources of neural variability are listed in Table 2.1.

TABLE 2.1
Sites and Levels of Neuronal Variation

A. Variation in genetic traits and developmental primary processes: cell division, migration, adhesion, differentiation, and death.

B. Variation in cell morphology
   1. Cell shape and size
   2. Dendritic and axonal aborizations
      a. Spatial distribution
      b. Branching order
      c. Length or branches
      d. Number of spines

C. Variation in connection patterns
   1. Number of inputs and outputs
   2. Connection order with other neurons
   3. Local vs. long-range connections
   4. Degree of overlap or arbors

D. Variation in cytoarchitectonics
   1. Number or density cells
   2. Thickness of individual cortical layers
   3. Relative thickness or supragranular, infragranular, and granular layers
   4. Position of somata
   5. Variation in columns
   6. Variation in strips or patches of terminations
   7. Variation in anisotropy of fibres

E. Variation in transmitters
   1. Between cells in a population
   2. Between cells at different times

F. Variation in dynamic response
   1. In synaptic chemistry and size of synapse
   2. In electrical properties
   3. In excitatory/inhibitory ratios and locations of these synapses
   4. In short-and long-term synaptic alteration
   5. In metabolic state

G. Variation in neuronal transport

H. Variation in interactions with glia

Note: Reprinted from Edelman, 1987 (with permission).

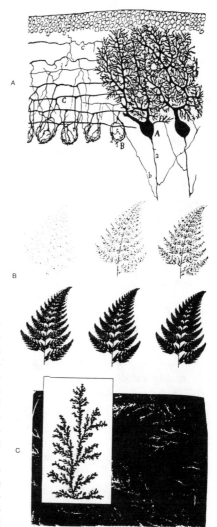

FIG. 2.2. The fractal-like structure of CNS neurons can be generated without instructions specifying each branch. A. Extensive arborization of cerebellar afferents, as drawn by the famed neuroanatomist Ramon y Cajal (from Ito, 1986). B. Computer-generated fern. A few simple rules and many reiterations produce an exact replica. C. Branching structures produced by electrical discharge and (inset) simulated aggregation of randomly moving particles (B and C from Gleick, 1987)

Indeed several authors have commented on the resemblance of neural arborization fields to mathematical and physical objects and processes called *fractals:* complex, high dimensional, nonlinear surfaces created by the iteration of initially simply dynamical laws (Fig. 2.2). Fractal properties are noted, for example, in the branching networks of the bronchial tubes of the lung and in the conducting fibers in heart (West, 1988). What is important about fractals and their self-similarity in scaling (as much complexity is revealed in the microstructure as in the macrostructure) is their potential for enormous behavioral richness and variability and for their ability to thus tolerate and modulate perturbations.

The variant, complex, and overlapping structure of the nervous system may also serve as a source of great adaptability (and of individual differences). I describe Edelman's view of how this structural indeterminancy may lead to adaptive behavior next.

Behavioral Development as a Dynamic and Selective Process

According to Edelman (1987), these primary neurogenic processes produce "surprisingly divergent terminal arborizations of afferents in many different regions of the nervous system" (p. 59) both within and between specific brain regions. This means that any neuron will receive inputs from a great number of connecting cells and regions, over a wide region in the brain or spinal cord and from a number of input modalities. Edelman calls this property *degeneracy,* and it is the very key to understanding how the nervous system makes sense of the world. A degenerate system is one where the many elements share sufficient characteristics to perform the same function but are not identical; that is, each of slightly different structures can carry out the same function more or less well. When these structures act cooperatively, a very high degree of accuracy can be obtained although none of the individual elements itself is very good. What degenerate systems can do—and what nervous systems do very well indeed—is to perceive and act both specifically and across a wide range of task inputs.

The primary structure of the nervous system is thus both widely distributed and highly parallel. According to Edelman, perceptual and action categories arise in such a system through *reentrant* signal processing. Incoming signals, from primary sensory feature detectors, for example, are sampled by many of these overlapping, but not identical, networks. All actions have a continual stream of multimodal sensory and motor consequences. Common features of that stream are extracted by the networks and correlated (because of the network overlap) and then reentered into the network to be compared with ongoing incoming signals. These signals, may in turn, be correlated with movement-related signals associated with the resulting action. Perceptual and motor features that are often associated and have multimodal commonalities become highly linked if their synaptic connections can become strengthened as a result of their frequent association. Thus, a group of functional networks are selected from the large number of possible interconnectivities strictly because they reflect common features in the real world, leading to more or less stable categories of action and perception. No a priori executives or decision-making machines are necessary to account for emerging regularities and rule-like aspects of behavior. Categories in mind emerge because they reflect the dynamic association of real-world features. From the enormous diversity laid down by epigenetic and dynamic processes, the system self-organizes into certain functionally driven attractor states characterized by frequently associated perceptual invariants and often performed motor actions.

This brief summary cannot do justice to Edelman's rich and generative theory. Nonetheless, it provides an outline for how developmental processes per se produce individual differences as a consequence of the open, nonlinear interactions between the organism and its surrounds:

1. In interaction with the genome, chemical and mechanical cellular mechanisms in embryogenesis and neurogenesis produce spatial and temporal organization. Because these processes are dynamic and contingent, they can generate local diversity within modal similarity, especially in the absence of strong ontogenetic constraints. Note that not all strong constraints are genetic; gravity and other physical laws constrain but do not prescribe the processes. Because open systems are entirely context sensitive, all constraints are logically equivalent in the process of developmental change. This diversity, in turn, builds the raw structures on which further epigenetic processes work.

2. Specific patterns of neural connectivity involving processes like synaptogenesis, migration, and cell death are likewise dynamic and contingent, depending on morphogenetic and topological features as well as patterns of activity. The fine structure of the nervous system offers ample overlap and degeneracy to provide a rich source of potential networks.

3. There is ample anatomical and behavioral evidence to suggest extensive multimodal interconnections; that is, every sensory input (exteroceptive and proprioceptive) is mapped onto multiple brain areas, and each brain area receives input from more than one modality. Every perception and every action, therefore, and all its minute variants are continually fed into multiple networks where common patterns can be extracted and correlated. Networks are strengthened whose inputs commonly co-occur, in a continual dynamic mapping and remapping. The formation of these categories is entirely stochastic; no privileged wiring links a specific input to a specific output.

Because the system is self-organizing and contingent, we would expect it to have the characteristics of other complex systems, that is, broadly resistant to perturbations within a range of parameter values at the same time as exquisitely sensitive to initial conditions at critical or sensitive boundaries. Thus, it is easy to imagine a developing system being set along a developmental pathway by an organizing internal or external event by these essentially chance events. Such a phase shift may be quite stable and may act as an attractor state for mild perturbations, leading to a continuity in individual type. On the other hand, at critical junctures, the system may indeed reorganize into a new attractor on the basis of both internal stability and/or changing external demands. Neither outcome may, *in principle,* be predictable because of the nonlinearity of the interaction of the intrinsic dynamics of the organism (not just its genome) and the minute variabilities of the organizing context.

DYNAMICAL SOURCES OF VARIABILITY
IN MOTOR DEVELOPMENT

To translate these abstract principles into the real domains of early human development, it is essential to view the organism as a self-organizing system of many parallel developing subsystems assembled strictly in response to the behavioral context (Fogel & Thelen, 1987; Thelen, 1986a, 1989). In this view, developmental change—the destabilization of existing attractors and the reformation of new stable states—can be equally driven by internal challenges to stability such as organic growth, anatomical differentiation, or shifting neuronal maps, as by external physical or social contexts. As each of the components in the complex system is itself "noisy" and changing, deviations from modal behavior are not only expected but inevitable.

It is instructive to cast early motor development within this dynamic and selectionist framework because the multiple contributing subsystems are relatively more obvious than those serving cognitive or perceptual development, for instance. I hypothesize the following: First, the processes of early neurogenesis establish primary tracts or maps, again globally similar, but locally variant, which provide the gross connectivity between the developing brain and spinal cord and the motorneurons at the periphery. At the same time, these tracts have overlapping and degenerate connections with all modes of sensory input tracts as well—visual, auditory, vestibular, chemosensory, and proprioceptive. These primary connectivities insure that at birth, and even prenatally, infants will exhibit certain preferred perceptual–perceptual, perceptual–motor, and motor–motor configurations. This means that given the anatomy of the fetus or infant at a particular stage in time and a particular patterned flow of energy through the system both as metabolic constraints and through the sense organs, natural behavior patterns will self-organize as stable solutions within that context. There are many examples of such early coordinations: motor coordinations such as sucking, rooting, and hand–mouth contact; perceptual motor coordinations such as head turning toward sound, or imitation of facial expressions seen visually, and intermodal perceptual coordinations such as the visual recognition of objects experienced through another modally (i.e., tactile receptors). What is important about these early topographies is their "soft-assembly," that is, each is assembled only when the infant is in a particular internal (state) and external context, and the components of each response, although preferred in that context, are not obligatory. As development proceeds, some of these early topographies will become more stable, others will destabilize and not be performed, whereas others will be replaced with other organizations as experience carves out more functionally appropriate categories.

The development of leg coordination is a case in point. At birth, and likely much earlier in gestation, infants kick their legs in a relatively coordinated fashion, producing not only regularities of movement within the segments of each limb, but between the two limbs as well (Heriza, 1986; Prechtl, 1986; Thelen, 1985). Studies of the patterns of muscle contraction and the modulation of forces at the joints have shown that the topography of the movement, its time and space trajectory, is a product not just of patterns of muscle firings alone, but of a complex interplay of active and passive components, including the effects of gravity, tissue elasticity, joint architecture, movements of the other segments, and the energy delivered to the legs (Schneider, Zernicke, Ulrich, Jensen, & Thelen, 1989). Patterns are emergent from contextual demands and the inherent structure of the neuromuscular system. Knowing the precise pattern of muscle contractions would not predict anything about the movement trajectory because of the importance of these other elements, whose contributions may be highly nonlinear. Thus, although the primary neural pathways provide the substrate on which the movement is built, the architectural details, so to speak, are emergent from the multicomponent complexity of the system.

This means that within this basic ground plan, variants of the basic kick pattern are inevitable, based on both the anatomical status of the infant, that is, his or her relative fatness, tissue density, muscle strength, joint construction, proportions, and so on, and the immediate context such as degree of motor excitation or variations in posture and support surface. Infants with round, chubby legs and low energy levels produce different kick trajectories than those who are thin, wiry, and tense. The same infant recruits different patterns of muscle contractions when kicking in supine than when reclined at 45° in an infant seat (Jensen, Ulrich, Thelen, Schneider, & Zernicke, 1988).

The second important requirement is that the motor system be in a continual active dialogue with the demands of the periphery. Recent evidence suggests that even at 1 month infants can detect and respond to the dynamic status of their limbs in an adaptive fashion. For example, infants at 6 weeks are able to adjust their interlimb kick pattern in response to a weight perturbation to one leg (Thelen, Skala, & Kelso, 1987). At 1 month, some infants produce well-coordinated, alternating stepping movements when placed on a moving treadmill (Thelen & Ulrich, 1988). Both of these abilities require a dynamic input–output linkage that suggests an exquisite sensitivity to the task environment.

In a selectionist view, then, the variability provides the population of movements from which functional categories are pruned, and the context sensitivity the means by which the pruning is accomplished. The degenerate nature of the primary mapping results in each movement and its variant feeding back into the central nervous system the multimodal sensory consequences of the action. Infants would remap, for example, the prioproception, how each kick "feels," in addition to the visual, tactile, and auditory feedback attendant to the action. Taken together, these would selectively strengthen particular neuronal groups where these common maps intersect. For example, after only a few minutes' exposure, infants whose legs have been tethered to a bright and noisy overhead mobile learn to associate their movements with the contingent actions of the mobile and adjust their kicking accordingly (Rovee-Collier, Morrongiello, Aron, & Kupersmidt, 1978; Thelen & Fisher, 1983).

The functional utility of kicking declines when infants spend more and more time sitting and standing, but in the first 6 months or so, infants do use these movement categories in a variety of functional configurations (Thelen, 1981). These include both expressive and instrumental actions. I presume, although it has not been systematically studied, that individual variability in the natural topographies of movement combined with the idiosyncratic nature of the task environment combine to produce differences in the adaptive motor categories and in their developmental changes. One striking example was an infant whose home had highly polished and slippery wood floors. This infant never crawled but scooted efficiently across the smooth surface on her bottom (Thelen, 1981). The category "scoot" was apparently a more stable attractor than "crawl" and was assembled with available components in response to the particular demands of the situation. The "soft-assembly" feature of the dynamic approach accounts for both these individual eccentricities—the appearance of new forms—and for the disappearance of no longer functional coordinations in the face of new tasks and capabilities.

The long-term motor skills acquired during the first year such as locomotion, postural support, reaching, or manipulation have such universal functions and constraints that it is not surprising that all intact infants reach these milestones. Nonetheless, it is well known that within the large stage-like sequences of motor acquisition there is considerable individual variability in the form and rate of these changes. The combination of dynamic and selectionist principles offers a process account for how both these universalities and these variations can arise. It is worthwhile to consider that such processes also underlie the puzzling acquisition of differences in temperament, cognition, and other traits distinguishing even individuals raised in the same family.

STABILITY AND INDIVIDUAL DIFFERENCES

Several issues are central to considering individual differences. In this chapter I have been concerned largely with how biological systems can develop so as to be globally similar and yet individually variant as a result of their intrinsic complexity and noisiness. Of more immediate psychological relevance are the implications of such dynamical processes to our real-world concerns, especially individual responses to nonoptimal medical, economic, and social conditions.

Stated baldly, a dynamical approach suggests that there will be real limits on our ability to predict long-range developmental outcome from any set of precursor variables, and that these limits are not a function simply of imperfect measurement instruments or incomplete statistical models. Consider again the weather example. Global climate is deterministic when viewed over the span of a year. Local weather is reasonably predictable within a few days, given good enough data. In the range between these extremes, the weather cannot be known. Even if we collect accurate data from all the weather stations in the world and use the largest computer to construct our model, we cannot predict the temperature and whether it will be raining in 2 weeks or 2 months.

Life is constructed from chance events. Dynamical theory says that the critical factors need not be major traumas but small changes in everyday factors at critical times. The chemical gradients of embryogenesis, the concentrations of nutrients and hormones during fetal life, the pepperoni pizza mom ate during her fifth month, the oxygen intake during delivery, the work needed to suckle at the breast—all the normal variation of living organisms—may act as each individual's "Butterfly effect."

This particular statement of sensitivity to initial conditions shares some features of a *critical* or *sensitive* period, or a time during ontogeny when the organism is especially or uniquely open to a specific environmental stimulus (e.g., Bornstein, 1989). There are, of course, many examples of species-typical developmental reorganizations at delimited epochs in the life cycle. Despite the attractiveness of this concept in the early ethological literature, a considerable body of evidence now attests to far more lability and context sensitivity than the original formulation would allow (for review, see Bateson, 1987). Even in the seemingly most "programmed" case—imprinting in birds—a number of endogeneous and exogenous factors dynamically coalesce to make some stimuli especially salient at certain times (Bateson, 1987). Sensitive periods are not precluded in a dynamical framework. An essential component of the approach is that, as development proceeds, the organism is differentially sensitive to internal and external conditions (Thelen, 1989). However, dynamical considerations add to the concept of critical periods by suggesting that, whereas some reorganizations lead to species-typical outcomes, others may, in principle, be unpredictable.

Accepting the inevitability of stochastic events does not, as Plomin and Daniels predict, doom our research efforts into a dead end. Quite the contrary. Dynamical systems theory, and specifically the concepts of stability and change, opens up a number of new ways to explore the developmental process. Instead of considering chance and variability as a problem plaguing our linear models, we can exploit the inherent noisiness of developing systems in a principled way to open windows on the dynamics of developmental change and to explore the limits of predictability. Dynamical systems principles change our fundamental views of the nature of variability in development. When we consider individual differences as noise, residual error, or the aggravating refusal of our subjects to cooperate, we design and interpret experiments that maximize global similarities and emphasize conventional statistical tests for the generalizability of results. When, however, we recast variability as not only the inevitable consequence of the developmental process *but the very pool from which change is sculpted,* we begin to look at the local indeterminancies as well as the global patterns.

These considerations lead to new strategies for conducting developmental research (see also Fogel, this volume).

Relative Stability of Behavior is Itself a Primary Variable of Interest

Recall that complex systems can self-organize into preferred configurations that are a function of the system components and their context. These configurations can be highly stable, as measured by their relative lack of variability and their tendency to return to that configuration when perturbed. The deep sleep of a newborn infant may be envisioned as such a particularly stable attractor (Thelen, Kelso, & Fogel, 1987). Attempts to awaken the infant may cause a temporary stirring, but the system "wants" to stay asleep and quickly returns to that state after the stimulation ceases. A drowsy infant, on the other hand, acts like an unstable attractor. At any point, the infant may be coaxed into wakefulness or may drift into sleep. We could determine the strength of the attractor by such measures as variability in behavioral measures and the time the system takes to settle down to less variable performance.

Dynamical systems theory makes several powerful predictions about complex systems and change. Specifically, the transition from one stable behavioral configuration to another involves a loss of stability. Thus, the transition between sleep and wakefulness can be detected in this unstable state of drowsiness, where the system is both variable and easily perturbed.

Behavioral performance on a developmental time scale may also be envisioned as a series of attractors, that is, coherent configurations that characterize performance. (Traditionally, developmentalists have recognized coherent performance as stages or phases.) *Transitions to new forms can thus be detected as the loss of stability in the developmental trajectory.*

The Individual is the Proper Unit of Analysis

The first requirement of a dynamical strategy, therefore, is to map the developmental trajectories of behaviors of interest to identify where the system reorganizes: where the stability of one state is disrupted and the system seeks a new stable topography.

As developing systems are multidetermined and highly sensitive to the perturbations of each of the component subsystems, the analysis of group outcomes will necessarily obscure the dynamics of the processes. The infant mentioned earlier who scooted but did not crawl eventually walked, climbed, and ran in a similar fashion and at comparable ages as other infants. Neurologically intact infants all learn a natural language, but their strategies of acquiring the language may vary considerably (Bates & MacWhinney, 1987). We learn little about how the system is assembled by studying walking in 18-month-olds or talking in 4-year-olds. In each of these cases, the variability in the strategies is the very key to understanding the convergence of the outcome. When considerable individual differences are expected in the outcome, it is even more crucial to use *individual developmental trajectories* as the primary data source. Once individual developmental paths are identified, it may then be possible to cluster subjects, not on the basis of outcome, but on the basis of route. This means that detailed longitudinal studies are necessary to capture the times of stability and change. Alternatively, it may be possible to conduct intensive observations over a relatively short, but rapidly changing, period, as suggested next.

Processes of Change Can Be Explored When the System Undergoes Transitions

Dynamical theory predicts that at these times of reorganization the system will be variable and highly sensitive to perturbations. At these times, it should be possible to identify those factors that disrupt or stabilize the system and to manipulate them using experimental methods. Here it is instructive to ask whether individuals differ on the parameters that shift them into new forms, and the relative stability or vulnerability of their behavior to individual elements of change.

For example, when infants are supported over a motorized treadmill, they produce well-organized, alternating stepping movements many months in advance of when they normally walk (Thelen, 1986b). The treadmill acts to "self-assemble" the system by providing the mechanical stretch of the leg backward, a skill that infants can do naturally when they can balance and support their weight. This treadmill manipulation identified an important parameter, the simultaneous shift of weight and leg stretch, that is essential for the onset of normal upright locomotion, and by artificially supplying that parameter, shifted the motor system into a new topography. Individual differences in the elicitation of treadmill stepping—some infants stepped as early as 1 month, whereas others were not proficient until 4 or 5 months—were partially a function of basic anatomical differences. Infants who remained in flexed posture and those who rotated inward could not benefit from the leg extension provided by the treadmill. Although all the infants studied by Thelen and Ulrich (1988) eventually stepped on the treadmill and indeed walked normally, there are surely behavioral domains where these early differences might skew the developmental trajectory toward another outcome. In other words, without both mapping the larger changes in behavior and dissecting the sensitive times of change, these convergences and divergences cannot be understood.

Variability is the Source of Adaptive Change

There is increasing evidence that constrained variability—mathematically known as *chaos*—is the source for adaptive flexibility in biological systems (Degn, Holden, Olsen, 1987; Gleick, 1987). This has been suggested for systems as diverse as heart rhythms (Goldberger & Rigney, 1988) and brain activity (Skarda & Freeman, 1987). Chaotic activity, somewhere between complete randomness and strict phase-locking, is believed to endow systems with some deterministic patterning, but with sufficient background variability to be able to instantly reorganize in the face of new, incoming demands. For example, highly rhythmical and synchronous activity is pathological in both heartbeats and brain waves.

It is intriguing to speculate that there is a relation between variability and flexibility on the developmental time scale as well. Is it possible that adaptive functioning is not so much a product of any specific style of response, but of the ability to reorganize quickly and smoothly as task demands change? Individuals may well differ in their ability to keep the system's integrity in the face of life's "butterflies."

The selectionist position has two consequences for research, therefore. The first is the prediction that positive outcomes would be associated with behavioral repertoires that are neither too random nor too rigid. The second prediction is that during ontogeny there ought to be a selective loss of forms as well as the overall increase in complexity. There is certainly evidence for such a process in some domains, mainly speech and language.

If a selectionist account is to be verified, that is, if children are truly pruning from a larger universe of behavior in response to functional demands, quantifying the changes in behavioral variability is essential. This means, then, not just disregarding the movements or responses that are disorganized or "wrong," but including them in the corpus of what is to be explained. This, of course, was the essence of Piaget's method, and it is used extensively by those studying language. A rigorous demonstration of the elimination of forms in other domains would go a long way to explain the dynamic processes of change in early life.

SUMMARY

It is through ontogenetic processes that all members of a species are both alike and different. I have argued here that differences are created through processes that can now be understood through the study of nonlinear dynamical systems and of the instantiation ont. The essential nonlinearity of dynamical systems means that sources of development cannot be partitioned into the static entities of genes and environment. Rather, the process itself must be the focus of investigation. The key to operationalizing dynamical principles is the mapping of stability and change and exploiting instabilities to explore how new forms emerge in both the individual and the species.

ACKNOWLEDGMENT

I am grateful to George Butterworth, Carol Eckerman, Alan Fogel, Susan Oyama, and the Editors, Jeff Fagen and John Colombo, for their most helpful comments on the first version of this chapter. These kind people are not responsible, however, for any remaining excesses. Preparation of this chapter was supported by a Research Scientist Development Award from the National Institutes of Mental Health.

REFERENCES

Bates, E., & MacWhinney, B. (1987). Competition, variation, and language learning. In B. MacWhinney (Ed.), *Mechanisms of language acquisition* (pp. 157–193). Hillsdale, NJ: Lawrence Erlbaum Associates.

Bateson, P. P. G. (1987). Imprinting as a process of competitive exclusion. In J. P. Raischecker & P. Marler (Ed.), *Imprinting and cortical plasticity* (pp. 151–168). New York: Wiley.

Bertalanffy, L. von (1968). *General system theory*. New York: Braziller.

Bornstein, M. H. (1989). Sensitive periods in development: Structural characteristics and causal interpretations. Psychological Bulletin, *105*, 179–197.

Brent, S. B. (1978). Prigogine's model for self-organization in nonequilibrium systems: Its relevance for developmental psychology. *Human Development, 21*, 374–387.

Cooke, J. (1986). Permanent distortion of positional system of *Xenopus* embryo by brief early perturbation in gravity. *Nature, 319*, 60–63.

Cowan, W. M. (1978). Aspects of neural development. *International Review of Physiology, 17*, 150–191.

Degn, H., Holden, A. V., & Olsen, L. F. (1987). *Chaos in biological systems*. New York: Plenum Press.

Edelman, G. M. (1987). *Neural Darwinism: The theory of neuronal group selection*. New York: Basic Books.

Falbo, T., & Polit, D. F. (1986). Quantitative review of the only child literature: Research evidence and theory development. *Psychological Bulletin, 100*, 176–189.

Fogel, A., & Thelen, E. (1987). The development of expressive and communicative action in the first year: Reinterpreting the evidence from a dynamic systems perspective. *Developmental Psychology, 23*, 747–761.

French, V., Bryant, P. J., & Bryant, S. V. (1976). Pattern regulation in epimorphic fields. *Science, 193*, 969–981.

Gierer, A. (1981). Generation of biological patterns and form: Some physical, mathematical, and logical aspects. *Progress in Biophysics and Molecular Biology, 37*, 1–47.

Gleick, J. (1987). *Chaos: Making a new science*. New York: Viking.

Goldberger, A. L., & Rigney, D. R. (1988). Sudden death is not chaos. In J. A. S. Kelso, A. J. Mandell, & M. F. Shlesinger (Eds.), *Dynamic patterns in complex systems* (pp. 248–264). Singapore: World Scientific.

Goodwin, B. C., & Trainor, L. E. H. (1985). Tip and whorl morphogenesis in *Acetabularia* by calcium-regulated strain fields. *Journal of Theoretical Biology, 117*, 79–106.

Heriza, C. (1986). *The organization of spontaneous movements in premature infants*. Unpublished doctoral dissertation, Southern Illinois University.

Horowitz, F. D. (1987). *Exploring developmental theories: Toward a structural/behavioral model of development*. Hillsdale, NJ: Lawrence Erlbaum Associates.

Ito, M. (1986). Neural systems controlling movement. *Trends in Neuro Sciences, 9*, 515–518.

Jensen, J. L., Ulrich, B. D., Thelen, E., Schneider, K., & Zernicke, R. F. (1988). Posture-related changes in lower limb intersegmental dynamics in spontaneous kicking in 3-month-old infants. *Abstracts*, Annual Meeting, Society for Neurosciences, Toronto.

Kelso, J. A. S., Mandell, A. J., & Shlesinger, M. F. (1988). *Dynamic patterns in complex systems*. Singapore: World Scientific.

Kitchener, R. F. (1982). Holism and the organismic model in developmental psychology. *Human Development, 25*, 233–249.

Kugler, P. N., & Turvey, M. T. (1987). *Information, natural law, and the self-assembly of rhythmic movement*. Hillsdale, NJ: Lawrence Erlbaum Associates.

Lerner, R. M. (1978). Nature, nuture, and dynamic interaction. *Human Development, 21*, 1–20.

Madore, B. F., & Freedman, W. L. (1987). Self-organizing structures. *American Scientist, 75*, 252–259.

Mittenthal, J. E. (1981). The rule of normal neighbors: A hypothesis for morphogenetic pattern regulation. *Developmental Biology, 88*, 15–26.

Overton, W. F. (1975). General systems, structure, and development. In K. F. Riegel & G. C. Rosenwald (Eds.), *Structure and transformation: Developmental and historical aspects* (pp. 61–81). New York: Wiley.

Oyama, S. (1985). *The ontogeny of information: Developmental systems and evolution*. Cambridge: Cambridge University Press.

Plomin, R., & Daniels, D. (1987). Why are children in the same family so different from one another? *Behavioral and Brain Sciences, 10*, 1–16.

Prechtl, H. F. R. (1986). Prenatal motor development. In M. G. Wade & H. T. A. Whiting (Eds.), *Motor skill development in children: Aspects of coordination and control* (pp. 53–64). Dordrecht (Netherlands): Martinus Nijhoff.

Prigogine, I., & Stengers, I. (1984). *Order out of chaos: Man's new dialogue with nature*. New York: Bantam Books.

Rasmussen, N. (1987). A new model of developmental constraints as applied to the *Drosophila* system. *Journal of Theoretical Biology, 127*, 271–299.

Rovee-Collier, C. K., Morrongiello, B. A., Aron, M., & Kupersmidt, J. (1978). Topographical response differentiation and reversal in 3-month-old infants. *Infant Behavior and Development, 1*, 323–333.

Sameroff, A. J. (1983). Developmental systems: Contexts and evolution. In P. H. Mussen (Ed.), *Handbook of child psychology, 4th ed. Vol. I. History, theory, and methods* (pp. 237–294). New York: Wiley.

Satoh, N. (1985). Recent advances in our understanding of the temporal control of early embryonic development in amphibians. *Journal of Embryology and Experimental Morphology, 89*, Supplement, 257–270.

Schneider, K., Zernicke, R. F., Ulrich, B. D., Jensen, J. L., & Thelen, E. (1989). Understanding movement control in infants through the analysis of limb intersegmental dynamics. Submitted for publication.

Schoner, G., & Kelso, J. A. S. (1988). Dynamic pattern generation in behavioral and neural systems. *Science, 239,* 1513–1520.

Skarda, C. A., & Freeman, W. J. (1987). How brains make chaos in order to make sense of the world. *Behavioral and Brain Sciences, 10,* 161–173.

Thelen, E. (1981). Kicking, rocking, and waving: Contextual analysis of rhythmical stereotypies in normal human infants. *Animal Behaviour, 29,* 3–11.

Thelen, E. (1985). Developmental origins of motor coordination: Leg movements in human infants. *Developmental Psychobiology, 18,* 1–22.

Thelen, E. (1986a). Development of coordinated movement: Implications for early human development. In M. G. Wade & H. T. A. Whiting (Eds.), *Motor skill development in children: Aspects of coordination and control* (pp. 107–124). Dordrecht (Netherlands): Martinus Nijhoff.

Thelen, E. (1986b). Treadmill-elicited stepping in seven-month-old infants. *Child Development, 57,* 1498–1506.

Thelen, E. (1989). Self-organization in developmental processes: Can systems approaches work? In M. Gunnar & E. Thelen (Eds.), *Systems and development: The Minnesota Symposium on Child Psychology* (Vol. 22, pp. 77–117). Hillsdale, NJ: Lawrence Erlbaum Associates.

Thelen, E., & Fisher, D. M. (1983). From spontaneous to instrumental behavior: Kinematic analysis of movement changes during very early learning. *Child Development, 54,* 129–140.

Thelen, E., Kelso, J. A. S., & Fogel, A. (1987). Self-organizing systems and infant motor development. *Developmental Review, 7,* 39–65.

Thelen, E., Skala, K., & Kelso, J. A. S. (1987). The dynamic nature of early coordination: Evidence from bilateral leg movements in young infants. *Developmental Psychology, 23,* 179–186.

Thelen, E., & Ulrich, B. D. (1988). *Hidden precursors to skill: The development of treadmill stepping during the first year.* In preparation.

Waddington, C. H. (1972). Form and information. In C. H. Waddington (Ed.), *Towards a theoretical biology* (Vol. 4, pp. 109–145). Edinburgh, Edinburgh University Press.

West, B. (1988). Fractal models in physiology. In J. A. S. Kelso, A. J. Mandell, & M. F. Shlesinger (Eds.), *Dynamic patterns in complex systems* (pp. 236–247). Singapore: World Scientific.

Wolff, P. H. (1987). *The development of behavioral states and the expression of emotions in early infancy: New proposal for investigation. Chicago: University of Chicago Press.*

Yates, F. E. (Ed.) (1987). *Self-organizing systems: The emergence of order.* New York: Plenum Press.

3   Genetic Contributions to Early Individual Differences

Lee A. Thompson
Case Western Reserve University

INTRODUCTION

Behavioral genetic concepts and theories have existed for well over 100 years but have only recently been applied to the study of infancy. Behavioral geneticists seek to explain variation in behavior as opposed to normative development. Developmental psychologists have not been interested in individual differences in infancy; therefore, research on these issues was sparse. The general lack of research on individual differences in infancy can be traced to two main factors. First, individual variation is less marked in infancy than later in life because of the highly canalized nature of infant development. Second, behavioral differences among infants are difficult to measure reliably and accurately. However, the last two decades have discovered that individual differences in infant behavior do exist and can be measured, as evidenced by this volume. Happily, behavioral genetics has also begun to pay increasing attention to the study of infancy.

The goal of this chapter is to provide empirical examples from ongoing studies that illustrate behavioral genetic approaches for explaining individual variation in development. The chapter foregoes a broad overview of the field and refers readers to Plomin's book, *Development, Psychology and Genetics* (1986a), which provides a complete and detailed explanation and overview of the field, and to a chapter by Scarr and Kidd (1983), which adds an evolutionary perspective. An exhaustive review of behavioral genetic research in infancy is not attempted; other encyclopedic reviews are available (see Plomin, 1987). Instead, this focus is on recent studies in the areas of language acquisition, temperament, and cognitive development. The studies serve as illustrations for the usefulness of behavioral genetic methodology in the pursuit of understanding the process of development. Several of these studies also provide good examples of the utility of structural equation modeling and multivariate analyses. Behavioral genetic research in infancy is accumulating rapidly, and this chapter also serves as an update.

DEVELOPMENTAL BEHAVIORAL GENETICS

Beginning in the 1970s behavioral genetic studies of infancy began to emerge; but, perhaps most important for the study of infancy was the birth of the interdisciplinary field of developmental behavioral genetics that explores genetic and environmental influences on individual differences across development. A key concept in the field is that of genetic change across the life-span. Behavior changes rapidly during infancy, providing a wonderful opportunity to study the interplay of genetic and environmental contributions. Furthermore, as developmental researchers began to explore variation in infancy, more detailed and reliable measures evolved thus allowing a wider variety of behaviors to be studied.

It is clear that the research conducted by developmental researchers has profound implications for the behavioral geneticist, but what has behavioral genetics offered the field of developmental psychology? This chapter provides evidence that behavioral genetics has made significant empirical contributions to the knowledge base on infant development as well as important theoretical and methodological contributions. One of the drawbacks of studying individual differences as opposed to normative development is the relative lack of theoretical guidance. Behavioral genetics, however, brings with it the maturity and completeness of quantitative genetic theory that can provide definite hypotheses about direction and size of effects (Plomin, 1987).

Methodologically, behavioral genetic designs provide the researcher with a great deal of power. Sample sizes must be large, careful attention must be paid to sample selection and distributions, and most behavioral genetic studies are multivariate, thus providing a rich source of data. Behavioral genetic analyses are characterized by powerful and sophisticated statistical techniques such as structural equation modeling and multivariate analyses. These techniques allow the data to be used to its fullest potential.

Behavioral geneticists strive to understand the role of both genes and environment on behavioral development. In fact, the field may have more promise for an in-depth understanding of the environment than it does for genetic effects (Scarr & McCartney, 1983; Wachs, 1983). Although a great deal of attention has been paid to the study of the environment, true environmental effects can only be seen if genetic effects are understood and accounted for first. Behavioral genetic designs provide this control.

Human behavioral genetic research uses naturally occurring populations to control the genetic similarity of individuals. The three basic designs most commonly used are the family, twin, and adoption studies. Each of the designs are briefly described. However, the interested reader should see Plomin, DeFries, and McClearn (1990) for an in-depth explanation of the designs and their assumptions.

Family Studies.   Family studies allow parents and their offspring, and siblings to be compared. Parent/offspring relationships are composed of additive genetic variance as well as shared family environmental experiences. Siblings share on average 50% of their additive genetic makeup, 25% dominance variation and shared environmental influences. In humans the family design does not allow genetic and environmental components to be separated, but familial resemblance is a prerequisite for the operation of genetic influences. Genetic influences and shared family environmental experiences make family members similar to each other. If family members do not resemble one another, then neither genetic nor shared family environment can be important.

Estimates of familiality (family resemblance) are typically calculated by regressing offspring scores on parent scores or by correlating one sibling with another. Assortative mating occurs when parents are similar to each other for a trait of interest and is easily assessed by examining spouse correlations. For instance, people tend to mate assortatively for height; in other words, tall men tend to marry tall women. If the parents are highly similar, then the single parent/offspring relationship becomes inflated because the relationship includes not only the genetic similarity between that parent and their child, but also a portion of the genetic similarity between the child and the other parent. However, if the parents' scores are averaged creating a midparent score, then assortative mating is no longer an issue (Falconer, 1973). The regression of the midparent score on the offspring score estimates 100% of the additive genetic variance plus shared family environmental influences.

Twin Studies.   Twin studies are more powerful than family studies in that genetic effects can be separated from the environment. The design hinges on the fact that identical twins share 100% of their genetic makeup and fraternal twins only share on average 50% of their genes. If a given trait is genetically influenced, then identical twins should resemble each other to a greater extent than fraternal twins; the identical twin correlation should be greater than the fraternal twin correlation. Heritability (h^2) represents the portion of variance due to genetic effects and can be estimated by subtracting the fraternal twin intraclass correlation from the identical twin correlation and doubling the difference. Identical twin similarity is due to both shared genes and shared environment. Shared family environmental influences (e_c^2) can be estimated by subtracting h^2 from the identical twin correlation. For example, if identical twins are correlated .75 for height and fraternal twin are correlated .50, then

$$h^2 = 2(.75 - .50) = 2(.25) = .50 \tag{1}$$

and,

$$e_c^2 = .75 - .50 = .25 \tag{2}$$

Table 3.1 summarizes the components of phenotypic covariance among relatives estimated by different designs.

The twin design assumes that environmental influences are shared to the same extent across the two twin types. Although the validity of the equal-environments assumption has been challenged, studies have failed to show that the assumption has compromised twin study result for major areas of interest such as intelligence and personality (Plomin et al., 1990).

Adoption Studies.   The adoption design also allows genetic and environmental effects to be separated and is one of the most powerful designs available for studying human behavior. The design compares an adopted child to biological parents who do not share any of the environmental experiences with the child, and with adoptive parents who do not share any genetic similarity with the child. If the child resembles biological relatives, then genetic influences are implicated. If the child resembles the adoptive relatives, then the effects of shared family environment are directly estimated. Adoption designs also allow unrelated siblings reared together to be studied.

Two major issues in adoption studies are the age of placement and selective placement. For the adoption design to be valid, adopted children should be

TABLE 3.1
Components of Phenotypic Covariance of Relatives

V_A = Additive Genetic
V_D = Dominance
V_{Ec} = Shared (Common) Family Environment

	V_A		V_D		V_{Ec}
parent/offspring	1/2	+	0	+	$V_{Ec(PO)}$
biological parent/ adopted away offspring	1/2	+	0	+	0
adoptive parent/ adopted offspring	0	+	0	+	$V_{Ec(PO)}$
full siblings	1/2	+	1/4	+	$V_{Ec(ES)}$
half siblings	1/4	+	0	+	$V_{Ec(HS)}$
unrelated siblings	0	+	0	+	$V_{Ec(US)}$
fraternal twins	1/2	+	1/4	+	$V_{Ec(DZ)}$
identical twins	1	+	1	+	$V_{Ec)MZ)}$

Adapted from Plomin et al. (1989).

TABLE 3.2
Summary of Behavioral Genetic Designs

Design	Issues	Studies in Infancy
Family	assortative mating	Eichorn (1969) McCall (1972) Nichols and Broman (1974) Wilson (1983) Daniels (1985) Plomin and DeFries (1985)
Twin	equal environments generalizability of results	Wilson (1983) Falkner et al. (1988) Thompson (1987)
Adoption	selective placement age of placement	Snygg (1938) Skodak and Skeels (1945) Casler (1976) Daniels (1985) Plomin and Defries (1985) Thompson (1987)

separated from their biological parents at birth or shortly thereafter. If the child has contact with the biological mother or father, then the estimates of genetic influence will be inflated. Selective placement, the matching of adoptive parents to biological parents, must also be assessed. Under selective placement, both genetic and environmental influences may be overestimated. If genetic influences are important, the adoptive parent/adoptive offspring relationship will be inflated and the effect of shared family environment will be overestimated. If shared environmental influences are important, the biological parent/offspring relationship will be inflated and the estimate of genetic influence will also be too large.

Table 3.2 summarizes each of the designs just described. Some are more easily conducted, for instance twins are easier to locate than adoptees. Ideally, a combination of data from all three designs should be sought for any research interest. Fortunately, three large ongoing research projects provide family, twin, and adoption data on infancy in several different domains. The three studies are the Louisville Twin Study, the Colorado Adoption Project, and the Colorado Infant Twin Project. Each of these studies is briefly described before data from each is presented.

Current Studies on Infancy

Louisville Twin Study (LTS). The oldest of the three studies, the LTS began in the 1950s and continues today (Wilson, 1983). Twins are first tested at 3 months of age and are followed every 3 months during the first year, every 6 months during the second and third years, and yearly until they reach 9 years of age. The twins receive their last testing at 15 years of age. During infancy, the primary tests administered are the Bayley Scales of Infant Development (Bayley,

1969) through 24 months of age, the Stanford–Binet (Terman & Merrill, 1973) at 30 and 36 months of age, and Bayley's Infant Behavior Record (Bayley, 1969). The study includes close to 500 pairs of twins. In addition to the twins, whenever possible both older and younger siblings of the twins were also included in the study.

Colorado Adoption Project (CAP).   Beginning in 1975, biological mothers were recruited through two Denver-area adoption agencies. All the biological mothers, about 25% of the biological fathers, and both adoptive parents of all the adopted children were tested on a 3-hour battery of cognitive and personality tests. In addition to the adoptive families, matched control families were also selected for testing based on sex of the child, father's age and occupation, and the number of children in the family. Currently, the sample consists of 245 adoptive families and 245 matched control families. Initially, the children in the CAP were tested twice during infancy at 1 and 2 years of age. The children are then followed longitudinally at 3, 4, and 7, phone interviews and tests are conducted at 9, 10, and 11, and plans are being made for subsequent testing until each child can be tested at age 16 years on the same battery that the parents initially received. Whenever possible, a younger sibling in both the adoptive and nonadoptive families is also included in the study. Beginning in 1982, the infants recruited into the study received the Fagan Test of Infant Intelligence (Fagan & Shepherd, 1986) at 5 and 7 months of age in addition to the rest of the testing. The infant tests administered at 1 and 2 years include: the Bayley Scales of Infant Development, Bayley's Infant Behavior Record, the Colorado Childhood Temperament Inventory (Rowe & Plomin, 1977), the Sequenced Inventory of Communication Development (Hedrick, Prather, & Tobin, 1975), maternal interviews, and videotaped assessments. Details about the CAP and extensive data analyses in infancy are reported in Plomin and DeFries (1985).

The Colorado Infant Twin Project (TIP).   The TIP, youngest of the three studies, began in 1985. Currently the study includes close to 200 pairs of twins tested at 7, 8, and 9 months of age. The twins receive a wide variety of tests that are described later, but each test was selected as a possible predictor of later intelligence. Both parents of the twins also receive extensive cognitive testing, including the Wechsler Adult Intelligence Scale (Wechsler, 1981) and a shortened form of the battery of cognitive tests used in the CAP. Further information on the TIP can be found in DiLalla, Thompson, Plomin, Phillips, Fagan, Haith, Cyphers and Fulker (1989).

The three large studies just described provide a wealth of data in infancy addressing many different issues in several domains. This section presents basic results from these studies on three main topics: cognition, language acquisition, and temperament. The next section then shows extensions of the results that lead to new insights through analyses of genetic continuity and correlations, structural equation modeling, and multivariate cross-domain analyses.

Cognitive Development

Conventional Infant Tests.   Bayley Mental Development Index (MDI) scores from the LTS indicate almost no genetic influence on individual differences in cognitive function during the first year and a half of life and little influence from 18 to 30 months of age (Wilson, 1983). Within-pair correlations are substantial but identical twins are not significantly more similar than fraternal twins. In fact, the twin correlations are greater than the age-to-age correlations for the same child; each twin predicts his cotwin's score better than the child her or himself at a later age. Figure 3.1 presents the twin correlations from 3–36 months of age. The mean twin correlations across 3, 6, 9, and 12 months of age are .69 and .63 for identical and fraternal twins, respectively. In contrast the same correlations across 18, 24, 30, and 36 months are .84 and .71. The pattern of correlations suggests that environmental factors are a strong determinant of twin similarity at these early ages with genetic influences beginning to play a small role after 18 months. Nontwin sibling correlations are also available for some of the ages. It is most striking that the sibling's resemble each other significantly less than the

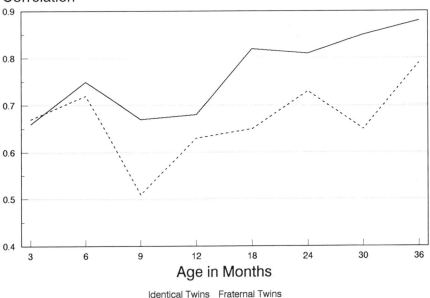

FIG. 3.1. Louisville Twin Study longitudinal correlations (data from Wilson, 1983).

fraternal twins, thus, suggesting that twins share environmental effects unique to twin pairs. Examples of such effects may be testing artifacts: Each twin is tested on the same day, whereas sibling tests are separated by at least a year; or perhaps more likely, twins share perinatal effects and are subject to perinatal problems more often than are singletons.

Another informative approach for studying cognitive development through twin data is to chart longitudinal changes or "spurts and lags" for individual twin pairs. These longitudinal profiles can be used to compute trend correlations for identical and fraternal twins. Figure 3.2 illustrates the pattern of change across three age groupings in the LTS. Trend correlations were computed (Wilson, 1983) for a combination of the 3, 6, 9, and 12 months Bayley MDI scores at .69 and .63 for identical and fraternal twins, respectively. Although these correlations show that twins are very similar in their developmental patterns, no genetic influence is indicated during the first year. Mental development scores at 12, 18, 24, and 36 months were correlated .80 for identical and .72 for fraternal twins ($p < .05$ for the difference between correlations), indicating that genetic factors begin to exert an influence during the second and third years of life. After the infancy period, combining across IQ at 3, 4, 5, and 6 years yields correlations of .87 for identical and .65 for fraternal twins. These trend results suggest that genetic factors become increasingly important after infancy through

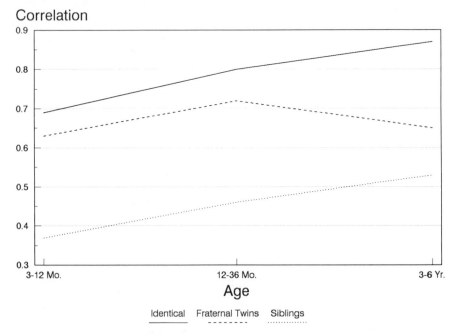

Correlation

FIG. 3.2.   Louisville Twin Study trend correlations (data from Wilson, 1983).

the transition into early childhood; but, once again implicate the role of shared family environment for the substantial twin similarities observed. The trend analyses for 35 pairs of infant siblings also support the previous single-age correlations in that they are significantly lower than the fraternal twin trend correlations during infancy. The 3-, 6-, 9-, and 12-month correlation is .37 and the 12-, 18-, 24-, and 36-month correlation is .46. However, the sibling trend correlation (.55) for early childhood is similar in magnitude to the fraternal twin correlation (.65), lending further support to the effect of perinatal influences that begin to wash out after infancy (Wilson, 1983).

The role of genetic influences on Bayley MDI scores during the first 2 years of life appear at best minimal in the LTS. Furthermore, developmental patterns of change and continuities, although very similar for twins, also appear to be unaffected by genetic factors.

Turning now to results from the CAP, parent/offspring resemblances are examined for 1- and 2-year Bayley MDI scores and parental general cognitive ability. In general the overall results are comparable to other adoption studies involving parent/infant comparisons (Plomin, 1987). The resemblances, separately for biological, adoptive, and nonadoptive mothers and fathers, are .12, .29, .12, .00, .04, and .09, respectively for 12-month Bayley scores and .06, .38, .10, .08, .22, and .21 for 24-month Bayley scores. Nonadoptive parent/offspring resemblance estimates familiality or an upper limit estimate for both genetic and environmental influences; biological parent/offspring resemblance directly estimates the impact of genetic effects, and adoptive parent/offspring resemblance indicates environmental influence. Again genetic influences appear to be minimal during the first year and slightly more important during the second year of life. However, the effect of parent/offspring shared environment also appears to be quite small. Maximum-likelihood model-fitting analyses allow these correlations to be simultaneously analyzed providing a more powerful approach to detect and explain some relationships. These analyses support a genetic hypothesis at 12 months and a combined effect of genes and shared family environment at 24 months of age (Fulker & DeFries, 1983). Plomin (1987) summarizes that about 20% of the variance in Bayley MDI scores is determined by genetic influences and about 10% of the variance can be accounted for by family environment shared by parents and infants.

Finding rather small parent/offspring correlations is not surprising. The interpretation of parent/offspring results requires a slightly different mind set than twin analyses. When twins and/or siblings are tested at the same age using exactly the same measure, it is clear that the resulting heritability and environmentality estimates pertain directly to the trait measured. However, in the case of parents and infant offspring, individuals are tested at drastically different ages on very different measures. When heritability estimates are obtained directly from these comparisons, isomorphism is assumed for the trait in question. This assumption may not be valid, especially in the case of infant intelligence where the predictive power of the infancy tests appears to be quite low especially during the first 12 months of life. The discovery of parent/infant resemblance becomes that much more remarkable, because in the case of the biological parent/offspring comparison it requires not only that genetic influences be important in infancy and in adulthood but that there be some degree of genetic continuity between the two ages. Genetic continuity is discussed later in the chapter.

The results discussed thus far have only involved general cognitive ability in infancy and in adulthood. The CAP data set can also be used to explore specific cognitive abilities and the process of differentiation in cognitive development (Plomin & DeFries, 1985). Four specific ability factor scores are available for each of the parents in the CAP representing Verbal and Spatial abilities, Perceptual Speed, and Memory. Bayley MDI scores relate only to parental general intelligence, not to these four factors. The next step taken was an attempt to isolate specific cognitive components from the items in the Bayley. Lewis (1983) reported on Spatial, Verbal, and Memory/Imitation scales derived from factor analyses of the Bayley items. These factors were created for the CAP infants and then compared to the parental factor scores as well as to general intelligence (Thompson, Plomin, & DeFries, 1985). Again, however, the results indicate that Bayley factors that relate to adult intelligence only relate to general intelligence and not to the specific abilities. These results suggest that infant intelligence is a global, undifferentiated ability, but this hypothesis requires further exploration. Perhaps specific abilities in infancy are very basic and are therefore not captured by the Bayley in enough detail to indicate differentiation. Similarly, perhaps the parental measures are themselves too complex to relate to specific infant skills. Further research is required to explore these issues.

Infant Information Processing. The combined results from the LTS and the CAP are very important and represent the best attempts to study genetic and environmental influences on infant cognitive development to date. However, as mentioned in the last paragraph, the measurement of infant intelligence is not an easy task and advances in test development have been made in the last decade that may shed further light on the etiology of individual differences in infant intelligence. Research on infant visual attention has led to a whole new approach to cognitive development in infancy (see also chapters by Rose and Feldman, Fagen, & Ohr, and Colombo & Mitchell, this volume). In particular, measures of visual novelty preference and habituation have been found to be predictive of later intelligence (Bornstein & Sigman, 1986; Fagan & McGrath, 1981; Lewis & Brooks-Gunn, 1981; Rose & Wallace, 1985) more so than conventional infant sensorimotor tests such as the Bayley. An information-processing approach has been taken to explain this continuity; visual attention measures tap basic information-processing abilities such as encoding, discrimination, categorization, and memory. All these abilities are important for performance on intelligence tests later in life (Fagan & Singer, 1983).

Beginning in 1982, the remaining infants recruited into the CAP were administered an early version of the Fagan Test of Infant Intelligence (Fagan & Shepherd, 1986) at 5 and 7 months corrected age. The Fagan Test uses a paired comparisons paradigm to measure visual recognition memory through infants' preferences for novel stimuli. Each of the infants received 4 problems of abstract patterns and photographs of faces at 5 months of age and 6 problems of photographs of faces at 7 months of age (Thompson, 1987). A total of 41 adopted infants and 95 nonadoptive infants were tested. In general, the 5-month Fagan Test did not relate to midparent general cognitive ability. The 7-month Fagan scores yielded midparent/infant regressions of .20, .19, and .16 for biological, adoptive, and nonadoptive parents, respectively. Although the samples are small, the results are encouraging. In general, both the adoptive parent/infant and the biological mother/infant correlations are higher than with the 12-month Bayley MDI scores, thus indicating more continuity mediated both by genetics and by environmental influences. Unfortunately, subject recruitment ended in the CAP in 1985 limiting the sample size for the early infancy measure.

The interesting results generated in the CAP involving the Fagan test prompted the Colorado Infant Twin Project conducted by David Fulker, Robert Plomin, Joseph Fagan, and Marshall Haith. The study began in 1985 and currently involves close to 200 pairs of infant twins and their parents. The primary goal of the study is to identify infant measures that are predictive of adult intelligence through the use of a midparent/midtwin design. In terms of additive genetic variance, the midparent (the average of both parents' IQ scores) to offspring correlation is the same as the longitudinal correlation for the same individual tested in infancy and in adulthood. The design therefore is like an "instant" longitudinal study and allows immediate validation of the infant measures. Using a midtwin score (the average of both twins' test score) rather than a single offspring's score increases the reliability of the infant measure similar to testing the same individual twice. An added advantage of the twin design is that estimates of heritability and shared family environmental influences can also be calculated for all the infant measures. The twins will also be followed longitudinally thus further testing both the predictive validities of the measures and the power of the midparent/midtwin design as a longitudinal model.

Each of the infant measures used in the TIP was selected to be predictive of later intelligence as indicated by previous developmental research. Twins were tested at 7 and 9 months corrected age in their homes on a 1.5-hour battery of tests summarized in Table 3.3. When the infants were 8 months corrected age, families were tested at the Institute for Behavioral Genetics where infants received a test of visual anticipation developed by Haith (Haith, Hazan, & Goodman, 1988). Haith's measure allows the assessment of both a complex visual attention measure, the anticipation of stimulus location, and a relatively simple cognitive-processing measure, reaction time. During this visit parents were also tested. They were administered the Wechsler Adult Intelligence Scale (WAIS; Wechsler, 1981) and a shortened version of the CAP adult battery of specific cognitive abilities (DeFries et al., 1981). The parental measures provide two measures of general cognitive ability, WAIS IQ and the first unrotated principal

TABLE 3.3
Summary of Infant Measures from the Colorado Infant Twin Project

7 and 9 Month Measures: Test	Description	Measure
Fagan Test of Infant Intelligence (Fagan & Shepherd, 1986) Immediate:	10 novelty preference problems	Mean Novelty Preference
Delayed Fagan:	same 10 novelty problems, 30 minutes later using 50% of the original familiarization times	Mean Delayed Novelty Preference

Lateralization:
    Forced choice
    of hand
	6 trials retrieving a toy
	through a hole in a shield
		Hand Preference

Reaching	6 trials reaching for a toy placed on a tray	Hand Preference
Holding (adapted from Caplan & Kinsbourne, 1976)	two identical toys placed in each hand, length of holding time recorded for each hand	Holding Ratio
Orientations	videotape of infant's response to an audiotape of 10 different sounds (dog bark, car horn, etc.)	Percent Trials Oriented
Vocalizations: during play	infant videotaped while playing with a toy alone and with a parent (5 minutes total)	Count of Vocalizations
during orientation videotape	number of vocalizations emitted during the orientation test	Count of Vocalizations
tester rating	tester records number of differ- ent syllable sounds emitted during the test session	Number of Different Vocalizations

Bayley Items:
(Bayley, 1969)
    bell
    rattle
    mirror
    paper play
	infant responds to a bell ring
	infant responds to a rattle
	infant responds to mirror image
	infant manipulates paper
		Pass/Fail
		Pass/Fail
		Pass/Fail
		Pass/Fail

Bayley's Infant Behavior Record (Bayley, 1969)	Tester rating of infant's test taking behaviors	Composite of All Items

component from the CAP battery (CAP IQ). Lengthy descriptions of each of the infant measures are not given here but can be found in the report by DiLalla et al. (1989).

Preliminary analyses are available for 83 of the twin families in the TIP. Each of the infant measures was regressed onto parental WAIS IQ and CAP IQ, where the mean twin score for each measure was regressed onto the mean parental score. The regression results are presented in Table 3.4. Thirteen of the 62 regressions were significant at the 5% level and 44 out of the 62 regressions were positive. The results for the Fagan Test were most striking. The average mid-parent/midtwin regression was .36. This relationship is comparable in magnitude

TABLE 3.4
Summary of Midparent/Midtwin Regressions from the TIP

Infant Measures	7 Months			9 Months		
	WAIS IQ	CAP IQ	N	WAIS IQ	CAP IQ	N
Fagan Test of Infant Intelligence:						
Immediate	0.11	0.08*	80	0.32***	0.40****	78
Delayed	0.16	0.02	58	0.42****	0.31*	60
Lateralization:						
Forced choice	0.04	-0.11	43	-0.02	-0.06	79
Reaching	0.02	0.06	81	0.02	-0.16	79
Holding	0.08	0.02	81	0.09	0.18	78
Orientations:						
Percent Trials Oriented	0.07	-0.02	31	0.00	-0.01	48
Vocalizations:						
Play	-0.05	-0.05	81	-0.02	-0.05	79
Orientation	0.17	-0.14	30	0.07	-0.15	48
Tester Rating	0.22*	0.20	81	0.20*	0.04	80
Bayley Items:						
Bell	0.09	0.23**	74	0.12	0.09	79
Rattle	0.14	0.26**	74	0.16*	0.15	79
Mirror	-0.06	0.00	74	0.05	0.08	79
Paper	0.04	0.04	75	0.03	0.02	79
Infant Behavior Record:						
Composite	0.22*	0.20	81	0.20*	0.04	80

	8 Months		
	WAIS IQ	CAP IQ	N
Haith's Visual Anticipation Test			
Percent Trials Anticipated	0.24*	0.32**	56
Reaction Time	0.11	-0.02	57
Attention	0.00	0.05	56

$*p < 0.05$ (1 tailed); $**p < 0.025$ (1 tailed); $***p < 0.01$ (1 tailed). Adapted from DiLalla et al. (1989).

to that found for the same individual tested in infancy and later in life (Fagan & Singer, 1983), supporting the validity of the midparent/midtwin approach for studying longitudinal relationships.

The most predictive measures from the battery of infant tests included the immediate and delayed Fagan Test, the IBR, total number of spontaneous vocalizations, the Bayley rattle item, a handedness holding ratio, and the percentage of trials accurately anticipated from the Haith test. Each of these test scores were z-scored and summed to form a simple composite score for each infant representing infant IQ. When the midtwin score for this infant IQ measure was regressed on midparent IQ, the relationship was very strong, .45 ($p < .01$) for WAIS IQ and .43 ($p < .01$) for CAP IQ. Although the sample is rather small for reliable calculation of heritability, the twin correlations estimate heritability at .30 and shared family environment at .24. The TIP results are in strong contrast with those reported for the Bayley Scales during the first year of life (Wilson, 1983) as previously discussed.

Language Acquisition

During the latter part of the infancy period one of the most important cognitive developments is the acquisition of language skills. Communicative development has been traditionally approached through a universals perspective, yet individual differences abound (Hardy-Brown, 1983). Behavioral genetics research has made important contributions toward the understanding of the origins of individual differences in the rate of communicative development.

Studies from the CAP have yielded some particularly interesting results. Infants in the CAP received the Bayley at 12 and 24 months of age, which contains many verbal items, a maternal report of the size of the infants vocabulary is recorded at 18 months, and the infants received the Sequenced Inventory of Communication Development (SICD; Hedrick, Prather, & Tobin, 1975) at 24 and 36 months of age.

Baker (1983) conducted a path analysis of verbal and nonverbal Bayley clusters at both 12 and 24 months of age. Parent/offspring results support the results discussed previously involving the Bayley factors (Lewis, 1983): Verbal and nonverbal Bayley clusters do not differentially relate to parental verbal and nonverbal skills. This pattern of results continues to suggest that infant cognitive skills are general and undifferentiated. Furthermore, genetic analyses suggest that the same genetic influences are operating to determine individual differences in verbal and nonverbal abilities at 12 months. At 24 months, the amount of genetic overlap is still large but suggests that some genetic differentiation begins to occur during the second year of life (Plomin & DeFries, 1985).

Although the Bayley does contain many verbal items, an entire test devoted to measuring communicative competence might allow a more accurate assessment of individual differences. Thompson and Plomin (1988) report a series of analyses involving the SICD at 2 and 3 years of age in the CAP. When the SICD was compared to measures of general cognitive ability, Bayley at 2 years and Stanford–Binet at 3 years, and other verbal measures, word diary at 18 months and a separate verbal ability test at 3 years, the SICD was significantly correlated with all the measures. However, the SICD was more highly correlated with general cognitive ability than with specific verbal tests.

Sibling correlations were also examined for the SICD. Although the sample size was small, related and unrelated sibling comparisons are interesting because they provide direct estimates of heritability and shared family environmental influences. Adoptive sibling pairs are genetically unrelated and any resemblance found between members of unrelated pairs must be due to shared family environment. Nonadoptive sibling pairs are on the average 50% genetically similar and also share the same rearing environment. The heritability of a trait can be estimated from sibling data as it is estimated from twin data (Plomin et al., 1990), by subtracting the unrelated sibling correlation (shared family environment estimate) from the related pair correlation and doubling the difference. For 70 pairs of related siblings and 56 pairs of unrelated siblings at year 2, the SICD correlations were .29 and .08, respectively, yielding an estimate of .42 for heritability at age 2. At 3 years, the 53 related pairs and 50 unrelated pairs were correlated at .21 and .10, providing an estimate of .22 for heritability. These results suggest that genetic influences are important for differences in the rate of language acquisition in infancy and early childhood.

Thompson and Plomin (1988) also explored parent/offspring resemblance for parental IQ and specific cognitive abilities as compared with offspring SICD scores. Although the SICD did relate to both IQ and verbal ability in the parents, the SICD/verbal relationship dropped out when IQ was controlled for, suggesting that communicative ability in infancy may be a good representation of general cognitive ability. Parent/offspring model-fitting analyses provide estimates of genetic and environmental influences on the "longitudinal" relationship between SICD and parental IQ. The results from these analyses yield small but significant estimates for genetic influence at age 2 ($h^2 = .19$) and a slightly higher estimate at age 3 ($h^2 = .38$).

The language measures discussed thus far have been widely used and are reliable but sample from a limited window of infant behavior as they assess language from a global perspective. Measures including detailed assessments from naturalistic observations may provide greater understanding of how communicative development is influenced by genes and by specific aspects of the environment. In a detailed analysis of language development, Hardy-Brown and Plomin (1985) examined a subsample of 50 adopted and 50 nonadopted CAP infants at 1 year of age. The assessment of the infants included analyses of videotapes involving mother/infant interactions during unstructured, semistructured, and structured situations. The variables that emerged from the videotaped situations included total vocalizations, vocal and physical imitation, syllable structure, communicative gestures, true words, and others. The videotape variables were combined with Bayley communication items and the word diary measure. A first unrotated principal component accounting for 29% of the variance of all these measures was used as an index of infant communicative behavior.

When the first principal component was related to parental IQ, the nonadoptive mother and father and the biological mother comparisons were significant thus strongly implicating genetic influences. Adoptive infants did not resemble their adoptive parents. Also of interest is the lack of relationship between the infant measure and parental specific abilities; again, general cognitive ability appears to be the most important determinant.

Although the adopted infants communicative ability did not relate to adoptive parents' IQ, some aspects of the language-learning environment were found to be important. Maternal variables that were assessed from the videotaped interactions included total vocalizations, sentence types, vocal imitation of the infant, contingent vocal responding, mean length of utterance, and others. Other measures of the home environment thought to be important for language development were also assessed, such as time reading books with the infant, presence of older siblings, and parental education and occupation. Although not as strong as the genetic effects, two interesting relationships emerged: nonadoptive and adoptive mothers' imitation of infant vocalizations and time spent reading books with the infant. Despite the small size of the environmental effect and the relatively small number of influential variables, these findings are important because they are estimates of "pure" environmental effects. Reports of significant effects of maternal interaction variables on infant behavior may in fact be indirectly determined by genetic factors unless the mother/child pairs are unrelated as in the CAP.

The acquisition of language skills has proven to be a fruitful area of study for behavioral geneticists. Adoption study results including sibling comparisons and parent/offspring comparisons indicate that genetic influences are an important determinant of early individual differences in communicative development. Furthermore, the results also suggest that it may be possible to identify specific environmental variables that affect the process of language acquisition. Language development and the link between other cognitive measures and temperament measures are discussed further later in this chapter.

Temperament

Although a great deal of research has been devoted to the study of cognitive development, perhaps temperament traits are where the most noticeable individual differences in infants and young children can be found. However, the study of temperament is a complex task. During infancy, understanding individual differences in temperament traits has been a challenge not only because of the difficulties inherent in infant testing but because of the lack of guidance to be found in terms of a generally accepted theoretical foundation (Goldsmith, 1983). Some degree of cohesion can be found among theorists beginning in the mid 1970s when temperament began to be viewed as the basic structure on which later personality traits are built. Four different approaches to the study of temperament were compared and contrasted in a roundtable discussion (Goldsmith, Buss, Plomin, Rothbart, Thomas, Chess, Hinde, & McCall, 1987); although these theories still did not agree on many aspects of temperament, most held that important characteristics for temperament traits include emergence early in life, some longitudinal stability, and to some extent genetic determination.

A temperament theory based on behavioral genetic principals is that of Buss and Plomin (1984), which requires that temperament traits be genetically influenced and stable over development. The theory nominates three general traits, emotionality, activity, and sociability (EAS), as the key facets of temperament. Plomin (1986b) presents a review of infancy research temperament from this perspective. Data on infant emotionality has been collected primarily from twin studies. Plomin reviewed four studies that clearly support the impact of genetic influences on emotionality. Parent/offspring adoption data only suggest slight genetic influence on the relationship between biological mothers' 16 PF neuroticism and a parental rating of the adopted-away infants' emotionality in the CAP. Turning to activity, Plomin summarizes the results from six twin studies, one family study, and one adoption study for activity. The studies included a mixture of parental and tester ratings. All the twin studies illustrate strong genetic influence on activity level, yet the parent/offspring data show little support for a genetic hypothesis. Plomin reviewed seven twin studies and one adoption study involving sociability. In infancy, shyness is usually assessed as opposed to sociability. Although the twin studies do not unanimously support the influence of genetic factors, genetic influences do appear to be important for individual differences in shyness early in life. The one adoption study indicates that genes and shared family environment are important for shyness. Plomin concludes that only the EAS traits indicate a consistent pattern of genetic influences across studies.

Goldsmith (1983) reviews studies examining genetic influences on personality in adults and in children. Goldsmith concludes that research supports the effect of moderate genetic influences across age with the strongest evidence found for the EAS dimensions as postulated by Buss and Plomin. However, he points out that the effect is somewhat weaker in infancy and discusses the problems of generalizing across studies where different instruments were used, where test reliability may be weak, and where small sample sizes were used as is the case with many infant temperament studies. Given the caveats outlined by Goldsmith and the thorough nature of his review, this chapter instead focuses again on the LTS and the CAP, two studies that avoid many of these problems.

The primary instrument used to assess temperament dimensions in the LTS is Bayley's IBR. The IBR is a particularly important assessment tool because it does not involve parental ratings of the infant's behavior; parental ratings may bias familial comparisons. The IBR is administered at 3, 6, 9, 12, 18, and 24 months of age, is a tester rating of the behaviors evidenced by the infant during the Bayley Scales, and yields three factors (Matheny, 1980): Task Orientation, Test Affect–Extraversion, and Activity. Within the LTS, interobserver reliabilities for the three factors were reported as .82, .87, and .79, respectively (Matheny, 1983).

To summarize the impact of genetic and environmental influences on the three IBR factors, Task Orientation shows significant genetic effects at all six ages, Affect Extraversion appears to be genetically influenced at 6, 12, 18, and 24 months, and Activity is genetically influenced at 18 and 24 months (Matheny, 1980). Although these single-age results are interesting, perhaps as with the cognitive data, patterns of continuity and change may be more informative. Matheny (1983) reports both the age-to-age correlations for the IBR factors as well as profile correlations. The matrix of age-to-age correlations indicates an overall simplex pattern for all three factors with significant but low-to-moderate correlations that increase in magnitude with age. The pattern of results suggests the importance of change especially during the early stages of infancy. The profile analyses indicate to what extent genetic differences determine differences in patterns of change over age. For all three factors across two overlapping age spans (6, 12, and 18 months; 12, 18, and 24 months), identical twins are more similar in their profiles than fraternal twins, thus indicating that genetic influences are at least in part helping to regulate developmental change and continuity.

In 1976, the LTS began to focus on the study of temperament rather than cognition (Wilson & Matheny, 1986). Videotaped laboratory assessments were incorporated into the testing sessions. Laboratory variables included emotional tone, attention, activity, and orientation to the staff. The laboratory variables when compared with variables from maternal questionnaire variables displayed a similar set of "core" temperament variables. Twin analyses indicate that genetic influences were minimal over the first year becoming significant at about 18 months of age. Although profile analyses followed the same pattern, with genetic influences showing the sharpest impact beginning at 18 months, overall the profiles indicated greater concordance for identical twins.

The results from the LTS suggest little stability for the IBR temperament measures even within the short infancy period. Age-to-age correlations in the CAP replicate these findings; 12 and 24 month IBR factors show only low correlations. This finding would predict that infant to adult comparisons, because they involve a much larger age span, will show no resemblance. Parent/offspring data from the CAP support this prediction (Plomin & DeFries, 1985). Parental personality measures in the CAP include Cattell's 16 Personality Factor Questionnaire (16PF; Cattell, Eber, & Tatsuoka, 1970) and self-report and mate ratings on the EASI Temperament Survey of Buss and Plomin (1975). Infant temperament ratings were collected using a parental rating, the Colorado Child-hood Temperament Inventory (CCTI; Rowe & Plomin, 1977), a synthesis of the EASI and New York Longitudinal Study (NYLS; Thomas & Chess, 1977), and tester ratings of the infants on the IBR. Another tester rating was collected by rating videotaped observations of mother/infant interactions using a modified version of the IBR (Plomin & DeFries, 1985). Parent personality measures are in general poor predictors of their infants' temperament characteristics. Little evidence was found for either genetic or environmental influence, and Plomin and DeFries report the overall average correlation for all the parental person-ality/infant temperament comparisons to be .08. It is interesting to note that this finding is true for infant behaviors as rated by the parents and by testers. As stated earlier, however, given the lack of stability from 12 to 24 months, the results are not surprising.

Despite the general finding of little continuity, a specific result did emerge that indicates some genetic influence for one temperament trait, sociability (Daniels & Plomin, 1985; Plomin & DeFries, 1985). Biological mother self-reported sociability is significantly related to 24-month-old adopted-away infant sociability (or shyness) as reported by the adoptive parents. Significant rela-tionships between adoptive parent sociability and infant sociability are found at both 12 and 24 months, indicating that environmental influences are also impor-tant. The control family relationships replicate these findings. These findings are noteworthy for two reasons. First, any glimmer of continuity in personality development from infancy to adulthood stands out because so little evidence has been found. Such continuity, even when relatively small, can be important because it implies some overlap in the genetic contributions to the trait at both ages. In other words, biological mother/infant resemblance requires that genetic influences are not only operating within each age but that a portion of the genetic influences operating in infancy continue to operate in adulthood. This issue is discussed in more depth in the next section. Second, shyness may be a particu-larly enduring aspect of personality.

Related to shyness, recent work by Kagan (Kagan, Reznick, & Snidman, 1986) has suggested that behavioral inhibition is manifested early in life, shows marked continuity across age, and is biologically based. A preliminary report from the LTS (Matheny, 1988) on ratings of twins' behaviors pertaining to behavioral inhibition across 18, 24, and 30 months indicate moderate stability and significant genetic influence. Furthermore, profile analyses indicate that genetic influences are also important for changes in inhibition across develop-ment.

McCall concludes in his summary of the roundtable discussion on tempera-ment (Goldsmith et al., 1987: p. 526).

This attempted synthesis of definitions suggests a specific empirical strategy. Mea-sures should be devised for all the major content domains embraced by the concept of temperament with the requirement that each be assessed in different situations and contexts and at different ages on the same individuals (and, ideally, on kinship groups to determine heritabilities). Factor-analytic methods should be applied within and across ages (e.g., three-mode factor analysis, structural equations) to describe the breadth of each temperamental dimension; possible differentiation over age; a common core of temperamental dimensions spanning the ages, if such exist in coherent fashion; and developmental changes in the structure of temperament. In the long run, such empirical description will be far more useful than a priori quibbling about many aspects of the definition.

Behavioral genetic studies of infant temperament have used an empirical strategy and have thus provided much useful information about the nature of temperament during infancy.

MODELS OF DEVELOPMENT

This chapter has thus far outlined genetic and environmental contributions to individual differences in three major areas of behavior in infancy: cognition, language acquisition, and temperament. However, the results have been presented at separate ages within each domain painting a static picture of individual differences. The appeal of developmental behavioral genetics is the dynamic nature of the approach. Delineating and dissecting behavioral changes and continuities across development will provide a more accurate and complete picture of the complexities involved. In this section empirical examples of genetic continuity and change, genetic correlations, and cross-domain relationships are explored.

Genetic Continuity

Twin data can estimate heritability and the effect of environmental influences at specific ages. Profile analyses from the LTS have illustrated the usefulness of longitudinal twin data for outlining continuities and changes across the period of infancy in terms of genetic influences. Parent/offspring adoption data provide estimates of genetic and environmental continuity from infancy to adulthood. As shown in the previous section, each of these correlational analyses has been informative. However, a model-fitting procedure involving maximum-likelihood estimations would allow the twin and adoption data to be analyzed simultaneously and would have greater power to detect relationships. Furthermore, model-fitting approaches require explicit specification of the genetic model and also allow alternative models to be accepted or rejected by comparing differences in goodness-of-fit estimates. DeFries, Plomin, and LaBuda (1987) developed a model that allows the simultaneous analysis of twin and adoption data.

The DeFries et al. model is primarily concerned with estimating the extent to which stability in cognitive development is determined genetically. Central to genetic stability is the concept of the genetic correlation (Plomin, 1986a). A genetic correlation represents the overlap in genetic variance for the same trait at two different ages. For instance, in the case of the biological parent/adopted infant comparison, phenotypic resemblance requires that the trait be genetically influenced both in infancy and in adulthood, and that some of the same genetic influences be operating at both ages. Therefore, the phenotypic correlation between a biological parent and their adopted-away offspring can be expressed as follows:

$$r_{pc} = .5h_c h_a r_G, \qquad (3)$$

where r_{pc} is the parent/offspring correlation, h_c and h_a are the square root of heritability in childhood and adulthood, respectively, and r_G is the genetic correlation from childhood to adulthood. Figure 3.3 illustrates the biological parent/offspring relationship assuming a genetic correlation of one on the left and allowing for genetic change on the right. To the extent that the genetic correlation is less than one, genetic change is implied. Notice in the third equation that

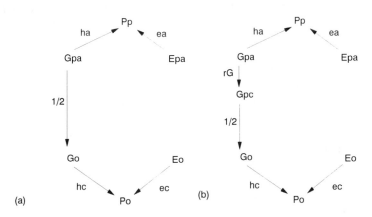

FIG. 3.3. Path diagrams illustrating complete genetic continuity and genetic change: (a) assumes that the genetic correlation is equal to 1, the same genes are influencing the trait in adulthood and in childhood; (b) allows for genetic change to be operating by estimating the genetic correlation (r_G). P_P, P_O = phenotypes of the parent and child; G_{Pa}, G_{Pc}, G_O = genotypes of the parent as an adult and as a child and of the offspring; E_{Pa}, E_O = environments of the parent and of the child; h_a, h_c = square root of the heritability of the trait in adulthood and in childhood; e_a, e_c = path coefficients for the effect of the environment in adulthood and in childhood; ½ = the degree of genetic resemblance between single parents and their offspring in the absence of assortative mating; r_G = genetic correlation between the trait in adulthood and in childhood.

the phenotypic correlation could be relatively small and the amount of genetic overlap (r_G) could still be substantial. Similarly, genetic influences operating in childhood could be minimal but, if the same genes are influential in adulthood, the genetic correlation would be quite large. For example, the reported correlation between biological parents general cognitive ability and their adopted-away infants' Bayley scores is around .10 (Plomin & DeFries, 1985). Infant twin data from the LTS yield an estimate of about .15 for the heritability of Bayley scores. Adult twin data estimate the heritability of adult IQ to be about .50. Using these estimates in the third equation provides an estimate for the genetic correlation between infant Bayley scores and adult IQ of .75 (DeFries, Plomin, & LaBuda, 1987). Although genetic correlations can be simply estimated from the third equation, the equation does not allow for either assortative mating or selective placement, both of which if significant would have a large impact on the results.

The DeFries et al. model is applied to Bayley MDI scores from the LTS (Wilson, 1983) and the CAP for ages 1–4 years, to CAP parental general cognitive ability, and to published adult twin correlations (.86 and .62 for adult identical and fraternal twins, respectively; Loehlin & Nichols, 1976). The model provides a thorough test of the twin and adoption data in that genetic correlations are modeled explicitly, the effects of both assortative mating and selective placement are accounted for, and a parameter for special twin environmental effects is provided.

Table 3.5 summarizes their results: Selective placement is negligible at all four ages, as is the impact of shared environmental influences as transmitted from parents to offspring. However, shared twin environment does have a large impact on twin similarity for cognitive development during the first 4 years. In other words, contemporaneous experiences and age-linked events play an important role for twin similarity early in life. Heritability estimates increase with age from .10 at age 1 to .26 at 4 years of age. The estimate of genetic stability, the genetic correlation parameter, also increases with age: .67, .85, .79, and .90 at ages 1–4, respectively. However, when the significance of the parameter esti-

TABLE 3.5
Summary of the Parameter Estimates for Genetic Stability in Cognitive Development in the CAP

Parameter	Children's Age in Years			
	1	2	3	4
Assortative mating	.22+.05	.20+.05	.22+.05	.23+.06
Special environment (adult twins)	.83+.02	.83+.02	.82+.03	.82+.03
Special environment (child twins)	.80+.03	.87+.02	.91+.01	.87+.02
Adult heritabilities	.74+.04	.73+.04	.74+.04	.74+.04
Child heritabilities	.32+.25	.41+.11	.43+.07	.51+.09
Genetic correlations	.42+.50	.61+.33	.56+.28	.75+.27

Note.   Adapted from DeFries et al. (1987).

mates are tested through a series of reduced models, the goodness-of-fit does not change appreciably when heritability and the genetic correlation are dropped at 1 year of age, thus, indicating that genetic influences are not significant for Bayley MDI scores during the first year of life.

The overall results from the DeFries et al. model-fitting analysis are striking in that substantial genetic stability is found to be operating for cognitive ability from the age of 2 years on into adulthood. It appears as if many of the same genes that are acting on cognitive development during the latter part of infancy and on into early childhood are also important for cognitive ability in adulthood; yet, heritability is low during infancy and increases with age. Are these results theoretically compatible? DeFries and Plomin (Plomin, 1986a; Plomin & De-Fries, 1985) propose an amplification model for cognitive development. The model predicts that the effects of a set of genes acting in infancy play a cumulative, increasingly important role across age. Genetic effects create relatively small differences in infancy that become magnified with age. The amplification model also appears to explain physical development and possibly some aspects of temperament as well (Plomin, 1986a).

Eaves, Long, and Heath (1986) propose a model that describes development in terms of genetic and environmental effects that either remain constant over time or are occasion specific. The model accounts for the cumulative impact of the phenotype at each age on the subsequent phenotype, whereas allowing for additional genetic and environmental factors to come into play at each age. The model can test various hypotheses about the course of development. Eaves et al. explain that different longitudinal patterns of correlations among relatives can imply the nature of gene and environment action. For instance, if the same genetic effects persist and accumulate over time, heritability will increase and environmental effects will diminish. Conversely, in a model where environmental effects are made continuous and cumulative, genetic effects will decrease if they do not produce comparable long-term effects through phenotypic changes. The Eaves et al. model was fit to twin data from the LTS, and they conclude that continuity in cognitive development and increasing heritability reflect the action of a single set of genes expressed throughout, and that shared family environment changes over time but also has a lasting effect on cognitive development. The Eaves et al. results support the results obtained with a different model previously discussed (DeFries et al., 1987) and also conform to the amplification model of development.

At a practical level, substantial genetic stability from infancy to adulthood seems counterintuitive. After all, the behaviors involved in cognition differ dramatically across development. Genetic stability does not necessarily assume isomorphism for the cognitive processes involved. The genetic effects in infancy and in adulthood may be manifested as different behaviors. DeFries et al. (1987, p. 11) give as an example, "For instance, 'childhood genes' might affect rate of language acquisition, whereas 'adult genes' might affect symbolic reasoning."

However, it is also possible that the same basic processes are involved whereas the level of measurement differs. As discussed earlier, new measures of infant visual attention provide an excellent example of this alternative explanation.

The DeFries et al. paper did not find evidence for genetic effects on Bayley MDI scores during the first year of life. Would a different pattern of results emerge if predictively valid measures of infant intelligence were used instead? Infant 7- and 9-month-old visual novelty preference and parental general cognitive ability scores from a combination of 41 adoptive, 95 nonadoptive families, and 83 twin families were analyzed with an adaptation of the DeFries et al. model (Thompson, 1989). Although the analyses are preliminary due to the small sample sizes involved, the results are promising. Heritability estimates for visual novelty preference during the first year of life greatly exceed the estimates previously found for Bayley MDI scores, and estimates of shared family environment as well as special twin environment are low. A moderate estimate for the genetic correlation is also found at .32. Additional twin family data is currently available and the analyses will be repeated. Meanwhile, the results are promising and strongly suggest that both continuity and change are operating at the process level for cognitive development, and that the continuity from early infancy to adulthood is in part genetically mediated.

Cross-Domain Relationships

Thus far, this chapter has focused on analyses within domains. Behavioral genetic methodology can also explore the etiology of cross-domain relationships. Genetic correlations assess not only the overlap of genetic effects for the same trait across age but can also be used to assess the overlap of genetic effects for different traits. Doubling the difference between identical and fraternal twin cross correlations (twin A's score on trait 1 correlated with twin B's score on trait 2) yields an estimate of the genetic contribution ($h_1 h_2 r_G$) to the phenotypic relationship (Plomin, 1986a; Plomin & DeFries, 1979). Data from related and unrelated sibling pairs can be used in exactly the same fashion. For example, given that language acquisition is an important ongoing process during late infancy and early childhood, to what extent is the relationship between early communication development and infant cognitive development mediated by the same genetic factors? Sibling data from the CAP suggest that the genetic correlation between SICD scores and Bayley MDI scores at 2 years of age is substantial (Thompson, Fulker, DeFries, & Plomin, 1988; Thompson & Plomin, 1988). The related and unrelated sibling cross-correlations are .31 and .13, respectively. Doubling the difference yields an estimate of .36 for the genetic chain of paths, $h_1 h_2 r_G$. Substituting actual estimates for the heritability of 2-year-old SICD and Bayley also derived from sibling correlations, .46 and .61, respectively, allows the genetic correlation to be directly estimated at .68.

Although the bivariate approach aforementioned is relatively straightforward and can be useful when a single variable best represents each trait, many times behaviors are more accurately characterized by a set of variables and a multivariate approach may be a better choice. The cross-domain relationship between temperament and cognitive measures is a good example of this situation. Understanding the interrelationships between cognitive ability, language, and temperament measures is extremely important when assessing infant behavior; yet we know very little about the links between these domains. Thompson et al. (1988) applied a multivariate model-fitting approach to CAP sibling data involving three temperament measures and two cognitive measures. The variables were all measured in 2-year-old related and unrelated siblings and included the Bayley MDI, the SICD, the Task Orientation and Affect factors from the IBR, and an index representing difficult temperament (Daniels, Plomin, & Greenhalgh, 1984). The measures for the most part are moderately intercorrelated. A multivariate genetic analysis proposed by Fulker, Baker, and Bock (1983) was adapted for application to sibling data. The model examined genetic and environmental influences through a components of covariance approach. LISREL IV (Jöreskog & Sörbom, 1978) was used to fit the model to the data and obtain maximum-likelihood estimates.

The results indicate that genetic influences are quite strong and the genetic correlation is high for the Bayley MDI and SICD scores, but not for the temperament measures. Furthermore, shared family environment does not play a strong role in this sample. Surprisingly, specific environmental influences appear to be structuring the cross-domain relationships at the phenotypic level. The pattern of results suggests that events idiosyncratic to each test session are influencing the infant's performance, thus creating the cross-domain relationships observed. In other words, experiences unique to each infant determine their reactions on the cognitive tests and temperament ratings. These experiences might involve previous encounters with strangers and novel situations, their feeding and eating schedules prior to the test session, or even previous parent/infant interactions. Comparable twin data might show an increase in shared environmental influences because twins are tested on the same day at the same time. Sibling tests are separated by several years and family environment might differ markedly for each sib.

Infant researchers realize that temperament has a profound effect on an infant's ability to respond appropriately in the testing situation. However, little research has attempted to tease apart the etiology of the effect. The analysis just described is one small attempt to further understand the nature of important cross-domain relationships. Future work should include comparable twin analyses, and the identification of specific variables that mediate the relationships. A great deal more needs to be done especially on understanding the interface between language, cognition, and temperament.

Genetic Mediation of the Environment

As mentioned previously, behavioral genetic methodology promises to study the effects of the environment as much as genetic effects. Infant research has provided an important example of environmental action. Plomin, Loehlin, and DeFries (1985) used data from the CAP to explore genetic mediation of environment-development relationships. Although the idea of genes influencing the environment sounds paradoxical, it is not hard to see how parental traits, which are in part genetically determined, contribute to environmental variables. For instance, the number of books in the home is correlated with parental IQ and is frequently used to estimate the level of intellectual stimulation provided by the home environment; yet, offspring IQ is also correlated with parental IQ. This effect is an example of passive genotype–environment correlation as described by Scarr and McCartney (1983). Adoptive families provide estimates of the environment-development relationship unconfounded by such genetic effects. While examining the correlations between indices of the home environment such as Caldwell and Bradley's (1978) Home Observation for Measurement of the Environment (HOME), and the Family Environment Scale (FES; Moos & Moos, 1981), and measures of infant cognition and temperament, Plomin et al. discovered that correlations in nonadoptive homes were sometimes significantly higher than those in adoptive homes. They examined 113 environment-development relationships in both adoptive and nonadoptive families. Of these, 34 were significant at the .05 level in either the adoptive or nonadoptive family, 28 of the 34 were greater in the nonadoptive family; 12 of the 28 were significantly greater. In nonadoptive homes, genetic resemblance between parents and their children enhances the relationship between aspects of the home environment and child development. Figure 3.4 illustrates genetic and environmental influences on the correlation between child measures and measures of the environment in adoptive and nonadoptive homes. Although the Plomin et al. findings implicate parental characteristics as the mediating factor for the environment-development relationships, specific parental characteristics were not identified. Furthermore, some environment-development relationships may be affected by genetic mediation more than others.

Thompson, Fulker, DeFries, and Plomin (1986) applied a multivariate extension of the model set forth by Plomin et al. to three environmental and three development variables. Again, the multivariate modeling approach has the added power of simultaneously analyzing the data and provides significance levels for goodness-of-fit. In addition, the environmental variables were chosen to represent different aspects of the environment: The first unrotated principal component for the HOME was used as a general home environment index; a measure of provision for exploration primarily evaluated the physical setting of the home (Gottfried, 1984), and a socioeconomic status measure of the adoptive and

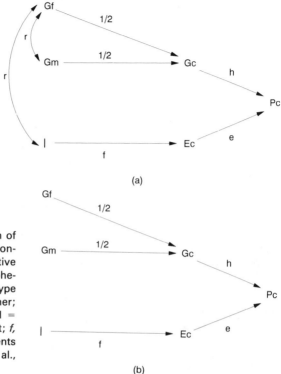

FIG. 3.4. Genetic mediation of environmental effects: (a) Non-adoptive Families; (b) Adoptive Families. P_c = child's phenotype; G_c, G_f, G_m = genotype of the child, father, and mother; E_c = child's environment; I = measure of the environment; *f, e, h,* ½ = path coefficients (adapted from Thompson et al., 1986).

nonadoptive fathers' prestige, income, and education (Hauser & Featherman, 1977) was used as a distal measure of home environment. The infant cognition measures include the Bayley MDI, the SICD, and the IBR's Task Orientation factor. The model-fitting results suggest that environmental measures are important independent of heredity, and that genetic influences sometimes mediate the relationship between environmental measures and measures of children's development. The relationship between the HOME and Bayley MDI and between the HOME and SICD scores appears to be mediated genetically. Interestingly, relationships between infant cognitive measures and the environmental indices tapping physical aspects of the home and socioeconomic status were not found to be genetically mediated. Plomin (1986a) suggests that future studies should focus on the determination of specific parental characteristics that contribute to the HOME index and further use of adoptive families to identify "pure" environmental influences. This analysis is just one example of behavioral genetic research on the environment, a topic that requires an entire chapter of its own.

IMPLICATIONS FOR FUTURE RESEARCH

The behavioral genetic research on infant development discussed thus far has contributed a great deal to the exploration of individual differences in cognition, language development, and temperament. Each of the three large contributing studies, the LTS, the CAP, and the TIP, use different designs yet maintain enough consistency at the measurement level to allow the results from each to be compared and contrasted. The combined power of longitudinal twin data, parent/offspring adoption data, adopted and nonadopted sibling data, and midparent/midtwin analyses provides impressive depth and scope in terms of issues that can be addressed.

A brief summary of the major findings discussed in this chapter include:

1. Twin and adoption studies agree that there is little evidence for genetic influence on cognitive development during the first year of life when conventional sensorimotor intelligence tests are used. Genetic influences become increasingly important during the second year and beyond. Model-fitting analyses support an amplification model of development.

2. In contrast to conventional tests, tests of infant visual attention may be significantly influenced by genetic factors during the first year of life.

3. Individual differences in language development are strongly genetically influenced by the second year of life and share a high genetic correlation with infant cognitive ability.

4. Twin data from the LTS indicate some genetic influence on temperament during the first 12 months of life but show a greater effect starting at about 18 months. Twin profile analyses indicate that patterns of change are determined in part by genetic factors. Parent/offspring adoption data show little continuity for temperament traits from infancy to adulthood with the possible exception of shyness.

5. Adoption data illustrate the importance of controlling for genetic effects when studying the environment. Genetic mediation of environment-development relationships is an important effect during infancy.

The field of behavioral genetics has just begun to be accepted into mainstream developmental psychology. Already, the merging of the two fields has resulted in advances that neither field could have obtained alone, and further collaboration will inevitably lead to further advancements. However, several specific research areas may be particularly fruitful.

Behavioral genetic methods and sophisticated modeling approaches are limited by the level of measurement. Behavioral genetic research will benefit immensely from newly developed infancy measures. The use of the Fagan Test in the CAP and TIP is a good example but should be just the beginning. Recent work in psychophysiological variables in infancy may yield particularly interesting results if collected within a behavioral genetic design. Whenever behavioral genetic studies have gone beyond routine standard assessment, new and interesting results have emerged.

Although behavioral geneticists will benefit from newly developed tests, test development efforts can take advantage of behavioral genetic approaches as well. The TIP has illustrated the usefulness of the midparent/midtwin design as an ''instant'' longitudinal study with the purpose of test validation. Predictive validities and longitudinal continuities can be immediately assessed and used to revise instruments.

Recent advances in the measurement of adult intelligence can be used to study infancy through a behavioral genetic design. Detterman et al. (1988) has recently devised a battery of elementary cognitive tasks that measures adult intelligence in terms of basic cognitive processes. Although research has indicated that infant intelligence is undifferentiated, perhaps basic processing indices in adulthood would allow a finer grained analysis. Comparison of elementary cognitive tasks in parents with newer infant information-processing measures may allow the identification of specific processing abilities in infancy.

Greater understanding of genetic variation can only benefit individual-differences research. Although this chapter has demonstrated that the last decade has found important collaborative efforts between behavioral genetics and developmental psychology, the study of infancy would benefit a great deal if the next decade included further collaboration.

ACKNOWLEDGMENTS

This work was conducted while the author was supported by a grant from NICHD (HD21947-02).

REFERENCES

Baker, L. A. (1983). *Bivariate path analysis of verbal and nonverbal abilities in the Colorado Adoption Project.* Unpublished doctoral dissertation, University of Colorado, Boulder.

Bayley, N. (1969). *Manual for the Bayley Scales of Infant Development.* New York: Psychological Corporation.

Bornstein, M. H., & Sigman, M. D. (1986). Continuity in mental development from infancy. *Child Development, 57,* 251–274.

Buss, A. H., & Plomin, R. (1975). *A temperament theory of personality development.* New York: Wiley-Interscience.

Buss, A. H., & Plomin, R. (1984). *Temperament: Early developing personality traits.* Hillsdale, NJ: Lawrence Erlbaum Associates.

Caldwell, B. M., & Bradley, R. H. (1978). *Home observation for measurement of the environment.* Little Rock: University of Arkansas.

Caplan, B., & Kinsbourne, M. (1976). Baby drops the rattle: Asymmetry of duration of grasp by infants. *Child Development, 47,* 532–534.

Casler, L. (1976). Maternal intelligence and institutionalized children's developmental quotients: A correlational study. *Developmental Psychology, 12,* 64–67.

Cattell, R. B., Eber, H., & Tatsuoka, M. M. (1970). *Handbook for the sixteen personality factor questionnaire (16PF).* Champaign, IL: IPAT.

Daniels, D. (1985). *Understanding the family environment: A study of adoptive and nonadoptive infant siblings.* Unpublished doctoral dissertation, University of Colorado, Boulder.

Daniels, D., & Plomin, R. (1985). Differential experience of siblings in the same family. *Developmental Psychology, 21,* 747–760.

Daniels, D., Plomin, R., & Greenhalgh, J. (1984). Correlates of difficult temperament in infancy. *Child Development, 55,* 1184–1194.

DeFries, J. C., Plomin, R., & LaBuda, M. C. (1987). Genetic stability of cognitive development from childhood to adulthood. *Developmental Psychology, 23,* 4–12.

DeFries, J. C., Plomin, R., Vandenberg, S. G., & Kuse, A. R. (1981). Parent-offspring resemblance for cognitive abilities in the Colorado Adoption Project: Biological, adoptive, and control parents and one-year-old children. Intelligence, 5, 121–130.

Detterman, D. K., Mayer, J. D., Caruso, D. R., Legree, P. J., Conners, F., & Taylor, R. (1988). *The assessment of basic cognitive abilities in relationship to cognitive deficits.* Manuscript submitted for publication.

DiLalla, L., Thompson, L. A., Plomin, R., Phillips, K., Fagan, J. F., Haith, M. M., Cyphers, L. H., & Fulker, D. W. (1989). *Infant predictors of preschool and adult IQ: A study of infant twins and their parents.* Manuscript submitted for publication.

Eaves, L. J., Long, J., & Heath, A. C. (1986). A theory of developmental change in quantitative phenotypes applied to cognitive development. *Behavior Genetics, 16,* 143–162.

Eichorn, D. H. (1969, August). *Developmental parallels in the growth of parents and their children.* Presidential address (Division 7) presented at the meeting of the American Psychological Association, Washington, DC.

Fagan, J. F., & McGrath, S. K. (1981). Infant recognition memory and later intelligence. *Intelligence, 5,* 121–130.

Fagan, J. F., & Shepherd, P. A. (1986). *The Fagan Test of Infant Intelligence: Training Manual.* Cleveland, OH: Infantest Corporation.

Fagan, J. F., & Singer, L. T. (1983). Infant recognition memory as a measure of intelligence. In L. P. Lipsitt (Ed.), *Advances in infancy research* (Vol. 2). Norwood, NJ: Ablex.

Falconer, D. S. (1973). *Introduction to Quantitative Genetics (2nd Ed.).* New York: Longman.

Fulker, D. W., Baker, L. A., & Bock, R. D. (1983). *DATA ANALYST: Communications in Computer Data Analysis, 1,* 5–8.

Fulker, D. W., & DeFries, J. C. (1983). Genetic and environmental transmission in the Colorado Adoption Project: Path analysis. *British Journal of Mathematical and Statistical Psychology, 36,* 175–188.

Goldsmith, H. H. (1983). Genetic influence on personality from infancy to adulthood. *Child Development, 54,* 331–335.

Goldsmith, H. H., Buss, A. H., Plomin, R., Rothbart, M. K., Thomas, A., Chess, S., Hinde, R., & McCall, R. B. (1987). Roundtable: What is temperament? *Child Development, 58,* 505–529.

Gottfried, A. W. (1984). *Home environment and early cognitive development: Longitudinal research.* New York: Academic Press.

Haith, M. M., Hazan, C., & Goodman, G. S. (1988). Expectation and anticipation of dynamic visual events by 3.5-month-old babies. *Child Development, 59,* 467–479.

Hardy-Brown, K. (1983). Universals and individual differences: Disentangling two approaches to the study of language acquisition. *Developmental Psychology, 19,* 610–624.

Hardy-Brown, K., & Plomin, R. (1985). Infant communicative development: Evidence from adoptive and biological families for genetic and environmental influences on rate differences. *Developmental Psychology, 21,* 378–385.

Hauser, R. M., & Featherman, D. L. (1977). *The process of stratification: Trends and analysis.* New York: Academic Press.

Hedrick, D. L., Prather, E. M., & Tobin, A. R. (1975). *Sequenced inventory of communication development.* Seattle: University of Washington Press.

Jöreskog, K. G., & Sörbom, D. (1978). *LISREL: Analysis of linear structural relationships by the method of maximum likelihood.* National Education Resources, Chicago.

Kagan, J., Reznick, J. S., & Snidman, N. (1986). Temperamental inhibition in early childhood. In R. Plomin & J. Dunn (Eds.), *The study of temperament: changes, continuities and challenges.* Hillsdale, NJ: Lawrence Erlbaum Associates.

Lewis, M. (1983). On the nature of intelligence: Science or bias? In M. Lewis (Ed.), *Origins of intelligence: Infancy and early childhood.* New York: Plenum Press.

Lewis, M., & Brooks-Gunn, J. (1981). Visual attention at three months as a predictor of cognitive functioning at two years of age. *Intelligence, 5,* 131–140.

Loehlin, J. C., & Nichols, R. C. (1976). *Heredity, environment, and personality.* Austin: University of Texas Press.

Matheny, A. P., Jr. (1980). Bayley's Infant Behavior Record: Behavioral components and twin analyses. *Child Development, 51,* 1157–1167.

Matheny, A. P., Jr. (1983). A longitudinal twin study of stability of components from Bayley's Infant Behavior Record. *Child Development, 54,* 356–360.

Matheny, A. P., Jr. (1988, June). *Behavioral-genetic analysis of toddler's inhibition across three situations and over three ages.* Paper presented at the meeting of the Behavior Genetics Association, Nijmegen, The Netherlands.

McCall, R. B. (1972). Similarity in developmental profile among related pairs of human infants. *Science, 178,* 1004–1005.

Moos, R. H., & Moos, B. S. (1981). *Family Environment Scale manual.* Palo Alto, CA: Consulting Psychologists Press.

Nichols, P. L., & Broman, S. H. (1974). Familial resemblance in infant mental development. *Developmental Psychology, 10,* 442–446.

Plomin, R. (1986a). *Development, genetics and psychology.* Hillsdale, NJ: Lawrence Erlbaum Associates.

Plomin, R. (1986b). Behavioral genetic methods. *Journal of Personality, 54,* 226–261.

Plomin, R. (1987). Developmental behavioral genetics and infancy. In J. D. Osofsky (Ed.), *Handbook of infant development* (2d ed.). New York: Wiley-Interscience.

Plomin, R., & DeFries, J. C. (1979). Multivariate behavioral genetic analysis of twin data on scholastic abilities. *Behavior Genetics, 9,* 505–517.

Plomin, R., & DeFries, J. C. (1985). *Origins of individual differences in infancy: The Colorado Adoption Project.* New York: Academic Press.

Plomin, R., DeFries, J. C., & McClearn, G. (1990). *Behavioral Genetics: A Primer (2d ed.).* San Francisco: W. H. Freeman.

Plomin, R., Loehlin, J. C., & DeFries, J. C. (1985). Genetic and environmental components of 'environmental' influences. *Developmental Psychology, 21,* 391–402.

Rose, S. A., & Wallace, I. F. (1988). Visual recognition memory: A predictor of later cognitive functioning in preterms. *Child Development, 56,* 843–852.

Rowe, D. C., & Plomin, R. (1977). Temperament in early childhood. *Journal of Personality Assessment, 41,* 150–156.

Scarr, S., & Kidd, K. K. (1983). Developmental behavior genetics. In P. H. Mussen (Ed.), *Handbook of child psychology (4th ed.): Vol. 2. Infancy and developmental psychobiology* (pp. 345–433). New York: Wiley.

Scarr, S., & McCartney, K. (1983). How people make their own environments: A theory of genotype environment effects. *Child Development, 54,* 424–435.

Skodak, M., & Skeels, H. M. (1949). A final follow-up of one hundred adopted children. *Journal of Genetic Psychology, 75,* 85–125.

Terman, L. M., & Merrill, M. A. (1973). *Stanford-Binet Intelligence Scale: 1972 norms edition.* Boston: Houghton-Mifflin.

Thomas, A., & Chess, S. (1977). *Temperament and development.* New York: Brunner/Mazel.

Thompson, L. A. (1987). *Prediction of Adult IQ from Infant Measures of Novelty Preference and Visual Anticipation: Twin and Adoption Data.* Unpublished doctoral dissertation, University of Colorado, Boulder.

Thompson, L. A. (1989). Developmental behavioral genetic research on infant information processing: Detection of continuity and change. In S. Doxiadis (Ed.), *Early Influences Shaping the Individual.* New York: Plenum Press.

Thompson, L. A., Fulker, D. W., DeFries, J. C., & Plomin, R. (1986). Multivariate genetic analysis of 'environmental' influences on infant cognitive development. *British Journal of Developmental Psychology, 4,* 347–353.

Thompson, L. A., Fulker, D. W., DeFries, J. C., & Plomin, R. (1988). Multivariate analysis of cognitive and temperament measures in 24-month-old adoptive and nonadoptive sibling pairs. *Personality and Individual Differences, 9,* 95–100.

Thompson, L. A., & Plomin, R. (1988). The sequenced inventory of communication development: An adoption study of two- and three-year-olds. *International Journal of Behavioral Development, 11,* 219–231.

Thompson, L. A., Plomin, R., & DeFries, J. C. (1985). Multivariate genetic analysis of 'environmental' influences on infant cognitive development. *British Journal of Developmental Psychology, 4,* 347–353.

Wachs, T. D. (1983). The use and abuse of environment in behavior-genetic research. *Child Development, 54,* 396–407.

Wechsler, D. (1981). *Examiner's Manual: Wechsler Adult Intelligence Scale-Revised.* New York: Psychological Corporation.

Wilson, R. C. (1983). The Louisville Twin Study: Developmental synchronies in behavior. *Child Development, 54,* 298–316.

Wilson, R. C., & Matheny, A. P., Jr. (1986). Behavior-genetic research in infant temperament: The Louisville Twin Study. In R. Plomin & J. Dunn (Eds.), *The study of temperament: Changes, continuities and challenges.* Hillsdale, NJ: Lawrence Erlbaum Associates.

4
Analyzing Individual Differences in Development: Correlations and Cluster Analysis

James A. Green
University of Connecticut

INTRODUCTION

Perhaps the most important role for individual differences in the study of development is to help generate and confirm hypotheses about processes of behavior change. Behavior change is the essence of development, yet the processes that effect change do not typically reveal themselves in tidy factorial experiments. Analysis of individual differences in behavior over time is one avenue that can lead toward a better understanding of the mechanisms of development.

To explore how individual differences can inform the study of developmental processes, a distinction must be made between analyses of *developmental functions* and analyses of *individual-difference stability* (see also Emmerich, 1964; McCall, 1977; Sackett, Sameroff, Cairns, & Suomi, 1981; Wohlwill, 1973). A functional relation between behavior and age (or, simply, a developmental function) is a plot of the relation of age to a particular characteristic of the developing organism (e.g., height, intelligence, sociability). Individual differences in developmental functions can suggest ways in which the causal network operates. For example, Sackett et al. (1981) used idealized plots of behavior change to suggest ways in which different developmental processes may be realized in different individuals or groups. McCall, Appelbaum, and Hogarty (1973) analyzed individual differences in developmental functions of IQ scores to find groups of children with similar patterns of change over age. Thus, individual differences in developmental functions can provide insights into differences in processes of change.

Studies of individual-difference stability, on the other hand, focus on the rank order of individuals on a particular behavior or characteristic. Stability, in this sense, indicates that the relative rank order of individuals remains consistent over time and is generally believed to provide empirical evidence of an enduring property, perhaps a fundamental behavioral disposition or trait. Equally important, characteristics that show individual-difference stability may be associated with different kinds of developmental processes than characteristics that are not stable.

Far more effort in longitudinal research has been devoted to the study of stability than to the study of individual differences in developmental functions. This imbalance is unfortunate, as the quest for stability is less directly relevant to developmental process than is analysis of developmental functions (see also Wohlwill, 1973). Perhaps the focus on stability results from the wide availability of methods for its assessment, particularly the Pearson correlation coefficient. In contrast, methods suitable to uncovering individual differences in patterns of behavior change over time are not so well known.

The goal of this chapter is to facilitate progress toward understanding the processes of behavior development by addressing statistical problems and solutions in analyses of individual differences. Problems in the assessment of individual-difference stability via correlations are addressed first. In particular, methods are discussed for testing the difference between two related and unrelated correlations and for testing the difference between two full matrices of correlations (both related and unrelated). The major focus of the chapter, however, is on hierarchical cluster analysis, a method of grouping individuals into relatively homogeneous sets. Cluster analysis is offered as one method of describing individual differences in developmental profiles, that is, individual differences in how behavior changes with time.

COMMON PROBLEMS IN ANALYZING INDIVIDUAL DIFFERENCE STABILITY

To assess individual-difference stability over time, developmental psychologists often use data of the following type: a sample of N individuals is measured on each of P variables at each of T time points. To evaluate whether subjects who score relatively high on a given variable also score relatively high on that variable at a subsequent point in time, the Pearson correlation coefficient is computed between two columns of this three-way data matrix (see Fig. 4.1).

Many of the tests and issues that follow have been discussed by Appelbaum and McCall (1983), Larzelere and Mulaik (1977), and Steiger (1980). Readers should consult these references for a more comprehensive discussion of testing correlations.

Properties of the Pearson Correlation Coefficient

It is worth reviewing briefly several properties of the Pearson correlation coefficient, r. First, r measures only the *linear* relation between two variables. Two

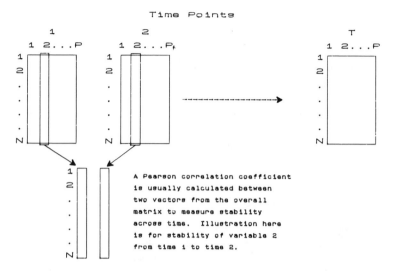

FIG. 4.1. Schematic three-way data matrix from a study with repeated measures.

variables can be strongly related and yet have a low Pearson r because the relation is nonlinear. The simplest way to evaluate the form of relation between two variables is to examine the scatterplot between the two variables. Inspection of the scatterplots can be followed, when necessary, by statistical methods for determining the form of the relation (see, e.g., Draper & Smith, 1981).

A second point to recall when using r to measure stability is that it ignores differences in the means and variances that may exist between the variables at the two time points. Recall that the correlation can be computed as the average cross-product of two variables *after* each has been *standardized,* namely

$$(\sum_{i=1}^{N} z_{ij}z_{ij'})/N,$$

where z_{ij} is the standardized score of subject i on variable j and $z_{ij'}$ is the standardized score of subject i on variable j'. Both variables have been transformed to have means of 0 and variances of 1. When r is used to measure stability, then, *changes over time* in the means and variances of the variables are not being addressed.

Finally, significance testing of r assumes that the variables come from a bivariate normal distribution. In other words, for the significance levels to be accurate, each variable should have a normal distribution by itself and at every value of the other variable (see, e.g., Hays, 1973). Recent studies have indicated, however, that r is robust to all but extreme violations of this assumption (e.g., Fowler, 1987). For aid in determining the sample size required for testing the significance of r at various levels of power, see Kraemer and Thiemann (1987).

Although these properties of r are covered in most introductory statistics books and courses, some of them are frequently ignored in published reports. Especially troublesome are the failure to examine scatterplots for nonlinear relations and the equating of no significant correlation with no association between variables. Another perennial problem is the interpretation of significant correlations, no matter what their magnitude. A correlation of .20, even though it is statistically significant because of a relatively large sample size, means that the variables share only 4% variance in common.

Testing For Significant Stability Across Time

The presence of individual-difference stability is usually assessed by testing whether the correlation between two time periods is significantly different from 0. There are several test statistics for this purpose (see, e.g., Edwards, 1976; Hays, 1973), and statistical software routinely print tests of the significance of r. (Note that some software prints p-values for one-tailed tests. In general, a two-tailed test is desirable, so users should select this option or look up the appropriate p level themselves.)

The most common problem in evaluating individual-difference stability is performing too many tests. It is not uncommon to see 10, 20, or 100 tests of individual correlations performed in a given study. The probability of rejecting the null hypothesis (i.e., no correlation in the population) when it is true (a Type I error) increases greatly when many individual tests are performed, especially when the correlations are related (Hays, 1973). One method of handling this problem is to interpret only patterns of significant relations and avoid interpreting single correlation coefficients. Replication also provides additional evidence of the robustness of the findings when many correlations are tested.

In other contexts, however, individual tests are interpreted only after a significant omnibus test (e.g., in ANOVA). There are similar solutions in testing many correlations, and two of them are reviewed briefly here. Presented first is the Bartlett test for whether an entire matrix of correlations is different from zero, and then a Bonferroni procedure is outlined that can be used for preplanned tests or as a follow-up procedure to the Bartlett test.

Controlling Type I Error in Testing for Stability

Testing an Entire Matrix of Correlations.   A matrix of correlations often occurs in two contexts: First, if multiple age points are studied, the stability of one variable may be assessed between each pair of time points (see Matrix A in Fig. 4.2). Second, a set of variables measured at any given time point may be intercorrelated (Matrix B in Fig. 4.2). This latter matrix is not directly relevant to

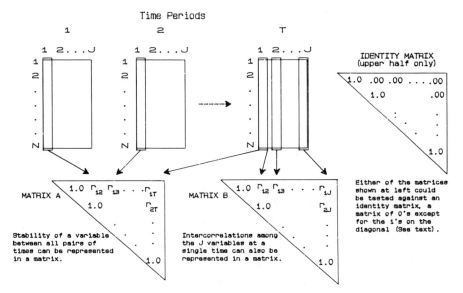

FIG. 4.2. Two different correlation matrices derived from a longitudinal study.

the study of individual-difference stability; however, it occurs frequently in the developmental literature as the basic input to a factor analysis of a set of variables.

Before testing whether each correlation in a matrix is different from zero, an omnibus test can be performed, that is, a test of the hypothesis that all the correlations (except those on the diagonal of the matrix) are zero. The null hypothesis is that the matrix of correlations, in the population, is an identity matrix (see Fig. 4.2). The test statistic for this hypothesis is calculated as $X^2 = -[(N - 1) - (2P + 5) / 6] \times \ln|\mathbf{R}|$. Note that "ln" denotes the natural logarithm, and $|\mathbf{R}|$ denotes the determinant of the sample correlation matrix. Many statistical packages will compute the determinant of a matrix, and several packages actually perform this test as part of their factor analysis procedures.

Under the assumption that the variables come from a multivariate normal distribution, this statistic is approximately distributed as a chi-square variable with $P \times (P - 1) / 2$ degrees of freedom (Bartlett, 1954). If the value is large, the result is significant and the null hypothesis is rejected. If the null hypothesis is rejected, tests that individual correlations are different from zero can be performed at the usual alpha level or the Bonferroni procedure (see following) can be used as a follow-up method.

A Bonferroni Procedure for Testing the Significance of Many Correlations. Another solution to the problem of testing too many correlations, the multistage Bonferroni procedure, was described in detail by Larzelere and Mulaik (1977). In this procedure, one first counts how many correlations are to be tested (for a typical correlation matrix this is $P \times (P - 1) / 2$) and then divides the desired alpha level (usually .05) by the total number of tests to be performed. For example, if one variable is measured at 5 times points, there are $(5 \times 4)/2$ or 10 stability correlations to be tested (Time 1 to Time 2, Time 1 to Time 3, etc.). Assuming that one desires an overall alpha level of .05, then the alpha level to be used in the first stage of the procedure is .05/10 or .005. If one or more correlations is significant at the first stage, then a second set of tests is performed, but with a new alpha level equal to the number of tests performed at the first stage minus the number of significant tests. Carrying forward the example, if four correlations were found significant at the .005 level, the remaining six correlations would be retested at stage 2 at alpha level .05/6 or .008. The process is repeated until no correlations are significant at a given stage. Using the multistage procedure, the probability of making a Type I error overall is less than or equal to .05.

Either the Bartlett test (often referred to as a test of "sphericity"; see Cooley & Lohnes, 1971) or the multistage Bonferroni procedure should be used to ensure that the alpha level is controlled when testing whether the individual correlations in a matrix are equal to 0. The Bartlett test assumes that the variables come from a multivariate normal distribution and is sensitive to sample size (notice from the preceding equation that the larger the N is, the larger the X^2 value will be). Therefore, the Bartlett test may not always be the most appropriate test for controlling Type I errors. Larzelere and Mulaik (1977) recommend using the Bonferroni procedure when there are preplanned tests of interest or as a follow-up procedure to the Bartlett test.

Testing for Similarity of Patterns of Stability Across Groups of Subjects

Independent Samples.   Often a question arises as to whether two groups of subjects (males and females, normal and abnormal, American and German) have similar patterns of stability across time. Perhaps the most used method of testing whether two independent groups have equal correlations is first testing whether the correlation in each group is different from zero and then comparing the results of the significance tests across groups. For example, the question may be whether measures of aggression are more stable for boys than girls during the preschool years. It is common to address such a question by testing separately whether the correlations for girls and boys are different from zero. This method, however, is insufficient; the correlations should be compared directly. For example, with sample sizes of 30, correlations of .10 and .30 are *not* significantly different from each other, yet only one of them (.30) is significantly different from zero. Procedures for testing the difference between two independent correlations can be found in most statistics textbooks (e.g., Hays, 1973); they are also reviewed by Appelbaum and McCall (1983).

When testing for the difference between many correlations from two independent groups, the question of overall alpha level again arises. Fortunately, the notion of testing for the difference between two independent correlations can be extended to test for the difference between entire *matrices* of correlations. A test of this hypothesis was given in Jennrich (1970); to perform Jennrich's test, one must be familiar with matrix algebra and be able to write a computer program to perform the test. An alternative is to use a program that estimates structural equations. LISREL VI (Jöreskog & Sörbom, 1984) is currently available at most universities and will be used to illustrate the procedure for testing the difference between two independent correlation matrices. (Other programs are available, including EQS (Bentler, 1985), and microcomputer versions of LISREL. Most programs that do structural equation modeling should be useful in this context, although some are easier to use than others!) The test described next is based on a procedure recommended by Werts, Rock, Linn, and Jöreskog (1976).

To test equality of correlation matrices using a structural equation modeling program, the observed variables must each be uniquely identified with an unobserved, or structural variable. Then, the equality of the correlations among the *structural* variables across groups is tested. This "trick" is necessary because the programs will not directly test equality of correlations among observed variables.

In LISREL, the model adopted for each variable in each group is that $X_j = \lambda_{jj}\xi_j + 0$ (see Fig. 4.3). In words, each observed variable, X_j, is represented as a

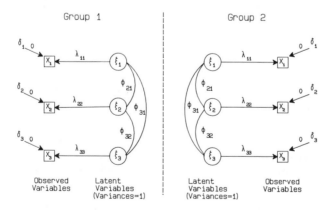

FIG. 4.3. A structural equation model for testing the equality of correlation matrices from two independent groups. The test is done by equating the correlations among the latent variables across the two groups. See text for further details and Table 4.1 for information on testing the model. Introductions to path and structural equation models can be found in Long (1983) and Pedhazur (1982).

weight, λ_{jj}, times one latent variable, ξ_j. By constraining the variances of the ξ's to be 1.0, the latent variable covariances become correlations, and they are contained in LISREL's Phi matrix. These correlations are, then, estimates of the correlations among the observed variables. To test the model, the correlations among the latent variables (in the Phi matrix) are constrained to be equal across the two groups. This procedure successfully tests the hypothesis that the correlations among the X's are identical in the two populations. (Werts et al., 1976 suggested this procedure for testing equality of correlation matrices, but they used *covariance* matrices as input to LISREL. The procedure, however, appears to be valid using correlation matrices as input as the underlying model is scale invariant; Cudeck, 1989.)

A simple model is shown in Fig. 4.3, where the stability of a variable across three time points is compared for two independent groups. Thus, X_1 is the variable at Time 1, and it is explained by a single latent variable, ξ_1. All ξ's have variances of 1.0. The path from ξ_1 to X_1 (namely, λ_{11}) is free to vary, but the path from the error term, δ_1, is set equal to zero. This is done for each time point in each group. Finally, the correlations among the latent variables must be constrained to be equal in the two groups. Thus, ϕ_{31} must be constrained to be equal in the two groups, as must all the other elements of the correlation matrix among the latent variables, namely ϕ_{21} and ϕ_{32}.

The LISREL VI control cards in Table 4.1 are used to test such a model. The data in Table 4.1 come from Pianta, Sroufe, and Egeland (1989) and are the stability correlations for maternal sensitivity across three time points. The two independent groups are girls (N = 74) and boys (N = 61). The stability correlations for girls are .16, .33, and .33, and for boys they are .29, .31, and .38. The question is whether these two sets of three correlations are different. (Note that the .16 correlation for girls is not significantly different from zero, whereas the .29 correlation for boys is significantly different from zero. Thus, one might be tempted to conclude, without directly testing for differences, that sensitivity is more stable from time 1 to time 2 for boys than for girls.)

LISREL VI provides a chi-square goodness-of-fit test of the model, as well as estimated model parameters and other diagnostic information (more of which can be requested on the OUTPUT card. Diagnostic information should be examined in accordance with recommendations in the LISREL manual). The chi-square test is a test of the hypothesis that the correlation matrices are equal. A large value of X^2, relative to the degrees of freedom, indicates that the two matrices are different.[1]

---

[1]The chi-square value in LISREL is affected by the sample size, so other methods should also be employed to evaluate the fit of the model to the data. LISREL VI prints a goodness-of-fit index, which probably ought to be above .90 for models that provide a good fit to the data, and a root mean square residual correlation, which probably ought to be less than .10 for models that fit. Bentler and Bonett (1980) provide other measures of fit and a more complete discussion of this issue. A recent review by Marsh, Balla, and McDonald (1988) discusses several measures of goodness-of-fit.

TABLE 4.1
Testing the Equality of Two Independent Correlation Matrices Using LISREL

The following LISREL analysis gives a chi-square test of the hypothesis that $\rho_1 = \rho_2$ where ρ_1 and ρ_2 are two population correlation matrices based on independent samples

Line	LISREL Statement	
1	TESTING EQUALITY OF TWO INDEPENDENT CORRELATION MATRICES	
2	DATAINFORMATION NI:no._of_variables_entered = 3	C
3	NO:no._of_observations = 74	C
4	NG:no._of_groups = 2	C
5	MA:type_of_matrix_to_analyze = KM:correlation matrix	
6	LABELS	
7	'6_MOS' '24_MOS' '42_MOS'	
8	KM:form_of_correlation_matrix_to_be_read SY:matrix_is_symmetric	
9	1.0	
10	.16 1.0	
11	.33 .33 1.0	
12	MODEL NX:no._of_observed_variables = 3	C
13	NK:no._of_latent_variables = 3	C
14	PH:covariances_of_latent_variables=ST:a_correlation_matrix	C
15	LX:form_of_paths_to_observed_variables=FU,FI:all_zeros	C
16	TD:covariance_matrix_among_errors=ZE:matrix_of_zeros	
17	FREE:set_these_lambdas_free_to_vary LX(1,1) LX(2,2) LX(3,3)	
18	OUTPUT MI:indices_for_improving_the_model	C
19	RS:predicted_and_residual_correlations	
20	TESTING EQUALITY OF TWO INDEPENDENT CORRELATION MATRICES	
21	DA NI=3 NO=61 NG=2 MA=KM	
22	LABELS	
23	'6_MOS' '24_MOS' '42_MOS'	
24	KM SY	
25	1.0	
26	.29 1.0	
27	.31 .38 1.0	
28	MODEL NX=3 NK=3 PHI=IN:set_phi_identical_to_Group_1 LX=FU, FI TD=ZERO	
29	FREE LX(1,1) LX(2,2) LX (3,3)	
30	OUTPUT MI RS	

The control cards in Lines 1-18 have been annotated (in lower case) to make clearer the function of each statement and parameter. These cards read in the first group's correlation matrix. Only the upper case statements are necessary to run the program, however. The minimal form of the statements is shown in lines 20-29, which read in the second group's correlation matrix.
The analysis yields a X^2 value of .80, based on [3X2/2] or 3 degrees of freedom, $p < .85$. The null hypothesis of equality of the population matrices is not rejected. Data were adapted from Table 1 of Pianta et al. (1989).

For the data in Table 4.1, the goodness-of-fit test from LISREL yields a value of .80, with 3 degrees of freedom, $p < .85$. Degrees of freedom are calculated as $P \times (P - 1) / 2$. Thus, the test suggests that the matrices for girls and boys are not different. Further, the Goodness-of-Fit-Index is .995, and the Root Mean Square Residual is .034, both indicating a very good fit of the model of equal correlations. Unless there were a priori specifications as to which individual correlations should differ, no individual tests of differences would be undertaken.

This test for the difference between two independent correlation matrices is predicated on several assumptions about the data, including the assumptions that the variables come from a multivariate normal distribution and that the sample size is large. Bentler and Chou (1988) discuss these and other practical issues in structural equation modeling.

Changes over time in the variances of the variables are ignored when the correlation matrices are tested. Therefore, it may be preferable to test for the equality of covariance matrices, which contain the variances as diagonal elements. An example outlined in the LISREL VI manual (Jöreskog & Sörbom, 1984) illustrates the test for differences between two covariance matrices (Example 13, p. V. 7).[2]

Dependent Correlations.   Special procedures for testing the differences between two correlations (and for testing equality of two correlation matrices) are required when the correlations are related, or dependent. Two correlations are related if the same subjects are used to compute both correlations. Related correlations may occur between different pairs of variables (e.g., comparing the stability across two time points of aggressive versus friendly behaviors on the same subjects) or because one variable is shared by the two correlations (e.g., comparing the correlation of home environment and aggression with the correlation of home environment and friendliness on the same subjects).

Steiger (1980) reviews research on the best methods for testing differences between correlations of each type. The tests he recommends can be done with hand calculators but seem to be unavailable in common statistical packages. Two of them are reviewed here.

Consider first the case of testing for the difference between two correlations that are calculated using the same group of subjects but do not share a common variable, r_{jk} and r_{hm}. (This test also applies to stability correlations of two different variables measured on the same subjects, such as might be obtained in a longitudinal study.) The steps in performing this test are shown in Table 4.2. First, it is necessary to calculate an estimate of $\psi_{jk,hm}$, which is a function of the covariance between r_{jk} and r_{hm}.

The next step is to calculate an estimate of the covariance of Fisher's z transformation of the two correlations. Finally, the test statistic, $\bar{Z}_2{}^*$, is calculated and compared with the distribution of z. (The notation $\bar{Z}_2{}^*$ is copied from Steiger, where several other variants of Z are proposed.) Although there are a number of calculations involved, this statistic is recommended as maintaining good control of Type I error rates in spite of the dependence of the correlations and with a relatively small N (a sample size of at least 20 is recommended when applying this test).

---

[2]To test for the equality of two covariance matrices, replace each KM by CM in Lines 5, 8, 21, and 24, use the variance–covariance matrices in Lines 9–11 and 25–27, change the ST in line 14 to SY, change FU,FI in lines 15 and 28 to ID, and delete lines 17 and 29. The procedure then tests whether all the variances and covariances in one group are equal to those in another group.

Note that if the procedure suggested by Werts et al. (1976) is to be strictly followed, then KM should be changed to CM in lines 5, 8, 21, and 24, and the covariance matrices should be placed in lines 9–11 and 25–27. The procedure then tests whether two correlation matrices are equal but using covariance matrices as input.

TABLE 4.2
Testing the Difference Between Two Dependent Correlations: Case 1

Data: Based on a sample of 103 subjects, the correlation between variables 1 and 2 is .50 and the correlation between variables 3 and 4 is .60. The same subjects are used to calculate both correlations. The correlations between the other pairs of variables must also be calculated; here $r_{13}=.80$, $r_{23}=.50$, $r_{14}=.50$, and $r_{24}=.70$.

Step 1: Calculate $\psi_{12,34} = \frac{1}{2} \{ [(r_{13} - r_{12}r_{23}) \times (r_{24} - r_{23}r_{34})] +$

$[(r_{14} - r_{13}r_{34}) \times (r_{23} - r_{12}r_{13})] +$

$[(r_{13} - r_{14}r_{34}) \times (r_{24} - r_{12}r_{14})] +$

$[(r_{14} - r_{12}r_{24}) \times (r_{23} - r_{24}r_{34})] \}$

Example: $\psi_{12,34} = \frac{1}{2} \{ [(.80 - .50 \times .50) \times (.70 - .50 \times .60)] +$

$[(.50 - .80 \times .60) \times (.50 - .50 \times .80)] +$

$[(.80 - .50 \times .60) \times (.70 - .50 \times .50)] +$

$[(.50 - .50 \times .70) \times (.50 - .70 \times .60)] \}$

$= \frac{1}{2} \{ [.55 \times .40] + [.02 \times .10] +$

$[.50 \times .45] + [.15 \times .08] \}$

$\psi_{12,34} = .2295$

Step 2: Calculate $\bar{s}_{12,34} = \dfrac{\psi_{12,34}}{\{ 1 - [\frac{1}{2}(r_{12}+r_{34})]^2 \}^2}$

Example: $\bar{s}_{12,34} = \dfrac{.2295}{\{ 1 - .55^2 \}^2}$

$\bar{s}_{12,34} = .4717$

Step 3: Calculate $\bar{z}_2^* = \dfrac{\sqrt{(n-3)} \times (z_{12} - z_{34})}{\sqrt{(2-2\bar{s}_{12,34})}}$

where $z_{12} = \frac{1}{2} \times \ln [(1 + r_{12})/(1 - r_{12})]$, namely, Fischer's r to z transformation.

Example: $\bar{z}_2^* = \dfrac{\sqrt{(103-3)} \times (.5493-.6931)}{\sqrt{(2-2 \times .4717)}}$

$= -1.40$

Step 4: Compare $\bar{z}_2^*$ to a standard normal distribution.

Example: The rejection region for P .05 from the standard normal distribution is $z \geq -1.96$ and $z \geq +1.96$. The obtained $\bar{z}_2^*$ value of -1.40 does not fall in the rejection region. Therefore, the null hypothesis is not rejected: There is insufficient evidence to support the hypothesis that the two correlations are different.

For testing the difference between two correlations that share a common variable, a different test statistic is proposed, one that has a t distribution with $N - 3$ degrees of freedom (again, N is the number of subjects on which the correlations are based). Illustration of the computation is contained in Table 4.3. Again, a sample size of 20 is desirable when performing this test.

Finally, it is often desirable to test whether two matrices of dependent correlations are the same. In developmental research, this situation would most commonly occur in longitudinal designs in which the question is whether a matrix of stability correlations is the same for two different variables or whether the intercorrelation of variables is the same at Time 1 as at Time 2. Rather than test each pair of dependent correlations one at a time (which, again, would increase the Type I error rate), the matrices as wholes should be compared. If the test

TABLE 4.3
Testing the Difference Between Two Dependent Correlations: Case 2

Data: Based on a sample of 103 subjects, the correlation between variables 1 and 2 is .50 and the correlation between variables 1 and 3 is .40.   The correlations are dependent, as the same variable appears in both.   The correlation between variables 2 and 3 is .10.

Step 1:

Calculate $|R| = (1 - r_{12}^2 - r_{13}^2) + (2Xr_{12}Xr_{13}Xr_{23})$.

Example: $|R| = (1 - .05^2 - .4^2 - .1^2) + (2X.5X.4X.1)$.

Step 2:

Calculate $T_2 = (r_{12} - r_{13}) \times \sqrt{\dfrac{(N-1)\ (1+r_{23})}{\{2[(N-1)/(N-3)]\}\ X\ |R| + \bar{r}^2 X\ (1-r_{23})^3}}$

where $\bar{r} = 1/2\ (r_{12}+r_{13})$

Example: $T_2 = (.5-.4) \times \sqrt{\dfrac{102 \times 1.1}{2[(102X100)]\ X\ .62 + .45^2(1-.1)^3}}$

$T_2 = (.1) \sqrt{\dfrac{112.2}{1.2648 + .1476}}$

$T_2 = .891.$

Step 3:   Compare T_2 to a t distribution with df = N - 3.

Example: The observed T_2 value is not greater than 1.98, which, based on 100 degrees of freedom, is the critical value for rejecting the null hypothesis at p < .05 (two-tailed).   Thus, the null hypothesis is retained as plausible; the correlations are not significantly different.

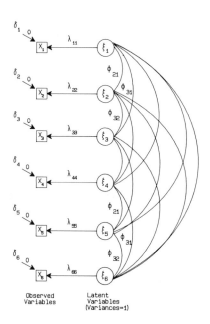

FIG. 4.4. A structural equation model for testing the equality of two dependent correlation matrices, each with three variables. All six variables are included in the model, but the appropriate correlations are constrained to be equal (note the identical subscripts of the labeled ϕ coefficients). All correlations indicated by curved lines are also estimated in this model (see Table 4.4 for information on testing the model).

indicates no change, there would generally be little point in trying to find structural differences across time (for example, via a factor analysis).

Although Steiger (1980) presents two tests for examining dependent correlation matrices, there is no readily available software to perform them. Again, a structural equation program is useful for this problem, and LISREL VI is used to illustrate the test.

As in the previous structural equation example, the model for each variable here is $X_j = \lambda_{jj}\xi_j + 0$. Each observed variable, X_j, is explained by one latent variable, ξ_j (see Fig. 4.4). Equality of correlations among the observed variables is then tested by equating the correlations among the ξ's (the correlations are contained in LISREL's Phi matrix).

The only "trick" in performing this test is that both correlation matrices must be entered as parts of a single large correlation matrix. The model in Fig. 4.4 is for testing the equality of two matrices of correlations among three variables. Note, however, that all six variables (15 correlations) are in the model. The test of interest is whether, simultaneously, $r_{12} = r_{45}$, $r_{23} = r_{56}$, and $r_{13} = r_{46}$. These equalities are forced by equating the latent variable correlations that correspond to the observed correlations: note that the correlation between ξ_1 and ξ_2 is equated to the correlation between ξ_4 and ξ_5. The other correlations among the latent variables are allowed to take on any value; this is signified in Fig. 4.4 by having unlabeled lines between all other pairs of latent variables. (Again, the paths from and the disturbances to the observed variables are fixed at zero.

TABLE 4.4
Testing the Equality of Two Dependent Correlation Matrices Using LISREL

The following LISREL analysis gives a x^2 test of the hypothesis that $\rho_1 = \rho_2$, where ρ_1 and ρ_2 are two population correlation matrices based on the same or related subjects (i.e., are dependent).

Line	LISREL Statements	
1	TESTING EQUALITY OF TWO DEPENDENT CORRELATION MATRICES	
2	DATAINFORMATION NI:no._of_variables_entered=6	C
3	NO:no._of_observations=368	C
4	MA:matrix_to_be_analyzed=KM:correlation_matrix	
5	LABELS	
6	'SOC-1' 'SOC-2' 'SOC-3' 'COMP-1' 'COMP-2' 'COMP-3'	
7	KM:form_of_correlation_matrix_to_be_read SY:matrix_is_symmetric	
8	1.0	
9	.641 1.0	
10	.387 .554 1.0	
11	.619 .332 .153 1.0	
12	.355 .488 .210 .681 1.0	
13	.273 .403 .459 .456 .558 1.0	
14	MODEL NX:no._of_observed_variables=6	C
15	NK:no._of_latent_variables=6	C
16	PH:covariances_of_latent_variables ST:a_correlation_matrix	C
17	LX:form_of_paths_to_observed_variables=FU,FI:all_zeros	C
18	TD:covariance_matrix_among_errors=ZE:matrix_of_zeros	
19	FREE:set_these_lambdas_free_to_vary LX(1,1) LX(2,2) LX(3,3)	C
20	LX(4,4) LX(5,5) LX(6,6)	
21	EQUAL: contrain_these_two_correlations_to_be_equal PHI(2,1) PHI(5,4)	
22	EQUAL: contrain_these_two_correlations_to_be_equal PHI(3,1) PHI(6,4)	
23	EQUAL: contrain_these_two_correlations_to_be_equal PHI(3,2) PHI(6,5)	
24	OUTPUT MI:indices_for-improving_the_model	C
	RS:predicted_and_residual_correlations	

Note. As in Table 4.1, the cards have been annotated (in lower case letters); only the statements in upper case are necessary to run the program. Data come from Table 1 of Mortimer et al. (1982). The x^2 value for testing the equality of the correlations yields a value of 3.1, based on 3 degrees of freedom. Thus, the correlation matrices specifying the cross-age stability of sociability and competence, respectively, are not significantly different.

The control cards shown in Table 4.4 test the model that two dependent correlation matrices are equal. The data come from Mortimer, Finch, and Kumka (1982) and are the stability across three time points (freshman year, senior year, and 10 years after graduation) of sociability and of competence as assessed by questionnaire. Thus, the question is whether sociability and competence, as aspects of self-concept, show similar patterns of stability across time. The stability correlations for sociability are .641, .387, and .554, whereas the correlations for competence are .681, .456, and .558. The remaining correlations in the matrix in Table 4.4 are the various synchronous and cross-lag correlations between sociability and competence.

Once the entire set of correlations is arrayed, the equivalence of the two sets of three correlations is tested by setting the appropriate elements of the Phi matrix equal to one another. This is done with the EQUAL command. In this case, we wish to set Phi(2,1) = Phi(5,4), Phi(3,1) = Phi(6,4), and Phi(3,2) = Phi(6,5). This allows us to test simultaneously whether .641 = .681, .387 = .456, and .554 = .558.

The chi-square goodness-of-fit is evaluated with P degrees of freedom, where P is the number of variables (at one of the time points), which is 3 in our example. For these data, the chi-square value is 3.1, which is not significant. (The adjusted goodness-of-fit index is .997 and the root mean square residual is .023.) Thus, the stabilities of sociability and competence across early adult years do not differ significantly.[3]

Summary of Procedures for Testing Individual-Difference Stability via Correlations

Although Pearson correlations are the most prevalent statistics for evaluating the stability of individual differences during development, many improvements are possible in the procedures typically used to evaluate them. When testing whether each one of a matrix of correlations is different from zero, the Type I error rate for the series of tests is higher than the alpha level employed in each individual test (.05, usually). Bartlett's chi-square test or the multistage Bonferroni procedure should be used in this circumstance to help control the overall error rate. If one is interested in whether two correlations are of the same magnitude, the pairwise tests reviewed by Steiger (1980) should be used for dependent correlations (Tables 4.2 and 4.3), and the standard z or t test (Hays, 1973) should be used for independent correlations.

Finally, it is relatively easy to test whether two entire matrices of correlations are different from one another using structural equation modeling. The procedures differ for independent versus dependent correlations (see Tables 4.1 and 4.4). If the overall test suggests that the matrices are not different, it is not advisable to go on and analyze differences in individual correlations, unless there are compelling theoretical reasons to do so.

---

[3]Again, it may be preferable to test for equality of covariances *and* variances, but this is easily accomplished by changing KM to CM in lines 4 and 7, and using the variance–covariance matrix in lines 8–13. In addition, the ST in lines 16 should be changed to SY, the FU,FI in line 17 should be ID, and lines 19–20 should be deleted. Finally, the variances must be equated. For the example in Table 4.4, this would be accomplished by adding three new lines after line 18, equating Phi(1,1) with Phi(4,4), Phi(2,2) with Phi(5,5), and Phi(3,3) with Phi(6,6).

In this brief survey of methods for testing correlations, many aspects of analyzing longitudinal data have been ignored. Readers are urged to consult Kenny and Campbell (1989) for tests of various kinds of structure in longitudinal correlation matrices, Hertzog and Nesselroade (1987), McArdle and Epstein (1987), and Rogosa and Willett (1985) for structural analysis based on growth curve and autoregressive models, and Law, Snyder, Hattie, and McDonald (1984) for analysis of three-mode data generally.

ANALYZING INDIVIDUAL DIFFERENCES
IN DEVELOPMENTAL FUNCTIONS

Two foci for the analysis of individual differences were outlined at the beginning of this chapter, namely differences in patterns of behavior change with development and the stability of individual difference. Issues in evaluating stability were discussed earlier. The rest of this chapter focuses on methods for discovering individual differences in patterns of behavioral change, especially hierarchical cluster analysis.

It is assumed that the investigator has collected data on the same subjects at several times (data like those of Fig. 4.1) such that he or she can plot *profiles* for each individual on one variable over time (see Fig. 4.5). The primary questions of interest are whether significant differences exist between the profiles and whether meaningful subgroups of individuals can be formed, based on their profiles.

One method of approaching these questions is via factor analysis of the profile data. Appelbaum and McCall (1983, pp. 461–463) provide a clear statement of Tucker's (1966) procedure for profile analysis, and an application of this technique can be found in McCall et al., (1973). More general introductions to and methods for factor analyzing longitudinal data can be found in Baltes and Nesselroade (1973), Bentler (1973), and Jöreskog (1979). An annotated bibliography of these and related approaches for analyzing longitudinal data is available (Abeles, 1986).

A second method for analyzing profile data is via cluster analysis. Cluster analysis is a generic term for a diverse set of methods whose goal is to represent the structure in a data matrix. This representation is often in the form of a dendrogram or tree (see Fig. 4.8) but may take other forms as well (see Hartigan, 1975). The user of cluster analysis seeks to place objects into relatively homogeneous groups or clusters, usually with little or no prior knowledge of what the grouping may be. (In our illustrations, the objects will always be individuals, although stimuli and variables can be clustered as well.) Only a few of the available clustering methods are covered in this review. Other resources on cluster analysis include texts by Anderberg (1973), Bijnen (1973), Everitt (1980), Hartigan (1975), Lorr (1983), Sneath and Sokal (1973), and Späth

(1980). (In particular, readers may wish to consult Hawkins, Muller, and ten Krooden (1982) for a different point of view regarding the clustering of profile data. Hawkins et al. advocate the use of partitioning and allocation methods, not hierarchical methods, when the distribution of the profiles is assumed to be multivariate normal.)

Cluster Analysis for Profile Data

At the outset of this discussion, it is important to note that cluster analysis is primarily a descriptive enterprise. There are few inferential tests and p levels to guide the decisions that must be made at various points in the analysis. Therefore, cautions about the use of clustering methods and critical reviews are easy to find (e.g., Cormack, 1971; Dubes & Jain, 1979). Nevertheless, there are few tasks so fundamental to science as the grouping together of similar objects. Perhaps this is why the area of cluster analysis has flourished, despite the limited statistical theory that has so far been developed in this area.

A general discussion of clustering is presented first, organized by the seven steps of clustering outlined in Milligan and Cooper (1987). Following this general discussion, two illustrations of cluster analysis are provided.

1. Selection of Individuals to be Clustered. As in most data analysis techniques, it is desirable in cluster analysis that subjects be representative of the population under consideration. In particular, the cluster structure in the population should be taken into account in the selection of subjects whenever possible (perhaps by a stratified sampling procedure); of course, prior information about cluster structure is usually not available.

A second consideration at this step of clustering is the identification of outliers in the data. An outlier is an individual with extreme values on one or more of the variables constituting the profile. The presence of outliers can affect the outcome of clustering, so decisions about who the outliers are and whether they should be kept in the data set ought to be made ahead of time. There is no agreed-upon method of detecting outliers, but users of cluster programs should examine the frequency distributions of each variable used in the profiles to find extreme cases. If some individuals are eliminated before clustering, it would seem wise to make an interpretation of the aberrant pattern they show. Edelbrock (1979) discusses the problem of outliers in cluster analysis.

2. Selection of Variables. In the developmental applications considered here (e.g., Fig. 4.7), there is one variable measured at several time points. Most often, that variable will have been selected for theoretical reasons, and there would appear to be no compelling reason to eliminate any measurement point from the analysis of the profiles.

When a profile score is calculated across many different variables at a single time point, however, variables that are irrelevant to the cluster structure (in the population) can degrade recovery of those clusters (Milligan, 1980). Thus, not all the variables measured in a given study should necessarily be used in the analysis. Selection of variables that are theoretically important, are reliably measured, and show some variance across subjects is recommended.

3. Standardizing the Variables.   When different variables are the basis for the profile, an important issue is whether they should be standardized. A major concern is that variables measured on different scales with different standard deviations will contribute differentially to some measures of proximity (see Step 4). It has been almost routine practice, therefore, to transform scores on all variables into z scores prior to computing profile similarity scores. A Monte Carlo study by Edelbrock (1979) indicates that, at least for some limited kinds of data, standardization makes only a modest improvement in cluster recovery.

For developmental profile data especially, it may be desirable to leave the variables in raw form, because greater influences of particular time points on the eventual grouping may be of interest. When one is not sure whether to standardize variables, clustering can be done both with and without variable standardization, so that the effect of this procedure on the final cluster solution can be evaluated.

4. Measuring the Similarity of Profiles.   Consider the three profiles in Fig. 4.5: How could one measure the similarity of the profiles to each other? The two most used measures are the Pearson correlation coefficient, *r,* and the Euclidean distance, *d.* The correlation is computed between the scores of two profiles across the several time points, using the usual formulas. Distance is calculated as the square root of the sum of the squared differences between the two profiles at each time point. Values for both *r* and *d* are shown in Fig. 4.5.

Much has been written about the appropriateness of each of these two measures. A classic paper by Cronbach and Gleser (1953) argued for using *d,* but others have argued against it (e.g., Overall, 1964). Some of the history of this issue, as well as proposed solutions to several problems inherent in measuring profile similarity, are reviewed in Cohen (1969) and Skinner (1978).

Inasmuch as *d* reflects differences across profiles in *elevation, scatter,* and *shape* (see Cronbach & Gleser, 1953), *d* would seem to be appropriate for developmental data because these three aspects of the profiles are potentially meaningful. Note that subjects A and B in Fig. 4.5, who have consistently different means (or elevations) on the variable at each time point (but the same scatter and shape), have a correlation of 1.0 between profiles. Thus, information about the difference in elevation of the profiles is lost when using *r.* For developmental data, however, the differences in elevation between profiles such as A and B may often be meaningful. The distance measure, *d,* reflects this difference in elevation.

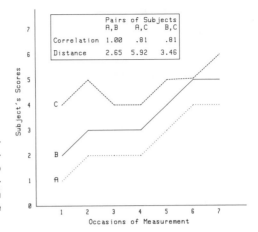

FIG. 4.5. Profiles for three subjects at seven occasions of measurement. Note that the two widely used similarity measures give different information about the similarity of the profiles.

The choice of a similarity measure depends, then, on what the investigator wants the measure to reflect. If differences between means and variances of profiles are important, d should be used. If shape is the only important attribute of the profile, then r should be used (or an alternate measure of shape, see Cohen, 1969; Skinner, 1978). It is critical at this step in the process that the profiles be carefully inspected in order to evaluate which aspects seem to characterize different subjects. An informed choice of similarity measure can then be made.[4]

5. Choice of a Clustering Technique.   Several hundred clustering algorithms have been proposed; for better or worse, only a few are used with any frequency. By far the most often-used techniques in psychology are the SAHN techniques (Sneath & Sokal, 1973). SAHN stands for sequential, agglomerative, hierarchical, and nonoverlapping. SAHN methods proceed in steps, beginning from the point at which each of N entities is its own cluster. The grouping process is agglomerative, with each step having one less cluster than the last step. Across steps, the groupings are hierarchical; that is, each new cluster is formed only by the joining of previous clusters, and clusters are not split once they are formed. Finally, the methods produce nonoverlapping clusters; no entity can be placed in more than one cluster.

Of the SAHN methods, the most frequent to appear in Monte Carlo simulation studies have been *Ward's* method (also known as the minimum variance method), the *group average* method (or the unweighted pair group method based on averages, UPGMA), the *complete link* method (maximum diameter, furthest

---

[4]Strictly speaking, r is a *similarity* measure because large values indicate greater similarity, whereas d is a *dissimilarity* measure because large values indicate less similarity. ''Similarity'' is used here to refer to both kinds of measures, unless explicitly stated otherwise.

neighbor, or compactness method), and the *single link* method (minimum diameter, nearest neighbor, or connectedness method). These four methods differ primarily in terms of the rule that governs which two clusters are joined at any step in the sequence (see Example 1 following).

There have been several Monte Carlo simulation studies to evaluate which clustering method is "best." These studies generally proceed by using each of several methods to cluster a sample of data from a population with a known number of clusters. The situations studied in Monte Carlo research may not generalize to "real" data, in that the clustering in the population is contrived and usually very strong. On the other hand, it can be argued that if a clustering method cannot recover the cluster structure in the population under these circumstances, it will likely not perform well in "real" data sets.

The outcomes of 11 comparative studies (reviewed by Milligan & Cooper, 1987) suggest that Ward's method consistently performs well, with the complete link method usually the next best. The group average method sometimes performs better than complete link and sometimes worse. Single link clustering generally did not perform as well as the others. Thus, if a SAHN method is desired, one of the first three methods would probably be selected. When the "true" configuration of the objects is of a certain type, however, single link clustering may be the best procedure, and it has many advocates (Sneath & Sokal, 1973).

A final consideration in choice of method involves the presence of ties in the distance matrix. The complete and single link methods break ties arbitrarily, and different rules for breaking ties can lead to different solutions. Therefore, the similarity data matrix should be examined carefully for ties and the results interpreted carefully if there are many ties. According to Jain and Dubes (1988), the complete link method is much more adversely affected by ties than the single link method. (Although the dendrogram does not typically provide a visual representation of tied similarity values, there are methods of graphical representation of the solution that do show ties; see Sneath & Sokal, 1973).

6. The Choice of Number of Clusters.   The SAHN methods produce as many different cluster solutions as there are entities to cluster, and the choice of which solution is best is not usually clear cut. With five individuals, for example, there are five cluster solutions, beginning with the solution in which all individuals are a cluster by themselves and proceeding to the solution in which all individuals are in one cluster. How does one decide whether to retain the 5-, 4-, 3-, 2-, or 1-cluster solution in this case?

Many "stopping" rules have been proposed to choose one solution from a hierarchy. Perhaps the oldest, and one of the easiest rules to apply, is the "stepsize" rule (see Example 1 following), in which the coefficients associated with each step in the solution are examined in a manner similar to the scree test (Cattell, 1978) in factor analysis. Other stopping rules involve calculating statistics that describe the similarity of each cluster solution to the input matrix. The solution with the largest value is usually taken as the best stopping place. A third class of stopping rules uses information about the within- and between-cluster sums of squares and cross-products matrices to select a solution that maximizes some function of the between-to-within variance.

Milligan and Cooper (1985) investigated the effectiveness of 30 different stopping rules. The easiest method, the stepsize rule, ranked 11th of the 30 methods; the errors made using stepsize almost always involved retaining fewer clusters than were present in the artificial data. The point biserial correlation, reviewed in Example 1 that follows, ranked 7th. Three of the criteria employed in SAS's PROC CLUSTER (SAS, 1985) ranked 1st, 2nd, and 6th of the 30 methods (the pseudo F, t, and cubic clustering criterion). No method was perfect, however, even for the artificial data generated in this study. The use of several rules would probably be useful in any given study. (Other methods of evaluating cluster solutions are reviewed in Dubes and Jain, 1979).

Stopping rules are usually applied jointly with less formal assumptions about what a desirable cluster solution might be. For example, there is little point in performing cluster analysis if the number of clusters retained is not smaller than the original number of entities, perhaps one-half the original number of objects (this rule was used in the Milligan & Cooper, 1985 study, for example). At the other extreme, solutions involving a very small number of clusters (e.g., one or two) are not desirable in most instances because the economy of description is too great. Interesting hypotheses about differences across clusters are less likely to be generated if one concludes that there are only one or two clusters. Thus, as long as there is a reasonably large number of entities in the analysis, the statistical rules are usually applied in addition to these informal constraints on the desirability of the final solution.

7. Interpretation, Testing, and Replication.   Because in most instances the investigator does not have a priori information about how many clusters are represented in the data, interpretation rests largely on the investigator's knowledge about the characteristics of the entities being clustered. In other words, interpretation is based on information *internal* to the clustering procedure. It is usually useful to examine the means and variances of each cluster on the original variables in order to help interpret the outcome. Some authors have recommended using discriminant function analysis to predict cluster group membership from the variables originally used to calculate the similarity coefficients. Milligan and Cooper (1987) warn against putting too much faith in the outcome of these analyses, as a discriminant function analysis will often show significant differences between clusters when the input data are random.

It is easy to recommend that several clustering methods be tried in order to evaluate the method-dependent characteristics of the solutions. It is not so easy, however, to recommend procedures for comparing cluster solutions to each other or for deciding which method is best for a given data set. As Kruskal (1977) notes, many data analysts believe that clustering methods give the best information about small distances in the input similarity matrices, and, hence, different methods are most likely to disagree after the first few joinings. Additional graphic aids for interpretation are suggested by Kruskal (1977) and Hartigan (1975).

Many authors recommend that cluster analysis and multidimensional scaling (methods for the spatial representation of structure in similarity data) be used together to provide complementary descriptions of the structure in the similarity matrix (e.g., Arabie, Carroll, & DeSarbo, 1988; Kruskal & Wish, 1978). Multidimensional scaling (MDS) uses the same kind of data matrix as input, namely a matrix of similarities between all pairs of objects, but gives the objects scale values (on one or more dimensions) as a solution, whereas cluster analysis simply provides groupings of the objects. Thus, MDS can sometimes provide a plot of the objects in two or three dimensions that is helpful in determining an appropriate clustering method to use or an acceptable number of clusters to retain (see Kruskal & Wish, 1978 and Fig. 4.9).

Summary of the Steps in Cluster Analysis. As is evident from this brief review of the steps involved in cluster analysis, there are many important decisions that do not involve the clustering method itself. The selection of subjects and variables and the issues of variable standardization and choice of similarity measure can have important effects on the conclusions of a cluster analysis.

Example 1: Clustering U.S. Cities Using Driving Distances

To illustrate the details of a typical cluster analysis, 12 U.S. cities were clustered on the basis of the driving distances between them. Driving distances were obtained from a road atlas and were used as input to complete link, Ward's, and group average cluster analyses[5]. Based on visual inspection of the "true" configuration of the cities (Fig. 4.6), it appears that there are four clusters of three cities each.

The driving distances were arrayed in a triangular matrix, similar to the standard correlation matrix (see Step 0, Table 4.5). This matrix served as input to the cluster analysis. At step 0, the two closest cities were New York (NY) and Philadelphia (PH). At Step 1, NY and PH (the most similar cities) have been merged to form a cluster of size 2. After this first joining, then, there are 11 clusters, one cluster consisting of [NY,PH] and 10 other clusters of single cities.

---

[5]This example, although it does not explicate individual differences, does provide an intuitively appealing method for grasping the relations between the distances used as input and the groupings obtained from the clustering methods.

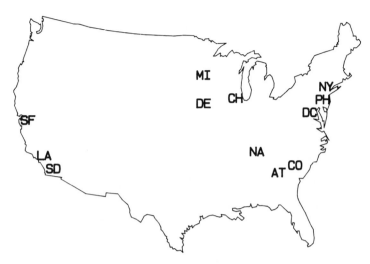

FIG. 4.6.   Driving distances between these 12 U.S. cities were clustered using several clustering methods (see text).

The alpha value (or gap or coefficient) associated with Step 1 is the distance between the cities joined at this step, in this case 106 miles between NY and PH.

Once NY and PH are joined at Step 1, the distances between this cluster and every other city (cluster) must be calculated. This is the point at which the SAHN methods diverge. How should we measure the similarity of the 11 clusters at Step 1?

In the complete link method, the similarity between two clusters is taken to be the maximum of all pairs of distances between them. For example, the distance between the cluster [NY, PH] and the cluster [LA] is taken to be the larger of the two distances NY to LA and PH to LA. These values are 2,794 miles and 2,703 miles, respectively. Therefore, the complete link method defines the distance between [NY, PH] and [LA] as 2,794, the maximum of the two values. The distance between each of the other 9 clusters and the [NY,PH] cluster is computed in a similar manner.

At Step 2, then, the process repeats. The 2 clusters with greatest similarity merge, and there is a total of 10 clusters. For the city data, LA and SD join at Step 2. The distances between all possible pairs of the 10 clusters are recalculated at Step 2, and it is determined that [AT] and [CO] have the greatest similarity. These are joined, and there are then 9 clusters at Step 3. The process repeats, with distances between clusters recalculated at each step, and the most similar clusters joined. At Step 10, there are 2 clusters, consisting of the 3 west coast cities and the 9 cities east of the Rockies. These 2 clusters are finally joined at Step 11 to form the final cluster containing all the objects.

The most important points about the SAHN methods are provided in Table

TABLE 4.5
Outline of Complete Link Cluster Solution for Driving Distances Between 12 U.S. Cities

STEP 0: Each city is its own cluster, and the distances between clusters
constitute the original data.

Alpha = 0 (The smallest possible distance.)

	AT	CH	CO	DE	LA	MI	NA	NY	PH	SD	SF	DC
Atlanta	0000											
Chicago	0708	0000										
Columbia	0214	0800	0000									
Des Moines	0955	0334	1112	0000								
Los Angeles	2191	2048	2420	1709	0000							
Minneapolis	1121	0410	1214	0245	1857	0000						
Nashville	0246	0486	0437	0693	2011	0833	0000					
New York	0854	0809	0717	1118	2794	1217	0900	0000				
Philadelphia	0748	0785	0611	1094	2703	1195	0787	0106	0000			
San Diego	2146	2093	2382	1766	0127	2001	1997	2803	2773	0000		
San Francisco	2483	2173	2768	1825	0387	1979	2325	2930	2902	0514	0000	
Washington DC	0618	0709	0481	1062	2646	1090	0659	0237	0131	2602	2843	0000

The clusters with the greatest similarity are NY and PH, with a distance of
106 miles. Hence, these clusters are combined and form a new cluster at
STEP 1.

STEP 1: NY and PH are joined to form a new cluster. Then, the distance
between each pair of clusters is recalculated, with the distance
between city X and the new cluster, [NY, PH] defined as the larger
of the distances NY to X and PH to X.

Alpha = 106 (The distance between the clusters joined at this step.)

At STEPs 2 through 10,   .
clusters are combined   .
in the same manner as at   .
STEP 1. Distances between   .
clusters are recalculated   .
at each STEP.   .
                                .

SUMMARY OF THE COMPLETE LINK CLUSTER SOLUTION

Step	Number of Clusters	Alpha Value	The Cluster Solution
0	12	0	[AT] [CH] [CO] [DE] [LA] [MI] [NA] [NY] [PH] [SD] [SF] [DC]
1	11	106	[AT] [CH] [CO] [DE] [LA] [MI] [NA] [SD] [SF] [DC] [NY,PH]
2	10	127	[AT] [CH] [CO] [DE] [MI] [NA] [SF] [DC] [NY,PH] [LA,SD]
3	9	214	[CH] [DE] [MI] [NA] [SF] [DC] [NY,PH] [LA,SD] [AT,CO]
4	8	237	[CH] [DE] [MI] [NA] [SF] [NY,PH,DC] [LA,SD] [AT,CO]
5	7	245	[CH] [NA] [SF] [NY,PH,DC] [LA,SD] [AT,CO] [DE,MI]
6	6	410	[NA] [SF] [NY,PH,DC] [LA,SD] [AT,CO] [DE,MI,CH]
7	5	437	[SF] [NY,PH,DC] [LA,SD] [AT,CO,NA] [DE,MI,CH]
8	4	514	[NY,PH,DC] [LA,SD,SF] [AT,CO,NA] [DE,MI,CH]
9	3	900	[NY,PH,DC,AT,CO,NA] [LA,SD,SF] [DE,MI,CH]
10	2	1217	[NY,PH,DC,AT,CO,NA,DE,MI,CH] [LA,SD,SF]
11	1	2930	[NY,PH,DC,AT,CO,NA,DE,MI,CH,LA,SD,SF]

4.5. The methods begin with each entity constituting a cluster of size 1. At each
step, the clusters that are most similar are joined, and the intercluster similarities
are recalculated. The alpha values are the distances between the clusters joined at
the last step. Where the SAHN methods differ is in which clusters are joined at
Step 1 and beyond.

The complete link method joins the two most similar clusters, with the similarity between cluster defined as the smallest similarity between pairs of entities
in the two clusters. The group average method also joins the two most similar

clusters but defines the similarity of two clusters as the average of the similarity values between pairs of objects in different clusters. In Ward's method (Ward, 1963), the two clusters that minimize a within-group sum of squares are joined at each step. Definitions of cluster similarity for single link, weighted group average methods, and other SAHN methods can be found in Sneath and Sokal (1973)[6].

Each of these methods of clustering seeks groupings that are homogeneous within but heterogeneous between the groups. This idea of homogeneity within and heterogeneity between clusters also forms the basis of many methods determining the number of clusters to retain as an optimal representation of the data.

Determining the Number of Clusters to Retain. In many applications, a dendrogram or tree describing the structure of the similarity data would suffice as a final solution (see Fig. 4.8 for an example). In other applications, however, a single grouping or partition of the subjects is desirable so that further analysis of the clusters can be conducted. The question addressed now is how many clusters of cities are present in the data?

To apply the *stepsize* criterion for number of clusters, the differences in alpha values between adjacent steps in the solution are calculated, and a large difference is sought. Recall that the purpose of clustering is to reduce the number of entities but not reduce the number too much. Thus, with 12 cities (a relatively small number of entities), we examine stepsizes in the range of 6 to 2 clusters. The alpha values, beginning at Step 6, are 410, 437, 514, 900, 1,217, and 2,930 miles (see bottom of Table 4.5). The first difference in alpha values that is much larger than previous differences is between Step 8 and Step 9, or between the 4- and the 3-cluster solution. A 4-cluster solution is thus a good candidate, because the alpha value associated with it (514 miles) is relatively small, compared with the next alpha value (900 miles). A 2-cluster solution is also a viable candidate for the same reason. The indeterminacy of which cluster solution to retain is understandable, given the location of the cities (Fig. 4.6). Although the cities were chosen to reflect 4 groups of 3 geographically close cities, there is also a clear East/West grouping. In many applications, however, 2 clusters would be considered too gross a grouping to retain as the final solution.

Another stopping rule that is relatively easy to apply employs the point-biserial correlation. For this rule, a correlation is calculated at each step of the solution that evaluates the similarity between the cluster solution at that step and

---

[6]Ward's method and the group average method compute means or sums of squares of the input data to determine which clusters to join at a given step. Thus, both methods assume that the input data (the similarity data) are interval scaled. Complete and single link methods, on the other hand, give invariant results under strictly monotonic transformations of the input data, and they are therefore more appropriate for similarity data that are ordinal. Consideration of the scaling of the similarity data is probably more important when the similarity data are obtained directly (e.g., by ratings or sorts) rather than by computing similarity coefficients across profiles.

the original data. The correlation is computed between each of the original [n ×
(n − 1) / 2] similarity measures and a vector of [n × (n − 1) / 2] zero's and
one's. In this vector, a pair of entities is assigned a value of one if they *are not*
clustered together and a zero if they *are* clustered together. The notion is that
entities with a score of one at a given step in the solution (because they are not in
the same cluster) should have higher *dis*similarity scores than entities with a
score of zero. The correlation is computed at each step in the solution. Applying
this method to the city data yields r values at steps 6 through 11 of .48, .53, .57,
.69, and .92. According to the point-biserial criterion, then, the two-cluster
solution is optimal for these data.

Interpreting the Cluster Solution.   The stepsize and the point-biserial correlation both suggest that a two-cluster solution best represents the structure in
the original driving distance matrix, although the stepsize criterion suggested that
the four-cluster solution would also be a reasonable representation. Such discrepancies occur more frequently than one would like, and interpretability of the
solutions often is the deciding factor. Interpretation of both the four- and the two-
cluster solution might be appropriate in this case. Because a known spatial
configuration exists for this clustering problem, the interpretation has already
been made, namely, cities that are close together geographically are clustered
together.

Example 2: Clustering Mother–Infant Dyads Based on Social Interactions

To illustrate the application of clustering to developmental profile data, the data
in Fig. 4.7 were clustered using three SAHN techniques. Fourteen profiles are
represented in the figure, one for each of 14 mother–infant dyads who were
observed at three ages during normal activities at home (see Green, Gustafson, &
West, 1980). For each dyad, the total number of social interactions (defined as
continuous periods of socially directed activity) were tallied across 80 minutes of
observation at each age. Figure 4.7 plots the frequency of social interactions,
standardized within each dyad, at each of the three ages; that is, the three scores
for each subject were transformed to z scores using the subject's own mean and
standard deviation.

Subjects' scores were standardized because the most interesting questions
concerned the *pattern* of changes in social interactions over age. One way to
ensure that pattern of change is examined is to eliminate differences between the
profiles in mean and variability (Cronbach & Gleser, 1953). After standardizing
each profile, the Euclidean distance, d, was calculated between the profiles of
every pair of subjects. (Using r as a measure of pattern similarity produced
similar results.)

The matrix of distances between subjects was clustered using Ward's method,

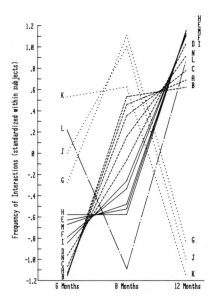

FIG. 4.7. Profiles for 14 mother–infant dyads at three ages. Dyads with similar types of lines were clustered into the same groups and show different patterns of change across age in the frequency of social interactions.

the group average method, and the complete link method. Complete link and Ward's method yielded identical hierarchies, except at the three-cluster level, and the group average solution shared many important features with the other two. The complete link solution is interpreted here, although the interpretation would not have been different using either of the other methods.

A dendrogram of the complete link solution is shown in Fig. 4.8. The dendrogram plots a history of the recursive procedure used to group the objects. At the bottom of the dendrogram, each object is its own cluster, and the associated alpha value is 0. The first two dyads to join are E and M; their distance (or alpha

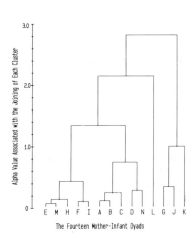

FIG. 4.8. Dendrogram of the complete link solution for the data shown in Fig. 4.7 (see text for further description).

value) is .06. Next, dyad F joins dyad I, with an alpha value of .09. The joining continues, and horizontal lines are drawn at the alpha level associated with the joining of the given clusters. Thus, the dendrogram summarizes the agglomerative sequence and also represents the stepsize values associated with the sequence. Large differences in alpha values (the basis of the stepsize criterion) are represented visually as long vertical lines between joinings. For this reason, the dendrogram is often a useful diagnostic aid in cluster analysis. Visual inspection of the dendrogram in Fig. 4.8 suggests that a four-cluster solution might be optimal; there appear to be two relatively compact clusters, namely, [E,M,H,F,I], [A,B,C,D,N], an isolate, [L], and a "looser" cluster of the dyads G, J, and K.

Several other criteria were used to help determine the optimal number of clusters to retain. As just mentioned, the visual inspection of the dendrogram suggested that four clusters were probably optimal. The stepsize criterion did not yield a clear-cut gap in alpha values. The point-biserial criterion suggested either five or two clusters as optimal, whereas a third criterion, the gamma coefficient (Hubert, 1974), suggested the two-cluster solution as optimal.

Thus, there is no solution that all criteria suggest as optimal, and the interpretability of the various solutions must be used as an aid to deciding the number of clusters. The most frequent solution that is suggested is the two-cluster solution, namely, the partition [G,J,K] and [A,B,C,D,E,F,H,I,L,M,N]. This solution clearly separates the dyads into those whose frequency of social interaction decreases from 8 to 12 months (dyads G, J, and K) and those whose frequency increase from 8 to 12 months (all others). The solution does not, however, capture any differences among dyads in changes from 6 to 8 months. Such changes are apparent in Fig. 4.7 between, for example, dyads A, B, C, D, and N, and dyads H, E, M, F, and I, who differ in rate of change between 6 and 8 months. Further, dyad L appears to be an outlier in that this dyad *decreases* from 6 to 8 months. Because of these apparent differences in the profiles, a four-cluster solution was chosen as maximally descriptive of these profiles. The four clusters are shown in Fig. 4.9, where the dyads are positioned in a two-dimensional space defined by nonmetric multidimensional scaling (see Kruskal & Wish, 1978). There is a clear separation of [G,J,K] and [L] from the other dyads.

To evaluate whether clustering revealed anything of interest about the dyads in addition to differences in patterns of change in the frequency of social interactions, several ANOVAs were performed. The dependent variables consisted of various measures of who initiated interactions at each age, how initiations were responded to, and the amount of infant fussing at each age (see Green et al., 1980, for further description of these measures). Each analysis was a 3 (Cluster) by 3 (Age) mixed model ANOVA; the isolate (dyad L) had to be eliminated from the analysis.

These analyses showed consistently that the patterns of change in frequency of social interactions shown in Fig. 4.7 were most closely related to changes in

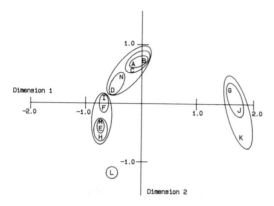

FIG. 4.9.   The four-cluster solution for the mother–infant data (Fig. 4.7 and 4.8) superimposed on the locations of the dyads in two-dimensional space. The spatial representation comes from a nonmetric multidimensional scaling of the same distance matrix used as input to the clustering methods.

mothers' initiations of interactions. There was a significant Age by Cluster effect for mothers' initiations, with mothers' initiations increasing most rapidly between 6 and 8 months for cluster [A,B,C,D,N] and less rapidly for cluster [H,E,M,F,U]. The reverse pattern held for these clusters between 8 and 12 months.

Thus, cluster analysis helped describe four groups of mother–infant dyads on the basis of changes in the frequency of social interactions across age. These groups, which differ in pattern of change in social interactions, differ also in changes in mothers' initiations over age. It may be, then, that mothers are primarily responsible for establishing the number of social contacts during this age range. (For a more detailed discussion of these issues, see Green et al., 1980).

Summary of Cluster Analysis for Profile Data

The preceding two examples have illustrated the procedures involved in performing cluster analysis, and the outline prepared by Milligan and Cooper (1987) serves as a useful framework for applying cluster analysis to a given data set. A point to reemphasize is that what the investigator does *before* applying a cluster method is as important as which method is employed. Especially when using profiles as the raw data for clustering, the selection of subjects and variables, the standardization of variables, and the choice of similarity measure can be as important as the choice of cluster method and stopping rule.

The SAHN methods are not the only clustering methods available. For either theoretical or practical reasons (e.g., computational cost with large numbers of objects), another clustering method may be preferred. Hartigan (1975), Lorr (1983), and Sneath and Sokal (1973) review K-means clustering, in which the user supplies the number of clusters desired a priori and a grouping of objects is formed that minimizes a within-cluster variance criterion. Thus, in K-means clustering, a single cluster solution is obtained, in contrast to the sequential methods. Models for overlapping clustering, such as ADCLUS and INDCLUS, allow for the possibility that an object may belong to more than one cluster (Arabie et al., 1988; Carroll & Arabie, 1983; Shepard & Arabie, 1979). Partitioning and allocation methods may be preferred when the profiles are assumed to be from a multivariate normal distribution (Hawkins et al., 1982). Whenever possible, the fit between the model and the investigator's theories about the data should be the primary concern in choice of a clustering technique.

As noted at the outset of this discussion, clustering methods are typically exploratory and have few significance tests and p levels. By their nature, then, these clustering methods do not often yield unambiguous solutions (as evident earlier in Example 2). Perhaps the most often asked question is "how many clusters are there?" This question reflects not only the difficulty that often arises in singling out one solution as "the" best solution but also the tendency to believe that the clusters are "real" groups that exist in the data. Clusters may indeed represent real groups, but it must also be remembered that clustering methods *always* yield a solution.

CONCLUSIONS

Two aspects of developmental research on individual differences have been reviewed. Several problems in analyzing individual-difference stability using correlation coefficients were addressed. In particular, solutions were offered to the problems of testing too many correlations for significance and of testing the equality of entire matrices of correlations. The analysis of individual differences in profiles was also discussed. The procedures of hierarchical cluster analysis were reviewed in detail. Clustering methods can be used to group together subjects with similar patterns of change over time.

The individual-differences analyses reviewed here can shed light on the mechanisms that effect behavior change during development. Both profile analysis and individual-difference stability methods, however, require longitudinal research designs. Although longitudinal research is time consuming, expensive, and fraught with methodological difficulties, it is required for the explication of processes of development (at least as a part of a comprehensive research program). In conjunction with longitudinal research, it is hoped that the procedures reviewed here can be applied toward the goal of understanding developmental processes.

ACKNOWLEDGMENTS

I wish to thank David Kenny for discussions of the structural equation models and Gwen Gustafson for comments on several previous versions of the chapter. Correspondence should be addressed to the author at Department of Psychology, University of Connecticut, 406 Babbidge Road, Storrs, CT, 06269-1020.

REFERENCES

Abeles, R. P. (1986). *Annotated bibliographies for longitudinal research methodologies* (Report from the Network on Methodological Issues in Longitudinal and Cohort Research). Washington, DC: National Institute on Aging and National Institute of Mental Health.

Arabie, P., Carroll, J. D., & DeSarbo, W. S. (1988). *Three-way multidimensional scaling and related techniques*. Newbury Park, CA: Sage.

Anderberg, M. R. (1973). *Cluster analysis for applications*. New York: Academic Press.

Appelbaum, M. I., & McCall, R. B. (1983). Design and analysis in developmental psychology. In W. H. Kessen (Ed.), *Handbook of child development* (Vol 1, pp. 415–476). New York: Academic Press.

Baltes P. B., & Nesselroade, J. R. (1973). The developmental analysis of individual differences on multiple measures. In J. R. Nesselroade & H. W. Reese (Eds.), *Life-span developmental psychology: Methodological issues* (pp. 219–251). New York: Academic Press.

Bartlett, M. S. (1954). A note on the multiplying factors for various χ^2 approximations. *Journal of the Royal Statistical Society* (Series B), *16*, 296–298.

Bentler, P. M. (1973). Assessment of developmental factor change at the individual and group level. In J. R. Nesselroade & H. W. Reese (Eds.), *Life-span developmental psychology: Methodological issues* (pp. 145–174). New York: Academic Press.

Bentler, P. M. (1985). *Theory and implementation of EQS: A structural equations program*. Los Angeles: BMDP Statistical Software.

Bentler, P. M., & Bonett, D. G. (1980). Significance tests and goodness of fit in the analysis of covariance structures. *Psychological Bulletin, 88*, 588–606.

Bentler, P. M., & Chou, C.-P. (1988). Practical issues in structural modeling. In J. S. Long (Ed.), *Common problems/proper solutions: Avoiding error in quantitative research* (pp. 161–192). Newbury Park, CA: Sage.

Bijnen, E. J. (1973). *Cluster analysis*. Tilburg, The Netherlands: Tilburg University Press.

Carroll, J. D., & Arabie, P. (1983). INDCLUS: An individual differences generalization of the ADCLUS model and the MAPCLUS algorithm. *Psychometrika, 48*, 157–169.

Cattell, R. B. (1978). *The scientific use of factor analysis*. New York: Plenum Press.

Cohen, J. (1969). r_c: A profile similarity coefficient invariant over variable reflection. *Psychological Bulletin, 71*, 281–284.

Cooley, W. W., & Lohnes, P. R. (1971). *Multivariate data analysis*. New York: Wiley.

Cormack, R. M. (1971). A review of classification. *Journal of the Royal Statistical Society* (Series A), *134*, 321–367.

Cronbach, L. J., & Gleser, G. C. (1953). Assessing similarity between profiles. *Psychological Bulletin, 50*, 456–473.

Cudeck, R. (1989). Analysis of correlation matrices using covariance structure models. *Psychological Bulletin, 105*, 317–327.

Draper, N. R., & Smith, H. (1981). *Applied regression analyses* (2d ed.). New York: Wiley.

Dubes, R., & Jain, A. K. (1979). Validity studies in clustering methodologies. *Pattern Recognition, 11*, 235–254.

Edelbrock, C. (1979). Comparing the accuracy of hierarchical clustering algorithms: The problem of classifying everybody. *Multivariate Behavioral Research, 14*, 367–384.

Edwards, A. L. (1976). *An introduction to correlation and regression.* New York: Freeman.

Emmerich, W. (1964). Continuity and stability in early social development. *Child Development, 35*, 311–332.

Everitt, B. (1980). *Cluster analysis* (2d ed.). New York: Wiley.

Fowler, R. L. (1987). Power and robustness of product-moment correlation. *Applied Psychological Measurement, 11*, 419–428.

Green, J. A., Gustafson, G. E., & West, M. J. (1980). Effects of infant development on mother–infant interactions. *Child Development, 51*, 199–207.

Hartigan, J. A. (1975). *Clustering algorithms.* New York: Wiley.

Hawkins, D. M., Muller, M. W., & ten Krooden, J. A. (1982). Cluster analysis. In D. M. Hawkins (Ed.), *Applied multivariate analysis.* Cambridge: Cambridge University Press.

Hays, W. L. (1973). *Statistics for the social sciences* (2d ed.). New York: Holt, Rinehart, & Winston.

Hertzog, C., & Nesselroade, J. R. (1987). Beyond autoregressive models: Some implications of the trait–state distinction for the structural modeling of developmental change. *Child Development, 58*, 93–109.

Hubert, L. (1974). Approximate evaluation techniques for the single-link and complete-link hierarchical clustering procedures. *Journal of the American Statistical Association, 74*, 698–704.

Jain, A. K., & Dubes, R. C. (1988). *Algorithms for clustering data.* Englewood Cliffs, NJ: Prentice Hall.

Jennrich, R. I. (1970). An asymptotic χ^2 test for the equality of two correlation matrices. *Journal of the American Statistical Association, 65*, 904–912.

Jöreskog, K. G. (1979). Statistical estimation of structural models in longitudinal-developmental investigations. In J. R. Nesselroade & P. B. Baltes (Eds.), *Longitudinal research in the study of behavior and development* (pp. 303–351). New York: Academic Press.

Jöreskog, K. G., & Sörbom, D. (1984). *LISREL VI: User's guide* (3rd. ed.). Mooresville, IN: Scientific Software.

Kenny, D. A., & Campbell, D. N. (1989). On the measurement of change in over-time data. *Journal of Personality, 57*, 445–481.

Kraemer, H. C., & Thiemann, S. (1987). *How many subjects?* Newbury Park, CA: Sage.

Kruskal, J. B. (1977). The relationship between multidimensional scaling and clustering. In J. Van Ryzin (Ed.), *Classification and clustering* (pp. 19–44). New York: Academic Press.

Kruskal, J. B., & Wish, M. (1978). *Multidimensional scaling* (Sage University Paper No. 07-011). Newbury Park, CA: Sage.

Larzelere, R. E., & Mulaik, S. A. (1977). Single-sample tests for many correlations. *Psychological Bulletin, 84*, 557–569.

Law, H. G., Snyder, C. W., Hattie, J. A., & McDonald, R. P. (1984). *Research methods for multimode data analysis.* New York: Praeger.

Long, J. S. (1983). *Covariance structure models.* Newbury Park, CA: Sage.

Lorr, M. (1983). *Cluster analysis for social scientists.* San Francisco: Jossey-Bass.

Marsh, H. W., Balla, J. R., & McDonald, R. P. (1988). Goodness-of-fit indexes in confirmatory factor analysis: The effect of sample size. *Psychological Bulletin, 103*, 391–410.

McArdle, J. J., & Epstein, D. (1987). Latent growth curves within developmental structural equation models. *Child Development, 58*, 110–133.

McCall, R. B. (1977). Challenges to a science of developmental psychology. *Child Development, 48*, 333–344.

McCall, R. B., Appelbaum, M. I., & Hogarty, P. S. (1973). Developmental changes in mental performance. *Monographs of the Society for Research in Child Development, 38* (No. 150).

Milligan, G. W. (1980). An examination of the effect of six types of error perturbation on fifteen clustering algorithms. *Psychometrika, 45,* 325–342.

Milligan, G. W., & Cooper, M. C. (1985). An examination of procedures for determining the number of clusters in a data set. *Psychometrika, 50,* 159–179.

Milligan, G. W., & Cooper, M. C. (1987). Methodology review: Clustering methods. *Applied Psychological Measurement, 11,* 329–354.

Mortimer, J. T., Finch, M. D., & Kumka, D. (1982). Persistence and change in development: The multidimensional self-concept. In P. B. Baltes & O. G. Brim (Eds.), *Life-span development and behavior* (pp. 263–289). New York: Academic Press.

Overall, J. G. (1964). Note on multivariate methods for profile analysis. *Psychological Bulletin, 61,* 195–198.

Pedhazur, E. J. (1982). *Multiple regression in behavioral research* (2d ed.). New York: Holt, Rinehart, & Winston.

Pianta, R. C., Sroufe, L. A., & Egeland, B. (1989). Continuity and discontinuity in maternal sensitivity at 6, 24, and 42 months in a high-risk sample. *Child Development, 60,* 481–487.

Rogosa, D. R., & Willett, J. B. (1985). Satisfying a simplex structure is simpler than it should be. *Journal of Educational Statistics, 10,* 99–107.

Sackett, G. P., Sameroff, A. J., Cairns, R. B., & Suomi, S. J. (1981). Continuity in behavioral development: Theoretical and empirical issues. In K. Immelmann, G. W. Barlow, L. Petrinovich, & M. Main (Eds.), *Behavioral development* (pp. 23–57). Cambridge: Cambridge University.

SAS Institute, Inc. (1985). *Sas user's guide: Statistics, version 5 edition.* Cary, NC: Sas Institute.

Shepard, R. N., & Arabie, P. (1979). Additive clustering: Representation of similarities as combinations of discrete overlapping categories. *Psychological Review, 86,* 87–123.

Skinner, H. A. (1978). Differentiating the contribution of elevation, scatter and shape in profile similarity. *Educational and psychological measurement, 38,* 297–308.

Sneath, P. H. A., & Sokal, R. R. (1973). *Numerical taxonomy.* San Francisco: Freeman.

Späth, H. (1980). *Cluster analysis algorithms.* New York: Wiley.

Steiger, J. H. (1980). Tests for comparing elements of a correlation matrix. *Psychological Bulletin, 87,* 245–251.

Tucker, L. R. (1966). Learning theory and multivariate experiment: Illustration by determination of generalized learning curves. In R. B. Cattel (Ed.), *Handbook of multivariate experimental psychology.* Chicago: Rand-McNalley.

Ward, J. H. (1963). Hierarchical grouping to optimize an objective function. *Journal of the American Statistical Association, 58,* 236–244.

Werts, C. E., Rock, D. A., Linn, R. L., & Jöreskog, K. G. (1976). Comparison of correlations, variances, covariances, and regression weights with or without measurement error. *Psychological Bulletin, 83,* 1007–1013.

Wohlwill, J. F. (1973). *The study of behavioral development.* New York: Academic Press.

II INDIVIDUAL DIFFERENCES IN NEUROBEHAVIORAL DEVELOPMENT

5 Behavioral States in Infants: Individual Differences and Individual Analyses

Evelyn B. Thoman
Mary P. Whitney
Biobehavioral Sciences Graduate Degree Program and Department of Psychology, University of Connecticut

INTRODUCTION

Behavioral states of sleep and wakefulness constitute a unique variable set for depicting individual differences among infants and for using these differences to make developmental predictions. An infant's states are ubiquitous—they are present at all times, over all ages, and, thus, they can be observed in the laboratory or in the home and under any environmental circumstances, naturally occurring or experimentally controlled. States are an expression of widespread integrative processes in the central nervous system, and deviancies in state characteristics are associated with deviancy in central nervous system functioning. Thus, it is reasonable to assume that state, as a fundamental neurobehavioral characteristic, should be most useful for assessment and prediction. However, studies of infants' states have not uniformly supported this assumption. Our research findings, which are described here, are based on new strategies for the study of states, and they clearly demonstrate that the assumption is a valid one.

We have approached these studies from the position that prediction for individuals differs from prediction for groups, and that the ultimate goal is to derive a developmental trajectory for each individual infant. Toward this end, we have focused on intensive study of state as a within-individual process, and we have found that state measures can reliably characterize individual infants from the earliest ages. From these studies, the organizational characteristics of the states of infants are described, and the adaptive significance of the earliest state system is considered.

The Importance of Definiteness in State Definitions

State is a concept that is operationally defined in various ways. By some investigators, states are defined as configurations of analog signals recorded from electrodes placed on the subject; they are defined by others as a mixture of such physiological signals along with behavioral variables; and by still others as configurations of behaviors. The latter procedure defines the behavioral states of sleep and wakefulness, which are the major focus of this chapter.

Behavioral researchers are in agreement on two major sleep states, Active (REM) Sleep and Quiet (Non-REM) Sleep; however, there is a general lack of agreement on categories and definitions of the states of wakefulness and the transition states (states that occur between the sleep states or between sleep and wakefulness). As a consequence of diversity in state taxonomies, it is very often not possible to make comparisons across studies of behavioral states (Ashton, 1973; Prechtl, 1982; Robinson, 1969). Stratton (1982) has spoken to this issue forcefully: "One of the unique features of working with human newborns is the attention which must be paid to their fluctuating behavioral states . . . it is a matter of some urgency that there should be a concensus over the definitions of the behavioural states. The use of idiosyncratic or undefined state ratings can only result in an uninterpretable and unusable literature" (p. 18).

The most commonly used behavioral state systems are those of Brazelton (1961), Prechtl and Beintema (1964), Thoman (1975, 1985), and Wolff (1966). These are markedly different in their conceptualization and in their classification of infants' states. For example, Prechtl proposes a state "scale," with five states identified by numbers, each defined by the presence or absence of criterial behaviors, including eye opening, gross body movements, regular respiration, and vocalization (Prechtl & O'Brien, 1982). By contrast, we propose states which are identified as coherent behavior patterns that are expressed by qualitative differences in visual attentiveness, motor activity, motor tone, breathing, and vocalization. Not only do researchers use one or another of these state classifications, but matters are further complicated because investigators often report that they used a "modification" of one of these state systems, whereupon Stratton's concern is aptly expressed.

It is often the case that state is not the major focus in an infant study and, in these instances, it would seem more appropriate to adopt rather than adapt, that is to rely on a state classification system that has already been demonstrated to meet psychometric requirements for reliability and validity. In this way, the researcher can avoid the extensive process of test development.

We have, of course, argued for the use of our state taxonomy and do so again in this chapter. Over two decades ago, Wolff's (1966) state classifications provided the starting point for our first state study—we adopted his states as our "standard." Over many years of state research, we have refined, modified, and extended the system of state categories and their definitions, and we have demonstrated measurement reliability for each state included in our final taxonomy. We have engaged in the serious business of instrument development.

The Importance of a Rationale for Classifying Infants' States

How one views states determines how one categorizes and defines them for study. At the same time, one's views of states is largely derived from their study. Epstein and Erskine (1983) stated: "The essence of the scientific method is that it involves a continuous interaction between observation and conceptualization, each influencing the other and, in the process, generating an increasingly differentiated, integrated, and accurate model of the world" (p. 133). Thus, the selection of taxonomic categories and their definitions must be a reflection of one's experienced perceptions of the nature of that which is being described. This is the reason that state theories and definitions have not been static over the years among those of us who have been intensely involved in state research.

Our own perceptions of infants' states have come from more than two decades devoted to observations of infants and their mothers while they were engaged in their typical daily activities in the home. For most of these studies, each day's observation was 7 hours in duration, with state and mother and baby behaviors recorded every 10 seconds throughout the day.

Our experience has led us to agree with Hobson (1977), that behavioral states are *qualitatively* different behavioral modes that express distinct but integrated central neural processes. These behavioral modes are expressed by a relatively limited number of behavioral patterns, or state themes (Iberall & McCulloch, 1969; Thoman, 1975, 1985). How many states are selected for a classificatory scheme is a function of the number of recurrent themes one discerns as common to most babies. There is obviously no such thing as "*the* states of infancy," a phrase that appears in the infancy literature. There are never absolutes in taxonomies of any kind.

We have selected categories of behavioral states, or prevailing behavioral themes, that are readily distinguishable and reliably recorded by observers, but also ones that are responded to distinctively by caregivers. For example, caregivers inevitably respond to their babys' crying. Neither parent nor researcher can ignore this state. But parents' responses are far more discriminating—for example, between fussing and crying, between alertness and nonalertness, and even between nonalertness and drowse. When the baby is in drowse, the parent is aware that the baby is about to go to sleep. Parents attend to their baby's alert looking, especially if the baby is returning their own gaze. In view of the role of state in providing cues to the baby's status, in modulating incoming stimulation, and in mediating the infant's responsiveness to the social input, the parents' sensitivity to the various states of their babies is of great significance for the developing relationship.

Some of the caregiver's responses to a baby's state are very subtle, others are not. For example, one father was noted to comment on his baby's way of looking, referring to what we call "nonalert wakefulness." He expressed his disappointment that the baby was never alert when he held her (his observation was quite accurate as this baby was rarely alert during any social-holding circumstance). Such recorded instances of parents' differential responses to their infants' behavioral states give a form of "face validity" to the categories we have included in our state taxonomy. As researchers, we have invented the concept of "state," and we may give names, or even numbers, to these behavioral patterns, but researchers neither created states nor discovered them. Evolution accomplished the first task, and parents the latter.

A Taxonomy of Infants' States

The following state classification system describes 10 sequentially recurring behavioral patterns that can be reliably observed in infants (Thoman, 1985)

Awake States

Alert. The infant's eyes are open, bright and shining, and attentive or scanning. Motor activity is typically low during the first 2 weeks of life, but the infant may be active.

Nonalert Waking. The infant's eyes are usually open, but dull and unfocused. Motor activity may vary but is typically high. The eyes may be closed during periods of high-level activity. Isolated fuss vocalizations may occur.

Fuss. Fuss sounds are made continuously or intermittently, at relatively low levels of intensity.

Cry. Intense vocalizations occur either singly or in succession.

Transition States Between Sleep and Waking

Drowse. The infant's eyes are either open but "heavy-lidded" or opening and closing slowly. The level of motor activity is typically low but may vary. This state usually occurs when the infant is going from waking to sleep.

Daze. The infant's eyes are open but glassy and immobile. The level of motor activity is typically low. Daze may occur between episodes of alertness or drowse as well as between sleep and waking.

Sleep–Wake Transition. The infant shows behaviors of both wakefulness and sleep. There is usually generalized motor activity; the eyes may be closed, or they may open and close rapidly. Isolated fuss vocalizations may occur. This state generally occurs when the baby is awakening from sleep.

Sleep States

Active Sleep. The infant's eyes are closed. Respiration is uneven and primarily costal in nature. Sporadic movements may occur, but muscle tone is low between movements. REMs occur intermittently, ranging from a brief, light flicker of the eyelids to prolonged intense REM storms accompanied by raising of the eyelids and occasional eye opening. Other behaviors that may be seen in Active Sleep include smiles, frowns, grimaces, mouthing, sucking, sighs, sigh–sobs, and twitching movements of the extremities. The baby may emit brief, high-pitched cries, as well as "straining" or grunting vocalizations during large stretching movements.

Quiet Sleep. The infant's eyes are closed. Respiration is relatively slow, regular, and abdominal in nature. A tonic level of motor tone is maintained, and motor activity is usually limited to occasional startles, sigh–sobs, or rhythmic mouthing. Brief periods of limb or body movements may occur (these are more frequent in preterm infants).

Transitional Sleep State

Active–Quiet Transition Sleep. This state typically occurs between periods of Active Sleep and Quiet Sleep. The eyes are closed, and there is little motor activity. Respiration is not as regular as Quiet Sleep, and more regular than Active Sleep. The baby shows mixed behavioral signs of Active Sleep and Quiet Sleep. Breathing may be abdominal or costal or mixed, muscle tone may vary, and isolated REMs may occur.

The distinct behavioral morphology of each of these states argues convincingly for the inclusion of all 10 categories in a complete taxonomy of behavioral sleep–wake states.

For many research and clinical purposes, 10 states are a large number to differentiate and record. It is reasonable to combine some of the states into clusters to reduce the number of categories for observation. The Summary State Set consists of six derived state clusters: *Alert; Nonalert Waking; Fuss or Cry; Drowse, Daze, or Sleep–Wake Transition; Active Sleep; Quiet Sleep or Active– Quiet Transition Sleep.* Note that this abbreviated classification scheme still includes all 10 of the original states.

This 6-state classification system has been used for full-term infants, premature infants during the preterm and postterm period (Thoman, 1985), and for infants throughout the first year of life (Acebo, 1987).

The Importance of Being Earnest
About Measuring State

Despite an emphasis on states as potential predictor variables, a number of researchers have concluded that infants are not sufficiently stable during the neonatal period to characterize individuals. For example, Anders (1979) reports that "most investigators have been largely unsuccessful . . . in determining reliable consistencies in individual infants' sleep patterns" (p. 47; also, see Anders & Keener, 1985). This conclusion would seem to describe the more recent state of state study. Using electrophysiological recordings, individual differences among neonates have been reported only in total sleep time (Brown, 1964; Parmelee, Schultz, & Disbrow, 1961); stability in Active and Quiet Sleep has been reported primarily over older age ranges (Anders & Keener, 1985; Dittrichova, Paul, & Vondracek, 1976; Hoppenbrouwers et al., 1978). If it were the case that one could reliably characterize an infant's states, there would be no reason to expect state measures to be useful for assessment or prediction for individuals.

Fortunately, this is not the case. In 1976 (Thoman, Korner, & Kraemer), we presented data indicating individual differences for some of the infants' behavioral states during the first 3 days of life. This report was based on only 2 hourly observations for each infant; and the results highlighted for us the necessity for more prolonged observations if one is interested in characterizing an infant's full repertoire of state strategies. Since that time, our studies have been based on extensive (i.e., 7-hour) observations of each infant in the home, as referred to

TABLE 5.1
Mean Percentage of Baby Alone Time in Each Primary State and Derived State,
F-Ratio for Individual Differences and Reliability Coefficient for Full-Term Infants

| | Primary States | | r_{tt} |
	Time	F	
Alert	6.7	3.45	0.71***
Nonalert wake	2.8	2.63	0.62***
Fuss	1.8	2.13	0.53**
Cry	1.7	4.17	0.76***
Drowse	4.3	2.38	0.58**
Daze	1.0	3.03	0.67***
S-W Transition	1.3	1.92	0.48*
Active Sleep	50.3	3.57	0.72***
Active-Quiet Tr. Sleep	1.9	2.50	0.60**
Quiet Sleep	28.1	2.78	0.64***
Derived States			
Alert	6.7	3.45	0.71***
Nonalert Wake	2.8	2.63	0.62***
Fuss or Cry	3.4	3.22	0.69***
Drowse, Daze, S-W Tr.	6.7	2.27	0.56**
Active Sleep	52.3	3.22	0.69***
Quiet Sleep	28.1	2.78	0.64***

*$p < .05$; **$p < .01$; $p < .001$.

TABLE 5.2
Mean Percentage of Baby Alone Time in Each Primary State and Derived State,
F-Ratio for Individual Differences and Reliability Coefficient for Premature Infants

	Primary States		
	Time	F	r_{tt}
Alert	8.9	4.24	0.76**
Nonalert Wake	7.2	4.68	0.79**
Fuss	2.8	4.78	0.79**
Cry	1.7	1.25	0.20
Drowse	4.4	5.09	0.80**
Daze	2.1	2.46	0.59
S-W Transition	3.7	1.52	0.34
Active Sleep	44.1	3.37	0.70*
Quiet Sleep	25.0	0.92	0.00
	Derived States		
Alert	8.9	4.24	0.76**
Nonalert Wake	7.2	4.68	0.79**
Fuss or Cry	4.5	3.34	0.70*
Drowse, Daze, S-W Tr.	10.3	4.71	0.79**
Active Sleep	44.1	3.37	0.70*
Quiet Sleep	25.0	0.92	0.00

$*p < .05; **p < .01.$

before. Data from such ecologically valid observations make it possible to describe each infant's state structure in the range of environmental conditions to which the infant is adapting.

From such intensive observations on repeated occasions, it has been possible to assess each state for consistency over weeks in the amount of time spent in that state. Using an analysis of variance for repeated measures, we have assessed individual differences in the amount of time spent in each state in various contexts, including the total 7-hour day, or periods of the day when the babies were alone, when they were with their mothers, when mothers were caregiving, etc.

The results of such analyses are given in Tables 5.1 and 5.2. Table 5.1 presents, for all portions of the 7-hour day when the babies were alone, the mean time 28 full-term babies spent in each state over postnatal weeks 2 through 5. Also presented are the F values from the ANOVAs for Individual Differences, and measurement reliability values, calculated as $r_{tt} = I - I/F$ (Denenberg 1979, 1982; Winer, 1971). In the top portion of Table 5.1, the results of these analyses are presented for the 10 primary states we have defined; and the bottom portion of the table presents the results for the six derived state clusters in the Summary Set. Notice that significant individual differences and measurement reliability are obtained for each of these states and state clusters. Thus, individual full-term infants are highly consistent over weeks in the amount of time they spend in each of the primary states as well as in each of the derived state clusters.

Table 5.2 presents the same analyses for eight prematurely born infants observed weekly when they were 2 to 5 weeks postterm (Davis & Thoman, 1987). Although this small sample of premature infants failed to show significant reliability on a number of the individual states, reliability was present on all the state clusters but Quiet Sleep. Thus, measures of time allocation to most of their states reliably describes individual infants, given four 7-hour observations.

There is considerable variability in the distribution and duration of periods babies spend alone within the day of an observation and over successive weekly observations. In addition, mothers and babies do not follow consistent temporal schedules throughout the day or on successive weeks. Despite these variations, individual differences and reliability of measures were obtained for both groups of infants aforementioned. Similar results were also obtained from such analyses of the states measured during portions of the day the infants were with the mother (Becker & Thoman, 1983).

The findings from these studies of normal and healthy prematurely born infants indicate an impressive degree of stability in central integrative controls for infants' states from the earliest postnatal age. It would seem, therefore, that marked deviations on these measures would have implications for abnormal CNS functioning. However, deviations in amounts of specific states have not been found to be associated with CNS and behavioral deviancy (e.g., Anders, Keener, Bowe, & Shoaff, 1983; Hoppenbrouwers et al., 1988). Once again, states have been viewed as failing to fulfill their promise as a tool for assessment. However, we propose that the search for predictors in variations in specific states derives from an overly simple view of states, and that it is necessary to consider states as expressing a complex, dynamic process that must be characterized over time in order to assess the functional status of the central nervous system.

States as a Behavioral System

Our view, and therefore our approach to the study of state, is best conceptualized within a General Systems Theory (GST) perspective (Bertalanffy, 1933, 1968; Weiss, 1969, 1971). We have found GST notions to be most relevant for developmental study and analysis at the level of the individual (Thoman, 1986). More specifically, GST is concerned with problems of organized complexity (Bertalanffy, 1968), which is precisely the issue for developmental research. Bertalanffy (1933) proposed that any theory of development and life in general must be a systems theory. Of major interest to systems theorists are the functions of the brain, as an hierarchically organized system, with multiple expressions, including overt behavior. Iberall and McCulloch (1969) asserted: "The function of the central nervous system, with its memory, communications, computational, and learning capabilities, is to provide algorithmic content capable of mediating the stability of internal chains, so that a satisfactory pattern of behavior emerges" (p. 290). The results of this regulation is behavioral patterning whose richness derives from this complexity at the level of the central nervous system; that is, the patterning of behaviors (i.e., state) is an emergent process from the organized processes of the central nervous system.

We have taken a relatively simple, nonmathematical, approach to the application of GST to our infant state research, mainly by applying the notions conceptually and thus using the characteristics of systems and the principles of their functioning as guidelines to our behavioral models. For example, the principle that a system functions to maintain its own equilibrium (Bunge, 1979; Weiss, 1971) provides the basis for investigation of overall state patterning, rather than specific, isolated states. A closely related principle is that systems processes occur over time and, thus, they must be studied over time. A single, time-frame, "snapshot" view of behavior cannot reveal the systems dynamics the developmentalist is interested in, either for assessing the current status of an individual or for prediction.

Even more, the objective of understanding the functional status of individual infants requires study of the system *within individuals*. In the following sections, we present several approaches to the study of infants' states from this perspective.

Relationships Among the States Within Individuals

If an infant's states are considered to be a system of integrated behavior patterns, the state categories selected and defined should show systematic relationships to each other. We have examined these relationships by studying the interlinkings among the states within individuals (Thoman, Davis, & Denenberg, 1987). *Intraperson* correlations were used rather than the usual *inter*person statistic, as the latter gives information only on the consistency of relative ranking of subjects within a group on any measure, whereas the former describes the relationship between state variables across time *within individuals*. The intraperson correlation tells us that there is covariation between two related states across the time domain of the four weekly observations; that is, related states are time locked so that they both change in parallel (directly or inversely) within infants on any day. The two correlational procedures are statistically and logically independent of each other.

Table 5.3 shows the intrainfant correlations among all pairings of nine of the 10 primary states (Active–Quiet Transitional Sleep was not differentiated for the subjects in this study). Significance levels have been adjusted, because percentage values were used, and these add up to 100%, forcing a negative average intercorrelation among the variables (Denenberg & Thoman, 1981).

These interlinkings among the states are also shown in Fig. 5.1. Not all the relationships comply with intuitive expectations. For example, *Quiet Sleep* is an almost completely isolated state, showing only a correlation with Drowse, and not a significant correlation to *Active Sleep*. These were surprising findings, and one can account for them only by speculation. First, the relationship between

TABLE 5.3

Intraperson Correlations Among the States

	Nonalert W. Active	Fuss	Cry	Drowse	Daze	Sleep-Wake Transition	Active Sleep	Quiet Sleep
Alert	.24*	.38**	.29*	.46**	.54***	.48**	-.76***	-.32
Nonalert		.36*	.23*	.47***	.27*	.28*	-.47*	-.21
Fuss			.70***	.48***	.52***	.06	-.56*	-.37
Cry				.32*	.12	-.03	-.44	-.28
Drowse					.57***	.18	-.46*	-.28
Daze						.44**	-.52*	-.60**
Sleep-Wake Transition							-.35	-.37
Active Sleep								-.29

Note. Based on portion of the day when infants were alone. From Thoman, Davis, and Denenberg (1987).

*$p < 0.05$; **$p < 0.01$; ***$p < 0.001$.

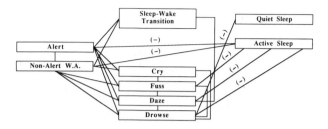

FIG. 5.1. Interlinking of the primary states, based on intrainfant correlations.

Quiet Sleep and Drowse can be seen as antecedent to the later ages when Drowse immediately precedes Quiet Sleep (i.e., Non-REM Sleep) rather than Active Sleep, as is the case in early infancy. In fact, in the adult, Drowse is often indistinguishable from Stage 1 Non-REM Sleep (Rechtschaffen & Kales, 1968). Thus, the linkage between these two states apparently begins before they are temporally sequential. Second, the lack of a correlation between Quiet Sleep and Active Sleep might be expected because they are temporally sequential and because the two sleep states are clearly related in the CNS at the cellular and biochemical levels (e.g., Hobson, Lydic, & Baghdoyan, 1986). The lack of a relationship between these states can be seen as reflecting the dramatic differences in the physiology of the two states (Jouvet, 1961; Orem & Barnes, 1980; Snyder, Hobson, Morrison, & Goldfrank, 1964).

Notice also that *Nonalert Waking Activity* has a unique pattern of relationships. This state is generally overlooked in infant research as it is often confused or combined with Alertness. It is characterized behaviorally by a vacant look in the baby's eyes. During this state, parents may comment about their babies being "spaced out." The importance of this state is indicated in our finding that the amount of time a baby spends in Nonalert Wakefulness is negatively correlated with an index of overall state stability (Becker & Thoman, 1982), which is described later. This relationship to overall state control, and its role in the social exchange, clearly suggest that Nonalert Wakefulness should be distinguished in observations of infant state, as it has significance for neurobehavioral functioning during early infancy, as well as for social adaptation.

The *Daze* state has not been differentiated except in our studies, although we have generally combined Daze and Drowse for data analysis. It is not clear whether other researchers combine the behavior patterns we call Daze and Drowse or if Daze is included with another waking state. In the intraindividual correlational analyses, Daze and Drowse are significantly correlated, but Daze also has a unique pattern of relationships with the other states. Thus, this state merits separate consideration.

The same is true of *Fuss* and *Cry*, which are highly correlated with each other but show distinct patterns of relations with other states.

The possibility of a negative correlation between *Alert* and *Active Sleep* was suggested by previous reports (Drucker-Colin & McGaugh, 1977; Hobson, 1977; McGinty & Siegel, 1983; Sterman, Lucas, & MacDonald, 1972) and confirmed by our study (Denenberg & Thoman, 1981). We interpret this relationship as support for the hypothesis proposed by Roffwarg, Muzio, and Dement (1966), namely that a primary function of Active Sleep during early infancy is to provide stimulation to the central nervous system at a time when the infant's capabilities for receiving stimulation from the environment are limited. Acebo (1987) reports that the linkage between these two states within individual infants persists at least through the first 6 months of life.

The evidence for extensive interlinkings among all the states clearly indicates that the sleeping and waking states constitute an integrated behavioral system. These results also indicate the degree to which the behavioral states express systems integration at the level of the central nervous system. Thus, the presence or absence of major linkages should be indicative of CNS functional status in individual infants.

An Alternative to Direct Observations of the Sleep States

Behavioral observations are very labor intensive, and they are not appropriate for study of large numbers of subjects observed for prolonged periods. For example, such observations are neither feasible nor appropriate for 24-hour recordings, which are essential for studies of diurnal rhythms. To extend our studies, both in terms of larger numbers of subjects and longer durations of observation, we have developed an automated monitoring procedure for continuous recording of the sleep states and the general category of wakefulness.

The recordings are accomplished by means of a pressure-sensitive crib mattress that produces a single channel of analog signals from the infant's respiration and body movements (Thoman & Glazier, 1987). We have shown that such a record of motility can be reliably scored for the sleep states and wakefulness in both human and animal infants (Thoman & Tynan, 1979; Thoman & Zeidner, 1979; Thoman, Zeidner, & Denenberg, 1981; Zeidner, Weyand, Thoman, & Denenberg, 1983). In the humans, recordings were validated from behavioral observations; and in the animals both behavioral observations and EEG recordings were used for validation. Using this nonintrusive procedure, we have carried out the first studies of infants' sleep from 24-hour recordings in the home.

From these automated recordings, it is possible to differentiate five states: Active Sleep, Quiet Sleep, Active–Quiet Transitional Sleep, Sleep–Wake Transition, and Wakefulness. Table 5.4 presents the mean time spent in each of these states by a group of 20 full-term infants, from weekly 24-hour recordings in the home at 1 through 5 weeks postnatally. The states were measured as a percentage of the portion of the 24-hour day the infants were in the crib. *F* values for

TABLE 5.4
Mean Percentage of Crib Time in Each State, F-Ratio for Individual
Differences and Reliability Coefficient for Fullterm Infants

State	Time	F	r_{tt}
Quiet Sleep	27.12	4.54**	0.78**
Active-Quiet Transition Sleep	1.34	6.25**	0.84**
Active Sleep	57.51	4.54**	0.78**
Sleep-Wake Transition	5.37	3.33**	0.70**
Wakefulness	8.73	7.69**	0.87**

$**p < 0.01$.

individual differences and measurement reliability values (r_{tt}) are also presented for each state. Table 5.5 presents the same analyses for 20 prematurely born infants recorded at 1 through 5 weeks postterm age (Pugsley, Acebo, & Thoman, 1988). For both groups of babies, each of the states measured by this procedure provides reliable description of individuals.

The sensor mattress recording procedure can be used to characterize temporal organization of infants' states, as described in the section that follows.

Sleep Cyclicity as a Characteristic of Individuals

States are sequentially recurring patterns of behavior. The temporal organization of sleep has long been of interest, especially with respect to rhythmicity, cyclicity, or periodicity, as it has variously been referred to. Although numerous studies report cyclicity during the early postterm period, findings have previously been so conflicting that some researchers have called into question the presence of cyclicity in infants' sleep. Anders and Keener (1985) did not find

TABLE 5.5
Mean Percentage of Crib Time in Each State, F-Ratio for Individual
Differences and Reliability Coefficient for Premature Infants

State	Time	F	r_{tt}
Quiet Sleep	29.15	2.78**	0.64**
Active-Quiet Transitional Sleep	1.25	9.09**	0.89**
Active Sleep	55.15	3.03**	0.67**
Sleep-Wake Transition	6.36	6.67**	0.85**
Wakefulness	8.12	2.50**	0.60**

$**p < 0.01$.

cyclicity to be typical throughout the first year. Likewise, Coons and Guilleminault (1984) report cycle lengths were so variable across age and within individual infants that, at least until 6 weeks, "sleep-state sequencing is relatively random" (p. 173). By contrast, the data described from our 24-hour recordings clearly demonstrate cyclicity from the earliest postnatal age (Thoman & McDowell, 1989).

Kraemer, Hole, and Anders (1984) proposed a statistical procedure that makes it possible to assess significance of rhythmicity in states. The procedure is based on an ordered sequence of tests for statistically significant nonrandom temporal organization in a state time series. We used this procedure to investigate cyclicity of Quiet Sleep in fullterm infants monitored in the home for 24-hour periods when they were 2, 3, 4, and 5 weeks old. In accordance with the requirements of the Kraemer et al. test, all sleep periods with at least four recurrences of Quiet Sleep were analyzed. A sleep period was delimited by 3 or more consecutive minutes of wakefulness, or time out of the crib.

Only 1 out of 20 subjects failed to have an analyzable sleep episode on any of the 4 weeks. More than half the subjects had analyzable sleep episodes each week; and 10 recordings showed 2 sleep episodes that met the criteria for cyclicity analysis. A total of 55 episodes were analyzable for all babies. For purposes of this analysis, the states in each sleep episode were categorized as either Quiet Sleep or Nonquiet Sleep (including Active Sleep, Transitional states, and Wakefulness less than 3 minutes). Significant cyclicity of Quiet Sleep was found in 49 of the 55 sleep episodes analyzed. Figure 5.2 shows a noncyclic sleep episode selected from one infant's record, and Fig. 5.3 shows a cyclic episode of another infant subject in the study. The mean Quiet Sleep recurrence

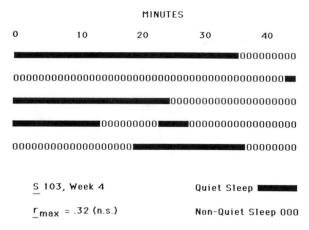

FIG. 5.2. Raster plot of sequences of Quiet Sleep and Nonquiet Sleep bouts in a sleep episode that does not show significant cyclicity (r_{max} = 0.32, n.s.).

MINUTES

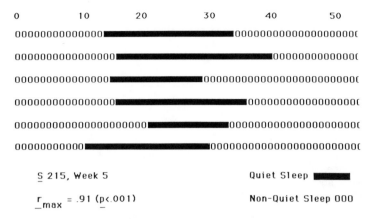

S 215, Week 5   Quiet Sleep ▬▬▬

r_{max} = .91 (p<.001)   Non-Quiet Sleep 000

FIG. 5.3.   Raster plot of sequences of Quiet Sleep and Nonquiet Sleep bouts in a sleep episode that shows significant cyclicity (r_{max} = 0.91, p < 0.001).

period was 63.2 minutes. Eighteen of the 20 infants exhibited cyclicity on 1 or more weeks (Thoman & McDowell, 1989). Likewise, in a study of 20 premature infants during the 5 postterm weeks, 19 of the 20 infants showed significant cyclicity on 1 or more weeks (Pugsley, Acebo, & Thoman, 1988). Thus, most infants are capable of showing significant cyclicity during the neonatal period.

A measure of degree of cyclicity over the 4 weeks for each infant was calculated as a summary of weighted weekly scores. These were based on the number of analyzable sleep episodes (those with four or more bouts of Quiet Sleep) and the number of episodes that showed significant cyclicity on each week. The cyclicity scores of full-term infants were found to be related to the State Stability Index (Thoman & McDowell, 1989), which is described in the following section.

Measurement of Stability in the State System in Individual Infants

We have used two methodological and statistical approaches to assessing stability in state patterning in individual infants.

Rate of State Change.   The first is a measure of rate of state change per hour during a sleep episode. A sleep episode was delimited by 3 or more consecutive minutes of wakefulness. A state change occurred only if the infant changed between Active Sleep, Quiet Sleep, or Nonsleep (defined as the states of

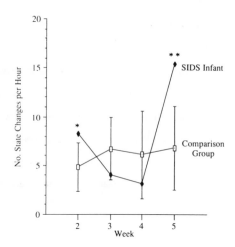

FIG. 5.4. Number of state changes per hour across weeks for one infant who later died of SIDS and a comparison group of normal infants (S.E.).

wakefulness, but including Drowse, and Sleep–Wake Transition). This measure reliably describes individual infants (Thoman, 1975).

Figure 5.4 presents the state changes of infants recorded weekly from direct behavioral observations on weeks 2 through 5. The mean for a group of 28 infants is presented, as well as the individual curve for one infant who was also apparently normal during these early weeks but died of SIDS at 3 months (Thoman & Becker, 1979; Thoman, Miano, & Freese, 1978; Thoman et al., in press; Waite & Thoman, 1981). This infant also showed other forms of neu-robehavioral instability (Thoman et al., in press) during the early weeks of life. Based on these findings, we proposed a model for SIDS risk, which was tested from predictions for siblings of SIDS (SSIDS) infants (Thoman et al., 1988). Of three SSIDS infants, two were predicted to develop normally and one was considered to be at risk. The first two infants developed uneventfully; the latter infant was a classical Near-miss infant who was hospitalized and was observed to have life-threatening apneas in the hospital. This infant also had unstable states over the early weeks, as measured by the following statistic.

The State Stability Index.   We have devised a statistic to assess the patterning of states over a series of observations (Thoman et al., 1981). Briefly, for the direct behavior observations in the Longitudinal study just described, the distribution of each infant's sleep and waking states within each of the four weekly 7-hour observations was determined, and weekly state profiles were thus obtained. Then a quantitative measure of consistency of these profiles was calculated using an ANOVA, yielding a single State Stability score (F = MS States/MS States × Weeks) for each infant for the four successive weekly observations. It should be noted that the State Stability F-value is used as a *descriptive* statistic to indicate relative degree of profile consistency, rather than using the F-ratio as an inferential statistic in the usual manner where a test of significant differences between groups is the objective. Thus the term State Stability Index.

To illustrate the stability of profiles found in some of the infants, Fig. 5.5 shows the four weekly profiles for four subjects with high Stability scores. The remarkable consistency in state profiles of these infants is obvious.

It should be noted that such consistency was present despite the fact that: (a) the total amount of time each baby spent alone from week to week varied, (b) the distribution of periods of the day when the baby was alone varied from week to week, and (c) each baby was observed by three different observers over the 4 weeks. These data provide strong evidence for the systems structure of states; that is, it is apparent that constraints imposed by the functioning of the CNS can be effective in maintaining a relative invariance in the apportionment of time to each state week after week.

State Stability Index as Predictor of Neurobehavioral Dysfunction

Not all infants are as stable over the early weeks as those shown in Fig. 5.5. Figure 5.6 presents weekly profiles for four infants with very low Stability (F-

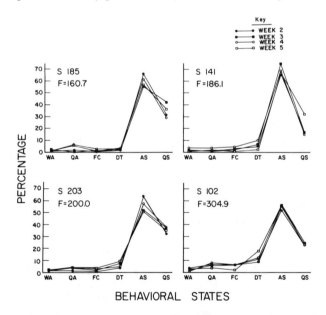

FIG. 5.5. Weekly behavioral state profiles for four infants with high State Stability scores. Along the X-axis are the behavioral states, and the Y-axis is the percentage of time spent in each state. WA: Waking Active; QA: Quiet Alert; FC: Fuss or Cry; DT: Drowse or Transition; AS: Active Sleep; QS: Quiet Sleep.

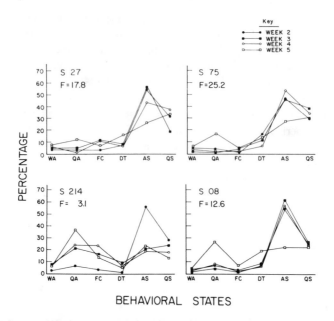

BEHAVIORAL STATES

FIG. 5.6. Weekly behavioral state profiles for four infants with very low State Stability scores. Along the X-axis are the behavioral states, and the Y-axis is the percentage of time spent in each state. WA: Waking Active; QA: Quiet Alert; FC: Fuss or Cry; DT: Drowse or Transition; AS: Active Sleep; QS: Quiet Sleep.

ratio) scores. Their erratic state patterning over weeks is clearly apparent. The looser constraints on the state system of these infants with lower Stability scores has major implications for the status of their CNS, as indicated by the fact that each of these four infants represented in Fig. 5.6 displayed either medical or behavioral dysfunction subsequently, as reported in Thoman et al. (1981). No infant with mental delay or developmental disability showed a Stability Score above the median value for the group. The findings depicted in Fig. 5.6 might immediately suggest that only 1 week, especially week 5, was responsible for the instability expressed in the F-score and, therefore, only that week is the critical one to observe. However, scrutiny of the figures for these infants indicates that week 5 was not the deviant week for all four infants. In addition, deviancy is based on the profiles for all 4 weeks for each individual baby, not on any group measure or profile. Thus, multiple recordings over this brief age span were necessary for determining deviancy, even in instances when it occurred primarily on a single week.

The findings of this study have been replicated in other laboratories, with full-term infants (Lombroso & Matsumiya, 1985) and with premature infants (Tynan, 1986). In addition, we have recently replicated these findings with a group of 50 premature infants monitored with the automated sleep recording procedure (Whitney & Thoman, unpub.).

Discussion: The importance of state as a reliable descriptor of babies, an index of functional status, and a predictor of development

The behavioral states are a system of species-specific behaviors that express CNS integration and serve endogenous needs of the organism. This is accomplished by two major functions of state. State functions as a gating mechanism for the infant's perception of internal processes and external events and as a modulating mechanism for the infant's behaviors. These functions are intimately linked to the role of state as an interface with the environment, primarily as a mediator of interactions between the infant and the caregiver. Thus, state functions in complex, dynamic ways to express the infant's neurobehavioral status while, at the same time, influencing the developmental course of that status. This perspective on state has major implications for state variables as predictors of development. It must be inferred that the individual infant has to be the unit of study if the potential of state variables for prediction is to be fulfilled. The states of infants have too often been assessed from group averages, a form of analysis that does not meaningfully represent the process in *any* individual (Wohlwill, 1973). Denenberg (1982) stated: "In the final analysis, if we wish to understand the individual, we can do so only by studying individuals, not by studying them as statistical actuarial averages" (p. 20). If we wish to predict for individuals, we must describe individuals.

In the studies described, state organizational characteristics and stability of these characteristics were statistically assessed for each individual, based on extensive data obtained over time. This is the appropriate basis for arriving at a developmental trajectory. Such an approach is consistent with General Systems Theory. For example, by comparing systems indices of an individual with those of a group, it is possible to obtain clues to disequilibrium, or subtle malfunctioning, in the individual. Such disequilibrium can have serious implications for an infant's developmental trajectory, as indicated by the developmental dysfunction found for infants with low State Stability scores.

A major methodological consideration is that it would not have been appropriate to use the individual systems statistics—the rate of state change, state stability, or cyclicity—for assessment purposes without first demonstrating measurement reliability for each of the component variables. Whether these indices were calculated from behavioral observations or the automated sleep recordings, they were based on extensive observations made on repeated occasions over a relatively brief age span to minimize effects from developmental changes. Clearly, briefer observations would yield lower reliabilities; and fewer observations would not characterize the infant's states as a dynamic, developing system that reflects competence of neural integrative processes. Accordingly, we conclude that intensive, time-span observations are required for assessing the functional status of individual infants and for deriving indices of future developmental status.

ACKNOWLEDGMENT

The preparation of this chapter was supported by Grant No. MH 41244 from the National Institute of Mental Health, Center for Prevention Research, Division of Prevention and Special Mental Health Programs.

REFERENCES

Acebo, C. (1987). *Naturalistic observations of mother and infant: Descriptions of mother and infant responsiveness and sleep–wake state development.* Dissertation at University of Connecticut.

Anders, T. F. (1979). Night-waking in infants during the first year of life. *Pediatrics, 63,* 860–864.

Anders, T., & Keener, M. (1985). The developmental course of nighttime sleep–wake patterns in full-term and premature infants. *Sleep, 8,* 173–192.

Anders, T., Keener, M., Bowe, T. R., & Shoaff, B. A. (1983). A longitudinal study of nightime sleep–wake patterns in infants from birth to one year. In J. Call, E. Galenson, R. Tyson (Eds.), *Frontiers of infant psychiatry.* New York: Basic Books.

Ashton, R. (1973). The state variable in neonatal research: A review. *Merrill–Palmer Quarterly, 19,* 3–20.

Becker, P. T., & Thoman, E. B. (1982). Intense rapid eye movements during active sleep in infants: An index of neurobehavioral instability. *Developmental Psychobiology, 15,* 203–210.

Becker, P. T., & Thoman, E. B. (1983). Organization of sleeping and waking states in infants: Consistency across contexts. *Physiology and Behavior, 31,* 405–410.

Bertalanffy, L. von. (1933). *Modern theories of development: An introduction to theoretical biology.* J. H. Woodger (Ed. and Trans.). London: Oxford University Press.

Bertalanffy, L. von. (1968). *General systems theory* (rev. ed.). New York: Brazilier.

Brazelton, T. B. (1961). Psychophysiologic reactions in the neonate. I. The value of observations of the neonate. *The Journal of Pediatrics, 58,* 508–512.

Brown, J. L. (1964). States in newborn infants. *Merrill-Palmer Quarterly, 10,* 313–327.

Bunge, M. (1979). *Treatise on basic philosophy: Vol. 4. Ontology II: A world of systems.* Dordrecht: Reidel.

Coons, S., & Guilleminault, C. (1984). Development of consolidated sleep and wakeful periods in relation to the day/night cycle in infancy. *Developmental Medicine and Child Neurology, 26,* 169–176.

Davis. D. H., & Thoman, E. B. (1987). Behavioral states of premature infants: Implications for neural and behavioral development. *Developmental Psychobiology, 20,*(1), 25–38.

Denenberg, V. H. (1979). Analysis of variance procedures for estimating reliability and comparing individual subjects. In E. B. Thoman (Ed.), *Origins of the infant's social responsiveness* (pp. 339–348). Hillsdale, NJ: Lawrence Erlbaum Associates.

Denenberg, V. H. (1982). Comparative psychology and single-subject research. In A. E. Kazdin &

A. H. Tuma (Eds.), *New directions for methodology of social and behavioral sciences: Single-case research designs* (No. 13, pp. 19–31). San Francisco: Jossey-Bass.

Denenberg, V. H., & Thoman, E. B. (1981). Evidence for a functional role for active (REM) sleep in infancy. *Sleep, 4,* 185–191.

Dittrichova, J., Paul, K., & Vondracek, J. (1976). Individual differences in infants' sleep. *Developmental Medicine and Child Neurology, 18,* 182–188.

Drucker-Colin, R. R., & McGaugh, J. L. (1977). *Neurobiology of sleep and memory.* New York: Academic Press.

Epstein, S., & Erskine, N. (1983). The development of personal theories of reality from an interactional perspective. In D. Magnusson & V. L. Allen (Eds.), *Human development: An interactional perspective.* New York: Academic Press.

Hobson, J. A. (1977). What is a behavioral state? In J. A. Ferrendelli (Ed.), *Society for neuroscience symposia. Vol. 3: Aspects of behavioral neurobiology.* Bethesda, MD: Society for Neuroscience.

Hobson, J., Lydic, R., & Baghdoyan, H. (1986). Evolving concepts of sleep cycle generation: From brain centers to neuronal populations. *The Behavioral and Brain Sciences, 9,* 371–448.

Hoppenbrouwers, T., Hodgman, J., Arakawa, K., Geidel, S., & Sterman, M. (1988). Sleep and waking states in infancy: Normative studies. *Sleep, 11*(4), 387–401.

Hoppenbrouwers, T., Hodgman, J., Arakawa, K., McGinty, D., Mason, J., Harper, R., & Sterman, M. (1978). Sleep apnea as a part of a sequence of events: A comparison of three month old infants at low and increased risk for sudden infant death syndrome (SIDS). *Neuropadiatrie, 9,* 320–337.

Iberall, A. S., & McCulloch, W. S. (1969). The organizing principle of complex living systems. *Journal of Basic Engineering,* 290–294.

Jouvet, G. I. (1961). Telencephalic and rhombencephalic sleep in the cat. In G. E. Wolstenholme & M. O'Connor (Eds.), *The nature of sleep.* London: Churchill.

Kraemer, H., Hole, W., & Anders. T. (1984). Detection of behavioral state cycles and classification of temporal structure in behavioral states. *Sleep 7,* 3–17.

Lombroso, C. T., & Matsumiya, Y. (1985). Stability in waking–sleep states in neonates as a predictor of long-term neurologic outcome. *Pediatrics, 76,* 52–63.

McGinty, D. J., & Siegel, J. M. (1983). Sleep states. In E. Satinoff & P. Teitelbaum (Eds.), *Motivation.* Handbook of Behavioral Neurobiology (pp. 108–181). New York: Plenum Press.

Orem, J., & Barnes, C. (1980). *Physiology in sleep.* New York: Academic Press.

Parmelee, A. H., Schultz, M., & Disbrow, M. P. (1961). Sleep patterns of the newborn. *Journal of Pediatrics, 58,* 241–250.

Prechtl, H. F. R. (1982). Assessment methods for the newborn infant: A critical evaluation. In P. Stratton (Ed.), *Psychobiology of the human newborn* (pp. 1–52). New York: Wiley.

Prechtl, H. F. R., & Beintema, D. (1964). *The neurological examination of the full-term newborn infant.* London: William Heinemann Medical Books.

Prechtl, H. F. R., & O'Brien, M. J. (1982). Behavioural states of the full-term newborn. The emergence of a concept. In P. Stratton (Ed.), *Psychobiology of the human newborn* (pp. 53–76). New York: Wiley.

Pugsley, M., Acebo, C., & Thoman, E. B. (1988). Sleep of preterm and fullterm infants from home monitoring. Sixth Biennial International Conference on Infant Studies, Washington, DC, on April 21–24. *Infant Behavior & Development, Special ICIS Issue, 11,* 263.

Rechtschaffen, A., & Kales, A. (1968). *A manual of standardized terminology, techniques and scoring systems for sleep stages of human subjects.* Washington, DC: U.S. Government Printing Office.

Robinson, R. J. (1969). Nomenclature of the stages of sleep. In *Brain & early behavior.* London: Academic Press.

Roffwarg, H. P., Muzio, J. N., & Dement, W. C. (1966). Ontogenetic development of the human sleep–dream cycle. *Science, 152,* 604–619.

Snyder, F. Hobson, J., Morrison, D., & Goldfrank, F. (1964). Changes in respiration, heart rate, and systolic blood pressure in human sleep. *Journal of Applied Physiology, 19,* 417.

Sterman, M. B., Lucas, E. A., & MacDonald, R. L. (1972). Periodicity within sleep and operant performance in the cat. *Brain Research, 38,* 327–341.

Stratton, P. (1982). Rhythmic functions in the newborn. In P. Stratton (Ed.), *Psychobiology of the human newborn* (pp. 119–145). New York: Wiley.

Thoman, E. B., (1975). Sleep and wake behaviors in neonates: Consistencies and consequences. *Merrill-Palmer Quarterly, 21,* 295–314.

Thoman, E. B. (1985). Affects of earliest infancy: The imperative for a biological model. In E. T. McDonald & D. L. Gallagher (Eds.), *Facilitating social-emotional development in multiple handicapped children* (pp. 9–27). Philadelphia, PA: Home of the Merciful Saviour for Crippled Children.

Thoman, E. B. (1986). The time domain in individual subject research. In J. Valsiner (Ed.), *The individual subject and scientific psychology* (pp. 181–200). New York: Plenum Press.

Thoman, E. B., & Becker, P. T. (1979). Issues in assessment and prediction for the infant born at risk. In T. Field, A Sostek, S. Goldberg, & H. H. Shuman (Eds.), *Infants born at risk* (pp. 461–483). New York: Spectrum.

Thoman, E. B., Davis, D. H., & Denenberg, V. H. (1987). The sleeping and waking states of infants: Correlations across time and person. *Physiology and Behavior, 41,* 531–537.

Thoman, E. B., Davis, D. H., Graham, S., Scholz, J. P., & Rowe, J. C. (1988). Infants at risk for sudden infant death syndrome: Differential prediction for three siblings of SIDS infants. *Journal of Behavioral Medicine, 11,* 565–583.

Thoman, E. B. Denenberg, V. H., Sievel, J., Zeidner, L., & Becker, P. T. (1981). State organization in neonates: Developmental inconsistency indicates risk for developmental dysfunction.*Neuropediatrics, 12,* 45–54.

Thoman, E. B., & Glazier, R. C. (1987). Computer scoring of motility patterns for states of sleep and wakefulness: Human infants. *Sleep, 10*(2), 122–129.

Thoman, E. B., Korner, A. F., & Kraemer, H. C. (1976). Individual consistency in behavioral states in neonates. *Developmental Psychobiology, 9,* 271–283.

Thoman, E. B., & McDowell, K. (1989). Sleep cyclicity in infants during the earliest postnatal weeks. *Physiology & Behavior, 45,*(3).

Thoman, E. B., Miano, V. N., & Freese, M. P. (1978). The role of respiratory instability in SIDS. *Developmental Medicine and Child Neurology, 19,* 748–756.

Thoman, E. B., & Tynan, W. D. (1979). Sleep states and wakefulness in human infants: Profiles from motility monitoring. *Physiology and Behavior, 23,* 519–525.

Thoman, E. B., & Zeidner, L. P. (1979). Sleep–wake states in infant rabbits: Profiles from motility monitoring. *Physiology and Behavior, 22,* 1049–1054.

Thoman, E. B., Zeidner, L. P., & Denenberg, V. H. (1981). Cross-species invariance in state related motility patterns. *American Journal of Physiology, 241,* R312–R315.

Tynan, W. D. (1986). Behavioral stability predicts morbidity and mortality in infants from a neonatal intensive care unit. *Infant Behavior and Development, 9,* 71–79.

Waite, S. P., & Thoman, E. B. (1981). Brief apneas and reliable assessment of respiratory instability. *Sleep, 4,* 61–69.

Weiss, P. (1969). The living system: Determinism stratified. In A. Koestler & J. R. Smythies (Eds.), *Beyond reductionism.* (pp. 3–42). Boston: Beacon.

Weiss, P. (Ed.). (1971). The basic concept of hierarchical systems. In *Hierarchically organized systems in theory and practice.* New York: Hafner.

Whitney, M. P., & Thoman, E. B. (Abstract). *Early sleep patterns of premature and fullterm infants monitored at home.* International Society for Developmental Psychobiology in Toronto, Canada, II/10/88–II/13/88.

Winer, B. J. (1971). Statistical principles in experimental design (2d ed.). New York: McGraw-Hill.

Wohlwill, J. F. (1973). *The study of behavioral development.* New York: Academic Press.

Wolff, P. H. (1966). The causes, controls and organization of behavior in the neonate. *Psychological Issues, 5,* 1–105.

Zeidner, L. W., Weyand, T., Thoman, E. B., & Denenberg, V. H. (1983). Comparisons of behavioral, motoric, and electrical criteria for assessment of sleep–wake states in the rabbit. *Physiology and Behavior, 31,* 273–278.

6 Behavioral Assessment of the Neonate

John Worobey
Rutgers—The State University

INTRODUCTION

Research on the origins of individual differences has been greatly advanced by the use of assessment techniques that focus specifically on the newborn, that is, the human infant in its first month of extrauterine life. In their recent review, Francis, Self, and Horowitz (1987) identified over two dozen assessment devices that have relevance to full-term infants in the newborn period. They grouped the instruments they surveyed under one of three headings, namely screening tests, neurological examinations, or behavioral assessments, and used this typology to describe the differential aims and applications of techniques employed with the neonate. Thus, the Apgar (1953) rating, the Prechtl (1977) scale, or the Graham (1956) test may be seen as addressing the distinct yet overlapping concerns of the physician, the neurologist, or the psychologist, respectively. Although derived from the intended purpose behind their administration, such a classification system is nevertheless somewhat arbitrary, insofar as each of these approaches rely on newborn *behavior* to determine viability, maturity, or individuality (Francis et al., 1987). An emphasis on behavior, however, reflects a recent perspective, as the earliest devices were rooted in pediatric neurology with the shift toward developmental psychology occurring relatively later.

Background

As documented in a number of review articles (Als, 1984; O'Donnell & Oehler, 1989; Parmelee, 1962; Prechtl, 1982; St. Clair, 1978), the identification of neonatal reflexes began in Europe in this century, with early efforts by Magitat

(1903), Moro (1918), and Magnus (1924) being catalogued by Peiper (1928). The Americans followed suit, with Dennis (1934), Dewey (1935), and McGraw (1943) describing additional reflexes and behavioral responses. Despite the detail of these compendia, they did not yet represent a formalized schedule for assessing the newborn (St. Clair, 1978).

By the 1950s, the first systematic examinations of the newborn appeared. The interest in neurological function that began in Europe was exemplified by Andre-Thomas and Saint-Anne Dargassies (1952) in France, and by Prechtl and Beintema (1964) in the Netherlands. To this day, the Prechtl (1977), Dubowitz and Dubowitz (1981), and Amiel-Tison and Grenier (1986) assessments reflect the vital European neurological tradition. Although a focus on identifying pathology has gradually given way to the detection of risk factors in general, for the most part these neurological approaches are used by neonatologists for clinical purposes. As such, they have not dwelled on measurement issues, although reliability across examiners is understood to be adequate.

In contrast to the neurological approach, efforts in the United States have been distinguished by their psychological orientation. In attempting to differentiate normal newborns from those with brain injuries, Graham (1956) developed a test that focused on observable behavior as an expression of neurological status. Continuing with this trend, Rosenblith (1961) and Brazelton (1973) extended Graham's work by formulating assessments that allowed not only for the description of early behavior, but the quantification of performance that would permit the analysis of individual differences for research ends (Als, 1984).

What has therefore evolved appears to be two types of neonatal assessment. The first tradition derives from pediatric neurology, in that reflexes are elicited to make clinical judgments about the newborn's viability or maturity. The European examinations are in this category, as well as the screening devices for full-term newborns (Apgar, 1953; Roberton, 1984). The second tradition owes more to psychology and psychometrics, as early behavior and its measurement are of interest. It is in this arena that the Americans have made their contribution, with behavioral assessments indexing postnatal status, predicting later development, and in some cases, serving as intervention devices.

Although this chapter addresses only these behaviorally based measures, it must be stated that the distinctions between these categories of assessment are sometimes more apparent than real. For example, the Graham (1956) test battery has been referred to as a neurological instrument by some, and as a behavioral assessment by others. Likewise, the Dubowitz and Dubowitz (1981) examination is termed a *neurological* assessment by psychologists (Francis et al., 1987), a *neuromotor* instrument by physical therapists (Harris & Brady, 1986), and a *neurobehavioral* device by those in the medical community (O'Donnell & Oehler, 1989).

In point of fact, the neurobehavioral approach has recently emerged as the favored method for assessing preterm and at-risk status (Kurtzberg et al., 1979; Lester, 1988). Korner and her associates (Korner, Kraemer, Reade, Forrest, &

Dimiceli, 1987; Korner et al., 1989) have developed an assessment procedure for testing the neurobehavioral maturity of the preterm infant. Gardner, Karmel, Magnano, and Norton (1989) have designed a neurobehavioral battery to characterize the effects of early brain insult in low-birth-weight infants. Finally, Als, Duffy, and McAnulty (1988a, 1988b) describe an assessment that measures preterm versus full-term differences in behavioral organization. Because the Als et al. (1988b) assessment can examine functional competence regardless of gestational age at birth, the neurobehavioral approach will likely characterize future work with full-term neonates (see also Riese, 1983).

Regardless of nomenclature, the reader is urged to consult any of the current reviews of neonatal assessment devices that are cited throughout these pages. The recent surveys by Als (1984) and O'Donnell and Oehler (1989), in particular, are quite comprehensive and include information on tests for the evaluation of preterm neonates that cannot be covered here.

The Graham/Rosenblith Behavior Test for Neonates (BTN)

The first behavioral examination was developed by Graham and her collaborators (Graham, 1956; Graham, Matarazzo, & Caldwell, 1956) for use at 1 to 14 days postpartum. Five areas were assessed in order to differentiate brain-injured from normal newborns, namely, pain threshold, general maturation, visual capacities, muscle tension, and irritability. Split-half reliability, computable only for pain threshold, was good (mean $r = .92$), with test–retest reliability averaging .61 for correlated estimates and 81% perfect agreement for the rating scales (Graham et al., 1956). Interrater agreement was satisfactory, with a number of reports indicating correlations in the high .70s through .90s, and levels of perfect agreement averaging 65% (Bench & Parker, 1970; Graham et al., 1956; Rosenblith & Lipsitt, 1959).

Concurrent validity for the exam was acceptable, as mean scores on the BTN discriminated normal newborns from those with trauma present (i.e., anoxia, mechanical trauma, erythroblastosis fetalis, hypoglycemia, or meningitis; Graham et al., 1956). Furthermore, test performance reflected the varying severity of clinical conditions within a group of anoxic infants (Graham, Pennoyer, Caldwell, Greenman, & Hartmann, 1957). However, prediction to 3- and 7-year developmental criteria was not encouraging (Corah, Anthony, Painter, Stern, & Thurston, 1965; Graham et al., 1957), with Graham herself doubting the predictive utility of the newborn behavior test (Graham, Ernhart, Thurston, & Craft, 1962).

After 2 years of studying the Graham (1956) test and its components, Rosenblith (1961) unveiled a modified version of the newborn examination. As did Graham, Rosenblith focused on behavior, incorporating age-normed data, measures of muscle tone, and responses to stimuli. In essence, she retained most of the original items, except the pain threshold test that required a special apparatus for administering electrotactual stimulation. In addition, she recommended that the newborn's best, as opposed to average, performance be scored when completing the examination.

Aside from her desire to improve the reliability and internal consistency of the Graham exam, Rosenblith's intent was to identify at-risk newborns who would warrant medical and psychological follow-up, with a procedure that could be administered in a brief time period (Rosenblith, 1979). The 30-minute BTN assesses behavior in the areas of general maturation, sensory responses, and irritability (Rosenblith, 1975). Maturation is determined via two scales, that is, a *motor* score that assesses muscle strength and coordination, and a *tactile adaptive* score that assesses adaptivity of the newborn's responses to tactile stimulation in the nose and mouth region. *Muscle tonus* is separately assessed by rating muscular tension, spontaneous activity, and trembling. The sensory scales allow for a *visual* score that taps visual fixation and pursuit of a moving object, and an *auditory* score based on responsiveness to a rattle and bicycle bell. Finally, *irritability* is based on the examiner's subjective impression over the entire exam, with a separate rating for discrete instances of *irritable behavior*.

Rosenblith (1961) reported 2-hour-test–retest correlation coefficients of .62 and above for the BTN, although estimates were not provided for auditory responsiveness. In comparison to her previous results with the Graham test (Rosenblith & Lipsitt, 1959), Rosenblith (1975) found that interscorer agreement improved for maturation and irritability but declined slightly for muscle tonus and the vision score. Bench and Parker (1970), however, found both forms of the test to be nearly equivalent in terms of interrater reliability. Other investigators have found agreement as high as 100% within 1 scale-point, and concurrent validity between the vision score and alertness during an observed feeding (Brown, Bakeman, Snyder, Fredrickson, Morgan, & Hepler, 1975).

Much information on the predictive validity of the BTN exists, although it is confined for the most part to reports by Rosenblith herself, through her work on the National Collaborative Perinatal Research Project (CPRP). Four cohorts of newborns were tested, comprising some 1,500 babies who were later seen at 4, 8, and 12 months, and again at 3 and 7 years (Rosenblith, 1979). Neonates who scored in the top quartile on the motor scale were unlikely to show any signs of abnormality in the first year, and those who were rated as irritable had suspect scores on a pediatric evaluation at 4 months and a temperament measure at 8 months (Rosenblith, 1975). Medium tactile-adaptive scores were related to more optimal outcomes at 8 months and at 4 and 7 years (Rosenblith, 1979), with the poorest scores being linked to occurrences of sudden infant death (Anderson-Huntington & Rosenblith, 1976). Neonatal muscle tonus was related to motoric performance and attention span at 4 years, predicted development at 7 years, and was said to be "the most powerful predictor of any aspect of the examination" (Rosenblith & Sims-Knight, 1985, p. 321).

Although it possesses satisfactory reliability and validity, the BTN has not seen frequent use beyond Rosenblith's efforts with the CRCP. Scoring the examination is confusing, with certain maneuvers graded on a scale of 1 to 9, others from 0 to 10, and still others from 1 to 5. Furthermore, the categorical assignment of irritability level prevents linear analysis. Nevertheless, as a true test of neonatal status, the BTN marks the beginning of the behavioral approach to newborn assessment. The reader may refer to Rosenblith (1979) for an extensive review of the BTN, as well as to Francis et al. (1987).

The Brazelton Neonatal Behavioral Assessment Scale (NBAS)

The increasing realization that *interactive* behavior, specifically that between the caregiver and newborn, may better predict later infant functioning than a singular focus on the neonate—no matter how rigorous the measure—led to the development and extensive use of the NBAS (Brazelton, 1973). The intent of Brazelton and his colleagues was to describe the separate functioning of the interactive, motoric, state, and autonomic systems, as well as their integration, within the healthy, normal, full-term newborn (Als, Tronick, Lester, & Brazelton, 1979).

Of primary concern is the newborn's level of arousal, as an expression of both internal organization and the ability to control reactions to external stimuli. Rosenblith (1961) also made note of states, although she does not score them. Brazelton (1984), however, argues that the newborn's pattern and movement across states may be the most useful predictor of future optimal outcome (see Thelen and Whitney, this volume). Also like Rosenblith, he suggests that best performance be credited, reasoning that it may serve to push the newborn to the limit, with the concomitant behavior being a better indicator of subsequent functioning than more typical responsivity.

The NBAS includes the assessment of reflexes but is overwhelmingly behavioral. It is appropriate for use with newborns from 36 to 44 weeks gestational age and takes approximately 25 minutes to administer and 15 minutes to score (Nugent & Sepkoski, 1984). The contents of the exam may be summarized through a variety of methods, with three techniques most often used, namely, the nonparametric (Adamson, Als, Tronick, & Brazelton, 1975), the factor-analytic (Aleksandrowicz & Aleksandrowicz, 1978; Kaye, 1978), and the conceptual–empirical clustering approach (Lester, Als, & Brazelton, 1982; Jacobson, Fein, Jacobson, & Schwartz, 1984). Choice is based on the needs of the clinician versus researcher; because this volume is primarily directed at a research audience, the clustering approach of Lester et al. (1982) is used to illustrate the contents of the NBAS.

Habituation describes the newborn's decreasing responses to redundant visual, auditory, and tactile stimuli. *Orientation* includes alertness, and the localization and pursuit of a rattle and the examiner's face and voice. *Motor* items include integrated motoric acts and overall muscle tonus. The newborn's *range of state* is based on the peak level, lability, and rapidity in buildup of states, whereas *regulation of state* is based on the newborn's success in modulating its own state control. Tremors, startles, and skin color changes reflecting physiological stress are grouped as *autonomic stability,* and *reflexes* are a simple count of the deviant reflex scores. Except for reflexes, higher scores for the clusters, derived from 9-point item ratings, are indicative of more optimal performance by the newborn (Lester et al., 1982).

The revised edition of the NBAS manual includes a listing of supplementary items for at-risk newborns (Brazelton, 1984). These additions reflect the revisions developed by Horowitz and her colleagues for their version of the test, titled the NBAS-K (for Kansas; Horowitz, Sullivan, & Linn, 1978; Lancioni, Horowitz, & Sullivan, 1980), as well as the precursors to the assessment model formulated by Als (1986) for specific use with preterm neonates.

The reliability and validity of both the NBAS and NBAS-K have been subjected to numerous reviews and evaluations (Brazelton, Nugent, & Lester, 1987; Francis et al., 1987; Lancioni et al., 1980; Sameroff, 1978). Reports of test–retest reliability on individual items (Kestermann, 1981; Leijon & Finnstrom, 1981) and factors (Kaye, 1978; Worobey, 1986), however, are at best low to moderate in magnitude. As any attempt at prediction would seem to be served by individual differences that may be reliably and repeatedly discerned, the issue of test–retest stability is addressed in detail later.

With regard to interrater agreement, Brazelton and colleagues report that high interobserver reliability is consistently attainable (Als et al., 1979; Brazelton et al., 1987). Concurrent validity has been demonstrated in literally dozens of studies that examine the negative impact of obstetric medication and maternal substance abuse on NBAS scores, document the performance of compromised infants, and showcase cross-cultural differences in newborns around the world. These studies are described in numerous publications (Als, 1984; Brazelton et al., 1987; Horowitz & Linn, 1984) and are not reviewed here.

Although these reports clearly document the effectiveness of the NBAS in distinguishing among normal newborn infants at the time of their assessment, the predictive value of the scale has been less than convincing. It is true that investigators have shown certain aspects of NBAS performance to be related to later infant behavior, for example, poor interactive or motoric processes and less responsiveness during feeding and play at 6 months (Vaughn, Taraldson, Crichton, & Egeland, 1980). Optimal state control has also been positively associated with mental development at 10 weeks (Sostek & Anders, 1977) and beyond (Vaughn et al., 1980). But correlations are sometimes found between NBAS clusters and behavioral dimensions that do not make implicit theoretical sense; witness the positive association between NBAS motor maturity and 3-month smiling but not activity (Crockenberg & Acredolo, 1983), or the linkage of NBAS–K assessed range of state to visual processing at 3 months, when orientation did not predict visual discrimination (Moss, Colombo, Mitchell, & Horowitz, 1988).

In spite of these inconsistencies, its less than ideal day-to-day reliability, and the training necessary to be certified to administer the procedure, the use of the NBAS has mushroomed in both the medical and psychological fields (Als, 1984). The reader is again urged to scan any of the recent reviews that exist for a fuller treatment of the NBAS and its use (Brazelton et al., 1987; Horowitz & Linn, 1982).

Prediction from the Newborn Period

Brazelton (1984) has recommended the repeated testing of newborns with the NBAS over the first weeks postpartum if one is specifically interested in making predictions to later behavior. For that matter, the use of repeated NBAS testing is virtually mandated in light of the low day-to-day stability reported in the literature (Sameroff, Krafchuk, & Bakow, 1978). Such dismaying accounts are partially explained by the use of correlational techniques, predominantly the Pearson r, which depend on the neonate's score maintaining its relative position over two or more occasions. As higher scores on the individualized NBAS items do not always reflect best performance, and recoding curvilinear items may mask the direction of nonoptimality (Jacobson et al., 1984), the use of correlational techniques becomes questionable. More importantly, when change within the organism is to be expected anyway, given the dynamic growth and maturation that characterize early infancy, the likelihood of attaining significant correlation coefficients is diminished (Sameroff, 1978). Indeed, one should not expect stability until 2- to 3-months postpartum (Prechtl, 1984), after the physiological disturbances accompanying birth have been attenuated (Woodson, 1983).

But if predicting from one NBAS assessment to a second or third cannot be reliably done, then how can long-term predictions to other measures be considered valid? In an attempt to resolve this dilemma, Lester (1984) describes how one may use recovery curves to gauge how neonates change over the first month of extrauterine life. Based on three NBAS examinations of the newborn, performance is plotted for each behavioral cluster, and the resulting profile curves are scored for *level, velocity,* and *acceleration.* In this manner, individual differences in patterns of change over repeated assessments reflect the development of behavioral processes over the neonatal period. Using this procedure, curve parameters have been related to infant mental outcomes at 18 months of age (Lester, 1984), with level of state regulation, velocity of habituation, and acceleration of motoric processes predicting mental abilities at 5 years (Lester, 1988; Sepkoski, 1986).

Behavioral Variability and Prediction

Because the developmental process involves the interaction of maturational and environmental forces, Lester (1984) suspects that the recovery curves have predictive power as they reflect the adaptations the neonate must make between endogenous mechanisms and exogenous demands. From this perspective, it is variability in early behavior that accounts for the neonate's adaptability. As Emde (1978) posits, a newborn characterized by variability of behavior across the first weeks of life may provide the new caregiver with greater opportunities for synchronization in early interaction. Rather than viewing measured change as error variance (Sameroff, 1978), an absence of early stability may instead be preferable, as it speaks for a newborn who is better equipped to adapt to its environment by organizing its own state, or eliciting state-organizing behaviors from its caregiver (Horowitz, 1987; see also Thoman & Whitney, this volume). The issue of stability as a dimension of individual difference, in and of itself, is addressed throughout the remainder of this chapter.

To illustrate, an alternate method of assessing consistency in newborn behavior over repeated testing is more direct. In essence, it involves identifying the number of scale items for which performance remains stable or changes from the first to second administrations. As described by Horowitz et al. (1978), corresponding items on each protocol are rated as in agreement if they are within one point of each other, and in disagreement if more than a point discrepant. The infant thus receives a reliability score that equals the number of items in agreement across the two exams divided by the total number of items tested.

The value of using such reliability estimates for predictive purposes was investigated by Linn and Horowitz (1983). After their correlational analysis revealed but one significant test–retest coefficient of the 27 computed, they used the agreement procedure to calculate reliability scores that ranged from less than .40 through .73. Splitting their sample at the .50 level of agreement, they discovered that the variable newborns (i.e., those whose reliability scores were .49 or less) were observed in more responsive interactions with their mothers than were the stable newborns (i.e., reliabilities of .50 or greater). Despite the NBAS assessments being restricted to the 2 days surrounding the observed feeding episode, these results support the hypothesis of change favoring outcome.

A Test of the Variability Hypothesis

In an attempt to replicate the Linn and Horowitz (1983) findings with a low-risk sample, I undertook my own investigation to see if the agreement method of determining reliability would be as predictive with mother–newborn dyads followed over 1 month. In that study (Worobey, 1986), 49 newborns were tested twice with the NBAS, at 2–4 days in the hospital and at 4–5 weeks in their own homes. Summary scores for each infant were derived by clustering newborn behaviors into the categories recommended by Lester et al. (1982). A traditional test–retest correlational analysis was then performed and revealed autonomic stability to be the only NBAS cluster that maintained consistency over 1 month.

The Horowitz et al. (1978) procedure for computing agreement was next employed, and the sample was subsequently split into variable (scores below .50) and stable (scores of .50 and above) newborns. Unlike the Linn and Horowitz (1983) sample, however, twice as many newborns were classified as stable compared to variable, so the stable group was further split into stable and extremely stable infants (scores of .64 and above).

I predicted that the variable infants would demonstrate greater responsivity during the naturalistic observation that also occurred at 1 month. In turn, I predicted that the stable infants would appear as less behaviorally active, followed by the extremely stable infants, that is, those who changed the least over the newborn period. Somewhat surprisingly, the results suggested a curvilinear relationship between degree of variability and observed outcome; that is, the extremely stable newborns were, relatively speaking, as high in their frequencies of behavior as the variable infants, with the middle, stable group as least adaptive on the behaviors observed.

These results gave partial support to the "variation as adaptation" hypothesis, but another question remained. Although the findings suggested that the newborns who were markedly stable across the first month of life were equivalent in outcome to those who changed, an inspection of the raw scores for the NBAS items revealed that the extremely stable newborns were indeed consistent but were comparatively higher in optimal performance at the time of the first assessment. Would such a curvilinear relationship result if certain of the infants were not favored at the outset?

To address this issue I selected, from those enrolled in the aforementioned study, infants who clearly represented the variable and stable classifications. But to avoid the possible confound between initial optimality and level of stability that may have characterized my earlier findings, infants were deliberately chosen to reflect midrange NBAS performance over the two assessments. The present analysis was thus performed in order to reexamine the predictive power of early variability on subsequent measures of infant functioning. As before, observations of infant behavior as seen in the home were included. In addition, ratings of the infants' temperament at 2 months were also obtained. The specifics of the procedures are outlined next.

The Variability Hypothesis Revisited

The pool of subjects consisted of the newborns and their mothers enrolled in our longitudinal project on early individual differences. Briefly, all the newborns were delivered at term and without abnormalities, weighed an average of well over 2,500 grams, and had Apgar scores of 8 and higher. The newborns were tested at 2–4 days of age in the hospital by one NBAS examiner, and again at 4–5 weeks of age in their own homes by a second, who was kept blind to their earlier performance.

Following the second NBAS examination, the newborns were observed with their mothers in a 20-minute naturalistic interaction. Behaviors were recorded every 10 seconds using a precoded listing, which allowed for a maximum frequency of 120 intervals checked. Specific infant behaviors included quiet and active alertness, looking at mother, cooing, sneezing/burping, arm and leg movements, fussing, and crying (Worobey & Belsky, 1982).

When the infants reached the age of 2 months, their mothers rated them on dimensions of temperament with the Infant Behavior Questionnaire (IBQ; Rothbart, 1981). The IBQ consists of 94 items, scored from 1 to 7, that concern the frequency of behaviors observed by the mother during the previous week. It includes the dimensions of activity level, smiling and laughter, fear, distress to limitations, soothability, and duration of orienting (see Rothbart, this volume).

As the first step in data reduction, the Horowitz et al. (1978) procedure was again used and resulted in reliability estimates ranging from .21 to .79. As before, a variable newborn was defined as having an agreement score less than .50, with stable newborns scoring at or above this percentage. Next, each infant's agreement records were inspected, and the number of NBAS items that were low (1–3), medium (4–6), and high (7–9) on the first assessment were noted. From the distribution of scores across these three levels, five high scores appeared to be a reasonable upper limit for assuring a medium level of initial functioning for each newborn. This criterion also allowed for equal representation from both the variable and stable groupings, as five newborns in each category had five or fewer NBAS scores of 7+ when first assessed. With this selection procedure, it thus became possible to directly test the variable–stable hypothesis, albeit in a relatively small sample of infants.

Having drawn the 10 infant subjects, their NBAS protocols at both times of assessment were reduced into the Lester et al. (1982) clusters, and their scores appear in Table 6.1. (Habituation was not included, due to an insufficient number of response decrement items scorable on the second NBAS.) The scores indicate that NBAS orientation, motor, and autonomic stability increased over 1 month for both groups of newborns, with state-related behaviors and deviant reflexes generally decreasing. These averages are consonant with NBAS cluster scores reported by others for infants of 40 and 44 weeks gestational age (Anderson, Boukydis, Pencker, & Lester, 1988). It further appears that the selection criteria produced two groups of functionally equivalent newborns, as based on their mean scores over 1 month.

With regard to the naturalistic observation, infant behaviors were first collapsed into the categories of alert, looks, vocalizes, movement, and crying (Worobey, 1986). In the extended report that tracked the larger cohort over their first year of development (Worobey & Blajda, 1989), we showed that infant alertness, looks at mother, and vocalizing were all positively and significantly correlated with each other. As the N-size of the present subsample made a confirmatory use of a correlational analysis impossible, it nevertheless seemed

TABLE 6.1
NBAS Behavioral Clusters by Variability-Stability Status

	Variable Newborns			Stable Newborns		
	NBAS 1	NBAS 2	Mean	NBAS 1	NBAS 2	Mean
	Mean (SD)	Mean (SD)		Mean (SD)	Mean (SD)	
Orientation	4.66 (1.18)	7.03 (.28)	5.84	5.16	6.26 (.77)	5.71 (1.09)
Motor	4.32 (.67)	6.16 (.52)	5.24	4.92 (.50)	5.24 (.48)	5.08
Range of State	4.15 (.42)	2.70 (1.25)	3.43	3.40 (.57)	3.50 (.40)	3.45
Regulation of State	6.09 (.99)	5.55 (.93)	5.82	5.95 (.91)	4.90 (1.79)	5.47
Autonomic Stability	5.73 (.43)	7.26 (1.01)	6.49	5.66 (.91)	6.33 (.97)	5.99
Reflexes	2.60 (.24)	2.40 (.15)	2.50	2.40 (.14)	2.20 (.25)	2.30

Note. For all clusters but reflexes, a higher score represents more optimal functioning.

useful to cluster these three behaviors into infant attentiveness and leave infant movement and crying intact.

Likewise, the temperament data were reduced beyond the six IBQ dimensions, given our findings with the larger pool of subjects. Specifically, infant responsivity was created by adding the frequency scores for smiling/laughter and duration of orienting. Activity level remained as initially computed. However, irritability was formed by combining fear, distress to limitations, and the inverse of the values for soothability. These combinations differ somewhat from Rothbart's (1986) clusters but, unlike hers, make use of all six IBQ dimensions (see Worobey & Blajda, 1989).

Results of the Analysis

The frequencies for both the observed behaviors and the temperament summary scores appear in Table 6.2. The limited N-size prevented the use of inferential statistics, but the pattern of the results is significant ($p < .05$, by sign test). The variable newborns were observed as higher in attentiveness and movement than were the stable newborns, but lower in the amount of crying they displayed. If one accepts the premise that increased attentiveness and movement characterize a more mature level of functioning, then the newborns who displayed variability were apparently favored. Conversely, few would argue that lessened crying would not facilitate early mother–infant interactions.

Similarly, mothers of variable newborns rated their babies relatively higher in responsivity and activity level, but lower in irritability. Again, maternal ratings

TABLE 6.2
Means for Observed Behaviors and Temperament Dimensions

	Variable	Stable
	Mean (SD)	Mean (SD)
Observed behaviors		
Attentiveness	130.00 (30.74)	85.40 (40.50)
Movement	105.20 (26.35)	84.60 (14.67)
Crying	41.00 (17.30)	63.00 (27.68)
Temperament dimensions		
Responsivity	6.28 (1.81)	6.06 (.95)
Activity level	3.69 (.94)	3.35 (.66)
Irritability	8.45 (1.48)	8.76 (.75)

of heightened responsivity and increased activity level indicate, at the very least, a perception of infants who are comparatively more mature. Although lower ratings of irritability do not infer greater maturation per se, such estimates suggest that the variable infants' behaviors were viewed by their mothers as less aversive.

What is particularly striking, besides the tendency toward greater maturity displayed for the variable infants relative to the stable babies, is the direct parallel between the observed behaviors and the mothers' ratings of the same. Observed infant attentiveness, as derived from alertness, looking at the mother, and vocalizing, is conceptually similar to the maternal ratings of infant responsivity, computed from the IBQ estimates for orienting and smiling/laughter. In turn, observer-scored arm and leg movements are virtually synonymous with the mother-rated activity level, and crying is most certainly comparable to the irritability score that was formed from the IBQ distress-related dimensions.

Activity, Responsivity, and Irritability

These results, although admittedly derived from the patterns displayed in a small sample of infants, nevertheless provide intriguing evidence for the use of the NBAS as a predictive tool in the study of individual differences. On both measures that reflected maturation, namely, activity level and attentiveness/responsivity, the infants who had demonstrated variability over the repeated NBAS assessments were higher at 1 month as observed at home and remained higher at 2 months as rated by their mothers. Conversely, the observed frequency of crying at 1 month, and the maternal estimates of distress at 3 months, were higher in infants who were deemed stable based on their NBAS performances.

Activity level is included in virtually every theory of temperament and instrument that purports to measure the construct. Although it increases with age and may be contextually influenced (Worobey & Anderson-Goetz, 1985), it is generally considered the dimension that shows the greatest continuity from infancy through childhood (Hubert, Wachs, Peters-Martin, & Gandour, 1982). Responsivity, alertness, orientation, attentiveness, or any other of a host of labels is usually acknowledged as slower in surfacing than activity level. However, its importance to the developing mother–infant interactive system is beyond question. In fact, its early recognition and expected improvement serve as the focal point for most NBAS-based interventions aimed at facilitating caregiving (Worobey, 1985). Finally, the infant's crying behavior, as an audible manifestation of distress, may be viewed as a core ingredient of difficultness (Bates, 1980).

Taken together, these three variables comprise what may prove to be the central dimensions of infant individuality. Buss and Plomin (1984), for example, specify activity, sociability, and emotionality as the three traits that constitute temperament. Given the favored outcomes evident in the variable subsample of infants, it seems reasonable to propose that stability itself may be viewed as an individual difference, or at the very least, a mediator of the more generally recognized dimensions of individual difference.

CONCLUSION

In this chapter, a distinction was made between neurological and behavioral assessments, and their roots in the fields of medicine and psychology were traced. The efforts of Graham (1956), Rosenblith (1961), and Brazelton (1973, 1984) were described, and evidence of the reliability and predictive validity of their tests were presented. Despite all three exams being psychometrically adequate, only one has seen steady and increasing use, namely, the NBAS. Although it has been cited or used in over 150 studies, a number of criticisms of the instrument have been raised, not the least of which has been the low stability of scores across repeated administrations of the exam. The issue of stability was discussed, a variability hypothesis was tested, and results showed that changes in newborn functioning across the first month of life have positive implications for infant behavior in a caregiving context.

There are many ways to define stability, however. The analysis presented herein employed a specific technique to determine stability, tailor made for the NBAS, and appropriate only for newborn infants. Moreover, the implications of the measured stability do not extend beyond 2 months of age. Within these constraints, however, the usefulness of repeated NBAS assessments is neverthe-less evident. Indeed, it is argued by some as absolutely necessary, given the possibility of measurement error (Asch, Gleser, & Steichen, 1986).

As Brazelton (1973) himself suggested at the outset, change in the infant over the first weeks postpartum is likely to be of greater value in describing neonatal functioning than relying on performance on any particular day (Kaye, 1978). Ironically, the use of repeated NBAS assessments to document patterns of change rather than stability, combined with other measures and settings for observation (Epstein, 1980), may best serve to strengthen our predictions from the newborn period to later development.

ACKNOWLEDGMENTS

The author wishes to thank the New Jersey Agricultural Experiment Station and Cook College of Rutgers University for support provided to this and related projects.

REFERENCES

Adamson, L., Als, H., Tronick, E. Z., & Brazelton, T. B. (1975). *A-priori profiles for the Bra-zelton Neonatal Assessment.* Mimeo. Child Development Unit. Boston: Children's Hospital.

Aleksandrowicz, M., & Aleksandrowicz, D. (1978). Precursors of ego in neonates: Factor analysis of Brazelton Scale data. *Journal of the American Academy of Children, 15,* 257–268.

Als, H. (1984). Newborn behavioral assessment. In W. J. Burns & J. V. Lavigne (Eds.), *Progress in pediatric psychology* (pp. 1–46). London: Grune & Stratton.

Als, H. (1986). A synactive model of neonatal behavioral organization: Framework for the assess-ment of neurobehavioral development in the premature infant and for support of infants and parents in the neonatal intensive care environment. *Physical and Occupational Therapy in Pedi-atrics, 6,* 3–53.

Als, H., Duffy, F. H., & McAnulty, G. B (1988a). Behavioral differences between preterm and full-term newborns as measured with the APIB system scores: I. *Infant Behavior and Develop-ment, 11,* 305–318.

Als, H., Duffy, F. H., & McAnulty, G. B. (1988b). The APIB, an assessment of functional competence in preterm and full-term newborns regardless of gestational age at birth: II. *Infant Behavior and Development, 11,* 319–331.

Als, H., Tronick, E., Lester, B. M., & Brazelton, T. B. (1979). Specific neonatal measures: The Brazelton neonatal behavioral assessment scale. In J. D. Osofsky (Ed.), *Handbook of infant development* (pp. 185–215). New York: Wiley.

Amiel-Tison, C., & Grenier, A. (1986). *Neurological assessment during the first year of life.* Oxford: Oxford University Press.

Anderson, L., Boukydis, C. F. Z., Pencker, M., & Lester, B. M. (1988, April). *Repeated analysis of Brazelton Scale (NBAS) performance of preterm infants at 36, 40 and 44 weeks conceptual age.* Paper presented at the International Conference on Infant Studies, Washington, DC.

Anderson-Huntington, R. B., & Rosenblith, J. F. (1976). Central nervous system damage as a possible component of unexpected deaths in infancy. *Developmental Medicine and Child Neurology, 18,* 480–492.

Andre-Thomas, & St.-Anne Dargassies, S. (1952). *Etudes neurologiques sur le nouveau-ne et le jeune nourisson.* Paris: Masson.

Andre-Thomas, C. Y., & St.-Anne Dargassies, S. (1952). *Etudes neurologiques sur le nouveau-ne et le jeune nourisson.* Paris: Masson.

Asch, P. A. S., Gleser, G. C., & Steichen, J. J. (1986). Dependability of Brazelton Neonatal Behavioral Assessment cluster scales. *Infant Behavior and Development, 9,* 291–306.

Bates, J. E. (1980). The concept of difficult temperament. *Merrill-Palmer Quarterly, 26,* 299–319.

Bench, J., & Parker, A. (1970). On the reliability of the Graham/Rosenblith Behavior Test for Neonates. *Journal of Child Psychology and Psychiatry, 11,* 121–131.

Brazelton, T. B. (1973). *Neonatal behavioral assessment scale.* Clinics in Developmental Medicine, # 50. London: Heinemann.

Brazelton, T. B. (Ed.). (1984). *Neonatal behavioral assessment scale* (2d ed.). Clinics in Developmental Medicine, # 88. London: Blackwell Scientific.

Brazelton, T. B., Nugent, J. K., & Lester, B. M. (1987). Neonatal behavioral assessment scale. In J. D. Osofsky (Ed.), *Handbook of infant development* (2d ed., pp. 780–817). New York: Wiley.

Brown, J. V., Bakeman, R., Snyder, P. A., Fredrickson, W. T., Morgan, S. T., & Hepler, R. (1975). Interactions of Black inner-city mothers with their newborn infants. *Child Development, 46,* 677–686.

Buss, A. H., & Plomin, R. (1984). *Temperament: Early developing personality traits.* Hillsdale, NJ: Lawrence Erlbaum Associates.

Corah, N., Anthony, E., Painter, P., Stern, J., & Thurston, D. (1965). Effects of perinatal anoxia after seven years. *Psychological Monographs, 32,* 1–34.

Crockenberg, S. B., & Acredolo, C. (1983). Infant temperament ratings: A function of infants, of mothers, or both? *Infant Behavior and Development, 6,* 61–72.

Dennis, W. A. (1934). A description and classification of the responses of the newborn infant. *Psychological Bulletin, 31,* 5–22.

Dewey, E. (1935). *Behavior development in infants: A survey of the literature on prenatal and postnatal activity, 1920–1934.* New York: Columbia University Press.

Dubowitz, L., & Dubowitz, V. (1981). *The neurological assessment of the preterm and full-term newborn infant.* Clinics in Developmental Medicine, # 79. London: Heinemann.

Emde, R. N. (1978). Commentary. In A. J. Sameroff (Ed.), Organization and stability of newborn behavior: A commentary on the Brazelton neonatal behavioral assessment scale (pp. 135–138). *Monographs of the Society for Research in Child Development, 43,* Serial # 177.

Epstein, S. (1980). The stability of behavior: Implications for psychological research. *American Psychologist, 35,* 790–806.

Francis, P. L., Self, P. A., & Horowitz, F. D. (1987). The behavioral assessment of the neonate: An overview. In J. D. Osofsky (Ed.), *Handbook of infant development* (2d ed., pp. 723–779). New York: Wiley.

Gardner, J. M., Karmel, B. Z., Magnano, C. L., & Norton, K. I. (1989). *Neurobehavioral indicators of early brain insult in high-risk neonates.* Manuscript under review.

Graham, F. (1956). Behavioral differences between normal and traumatized newborns: I. The test procedures. *Psychological Monographs, 70,* 1–16.

Graham, F., Ernhart, C., Thurston, D., & Craft, M. (1962). Development three years after perinatal anoxia and other potentially damaging newborn experiences. *Psychological Monographs, 76,* 1–53.

Graham, F., Matarazzo, R., & Caldwell, B. M. (1956). Behavioral differences between normal and traumatized newborns: II. Standardization, reliability and validity. *Psychological Monographs, 70,* 17–23.

Graham, F., Pennoyer, M. M., Caldwell, B. M., Greenman, M., & Hartmann, A. F. (1957). Relationship between clinical status and behavior test performance in a newborn group with histories suggesting anoxia. *Journal of Pediatrics, 50,* 177–189.

Harris, S. R., & Brady, D. K. (1986). Infant neuromotor assessment instruments: A review. *Physical and Occupational Therapy in Pediatrics, 6,* 121–153.

Horowitz, F. D. (1987). *Exploring developmental theories: Toward a structural/behavioral model of development.* Hillsdale, NJ: Lawrence Erlbaum Associates.

Horowitz, F. D., & Linn, P. (1984). The Neonatal Behavioral Assessment Scale. In M. Wolraich & D. K. Routh (Eds.), *Advances in developmental pediatrics* (pp. 223–256). Greenwich, CT: JAI Press.

Horowitz, F. D., Sullivan, J., & Linn, P. (1978). Stability and instability in the newborn infant: The quest for elusive threads. In A. J. Sameroff (Ed.), Organization and stability of newborn behavior: A commentary on the Brazelton neonatal behavioral assessment scale (pp. 29–45). *Monographs of the Society for Research in Child Development, 43,* Serial # 177.

Hubert, N. C., Wachs, T. D., Peters-Martin, P., & Gandour, M. (1982). The study of early temperament: Measurement and conceptual issues. *Child Development, 53,* 571–600.

Jacobson, J. L., Fein, G. G., Jacobson, S. W., & Schwartz, P. M. (1984). Factors and clusters for the Brazelton Scale: An investigation of the dimensions of neonatal behavior. *Developmental Psychology, 20,* 339–353.

Kaye, K. (1978). Discriminating among normal infants by multivariate analysis of Brazelton scores: Lumping and smoothing. In A. J. Sameroff (Ed.), Organization and stability of newborn behavior: A commentary on the Brazelton neonatal behavioral assessment scale (pp. 60–80). *Monographs of the Society for Research in Child Development, 43,* Serial # 177.

Kestermann, G. (1981). Assessment of individual differences among healthy newborns on the Brazelton Scale. *Early Human Development, 5,* 15–27.

Korner, A. F., Brown, B. W., Dimiceli, S., Forrest, T., Stevenson, D. K., Lane, N. M., Constantinou, J., & Thom, V. (1989). Stable individual differences in developmentally changing preterm infants: A replicated study. *Child Development, 60,* 502–513.

Korner, A. F., Kraemer, H. C., Reade, E., Forrest, T., & Dimiceli, S. (1987). A methodological approach to developing an assessment procedure for testing the neurobehavioral maturity of preterm infants. *Child Development, 58,* 1478–1487.

Kurtzberg, D., Vaughan, H. G., Daum, C., Grellong, B. A., Albin, S., & Rotkin, L. (1979). Neurobehavioral performance of low-birthweight infants at 40 weeks conceptual age: Comparison with normal fullterm infants. *Developmental Medicine and Child Neurology, 21,* 590–607.

Lancioni, G. E., Horowitz, F. D., & Sullivan, J. W. (1980). The NBAS-K:1. A study of its stability and structure over the first month of life. *Infant Behavior and Development, 3,* 341–359.

Leijon, I., & Finnstrom, O. (1981). Studies on the Brazelton Neonatal Behavioral Assessment Scale. *Neuropediatrics, 12,* 242–253.

Lester, B. M. (1984). Data analysis and prediction. In T. B. Brazelton (Ed.), *Neonatal behavioral assessment scale* (2d ed., pp. 85–96). London: Blackwell Scientific.

Lester, B. M. (1988). Neurobehavioral assessment of the infant at risk. In P. M. Vietze & H. G. Vaughan (Eds.), *Early identification of infants with developmental disabilities* (pp. 96–120). Philadelphia: Grune & Stratton.

Lester, B. M., Als, H., & Brazelton, T. B. (1982). Regional obstetric anesthesia and newborn behavior: A reanalysis of synergistic effects. *Child Development, 53,* 687–692.

Linn, P. L., & Horowitz, F. D. (1983). The relationship between infant individual differences and mother–infant interaction during the neonatal period. *Infant Behavior and Development, 6,* 415–427.

Magitat, A. (1903). L'apparition prococe reflexe photomeur au cours du development foetal. *Annales d'Oculistique, 141,* 161.

Magnus, R. (1924). *Korperstellung.* Berlin: Julius Springer.

McGraw, M. (1943). *The neuromuscular maturation of the human infant.* New York: Columbia University Press.

Moro, E. (1918). Das erste Trimenon. *Munchener Medizinischer Wochenschrift, 65,* 1147–1150.

Moss, M., Colombo, J., Mitchell, D. W., & Horowitz, F. D. (1988). Neonatal behavioral organization and visual processing at three months. *Child Development, 59,* 1211–1220.

Nugent, J. K., & Sepkoski, C. (1984). The training of NBAS examiners. In T. B. Brazelton (Ed.), *Neonatal behavioral assessment scale* (2d ed., pp. 78–84). London: Blackwell Scientific.

O'Donnell, K. J., & Oehler, J. M. (1989). Neurobehavioral assessment of the newborn infant. In D. B. Bailey & M. Wolery (Eds.), *Assessing infants and preschoolers with handicaps* (pp. 166–201). Columbus: Merrill.

Parmelee, A. H. (1962). European neurological studies of the newborn. *Child Development, 33,* 169–180.

Peiper, A. (1928). *Die hirntatigkeit des suglings.* Berlin: Springer.

Prechtl, H. F. R. (1977). *The neurological examination of the full term newborn infant* (2d ed.). Clinics in Developmental Medicine, # 63. London: Heinemann.

Prechtl, H. F. R. (1982). Assessment methods for the newborn infant, a critical evaluation. In P. Stratton (Ed.), *Psychobiology of the human newborn.* London: Wiley.

Prechtl, H. F. R. (1984). Epilogue. In H. F. R. Prechtl (Ed.), Continuity of neural functions from prenatal to postnatal life. *Clinics in Developmental Medicine,* # 94. London: Blackwell Scientific.

Prechtl, H. F. R., & Beintema, D. (1964). *The neurological examination of the full term newborn infant.* Clinics in Developmental Medicine, # 28. London: Heinemann.

Riese, M. L. (1983). Assessment of behavioral patterns in neonates. *Infant Behavior and Development, 6,* 241–246.

Roberton, N. R. C. (1984). The routine neonatal clinical examination. In N. J. Wald (Ed.), *Antenatal and neonatal screening.* Oxford: Oxford University Press.

Rosenblith, J. F. (1961). The modified Graham Behavior Test for Neonates: Test–retest reliability, normative data, and hypotheses for future work. *Biologia Neonatorum, 3,* 174–192.

Rosenblith, J. F. (1975). Prognostic value of neonatal behavioral tests. In B. Z. Friedlander, G. M. Sterritt, & G. E. Kirk (Eds.), *Exceptional infant* (pp. 157–172). New York: Brunner/Mazel.

Rosenblith, J. F. (1979). The Graham/Rosenblith behavioral examination for newborns: Prognostic value and procedural issues. In J. D. Osofsky (Ed.), *Handbook of infant development* (pp. 216–249). New York: Wiley.

Rosenblith, J. F., & Lipsitt, L. P. (1959). Interscorer agreement for the Graham Behavior Test for Neonates. *Journal of Pediatrics, 54,* 200–205.

Rosenblith, J. F., & Sims-Knight, J. E. (1985). *In the beginning: Development in the first two years of life.* Monterey: Wadsworth.

Rothbart, M. K. (1981). Measurement of temperament in infancy. *Child Development, 52,* 569–578.

Rothbart, M. K. (1986). Longitudinal observation of infant temperament. *Developmental Psychology, 22,* 356–365.

St. Clair, K. L. (1978). Neonatal assessment procedures: A historical review. *Child Development, 49,* 280–292.

Sameroff, A. J. (1978). Summary and conclusions: The future of newborn assessment. In A. J. Sameroff (Ed.), Organization and stability of newborn behavior: A commentary on the Brazelton neonatal behavioral assessment scale (pp. 102–117). *Monographs of the Society for Research in Child Development, 43,* Serial # 177.

Sameroff, A. J., Krafchuk, E. E., & Bakow, H. A. (1978). Issues in grouping items from the neonatal behavioral assessment scale. In A. J. Sameroff (Ed.), Organization and stability of newborn behavior: A commentary on the Brazelton neonatal behavioral assessment scale (pp. 46–59). *Monographs of the Society for Research in Child Development, 43,* Serial # 177.

Sepkoski. C. (1986, April). *The relationship between NBAS profiles, 1-year Bayley and 5-year McCarthy scores.* Paper presented at the International Conference on Infant Studies, Los Angeles.

Sostek, A. M., & Anders, T. F. (1977). Relationships among the Brazelton neonatal scale, Bayley infant scales and early temperament. *Child Development, 48,* 320–323.

Vaughn, B. E., Taraldson, B., Crichton, L., & Egeland, B. (1980). Relationships between neonatal behavioral organization and infant behavior during the first year of life. *Infant Behavior and Development, 3,* 47–66.

Woodson, R. H. (1983). Newborn behavior and the transition to extrauterine life. *Infant Behavior and Development, 6,* 139–144.

Worobey, J. (1985). A review of Brazelton-based interventions to enhance parent–infant interaction. *Journal of Reproductive and Infant Psychology, 3,* 64–73.

Worobey, J. (1986). Neonatal stability and one-month behavior. *Infant Behavior and Development, 9,* 119–124.

Worobey, J., & Anderson-Goetz, D. (1985). Maternal ratings of newborn activity: Assessing convergence between instruments. *Infant Mental Health Journal, 6,* 68–75.

Worobey, J., & Belsky, J. (1982). Employing the Brazelton scale to influence mothering: An experimental comparison of three strategies. *Developmental Psychology, 18,* 736–743.

Worobey, J., & Blajda, V. M. (1989). Temperament ratings at two-weeks, two-months and one year: Differential stability of activity and emotionality. *Developmental Psychology, 25,* 257–263.

III INFORMATION PROCESSING AND OUTPUT

7 Individual Differences in Infant Conditioning and Memory

Jeffrey W. Fagen
Phyllis S. Ohr
St. John's University

INTRODUCTION

Infant researchers have long since abandoned the view that learning (conditioning) is not possible in early infancy. Rather, both classical and operant conditioning have been shown to be obtainable in the human newborn and possibly before birth (for reviews of this literature see, for example, Brackbill & Koltsova, 1967; Fitzgerald & Brackbill, 1976; Fitzgerald & Porges, 1971; Horowitz, 1968; Hulsebus, 1973; Lipsitt, 1963, 1971, 1982; Olson & Sherman, 1983; Rovee-Collier, 1983, 1986, 1987; Rovee-Collier & Gekoski, 1979; Rovee-Collier & Lipsitt, 1982; Sameroff, 1972; Sameroff & Cavanagh, 1979). The need to demonstrate that young infants could be conditioned has occupied the time of investigators for several decades as researchers have asked questions revolving around the issues of when the infant learns, how he or she learns, and what experimental manipulations affect learning (Horowitz, 1969). More recently, investigators have begun to use conditioning procedures to study infant memory, designing their research to address questions of can the infant remember, at what age, for how long, and under what conditions (Rovee-Collier, 1984; for reviews see Fagen & Rovee-Collier, 1982; Rovee-Collier, 1983, 1984, 1987; Rovee-Collier & Fagen, 1981; Rovee-Collier & Hayne, 1987; Rovee-Collier & Lipsitt, 1982). Faced with the need to answer these overriding questions, little energy has been devoted to questions of individual differences (see also Wachs, 1984).

Conditioning studies have generally relied on two basic research strategies: the group-comparison design and the single-subject design. All of psychology uses the former design, which, in its simplest version, involves exposing relatively large numbers of subjects to one of two treatments and statistically comparing the groups' means and variances. Individual differences in behavior are the bane of this design because they increase the within-groups variance making statistical rejection of the null hypothesis of no group differences more difficult. The single-subject design, the mainstay of many operant conditioning researchers, also has as one of its goals the "elimination" of performance differences between subjects. For example, in discussing the "problem" of individual differences, Sidman (1960), one of the foremost proponents of the single-subject design, concluded that with regard to individual differences, "nobody really cares . . . [individual differences] only tells him [the experimenter] that he does not possess the information and technical skill to obtain the data in which he is *really* interested'' (p. 51, emphasis added). This attitude reflects the bias of most investigators that differences between individuals under study are primarily due to measurement errors or reflect "chance" or "random" factors that need to (or should have been) controlled. Although by and large this is correct, there is still a portion of behavioral variance that can be explained by variables other than those being manipulated.

This chapter reviews the handful of studies that have questioned why all infants receiving the same treatment in a classical or operant conditioning study do not perform the same. In general, these studies have looked to explain individual differences by examining the relation of behavioral (e.g., temperament, responsivity), biomedical (e.g., prematurity, Down syndrome), or neurological (e.g., hydranencephaly) factors to conditioning and memory. Others have examined questions of stability between performance at Time 1 and Time 2, whereas a third group has investigated whether conditioning performance can be predicted by, or is predictive of, performance on other tasks. In addition, we present data from our own research that have addressed some of these issues. Noticeably absent from this list is the age variable. This is because longitudinal studies of infant conditioning and memory are extremely rare and although several investigators have made age-to-age comparisons based on cross-sectional data, the utility of these studies for answering questions of stability and prediction is questionable (see also McCall, 1977). Furthermore, developmental studies of conditioning during the first year of life are faced with the difficulty of assessing age-related changes in performance against developmental changes in responsiveness, motivation, reinforcement value, and response requirements (Rovee-Collier & Lipsitt, 1982; Siqueland, 1970).

CLASSICAL CONDITIONING

Until recently, definitions of classical conditioning focused on the process by which a neutral stimulus, the conditioned stimulus (CS), eventually evokes a response that was previously elicited by another stimulus, the unconditioned stimulus (US), due to the repeated pairing of the two stimuli. Such a mechanistic definition has given way to a modern view of classical conditioning as "the learning of relations among events that are complexly represented" (Rescorla, 1988, p. 158) or the acquisition of "expectancies" regarding predictive relations among stimuli (Bolles, 1979, p. 160). In spite of this modern conceptualization, classical conditioning research with infants, which enjoyed a flurry of activity in the 1960s and early 1970s, is scarce today although there is hope for its recovery (for some notable recent studies see Blass, Ganchrow, & Steiner, 1984; Hoffman, Cohen, & DeVito, 1985; Little, Lipsitt, & Rovee-Collier, 1984). As Rovee-Collier (1986) noted:

> Current perspectives of classical conditioning focus on the nature of what is learned, its functional significance, how it is represented, and under what conditions it is expressed. These perspectives should provide an impetus for innovative research with infants. In addition, classical conditioning as a paradigm permits an elegant and precise assay of infant sensation and perception, learning and memory, neurological development and function, and perhaps even the underlying "deep" structure of behavior. In the hands of a skilled experimenter, it is one of our finest and most powerful experimental tools. (p. 140)

Given the preceding assertions, the classical conditioning paradigm seems ripe for the study of individual differences in infant behavior and development. Unfortunately, little has changed in the 20-plus years since Brackbill and Koltsova (1967) pointed out that, unlike Pavlov, most infant classical conditioning researchers have little interest in individual differences. Thus, according to Brackbill and Koltsova (1967), it is still true that "a primary goal among American experimenters when planning [classical conditioning] research is to reduce to the maximum extent, variance due to between-subject differences, and the tacitly understood policy when, despite all, individual differences in results do appear, is to ignore the fact" (p. 213).

Pavlov's interest in individual differences resulted from, among other things, the fact that he repeatedly used the same dogs for many experiments and became convinced that the differences he observed among them were due to "the constitutionally determined status of excitation and inhibition" (Brackbill & Koltsova, 1967, p. 214). In essence he was referring to temperamental differences among his dogs that Pavlov believed could be described in terms of an individual's balance (or lack of balance) between excitatory and inhibitory tendencies. In spite of this interest, however, most Soviet investigators of infant classical conditioning, many of whom studied under Pavlov, have not systematically studied questions of individual differences. Kasatkin and Levikova (1935), for example, reported data for individual infants yet only noted but did not discuss the variability among them. Instead, Soviet investigators have focused on a hypothesized (and essentially incorrect) developmental sequence in which conditioned responses can be established based on the modality, duration, and intensity of the unconditioned stimulus. Thus, for example, in one of the earliest Soviet studies, Krasnogorskii (1913, cited in Lipsitt, 1982) concluded that classical conditioning was not possible in the first 6 months of life because of the infant's cortical immaturity. We now know, however, that not only is classical conditioning possible in the newborn (e.g., Lipsitt & Kaye, 1964), but infants born without any discernible cerebral cortex can also be classically conditioned (e.g., Tuber, Berntson, Bachman, & Allen, 1980). In a major review, Fitzgerald and Brackbill (1976) concluded that age accounts for little of the variance in conditioned response formation. Rather, it appears that, regardless of age, somatic responses (e.g., eye blinking, sucking) are more readily associated with tactile, visual, or auditory conditioned stimuli whereas autonomic responses (e.g., the pupillary reflex, heart rate) are more likely to become associated with a temporal conditioned stimulus.

Individual Differences in Orienting and Conditionability

The 1963 English-language publication of Sokolov's *Perception and the conditioned reflex* (Sokolov, 1963) helped to focus investigators' attention on the role played by the infant's initial response to the CS in determining the success of classical conditioning procedure. Sokolov maintained that the cortex functions to extrapolate information from incoming stimuli. Graham (1973) asserted that a stimulus presented to the infant is believed to elicit the orienting reflex (OR) (Pavlov's "what is it" reflex; Pavlov, 1927); "a generalized system of responses which includes central, motor, and ANS [autonomic nervous system] components that enhance stimulus reception" (p. 166). Repeated presentation of the same stimulus in the same context leads to the construction of an internal representation of the stimulus to which subsequent stimulus encounters are compared. This comparison process continues until a match occurs between the incoming stimulus information and the internal model, at which time habituation occurs and attention is directed elsewhere. Implicit in the aforementioned is Sokolov's (1963) contention that (a) the OR is necessary for conditioning to occur and (b) the magnitude of the OR is related to individual differences in the speed of conditioning.

Ingram and Fitzgerald (1974) were the first to explore the relation between infant orienting and conditionability using the skin potential response. Three-month-old infants received repeated presentations of one of two tones paired with a puff of air to the cheek (the US). Prior to conditioning, each infant also received random presentations of each tone until a criterion of habituation was achieved. Conditioning consisted of two parts: discrimination and reversal. During the 2-day discrimination phase, presentations of one tone (the CS$^+$) were followed by the US whereas presentations of the other (the CS$^-$) were not. One day later, the CS$^+$ and CS$^-$ were reversed. Although one-half the subjects responded more to the CS$^+$ than to the CS$^-$ during discrimination training, an analysis based on the magnitude of the infants' first response during the habituation phase (OR) indicated that five of the six "high" OR infants (determined by a median split) demonstrated conditioning whereas only one of the six "low" OR subjects did. Furthermore, OR magnitude was related to conditionability ($r = .66$) and, within the group that successfully acquired the discrimination, negatively related to the number of trials necessary to achieve the criterion of conditioned discrimination ($r = -.71$). Although no relation between OR magnitude and discrimination reversal was reported, infants who habituated most rapidly were also those who most rapidly acquired the reversal ($r = .66$). Ingram (1978) replicated the relation between OR magnitude and discrimination learning and also found that high OR subjects showed a greater decrease in responding during extinction. Ingram interpreted the latter as reflecting faster habituation by the high OR subjects; however, the lack of response decrease in the low OR subjects probably resulted from a "floor effect" due to their low response magnitude, both at the end of acquisition and throughout extinction.

Stamps and his colleagues (Stamps, 1977; Stamps & Porges, 1975; Turco & Stamps, 1980) have conducted a series of studies on the relation between heart rate variability, sex, and conditionability. Although Sokolov did not consider heart rate change, an unconditioned response to stimulation, as an element of the OR, it is generally agreed that heart rate deceleration is a component of this response (see Graham & Clifton, 1966; Graham & Jackson, 1970). Furthermore, heart rate variability is directly related to the attentional component of the OR; greater heart rate variability is associated with better performance on attentional tasks as well as consistency of the heart rate response to changes in stimulation (see Porges, 1974). Stamps and Porges (1975) presented newborn infants with a tone CS paired with a US consisting of a pattern of blinking lights. The use of a trace paradigm (i.e., the CS terminated 10 sec prior to the onset of the US), and both CS-only and extinction trials, allowed them to measure the infants' responses to the CS, in anticipation of the US, and to the absence of the US. Heart rate variability was related to the first measure in that only high-variance subjects (determined by a median split based on pretraining heart rate variability) showed a conditioned deceleration and change in response over CS–US trials. When these data were analyzed for sex differences, only the females exhibited conditioned heart rate deceleration in response to the tone. It is unclear, however, whether there was any interaction between these two factors. There was a sex difference but no heart rate variability difference in US anticipation with only females exhibiting a deceleration. Finally, neither sex nor heart rate variability affected infants' responsiveness when the US was omitted. Stamps (1977) replicated the sex difference in US anticipation using a temporal conditioning procedure in which the US (a buzzer) was presented every 20 sec. In addition, female infants had a higher level of spontaneous heart rate variability. Using older infants and a visual CS, but no measure of prestimulus heart rate, Turco and Stamps (1980) found that only male infants showed anticipatory heart rate deceleration whereas only females showed a deceleration on CS-only trials.

The preceding studies suggest that both infant sex and heart rate variability are important individual-difference variables for determining the conditionability of infant autonomic responses. It appears, however, that the relation between sex and conditionability is an indirect one, mediated by the fact that in both the Stamps and Porges (1975) and Stamps (1977) studies, females tended to also have higher rates of spontaneous heart rate variability.

If, as is now believed, classical conditioning involves the acquisition of expectancies regarding predictive relations between stimuli, then it follows that differences in attention to the initially "meaningless" CS should aid in this process. Infants who initially orient to the CS are afforded sufficient time to process information regarding the details of that stimulus. The rapidity with which the infant habituates to the CS also appears to aid in conditioned response formation. Although this may simply be due to the "fact" that habituation is also a form of conditioning (see Flaherty, 1985), it seems more likely that it too reflects attentional differences between infants.

In discussing the relation between habituation and conditionability, Kimmel (1973) proposed the existence of two classes of reflexes: positive feedback reflexes and negative feedback reflexes. The former reflect orienting and other responses (e.g., searching) designed to increase afferent input to the central nervous system (CNS). Thus, they not only direct the sense organs to the source of stimulation but also aid the CNS in processing information obtained through these sensory inputs. Furthermore, positive feedback reflexes are plastic and should habituate rapidly. Negative feedback reflexes (e.g., postural, protective, ingestive) reduce afferent input to the CNS, are generally nonhabituable, and can function as reinforcers. As Kimmel (1973) stated, "the easiest way of establishing a conditioned response of the Pavlovian [classical] type is to pair any member of the plastic, positive feedback reflexes with any member of the nonhabituating, negative reflexes" (p. 231). This is true, however, only to the extent that the subject initially orients to and subsequently habituates to the stimulus that elicited the positive feedback stimulus (i.e., the CS) during the CS–US interval (see also Fitzgerald & Brackbill, 1976; Rovee-Collier & Lipsitt, 1982). Lack of orienting will preclude elicitation of the positive feedback reflex; lack of habituation will result in the CS gaining rather than losing strength to the point that classical conditioning may be impossible or, at best, retarded.

This account of the role of the OR and its habituation in infant classical conditioning does not, however, aid in understanding the reason and/or significance of the reported individual differences in OR magnitude and heart rate variability. Do these represent interindividual differences in maturational status, responsiveness to stimulation, general inhibitory ability, sensitization (see Kaplan & Werner, 1987), or even personality characteristics such as introversion–extroversion (Ingram & Fitzgerald, 1974)? Are they related to other aspects of infant behavior, such as temperament (Fagen & Ohr, 1985)? Are they predictive of future inter- and intraindividual differences in learning or other cognitive behaviors? We can only hope that future investigators of human development heed Rovee-Collier's (1986) timely call for a resurgence of research on infant classical conditioning.

Classical Conditioning in Compromised Infants

Decerebrate Infants.   Related to the previous discussion of orienting, habituation, and conditionability are a handful of studies that have examined these behaviors in anencephalic and hydranencephalic infants. These infants are born without a cerebral cortex and therefore provide a test for Sokolov's (1963) position that orienting and conditioning are related *cortical* functions. However, both orienting and habituation have been obtained in a handful of these infants (Aylward, Lazzara, & Meyer, 1978; Berg, Clarkson, Eitzman, & Setzer, 1981; Graham, Leavitt, Strock, & Brown, 1978; cf. Brackbill, 1971).

Two studies have been successful at classically conditioning hydranencephalic infants. Tuber et al. (1980) compared a pair of premature twins, one hydranencephalic and the other normal, using a tone as the CS and a flash of light directed at the infant's face as the US. Both infants received 162 paired CS-US trials and 18 CS-only trials over four sessions separated by an average of 7 days. Training began when the infants were 40 days of age (they had been born 2 months prematurely). Measures of heart rate (HR) indicated that both infants responded to the CS-US pairings with HR deceleration and to the CS-only trials with a long-latency HR acceleration. In addition, extinction trials given after each session revealed a rapid diminution of the acceleratory HR response to the tone in both infants. Interestingly, it appears from the data presented by Tuber et al. (1980) that the hydranencephalic infant exhibited a larger orienting response on the two CS-only trials presented at the outset of each session. In a subsequent study using the same basic procedure, Berntson, Tuber, Ronca, and Bachman (1983) reported successful classical conditioning in two of three hydranencephalic infants.[1] The one infant who did not condition also failed to habituate to the CS.

These studies provide additional support for the notion that attention to the CS is a necessary prerequisite for classical conditioning, and that individual differences in orienting are related to individual differences in conditionability. They do not suport Sokolov's contention that classical conditioning processes are mediated cortically; rather, it appears that they may be mediated by subcortical circuits. In addition, however, the work with these hydranencephalic infants suggests a potentially useful role for classical conditioning procedures in the study of individual differences in a wide variety of infant groups (e.g., preterms, those suffering from anoxia, infants with Down syndrome, etc.).

---

[1]It appears from the description of the subjects and the data presented that one of the infants in this study was the hydranencephalic twin of Tuber et al. (1980).

Premature infants. Traditionally, Soviet and Eastern European researchers have been interested in classical conditioning in premature infants because they have viewed the preterm infant as a natural "preparation" for studying the role of cortical development in conditioning. Also, consistent with their emphasis on the relation between age and conditionability, these investigators have sought to determine if the extrauterine environment has any facilitating effect. Thus, Kasatkin (1969) concluded that his early work with preterms supported the contention that maturation plays a minor role in determining conditionability. Specifically, he reviewed evidence that classical conditioning is not possible in preterm infants until the first half of their second month of life regardless of their degree of prematurity or the age at which conditioning was begun. Furthermore, this was the same age at which conditioning was first obtainable in full-term infants. More recent research, however, has failed to support this and has indicated that the degree of prematurity does have an effect. For example, Polikanina (1961) tested 14 infants born between 1 and 3 months premature. Conditioning began when the infants were between 11 and 20 days of age and consisted of repeated pairings of a tone (CS) with ammonia vapor (US). Measures of respiration, pulse, and various somatic responses (grimaces, blinking, swallowing, and sucking) all indicated that the speed of conditioning was a function of gestational age at birth (see Fig. 7.1). Furthermore, premature infants who began the conditioning procedure later in life (at an average age of 75 days) acquired the conditioned response at about the same age as those started in the first 20 days. In addition,

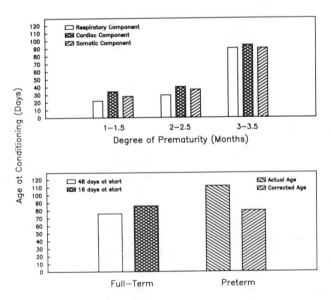

FIG. 7.1. Mean age on reaching criterion for subjects in Polikanina (1961) (top panel) and Ianosh (1959) (bottom panel).

the average correlation between birthweight (range = 1180–2300 g) and the three measures of conditioning was −.72.

The preceding study suggests that, consistent with what most investigators now believe, chronological age is an inappropriate metric against which to measure conditionability (or just about anything else) in preterm infants. Ianosh (1959) has provided direct evidence in support of this. He used a group of preterm infants and two groups of full-term infants: one matched to the preterms in average chronological age at the beginning of conditioning (preterms = 53.7 days; full terms = 47.8 days) and the other matched to the preterms average "corrected" age (preterms = 21.4 days; full-terms = 16.1 days). As shown in Fig. 7.1, the age at which the two full-term groups achieved criterion (five consecutive responses in a single session) did not differ. More importantly, however, these groups' means were not different from the preterms corrected-age mean but were significantly below the preterms chronological age mean.

The past 20 years has seen an explosion of interest on the part of Western researchers in studying the behavior and development of the premature infant. Unfortunately, these investigators have not compared preterm and full-term infants on measures of classical conditioning. The Soviet studies, although commendable, are of limited value because (a) they have focused exclusively on defensive reflexes and have not explored appetitive or other approach responses, and (b) they lack the control groups necessary to conclude that classical conditioning rather than sensitization or pseudoconditioning has occurred (see Rescorla, 1967). Furthermore, nothing is known about the influence of various physiological factors commonly associated with prematurity (e.g., respiratory distress, intraventricular hemorrhage, etc.); factors that are more relevant predictors of individual differences in developmental outcome than prematurity per se.

INSTRUMENTAL CONDITIONING

As with the definition of classical conditioning, modern definitions of instrumental (operant) conditioning focus on the contingency between events in the organism's environment. Unlike classical conditioning, however, in which the organism acquires information regarding the predictive relations among stimuli, the major predictive relation in instrumental conditioning involves the organism's own behavior and a stimulus, typically a reward. A second distinction that can be drawn between these two conditioning procedures is that classical conditioning involves elicited behaviors whereas instrumental conditioning involves emitted behaviors; behaviors that must precede the occurrence of the reward stimulus.

In a recent review, Rovee-Collier (1987) traced the history of investigators' interest in infant instrumental conditioning. In the 1960s, the chief concern was to establish that infants could be instrumentally conditioned and the earliest ages at which conditioning was possible. In the 1970s, the concern shifted to questions regarding interactions among responses, reinforcers, schedules, and ages. Thus, the typical 1970's question was something like: Can a 3-month-old be conditioned to produce a 2-sec exposure of a two-dimensional face stimulus via sucking with a 1-sec delay of reward on a continuous reinforcement schedule? In the 1980s, researchers began to *use* the instrumental conditioning paradigm as a means of studying other aspects of infant behavior and development such as perception, information processing, and memory. Also in this decade, investigators began to take their first systematic looks at questions of individual differences in infant instrumental conditioning. Thus, it is here that a sprinkling of studies have appeared that have compared conditioning performance in various infant groups (e.g., preterms vs. full-terms) or have looked at the relation of other variables (e.g., temperament) to conditioning.

Inter- and Intratask Relationships

In one of the few existing long-term (but not longitudinal) studies of infant instrumental conditioning, Papousek (1967a, 1967b, 1977) attempted to condition infant head-turning for milk reinforcement in newborns and 3- and 5-month-olds. Infants received daily conditioning sessions (except weekends) consisting of 10 trials in which a bell was sounded for 10 sec signaling the availability of milk contingent upon a left head turn within the 10-sec interval.[2] Following the attainment of a learning criterion (five consecutive responses in a single session), infants received an extinction phase in which head turns in the presence of the bell were no longer reinforced. Once the infant failed to respond on five consecutive trials, infants were reconditioned and then conditioned to turn their heads to the left when the bell sounded but to turn to the right when a buzzer was presented. Achievement of a criterion of six consecutive correct responses was followed by a reversal of the left–right discrimination.

Papousek (1967b) reported that, for the newborn group, there was no relation between the occurrence of the first head-turn and the number of trials to criterion. Significant correlations were obtained, however, between trials to criterion and the occurrence of the first two ($r = .71$) and three ($r = .86$) correct responses. In addition, there was a negative correlation ($r = -.66$) between the number of trials to conditioning and extinction (i.e., infants who conditioned faster extinguished slower). Papousek did not, however, report any of the preceding correlations for the 3- or 5-month old groups. A small but significant correlation

---

[2]If the infant did not respond, the experimenter attempted to elicit head turning by perioral stimulation and, if that failed, the infant's head was turned manually. Because reinforcement was presented on every trial regardless of the infant's behavior, Papousek's procedure may be considered a classical conditioning one. We have included it here because (a) it required that a response occur prior to the delivery of the reinforcement, and (b) responses were counted as "correct" only if the infant initiated the head turn.

($r = .38$) was reported for the total sample between the number of trials to conditioning and reconditioning. In addition, although all his subjects were full term, he reported that there were no significant correlations between any conditioning measure and measures of birthweight, birth length, head and chest circumference, or increases in weight or length during the first 3 months. In newborns there was a negative correlation ($r = -.67$) between response latency and chest circumference indicating that stouter newborns made faster head turns. Finally, there was a correlation in both newborns ($r = .59$) and 3-month-olds ($r = .63$) between the number of trials to criterion and daily food intake (i.e., infants who had lower daily intakes of milk conditioned faster).

The correlations reported by Papousek demonstrate that, at least in the first month of life, infants maintain their rankings with respect to the rapidity with which they achieve various conditioning landmarks. Whether (or why) this consistency decreases with age cannot be determined either from Papousek's data or from his procedure. As mentioned earlier, age-to-age comparisons of conditioning performance are difficult to make. In Papousek's research, for example, the reinforcing value of milk may have increased or decreased not only across ages but across the several daily sessions used at each age. Furthermore, it appears from the data he presented that there were age-related differences in the pretraining baseline rates of head turning and the ease with which the infants made the operant response (a head-turn from midline of at least 30°). Nevertheless, Papousek's research represents a milestone in terms of both the study of infant instrumental conditioning in general and the search for intratask consistency in particular.

Papousek (Janos & Papousek, 1977) has also been one of the few infant investigators to question whether performance during instrumental conditioning is related to that during another learning task. Infants from 3 to 150 days of age were first trained in the left-head-turn-for-milk procedure discussed earlier and then received classical conditioning training. The latter involved paired presentations of a tone and a flash of light designed to elicit eyeblinking. A correlation of .84 was obtained between the number of trials to criterion in both procedures. To our knowledge, this is the only study that has attempted to compare infant classical and instrumental conditioning. The relatively high correlation obtained suggests that these two types of conditioning may be mediated by similar processes in the infant, but additional research is obviously needed.

Gekoski (1977) has conducted what we believe to be the only study comparing infant habituation and instrumental conditioning. Her habituation task involved repeated presentations of either a bulls-eye or checkerboard stimulus. Conditioning involved 2 days of training in the mobile conjugate reinforcement task (Rovee & Rovee, 1969) in which footkicks produced proportional movement in an overhead crib mobile containing six brightly colored or achromatic objects. Gekoski found that rate of visual habituation at 12 and 15 weeks was not related to any measure of conditioning (speed of acquisition, magnitude of extinction, or changes in responding accompanying changes in the mobile during the second conditioning session). Only one significant correlation was obtained in this study: At 12 weeks there was a negative correlation ($r = -.66$) between the magnitude of response recovery to the presentation of a novel stimulus following habituation and the response rate following the change in reinforcers. Infants who looked longer at the novel stimulus following habituation exhibited a larger decrease in kicking following the introduction of a novel mobile. The general lack of consistency between measures obtained in the two tasks may have been precluded, however, by the lack of variability in the rapidity with which infants in this study habituated. Given the relations cited in the previous section between orienting, habituation, and classical conditioning, one would expect to find a greater degree of consistency across a variety of habituation and instrumental conditioning tasks. However, because habituation, unlike conditioning, does not involve the establishment of any *predictive* relations between events (stimuli or responses), we would also assume that the habituation-conditioning correlation will not prove to be as strong as either the intra- or interconditioning correlations. In other words, unlike in the habituation procedure, infants in instrumental conditioning tasks are motivated to solve the ''problem'' at hand (see also Fagen & Rovee-Collier, 1982).

Support for the hypothesis of increased individual stability with increased environmental control can be found in a study by Milewski and Siqueland (1975). This study used the high-amplitude sucking technique (HAS) in which criterion sucks on a nonnutritive nipple control the onset and duration of a visual stimulus. Using 1-month-olds they found that operant responding first increased and then decreased across a single conditioning session. Following the response decrease (''habituation''), infants were reinforced with a novel visual stimulus. Correlational analysis revealed a significant relation between the magnitude of operant response decrement during the first phase and the amount of response recovery to the novel stimulus (Experiment 1: $r = .55$; Experiment 2: $r = .69$). Using a paired-comparison technique, however, Fagan (1972, 1973) has consistently reported negligible correlations (in older infants) between the duration of visual attention during a 2-min familiarization period and responsiveness to a novel stimulus.

Temperament

Although there is no consensus regarding precise conceptual or operational definitions of infant temperament, most investigators subscribe to the view that temperament is a stable characteristic which, at the very least, involves individual differences in arousal and emotional expression (Campos, Barrett, Lamb, Goldsmith, & Sternberg, 1983; see also chapters by Rothbart and Mauro and Gunnar in this volume). Research has shown that aspects of infant temperament are correlated with various cognitive measures such as the level of sensorimotor development (Wachs & Gandour, 1983) or performance on standardized tests of infant functioning such as the Bayley Scales of Infant Development (e.g., Fagen, Singer, Ohr, & Fleckenstein, 1987; Roth, Eisenberg, & Sell, 1984). In addition, a few studies have questioned whether aspects of temperament are related to conditioning.

Krafchuk, Sameroff, and Bakow (1976, cited in Sameroff & Cavanagh, 1979) hypothesized that newborn conditionability in a head-turn paradigm would be related to alertness as measured by the Brazelton Neonatal Assessment Scale. Surprisingly, however, this was not the case but increased responding during training was highly correlated with high activity level and muscle tonus scores.

Two studies exist that have compared older infants' performance in the mobile conjugate reinforcement task (Rovee & Rovee, 1969) with various temperamental characteristics as determined by maternal reports. Dunst and Lingerfelt (1985) had mothers of their 2- to 3-month-old subjects complete the Carey and McDevitt Revised Infant Temperament Questionnaire that yields scores on nine temperament dimensions: activity, rhythmicity, approach, adaptability, intensity, mood, persistence, distractibility, and threshold. None of the 63 correlations between these dimensions and the rate of responding (kicking) during baseline and various phases of conditioning were significant. Rhythmicity and persistence were, however, correlated with the rate of learning (rate of response during conditioning minus the rate during baseline) (average $r = -.44$). Thus, faster conditioning occurred in infants rated by their mothers as more predictable in terms of their daily sleeping and feeding patterns and having longer "attention-spans." This relation between attention, as measured during a noncontingent baseline phase, and conditioning performance has also been reported by Hayes, Ewy, and Watson (1982). In fact, in that study, infants with low attention ratings at the end of a 5-min baseline period failed to acquire the instrumental contingency.

In a recent paper, Worobey and Butler (1988) employed two conditioning sessions separated by 24 hr with 3-month-olds whose mothers completed the Rothbart Infant Behavior Questionnaire (IBQ). This 94-item questionnaire produces scores on six scales: activity level, smiling and laughter, fear (distress and latency to approach sudden or novel stimuli), distress to limitations, soothability, and duration of orienting. Consistent with the results of Dunst and Lingerfelt (1985), duration of orienting was related to a measure of the speed of conditioning (the number of minutes necessary to achieve a level of responding greater than or equal to 150% of an infant's baseline response rate) ($r = -.23$). In addition, speed of conditioning was positively correlated with fear ($r = .30$) and negatively correlated with smiling and laughter ($r = -.25$).

The use of a second conditioning session allowed Worobey and Butler (1988) to examine not only the relation between temperament and conditioning but between temperament and session-to-session memory as well. This was done by calculating two retention scores for each infant (see Rovee-Collier & Fagen,

1981). The first, the retention ratio, reflected the proportional change in responding between 3-min nonreinforcement phases given at the end of the first session and the beginning of the second. The second, the baseline ratio, indexed the percentage of the baseline response rate that the infants continued to exhibit during the 3-min nonreinforcement phase at the outset of the second session. The many correlations between these measures and the six measures of temperament were nonsignificant.

The studies just cited suggest that a small amount of variance in contingency acquisition can be accounted for by various aspects of individual differences in infant temperament. These relations, however, seem to be fleeting and inconsistent. For example, we have examined the correlations between 84 of our subjects who were trained with the mobile conjugate reinforcement task and whose mothers completed the IBQ. Unlike the previous two studies, we found that the duration of orienting was correlated with the number of responses during the acquisition and extinction phases of the first day of training but not with the number of minutes to criterion (our measure was the same as that used by Worobey and Butler) (see Table 7.1). Also, unlike Worobey and Butler (1988), neither fear nor smiling and laughter was related to acquisition speed. Looking at 24-hr retention, we found that one measure of temperament, activity level, was correlated with the retention ratio but not with the baseline ratio. Two of the six temperament dimensions, activity level and duration of orienting, were negatively correlated with the number of responses during the Day 2 extinction phase.

We have also examined the relation between older infants conditioning performance and temperament. Infants have been trained with two different operant conditioning tasks at 7 and 11 months of age. At 7 months, the infant was placed in a highchair and learned to activate a musical toy (Fisher-Price "Change-A-Tune" carousel) and a bank of 10 lights via an arm-pull response. At 11 months, a bar-press response activated this toy in a different enclosure containing a red and a green light. As shown in Table 7.1, the vast majority of correlations between the IBQ scores and the learning and retention measures have been low and nonsignificant and, as with 3 months, even the significant correlations generally account for less than 10% of the variance.

Other research from our laboratory has examined the relation between infant temperament, as measured by the IBQ, and crying during instrumental conditioning. As Campos et al. (1983) noted: "Although differences in crying may at times reflect hunger or illness, temperamental influences likely exert more profound and pervasive effects upon individual differences in crying" (p. 831). In our first study (Fagen & Ohr, 1985), infants were trained with the mobile conjugate reinforcement task to produce movement in an overhead crib mobile containing 10 components and were subsequently shifted to a mobile containing only two of these components during a third daily conditioning session. This change in mobile reinforcers led to crying in 55% of the infants. Comparisons of the maternal ratings on the six IBQ scales indicted that the criers were rated as

TABLE 7.1
Correlations Between Temperament Dimensions and Conditioning Measures
at 3, 7, and 11 Months-of-Age

Conditioning Measure	Activity Level	Distress to Limitations	Fear	Duration of Orienting	Smiling and Laughter	Soothability
3 Months[a]						
Day 1 Baseline	.09	.03	.13	-.19	.05	.19
Day 1 Reinforcement	.01	-.10	.03	-.22*	-.08	.02
Day 1 Extinction	-.15	.07	.04	-.21*	-.13	-.05
Day 2 Baseline	-.02	.07	.03	-.11	-.02	.05
Day 2 Reinforcement	-.12	.01	-.01	-.14	.02	.08
Day 2 Extinction	-.32**	.10	-.19	-.28**	-.02	.07
Minutes to Criterion	-.04	.20	.12	-.05	.03	.02
Day 2 Retention Ratio	.23*	-.02	-.01	-.01	.07	.04
Day 2 Baseline Ratio	-.06	.13	-.06	.09	-.05	-.12
7 Months[b]						
Day 1 Baseline	.30*	-.04	.12	-.02	-.06	.10
Day 1 Reinforcement	.27*	.02	-.01	-.09	.05	.25*
Day 1 Extinction	.15	.04	-.21	-.25*	.13	.01
Day 2 Baseline	.16	-.03	-.06	-.08	.05	-.04
Day 2 Reinforcement	.24*	.13	-.03	-.20	.12	.03
Day 2 Extinction	.12	.12	.04	-.13	-.04	.06
Minutes to Criterion	.15	.02	.30*	.24*	-.11	-.01
Day 2 Retention Ratio	.05	.01	.14	.15	-.03	-.05
Day 2 Baseline Ratio	-.15	.01	-.13	.05	.10	-.14
11 Months[c]						
Day 1 Baseline	-.16	-.05	-.18	-.21	-.09	-.14
Day 1 Reinforcement	.02	.03	-.12	-.16	.14	.08
Day 1 Extinction	.21	.31*	.08	-.20	-.13	.09
Day 2 Baseline	-.03	-.23	-.15	-.15	.09	.05
Day 2 Reinforcement	.10	.06	-.09	-.16	-.05	-.01
Day 2 Extinction	.03	.15	.02	-.14	-.22	-.01
Minutes to Criterion	-.12	-.01	.07	.06	-.27	-.12
Day 2 Retention Ratio	-.11	-.30*	-.20	.08	.30*	.02
Day 2 Baseline Ratio	.15	-.10	.01	.02	.15	.12

Note.   At 3 months the daily baseline and extinction phases lasted 3 min each
and the daily reinforcement phases were each 9 min in duration.   At 7 and 11 mos
the daily baseline and extinction phases lasted 1 min each and the daily reinforcement phases were 6 min each.
[a] n = 84; [b] n = 64; [c] n = 45.
*p < .05; **p < .01; two-tailed.

more active and fearful than the noncriers. A stepwise discriminant function
analysis revealed that these two measures of temperament, plus the duration of
orienting and the number of reinforced foot-kicks, reliably predicted membership
in these two groups (R = .42). Fagen, Ohr, Singer, and Fleckenstein (1987)
examined the relation between temperament and the failure to complete the 2-day
training phase of the mobile conjugate reinforcement task because of continuous
crying. A discriminant function analysis revealed that female infants who cried
could be discriminated from those who did not based on IBQ scores for duration
of orienting and fear (R = .36). No reliable discriminant function was obtained
for males.

   The picture that emerges from the studies discussed in this section is far from
clear. It would be wrong to conclude that individual differences in temperament
have no relation to instrumental conditioning performance, but it is premature to
draw specific conclusions regarding the nature of whatever relationship does

exist. It is not too surprising that behavioral and maternal ratings of infant orienting are related to conditionability. As we have seen, attention to stimulus details is an important predictor of success in both classical and instrumental procedures. The relation between fear and conditioning, when coupled with that between attention span and conditioning, is consistent with the theorizing of Rothbart and Derryberry (1981), who hypothesized that these two dimensions of temperament interact as behavioral processes designed for self-regulation (see also Rothbart & Mauro, this volume).

Instrumental Conditioning in Compromised Infants

Premature Infants.   Solkoff and Cotton (1975) made one of the first reported attempts to instrumentally condition preterm infants (neonates) using a modified version of the mobile conjugate reinforcement task. Although the authors reported that there was some evidence of conditioning, no data or statistics were presented and the authors themselves concluded that the findings were "difficult at present to interpret" (p. 710). Rovee-Collier and Lipsitt (1982) pointed out that the general negative results obtained by Solkoff and Cotton are not too surprising in light of the response chosen as the operant. High-energy responses such as kicking typically are not conditionable until after the first month of life when the infant achieves physiological control over body temperature. Given that thermoregulation takes longer to achieve in the premature infant, one would expect a similar delay in the chronological age (but not the conceptional age) at which such responses could be conditioned in the premature infant. This hypothesis, however, remains to be tested.

One prediction that can be derived from the aforementioned is that even the premature newborn is capable of being instrumentally conditioned if the investigator reinforces a low-energy response. Direct support for this can be found in the work of Siqueland (1981; Werner & Siqueland, 1978) using the HAS technique. In several studies he has reported successful instrumental conditioning in preterm infants from birth to approximately 8 weeks of age. Unfortunately, Siqueland did not include groups of full-term infants in this research and so preterm/full-term comparisons cannot be made. Also, because Siqueland's primary interest was not in the acquisition of the HAS contingency but in the variables that control the recovery of the sucking response when the visual reinforcer is changed, no data, other than group data, were reported for the contingency acquisition phase of this research. Siqueland (1981) did report that response recovery was negatively related to the frequency of maternal birth complications and positively correlated with conceptional but not chronological age at testing.

Gekoski, Fagen, and Pearlman (1984) compared 3-month-old (corrected) preterm and full-term infants' acquisition and retention of the mobile conjugate reinforcement contingency. As shown in Fig. 7.2, the full-term infants demon-

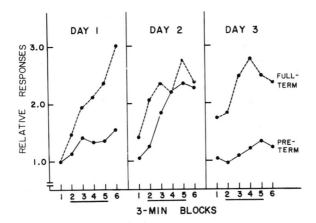

FIG. 7.2. Mean relative response scores per minute over successive 3-min blocks during training (Days 1 and 2) and a 7-day long-term retention session (Day 3) for 3-month-old preterm and full-term infants. Blocks 1 and 6 on each day are nonreinforcement periods; Blocks 2–5 on each day represent reinforcement (from Gekoski et al., 1984).

strated a response increase from pretraining baseline during the first daily conditioning session, whereas the preterms did not achieve this criterion until the second session. The full-term infants also had superior 1-week retention; their baseline ratio averaged 1.73 compared with 1.02 for the preterms (a baseline ratio of 1.00 reflects a return to operant level). Measures of pre- and perinatal complications, as determined by Littman and Parmelee's (1974) Obstetric Complications and Postnatal Factors Scales, indicated that, regardless of term, retention was related to perinatal risk as determined by the infants' Postnatal Factors Score ($r = .40$). We conducted a multiple regression analysis of the Gekoski et al. data, entering the term variable first followed by the two Littman and Parmelee scale scores. By itself, the categorization of preterm/full-term accounted for 19% of the variance in the 1-week baseline ratios; adding the additional information concerning pregnancy and neonatal status increased the R^2 to .41 ($F(3,16) = 3.72 \ p < .05$).

Finally, as part of a dissertation being conducted in our laboratory, Marie Ribarich is examining the conditioning and 1-week retention of 7-month-old (corrected) preterm and full-term infants using the panel-press apparatus previously described in the section on temperament. The preterms in this study are all generally "healthy" (e.g., no intraventricular hemorrhages) with gestational ages between 28 and 36 weeks and birthweights between 1000 and 2500 gm. Her preliminary results, presented in Fig. 7.3, suggest that, as Gekoski et al. (1984) observed at 3 months, the preterm infants are slower to learn the contingency. Unlike at 3 months, however, the preterms' performance at 7 months never reached the level of the full-terms'.

FIG. 7.3. Mean relative response scores per minute during training (Panels 1 and 2) and a long-term retention session (Panel 3) for 7-month-old preterm and full-term infants. Minutes 1 and 8 for each session are nonreinforcement periods; Minutes 2–7 represent reinforcement.

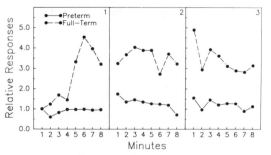

The preceding studies represent the extent of our knowledge regarding instrumental conditioning in preterm infants. It appears that the health of the preterm at birth, not prematurity per se, is important in determining both the acquisition and retention of instrumental contingencies. Support for this conclusion can also be found in a recent study by Millar (1985), who compared 6- and 12-month-old "normal" infants with two groups of infants labeled *high-risk:* one based on CNS-related risk (e.g., hypoxia, asphyxia, apnea) and the other due to various non-CNS-related risk factors (e.g., hypotonia, jaundice). Only a few infants in either group, however, were premature. The conditioning task, which lasted only 3 min, involved the delivery of a 1-sec audio/visual reinforcer contingent upon touching a small cylinder. The reinforcer was delivered either at the canister (proximal condition) or from a second canister positioned 60° to the infant's left or right (distal condition). At 6 months, only the normal infants acquired the contingency in the proximal condition whereas none of the infants in the distal group did so. At 12 months, successful conditioning was observed in all groups in the proximal condition. In the distal condition, the response rate of the normal infants surpassed that of the two high-risk groups; however, there was evidence of conditioning in the CNS-related risk group by the final minute of acquisition. Not known, however, is whether the differences between the at-risk and normal groups would have disappeared if the acquisition period had been longer.

Why should infants, either preterm or full-term, who experience various types and degrees of perinatal complications, condition slower or show poorer long-term retention than "normal" infants? Are these differences and/or deficiencies related solely to the instrumental conditioning procedures used or are they indicative of more global information-processing difficulties? Preterms, as a group, suffer lags in their motor development even when adjustments are made for their prematurity (e.g., Field, Hallock, Ting, Dempsey, Dubiri, & Shuman, 1978). This, coupled with Siqueland's success with the HAS technique, suggests that comparisons between full-term and preterm infants based on high-energy operants such as kicking or reaching may be inappropriate. However, it should be noted that in both the Gekoski et al. (1985) and Ribarich studies the preterms' operant level of responding was higher than that of the full-terms', although in neither study was this difference significant. Furthermore, in both studies, subsequent changes in performance were assessed in relation to each infant's own baseline response rate. We conclude, therefore, that the performance differences do reflect underlying differences in information processing abilities; a conclusion that is supported by research using the habituation and paired-comparison paradigms (e.g., Caron & Caron, 1981; Rose & Feldman, this volume; Rose, Feldman, McCarton, & Wolfson, 1988).

Down Syndrome.   Down syndrome is a genetic disorder which, in its pure form (Trisomy 21), is caused by the presence of an extra 21st chromosome. Behaviorally, one of the defining characteristics of this condition is moderate to severe mental retardation. Historically, infants with Down syndrome have been characterized as being very similar to normal infants on standardized measures of development, but by school age they are substantially behind their nonhandicapped peers in level of abilities and attainment of skills as reflected by IQ scores. Kopp and Parmelee (1979) hypothesized that both the decline and the differences result from the fact that infants with Down syndrome have difficulty processing information.

Most of the research on information processing in infants with Down syndrome has been conducted using the habituation or paired-comparison techniques (e.g., Lewis & Brooks-Gunn, 1984; Miranda & Fantz, 1973, 1974). In general, this research has shown that infants with Down syndrome have difficulty discriminating among stimuli and in processing visual information (see Cohen, 1981; Fantz, Fagan, & Miranda, 1975). Brinker and Lewis (1982), however, found that infants with Down syndrome could be instrumentally conditioned. Four infants with Down syndrome, ranging in age from 3.5 to 6.5 months, learned to produce auditory, visual, or tactual feedback by kicking a panel or pulling a string. During initial training, both manipulands were available; however, only one produced any contingent consequences. After each infant learned one response at a steady rate of at least 25% above the baseline level, a reversal was instituted. Large individual differences were noted among the four infants: two exhibited immediate differentiation of the reinforced from the nonreinforced responses whereas for the other two infants the differentiation was more gradual.

Vietze, McCarthy, McQuiston, MacTurk, and Yarrow (1983) conducted a large-scale study of cognitive development in 6-, 8-, and 12-month-old infants with Down syndrome. Infants received a total of 12 tasks, 4 of which (the "effect production" tasks) were instrumental conditioning tasks involving auditory and/or visual stimulation contingent upon responding to various manipulands. Although no response-rate data were presented, the authors reported that "mastery behavior" on these tasks did increase with age although the infants with Down syndrome never achieved the level of performance previously observed in nonhandicapped infants. Furthermore, at 12 months, but not at earlier ages, mastery behavior was highly correlated with the Bayley Mental Development Index ($r = .87$). Vietze et al. (1983) concluded that:

> It is clear that infants with Down's syndrome do explore objects and toys appropriately and are able to solve problems with them. The major difference between their performance and that of normal infants is in the level of behavior—the amount of time they spend in more instrumental behaviors such as manual exploration, or what we have called mastery behavior. (p. 266)

Poulson (1988) presented an operant learning model of infant vocal development in infants with Down syndrome using a single subject repeated-reversal experimental design. She observed three infants (2.7, 5, and 8.2 months of age) one to three times a week for 12 to 32 12-min sessions. Vocalization rates were compared when the mothers provided social reinforcement for their infants' vocalizations under two reinforcement schedules: continuous reinforcement for vocalization (CRF) and differential reinforcement of other-than-vocalization (DRO). Poulson (1988) found that infant vocalization rates during the CRF condition were systematically higher than during the DRO condition, a finding which replicated earlier results with nonhandicapped infants (Poulson, 1984).

Ohr (1989) conducted a study of instrumental learning in 3-month-old infants with Down syndrome using the mobile conjugate reinforcement task. She found it necessary, however, to use a sling-type infant seat placed inside the infant's crib to compensate for the hypotonia characteristic of the infant with Down syndrome. Twenty infants with Down syndrome and 20 normal infants received two daily 14-min training sessions with a procedurally identical retention-test session 7 days later. As shown in Fig. 7.4, both groups increased their rate of kicking during the first session as compared to their baselines. An analysis of when operant responding first exceeded baseline indicated that the groups did not differ with both evidencing a reliable increase at the third 2-min block of training (Fig. 7.4, Block 4). In addition to this measure of contingency acquisiton, the number of minutes to reach a learning criterion (acquisition speed) was calculated for each infant. The criterion was defined as the number of reinforced

FIG. 7.4. Mean kicks per minute over successive 2-min blocks during training (Sessions 1 and 2) and a 7-day long-term retention session (Session 3) for 3-month-old infants with Down syndrome and nonhandicapped infants. Blocks 1 and 7 on each day are nonreinforcement periods; Blocks 2–6 represent reinforcement.

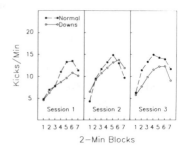

minutes during training it took an infant to achieve a level of responding equal to or greater than 1.5 times that infant's pretraining baseline level for 2 of 3 consecutive minutes. Eighteen of the 20 infants in each group successfully met this criterion and, furthermore, an analysis conducted on these acquisition speed scores indicated that the groups did not differ. The only difference to emerge between the two groups was that the normal infants maximum response increase from baseline during any single training minute exceeded that of the infants with Down syndrome. Given that both groups learned the contingency, however, the meaning of this finding loses significance. It may simply be that, relative to the normal infant, conditioning in the infant with Down syndrome is more subtle and large changes in the performance of the operant response are not seen.

To measure retention following the 1-week interval between sessions 2 and 3, retention and baseline ratios were calculated for each infant. As mentioned previously, the retention ratio reflects the change in performance, if any, between the end of session 2 and the beginning of session 3, whereas the baseline ratio indicates the extent to which the response rate at the outset of session 3 has remained above an infant's operant level. Retention ratios of 1.00 result when performance has not changed following the retention interval (i.e., retention), whereas baseline ratios greater than 1.00 are indicative of retention. As illustrated in Fig. 7.5, neither the retention nor baseline ratios of the two groups differed. Furthermore, both groups' average baseline ratio was significantly above 1.00, whereas neither groups' retention ratio was below this value. Thus, 1-week retention was excellent in both the infants with Down syndrome and the normal infants.

Ohr (1989) revisited 10 of the infants with Down syndrome and 10 of the normal infants when they were 9 months of age. The infants received 2 days of training (10 min/day) using the arm-pull conditioning apparatus described in the temperament section and a 10-min retention test session 1 week later. Unlike at 3 months, only the normal 9-month-old infants exhibited a reliable and sustained increase in their baseline level of arm-pulling during acquisition training and the retention test. On the other hand, neither the actual nor the relative response rates of the infants with Down syndrome showed any change from their pretraining levels.

In summary, it appears from the limited research that infants with Down syndrome can successfully master instrumental contingencies. Whether the age

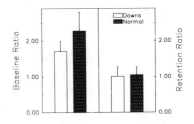

FIG. 7.5. Mean 1-week baseline and retention ratios for 3-month-old infants with Down syndrome and nonhandicapped infants.

changes observed by Ohr (1989) reflect a decline in conditionability with age or are simply due to differences in the conditioning task and/or parameters used at 3 and 9 months remains to be seen. When comparing the contingency learning of the 3- and 9-month-olds who participated in both tasks, Ohr (1989) found that the overall relative response rate and maximum increase in responding over baseline was significantly greater for both the infants with Down syndrome and the normal infants during the 3-month learning task. This suggests that, even for the normal infants, the differences in the two tasks had some significant effect. Although both tasks required the infant to form an association between his or her behavior and an event contingent on that behavior, the mobile task used at 3 months was a conjugate reinforcement task but the carousel task was not (i.e., neither the speed nor the intensity of the carousel or the lights varied proportionally with the infants' rate or vigor of responding). Perhaps the conjugate nature of the learning task was a crucial part of the learning experience for the infants with Down syndrome, without which, contingency learning was not possible (see also Rovee-Collier & Gekoski, 1979). On the other hand, both Carr (1988) and Dicks-Mirieux (1972) have reported that, during the first year of life, the cognitive development of the infant with Down syndrome shows a marked divergence from that of the normal infant beginning at about 6 months of age.

CONDITIONING AND MEMORY:
STABILITY AND PREDICTION

In 1983, we began a longitudinal study of instrumental conditioning and memory in the first year of life. Our aim was threefold: First, we wanted to determine if there was any relation between measures of infant conditioning and memory and scores on the Bayley Scales of Infant Development. Second, we questioned whether measures such as the speed of acquisition or the retention and baseline ratios were stable from one age to the next in spite of the fact that our conditioning task changed. Third, we sought to determine if our conditioning and memory measures were correlated with future performance on standardized tests of preschool intelligence (e.g., the Stanford-Binet Intelligence Scale or the Peabody Picture Vocabulary Test).

In commenting on the relation between early learning and intelligence, Watson and Ewy (1983) pointed out that such a relation could take one of three forms: (1) early learning could be a determinant of intelligence, (2) intelligence could be a determinant of early learning, and (3) early learning might be a means of predicting later intelligence. The first of these is not directly related to our research because it deals primarily with correlations between early environmental experiences and mental test performance. It is interesting to note, however, that studies have found a positive relation between the amount and variety of environmental stimulation in the home, especially from responsive toys that the infant can operate upon, and mental test performance (e.g., Bradley, Caldwell, & Elardo, 1977, 1979).

The remaining two forms of the hypothesized learning-intelligence relation are directly related to our research. These are certainly not new concerns in infant psychology, having been espoused as early as 1944 by Morgan and Morgan. But, as Watson and Ewy (1983) noted:

> So why does there appear to be no single study in which the mental age (MA) or IQ scores of infants have been related to some aspect of their performance in a standard learning situation (e.g., operant or classical conditioning)? . . . The point remains that regardless of the difficulty in arriving at a data set that will allow some form of conclusive statement, the question of the relationship between intelligence and early learning is of basic concern in the study of the development of mental behavior. . . . While few if any researchers have been moved to invest energy in studying the relations between an infant's intelligence and his or her developing learning capacities, this area of study would seem to be a potentially fruitful one for both the practical objective of finding early measures of intelligence and the theoretical objective of charting the early relations between intelligence and the capacity to learn. (pp. 229–232)

In our research we are using the mobile conjugate reinforcement task at 3 months and the previously described arm-pull and panel-press tasks at 7 and 11 months, respectively. At each age infants receive 2 days of training separated by 24 hr and a retention test session 1, 7, or 14 days later. Once assigned to a particular retention interval, an infant is tested at that interval at each age. All sessions take place in the infant's own home. Each session begins and ends with a nonreinforcement phase that lasts 3 min at 3 months and 1 min at 7 and 11 months. At 3 months, nonreinforcement means that the mobile is in the infant's view but is not responsive to his or her kicking (i.e., it is hung from a second mobile stand to which no ankle ribbon is attached). At 7 and 11 months, nonreinforcement involves turning off the toy and lights so that the infant's arm-pull (7 months) or panel-press (11 months) responses do not produce any contingent visual or auditory reinforcement. Reinforcement at 3 months consists of suspending the mobile from the stand to which the ribbon is attached for 9 min so that kicking produces movement in a conjugate manner. At 7 and 11 months, reinforcement lasts for 6 min during which each response is immediately followed by a brief activation of the toy and lights. At each age, in addition to the number of responses per minute, we assess each infant's speed of acquisition (a response rate greater than or equal to 1.5 times the baseline rate in 2 of any 3 successive min of a training-session reinforcement phase) and baseline and retention ratios.

Stability.   A total of 118 infants (67 males, 51 females) have contributed data to this study. Complete data are available for 98 3-month-olds, 76 7-month-olds, and 71 11-month-olds. Missing data have resulted primarily from illness, the inability to complete all testing sessions at a particular age for various reasons, and parents moving from the area or not wanting to continue their participation. In addition to receiving one of the instrumental conditioning tasks, at each age the Bayley Scales of Infant Development was administered. At no age, however, were the correlations between either the mental (MDI) or motor (PDI) development indexes and the measures of conditioning speed or retention significant.

Table 7.2 presents the age-to-age correlations for the learning and retention measures as well as the Bayley Scales. Individual differences in acquisition speed were not stable across any of the ages. It should be noted, however, that our conditioning tasks were purposefully chosen as to be readily acquired by all "normal" infants and, indeed, there was very little variability in the rapidity with which different infants acquired them at each age. The two retention measures were significantly correlated between 3 and 7 and 7 and 11 months, but only the baseline ratio was stable from 3 to 11 months. Although uncorrelated with Bayley performance, the degree of stability for the retention measures was equivalent to that obtained with this standardized developmental index.

Prediction. During the last half century, numerous attempts have been made to relate scores obtained on "intelligence" tests administered during infancy to those obtained in later life. Several reviews of the literature, however, have all arrived at the conclusion that scores obtained on standardized infant tests such as the Bayley Scales of Infant Development, Gesell Developmental Schedules, and Cattell's Infant Intelligence Scale have little if any predictive validity (see, for example, Bayley, 1970; Lewis & McGurk, 1972; McCall, 1976, 1979a; McCall, Hogarty, & Hurlburt, 1972). It is our belief that this lack of predictive validity results from the type of behavior assessed by the standardized infant tests (see also Fagan & Singer, 1983; Rose, 1981; Rose & Feldman, this volume). By and large, the infant scales are composed of items designed to assess simple sensory and motor skills. Childhood IQ tests, on the other hand, are primarily verbal in nature and measure the child's ability to reason, as well as his or her abilities in such areas of intellectual competence as learning and remembering. Thus, if there is consistency in mental development, we should assess the same underly-

TABLE 7.2
Stability Correlations

Measure	Ages (Months)		
	3 to 7	7 to 11	3 to 11
Acquisition speed	.09	.18	-.07
Retention ratio	.31**	.39**	.10
Baseline ratio	.42**	.46**	.29*
Bayley mental	.38**	.31**	.34**
Bayley motor	.29*	.48**	.21

Note. Correlations for retention and baseline ratios are pooled within-cell correlations adjusted for retention interval.

$*p < .05$; $**p < .01$; two-tailed.

ing processes in the infant that will later be examined as the child develops. Although the behavioral expression of intelligence may change from one age to another, its underlying processes should remain invariant. According to McCall (1979b):

> Consistency is more likely to be found in the biological function of mental behavior (i.e., its adaptive significance for the organism and species) than in its specific behavioral manifestations . . . One function is the *acquisition of information*, its intake, storage, and retrieval. A second but corollary function is *to influence the environment*, both animate and inanimate. (p. 191)

Faced with the questionable usefulness of total infant test scores, a few investigators have begun to look for predictive validity in some of the specific behaviors tapped by the standardized infant tests. Most notable among these has been the work of McCall (McCall et al., 1972; McCall, Eichorn, & Hogarty, 1977), in which individual items on the Gesell tests administered at 6, 12, 18, and 24 months of age were subjected to separate principal components analyses at each age. These components were used to determine correlations between independent "skill areas" within ages and then the components were correlated across ages and with childhood IQ scores. The data presented by McCall et al. (1972) revealed that during early infancy the items that loaded on the first principal component appeared to reflect the infant's active attempt to produce contingent change in the environment. According to McCall et al. (1972): "Many of these behaviors involve the manipulation of objects that yield perceptual contingencies, behavior that has been called 'the game' (Watson, 1972), or involve conjugate reinforcement (Rovee & Rovee, 1969)" (p. 740).

It thus appears that although the expression of intellectual functioning during the first year of life cannot be found in a total test score, learning tasks may offer a more fruitful approach to the problem of predicting later cognitive functioning from infancy. As Watson and Ewy (1983) pointed out, however, "We could find no specific application of this principle of learning as an 'exposing agent' in the attempt to predict later intelligence" (p. 249).

In addition to early learning, infant memory has been implicated as a potentially useful predictor of later intelligence. For example, Fagan (1979, 1981, 1984; Fagan & McGrath, 1981; Fagan & Singer, 1983) familiarized 4- to 7-month-old infants with one visual target and then exposed these infants to the familiar target paired with a novel one. Immediate recognition memory for the familiar target was inferred from the percentage of total fixation time that was allocated to the novel stimulus. At 3, 4, 5, or 7 years of age, moderate but significant correlations ranging from .37 to .57 were obtained between the "percent novelty" scores and the scores on the Peabody Picture Vocabulary Test.

Other studies have also implicated the infants response-to-novelty as a reliable predictor of some underlying cognitive competence. Yarrow, Klein, Lomonoco, and Morgan (1975) permitted a group of 6-month-old lower class Black infants to manipulate a toy bell for 10 min. Following this familiarization period, each infant's responses were observed when the bell was paired with each of 10 novel objects. Responsiveness to novelty (the amount of time the infant spent handling or mouthing the novel object) was found to be significantly related to Stanford-Binet IQ at 3 years ($r = .35$). Lewis and Brooks-Gunn (1981) tested two samples of infants at 3 and 24 months of age. At 3 months each infant received six 30-sec presentations of the same slide followed by a 30-sec exposure to a novel stimulus. They found that the magnitude of the recovery of the fixation response to the novel stimulus reliably predicted scores on the Bayley Scales at 24 months (Sample 1: $r = .52$; Sample 2: $r = .40$). Fagan (1985) reported that the mean predictive validity coefficient based on his samples as well as those of Lewis and Brooks-Gunn (1981) and Yarrow et al. (1975) is .44. Bornstein and Sigman (1986) conducted a meta-analysis using 11 studies that compared the response to novelty in infancy with various measures of cognitive functioning obtained between 2 and 7.5 years of age. This analysis indicated that infancy and childhood measures share 22% of common variance. Finally, Rose, Feldman, and Wallace (1988) recently reported data from a combined sample of preterm and full-term infants exposed to a series of 11 novelty-preference tasks of visual recognition memory and tactual-to-visual transfer. Infants were tested on these tasks at 6, 7, and 8 months of age and received the Stanford-Binet at 3 years. Summary scores based on the preference for novelty across similar and dissimilar tasks at each age yielded correlations to 3 year IQ that ranged from .37 to .63; multiple correlations across the three infant assessments ranged from .68 to .72.

The working hypothesis of our longitudinal research has been that operant conditioning procedures offer a means of assessing differences in cognitive processes early in life; processes that are both stable and predictive of later intellectual functioning. By placing infants in settings where they produce changes in the environment, we can measure how well an infant learns a task and how long, and under what conditions, he or she retains it. An operant conditioning approach to early assessment has the added advantage of going beyond measurement of basic cognitive competencies to bridge the gap between cognitive and motivational factors in early development (cf. Yarrow et al., 1975). As Horowitz and Dunn (1978) have written:

> After all, it is quite possible that our most fruitful approach to understanding infant development and the prevention of developmental delay lies in an analysis that views the infant as a processor of environmental information who, in the exercise of processing strategies, functionally affects the amount, kind, duration, and timing of stimulus information made available to him or her. (p. 32)

The correlations between our infant conditioning and memory measures and intelligence-test performance at 2 and 3 years of age are presented in Table 7.3. At 2 years, subjects received a final administration of the Bayley Scales as well as a first administration of the Stanford-Binet Intelligence Scale. At 3 years of

TABLE 7.3
Correlations Between Infant and Preschool Measures

Infant Measures	MDI2	PDI2	SB2	SB3	PPVT3	K-ABC3 SeqPro	K-ABC3 SimPro	K-ABC3 Achiev
			Preschool Intelligence Test Scores					
3 Months[a]								
AS	.09	.11	-.03	.26*	.21	-.09	.16	.05
RR	.41**	.09	.43**	.42**	.44**	.39**	.31*	.40**
BLR	.33**	-.02	.39**	.32*	.38**	.39**	.30*	.35**
MDI	.35**	.28*	.27*	.23	.26*	.22	.09	.31*
PDI	.31**	.22*	.26*	.22	.24	.13	.06	.14
7 Months[b]								
AS	.12	-.03	.26*	.17	.24	.13	.09	.09
RR	.51**	.05	.49**	.44**	.40**	.47**	.32*	.46**
BLR	.31*	.08	.39**	.36**	.39**	.41**	.33*	.37**
MDI	.37**	.26*	.37**	.34*	.32*	.36**	.13	.33*
PDI	.31*	.33**	.34**	.15	.13	.16	-.09	.13
11 Months[c]								
AS	.09	-.15	.10	.03	.11	.12	.02	-.05
RR	.66**	.08	.54**	.41**	.45**	.43**	.19	.39**
BLR	.59**	-.12	.44**	.38**	.41**	.34*	.16	.34*
MDI	.42**	.33**	.40**	.37**	.34*	.33*	.19	.34*
PDI	.34**	.28*	.26*	.17	.18	.04	-.01	-.11

Note. For infant measures, AS = Acquisition Speed; RR = Retention Ratio; BLR = Baseline Ratio; MDI = Bayley Mental Development Index; PDI = Bayley Psychomotor Development Index. For preschool intelligence test scores, MDI2 = Bayley Mental Development Index at 2 years of age; PDI2 = Bayley Psychomotor Development Index at 2 years of age; SB2 and SB3 = Stanford-Binet Intelligence Test Scores at 2 and 3 years of age, respectively; PPVT3 = Peabody Picture Vocabulary Test score at 3 years of age; K-ABC3 SeqPro = Kaufman Assessment Battery for Children Sequential Processing score at 3 years of age; K-ABC3 SimPro = Kaufman Assessment Battery for Children Simultaneous Processing score at 3 years of age; K-ABC3 Achiev = Kaufman Assessment Battery for Children Achievement score at 3 years of age. Correlations between infant retention measures (i.e., RR and BLR) and preschool test scores are pooled within-groups correlations adjusted for retention interval (1, 7, or 14 days).
[a] n = 85 at 2 years and 63 at 3 years.
[b] n = 62 at 2 years and 54 at 3 years.
[c] n = 59 at 2 years and 52 at 3 years.
*$p < .05$; **$p < .01$; two-tailed.

age, the Stanford-Binet was again administered as well as the Kaufman Assessment Battery for Children (K-ABC) and the Peabody Picture Vocabulary Test (PPVT-R).

In general, the rapidity with which the infants acquired the conditioning tasks is not correlated with the measures of preschool intelligence. Although two of the individual correlations between acquisition speed and the preschool measures are reliable, the average correlation at 2 years of age is only .06 whereas that at 3 years is .10. Again, however, we are not ready to accept the null hypothesis of no predictability for this measure until conditioning tasks that yield greater variability in acquisition speed (e.g., discrimination tasks) have been used.[3] Our

_____

[3]Alternatively, we expect that preschool follow ups of our Down syndrome and preterm samples, who exhibit greater variability in acquisition speed, will reveal the predictive validity of this measure for developmental delay.

retention measures, on the other hand, are consistently correlated with the various preschool intelligence measures. Specifically, the average correlation between the 3-, 7-, and 11-month retention ratios and the 2-year assessments is .51 whereas that between these ratios and the various 3-year measures is .39. For the baseline ratio, the average correlation from 3, 7, and 11 months to the Bayley MDI and Stanford-Binet score at 2 years is .41 whereas at 3 years the average correlation to the Stanford-Binet and Kaufman is .35. These correlations are higher than the average obtained between the Bayley MDI at 3, 7, and 11 months and the 2-year MDI and Stanford-Binet IQ scores, which is .36, or between the infancy assessments and the 3-year scores, the average of which is .28. More important than the differences in the magnitudes of these correlations is the fact that our retention measures are uncorrelated with concurrent Bayley MDI scores, and that each shares a unique amount of variance with the preschool assessments.

The results from this study indicate that our tasks are tapping a cognitive ability, memory, that is relatively stable and, especially with respect to the retention ratio measure, accounts for a fair amount of the variance in future intellectual functioning. Furthermore, when coupled with the stability findings, it appears that we are measuring skills during the first year of life that are different from those measured by the Bayley Scales. By using the same basic operant conditioning procedure at each age, we have successfully overcome a major problem in previous attempts to assess infant intellectual functioning, namely, that the infant's behavioral repertoire changes during the first year of life. Our tasks permit us to adapt to the developing infant while focusing on the same cognitive processes at each age.

SUMMARY

In this chapter we have reviewed studies of classical and instrumental conditioning with infants that have focused on questions of individual differences in acquisition and retention. It appears that classical conditioning researchers have not only abandoned Pavlov's theoretical account of classical conditioning but his interest in individual differences as well. Even those investigators who have focused on the orienting-conditioning relationship have accepted OR differences as a given (albeit an important one) but have not examined either the reasons for the obtained differences or their reliability, stability, and/or predictiveness. This is unfortunate given the success that other areas of psychology (e.g., animal learning and memory, sensation and perception, developmental psychobiology) have had with the classical conditioning paradigm. The small amount of work with decerebrate and premature infants is encouraging but it is only a start.

The picture for instrumental conditioning is a bit brighter but here too researchers (including ourselves; see Rovee-Collier & Fagen, 1981) have generally ignored the individual differences they have obtained. Too little is known about the relations between instrumental conditioning performance and performance on other cognitive or perceptual tasks and, with the exception of temperament, not much effort has been expended to account for some of the variance in conditioning performance and/or retention. Risk factors that might affect learning or memory have also generally been ignored.[4] We are encouraged by our own ongoing longitudinal research that has shown that measures of infant contingency retention are both stable and predictive. Memory is a major process tapped by childhood intelligence tests and we now have a measure of this process in the infant that has some predictive validity to at least 3 years of age.

ACKNOWLEDGMENTS

This research was aided by Social and Behavioral Sciences Research Grant No. 12–111 from the March of Dimes Birth Defects Foundation. We thank Lori Fleckenstein, Jayne Singer, Carol Miskiv, Sandra Caputo, Kathryn Garten, Marie Ribarich, Brenda Shapiro, Liane Pioli, and Susan Klein for assistance with the collection and analysis of the data reported in this chapter and Philip Lipsitz, Barbara Lenihan, Lois Fink, Wendy Doret, Pamela Matheson, and Audrey Heimler for assistance with subject recruitment.

REFERENCES

Aylward, G. P., Lazzara, A., & Meyer, J. (1978). Behavioral and neurological characteristics of a hydranencephalic infant. *Developmental Medicine and Child Neurology, 24,* 211–217.

Bayley, N. (1970). Development of mental abilities. In P. H. Mussen (Ed.), *Carmichael's manual of child psychology* (Vol. 1, pp. 1163–1209). New York: Wiley.

Berg, W. K., Clarkson, M. G., Eitzman, D. V., & Setzer, E. (1981, April). *Habituation in infants lacking a cortex.* Paper presented at the meeting of the Society for Research in Child Development, Boston.

Berntson, G. G., Tuber, D. S., Ronca, A. E., & Bachman, D. S. (1983). The decerebrate human: Associative learning. *Experimental Neurology, 81,* 77–88.

Blass, E. M., Ganchrow, J. R., & Steiner, J. E. (1984). Classical conditioning in newborn humans 2–48 hours of age. *Infant Behavior and Development, 7,* 223–235.

Bolles, R. C. (1979). *Learning theory* (2nd ed.). New York: Holt, Rinehart, & Winston.

Bornstein, M. H., & Sigman, M. D. (1986). Continuity in mental development from infancy. *Child Development, 57,* 251–274.

Brackbill, Y. (1971). The role of the cortex in orienting: Orienting reflex in an anencephalic human infant. *Developmental Psychology, 5,* 195–201.

Brackbill, Y., & Koltsova, M. M. (1967). Conditioning and learning. In Y. Brackbill (Ed.), *Infancy and early childhood* (pp. 206–286). New York: The Free Press.

---

[4]Lipsitt (1978; Rovee-Collier & Lipsitt, 1982) has taken the risk/learning relation a step further by hypothesizing that the infant's failure to learn certain responses that normally prevent respiratory occlusion may be a contributory factor to sudden infant death syndrome.

Bradley, R. H., Caldwell, B., & Elardo, R. (1977). Home environment, social status and mental test performance. *Journal of Educational Psychology, 69,* 697–701.

Bradley, R. H., Caldwell, B., & Elardo, R. (1979). Home environment and cognitive development: A cross-lagged panel study. *Developmental Psychology, 15,* 246–250.

Brinker, R. P., & Lewis, M. (1982). Contingency intervention in infancy. In J. Anderson & J. Cox (Eds.), *Curriculum materials for high risk and handicapped infants* (pp. 37–41). Chapel Hill, NC: Technical Assistance Development Systems.

Campos, J. J., Barrett, K. C., Lamb, M. E., Goldsmith, H. H., & Stenberg, C. (1983). Socioemotional development. In M. M. Haith & J. J. Campos (Eds.), P. H. Mussen (Series Ed.), *Handbook of child psychology: Vol. 2. Infancy and developmental psychobiology* (pp. 783–915). New York: Wiley.

Caron, A. J., & Caron, R. F. (1981). Processing of relational information as an index of risk. In S. L. Friedman & M. D. Sigman (Eds.), *Preterm birth and psychological development* (pp. 219–240). New York: Academic Press.

Carr, J. (1988). Six weeks to twenty-one years old: A longitudinal study of children with Down's syndrome and their families. *Journal of Child Psychology and Psychiatry, 29,* 407–431.

Cohen, L. B. (1981). Examination of habituation as a measure of aberrant infant development. In S. L. Friedman & M. D. Sigman (Eds.), *Preterm birth and psychological development* (pp. 241–253). New York: Academic Press.

Dicks-Mirieux, M. J. (1972). Mental development of infants with Down's syndrome. *American Journal of Mental Deficiency, 77,* 26–32.

Dunst, C. J., & Lingerfelt, B. (1985). Maternal ratings of temperament and operant learning in two- to three-month-old infants. *Child Development, 56,* 555–563.

Fagan, J. F. (1972). Infants' recognition memory for faces. *Journal of Experimental Child Psychology, 14,* 435–476.

Fagan, J. F. (1973). Infants' delayed recognition memory and forgetting. *Journal of Experimental Child Psychology, 16,* 424–450.

Fagan, J. F. (1979, March). *Infant recognition memory and later intelligence.* Paper presented at the meeting of the Society for Research in Child Development, San Francisco.

Fagan, J. F. (1981, April). *Infant memory and the prediction of intelligence.* Paper presented at the meeting of the Society for Research in Child Development, Boston.

Fagan, J. F. (1984). The relationship of novelty preferences during infancy to later intelligence and later recognition memory. *Intelligence, 8,* 339–346.

Fagan, J. F. (1985). A new look at infant intelligence. In D. K. Detterman (Ed.), *Current topics in human intelligence. Vol. 1: Research methodology* (pp. 223–246). Norwood, NJ: Ablex.

Fagan, J. F., & McGrath, S. K. (1981). Infant recognition memory and later intelligence. *Intelligence, 5,* 121–130.

Fagan, J. F., & Singer, L. T. (1983). Infant recognition memory as a measure of intelligence. In L. P. Lipsitt (Ed.), *Advances in infancy research* (Vol. 2, pp. 31–78). Norwood, NJ: Ablex.

Fagen, J. W., & Ohr, P. S. (1985). Temperament and crying in response to the violation of a learned expectancy in early infancy. *Infant Behavior and Development, 8,* 157–166.

Fagen, J. W., Ohr, P. S., Singer, J. M., & Fleckenstein, L. K. (1987). Infant temperament and subject loss due to crying during operant conditioning. *Child Development, 58,* 497–504.

Fagen, J. W., & Rovee-Collier, C. K. (1982). A conditioning analysis of infant memory: How do we know they know what we know they knew? In R. L. Isaacson & N. E. Spear (Eds.), *The expression of knowledge* (pp. 67–111). New York: Plenum Press.

Fagen, J. W., Singer, J. M., Ohr, P. S., & Fleckenstein, L. K. (1987). Infant temperament and performance on the Bayley Scales of Infant Development at 4, 8, and 12 months of age. *Infant Behavior and Development, 10,* 505–512.

Fantz, R. L., Fagan, J. F., & Miranda, S. B. (1975). Early visual selectivity. In L. Cohen & P.

Salapatek (Eds.), *Infant perception: From sensation to cognition* (Vol. 1, pp. 249–346). New York: Academic Press.

Field, T., Hallock, N., Ting, G., Dempsey, J., Dabiri, C., & Shuman, H. H. (1978). A first-year follow-up of high-risk infants: Formulating a cumulative risk index. *Child Development, 49,* 119–131.

Fitzgerald, H. E., & Brackbill, Y. (1976). Classical conditioning in infancy: Development and constraints. *Psychological Bulletin, 83,* 353–376.

Fitzgerald, H. E., & Porges, S. W. (1971). A decade of infant conditioning and learning research. *Merrill-Palmer Quarterly, 17,* 79–117.

Flaherty, C. F. (1985). *Animal learning and cognition.* New York: Knopf.

Gekoski, M. J. (1977). Visual attention and operant conditioning in infancy: A second look. (Doctoral dissertation, Rutgers University, 1977), *Dissertation Abstracts International, 38,* 875b. (University Microfilms No. 77-17, 533)

Gekoski, M. J., Fagen, J. W., & Pearlman, M. A. (1984). Early learning and memory in the preterm infant. *Infant Behavior and Development, 7,* 267–276.

Graham, F. K. (1973). Habituation and dishabituation of responses innervated by the autonomic nervous system. In H. V. S. Peeke & M. J. Herz (Eds.), *Habituation. Vol. 1: Behavioral studies* (pp. 163–218). New York: Academic Press.

Graham, F. K., & Clifton, R. K. (1966). Heart-rate change as a component of the orienting response. *Psychological Bulletin, 65,* 305–320.

Graham, F. K., & Jackson, J. C. (1970). Arousal systems and infant heart rate response. In L. P. Lipsitt & H. W. Reese (Eds.), *Advances in child development and behavior* (Vol. 5, pp. 59–117). New York: Academic Press.

Graham, F. K., Leavitt, L. A., Strock, B. D., & Brown, J. W. (1978). Precocious cardiac orienting in a human anencephalic infant. *Science, 199,* 322–324.

Hayes, L. A., Ewy, R. D., & Watson, J. S. (1982). Attention as predictor of learning in infants. *Journal of Experimental Child Psychology, 34,* 38–45.

Hoffman, H. S., Cohen, M. E., & DeVito, C. J. (1985). A comparison of classical eyelid conditioning in adults and infants. *Infant Behavior and Development, 8,* 247–254.

Horowitz, F. D. (1968). Infant learning and development: Retrospect and prospect. *Merrill-Palmer Quarterly, 14,* 101–120.

Horowitz, F. D. (1969). Learning, developmental research, and differences. In L. P. Lipsitt & H. W. Reese (Eds.), *Advances in child development and behavior* (Vol. 4, pp. 83–126). New York: Academic Press.

Horowitz, F. D., & Dunn, M. (1978). Infant intelligence testing. In F. D. Minifie & L. L. Lloyd (Eds.), *Communicative and cognitive abilities: Early behavioral assessment* (pp. 21–36). Baltimore: University Park Press.

Hulsebus, R. E. (1973). Operant conditioning of infant behavior: A review. In H. W. Reese (Ed.), *Advances in child development and behavior* (Vol. 8, pp. 111–158). New York: Academic Press.

Ianosh, O. (1959). Development of higher nervous activity in premature infants. *Pavlov Journal of Higher Nervous Activity, 9,* 760–767.

Ingram, E. M. (1978). The interstimulus interval in classical autonomic conditioning of young infants. *Developmental Psychobiology, 11,* 419–426.

Ingram, E. M., & Fitzgerald, H. E. (1974). Individual differences in infant orienting and autonomic conditioning. *Developmental Psychobiology, 7,* 359–367.

Janos, O., & Papousek, H. (1977). Acquisition of appetitional and palpebral conditional reflexes by the same infants. *Early Human Development, 1,* 91–97.

Kaplan, P. S., & Werner, J. S. (1987). Sensitization and dishabituation of infant visual fixation. *Infant Behavior and Development, 10,* 183–197.

Kasatkin, N. I. (1969). The origin and development of conditioned reflexes in early childhood. In

M. Cole & S. I. Maltzman (Eds.), *A handbook of comtemporary soviet psychology*. New York: Basic Books.

Kasatkin, N. I., & Levikova, A. M. (1935). On the development of early conditioned reflexes and differentiations of auditory stimuli in infants. *Journal of Experimental Psychology, 18*, 1–19.

Kimmel, H. D. (1973). Habituation, habituability, and conditioning. In H. V. S. Peeke & M. J. Herz (Eds.), *Habituation. Volume 1: Behavioral studies* (pp. 219–238). New York: Academic Press.

Kopp, C. B., & Parmelee, A. H. (1979). Prenatal and perinatal influences on infant behavior. In J. D. Osofsky (Ed.), *Handbook of infant development* (pp. 29–75). New York: Wiley.

Lewis, M., & Brooks-Gunn, J. (1981). Visual attention at three months as a predictor of cognitive functioning at two years of age. *Intelligence, 5*, 131–140.

Lewis, M., & Brooks-Gunn, J. (1984). Age and handicapped group differences in infant visual attention. *Child Development, 55*, 858–868.

Lewis, M., & McGurk, H. (1972). The evaluation of infant intelligence: Infant intelligence scores—true or false? *Science, 178*, 1174–1177.

Lipsitt, L. P. (1963). Learning in the first year of life. In L. P. Lipsitt & C. C. Spiker (Eds.), *Advances in child development and behavior* (Vol. 1, pp. 147–195). New York: Academic Press.

Lipsitt, L. P. (1971). Infant learning: The blooming, buzzing, confusion revisited. In M. E. Meyer (Ed.), *Second western symposium on learning: Early learning*. Bellingham, WA: Western Washington State College.

Lipsitt, L. P. (1978). Perinatal indicators and psychophysiological precursors of crib death. In F. D. Horowitz (Ed.), *Early developmental hazards: Predictors and precautions* (pp. 11–29). Boulder: Westview Press.

Lipsitt, L. P. (1982). Infant learning. In T. M. Field, A. Huston, H. C. Quay, L. Troll, & G. E. Finley (Eds.) *Review of human development* (pp. 62–78). New York: Wiley.

Lipsitt, L. P., & Kaye, H. (1964). Conditioned sucking in the human newborn. *Psychonomic Science, 1*, 29–30.

Little, A. H., Lipsitt, L. P., & Rovee-Collier, C. (1984). Classical conditioning and retention of the infant's eyelid response: Effects of age and interstimulus interval. *Journal of Experimental Child Psychology, 37*, 512–524.

Littman, B., & Parmelee, A. H. (1974). *Obstetric complications scale and postnatal factors scale*. Unpublished manuscript, University of California at Los Angeles.

McCall, R. B. (1976). Toward an epigenetic conception of mental development in the first year of life. In M. Lewis (Ed.), *Origins of intelligence* (pp. 97–122). New York: Plenum Press.

McCall, R. B. (1977). Challenges to a science of developmental psychology. *Child Development, 48*, 334–344.

McCall, R. B. (1979a). The development of intellectual functioning in infancy and the prediction of later IQ. In J. D. Osofsky (Ed.), *Handbook of infant development* (pp. 707–741). New York: Wiley.

McCall, R. B. (1979b). Quantitative transitions in behavioral development in the first two years of life. In M. H. Bornstein & W. Kessen (Eds.), *Psychological development from infancy: Image to intention* (pp. 183–224). Hillsdale, NJ: Lawrence Erlbaum Associates.

McCall, R. B., Eichorn, D. H., & Hogarty, P. S. (1977). Transitions in early mental development. *Monographs of the Society for Research in Child Development, 42*, (3, Serial No. 147).

McCall, R. B., Hogarty, P. S., & Hurlburt, N. (1972). Transitions in infant sensorimotor development and the prediction of childhood IQ. *American Psychologist, 27*, 728–748.

Milewski, A. E., & Siqueland, E. R. (1975). Discrimination of color and pattern novelty in one-month human infants. *Journal of Experimental Child Psychology, 19*, 122–136.

Millar, W. S. (1985). The effect of proximal and distal feedback on the contingency learning of 6- and 12-month-old normal and perinatally compromised infants. *Journal of Child Psychology and Psychiatry, 26*, 789–800.

Miranda, S. B., & Fantz, R. L. (1973). Visual preferences of Down's syndrome and normal infants. *Child Development, 44,* 555–561.

Miranda, S. B., & Fantz, R. L. (1974). Recognition memory in Down's syndrome and normal infants. *Child Development, 45,* 651–660.

Morgan, J. J. B., & Morgan, S. S. (1944). Infant learning as a developmental index. *The Journal of Genetic Psychology, 65,* 281–289.

Ohr, P. S. (1989). *Learning and memory in Down syndrome infants.* Unpublished doctoral dissertation, St. John's University, New York.

Olson, G. M., & Sherman, T. (1983). Attention, learning, and memory in infants. In M. M. Haith & J. J. Campos (Eds.), P. H. Mussen (Series Ed.), *Handbook of child psychology: Vol. 2. Infancy and developmental psychobiology* (pp. 1001–1080). New York: Wiley.

Papousek, H. (1967a). Conditioning during postnatal development. In Y. Brackbill & G. G. Thompson (Eds.), *Behavior in infancy and early childhood: A book of readings* (pp. 259–274). New York: Free Press.

Papousek, H. (1967b). Experimental studies of appetitional behavior in human newborns. In H. W. Stevenson, E. H. Hess, & H. L. Rheingold (Eds.), *Early behavior: Comparative and developmental approaches* (pp. 249–277). New York: Wiley.

Papousek, H. (1977). The development of learning ability in infancy. In G. Nissen (Ed.), *Intelligence, learning, and learning disturbances* (pp. 75–93). Berlin: Springer-Verlag.

Pavlov, I. P. (1927). *Conditioned reflexes.* London: Oxford University Press.

Polikanina, R. I. (1961). The relationship between autonomic and somatic components during the development of a defensive conditioned reflex in premature children. *Pavlov Journal of Higher Nervous Activity, 11,* 72–82.

Porges, S. W. (1974). Heart rate indices of newborn attentional responsivity. *Merrill-Palmer Quarterly, 20,* 231–254.

Poulson, C. L. (1984). Operant theory and methodology in infant vocal conditioning. *Journal of Experimental Child Psychology, 38,* 103–113.

Poulson, C. L. (1988). Operant conditioning of vocalization rate of infants with Down syndrome. *American Journal of Mental Retardation, 93,* 57–63.

Rescorla, R. A. (1967). Pavlovian conditioning and its proper control procedures. *Psychological Review, 74,* 71–80.

Rescorla, R. A. (1988). Pavlovian conditioning: It's not what you think it is. *American Psychologist, 43,* 151–160.

Rose, S. A. (1981). Lags in the cognitive competence of prematurely born infants. In S. L. Friedman & M. Sigman (Eds.), *Preterm birth and psychological development* (pp. 255–269). New York: Academic Press.

Rose, S. A., Feldman, J. F., McCarton, C. M., & Wolfson, J. (1988). Information processing in seven-month-old infants as a function of risk status. *Child Development, 59,* 589–603.

Rose, S. A., Feldman, J. F., & Wallace, I. F. (1988). Individual differences in infants' information processing: Reliability, stability, and prediction. *Child Development, 59,* 1177–1197.

Roth, K., Eisenberg, N., & Sell, E. R. (1984). The relation of preterm and full-term infants' temperament to test-taking behaviors and developmental status. *Infant Behavior and Development, 7,* 495–505.

Rothbart, M. K., & Derryberry, D. (1981). Development of individual differences in temperament. In M. K. Lamb & A. L. Brown (Eds.), *Advances in developmental psychology* (Vol. 1, pp. 37–86). Hillsdale, NJ: Lawrence Erlbaum Associates.

Rovee, C., & Rovee, D. (1969). Conjugate reinforcement of infant exploratory behavior. *Journal of Experimental Child Psychology, 8,* 33–39.

Rovee-Collier, C. (1983). Learning and memory in infancy. In M. M. Haith & J. J. Campos (Eds.), P. H. Mussen (Series Ed.), *Handbook of child psychology: Vol. 2. Infancy and developmental psychobiology* (pp. 98–148). New York: Wiley.

Rovee-Collier, C. (1984). The ontogeny of learning and memory in human infancy. In R. Kail & N. E. Spear (Eds.), *Comparative perspectives on the development of memory* (pp. 103–134). Hillsdale, NJ: Lawrence Erlbaum Associates.

Rovee-Collier, C. (1986). The rise and fall of infant classical conditioning research: Its promise for the study of early development. In L. P. Lipsitt & C. Rovee-Collier (Eds.), *Advances in infancy research* (Vol. 4, pp. 139–159). Norwood, NJ: Ablex.

Rovee-Collier, C. (1987). Learning and memory in infancy. In J. D. Osofsky (Ed.), *Handbook of infant development* (2nd ed., pp. 98–148). New York: Wiley.

Rovee-Collier, C. K., & Fagen, J. W. (1981). The retrieval of memory in early infancy. In L. P. Lipsitt (Ed.), *Advances in infancy research* (Vol. 1, pp. 225–254). Norwood, NJ: Ablex.

Rovee-Collier, C. K., & Gekoski, M. J. (1979). The economics of infancy: A review of conjugate reinforcement. In H. W. Reese & L. P. Lipsitt (Eds.), *Advances in child development and behavior* (Vol. 13, pp. 195–255). New York: Academic Press.

Rovee-Collier, C., & Hayne, H. (1987). Reactivation of infant memory: Implications for cognitive development. In H. W. Reese (Ed.), *Advances in child development and behavior* (Vol. 20, pp. 185–238). New York: Academic Press.

Rovee-Collier, C. K., & Lipsitt, L. P. (1982). Learning, adaptation, and memory in the newborn. In P. Stratton (Ed.), *Psychobiology of the human newborn* (pp. 147–190). Chichester: Wiley.

Sameroff, A. J. (1972). Learning and adaptation in infancy: A comparison of models. In H. W. Reese (Ed.), *Advances in child development and behavior* (Vol. 7, pp. 169–214). New York: Academic Press.

Sameroff, A. J., & Cavanagh, P. J. (1979). Learning in infancy: A developmental perspective. In J. D. Osofsky (Ed.), *Handbook of infant development* (pp. 344–392). New York: Wiley.

Sidman, M. (1960). *Tactics of scientific research*. New York: Basic Books.

Siqueland, E. R. (1970). Basic learning processes: I. Classical conditioning. In H. W. Reese & L. P. Lipsitt (Eds.), *Experimental child psychology*. New York: Academic Press.

Siqueland, E. R. (1981). Studies of visual recognition memory in preterm infants: Differences in development as a function of perinatal morbidity factors. In S. L. Friedman & M. Sigman (Eds.), *Preterm birth and psychological development*. New York: Academic Press.

Sokolov, E. N. (1963). *Perception and the conditioned reflex*. New York: Macmillan.

Solkoff, N., & Cotton, C. (1975). Contingency awareness in premature infants. *Perceptual and Motor Skills, 41,* 709–710.

Stamps, L. E. (1977). Temporal conditioning of heart rate responses in newborn infants. *Developmental Psychology, 3,* 624–629.

Stamps, L. E., & Porges, S. W. (1975). Heart rate conditioning in newborn infants: Relationships among conditionability, heart rate variability, and sex. *Developmental Psychology, 11,* 424–431.

Tuber, D. S., Berntson, G. G., Bachman, D. S., & Allen, J. N. (1980). Associative learning in premature hydranencephalic and normal twins. *Science, 210,* 1035–1037.

Turco, T. L., & Stamps, L. E. (1980). Heart rate conditioning in young infants using a visual conditional stimulus. *Journal of Experimental Child Psychology, 29,* 117–125.

Vietze, P. M., McCarthy, M., McQuiston, S., MacTurk, R., & Yarrow, L. J. (1983). Attention and exploratory behavior in infants with Down's syndrome. In T. Field & A. Sostek (Eds.), *Infants born at risk: Physiological, perceptual, and cognitive processes* (pp. 251–268). New York: Grune & Stratton.

Wachs, T. D. (1984). Individual differences in infant memory: Forgotten but not gone. In R. Kail & N. E. Spear (Eds.), *Comparative perspectives on the development of memory* (pp. 209–226). Hillsdale, NJ: Lawrence Erlbaum Associates.

Wachs, T. D., & Gandour, M. J. (1983). Temperament, environment, and six-month cognitive-intellectual development: A test of the organismic specificity hypothesis. *International Journal of Behavioral Development, 6,* 135–152.

Watson, J. S., & Ewy, R. D. (1983). Early learning and intelligence. In M. Lewis (Ed.), *Origins of intelligence* (2nd ed., pp. 225–254). New York: Plenum Press.

Werner, J. S., & Siqueland, E. R. (1978). Visual recognition memory in the preterm infant. *Infant Behavior and Development, 1,* 79–94.

Worobey, J., & Butler, J. (1988, April). *Memory, learning, and temperament in early infancy.* Paper presented at the International Conference on Infant Studies, Washington, DC.

Yarrow, L. J., Klein, R. P., Lomonoco, S., & Morgan, G. A. (1975). Cognitive and motivational development in early childhood. In B. X. Friedlander, G. M. Stenritt, & G. E. Kirk (Eds.), *Exceptional infant* (Vol. 3, pp. 491–503). New York: Bruner/Mazel.

Individual Differences in Early Visual Attention: Fixation Time and Information Processing

8

John Colombo
D. Wayne Mitchell
The Department of Human Development
The University of Kansas

There are at least two reasons why individual differences in infant visual attention during infancy are important to the field of psychology. The first is based on Underwood's (1975) concept of individual differences as a proving ground for psychological theory. Given an objective measure of an unseen psychological activity and a measure of the manifest outcome or performance of that activity, a correlation within individuals between the process and performance measures provides confirmatory theoretical support for the operation of the underlying activity. Because visual attention has long been proposed to reflect cognitive activity in the preverbal human (McCall, 1971), individual differences in visual attention and the habituation of that attention should be amenable to such a process–performance analysis (Colombo & Mitchell, 1988).

The second reason is more applied in nature and is based on the desire to predict later development from infancy.[1] Given that infant visual attention may reflect cognitive activity deemed critical to later intellectual development, such measures might provide better prediction of developmental outcome than the traditional tests of infant development (e.g., the Bayley or Gesell Scales) whose predictive validity is of dubious value (McCall, 1979b,c; McCall, Eichorn, & Hogarty, 1977). Although the failure of traditional tests has been attributed to the presence of "discontinuity," or qualitative transitions in intellectual development from infancy (McCall, 1979b,c, 1981; McCall, Appelbaum, & Hogarty, 1973), it is possible that such tests tap behavioral domains that are not particu-

---

[1]It is of some importance to note that the predictive validity of parameters of infant visual attention for later cognitive or intellectual development may be seen as a special instance of a process-performance relationship.

larly relevant to mental function at subsequent points during the life-span (Brooks & Weinraub, 1976; Honzik, 1976).

The purpose of this chapter is to examine individual differences in infant visual attention and habituation (in this volume, see also coverage of early learning and conditioning by Fagen and Ohr and recognition memory–novelty preference by Rose and Feldman). Theoretical and measurement issues with regard to individual differences in early visual attention are outlined, followed by a summary of the literature on these individual differences with respect to individual consistency and process–performance relationships, with a special emphasis on the variable of fixation duration. We conclude with a discussion of what this variable may represent in terms of cognitive processes and of what directions might prove most fruitful for future investigation.

INFANT VISUAL ATTENTION AND
HABITUATION: A BRIEF SKETCH

The Phenomenon

During the 1950s and 1960s, theoretical accounts of behavior in terms of the internal processes occurring between stimulus and response were offered with increasing frequency in the field of psychology. One of the first places researchers looked for empirical confirmation of such processes were the eyes of their subjects. For example, Wyckoff (1952) noted the usefulness of "observing responses" in the study of adult attention and learning (see also White & Plum, 1964), and Hess (e.g., 1975) studied adult pupillary reactions to various visual stimuli as an unobtrusive measure of autonomic response. It was a student of Hess, Robert Fantz, who developed a preferential fixation technique for use with newly hatched chicks (Fantz, 1956), with chimpanzees (see Fantz, 1961), and eventually with human infants (Fantz, 1958, 1961, 1963; see also Berlyne, 1958; Stirnimann, 1944; Valentine, 1913) that presaged the proliferation of research into early perceptual-cognitive development.

Although differences in the rate with which human infants and chimpanzees became "bored" with visual stimuli were noted anecdotally by Fantz in 1961, the decline of infants' attention to repetitive presentations of visual stimuli was first published by Fantz in 1964. In that elegant study, 2- to 6-month-old infants were exposed to pairs of stimuli for ten 1-min periods. One of the pair was always different, whereas the other was always the same. Analyses of infants' fixation to the two targets showed that infants older than 2 months of age reliably decreased their attention to the repeatedly exposed target. The parallels between the topography of this attentional decline and that of neural habituation (Thompson & Spencer, 1966) were such that within several years infant visual habituation had become a central measure of early stimulus encoding and processing

(Caron & Caron, 1968; Cohen, 1969; Lewis, 1969; Lewis, Kagan, & Kalafat, 1966; McCall & Kagan, 1967), and the recovery of the fixation response to a new stimulus was a routine measure of stimulus discrimination (Pancratz & Cohen, 1970; Saayman, Ames, & Moffitt, 1964).[2]

THEORETICAL INTERPRETATIONS

Comparator Theory

The most widely accepted theoretical account for infant visual habituation is the comparator model, which was adapted from Sokolov's (1963) analysis of changes in the orienting reflex. This theory posits that the magnitude of the orienting reflex (OR) reflects both the process of forming an "engram" of the actual stimulus, and of continual comparisons between that internal representation and the actual stimulus. At first, when there is no such representation, the magnitude of the OR (i.e., the duration of the fixation) is large. With successive presentations of the stimulus, however, the form of the representation proceeds toward an approximation of the actual stimulus. As a function of the reduction of the difference between the internal representation and the actual stimulus, the magnitude of the OR declines.

The Serial Habituation Model.   The comparator model is not without weakness. In addition to its nonspecific nature, it is unclear from this model why an infant would look away from a stimulus at any time during the presentation sequence before habituation occurred. To account for this, it was proposed that infants habituated to specific features of the stimulus at different times during the habituation sequence (Jeffrey & Cohen, 1971; Olson, 1976). These theories suggest that infants encode individual features of the stimulus serially, in order of each features' relative salience. This "serial" habituation hypothesis (Miller, 1972; Miller, Ryan, Sinnott, & Wilson, 1976; but see Lasky, 1979) implies that significant amounts of stimulus encoding could occur within the constraints of a single fixation, and that the attainment of habituation should signal the infant's processing of the entire stimulus.

Other Theories

Dual-Process Theory.   Thompson and Glanzman (1976) noted that the procedures employed to induce habituation of a response also produce a transitory increase in excitability, called sensitization. It has been argued that overall

---

[2]The relevance of habituation to infant audition (e.g., Bartoshuk, 1962; Bridger, 1961) and olfaction (Engen, Lipsitt, & Kaye, 1963) briefly preceded its application to visual behavior.

response decrement may be best accounted for in terms of the interaction of the dual processes of habituation and sensitization (Groves & Thompson, 1970). Within the context of infant attention, sensitization should produce a brief increase in attention after initial presentation of a moderately strong stimulus (Bashinski, Werner, & Rudy, 1985; Kaplan, Werner, & Rudy, 1988). Furthermore, recovery of fixation to a novel stimulus should more closely reflect sensitization rather than habituation (Thompson & Spencer, 1966). Some of the predictions of dual-process theory have been tested and confirmed in recent research with infants (Bashinski et al., 1985; Kaplan & Werner, 1986, 1987; Kaplan et al., 1988; Kaplan, Scheuneman, Jenkins, & Hilliard, 1988), although some older data (e.g., Miller, 1972; Wetherford & Cohen, 1973) seem to counter its contentions with respect to fixation recovery.

Learning-Theory Models.   Habituation has also been variously interpreted in terms of learning theory, which eschews the invocation of any mental representation or schema in favor of concepts derived from classical (Pearce & Hall, 1980; Rescorla & Wagner, 1972) or operant (Malcuit, Pomerleau, & Lamarre, 1988a; Watson, 1968) conditioning. Such accounts are generally designed to avoid the complications inherent in the modeling and measurement of internal processes and are appealing in their simplicity and precision. However, their success in escaping hypothetical internal processes is equivocal (Colombo & Mitchell, 1988).

Adaptive Significance.   Finally, Rovee-Collier (1987, 1988) has repeatedly stressed that infant visual habituation should be regarded from an evolutionary perspective and analyzed in terms of its functional significance to the individual. Whereas this point of view does not provide a detailed model of operation for the microanalysis of habituation, it does suggest that habituation may be best considered at the level of the stimulus, or the stimulus-by-individual interaction.

SUMMARY

The distribution of visual attention has long been assumed to allow access to the cognitive abilities of young infants (Fantz, 1964; McCall, 1971), and much empirical research accumulated over the past three decades supports this assumption. At this time, however, perhaps the only theoretical consensus on the process or processes that control infants' attentional responses may be that the existing theories are inadequate.

Despite its difficulties, the comparator model is the most popular theoretical account of visual habituation among developmental scientists, and as such the discussion that follows is based largely on its tenets and assumptions. Although dual-process theory clearly has potential for furthering progress in the area of early attention, further empirical evaluation of its predictions is awaited. The learning-theory models, especially those based on the waning of the stimulus' reinforcement value (Malcuit et al., 1988a, 1988b), have serious difficulty in accounting for developmental changes in the habituation function and avoiding the postulation of unseen internal processes (e.g., McCall, 1988; Rovee-Collier, 1988). However, some behavioral models have merit in the rigor of their analysis of the phenomenon (Colombo & Mitchell, 1988).

TECHNICAL ISSUES

The value of the habituation paradigm for characterizing infants' visual-processing capabilities has led to its widespread use among researchers interested in early cognitive processes. One consequence of such popularity, however, is wide variability in procedure, measurement, and in the calculation of habituation. In contrast to the study of habituation in the physiological and animal-learning arenas (Denny & Ratner, 1970), infant visual habituation has not been subject to rigorous parametric examination, and so little is known about the effects of such procedural variations. If we are to understand individual differences in infant cognitive processing through the use of visual habituation, such information is needed to understand accurate measurement of the processes that habituation is purported to represent—which is to determine whether particular effects we observe can be attributed to underlying processes or to procedural constraints. Next we review refinements in the measurement of infant visual habituation (see Olson & Sherman, 1983; Werner & Perlmutter, 1979) and parametric data currently available on the paradigm.

PROCEDURAL REFINEMENTS

Fixed Trial Procedures

In early studies of infant habituation, attention was typically assessed during some predetermined number of repetitive presentations of the stimulus, with each presentation lasting for some predetermined length of time. Whereas this "fixed trial" procedure is easily run and yields data that are easily analyzed, the procedure suffers from several limitations. First, because the availability of the stimulus for fixation is determined by the experimenter, some infants may not habituate in the time or presentations allowed (Lewis, 1969). On the other hand, some infants will habituate quickly and thus endure presentations past the point of habituation. Theoretically, this increases the amount of between-subject variability in processing both within ages (see DeLoache, 1976) and across ages (Lewis, 1969). Under such circumstances the group habituation function may not be considered representative of the individual function (Bornstein, 1985; Cohen & Menten, 1981). Second, in comparing memory and encoding for various types of stimuli, the group function cannot adjust for the possibility that such stimuli may be differentially salient or take varying amounts of time to process. Third, as Cohen (1976) has noted, the total fixation time per trial (the most widely used datum from the procedure) can be misleading because the same amount of per-trial fixation time (e.g., 10 s) may be accumulated in very different ways (one 10 s look, or five 2 s looks).

Variations in Intertrial Interval. Lewis (1969) presented a visual stimulus for four 30 s trials but also varied the length of the intertrial interval (0 s, 5 s, and 15 s). Only the 0 s and 5 s interval conditions resulted in a response decrement. These findings suggest that, with fixed trial paradigms, shorter intertrial intervals will be more successful at eliciting habituation and that habituation will occur with shorter overall fixation times.

Criterion-Based Paradigms

Stimulus-Presentation Issues. In response to the limitations of fixed-trial procedures, criterion-based habituation paradigms were introduced (Horowitz, Paden, Bhana, & Self, 1972b; see also Cohen, 1972). Early forms of the criterion-based procedures simply involved the extension of experimenter-determined stimulus presentations until some habituation criterion for looking time per trial was met. In true "infant-controlled" paradigms (Horowitz et al., 1972b), stimulus presentation was contingent on the infant's behavior; data were not collected until the infant fixated the stimulus, and presentation ended when the infant looked away from it. The habituation criterion could then be calculated from data that more closely reflected the infant's ad lib inspection of the stimulus. However, even though criterion-based paradigms are widely accepted, procedural variability has not been appreciably reduced.

Criterion-Calculation Issues. First, the nature of the habituation criterion may vary. In some studies (Friedman, Bruno, & Vietze, 1974; McCall, Hogarty, Hamilton, & Vincent, 1973; McCall, Kennedy, & Dodds, 1977), the criterion is an attentional decline to some *absolute* fixation level (e.g., two trials at 4 s or less). However, more often, a *relative* criterion is employed that is operationalized as a 50% decrement from some previous level of fixation during the session. With a relative criterion, the processing of the stimulus is theoretically equated within or between ages before a subsequent test for stimulus discrimination. For example, if an infant's initial fixation level is 20 s, two consecutive looks at 10 s or below might be necessary to meet the habituation criterion; if the initial level is 40 s, two looks at or below 20 s are necessary to reach criterion.

Furthermore, the "previous level" from which the criterion is calculated may also vary. It may refer to the initial portion of the session, such as the duration of the first fixation, or the mean of the first two (Bornstein & Benasich, 1986) or first three (Pecheaux & Lecuyer, 1983) fixations. However, long fixations that occur relatively late in the sequence (Colombo, Mitchell, O'Brien, & Horowitz, 1987a; McCall, 1979a) are ignored with such a procedure. To address this, a "floating point" procedure (Mitchell & Steiner, 1984; Nelson & Horowitz, 1983) may be used in which the criterion is recalculated if long fixations are encountered anywhere in the habituation sequence. Finally, the criterion may be derived from a combination of parameters. For example, Bushnell (1979) employed a 25% floating-point decrement, conditional on each infant having at least one 15 s fixation and a minimum of 2 min of familiarization (see also Caron & Caron, 1981).

Fixation Parameters.   Additionally, differences in the operational definition of the fixation may vary in the infant-controlled procedure. For example, in some cases *any* look to the stimulus is counted as a fixation, and *any* look away from the stimulus is sufficient to terminate the fixation (McCall et al., 1973). In other cases, the look to the stimulus that begins the fixation (the "onset"), and the look away from the stimulus that terminates it (the "offset"), must be of a particular length (e.g., 1 s) to be counted (e.g., Colombo et al., 1987a, 1987b). We have briefly examined the effects of such temporal factors (Colombo & Horowitz, 1985). Although differences in fixation onsets of .5 s and 1 s did not affect various habituation measures (e.g., number of fixations to criterion, total fixation time, average fixation duration, location of peak fixation), offsets of 0 s (i.e., *any* look-away terminating the fixation) versus 2 s produced large differences. The total and average duration of infants' fixations were doubled in the 2 s offset condition, relative to the 0 s offset condition, with no observable improvement in discrimination performance. This suggested that infants were accumulating unneeded fixation to the visual stimuli under the long offset, a point borne out in higher rates of fussiness and state-related attrition in the long offset condition, relative to the shorter offset. However, it should be noted that the trade-off for very short onsets and offsets is lower interobserver reliability (Colombo & Horowitz, 1985).

SUMMARY

The point of this brief procedural review is that individual differences in infant attention and visual habituation must be considered in the context of the procedure in which the data are collected (Dannemiller, 1984) because it is likely that such procedures strongly influence the observed attentional profile of the infant. For example, "slow-" or "nonhabituating" infants as assessed under fixed-trial procedures may be labeled as "long lookers" when assessed under infant control procedures, whereas "rapid habituators" are likely to be characterized as "short lookers" in these respective paradigms (Colombo, Mitchell, & Horowitz, 1988; McCall, 1973; McCall et al., 1973; McCall & Kagan, 1970). Duration and decrement have frequently been treated as distinct components of the habituation function (Bornstein, 1988; Bornstein & Sigman, 1986; Tamis-Lemonda & Bornstein, 1989); such duality in the literature has been interpreted as a theoretical weakness (e.g., Malcuit, Pomerleau, & Lamarre, 1988b) when in fact it is likely attributable to the procedural influence on the derivation of attentional measures. We tend toward the view that individual differences in duration and decrement vary and thus actually represent a unitary attentional profile; that is, the rapidity of decrement, or habituation rate, under fixed-trial procedures will be directly and inversely related to the duration of fixation under criterion-based procedures.

Furthermore, because habituation is sensitive to temporal variables (see also Ames, Hunter, Black, Lithgow, & Newman, 1978; Greenberg & Weizmann, 1971; Haaf, Smith, & Smitley, 1983; Mitchell & Horowitz, 1987), such factors should be seriously considered when individual differences are the primary research topic. For example, Haaf et al. (1983) have taken issue with the purported ease of administration of the infant control procedure (Horowitz et al., 1972b), but their claims must be qualified by their use of a long (i.e., 2 s) fixation offset, which is the direct cause of increased attrition.

DEVELOPMENTAL AND INDIVIDUAL DIFFERENCES IN VISUAL HABITUATION

Combined with the expectation that information processing should improve as a function of age (or as a function of the experience that accompanies age), the comparator model makes some fairly straightforward predictions for developmental trends and individual differences in infant visual habituation (see Fig. 8.1 for a representative infant-control habituation sequence and variables of interest). For example, if processing improves with age, then those habituation variables purported to reflect processing (rapidity of the attainment of the criterion, the magnitude of the OR, or the magnitude of the decrement of the OR) should show prescribed directional changes; that is, older infants should show fewer numbers of fixations to meet criterion, steeper decrements, and shorter fixation durations, relative to younger infants. A corollary to this set of predictions is that, within ages, those infants with such attentional profiles might also exhibit an advantage in other aspects of stimulus processing. Furthermore, if one accepts the possibility of longitudinal continuity in psychological ability from infancy, this profile might also be associated with superior cognitive or intellectual development later in childhood. We address these predictions in a review of the available literature on these measures, including data collected in our own laboratory.

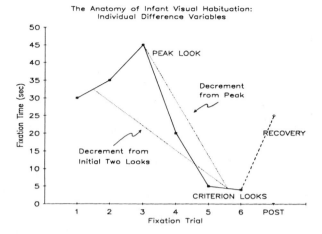

The Anatomy of Infant Visual Habituation:
Individual Difference Variables

FIG. 8.1.   The anatomy of infant visual habituation. Measures available for individual difference and developmental analysis include the number of fixations to meet criterion (here, the infant has taken 6 looks), various measures of fixation duration (total fixation of 139 s, partitioned into a peak fixation of 45 s, and 5 nonpeak fixations that sum to 94 s), a decrement measure (the decrements or slopes yielded by this curve is −10.1 from the peak fixation to the mean of the 2 criterion looks, and −4.7 from mean of the first 2 looks to the mean of the criterion looks). Additionally, this curve indicates response recovery to a new stimulus (POST).

Developmental Course

Fixed-Trial Data.   The developmental course of infant visual attention has been the direct focus of surprisingly little research, although some experimental work with the fixed-trial paradigm 10 to 15 years ago has yielded information relevant to this issue. Generally speaking, within the fixed-trial paradigm, the amount of fixation time to a stimulus decreases with age (Barten & Ronch, 1971; Horowitz, Paden, Bhana, Aitchison, & Self, 1972a; Lewis, 1969, 1975; Schaffer, Greenwood, & Parry, 1972; Wetherford & Cohen, 1973), whereas habituation decrement increases with age (Cohen, 1969; Fantz, 1964; Lewis, 1969; Martin, 1975; see Fig. 8.2). Lewis (1975) also reported age-related increases in the degree of recovery to a new stimulus.

This general trend is further supported by studies of newborn habituation within the fixed-trial paradigm that show long fixation times and, on average, very little decrement to the stimulus (Friedman et al., 1974; but see Slater, Morison, & Rose, 1984).

Criterion-Based Paradigm Data.   Rose, Slater, and Perry (1986) reported some developmental trends for infant-controlled habituation data with correla-

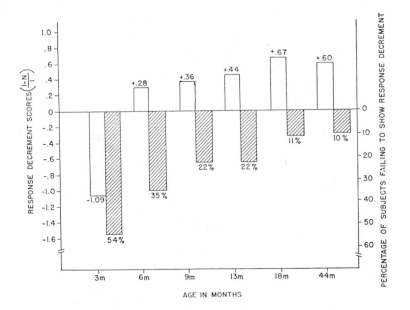

FIG. 8.2. Developmental trends in decrement and habituation across 5 30 s presentation trials (from Lewis, 1969). The left-hand axis represents a measure of the proportion of decrement and corresponds to the open bars; The right-hand axis is the percentage of infants who actually habituated within the limits of the procedure. Decrement appears to increase with development, but even at older ages sizeable percentages of the sample do not habituate within the constraints of the fixed-trial procedure. (Reprinted with permission of the author and the Society for Research in Child Development.)

tional analyses. All duration measures were negatively correlated with age, and trials to criterion were slightly but positively correlated with age. Finally, the correlation between recovery to a new stimulus and age was negative. Although this last finding is counter to the expectation that older infants should exhibit better discrimination skills, it is most likely due to the negative correlation between duration measures and age; because recovery magnitude is positively correlated with fixation duration, infants who look for shorter durations (e.g., older infants) will likely show lower recovery magnitudes. Bornstein and Pecheaux (1986) have also reported a drop in total fixation time in a single infant tested weekly from 3 to 7 months of age.

Extensive data on the developmental course of visual habituation in the infant-control procedure, however, are available from a project conducted on individual differences in habituation across the first year of life (Colombo et al., 1987a; Colombo & Mitchell, 1989). This study included cross-sectional age groups of

3, 4, 7, and 9 months of age tested twice within ages, and a longitudinal group tested once each at 3, 4, 7, and 9 months of age. Infants were habituated to color photographs of faces using a floating-point 50% decrement criterion and 1 s onset and offset parameters. These developmental data largely contradict both earlier findings within the fixed-trial paradigm and some of the predictions of the comparator model. First, the number of fixations to meet criterion, which the comparator model predicts should decrease with age, actually *increases* significantly (see Fig. 8.3).

More surprisingly, the decrement of the habituation curve, which the comparator model predicts should increase (i.e., become steeper) with age, actually *decreases* (i.e., becomes shallower) with age. This is true whether decrement is calculated from initial fixation levels (Bornstein & Benasich, 1986) or from the floating-point peak fixation (Mitchell & Steiner, 1984). McCall (1979a) reported similar findings in comparing the habituation of 5- and 10-month-olds in a fixed-trial procedure.

One finding consistent with both the comparator model and past fixed-trial research is a drop in duration of fixation time with age. Every duration-based measure we examined shows a substantial decline (see Fig. 8.5 for data on the peak fixation and the sum of nonpeak fixations).

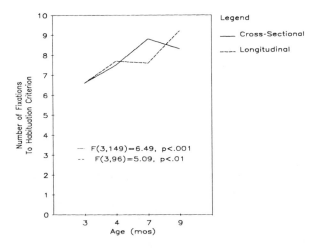

FIG. 8.3. Developmental changes in number of trials to meet habituation criterion under the infant-control procedure. The cross-sectional curve represents the average from two within-age habituation sessions using different stimulus faces with independent samples for each age group; the longitudinal curve represents the same infants tested at each age.

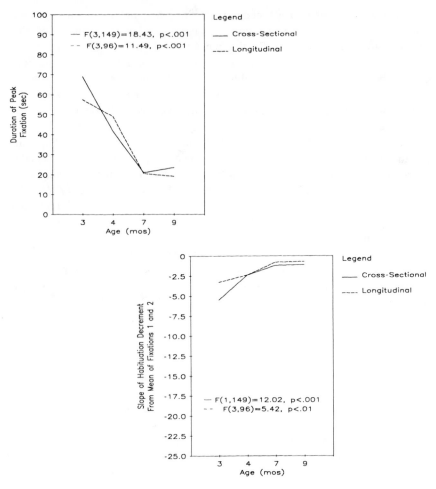

FIG. 8.4.   Developmental changes in the slope (decrement) of decrement under the infant-control procedure. Large negative numbers indicate steep slopes; shallower slopes are indicated as values approach
zero. Decrement is calculated from the mean of the first two fixations
(a) and from the peak fixation of the sequence (b); both are shown on
the same scale to facilitate direct comparison. Cross-sectional curves
represented the average of two within-age assessments, as in Fig. 8.3.

Duration and Decrement

Because the duration of infants' fixations determines the criterion for habituation
and figures arithmetically into equations for deriving decrement scores, we
suspected that developmental changes in both number of fixations to criterion and
for decrement variables observed here may be attributable to the decline in fixation
duration per se. For example, infants beginning the habituation sequence with a

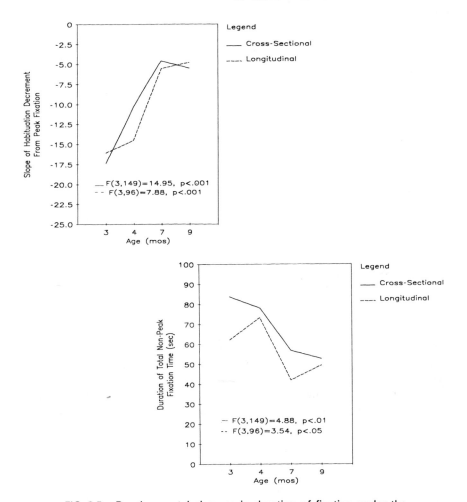

FIG. 8.5. Developmental changes in duration of fixation under the infant-control procedure. Presented here are data for the longest or "peak" fixation from the habituation sequence (a) and for the sum of the other nonpeak fixations (b). Again, the cross-sectional curve is the average of two within-age assessments.

long-duration fixation might find it easier to meet the 50% decrement criterion than those infants who begin with a short fixation; an infant beginning a sequence with a 100 s fixation can meet criterion with looks ranging from 0 to 50 s, whereas an infant who begins a sequence with a 10 s fixation can only meet criterion with looks between 0 and 5 s. Those infants who begin with short fixations may either continue on in the procedure until meeting the requirement for consecutive brief criterion looks or, if a floating-point criterion is used, may eventually fixate the stimulus long enough to cause a recalculation of the criterion. This scenario

TABLE 8.1
Correlations Between Number of Fixations to Criterion
and the Duration of First Through Fifth Fixations

		Ordinal Fixation				
Age	N	First	Second	Third	Fourth	Fifth
Cross-Sectional Sample						
3 months	34	-.30*	-.10	-.21	+.04	-.07
4 months	34	-.35*	-.33*	-.29	+.04	+.33*
7 months	50	-.46**	-.33**	-.44**	-.36**	+.03
9 months	34	-.25	-.23	+.09	-.02	+.05
All ages	182	-.35***	-.29***	-.28***	-.15*	-.02
Longitudinal Sample						
3 months	68	-.41**	-.26**	-.07	-.05	+.19
4 months	57	-.27*	-.26*	-.20	-.01	+.18
7 months	49	-.31*	-.19	-.05	+.03	+.14
9 months	38	-.25	-.26	-.25	-.21	-.06
All ages	38	-.52**	-.21	-.03	-.24	+.20

*$p < .05$; **$p < .01$; ***$p < .001$.

predicts that the number of fixations to criterion would be negatively correlated with the first two or three fixations of the sequence. We examined our data for this possibility (see Table 8.1). Although the magnitude of the relationships vary somewhat across ages and samples, the direction and pattern is exactly as predicted for every age and sample tested. This finding is also consistent with Dannemiller's (1984) statistical simulations that suggest "faster" habituators (i.e., those infants with short fixation durations) might in fact show more trials to criterion than "slower" habituators.

We believe that the decrease in decrement with age is attributable to the drop in fixation time as well. Decrement measures are very highly correlated with duration measures, so that infants with long fixations will have large decrements (see also Tamis-LeMonda & Bornstein, 1989). Across ages from our data, the lowest correlation between peak fixation and decrement from the peak fixation was +.96, and the lowest correlation between the mean of the first two fixations and the decrement from that mean was +.94. Most interestingly, if duration measures from which the decrement measures are derived are covaried in developmental analyses, the robust age effects reported for decrement variables disappear for both cross-sectional and longitudinal samples.

Developmental Function and Infant Background

Given the findings that suggest shorter fixation times might reflect greater speed or efficiency in information processing, the profile of the individual infant's

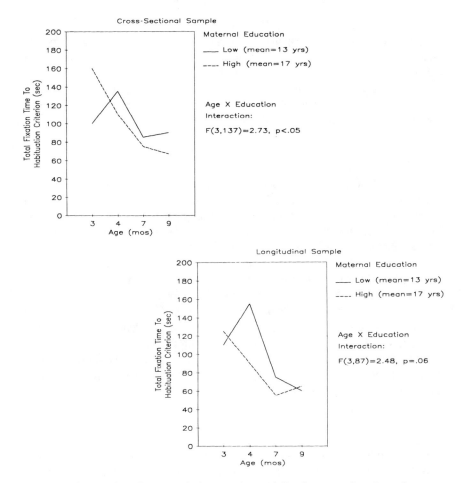

FIG. 8.6. Developmental changes in total fixation as a function of maternal education for the cross-sectional (a) and longitudinal (b) samples (cross-sectional data again averaged across two within-age visits). As the figures show, the Age × Maternal Education interaction is statistically significant for the cross-sectional sample, and marginally significant for the longitudinal sample.

developmental change in fixation time might be expected to vary as a function of his or her background. We tested this hypothesis in developmental analyses of fixation duration in infants from backgrounds of high- versus low-maternal education (Colombo & Mitchell, 1989). Figure 8.6 shows that in both samples infants whose mothers had attained a higher level of education showed a more accelerated and pronounced drop in fixation time from 3 to 9 months of age, whereas infants whose mothers were less educated showed a decline in fixation time only after 4 months of age.[3] Given the crudity of the maternal education variable, the mechanism responsible for such differences is obviously open to question. This may be attributable to genetic sources, or to greater stimulation or experiential variability that may exist in the homes of higher educated families. However, the data further implicate fixation time as a measure that is sensitive to both intrinsic and extrinsic influences and also suggest that the developmental function may be of interest to individual-difference researchers.

Summary

The data on the developmental course of infant visual habituation vary as a function of the paradigm involved. With fixed-trial procedures, older infants will show shorter looking times and steeper decrements with age than young infants. The age effects for decrement are quite likely attributable to the failure of a substantial number of young infants to habituate under fixed-trial procedures rather than to a true developmental effect for decrement.

In criterion-based paradigms, however, only fixation time yields a developmental course in line with the predictions of comparator theory. Under such conditions, where visual habituation actually occurs for every individual, the developmental course of measures of habituation ''rate'' (decrement and number of fixations to criterion) contradicts comparator theory. We believe that this occurs in criterion-based paradigms because these measures are closely related to fixation duration, and that measures of fixation duration most strongly characterize the habituation function.

Individual Differences

Studies of individual differences in infant visual attention have taken two forms. The first documents the degree to which various measures of attention reflect some characteristic of the individual infant by assessing the within-subject consistency (i.e., reliability or stability) of these measures across time. The second type of study examines the concurrent or lagged prediction of infants' perceptual, cognitive, or intellectual performance from their attentional characteristics.

Individual Consistency of Visual Attention

If visual attention and habituation are thought to signify cognitive processes that are a characteristic trait of the individual, then those attentional measures should

---

[3]It should be noted that these effects were obtained with from a highly educated upper middle-class population (mean education = 15.0 years). This constraint may limit the generality of the effect, although one would expect that such homogeneity and restricted range would attenuate rather than exaggerate the size of this effect. See also a similar trend reported by Cohen (1981, p. 250).

also be trait like; that is, they should be consistent within individuals across time. The following sections review the evidence for such consistency from a loosely chronological framework.

Consistency Within Ages.   Interestingly, one of the first within-age reliability studies of infant attention examined neither habituation nor fixation time. Barten, Birns, and Ronch (1971) tested for the reliability of ocular tracking across a 24-hr period ($N = 12$). They found strong individual consistency for newborns' oculocephalic pursuit to a schematic face ($r = +.56$) and a blank card ($r = +.59$), and for simple ocular pursuit for the face ($r = +.65$). Subsequently, Barten and Ronch (1971) reported within-session reliability of fixation duration ($N = 24$) across two stimuli for 3- ($r = +.61$) and 4-month-olds ($r = +.39$).

Fenson, Sapper, and Minner (1974) examined the within-age reliability of habituation in 12-month-olds. Individual differences in the duration of infants' attention to various stimuli within fixed-trial habituation sessions showed correlations mostly in the $+.40$ to $+.60$ range ($N = 52$), and a subsample of these ($n = 18$) retested across an interval of 3 weeks showed good reliability for the duration of both first ($+.64$) and total ($+.74$) fixation. Fenson et al. (1974) reported the reliability of decrement across the same 3-week interval to be positive ($r = +.31$) but not statistically significant.

Mitchell and Steiner (1984) sequentially habituated 3-month-olds to three stimuli with an infant-control procedure. Within-session reliability was $+.48$ for total looking time to criterion and $+.54$ for duration of peak fixation. Also using an infant-control procedure, Pecheaux and Lecuyer (1983) computed consistency of 4-month-olds' total looking time and number of fixation to habituation criterion across four different stimuli presented in two sessions 1 week apart. Although the mean reliability of number of fixations to criterion was only $+.19$, the mean reliability of total looking time was $+.58$. Ritz, Woodruff, and Fagen (1984) also reported a reliability of $+.48$ for total looking time across a 1-week period for 4-month-olds.

Bornstein and Benasich (1986) tested for the reliability of habituation measures at 5 months of age across a 1-week period. Although they reported low reliability (r's $< +.20$) for various single measures of habituation, an habituation "factor" score derived from factor analysis showed moderate week-to-week reliability ($+.31$) that was statistically significant. Additionally, these authors found that the pattern of habituation was also a reliable measure across the 2 weeks. Rose et al. (1986) also reported test–retest reliabilities for various measures of infant-controlled habituation across three sessions 24 hours apart ($N = 16$). Although their sample included infants across a wide age range, age was partialled from the test–retest correlations. Total fixation time had the best reliability (mean $r = +.65$ across all three assessments) across all ages. Other duration measures, such as duration of first fixation and average fixation duration, were positively correlated across at least two of the three sessions, and number of trials to criterion was correlated across one. Recovery of fixation to a novel stimulus was not reliable.

Colombo et al. (1987a) studied the within-age reliabilities of 12 measures of infant habituation and recovery to faces at 3, 4, 7, and 9 months of age under infant-control procedures. The mean interval between assessments was about a week. The results indicated that ordinal measures of habituation were not reliable within any of the ages tested; the respective reliabilities for number of fixations to habituation, location of peak fixation, and habituation pattern were +.17, +.09, and −.13. Measures of habituation decrement were found to be reliable (+.38 for decrement from looks 1–2 and +.48 for decrement from the peak fixation), but this reliability was directly attributable to the reliability of the duration measures that were entered into the decrement calculations. The reliabilities for duration of peak, first fixation, and total fixation time averaged +.47; the reliability of the average nonpeak fixation was +.36. Finally, neither the magnitude nor the presence of recovery to a novel stimulus was reliable within ages, suggesting that the measure most often used as a group measure of visual discrimination in infancy was not a reliable indicator of individual discrimination abilities. Although 3-month-olds' habituation measures were consistently lower than that observed for older infants, we subsequently traced this to variation in stimulus pairs (Colombo, Mitchell, O'Brien, & Horowitz, 1987b). Reliability assessed across a 1-week interval for 22 3-month-olds with stimulus pairs more closely equated for amount of contrast at the hairline (Melhuish, 1982) yielded the same pattern of results observed for older infants in Colombo et al. (1987a).

Consistency Across Ages.   The stability of infant visual attention has attracted sporadic interest from researchers beginning in the late 1960s. Generally speaking, stability of visual attention across longer periods of infancy is more elusive than within-age reliability but shows the same pattern of results; nominal or ordinal variables are not stable, but moderate stability often is observed for measures of duration and decrement. In the infant-controlled habituation paradigm, however, the stability of decrement again appears to be attributable to the stability of duration measures alone.

Kagan and Lewis (1965) were among the first to report on the cross-age consistency of infant attention. Total fixation time to various stimuli from 6 to 13 months of age in a fixed-trial procedure ranged from about zero to +.60; the degree of stability interacted with the sex of the infant and the stimulus involved. More than a decade later, McCall (1979a) published data on the stability of attentional measures from 5 to 10 months of age, also within a fixed-trial procedure. Individual infants were clustered as exhibiting one of three particular habituation patterns (see also Bornstein & Benasich, 1986; Colombo et al., 1987a), but there was no stability in cluster membership across this 5-month period, nor was there any stability in recovery of fixation to a novel stimulus;

stabilities for other habituation measures were not reported. In the same year, Miller et al. (1979) published data on the stability of fixed-trial decrement ratios collected at 2 to 4 months of age and at 27 and 39 months. The stabilities of these ratios were positive, but moderately low, ranging from $+.10$ to $+.32$. Moreover, when studied in the fourth year of life (Miller et al., 1980), evidence for the stability of decrement was equivocal.

Using an infant-control procedure with a multiple-stimulus habituation sequence, Byrne, Clark-Tousenard, Hondas, and Smith (1985) reported significant stability for duration of first look ($+.44$), total looking time ($+.37$), average look ($+.53$), and decrement ($+.41$) in a sample of 24 infants followed longitudinally from 4 to 7 months of age. Interestingly, this study is the only one in which magnitude of recovery to a novel stimulus was found to be reliable ($+.48$).

Colombo et al. (1987a) reported stability from 3 to 9 months in a sample of 69 infants followed longitudinally. The results from this cross-age sample echo those from the within-age sample reviewed earlier. Ordinal measures were not stable across ages, whereas fixation duration measures (particularly the longest or "peak" fixation) were stable, with longitudinal correlations ranging from a low of $+.20$ from 4 to 9 months to a high of $+.49$ from 7 to 9 months. Decrement measures are also relatively stable, although again the stability of these measures is attributable to the stability of the duration measures used in their derivation.

Lastly, in a study with a somewhat different focus, Barten and Ronch (1971) examined the continuity of infant visual behavior across different measures from the newborn period. They found that the proficiency of newborn visual pursuit correlated positively with vertical pursuit at 1 month ($r = +.43$), but negatively with fixation duration to two-dimensional stimuli at 3 and 4 months of age (mean $r = -.42$). These authors concluded that high visual attentiveness during the neonatal period (as reflected by visual pursuit) was conducive to the rapidity of stimulus processing later in infancy (as signified by shorter fixation durations).

Summary

The results of these studies provide evidence that support the individual consistency of measures of infant visual attention and habituation. The degree of consistency generally varies with the test–retest interval (Bornstein, 1988), as findings of inconsistency are much more common in studies of cross-age stability (e.g., McCall, 1979a) than within-age reliability (Colombo et al., 1987a, 1978b).

Consistency also varies as a function of the measure observed. For example, measures of fixation duration are most reliable. Measures of fixation decrement are also reliable, although, at least within criterion-based procedures, this reliability appears dependent on the reliability of the duration measures from which they are derived. Empirical tests of the consistency of other ordinal measures (e.g., number of fixations to criterion, location of peak fixations) have confirmed the results of Dannemiller's (1984) simulations, which predicted their unreliability.

Infant Attention: Process–Performance Correlations

Following Underwood's (1975) process-product framework, the following sections examine the covariation between parameters of infant visual habituation and outcome measures of the processes they are purported to reflect.

Concurrent Stimulus Processing.   Comparator theory posits that infant visual attention to a stimulus is driven by the processing of the informational content of that stimulus. Attentional measures should therefore correlate with independent measures of how well, how much, or how quickly that stimulus has been processed. A number of studies have sought to document relationships between habituation/attentional measures and information-processing performance, as indexed by recovery of fixation to a novel stimulus, preference for a novel stimulus in a paired-comparison paradigm, or performance in operant conditioning paradigms.

Early studies using fixed-trial paradigms focused on "slow" versus "fast" habituators. For example, both McCall (1973; McCall et al., 1973; McCall & Kagan, 1970) and Miller (1972) showed that dividing infants as a function of the amount of decrement shown in a fixed-trial procedure yielded differential results for recovery to a novel stimulus. As might be expected under such conditions, "fast" habituators perform better than "slow" habituators. However, because "slow" habituators may not really have habituated under fixed-trial conditions (indeed, Cohen, DeLoache, & Pearl, 1977, more accurately classify infants as "habituators" or "nonhabituators"), it is difficult to justify testing for recovery (Bridger, 1961). To address this issue, DeLoache (1976) examined the recovery of fast and slow habituators under an infant-controlled procedure and found no differences in the recovery to stimuli discrepant from the standard. However, McCall, Kennedy, and Dodds (1977) found fast habituators' recovery performance superior to that of slow habituators under infant-controlled conditions. These studies differed on two procedural details that may explain the contradiction. First, DeLoache (1976) used a relative criterion, whereas McCall et al. (1977) used an absolute calculation. Second, although "distractor" stimuli were used in both studies between the attainment of the habituation criterion and the test trials, DeLoache (1976) presented the distractor for a greater number of trials than did McCall et al. (1977). This may have handicapped fast habituators' performance more than slow habituators, because fast habituators have been shown to encode such distractors more quickly than slow habituators (e.g., Cohen et al., 1977).

Several other studies have examined concurrent information-processing performance during infancy from the framework of fixation duration. Colombo et al. (1988) examined the recognition memory performance of short-versus long-looking infants within the paired-comparison paradigm with simple stimuli. Fixation duration was assessed using a measure of infants' rate of looking during fixed familiarization phases (such a measure under fixed time exposures should be inversely proportional to the duration of fixations made by the infant) and significantly predicted novelty preferences at both 4 ($r = +.40$) and 7 ($r = +.36$) months of age. These results are in concordance with an earlier study by Caron, Caron, Minichiello, Weiss, and Friedman (1977), who examined infants' novelty preferences in terms of a measure of "decrement" during familiarization phases that should relate directly to the rate measure used by Colombo et al. (1988).

Mitchell and Horowitz (1988) recently demonstrated differential performance by long and short lookers within the infant-control paradigm. Three- and 4-month-old infants were habituated to a stimulus comprised of an array of large dark blue triangles and smaller light blue circles on a pink background. Following habituation, infants were tested for recognition of the triangular and circular components presented alone. Four-month-olds recognized both components, but as a group, 3-month-olds failed to demonstrate recognition of the circles. Closer examination of individual data indicated that actually half the 3-month-old sample did recognize the circles, whereas the other half did not; those 3-month-olds who failed to recognize the circles looked nearly twice as long as those who did recognize them.

Learning Performance.   Given that habituation is considered to be a simple form of learning, it might be expected that proficiency in the processes underlying visual habituation (as reflected by, for example, shorter fixation times) might predict performance in other learning paradigms. In fact, several studies have examined the correlation between infants' attentional patterns and performance on operant learning tasks (see also Fagen & Ohr, this volume). Lewis (1969) reported two experiments in which the extent of visual decrement to a series of curved lines at 44 months of age was positively related to performance in learning (i.e., concept formation and discrimination learning) tasks at the same age. In two experiments, Hayes, Ewy, and Watson (1982) assessed 3.5-month-olds' attentiveness to visual displays before a session in which they learned to kick for a visual reinforcer. In both experiments, attentiveness was measured in terms of the frequency of fixations within a fixed period (i.e., infants making more fixations per period were classified as being more attentive), and in both studies, infants who made a higher number of fixations within the time period exhibited greater increases in kicking from baseline. Although attention was not quantified as fixation duration or habituation, a higher number of fixations per fixed period may reflect patterns of shorter fixation duration, as in Colombo et al. (1988). Lamarre and Pomerleau (1985) also examined the relationship between habituation and learning. Fast habituators did not learn any better or faster than slow habituators, but they did have shorter latencies and faster responses in an operant head-turning task than did slower habituators.

Recently, Mitchell and Colombo (1989) assessed 3- and 4-month-olds' looking times and then trained these subjects on a visual discrimination based on the circular stimulus component previously shown to be differentially processed by long and short lookers at 3 months of age by Mitchell and Horowitz (1988, aforementioned). Infants were reinforced in fixate stimuli based on the presence or absence of this cue using a synchronous reinforcement paradigm (Colombo, Mitchell, Coldren, & Atwater, 1990). After training, infants were tested for retention of the discrimination and transfer. Retention was assessed via the maintenance of fixation to the reinforced target when reinforcement was withdrawn; transfer was measured by retraining the discrimination with the previously reinforced component set in a novel stimulus context. In both the 3- and 4-month-old samples, the length of infants' average look during the looking-time pretest predicted retention of the discrimination (the respective r's were $-.47$ and $-.39$) and transfer (respective r's were $-.38$ and $-.42$), with short-looking infants showing superior performance. Also, 4-month-olds' peak duration predicted performance level during training ($r = -.42$). Once again, shorter fixations predicted superior performance.

Later Language, Cognitive Development, and Intelligence.   Studies of the long-term predictive validity of infant visual attention and habituation were driven by the assumption that such measures tap some component of the cognitive domain shared by assessments of language, cognitive development, and IQ.

The first longitudinal studies on the predictive value of habituation measures were published by Miller, which consistently relate steeper decrements under fixed-trial conditions to superior cognitive development. Miller, Sinnott, Short, and Hains (1976) first observed a correlation of $+.51$ between 4-month fixed-trial habituation decrement scores and performance on an object permanence task at 14 months ($N = 15$). In subsequent papers, Miller et al. (1977, 1979, 1980) reported on the longitudinal follow-up of a larger sample ($N = 48$) of 2-, 3-, and 4-month-old infants (from Miller et al., 1976) on tasks from the Uzgiris and Hunt (1975) cognitive development scale, showing infants with steeper decrements outperforming those with shallower decrements. The sample was reported on again at 27 and 39 months of age (Miller et al., 1979) and finally at 51 months of age (1980). Faster decrements were related to cognitive and linguistic development in the third and fourth year of life (Miller et al., 1979), a trend echoed at 51 months (85% of the relationships between decrement and cognitive tasks were in the expected direction), although few of the correlations attained statistical significance (Miller et al., 1980).

Two studies document correlations between decrement from fixed-trial habituation procedures and subsequent Bayley scores. Lewis and Brooks-Gunn

(1981) reported a +.61 correlation between decrement at 3 months and 24-month Bayley scores. Ruddy and Bornstein (1982) also found larger decrements at 4 months predicting higher Bayley scores ($r = +.46$), and productive vocabulary ($r = +.52$) at 12 months of age. When maternal variables assessed at 4 months were factored into the predictive equation, nearly 60% of the variance in 12-month vocabulary was accounted for (see also Bornstein & Ruddy, 1984).

In a more recent longitudinal study of the development of 35 mother–infant dyads, Tamis-LeMonda and Bornstein (1989) re-examined the predictive power of the combination of infant habituation measures and maternal skill. The most significant change from the Ruddy and Bornstein (1982) study, however, was the use of an infant-control procedure for the assessment of habituation at 5 months of age, which accounts for a somewhat different pattern of prediction. Tamis-LeMonda and Bornstein (1989) found shorter looking times and shallower decrements at 5 months to predict representational competence at 13 months; the factor scores correlate at −.59. Finally, Krinsky (1988) reported negative correlations between the location of the peak fixation and number of fixations to criterion at 5 months and expressive and comprehensive language at 24 months. This finding is qualified by the poor psychometric properties of these two variables (Colombo et al., 1987a, 1987b)[4] and r's reported separately for boys ($n = 15$) and girls ($n = 8$).

Lastly, three studies document direct relationships between infant habituation and later performance on standardized intelligence tests. Bornstein (1984) found 4-month decrement scores from a fixed-trial procedure to predict intelligence test (WPPSI) performance at 4 years ($r = +.54$; $N = 14$). Using a fixed-trial procedure with 4-month-olds, Sigman, Cohen, Beckwith, and Parmelee (1986) found larger decrements predicting higher intelligence at 5 years of age ($r = +.44$). An earlier presentation of these data (Sigman, Cohen, Beckwith, & Parmelee, 1985), reported in terms of fixation duration, showed a large negative correlation ($r = −.69$) between duration measures and intelligence at 5 and 8 years. Rose et al. (1986) reported the only results involving habituation as assessed in an infant-control procedure and later intelligence. These show sizeable negative correlations (r's range from −45 to −.85 between duration measures and various standardized American and British intelligence scales) at 4.5 years of age.

Exploration and Play.   Given that visual inspection may simply reflect an exploratory resp͡ ıse, one might posit a correlation between visual attention to the environment and exploration or tempo in free-play situations. Kagan and Lewis (1965) first examined the relationships between various attentional mea-

---

[4]It is of further interest that short-term reliability data available for the Krinsky (1988) sample (reported in Bornstein & Benasich, 1986) also failed to indicate the existence of any test–retest reliability for these variables.

sures at 6 and 13 months and the amount of free-play locomotor activity at 13 months. Although qualified by a small sample and by results reported separately for boys and girls, the few substantial correlations indicated that infants with long fixation times at 6 and 13 months were more sedentary during free play. Fenson et al. (1974) found that the duration of 12-month-olds' visual attention was negatively correlated with preferences for novel toys in a free-play session, although the finding was much stronger for girls (mean $r = -.60$) than for boys ($r = -.15$). Pecheaux and Lecuyer (1983) reported similar findings for a sample of 24 4-month-olds, whose fixation time was positively correlated ($+.47$) with their visual exploration of a toy (sex differences were not analyzed).

Colombo, Mitchell, Dodd, Coldren, and Horowitz (1989) did not find any correlation between long- versus short-fixation patterns at 4 and 7 months and exploratory behavior at 16 months ($N = 23$). One last set of findings, which may relate to the generality of visual attention to exploratory situations, are significant correlations between individual differences in infants' attention to stimuli in laboratory tasks and their attention to mother in face-to-face interaction sessions reported for 3-month-olds (Coldren, 1987) and 4-month-olds (Sigman, Cohen, Forsythe, 1981). However, this relationship was not found at 6 months (Coldren, 1988).

SUMMARY AND CONCLUSIONS

Fixation Duration as a Measure of Infant Information Processing

In this chapter, we have examined the evidence on individual differences in infant visual attention. Although initial theoretical formulations based on the Sokolovian (1963) model would have proposed that measures of habituation rate (slope, decrement, number of trials to criterion) would best reflect the underlying cognitive processes, we contend that, under conditions in which the infant actually habituates, fixation duration provides a better index of these processes. Our case is based on three points.

First, fixation duration shows that the most robust and consistent developmental change across infancy, as attention to a visual stimulus will shorten with age during the first year; developmental changes in other attentional variables (e.g., decrement, number of trials to criterion) can be traced to the observed changes in duration. Second, duration variables exhibit the best individual consistency across both short- and long-test–retest intervals; once again, the consistency of other attentional measures appears to be attributable to the consistency of the duration variables from which they were derived. Third, measures of fixation duration predict infant performance on feature encoding, recognition memory, learning, and childhood performance on standardized language and intelligence tests. The established reliability and predictive validity of fixation time measures suggest to us that these measures best reflect developmental and individual differences in "process."

These contentions concerning the validity of fixation duration measures are further bolstered by the results of research with infants at varying amounts of risk for later cognitive deficits. Preterm infants have been reported to look longer at visual stimuli than full-term infants (Fantz & Fagan, 1975) and to need more fixation time to process stimuli than full terms (e.g., Rose, 1981). Down syndrome infants are reported to have longer mean fixation times than matched samples of normal infants (Cohen, 1981; Fantz, Fagan, & Miranda, 1975); although, based on the number of trials to habituation criterion, they habituate just as rapidly as normals (Cohen, 1981). Down syndrome infants are also reported to need longer amounts of fixation to process stimuli (Fantz et al., 1975; Miranda & Fantz, 1970).

The Process Question: What Does Duration Represent?

Despite encouraging findings that link fixation time to information-processing performance and later developmental status, it is important to note that it is still unclear what behavioral process or processes fixation duration might represent.

Exploration. First, individual and developmental differences in infant visual fixation time may reflect the propensity to explore the visual environment (Pecheaux & Lecuyer, 1983). Such a relationship has been broadly proposed to account for the correlation between infant novelty preferences and childhood IQ (Berg & Sternberg, 1985; Fagan, 1984) and may also well explain the relationship between fixation duration and novelty preferences with simple visual stimuli and brief familiarizations (Caron et al., 1977; Colombo et al., 1988). It also is relevant to claims that infant habituation and temperament are related (Wachs & Smitherman, 1985). Although this hypothesis is certainly plausible, it is hard put to explain the relationships between looking time and measures of cognitive performance such as stimulus processing (Mitchell & Horowitz, 1988) and learning (Lewis, 1969; Mitchell & Colombo, 1989).

Speed of Processing. Second, fixation time may reflect individual differences in the speed of stimulus or information processing, such that short-looking infants may process faster than long-looking ones (Colombo et al., 1987a, 1988; Colombo & Mitchell, 1989; Morrongiello, 1988). In our view, this possibility is widely supported by available data. Furthermore, this might both accommodate and supersede the observed correlations between fixation time and exploration, because infants and children who are more efficient processors might be more likely to show greater exploration or movement in novel situations; given that, they will be ready to "move on" to new things in their environment more quickly and more frequently than children who process more slowly. Finally, because speed or efficiency of processing is modestly related to adult IQ performance (Campione, Brown, & Ferrara, 1982; Cooper & Regan, 1982), we might expect that fixation time would also relate modestly to later childhood performance on standardized assessments (cf. Bornstein & Sigman, 1986; Rose et al., 1986; Sigman et al., 1986).

Whereas speed of processing is one aspect of information processing that varies with age (e.g., Kail, 1986; Kail & Siegel, 1977) and is believed to underlie many and varied aspects of cognitive function (Bjorklund, 1989), it is very important to note that, like the age variable in developmental research, "speed of processing" per se cannot be regarded as an explanatory construct.[5] As we use it, it refers only to the time necessary to process a visual stimulus, as accessed via fixation time during infancy. As such, one may attribute developmental and individual differences in processing speed to several determinants (e.g., Kail, 1986).

Structural Determinants of Processing Speed.   Such determinants may be termed *structural* in that they reflect some characteristic of the infant's CNS. An example of such a characteristic might be neural transmission rate, which may increase as a function of postnatal myelination or synaptogenesis. Short-looking infants may therefore simply have a more developmentally advanced or integrated CNS. Such a possibility is supported by negative correlations between fixation time and motor development (Colombo et al., 1987b), and positive correlations between fixation time and reaction time during operant conditioning (Lamarre & Pomerleau, 1985). In a global sense, this possibility is also supported by the "spurts" in the developmental course of fixation time that coincide with biobehavioral reorganizations during the first year (Emde, Gaensbauer, & Harmon, 1976), which are presumably behavioral manifestations of CNS maturation.

Operational Determinants of Processing Speed.   It is also possible, however, that differences in speed of processing in infancy as reflected by fixation time are due to differences in the operation of particular information-processing components. Short-looking infants may employ more efficient or mature "strategies" for acquiring visual information than long lookers. One specific type of strategy might involve attention to global versus local stimulus features. Because the processing of visual stimuli appears to proceed in a global-to-local sequence even in infancy (Ghim & Eimas, 1988), it is possible that short lookers might be better at the analysis of local stimulus features than long lookers. Such a possibility would account for short-lookers' better recognition performance than long lookers with letter stimuli (Colombo et al., 1988), given that letters have

---

[5]We acknowledge and thank George Kellas for bringing this point to our attention.

served as feature-detection prototypes in experiments with adults (Garner, 1979). It would also account for long-lookers' failure to completely process compound visual arrays (Mitchell & Horowitz, 1988).[6] This processing account is indirectly supported by robust developmental differences in visual scanning during infancy (e.g., Salapatek, 1975), which may be taken to indicate different "input" strategies at different times of development. Other variants of input strategies, such as the dimensionalization of visual stimuli (e.g., Smith, 1989) might also covary with infants' attentional patterns.

One corollary of this position is that speed–accuracy tradeoffs commonly observed with adult subjects (e.g., Cooper & Regan, 1982) should be observed with short- and long-looking infants in more complex processing tasks; that is, if the operational position is correct, we might expect long-looking infants to perform better on cognitive tasks that demand more time. Such an interaction of task and looking pattern remains untested.

Experiential Determinants of Processing Speed. A final possibility is that experience, or more accurately information stored as a function of experience, may bear on differences in speed of processing during infancy. Short-looking infants may simply have a larger "knowledge base" of stored stimulus features on which to draw. Such a base would reduce the amount of attentional effort necessary for the engram formation and stimulus comparison processes proposed to occur during habituation and thus might yield a mode of stimulus processing that is more "automatic," and thus take place in less time. Because such a knowledge base is acquired as a function of experience, it could account for both between- and within-age differences.

We have examined the cross-sectional and longitudinal samples described earlier to test for the possibility that infants' fixation times might decrease simply as a function of repeated testings within or across ages. However, significant decreases were not observed for looking time across weeks in the cross-sectional sample, nor were there differences in the fixation levels of the longitudinal and cross-sectional sample at the older ages tested. Perhaps the amount of "experience" we provided in this design was not extensive enough to produce the predicted experiential-based drop in fixation duration. When more extensive experience has been provided in other studies (Greenberg, 1971; Greenberg & Blue, 1977; Greenberg, O'Donnell, & Crawford, 1973; Horowitz et al., 1972a), the expected decrease in attention is observed. For example, Horowitz et al. (1972a) administered repeated fixed-trial sessions at weekly intervals from 3 to

---

[6]Perhaps the characterization of this stimulus analysis is better based on the contrast sensitivity function. Long lookers may be simply more susceptible to visual "capture" by high-salience stimuli (e.g., Cohen & Gelber, 1975), such as low spatial frequencies. We are indebted to discussions with Dr. Mary Williams and Dr. Genie Hartmann of the University of New Orleans for the articulation of this possibility.

14 weeks of age. Infants from this longitudinal sample exhibited a mean fixation ($M = 46.6$ s, averaged across a series of checkerboards) at 14 weeks that was nearly half of that observed for 14-week-olds seeing the same stimuli the first time ($M = 79.0$ s).

Directions for Future Research

Clearly, we favor research whose focus is the determination of what processing components contribute to individual and developmental variance in infant attention, and the manner in which they contribute to that variance (e.g., Cohen, 1988; Colombo & Mitchell, 1988). One profitable strategy toward this end would be the use of convergent measures in tandem with visual fixation. One example of this is Richards' (Casey & Richards, 1988; Richards, 1985a, 1985b, 1987, in press) excellent work on the interplay between early sustained attention and cardiac–respiratory responses. For example, Casey and Richards (1988) have shown infants to be less distractible during attentional periods defined by particular heart rate patterns. Additionally, links between duration of attention and patterns of visual scanning (e.g., Haith, 1980), which have not been actively pursued, would also be of interest to those looking to explicate more precisely the meaning of individual differences in early visual attention.

The limited amount of variance accounted for by measures of infant attention in concurrent and lagged predictions has been used to question the connection between attentional measures and early cognition (Malcuit et al., 1988a, 1988b; McCall, 1988). Instead, we believe that these correlations demonstrate the feasibility of functional relationships (see Abelson, 1985) between early attention and cognitive performance and set the stage for more controlled inquiry into the effortful cognitive operations (Kahneman, 1973) that must occur during infants' visual fixations.

ACKNOWLEDGMENTS

The research summarized in this chapter was supported by federal grants 5T32-HD07173, RO3-MH41395, RO3-MH43246, RO1-HD18290, University of Kansas Biomedical Research Support, and by the KU Mental Retardation Research Center.

We thank the staff of the University of Kansas Infant Study Center (especially Carla Dykeman, Paula Seikel, and Michelle Knoll) for assistance in subject recruitment and data collection, Mary Gersh and the staff of the University of Kansas Regents Center for cooperation and assistance, and the families of suburban Kansas City for their support of our research. We are grateful for the continued consultation and support of Frances Degen Horowitz. Constructive feedback on an earlier draft was provided by Robert McCall, Jeff Fagen, Jeff

Coldren, and Herb Gingold; George Kellas and John Belmont provided very helpful opinions on the speed of processing construct. Laura Maag proofread the manuscript and checked our references.

REFERENCES

Abelson, R. P. (1985). A variance explanation paradox: When a little is a lot. *Psychological Bulletin, 97,* 129–133.

Ames, E. W., Hunter, M. A., Black, A., Lithgow, P. A., & Newman, F. M. (1978). Problems of observer agreement in the infant control procedure. *Developmental Psychology, 14,* 507–511.

Barten, S., Birns, B., & Ronch, J. (1971). Individual differences in the visual pursuit behavior of neonates. *Child Development, 42,* 313–319.

Barten, S., & Ronch, J. (1971). Continuity in the development of visual behavior in young infants. *Child Development, 42,* 1566–1571.

Bartoshuk, A. K. (1962). Human neonatal cardiac acceleration to sound: Habituation and dishabituation. *Perceptual and Motor Skills, 15,* 15–27.

Bashinski, H., Werner, J., & Rudy, J. (1985). Determinants of infant fixation: Evidence for a two-process theory. *Journal of Experimental Child Psychology, 39,* 580–598.

Berg, C. A., & Sternberg, R. J. (1985). Response to novelty: Continuity vs. discontinuity in the developmental course of intelligence. In H. W. Reese (Ed.), *Advances in child development and behavior* (Vol. 15, pp. 1–47). New York: Academic Press.

Berlyne, D. E. (1958). The influence of complexity and albedo of stimuli on visual fixation in the human infant. *British Journal of Psychology, 49,* 315–318.

Bjorklund, D. F. (1989). *Children's thinking: Developmental function and individual differences.* New York: Brooks-Cole.

Bornstein, M. H. (1984, April). *Infant attention and caregiver stimulation: Two contributions to early cognitive development.* International Conference on Infant Studies, New York.

Bornstein, M. H. (1985). Habituation of attention as a measure of visual information processing in human infants: Summary, systematization, and synthesis. In G. Gottlieb & N. A. Krasnegor (Eds.), *Measurement of vision and audition in the first year of life* (pp. 253–301). Norwood, NJ: Ablex.

Bornstein, M. (1988). Answers to three prominent questions about habituation. *European Bulletin of Cognitive Psychology/Cahiers de Psychologie Cognitive, 8,* 531–538.

Bornstein, M. H., & Benasich, A. A. (1986). Infant habituation: Assessments of individual differences and short-term reliability at five months. *Child Development, 57,* 87–99.

Bornstein, M. H., & Pecheaux, M.-G. (1986). *The ontogenesis of habituation, novelty preference, and recognition memory.* Unpublished manuscript, New York University.

Bornstein, M. H., & Ruddy, M. (1984). Infant attention and maternal stimulation: Prediction of cognitive and linguistic development in singletons and twins. In H. Bouma & D. Bouwhuis (Eds.), *Attention and performance X: Control of language processes* (pp. 433–445). London: Lawrence Erlbaum Associates.

Bornstein, M. H., & Sigman, M. D. (1986). Continuity in mental development from infancy. *Child Development, 57,* 251–274.

Bridger, W. H. (1961). Sensory habituation and discrimination in the neonate. *American Journal of Psychiatry, 117,* 991–996.

Brooks, J., & Weinraub, M. (1976). A history of infant intelligence testing. In M. Lewis (Ed.), *Origins of intelligence* (pp. 19–58). New York: Plenum Press.

Bushnell, I. W. R. (1979). Modification of the externality effect in young infants. *Journal of Experimental Child Psychology, 28,* 211–229.

Byrne, J. M., Clark-Tousenard, M. E., Hondas, B. J., & Smith, I. M. (1985, April). *Stability of individual differences in infant visual attention.* Society for Research in Child Development, Toronto, Ontario.

Campione, J. C., Brown, A. L., & Ferrara, R. A. (1982). Mental retardation and intelligence. In R. J. Sternberg (Ed.), *Handbook of human intelligence* (pp. 392–492). Cambridge: Cambridge University Press.

Caron, R. F., & Caron, A. J. (1968). The effects of repeated exposure and stimulus complexity on visual fixation in infants. *Psychonomic Science, 10,* 207–208.

Caron, A. J., & Caron, R. F. (1981). Processing of relational information as an index of infant risk. In S. L. Friedman & M. D. Sigman (Eds.), *Preterm birth and psychological development* (pp. 219–240). New York: Academic Press.

Caron, A. J., Caron, R. F., Minichiello, M. D., Weiss, S. J., & Friedman, S. L. (1977). Constraints on the use of the familiarization–novelty method in the assessment of infant discrimination. *Child Development, 48,* 747–762.

Casey, B. J., & Richards, J. E. (1988). Sustained visual attention in young infants measured with an adapted version of the visual preference paradigm. *Child Development, 59,* 1514–1521.

Cohen, L. B. (1969). Observing responses, visual preferences, and habituation to visual stimuli in infants. *Journal of Experimental Child Psychology, 7,* 419–433.

Cohen, L. B. (1972). Attention-getting and attention-holding processes of infant visual preferences. *Child Development, 43,* 869–879.

Cohen, L. B. (1976). Habituation of infant visual attention. In T. Tighe & R. Leaton (Eds.), *Habituation* (pp. 207–238). Hillsdale, NJ: Lawrence Erlbaum Associates.

Cohen, L. B. (1981). Examination of habituation as a measure of aberrant infant development. In S. L. Friedman & M. D. Sigman (Eds.), *Preterm birth and psychological development* (pp. 241–253). New York: Academic Press.

Cohen, L. B. (1988). The relationship between infant habituation and infant information processing. *European Bulletin of Cognitive Psychology/Cahiers de Psychologie Cognitive, 8,* 442–444.

Cohen, L. B., DeLoache, J. S., & Pearl, R. D. (1977). An examination of interference effects in infants' memory for faces. *Child Development, 48,* 88–96.

Cohen, L. B., & Gelber, E. C. (1975). Infant visual memory. In L. Cohen & P. Salaptek (Eds.), *Infant perception: From sensation to cognition* (Vol. 1, pp. 347–404). New York: Academic Press.

Cohen, L. B., & Menten, T. G. (1981). The rise and fall of infant habituation. *Infant Behavior and Development, 4,* 269–280.

Coldren, J. T. (1987, April). *The relationship of infant attention across laboratory and social interaction tasks.* Society for Research in Child Development, Baltimore.

Coldren, J. T. (1988, April). *Habituation of infant attention during social interaction tasks.* International Conference on Infant Studies, Washington, DC.

Colombo, J., & Horowitz, F. D. (1985). A parametric study of the infant control procedure. *Infant Behavior and Development, 8,* 117–121.

Colombo, J., & Mitchell, D. W. (1988). Infant visual habituation: In defense of an information processing analysis. *European Bulletin of Cognitive Psychology/Cahiers de Psychologie Cognitive, 8,* 455–461.

Colombo, J., & Mitchell, D. W. (1989, April). *The development of infant visual habituation.* Society for Research in Child Development, Kansas City, MO.

Colombo, J., Mitchell, D. W., Coldren, J. T. & Atwater, J. D. (1990). Discrimination learning during the first year: Stimulus and positional cues. *Journal of Experimental Psychology: Learning, Memory, & Cognition, 16,* 98–109.

Colombo, J., Mitchell, D. W., Dodd, J., Coldren, J. T., & Horowitz, F. D. (1989). Longitudinal correlates of infant visual behavior in the paired-comparison paradigm. *Intelligence, 13,* 33–42.

Colombo, J., Mitchell, D. W., & Horowitz, F. D. (1988). Infant visual behavior in the paired-comparison paradigm: Test–retest and attention–performance relations. *Child Development, 58,* 1198–1210.

Colombo, J., Mitchell, D. W., O'Brien, M., & Horowitz, F. D. (1987a). The stability of visual habituation during the first year of life. *Child Development, 57,* 474–488.

Colombo, J., Mitchell, D. W., O'Brien, M., & Horowitz, F. D. (1987b). Stimulus and motoric influences on visual habituation to facial stimuli at three months of age. *Infant Behavior and Development, 10,* 173–181.

Cooper, L. A., & Regan, D. T. (1982). Attention, perception, and intelligence. In R. J. Sternberg (Ed.), *Handbook of human intelligence* (pp. 123–224). Cambridge: Cambridge University Press.

Dannemiller, J. L. (1984). Infant habituation criteria: I. A Monte Carlo study of the 50% decrement criterion. *Infant Behavior and Development, 7,* 147–166.

Denny, M. R., & Ratner, S. C. (1970). *Comparative psychology: Research in animal behavior.* Homewood, IL: Dorsey.

DeLoache, J. S. (1976). Rate of habituation and visual memory in infants. *Child Development, 47,* 145–154.

Emde, R., Gaensbauer, T., & Harmon, R. J. (1976). Emotional expression in infancy: A bio-behavioral study. *Psychological Issues: Monograph Series, 10.*

Engen, T., Lipsitt, L. P., & Kaye, H. (1963). Olfactory responses and adaptation in the human neonate. *Journal of Comparative and Physiological Psychology, 56,* 73–77.

Fagan, J. F. (1984). The relationship of novelty preferences during infancy to later intelligence and recognition memory. *Intelligence, 8,* 339–346.

Fantz, R. L. (1956). Form preferences in newly hatched chicks. *Journal of Comparative and Physiological Psychology, 50,* 422–430.

Fantz, R. L. (1958). Pattern vision in young infants. *Psychological Record, 8,* 43–49.

Fantz, R. L. (1961). The origin of form perception. *Scientific American, 204,* 66–72.

Fantz, R. L. (1963). Pattern vision in newborn infants. *Science, 140,* 296–297.

Fantz, R. L. (1964). Visual experience in infants: Decreased attention to familiar patterns relative to novel ones. *Science, 146,* 668–670.

Fantz, R. L., & Fagan, J. F. (1975). Visual attention to size and number of pattern details by term and preterm infants during the first six months. *Child Development, 46,* 3–18.

Fantz, R. L., Fagan, J. F., & Miranda, S. B. (1975). Early visual selectivity. In L. Cohen & P. Salapatek (Eds.), *Infant perception: From sensation to cognition* (Vol. 1, pp. 249–346). New York: Academic Press.

Fenson, L., Sapper, V., & Minner, D. G. (1974). Attention and manipulative play in the one-year-old child. *Child Development, 45,* 757–764.

Friedman, S., Bruno, L. A., & Vietze, P. (1974). Newborn habituation to visual stimuli: A sex difference in novelty detection. *Journal of Experimental Child Psychology, 18,* 242–251.

Garner, W. R. (1979). Letter discrimination and identification. In H. Pick (Ed.), *Perception and its development: A tribute to Eleanor Gibson* (pp. 111–144). Hillsdale, NJ: Lawrence Erlbaum Associates.

Ghim, H.-R., & Eimas, P. (1988). Global and local processing by 3- and 4-month-old infants. *Perception and Psychophysics, 43,* 165–171.

Greenberg, D. J. (1971). Accelerating visual complexity levels in the human infant. *Child Development, 42,* 905–918.

Greenberg, D. J., & Blue, S. Z. (1977). The visual preference-technique in infancy: Effect of number of stimuli presented upon experimental outcome. *Child Development, 48,* 131–137.

Greenberg, D. J., O'Donnell, W. J., & Crawford, D. (1973). Complexity levels, habituation, and individual differences in early infancy. *Child Development, 44,* 569–574.

Greenberg, D. J., & Weizmann, F. (1971). The measurement of visual attention in infants: A comparison of two methodologies. *Journal of Experimental Child Psychology, 11,* 234–243.

Groves, P. M., & Thompson, R. F. (1970). Habituation: A dual-process theory. *Psychological Review, 77,* 419–450.

Haaf, R. L., Smith, P. H., & Smitley, S. (1983). Infant response to facelike patterns under fixed-trial and infant-control procedures. *Child Development, 54,* 172–177.

Haith, M. M. (1980). *Rules that babies look by.* Hillsdale, NJ: Lawrence Erlbaum Associates.

Hayes, L. A., Ewy, R. D., & Watson, J. S. (1982). Attention as a predictor of learning in infants. *Journal of Experimental Child Psychology, 34,* 38–45.

Hess, E. H. (1975). *The tell-tale eye.* New York: Van Nostrand Reinhold.

Honzik, M. P. (1976). Value and limitations of infant tests: An overview. In M. Lewis (Ed.), *Origins of intelligence* (pp. 59–122). New York: Plenum Press.

Horowitz, F. D., Paden, L. Y., Bhana, K., Aitchison, R., & Self, P. A. (1972a). Developmental changes in infant visual fixation to differing complexity levels among cross-sectionally and longitudinally studied infants. *Developmental Psychology, 7,* 88–89.

Horowitz, F. D., Paden, L. Y., Bhana, K., & Self, P. A. (1972b). An infant control procedure for the study of infant visual fixations. *Developmental Psychology, 7,* 90.

Jeffrey, W. E., & Cohen, L. B. (1971). Habituation in the human infant. In H. W. Reese (Ed.), *Advances in child development and behavior* (Vol. 2, pp. 63–97). New York: Academic Press.

Kagan, J., & Lewis, M. (1965). Studies of attention in the human infant. *Merrill-Palmer Quarterly, 11,* 95–127.

Kahneman, D. (1973). *Attention and effort.* Engelwood Cliffs, NJ: Prentice Hall.

Kail, R. V. (1986). Sources of age differences in speed of processing. *Child Development, 57,* 969–987.

Kail, R. V., & Siegel, A. W. (1977). Mnemonic encoding in children. In R. V. Kail & J. W. Hagen (Eds.), *Perspectives on the development of memory and cognition* (pp. 61–88). Hillsdale, NJ: Lawrence Erlbaum Associates.

Kaplan, P. S., Scheuneman, D., Jenkins, L., & Hilliard, S. (1988). Sensitization of infant visual attention: Role of pattern contrast. *Infant Behavior and Development, 11,* 265–276.

Kaplan, P. S., & Werner, J. S. (1986). Habituation, response to novelty, and dishabituation in human infants: Tests of a dual-process theory of visual attention. *Journal of Experimental Child Psychology, 42,* 199–217.

Kaplan, P. S., & Werner, J. S. (1987). Sensitization and dishabituation of infant visual attention. *Infant Behavior and Development, 10,* 183–197.

Kaplan, P. S., Werner, J. S., & Rudy, J. W. (1988). Habituation, sensitization, and infant visual attention. In C. Rovee-Collier (Ed.), *Advances in infancy research.* Norwood, NJ: Ablex.

Krinsky, S. (1988, April). *Measures of infant habituation at five months and language proficiency at 24 months.* International Conference on Infant Studies, Washington, DC.

Lasky, R. E. (1979). Serial habituation or regression to the mean? *Child Development, 50,* 568–570.

Lamarre, G., & Pomerleau, A. (1985, July). *The meaning of individual differences in early habituation.* International Society for the Study of Behavioral Development, Tours, France.

Lewis, M. (1969). A developmental study of information processing within the first three years of life: Response decrement to a redundant signal. *Monographs of the Society for Research in Child Development, 34*(9, Whole #133).

Lewis, M. (1975). The development of attention and perception in the infant and young child. In W. M. Cruickshank & D. P. Hallahan (Eds.), *Perceptual and learning disabilities in children* (Vol. 2, pp. 137–162). Syracuse, NY: Syracuse University Press.

Lewis, M., & Brooks-Gunn, J. (1981). Visual attention at three months as a predictor of cognitive functioning at two years of age. *Intelligence, 5,* 131–140.

Lewis, M., Kagan, J., & Kalafat, J. (1966). Patterns of fixation in the young infant. *Child Development, 37,* 63–71.

Malcuit, G., Pomerleau, A., & Lamarre, G. (1988a). Habituation, visual fixation, and cognitive activity in infants: A critical analysis and attempt at a new formulation. *European Bulletin of Cognitive Psychology/Cahiers de Psychologie Cognitive, 8,* 415–440.

Malcuit, G., Pomerleau, A., & Lamarre, G. (1988b). Author's response. *European Bulletin of Cognitive Psychology/Cahiers de Psychologie Cognitive, 8,* 539–547.

Martin, R. M. (1975). Effects of familiar and complex stimuli on infant attention. *Developmental Psychology, 11,* 178–185.

McCall, R. B. (1975). Attention in the infant: Avenue to the study of cognitive development. In D. Walcher & D. L. Peters (Eds.), *Early childhood: The development of self-regulatory mechanisms* (pp. 107–137). New York: Academic Press.

McCall, R. B. (1973). Encoding and retrieval of perceptual memories after long-term familiarization and the infant's response to discrepancy. *Developmental Psychology, 9,* 310–318.

McCall, R. B. (1979a). Individual differences in the pattern of habituation at 5 and 10 months of age. *Developmental Psychology, 15,* 559–569.

McCall, R. B. (1979b). Qualitative transitions in behavioral development in the first two years of life. In M. Bornstein & W. Kessen (Eds.), *Psychological development from infancy* (pp. 183–224). Hillsdale, NJ: Lawrence Erlbaum Associates.

McCall, R. B. (1979c). The development of intellectual functioning in infancy and the prediction of later IQ. In J. Osofsky (Ed.), *Handbook of infant development* (pp. 707–741). New York: Wiley.

McCall, R. B. (1981). Toward an epigenetic conception of mental development in the first year of life. In M. Lewis (Ed.), *Origins of intelligence* (pp. 97–122). New York: Plenum Press.

McCall, R. B. (1988). Habituation, response to new stimuli, and information processing in human infants. *Cahiers de Psychologie Cognitive/European Bulletin of Cognitive Psychology, 8,* 481–488.

McCall, R. B. (in press). Individual differences in infancy. *Merril-Palmer Quarterly.*

McCall, R. B., Appelbaum, M., & Hogarty, P. (1973). Developmental changes in mental performance. *Monographs of the Society for Research in Child Development, 38*(3, Whole #150).

McCall, R. B., Eichorn, D., & Hogarty, P. (1977). Transitions in early mental development. *Monographs of the Society for Research in Child Development, 42*(3, Whole #171).

McCall, R. B., Hogarty, P. S., Hamilton, J. S., & Vincent, J. H. (1973). Habituation rate and the infant's response to visual discrepancies. *Child Development, 44,* 280–287.

McCall, R. B., & Kagan, J. (1967). Stimulus-schema discrepancy and attention in the infant. *Journal of Experimental Child Psychology, 5,* 381–390.

McCall, R. B., & Kagan, J. (1970). Individual differences in the infant's distribution of attention to stimulus discrepancy. *Developmental Psychology, 2,* 159–170.

McCall, R. B., Kennedy, C. B., & Dodds, C. (1977). The interfering effect of distracting stimuli on the infant's memory. *Child Development, 48,* 79–87.

Melhuish, E. C. (1982). Visual attention to mother's and stranger's faces and facial contrast in 1-month-old infants. *Developmental psychology, 18,* 229–231.

Miller, D. J. (1972). Visual habituation in the human infant. *Child Development, 43,* 481–493.

Miller, D. J., Ryan, E. B., Aberger, E., McGuire, M. D., Short, E. J., & Kenny, D. A. (1979). Relationships between assessments of habituation and cognitive performance in the early years of life. *International Journal of Behavioral Development, 2,* 159–170.

Miller, D. J., Ryan, E. B., Short, E. J., Ries, P. G., McGuire, M. D., & Culler, M. P. (1977). Relationships between early habituation and later cognitive performance in infancy. *Child Development, 48,* 658–661.

Miller, D. J., Ryan, E. B., Sinnott, J. P., & Wilson, M. A. (1976). Serial habituation in two-, three-, and four-month-old infants. *Child Development, 47,* 341–349.

Miller, D. J., Sinnott, J. P., Short, E. J., & Hains, A. A. (1976). Individual differences in habituation rates and object concept performance. *Child Development, 47,* 528–531.

Miller, D. J., Spiridigliozzi, G., Ryan, E. B., Callan, M. P., & McLaughlin, J. E. (1980). Habituation and cognitive performance: Relationships between measures at four years of age and earlier assessments. *International Journal of Behavioral Development, 3*, 131–146.

Miranda, S. B., & Fantz, R. L. (1970). Recognition memory in Down's Syndrome and normal infants. *Child Development, 45*, 651–660.

Mitchell, D. W., & Colombo, J. (1989, April). *Fixation time as a predictor of 3- and 4-month-olds' learning, retention, and transfer.* Society for Research in Child Development, Kansas City, MO.

Mitchell, D. W., & Horowitz, F. D. (1987, April). *Recognition and recall: A comparison of two procedures for assessing infant visual memory.* Society for Research in Child Development, Baltimore.

Mitchell, D. W., & Horowitz, F. D. (1988, April). *Processing of high- and low-saliency stimulus features by 3- and 4-month-old infants.* International Conference on Infant Studies, Washington, DC.

Mitchell, D. W., & Steiner, L. (1984, April). *Individual differences in habituation performance: Implications for recovery behavior.* International Conference on Infant Studies, New York.

Morrongiello, B. A. (1988). Habituation, visual fixation, and cognitive activity: Another "look" at the evidence. *European Bulletin of Cognitive Psychology/Cahiers de Psychologie Cognitive, 8*, 482–488.

Nelson, C., & Horowitz, F. D. (1983). The perception of facial expressions and stimulus motion by two- to five-month-old infants using holographic stimuli. *Child Development, 54*, 868–877.

Olson, G. M. (1976). An information-processing analysis of visual memory and habituation in infants. In T. Tighe & R. Leaton (Eds.), *Habituation* (pp. 239–277). Hillsdale, NJ: Lawrence Erlbaum Associates.

Olson, G. M., & Sherman, T. (1983). Attention, learning, and memory in infants. In M. M. Haith & J. J. Campos (Eds.), P. H. Mussen (Series Ed.), *Handbook of child psychology* (Vol. 2, pp. 1001–1080). New York: Wiley.

Pancratz, C., & Cohen, L. B. (1970). Recovery of habituation in infants. *Journal of Experimental Child Psychology, 9*, 208–216.

Pearce, J. M., & Hall, H. (1980). A model for Pavlovian learning: Variations in the effectiveness of conditioned but not of unconditioned stimuli. *Psychological Review, 87*, 532–552.

Pecheaux, M-G., & Lecuyer, R. (1983). Habituation rate and free exploration tempo in 4-month-old infants. *International Journal of Behavior Development, 6*, 37–50.

Rescorla, R. A., & Wagner, A. R. (1972). A theory of Pavlovian conditioning: Variations in the effectiveness of reinforcement and nonreinforcement. In A. H. Black & W. F. Prokasy (Eds.), *Classical conditioning II: Current research and theory.* New York: Appleton-Century-Crofts.

Richards, J. E. (1985a). Respiratory Sinus Arrhythmia predicts heart rate and visual responses during visual attention in 14 and 20 week old infants. *Psychophysiology, 22*, 101–109.

Richards, J. E. (1985b). The development of sustained visual attention in infants from 14 to 26 weeks of age. *Psychophysiology, 22*, 409–416.

Richards, J. E. (1987). Infant visual sustained attention and respiratory sinus arrhythmia. *Child Development, 58*, 488–496.

Richards, J. E. (in press). Heart rate changes and heart rate rhythms and infant visual sustained attention. In P. H. Ackles, J. R. Jennings, & M. G. H. Coles (Eds.), *Advances in psychophysiology* (Vol. 3). Greenwich, CT: JAI Press.

Ritz, E., Woodruff, A. B., & Fagen, J. W. (1984). Short- and long-term stability of habituation rate and looking time in four-month-old infants. *Journal of Genetic Psychology, 144*, 285–286.

Rose, S. A. (1981). Lags in the cognitive competence of prematurely born infants. In S. L. Friedman & M. D. Sigman (Eds.), *Preterm birth and psychological development* (pp. 255–270). New York: Academic Press.

Rose, D., Slater, A., & Perry, H. (1986). Prediction of childhood intelligence from habituation in early infancy. *Intelligence, 10*, 251–263.

Rovee-Collier, C. K. (1987). Learning and memory in infancy. In J. D. Osofsky (Ed.), *Handbook of infant development* (pp. 98–148). New York: Wiley.

Rovee-Collier, C. K. (1988). The adaptive significance of habituation in infancy. *European Bulletin of Cognitive Psychology/Cahiers de Psychologie Cognitive, 8*, 503–511.

Ruddy, M., & Bornstein, M. H. (1982). Cognitive correlates of infant attention and maternal stimulation over the first year of life. *Child Development, 53*, 183–188.

Saayman, G., Ames, E. W., & Moffitt, A. (1964). Response to novelty as an indicator of visual discrimination in the human infant. *Journal of Experimental Child Psychology, 1*, 189–198.

Salapatek, P. (1975). Pattern perception in early infancy. In L. Cohen & P. Salapatek (Eds.), *Infant perception: From sensation to cognition* (Vol. 2, pp. 133–248). New York: Academic Press.

Schaffer, H. R., Greenwood, A. R., & Parry, M. H. (1972). The onset of wariness. *Child Development, 43*, 165–175.

Sigman, M. D., Cohen, S. E., Beckwith, L., & Parmelee, A. H. (1985, July). *Infant attention in relation to intellectual abilities in childhood*. International Society for the Study of Behavioral Development, Tours, France.

Sigman, M. D., Cohen, S. E., Beckwith, L., & Parmelee, A. H. (1986). Infant attention in relation to intellectual abilities in childhood. *Developmental Psychology, 22*, 431–437.

Sigman, M. D., Cohen, S. E., & Forsythe, A. B. (1981). The relation of early infant measures to later development. In S. L. Friedman & M. Sigman (Eds.), *Preterm birth and psychological development* (pp. 313–327). New York: Academic Press.

Slater, A., Morison, V., & Rose, D. (1984). Habituation in the newborn. *Infant Behavior and Development, 7*, 183–200.

Smith, L. B. (1989). A model of perceptual classification in children and adults. *Psychological Review, 19*, 1–20.

Sokolov, E. (1963). *Perception and the conditioned reflex*. Oxford: Pergamon.

Stirnimann, F. (1944). Ubr das forbenempfinden neugeborener. *Annales Paediatrici, 163*, 1–25.

Tamis-LeMonda, C. S., & Bornstein, M. H. (1989). Habituation and maternal encouragement of attention in infancy as predictors of toddler language, play, and representational competence. *Child Development, 60*, 738–751.

Thompson, R. F., & Glanzman, D. L. (1976). Neural and behavioral mechanisms of habituation and sensitization. In T. Tighe & R. Leaton (Eds.), *Habituation* (pp. 49–93). Hillsdale, NJ: Lawrence Erlbaum Associates.

Thompson, R. F., & Spencer, W. A. (1966). Habituation: A model phenomenon for the study of neuronal substrates of behavior. *Psychological Review, 73*, 16–43.

Underwood, B. J. (1975). Individual differences as a crucible for theory construction. *American Psychologist, 30*, 128–134.

Uzgiris, I. C., & Hunt, J. McV. (1975). *Assessment in infancy*. Urbana, University of Illinois Press.

Valentine, C. W. (1913). The colour perception and colour preferences of an infant during its fourth and eighth months. *British Journal of Psychology, 6*, 363–386.

Wachs, T., & Smitherman, S. (1985). Infant temperament and subject loss in an habituation procedure. *Child Development, 56*, 861–867.

Watson, J. S. (1968). Operant fixation in visual preference behavior of infants. *Developmental Psychology, 1*, 508–516.

Werner, J. S., & Perlmutter, M. (1979). Development of visual memory in infants. In H. W. Reese & L. P. Lipsitt (Eds.), *Advances in child development and behavior* (Vol. 14). New York: Academic Press.

Wetherford, M. J., & Cohen, L. B. (1973). Developmental changes in infant visual preferences for novelty and familiarity. *Child Development, 44*, 416–424.

White, S., & Plum, G. (1964). Eye movement photography during children's discrimination learning. *Journal of Experimental Child Psychology, 1*, 327–338.

Wyckoff, L. B. (1952). The role of observing responses in discrimination learning. *Psychological Review, 59*, 431–442.

9 Infant Cognition: Individual Differences and Developmental Continuities

Susan A. Rose
Judith F. Feldman
Albert Einstein College of Medicine

BACKGROUND

Research on the nature of infant cognition and the existence of continuities in cognitive development has recently generated considerable interest and controversy. Until the past few years, the preponderance of evidence suggested that the relation between early infant competence and later cognitive performance was poor at best. In a review article, Kopp and McCall (1982) reported that the median correlation between developmental tests administered in the first 6 months of life and IQ scores at 2–4 years is only $r = .21$; the correlation drops to near zero when IQ scores at 5–7 years are the outcome variable. In unselected groups of normal infants, prediction improves beginning around 2 years, although it is still relatively poor; for example, the correlation between 2- and 5-year scores is only $r = .32$ (Honzik, Macfarlane, & Allen, 1948). By contrast, correlations obtained over a similar 3-year age span in later childhood are much higher (e.g., IQs assessed at 9 and 12 years correlate in the neighborhood of $r = .85$).

Overall, the classic longitudinal studies in the field have all indicated a lack of continuity in cognitive development between the first years of life and later childhood. As Bornstein (1988) observed: "these findings exerted a profound impact on psychological theorizing in the sense that they gave rise to general conclusions about instability in the nature and development of the human mind" (pp. 535–536).

A closer examination of the content of tests of mental development suggests, however, that the observed discontinuities between infancy and childhood might have more to do with the nature of the tasks that comprise these tests than with

229

the nature of intellectual development itself. Later tests of mental abilities depend heavily on complex cognitive processes, whereas the standard infant tests, such as the Bayley and Gesell, primarily assess imitation and sensory-motor competence. Measures assessing specific aspects of information processing in infancy might prove more appropriate for evaluating the presence or absence of cognitive continuities.

Many of the individual-difference studies have taken as their point of departure the innovative work in infant cognition where demonstrations of memory, categorization, abstraction, and the like are increasingly common (Olson & Sherman, 1983; Rose & Ruff, 1987; Rovee-Collier & Gekoski, 1979). Examination of encoding and retrieval skills currently occupy a central role in these studies. Such studies generally rely on the habituation or paired-comparison paradigm, both of which take advantage of the infant's tendency to respond differentially to novel and familiar stimuli. In the habituation paradigm, a visual stimulus is successively presented until the infant's attention to it wanes; then, during the dishabituation phase, a novel stimulus is presented. Attention generally increases to the novel stimulus. In the paired-comparison paradigm, the infant is first exposed to a visual stimulus for a fixed period of familiarization; then, in the test phase, the infant is shown the original stimulus paired with a novel one. Here, too, infants typically spend more time inspecting the novel member of the pair. In line with formulations put forth by Sokolov (1963), it is generally assumed that an engram or trace of the stimulus is formed during the familiarization or habituation phase. When the new stimulus is presented in the test phase, the infant is presumed to compare the new image either directly with the old one, or, in the case of habituation, with the memory trace of the old stimulus.

Although these paradigms initially were developed for laboratory studies of cognition, in the past few years they have been successfully adapted to the study of individual differences in cognitive ability (e.g., Caron, Caron, & Glass, 1983; Colombo & Mitchell, this volume; Colombo, Mitchell, & Horowitz, 1988; Colombo, Mitchell, O'Brien, & Horowitz, 1987; Fagan & McGrath, 1981; Fagan, Singer, Montie, & Shepherd, 1987; Fagan, Shepherd, & Montie, 1987; Lewis & Brooks-Gunn, 1981; Rose, Slater, & Perry, 1986). Two lines of investigation have most frequently been pursued. In one, groups of infants at risk for later cognitive deficit have been compared to nonrisk infants in their performance on these infant measures. In the other, the predictive validity of infant measures for later cognitive functioning has been examined directly.

Normal versus Risk Groups

There are now several studies showing that children expected to differ in intelligence later in life differ during infancy in their ability to recognize visual stimuli. These include infants suffering from Down syndrome (Cohen, 1981;

Miranda & Fantz, 1974), prematurity (Caron & Caron, 1981; Sigman, 1977; Sigman & Parmelee, 1974), failure to thrive (Fagan & Singer, 1983), nonoptimal perinatal events (Caron, Caron, & Glass, 1983), and exposure to chemical teratogens, such as PCB (Jacobson, Fein, Jacobson, Schwartz, & Dowler, 1985). Preterms have also been found to be slower to visually inspect and manually explore new objects (Sigman, 1977), more likely to use immature strategies of exploration (Ruff, McCarton, Kurtzberg, & Vaughan, 1984), and more likely to respond to the local features of a stimulus instead of the total pattern or configuration (Caron & Caron, 1981).

In a series of investigations from our own laboratory, we found that preterms often performed poorly on information-processing tasks relative to full terms. In one of these studies (Rose, 1980), 6-month-old-full term and preterm infants were tested on three problems of visual recognition memory. (The preterm groups used in this study had mean gestational ages of approximately 33 weeks, and mean birth weights of around 1,630 g.) In the first of two experiments reported in that study, preterms (N = 18) failed to differentiate between novel and familiar test stimuli on any of the problems, whereas full terms (N = 18) showed significant novelty preferences on two of the three. In a second experiment, the poor performance of preterms was replicated (N = 18). Of particular interest was the fact that the performance of preterms improved dramatically for a group (N = 18) given substantially increased familiarization times. This success suggests that, in general, the preterms were unable to encode the information as quickly as the full terms.

We replicated and extended these findings in a study where we introduced parametric variations in familiarization time, using 10, 15, 20, and 30 sec of familiarization (Rose, 1983). This study was carried out with 6- and 12-month-old full term and preterm infants (N = 20 in each of the 4 groups). (Both preterm groups had mean gestational ages of approximately 34.5 weeks and mean birth weights slightly greater than 1,800 g.) Although the older infants required less familiarization time than the younger ones, preterms of both age groups required considerably longer familiarization than full terms. At 6 months, full terms achieved significant scores with only 15 sec of familiarization, whereas preterms needed 30 sec; at 12 months, full terms achieved significant scores with as little as 10 sec of familiarization (the briefest interval used), whereas preterms required 20 sec. These results suggest that there are persistent differences between preterms and full terms throughout at least the first year of life in this very fundamental aspect of cognition.

These findings were further buttressed by results from a study of cross-modal transfer in 12-month-olds. In this study (Rose, Gottfried, & Bridger, 1978), we investigated infants' ability to recognize an object visually when the initial inspection or familiarization had been either tactual or oral—the infant must visually recognize a stimulus never seen, but only felt or mouthed. On these problems, middle-class full terms (N = 39) achieved successful transfer, whereas preterms (N = 28) and lower SES full terms (N = 27) did not. In other words, the preterms either failed to gain knowledge about the shape of an object by feeling it and mouthing it or were unable to make this information available to the visual system.

Preterms also seem to have more difficulty than do full terms in another aspect of intersensory functioning, namely, extracting visual information from objects that are explored in a multimodal fashion—by visual regard, touch, mouthing, and manipulation (Rose, Gottfried, & Bridger, 1979). Contrary to our expectations, a brief period of such multimodal exploration turned out to impede rather than facilitate subsequent visual recognition. Whereas this was true at more than one age, and for full terms as well as preterms, the negative effect was decidedly more pronounced for preterms.

Overall, studies from many laboratories are now beginning to provide a replicated network of findings to suggest that, even during the early months of life, "at-risk" infants are less capable than normal infants in learning about their world.

Prediction Studies

With respect to the predictive validity of infant measures, a number of recent studies have examined the relation of infant abilities to more standard measures of later cognition. Additionally, various measures of infant recognition memory, selective attention, habituation, and cross-modal transfer are proving to have good predictive validity (e.g., Caron, Caron, & Glass, 1983; Cohen & Parmelee, 1983; Fagan, 1984; Fagan & McGrath, 1981; Fagan & Singer, 1983; Fagan et al., 1986; O'Connor, Cohen, & Parmelee, 1984; Sigman, 1983; Sigman, Beckwith, Cohen, & Parmelee, 1986). Infants who habituate quickly, recognize new stimuli readily, or transfer information across modalities tend to perform well on traditional assessments of cognitive competence in later childhood. Fagan and Singer (1983) reported a median correlation of $r = .40$ between novelty scores (representing infants' differential attention to novel stimuli) and later outcome, and Bornstein and Sigman (1986), in a subsequent review, reported a median predictive correlation of $r = .46$ between later mental outcome and measures of habituation, dishabituation, and response to novelty. Other measures such as exploratory manipulation in 9-month-olds, visual attention in neonates, and auditory habituation in 4-month-olds were also related to later outcome (O'Connor, Cohen, & Parmelee, 1984; Ruff et al., 1984; Sigman, 1983; Sigman et al., 1986).

In two preliminary prediction studies from our laboratory, we found similar results. These studies were made possible when we discovered that some of the children who had participated in two of our experimental investigations of infant cognition were included in longitudinal studies being conducted by other investigators at our Kennedy Center. Follow-up developmental assessments included the Bayley scales at 12 and 24 months, the Stanford–Binet IQ at 34 and 40 months, and the WISC-R at 6 years. In the first of these studies (Rose & Wallace 1985a), we found strong positive correlations between novelty scores from 6-month-olds (N = 35) and the outcomes of those who returned for follow-up at 24 months (N = 28), 34 months (N = 14), 40 months (N = 17), and 6 years (N = 19): Correlations through 6 years ranged from .53 to .66. By contrast, early Bayley scores (at either 6 or 12 months) failed to predict these same outcomes. Although parental education also correlated strongly with outcome beginning at 2 years (rs = .32 to .68), when considered together in multiple correlations, it was clear that novelty scores significantly improved prediction, accounting independently for 20 to 28% of the variance in 2–6 year outcomes.

In the second study (Rose & Wallace, 1985b), similar follow-up data were available for a number of preterms (N = 33) who had participated in a study of cross-modal transfer and intramodal transfer (visual recognition memory) at 12 months. (One year follow-up data were also available for a group of 25 full terms tested on these same tasks at 12 months.) Both measures showed similar and reasonably strong relations to the outcomes of those who returned for follow-up at 24 months (N = 26), 34 months (N = 16), 40 months (N = 19), and 6 years (N = 21): Correlations through 6 years ranged from r = .38 to .64. As in the previous study, these early information-processing measures were unrelated to contemporaneous Bayley scores. Once again, they significantly predicted variance in outcome over and above that accounted for by parental education.

These early results are promising; even more so because correlations of the early information-processing measures with later outcome are uniformly higher than correlations obtained between performance on psychometric tests of early competence, such as the Bayley or Gesell, and measures of later outcome (Fagan & McGrath, 1981; Fagan & Singer, 1983; Fagan et al., 1986; Kopp & McCall, 1982; McCall, 1979). Even where early Bayley scores are predictive, as they turned out to be for one of the two samples in our current longitudinal study, they account for no unique variance; that is, when Bayley and early novelty scores are both entered into regressions predicting later IQ, only the latter contribute significantly to prediction (Rose et al., 1988).

CURRENT LONGITUDINAL STUDY

In the remainder of this chapter, we review some of our most recent work concerning individual differences and developmental continuities in infant information processing. This work comes from a prospective longitudinal study of high-risk preterms (birth weights < 1,500 g) and a comparison group of full terms of the same social status. Initially, the children were seen at 7 and 12 months (with subgroups seen additionally at 6, 8, and 11 months), then semiannually through 3 years, and annually thereafter through age 6. In infancy the children were tested for visual recognition memory and cross-modal transfer; on follow-up they received a battery of cognitive and behavioral assessments. Detailed results through 5 years have been presented elsewhere (Rose & Feldman, 1987; Rose, Feldman, McCarton, & Wolfson, 1988; Rose, Feldman, & Wallace, 1988, 1989; Rose, Feldman, Wallace, & McCarton, 1989). Here, we summarize some of the findings relevant to (a) the effect of developmental risk on infant performance, (b) the psychometric soundness of the infant measures, and (c) developmental continuities in certain facets of cognition. Finally we raise some questions about the link between infant performance and later intelligence, suggesting some future direction for this research.

Sample

The entire cohort, which has been studied from 7 months to 6 years, consists of 109 subjects, 63 preterms (9 of whom were not enrolled until 12 months), and 46 full terms. All subjects were drawn from the Bronx Municipal Hospital Center, a public hospital that serves a population that is largely minority, poor, and of lower social class.

Although the preterms have a higher percentage of females than do the full terms (62 vs. 41%) the two groups are similar in all other demographic factors: birth order, ethnicity, maternal age, maternal education, and SES. Most of the sample are black and hispanic, and more than 60% came from families in the two lowest social strata (unskilled and semiskilled). Because we invited into the study all eligible subjects born within a given time period, the resulting sex difference is due to happenstance. (There was no sex difference in acceptance rate.)

The full terms were not at medical risk, as they were selected on the basis of normal, healthy births. Preterms, on the other hand, were selected as a prototypic risk group: All were born weighing <1,500 g. Their birth weight actually averaged <1,200 g, and their gestational age averaged <32 weeks; 44% were small-for-gestational-age (SGA), and 73% suffered Respiratory Distress Syndrome (RDS). Because ultrasonography was not routinely available at the time these children were born, no grading of the severity of intraventricular hemorrhage was made. Given the low SES of these cohorts, the preterms could be considered as infants at "double hazard" (i.e., at both biologic and social risk; Escalona, 1982).

To date, the developmental outcomes indicate that the low birth-weight infants show persistent deficits. Preterms had lower scores than the full terms in virtually all developmental assessments of MDI/IQ; the mean difference between the two groups after 2 years of age ranged from 6 to 10 points, with the means of the preterm group generally in the 80s. Preterms were also poorer in language comprehension at 3 and 4 years. In comparison with full terms of the same SES, these children started out with a handicap that has persisted to the present day.

Note that these deficits are found even though preterms were tested at corrected age (i.e., age from expected date of birth). These data are of particular interest because they track performance over a lengthy time span (7 months–5 years), and because, unlike many earlier reports (which failed to include control groups), they indicate that the deficits found in low birth-weight preterms are not an artifact of these children's predominantly low SES.

Measures from Infancy

The measures from infancy that are of primary concern are those of visual recognition memory, visual attention, and cross-modal transfer. All were obtained when the children were 7 months of age. (Data on similar measures is available at older ages as well but has not yet been fully analyzed.)

Visual Recognition Memory. The major measure of visual recognition memory at 7 months is based on nine problems: Three used two-dimensional Abstract Patterns as stimuli, three used achromatic photographs of Faces, and three used three-dimensional Geometric Forms (as shown in Fig. 9.1 & 9.2 of Rose, Feldman, & Wallace, 1988). Each problem consists of a brief familiarization (5–20 sec, depending on the type of problem), followed by a 10- or 20-sec test in which the familiar is paired with a novel stimulus. Controls have been introduced to avoid positional biases, minimize procedural variance, and rule out observer bias. Novelty percentages were computed for each problem by dividing the time spent looking at the novel target on test by the time spent looking at both stimuli, and then multiplying by 100. Although aggregates of various sizes were examined, in the final analysis a single aggregate of all nine problems has turned out to be most useful and most strongly related to outcomes.

Visual Attention. Attention was measured indirectly by exposure-time scores. These scores index the time required to reach a predetermined amount of looking in the familiarization phase, that is, the time the stimulus was on display before the infant actually accumulated the requisite amount of looking. More attentive infants require shorter exposure time. Scores from the nine visual recognition problems were log transformed (because distributions were highly skewed), standardized, and averaged. This score and associated variables (shifts, pauses, fixations) has been useful for isolating differences in information gathering strategies used by preterms and full terms; moreover, unusually long exposure times are associated with compromised outcome.

Cross-Modal Transfer. At 7 months, there were only two problems. Both used three-dimensional geometric forms as stimuli, and each consisted of a tactual familiarization and visual test. These problems used the paired-comparison paradigm and differed from those of visual recognition memory only in that the familiarization was tactual instead of visual. For familiarization, the stimulus was placed in one of the infant's hands; the experimenter kept her hand cupped around the infant's hand to shield the object from the infant's view. Novelty scores were computed for each problem and averaged.

PRINCIPAL FINDINGS

Information Processing at 7-Months: Concurrent Validity

In the absence of a criterion measure for cognition in infancy, concurrent validity is often assessed by comparing normal infants with those thought to be at risk for cognitive deficits later on. Here then, we compared the performance of preterm infants to that of full terms on the 11 problems used at 7 months. These included nine problems of visual recognition memory and two of cross-modal transfer (Rose, Feldman, McCarton, & Wolfson, 1988). Novelty scores, which reflect the relative amount of time infants look at a new stimulus compared with a familiar one, were computed for each problem and aggregated over problems (with the size of the aggregate depending on the question being addressed). Exposure time was also scored to index the time required to reach the duration of looking required for the familiarization phase. These scores were considered a measure of attention (with more attentive infants having shorter exposure times).

On the visual problems, preterms had lower novelty scores than full terms (M = 51.6% vs. M = 55.2%), and required longer exposure times (primarily because of longer pauses between looks). In addition to spending more time off-target, preterms displayed less comparison behavior, as indexed by fewer shifts in gaze between paired targets. On the cross-modal problems, both groups exhibited significant preferences for the familiar stimuli (M = 42.9% and M = 41.5%). This latter finding is theoretically meaningful and suggests that the problems were relatively difficult, independent of risk status (Rose, Gottfried, Melloy-Carminar, & Bridger, 1982).

Among the various medical complications evaluated for preterms, gestational age, obstetrical complications, and Respiratory Distress Syndrome proved to be related to performance. Infants with higher novelty scores had higher gestational ages at birth ($r = .36$), fewer obstetrical complications ($r = .29$), and were less likely to have suffered severe RDS ($r = .44$). The relation between RDS and novelty remained significant even when other complications were partialled out. Lower exposure-time scores (particularly on Geometric Forms) were similarly related to these same risk factors.

Overall, the results of this study substantiate earlier findings of delays or deficits in visual recognition memory among preterms and extend them to a group at particularly high risk (those born weighing <1,500 g). In addition to deficits in visual recognition memory, these high-risk preterms exhibited difficulty in recruiting, maintaining, and shifting attention. Because the measures of recognition memory and attention are unrelated to one another and both show moderate stability (Rose & Feldman, 1987), each may reflect a different process that has some enduring significance for the infant.

Stability and Reliability of Early Infancy Measures

In adapting the infant measures from experimental work to the study of individual differences, issues concerning their psychometric soundness assume considerable importance. To be useful for assessing individual differences measures must show stability; that is, they must reflect a genuine characteristic that persists over time. They must also be reliable because reliability sets an upper limit to a measure's ability to correlate with other measures; specifically, the maximum correlation that can be expected between two measures is the square root of the product of their associated reliability coefficients.

Although recruitment for our longitudinal study was initially targeted to the infant's 7-month birthday, additional sessions were introduced at 6 and 8 months to assess short-term stability. Because these additional sessions were instituted only after testing was well underway (particularly for preterms, whose recruitment had begun prior to that of full terms), not all subjects were seen at all three time points.

Our first study of stability (Rose & Feldman, 1987) was based on those full terms who had complete data at each of the three ages on the first series of six problems (visual recognition memory for Abstract Patterns and Faces). Stability was moderate for the novelty scores, with cross-age correlations ranging from .30 to .50 across the 1- and 2-month period, and for exposure-time scores, with cross-age correlations ranging from .32 to .38. These measures were not correlated with one another, nor with contemporaneous 7-month Bayley scores, indicating that neither visual measure is simply mirroring the infant's overall developmental status. Instead, each reflects a different, and independent, component of infants' information processing. As discussed in the previous section, even though independent, both measures proved sensitive to the same medical risk factors (Rose, Feldman, McCarton, & Wolfson, 1988).

Stability coefficients were also computed for novelty scores using data for the entire cohort (Rose, Feldman, & Wallace, 1988), and including the second series of five problems (the three visual problems using geometric forms and the two cross-modal). In general, cross-age correlations again ranged from .30 to .50 and were similar whether the aggregates consisted of 6, 9, or all 11 problems.

Novelty scores are traditionally interpreted as a measure of recognition memory. We see the exposure-time scores as a measure of the infant's capacity to sustain attention: Infants with shorter exposure times are those who look at the stimulus more steadily (i.e., they have fewer pauses than those with longer exposure times). It would seem probable that the stability of these differences in concentrated versus dispersed looking patterns represents an important difference among infants in information-gathering styles or strategies.

Although the infant measures showed moderate stability over 1- and 2-month intervals, their internal consistency, as indexed by Chronbach's alpha, was surprisingly low. At 6, 7, and 8 months, alphas for the novelty scores did not exceed .24, even for composites containing up to 11 problems; the alphas were slightly higher when the four means (one for each type of problem) were used as components of the larger composites. Given that internal consistency is often used as an estimate of reliability, these findings were initially surprising. Apparently, more variance is unique to each problem than is shared among problems. In line with this notion, cross-age correlations involving identical problems proved to be consistently higher than those involving different problems.

Although it is puzzling that so little variance is shared across problems, it is by now a fairly common finding (Colombo, Mitchell, & Horowitz, 1988; Fagan & McGrath, 1981; Fagan & Singer, 1983). There are basically two reasons why this may have occurred. First, the stimuli may not have actually belonged to the same task domain. To achieve good internal consistency, it will be necessary to delineate more carefully the characteristics of stimuli that belong to a unitary domain. Yet it should be noted that interitem correlations were found to be surprisingly low even with stimuli that appear to have been well specified and homogeneous (Colombo et al., 1988). Second, it may be that interitem correlations will be low no matter now homogeneous the stimuli. Because each problem samples such a small fraction of infant behavior, moment-to-moment fluctuations in attention can carry considerable weight. If the vagaries in infant attention could be better controlled, or variations in attention were carefully assessed, and their effects removed, error variance might be reduced and the percentage of shared variance increased.

Because measures that are unreliable cannot correlate highly with anything else (and these measure do), the stability figures would leave one to conclude that, unless interitem correlations can be substantially improved, reliability for such measures is better estimated by test–retest methods.

Predictive Validity of Early Measures for Later Cognition

In the first of two prediction studies (Rose, Feldman, & Wallace, 1988), scores for aggregates of 6–11 problems were obtained at 6, 7, and 8 months and then correlated with 3-year IQ. At all three ages, these scores were significantly related to later IQ. Correlations ranged from .37 to .63 and clustered between .50 and .60. The predictive relations were similar for both groups, and it made little difference at which of the three ages the infant assessments had been obtained. However, in multiple regressions, aggregates from different ages often contributed independently of one another to the prediction of outcome, as indicated by the semipartial correlations. Using measures from two or three ages led to multiple correlations as high as R = .72. In addition, cutoffs for predicting children at risk for mental retardation (IQ <70) or cognitive delay (IQ <85) showed reasonable sensitivity and specificity.

In the second study (Rose, Feldman, Wallace, & McCarton, 1989), the 7-month aggregate comprised of all nine problems of visual recognition memory was used to predict MDI/IQ outcomes across the first 5 years of life—at 1, 1.5, 2, 3, 4, and 5 years. Novelty scores were significantly and consistently related to outcome beginning at 2 years. Correlations ranged from .37 to .65 and were similar for both preterms and full terms. Ability to sustain attention during the familiarization phase was also related to outcome: Infants who took longer to reach the looking criteria had lower MDI/IQ scores. By contrast, none of the correlations between concurrent (7-month) Bayley scores and outcomes were significant for full terms and, with one exception, none were significant beyond 1.5 years for preterms. This standard infant test had some predictive value for the more high-risk children (preterms), but its value decreased with age. Novelty scores were related to later intelligence independently of SES, maternal education, and medical risk. Correlations of novelty scores with outcome could not be accounted for by the inclusion of the few children with neurological handicaps (N = 5) or very low IQ (<70), because the associations remained high when they were omitted from the analyses. The relation of novelty score to outcome appears to be robust with respect to sample characteristics, medical risk, and age of outcome, at least through the preschool years.

Novelty Scores, Language, and IQ

The findings emerging from studies of infant visual recognition memory, habituation, and cross-modal transfer point to a link with later intelligence. For the following reasons it was thought that this relation might be due to variance that the early and later measures share with language: (a) many of the intelligence tests are themselves highly dependent on linguistic skills; (b) early measures actually predict later language proficiency as well as IQ; and (c) it has been suggested that both the infant measures and language tap the same fundamental cognitive process, namely categorization (Bornstein & Sigman, 1986). Unlike earlier studies, we had included an assessment of language, the Reynell Developmental Language Scale (Reynell, 1969), as well as intelligence at ages 3 and 4 years so we could examine this issue directly.

The 7-month novelty scores were nearly as strongly related to 3- and 4-year language scores as they were to IQ (Rose, Feldman, & Wallace, 1989). This was true for both groups and for both aspects of language: comprehension and expression. Although the correlations with IQ were somewhat reduced when the variance shared with language was partialled out, for the most part, they remained significant and moderately high (*pr* = .28 to *pr* = .53). This result supports the notion that IQ consists of two components—a language component plus a language-free component—and that infants' novelty scores predict both. On the other hand, with IQ removed from language, the novelty-language relations were considerably reduced in magnitude. Thus a substantial portion of the novelty-IQ relation is independent of language (i.e., language-free, but the reverse is not the case).

Summary

In summary, the results to date indicate that the early measures of information processing from infancy (a) show modest cross-age stability; (b) consistently predict later cognitive status, at least through the age of 5 years; (c) uniquely predict variance in IQ and language proficiency not accounted for by early Bayley scores, SES, or medical risk; (d) have reasonably high sensitivity and specificity for predicting IQ; and (e) predict IQ even after variance shared with language is partialled out.

CONCLUSIONS

Overall, there is now growing evidence that cognitive abilities can be assessed in infancy, and that individual differences in these abilities have greater import for later cognitive status than previously believed. Indeed, there appears to be a strong thread of continuity in intellectual functioning extending from infancy onwards. Although these are exciting initial findings, they throw into bold relief how little we know about the nature of early cognition, its developmental course, and the qualities of mind that form the basis for the longitudinal relations observed. In this regard, the measures of cognition used to assess infant functioning and those used to assess outcome both require closer examination.

To better understand developmental continuities, it is essential to identify more specific aspects of the mental processes involved. For example, let's consider novelty scores. Although they have generally been viewed as measures of short-term memory (Fagan & McGrath, 1981), it is clear that they subsume a diversity of processes. To respond preferentially to a novel stimulus in the paired-comparison paradigm, the infant must have encoded the initial information during the familiarization phase, stored it in memory, accessed that memory during the test phase, and then compared and discriminated the old from the new. These acts implicate the processes of encoding, storage, retrieval, discrimination, and comparison. Variation in any one of these could differentially affect novelty scores. To determine the relative importance of these component processes, each needs to be measured separately. Such measures could then be related to measures of the same cognitive processes at later ages.

Alternatively, overarching or more general processes may be involved. For example, Fagan (1984) has suggested that the link between novelty preference and cognition may consist of some general "g"-like factor related to speed of processing. Such a factor could encompass individual differences in the rate or efficiency of encoding, storing, and/or retrieving information. Deary (1988) notes that, historically, attempts to correlate speed of encoding with estimates of intelligence, although few in number, have been relatively successful. Another possibility, suggested by Bornstein and Sigman (1986), is that mental representation may be a common thread for continuity. The formation of percepts and categories involves the extraction of salient features, commonalities, or invariances from the perceptual flux. Perhaps these processes lie at the heart of various infant competencies and later intelligence.

A further possibility is that noncognitive factors, such as motivation or arousal, may play a role in infant-to-child correlations (see Bornstein & Sigman, 1986). For example, novelty scores could reflect variations in infants' proclivity to attend to new events, rather than variations in their short-term memory or encoding speed (see e.g., Berg & Sternberg, 1985; Colombo, Mitchell, & Horowitz, 1988). In other words, some infants may fail to attend to novel stimuli because of a tendency to shun change, not because of poorer memories. The individual's characteristic level of arousal could also play a role. As Sigman (1988) notes, "The infant who is able to regulate states of arousal so as to attend effectively may maintain this capacity for self regulation so that attending and learning are easier in childhood" (p. 513). If variations in the capability for self-regulation were to remain stable, they could underpin stabilities between infant and childhood measures.

To understand what the infant measures mean, it will also be necessary to move in new directions on the outcome end. Most prediction studies have used a single type of outcome measure, generally a traditional intelligence test, such as the Stanford–Binet or WISC–R. These tests consist of a variety of tasks, each of which tap various functions, such as digit span, short-term memory, verbal comprehension, the perception and manipulation of geometric patterns, etc. The intelligence quotient, commonly referred to as IQ, is a weighted composite of scores on these separate tasks. Such tests were a logical choice as an initial outcome measure because they estimate well the variance common to most tests of mental ability. They provide a quantitative perspective on the nature of intellectual growth that allows for a meaningful comparison of individual children.

Whereas there is no doubt that intelligence tests provide a highly reliable estimate of global mental ability, they have two important limitations in terms of what they tell us about the nature of intellectual functioning. First, although made up of tasks that are presumably unrelated, these various components are nearly always highly intercorrelated. Thus, they do not represent specific abilities, as demonstrated by the fact that they generally load highly on the first principal component that emerges in factor analytic studies (Detterman, 1987a,

1987b; Jensen, 1987). Spearman (1927) speculated that this strong first principal component was due to a single underlying variable. In other words, a single ability would appear to determine performance on what are ostensibly very different tasks (Hunt, 1983). Others have suggested that the high loadings on a single factor are not a fundamental characteristic of intelligence as much as how it has been measured (e.g., Detterman, 1987a). In Detterman's conceptualization, intelligence can be thought of as consisting of components that (a) are relatively independent of one another and that (b) when taken together account for most of the variance in IQ. Detterman has obtained empirical findings compatible with this conceptualization.

Second, factors derived from the popular factor-analytic approach have no psychological reality as components of intelligence. They are statistical abstractions and not a measure of any definable mental ability (Hunt, 1983; Sternberg, 1977, 1985). They do not identify any aspect of individual performance that would be important on theoretical grounds, such as memory strategies, inferential abilities, symbol manipulation, capacity factors, the representation of information, problem-solving strategies, etc. In contrast to traditional approaches, information-processing theorists seek to identify and study precisely such basic processing skills (Cooper & Regan, 1982).

We would like to suggest that, if we are to account for infant-to-child continuities, it will be necessary to bring developmental and information-processing theorists together. The developmental approach is essential for specifying change and continuity in individual differences. Because development is not always a linear process but is frequently characterized by transitions or abrupt changes in capability, this will be no easy task. As a first step, developmental transitions will have to be identified and understood. In particular, it is not clear whether the processes involved in memorial organization, storage, and retrieval are fundamentally the same across age. The observed continuities in development could reflect stabilities in one or more underlying processes, or they could come about because skilled execution of one process at an early age sets the stage for skilled execution of a different process at a later age. We need to elucidate the nature of the infant measures, specify more precisely their relation to later measures, and identify the component mental processes. A careful investigation of such issues will enrich our understanding of individual differences and of the nature of the human mind.

ACKNOWLEDGMENTS

This work was supported by a Social and Behavioral Sciences Research Grant from the March of Dimes Birth Defects Foundation, by Grants HD 13810 and HD 01799 from the National Institute of Child Health and Human Development, and by NIMH Postdoctoral National Research Service Award MH 15151. We would like to express our appreciation to Frances Goldenberg, Patricia Melloy-Carminar, and Johanna Wolfson for their assistance in testing subjects, to Cecelia M. McCarton and Ina F. Wallace for their collaboration in much of the work presented here, and to Robert R. Golden for his helpful discussions of statistical issues. This work was facilitated by Grant HD10799 to the Rose F. Kennedy Center For Research and Human Development.

REFERENCES

Berg, C. A., & Sternberg, R. J. (1985). Response to novelty: Continuity versus discontinuity in the developmental course of intelligence. In H. W. Reese (Ed.), *Child development and behavior* (Vol. 19, pp. 1–47). New York: Academic Press.

Bornstein, M. H. (1988). Answers to three prominent questions about habituation. *Cahiers de Psychologie Cognitive/European Bulletin of Cognitive Psychology, 8,* 415–440.

Bornstein, M. H., & Sigman, M. D. (1986). Continuity in mental development from infancy. *Child Development, 57,* 251–274.

Caron, A. J., & Caron, R. F. (1981). Processing of relational information as an index of infant risk. In S. L. Friedman & M. Sigman (Eds.), *Preterm birth and psychological development.* New York: Academic Press.

Caron, A. J., Caron, R. F., & Glass, P. (1983). Responsiveness to relational information as a measure of cognitive functioning in nonsuspect infants. In T. Field & A. Sostek (Eds.), *Infants born at risk: Physiological, perceptual and cognitive processes.* New York: Grune & Stratton.

Cohen, L. B. (1981). Examination of habituation as a measure of aberrant infant development. In S. L. Friedman & M. Sigman (Eds.), *Preterm birth and psychological development.* New York: Academic Press.

Cohen, S. E., & Parmelee, A. H. (1983). Prediction of five-year Stanford–Binet scores in preterm infants. *Child Development, 54,* 1242–1253.

Colombo, J., Mitchell, D. W., & Horowitz, F. D. (1988). Infant visual behavior in the paired-comparison paradigm: Test–retest and attention–performance relations. *Child Development, 59,* 1198–1210.

Colombo, J., Mitchell, D. W., O'Brien, M., & Horowitz, F. D. (1987). The stability of visual habituation during the first year of life. *Child Development, 58,* 474–487.

Cooper, L. A., & Regan, D. T. (1982). Attention, perception and intelligence. In R. J. Sternberg (Ed.), *Handbook of human intelligence* (pp. 123–169). New York: Cambridge University Press.

Deary, I. J. (1988). Intelligence and encoding speed in infants, adults and children. *Cahier de Psychologie Cognitive/European Bulletin of Cognitive Psychology, 8,* 462–468.

Detterman, D. K. (1987a). Theoretical notions of intelligence and mental retardation. *American Journal of Mental Deficiency, 92,* 2–11.

Detterman, D. K. (1987b). What does reaction time tell us about intelligence? In P. A. Vernon (Ed.), *Speed of information processing and intelligence* (pp. 177–199). Norwood, NJ: Ablex.

Escalona, S. K. (1982). Babies at double hazard: Early development of infants at biologic and social risk. *Pediatrics, 70,* 670–676.

Fagan, J. F. (1984). The relationship of novelty preferences during infancy to later intelligence and recognition memory. *Intelligence, 8,* 339–346.

Fagan, J. F., & McGrath, S. K. (1981). Infant recognition memory and later intelligence. *Intelligence, 5,* 121–130.

Fagan, J. F., & Singer, L. T. (1983). Infant recognition memory as a measure of intelligence. In L. P. Lipsitt (Ed.), *Advances in infancy research* (Vol. 2, pp. 31–78). Norwood, NJ: Ablex.

Fagan, J. F., Shepherd, P. A., & Montie, J. E. (1987). A screening test for infants at risk for mental retardation. *Journal of Developmental and Behavioral Pediatrics, 8,* 118.

Fagan, J. F., Singer, L. T., Montie, J. E., & Shepherd, P. A. (1986). Selective screening device for the early detection of normal or delayed cognitive development in infants at risk for later mental retardation. *Pediatrics, 78,* 1021–1026.

Honzik, M. P., Macfarlane, J. W., & Allen, L. (1948). The stability of mental test performance between two and eighteen years. *Journal of Experimental Education, 18,* 309–324.

Hunt, E. (1983). On the nature of intelligence. *Science, 219,* 141–146.

Jacobson, S. W., Fein, G. G., Jacobson, J. L., Schwartz, P. M., & Dowler, J. K. (1985). The effect of intrauterine PCB exposure on visual recognition memory. *Child Development, 56,* 853–860.

Jensen, A. R. (1987). Individual differences in the Hick paradigm. In P. A. Vernon (Ed.), *Speed of information-processing and intelligence,* Norwood, NJ: Ablex.

Kopp, C. B., & McCall, R. B. (1982). Predicting later mental performance for normal, at-risk, and handicapped infants. In P. B. Bates & O. G. Brim (Eds.), *Life-span development and behavior* (Vol. 4, pp. 33–61). New York: Academic Press.

Lewis, M., & Brooks-Gunn, J. (1981). Visual attention at three months as a predictor of cognitive functioning at two years. *Intelligence, 5,* 131–140.

McCall, R. B. (1979). The development of intellectual functioning in infancy and the prediction of later IQ. In J. D. Osofsky (Ed.), *Handbook of infant development* (pp. 704–741). New York: Wiley.

Miranda, S. B., & Fantz, R. L. (1974). Recognition memory in Down's syndrome and normal infants. *Child Development, 45,* 651–660.

O'Connor, J. J., Cohen, S., & Parmelee, A. H. (1984). Infant auditory discrimination in preterm and full-term infants as a predictor of 5-year intelligence. *Developmental Psychology, 20,* 159–165.

Olson, G. M., & Sherman, T. (1983). Attention, learning and memory in infants. In M. M. Haith & J. J. Campos (Eds.), P. H. Mussen (Series Ed.), *Handbook of child psychology: Vol. 2. Infancy and developmental psychobiology* (pp. 1001–1080). New York: Wiley.

Reynell, J. K. (1969). *The Reynell Developmental Language Scales.* Slough, Bucks: NFER.

Rose, D. H., Slater, A., & Perry, H. (1986). Prediction of childhood intelligence from habituation in early infancy. *Intelligence, 10,* 251–263.

Rose, S. A. (1980). Enhancing visual recognition memory in preterm infants. *Developmental Psychology, 16,* 85–92.

Rose, S. A. (1983). Differential rates of visual information processing in fullterm and preterm infants. *Child Development, 54,* 1189–1198.

Rose, S. A., & Feldman, J. F. (1987). Infant visual attention: Stability of individual differences from six to eight months. *Developmental Psychology, 23,* 490–498.

Rose, S. A., Feldman, J. F., McCarton, C. M., & Wolfson, J. (1988). Information processing in seven-month-old infants as a function of risk status. *Child Development, 59,* 589–603.

Rose, S. A., Feldman, J. F., & Wallace, I. F. (1988). Individual differences in infant information processing: Reliability, stability and prediction. *Child Development, 59,* 1177–1197.

Rose, S. A., Feldman, J. F., & Wallace, I. F. (1989). *Language: A partial link between infant attention and later intelligence.* Manuscript submitted for publication.

Rose, S. A., Feldman, J. F., Wallace, I. F., & McCarton, C. M. (1989). Infant visual attention: Relation to birth status and developmental outcome during the first five years. *Developmental Psychology, 25,* 560–576.

Rose, S. A., Gottfried, A. W., & Bridger, W. H. (1978). Cross-modal transfer in infants: Relationship to prematurity and socio-economic background. *Developmental Psychology, 14,* 643–652.

Rose, S. A., Gottfried, A. W., & Bridger, W. H. (1979). Effects of haptic cues on visual recognition memory in full-term and preterm infants. *Infant Behavior and Development, 2,* 55–67.

Rose, S. A., Gottfried, A. W., Melloy-Carminar, P. M., & Bridger, W. H. (1982). Familiarity and novelty preferences in infant recognition memory: Implications for information processing. *Developmental Psychology, 18,* 704–713.

Rose, S. A., & Ruff, H. A. (1987). Cross-modal abilities in human infants. In J. D. Osofsky (Ed.), *Handbook of infant development* (2d ed., pp. 318–362). New York: Wiley.

Rose, S. A., & Wallace, I. F. (1985a). Cross-modal and intra-modal transfer as predictors of mental development in fullterm and preterm infants. *Developmental Psychology, 21,* 949–962.

Rose, S. A., & Wallace, I. F. (1985b). Visual recognition memory: A predictor of later cognitive functioning in preterms. *Child Development, 56,* 843–852.

Rovee-Collier, C. K., & Gekoski, M. J. (1979). The economics of infancy: A review of conjugate reinforcement. In H. W. Reese & L. P. Lipsitt (Eds.), *Advances in child development* (Vol. 13, pp. 195–255). New York: Academic Press.

Ruff, H. A., McCarton, C., Kurtzberg, D., & Vaughan, H. G. (1984). Preterm infants' manipulative exploration of objects. *Child Development, 55,* 1166–1173.

Sigman, M. (1977). Early development of preterm and fullterm infants: Exploratory behavior in eight-month-olds. *Child Development, 47,* 606–612.

Sigman, M. (1983). Individual differences in infant attention: Relation to birth status and intelligence at five years. In T. Field & A. Sostek (Eds.), *Infants born at risk: Physiological, perceptual and cognitive processes.* New York: Grune & Stratton.

Sigman, M. (1988). Infant attention: What processes are measured? *Cahier de Psychologie Cognitive/European Bulletin of Cognitive Psychology, 8,* 512–516.

Sigman, M., Beckwith, L., Cohen, S. E., & Parmelee, A. H. (1986). Infant attention in relation to intellectual abilities in childhood. *Developmental Psychology, 22,* 788–792.

Sigman, M., & Parmelee, A. H. (1974). Visual preferences of four-month-old premature and fullterm infants. *Child Development, 45,* 959–965.

Sokolov, E. N. (1963). *Perception and the conditioned reflex.* New York: Macmillan.

Spearman, C. (1927). *The abilities of man.* London: Macmillan.

Sternberg, R. J. (1977). *Intelligence, information processing, and analogical reasoning: The componential analysis of human abilities.* Hillsdale, NJ: Lawrence Erlbaum Associates.

Sternberg, R. J. (1985). *Beyond IQ: A triarchic theory of human intelligence.* New York: Cambridge University Press.

10 Individual Differences in Sustained Attention during Infancy

Holly A. Ruff
Albert Einstein College of Medicine

Attention refers to the orienting of the perceptual apparatus toward some specific aspect of the environment; in addition, the term *sustained attention* implies that effort is expended for the purpose of gathering information, acting on the information, and, frequently, progressing toward a goal (Kahneman, 1973). Some argue that attention overlaps with awareness (Posner, 1978) and can be directed covertly as well as overtly to locations in the environment. In some ways, attention can be considered a state that makes the organism more receptive to environmental events and more likely to engage in effortful activity; the state may be reflected in behavioral indices (e.g., Anderson, Choi, & Lorch, 1987; Campbell, 1985; Elliot, 1970; Ruff, 1986; Ruff & Lawson, 1990), in aspects of autonomic functioning (Porges, 1972, 1976; Richards, 1988), and in the functioning of neurons in the central nervous system (Näätänen, 1982; Spitzer, Desimone, & Moran, 1988). The major questions addressed in this chapter are whether there are, in the first year or two of life, stable individual differences in the tendency to maintain attention over time, and if so, what the origins and consequences of the differences are.

What measures are likely to reflect the underlying construct of sustained attention? The most common is a measure of the *duration* of time that children spend oriented to pictures, toys, tasks, or locations. It may be important, however, to gather information about the intensity or degree of effort that is involved (Berlyne, 1970; Kahneman, 1973) and not assume that all activity directed toward a target is equally concentrated. Richards (1988) has differentiated between looking at objects and more active attention by using heart rate as well as behavioral measures. Ruff and Lawson (1990; see also Ruff, 1986, 1988) have found it useful to differentiate behaviorally between the durations of more concentrated and more casual attention during play. In the mastery motivation literature, the different levels of mastery behavior can also be seen as different intensities of engagement in the task (Messer, McCarthy, McQuiston, MacTurk, Yarrow, & Vietze, 1986). Because attention is a quality of interaction between the individual and the environment (Gibson & Rader, 1979), global qualitative ratings, such as ''very attentive'' or ''very inattentive,'' may be useful in capturing the intensity or degree of attention (Ruff, Lawson, Parrinello, & Weissberg, 1990; Wenar, 1976).

We also have to consider that attention occurs in the context of specific activities and particular goals. The maintenance of attention in infancy, therefore, can be and has been studied in a wide variety of situations: infants' observation of static and moving objects and events (Richards, 1988; Cohen, DeLoache, & Strauss, 1979); exploration and play with objects (e.g., McCall, 1974; Ruff, 1986; Ruff et al., 1990); activity in goal-oriented situations (Jennings, Harmon, Morgan, Gaiter, & Yarrow, 1979; Yarrow, McQuiston, MacTurk, McCarthy, Klein, & Vietze, 1983); searching for hidden objects (Goldfield & Dickerson, 1981; Horobin & Acredolo, 1986); and simply waiting for expected events (Donohue & Berg, 1988; Ruff, Capozzoli, Dubiner, & Parrinello, 1990). The fact that attention has been measured under such different conditions raises the question of whether the attention observed in these different contexts reflects a unitary phenomenon, or whether there are multiple processes involved in attention, only some of which may be called on in any given situation (Posner & Boies, 1971; Pribram & McGuinness, 1975). The possible existence of multiple processes underlying sustained attention has important implications for the issue of individual differences; that is, we may find evidence for stable individual differences in attention that transcend particular situations, or we may find individual differences only in specific situations with little cross-situational consistency. Our understanding of individual differences in attention will clearly depend on a systematic study of the effects of different objects, different circumstances, and different demands on the infant's attention.

From a methodological point of view, individual differences are searched for and discovered in correlations of the same behavior over time, and in correlations of related and concurrently measured constructs. The infant, however, is a rapidly developing organism, and individual differences have to be seen in the framework of the developmental changes that occur. These changes are likely to affect what is attended to as well as the extent to which attention is maintained in different situations.

The goal of this chapter is to discuss (a) the contexts in which sustained attention occurs, (b) the extent to which maintenance of attention can be considered a stable individual characteristic, (c) the relationship of attention to temperamental characteristics, (d) the potential consequences of such differences, and (e) possible contributing factors to such differences. At the end of the chapter, I summarize the discussion by suggesting a number of directions for further research.

OBSERVED DIFFERENCES
IN ATTENTION AND PERSISTENCE

This section addresses two questions simultaneously: In what ways and in what contexts does variation in infants' attention occur, and are the observed differences among individuals stable across time and across situation? Much of the research on attention in infants has involved presenting infants with pictures or objects and observing the duration of looking, the rate of habituation to repeated presentations, and the response to novelty. However, because another chapter is devoted to individual differences in this context, I do not cover it here (see Colombo and Mitchell's chapter in this volume).

Manipulative Exploration.   Much research relevant to the issue of sustained attention has been conducted in the context of infant's manipulation and exploration of objects. Even though objects differ in the extent to which they elicit attention (McCall, 1974; Ruff, 1984), for any one object there is an impressive range of variation across infants in the duration and types of activity involved in interacting with it. Using duration of mouthing, manipulation with visual regard, length of play session, number of appropriate activities, number of secondary and tertiary circular reactions, the frequency of parallel play with two objects, and the average duration of interaction with any one object, McCall (1974) found that many of a group of 9.5-month-olds could be clustered into four types. He writes:

> One group played all of the available time and were characterized by sustained interaction with individual objects and a mature, businesslike style of play enriched with substantial amounts and variety of appropriate and creative behavior. A second group, mostly males, played a long time in the session but lacked persistence with specific toys. Their play also involved relatively less creativity and imagination and was more keyed to the raw sensorimotor feedback provided by the toys, especially loud sounds produced by roughly casting the toys about. A third group played a shorter time in the session, and they appeared to be quick, superficial, and unimaginative in their interaction with the toys. (p. 77)

A fourth group played very little in any way. It is important to note that the analysis left out about 50% of the sample who did not share a particular profile of play with other children. Looking at the behavioral measures individually, McCall found relatively little consistency across situations with simple and complex toys and relatively little stability across the age range of 8.5 to 11.5 months.

Tempo of play seems to be an important component of the groups formed in

McCall's analysis; it is a characteristic also studied by Kagan and his colleagues (Kagan, McCall, Repucci, Jordan, Levine, & Minton, 1971) and can be measured by the frequency of toy changes as well as by the average duration of contact with a given toy as was the case in the McCall (1974) study. In a longitudinal study of infants seen at 4, 8, 13, and 27 months (Kagan et al., 1971), the number of toy changes was not particularly stable from 8 to 13 months. Wenckstern, Weizmann, and Leenaars (1984), however, did find shorter term stability from 8 to 8.5 months in a measure of tempo related to those of McCall (1974) and Kagan et al. (1971). They examined the number of toy changes over the total contact time during free play at 8 months and then 1 to 2 weeks later. This measure was quite stable for play with a set of simple toys (r = .55) and for play with a set of complex toys (r = .60). In another longitudinal study (Ruff et al., 1990), a related measure was used in scoring free play with both single and multiple objects at 12 months. This measure was the number of times the infant changed activities regardless of whether there was a change in object; that is, examining an object, mouthing it, examining it, and then banging it against the table would be scored as three changes of activity. In this study, there was considerable individual variation in the number of changes, but no data relevant to the issue of short-term stability.

As already noted, tempo is reflected in the extent to which an infant is willing and interested in remaining in contact with individual toys, or in sustaining a particular activity. Power, Chapieski, and McGrath (1985) tested 12- to 24-month-old children twice within a 2-week period to assess individual differences along these dimensions. From a period of free play, they obtained measures of total duration of exploratory play with the objects and the longest periods of uninterrupted involvement with an object, and from the child's encounter with a very difficult task, they obtained a measure of persistence. These measures showed correlations of .64, .61, and .55 between Day 1 and Day 2 with age partialled out. In addition, these measures that were quite highly intercorrelated tended not to be related to developmental level, as measured during play with the McCune-Nicolich system (1981); this pattern of correlations suggests that individual differences in attention span or persistence is a construct independent of the child's relative developmental status.

All the duration measures used here refer to general orientation toward objects. It is possible, however, to consider the stability of particular behaviors within the category of general manipulative play. One of the most stable activities seems to be mouthing, despite a dramatic decline in the duration of mouthing from 5 to 12 months (Ruff, 1984); stability has been found in a number of studies across a wide age range (Ruff & Dubiner, 1986, 5 to 7 months; Wenckstern et al., 1984, 8 to 8.5 months; McCall, 1974, 8.5 to 11.5 months; Cox & Campbell, 1968, 14 to 15 months). Ruff and Dubiner (1987) observed the same infants at 9, 9.5, and 12 months of age while they played freely with a series of objects presented one at a time. The objects were part of a familiarization and response to novelty paradigm so that for each "problem" the infant was presented with one object for three 30-second trials and then presented with an object that was discrepant from the first in texture, weight, or shape (see Ruff, 1984). The categories of manipulative activity were the durations of looking, rotating or turning the object around, fingering, mouthing, banging, and the frequency of transferring and dropping or throwing the object. All the behaviors except transferring were stable in the familiarization period from 9 to 9.5 months (see Table 10.1); looking, fingering, mouthing, and dropping were stable in the test periods. Because the data from the two 9-month visits were well correlated, a mean for duration or frequency of each behavior was obtained on the grounds that it would be a more reliable estimate of the child's tendency to engage in particular activities than the scores from either visit alone. Using these combined scores, fingering, mouthing, banging, and dropping were stable from 9 to 12 months in the familiarization period; for the test period, only looking and dropping showed any stability. These data suggest that there is moderate to substantial stability within individuals in the extent to which they engage in particular activities.

What is the relationship between these behaviors and attention? In other work (Ruff, 1986), focused attention or examining has been scored in this same context. Observers who are told only to record the times when the infant seems to be concentrating attention on the object can record the duration of these episodes with high reliability ($>.90$); they claim to be using clues from the infant's facial expression as well as from the nature of the activity. When two observers simultaneously, but independently, coded several interactions, with one observer recording looking and the other recording fingering and rotating, the duration of time that looking overlapped with one of those manipulations agreed very well with the duration of time the infants are judged to be concentrating ($r = .92$). It is

TABLE 10.1
Correlations Between Ages
Manipulative and Exploratory Activities

Activity	Familiarization		Test	
	9/9.5 Mos	9/12 Mos	9/9.5 Mos	9/12 Mos
Look	.41*	.30	.44*	.50*
Rotate	.42*	.04	.25	.20
Finger	.39*	.49*	.55**	.24
Mouth	.64**	.44*	.58**	.12
Bang	.38*	.58*	.08	.30
Transfer	-.06	.35	.02	-.11
Drop/Throw	.81**	.64**	.61**	.48*
n	29	20	29	20

*$p < .05$; **$p < .01$.

Note: From Ruff and Dubiner (1987). Stability of individual differences in infant's manipulation and exploration of objects. *Perceptual and Motor Skills, 64*, 1095-1101. Reprinted by permission of the publishers.

not surprising, then, that these behaviors that are most closely related to measures of focused attention are those that are used differentially to explore novel characteristics of objects and that decline over time; the decline over time suggests that these behaviors and the attention that accompanies them are instrumental in helping the child learn about the physical characteristics of the objects (Ruff, 1989). In contrast, from 9 to 12 months, behavior such as mouthing, banging, and dropping are used less differentially for novel characteristics and do not decline over time (Ruff, 1984). As a consequence, in the study of individual differences, we (Ruff & Dubiner, 1987) combined looking, fingering, and rotating into an exploratory score and mouthing, banging, and dropping into a nonexploratory score. When the scores for the 20 infants who were seen at all ages were correlated across age, both exploratory and nonexploratory summary scores were stable from 9 to 9.5 months, r's $= .59$ and $.65$. Only the combined nonexploratory score (9 and 9.5 months combined) was related to the equivalent score at 12 months. It appears that the nonexploratory behaviors not associated with concentrated attention may be more stable than the more exploratory attentive behaviors, a possibility to which I return later.

Studies of mastery motivation also involve observations of children during play; unlike the studies of attention and exploration of objects, studies of mastery motivation are more likely to employ "problems," for example, asking the child to get an attractive toy from behind a plexiglass barrier, or to use toys that invite the child to produce particular effects (Yarrow et al., 1983). Even so, the investigators score (a) visual attention only, (b) exploratory behavior (the definition of which is more general than the one I use), and (c) persistence in solving the problem, producing the effects, or engaging in particular sensorimotor sequences. In a longitudinal study of 6- and 12-month-old infants, Yarrow et al. (1983) found significant changes over age in most of the measures but still found significant correlations across age in two measures: persistence in producing effects, and exploratory behavior during the sensorimotor tasks.

Anticipatory Attention and Response Preparation.   Both attention to events in which the infant does not participate and attention to the objects that are being manipulated potentially involve the acquisition of information about the objects and events. In other contexts, however, attention may be paid to an absent object for the purposes of responding to it when it does appear. Vigilance, as measured in adults, refers to the combination of maintaining alertness for an expected event and preparation to respond to it. In the typical paradigm the subject is instructed to listen or watch for a signal and to respond in a specific way (e.g., lifting a finger from a switch) as soon as the signal occurs. Such a paradigm, of course, cannot be used with infants, but if the expectation of a salient event can be developed, then vigilance should be observable. The expectation that an event is going to reoccur is a very simple one. There is considerable evidence that even more complex expectations can be formed early in development (Cornell &

Heth, 1979; Haith, Hazan, & Goodman, 1988), and Donohue and Berg (1988) have shown that infants of 7 months demonstrate the typical adult anticipatory heart rate deceleration prior to an expected event that occurs in predictable intervals from a warning signal. Little work has been done, however, on the extent to which infants are willing to sustain attention in waiting for an expected event.

In two studies, one with 10-month-old infants and another with 5- to 11-month-old infants, my colleagues and I (Ruff et al., 1990) have found that infants would indeed attend to the place where a lively and interesting puppet had been. In the first study, the puppet appeared, called the infant by name, and moved up and down for about 5 seconds. The puppet then disappeared. After 5 seconds, it reappeared for a short time, talking and moving as before, and then disappeared for 20 seconds. This last cycle was repeated two more times. Although the observed anticipatory attention waned somewhat with the repetition of the event, as one might expect on the basis of habituation to the event itself, the striking finding was the degree of variability among the infants. All these infants were the same age, 10 months, but the mean amount of time spent looking for the puppet during the 20-second intervals between events varied from .4 to 15 seconds per interval. When the durations of anticipatory looking in the three 20-second intervals were correlated, it was found that there was substantial consistency across trials, .61, .67, and .77, for trials 1 and 2, 1 and 3, and 2 and 3, respectively.

In the next study, the events varied from trial to trial, and the intervals between events varied unpredictably from 5 to 25 seconds. Whereas the anticipatory looking of the older infants tended to be more spread out in time and more specific to the place where the puppets entered and disappeared from the stage, there was no significant change from 5 to 11 months in the overall amount of anticipatory looking observed. As in the previous study, the interindividual variability was striking; infants showed anticipatory looking for as little as 3% of available time during the interevent intervals and as much as 68%. Because there was no decline in anticipatory looking with time, as expected because of the change in puppets from event to event, the first 6 trials were correlated to the last 6 trials; the correlations were .84, .84, .70, and .75 for the 5-, 7-, 9-, and 11-month-olds, respectively.

Both of these studies suggest that individual infants vary widely in the extent to which they will pay attention in anticipation of an expected event, and that, within a session, the infants are consistent. We do not know, however, how stable this form of attention is from one day to the next. Research with adults suggests that individual differences in vigilance performance and in vigilance decrement do show short-term stability (Davies, Jones, & Taylor, 1984); there are, however, many other factors at work in an adult vigilance task, and we cannot assume that short-term stability will also be found in infancy.

There are other contexts in which a similar kind of attention may be observed.

Several investigators have measured the amount of visual attention an infant will pay to hiding places in searching for hidden objects. In several studies, a delay is imposed between the hiding of the object and the infant's being allowed to search for it, sometimes with the infant being moved relative to the object during the delay period; how much attention the infant pays to the hiding place is significantly related to the ability to search correctly for objects (Acredolo, Adams, & Goodwyn, 1984; Goldfield & Dickerson, 1981). There is a tendency for infants to attend more when they are moving under their own steam than when they are passively moved (Acredolo et al., 1984), raising the possibility also that the onset of self-produced locomotion leads to increases in attention to spatial locations and relationships in the environment (see also Bertenthal, Campos, & Barrett, 1984). Horobin and Acredolo (1986) tested 56 9-month-olds in an "A not B" paradigm; they found that performance on B hidings was linked to the degree to which the infant attended to the B location. Fourteen were attentive to B throughout the delay period in all conditions, 18 were inattentive in all conditions, and 24 showed attention in some conditions and not others. There were significant differences in the average length of time the three groups had been sitting independently, and the two extreme groups were different on the amount of time since the emergence of independent locomotion. As is the case for anticipatory attention in the Ruff et al. study, attention in the hiding situation is also directed, in part, to an unseen object and is related to a preparation to respond when the object is uncovered.

A similar kind of attention could be observed in the "strange situation" (Ainsworth, 1973), but a search of representative studies did not reveal any attempts to measure the amount of time the infants spent looking at the door through which their mothers had disappeared. For some infants, this may be a more salient event than the puppets or the hidden object. To understand vigilance or anticipatory attention and the processes underlying it, there needs to be systematic research into the influences of different types of objects and events, and the relationship of attention to other aspects of development.

Summary.   There are, theoretically, at least two kinds of sustained attention that are tested in two different situations and may have different underlying processes. One is attention maintained on an object, event, or task for the purpose of learning more about it and/or reaching a goal. The other is attention maintained in anticipation of an event for the purpose of responding to the event when it occurs. The correlations between attention during manipulative exploration of objects and anticipatory attention are generally low and nonsignificant (Ruff et al., 1990), which may suggest that they are relatively independent of each other. On the other hand, we have as yet very little information about convergent validity, that is, positive correlations among situations theoretically tapping the same kind of attention. It is just as possible that attention during free play with objects may be based on somewhat different processes than attention during problem solving. Any taxonomy as it applies to infants must, therefore, be considered quite tentative.

Long-Term Stability

Although more research is clearly needed, the evidence points to short-term stability in at least some measures of sustained attention. Another way of addressing the issue of whether the observed differences are due to stable differences in the propensity to attend in various situations is to examine long-term stability. In this case, the evidence is also suggestive of some stability over relatively long periods of time.

Using the rating of attention span from the Bayley Infant Behavior Record, Heinicke, Diskin, Ramsey-Klee, and Oates (1986) found a zero-order correlation of .60 between the rating at 6 months and the one at 24 months; in a path analysis with other variables controlled, the correlation was still .45 between these two times. Kagan et al. (1971) found that the duration of episodes of "sustained directed activity" at 27 months was significantly and negatively related to the number of object changes at 8 months. In a longitudinal study, we (Ruff et al., 1990) examined the relationships among measures of tempo, inattention, and focused attention at 1, 2, and 3.5 years. With regard to tempo, we found that number of changes of activity at 1 year was positively related to active inattention for preterms at 3.5 years. Measures of inattention at 2 years were strongly related to equivalent measures at 3.5 years. We found no stability of the duration of focused attention between any two time points. These data suggest, as the data on short-term reliability did, that measures of inattention may be more stable than those of attention, at least more concentrated and focused attention.

The lack of evidence for stability in focused attention might be due to unreliable measurement at any time point, or to the possibility that intensity of attention is sensitive to temporary organismic and contextual factors. Another possibility, however, is that stability would be more likely at the extremes of the distribution than in the middle ranges. To address this possibility, each of our study children at 1 year was given a global and qualitative rating by an individual observing the videotapes of that session. The rating scale was simply: (a) very low attentiveness, (b) average attentiveness, and (c) very high attentiveness. A second observer made the same kind of ratings on the basis of the videotapes of the children in their 2-year lab sessions. The observers' global, qualitative ratings were quite strongly related to the quantitative behavioral measures of focused attention and inattention taken from the same segments of videotape (Ruff et al., 1990).

We then selected the children who were very attentive at both ages (n = 5), and the children who were very inattentive at both ages (n = 6); these subgroups therefore represented children who were consistent and extreme. We compared the "high attenders" and "low attenders" on our attention measures at 3.5

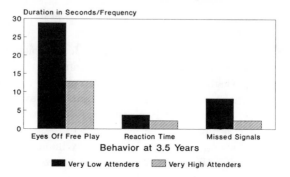

Comparison of Extreme Groups
Inattention at 3.5 Years

FIG. 10.1. Comparison of low attenders and high attenders on measures of inattention at 3.5 years.

years, measures that were completely independent of the basis for forming the groups in the first place. The high attenders showed more focused attention during free play and were more attentive than average, whereas the low attenders were less attentive than average. During a more structured reaction-time task, the low attenders were less attentive than average, that is, they had slower reaction times and made more errors of omission than either the high or average attenders (see Fig. 10.1). These data suggest that extremely attentive and inattentive children can be identified in the first 2 years, and that they continue to be significantly different along relevant dimensions 1.5 years later (Ruff & Lawson, 1988). There may, therefore, be some long-term stability for some individuals that is hard to capture in correlations involving the whole range of variation.

Summary.   The data suggest that some measures of sustained attention and persistence may be stable over quite long periods, particularly for children who fall at the extremes. There is no information about stability of anticipatory attention or of attention in more structured, constrained tasks. In addition, how general the observed differences are across situations and across time is still not known.

Relationship of Attention to Measures of Temperament

Most temperament scales include questions concerning the relative length of time a child will attend to or persist in an activity; the Carey Infant and Toddler Scales (Carey & McDevitt, 1978; Fullard, McDevitt, & Carey, 1978) both have subscales for "attention span/persistence," and the Rothbart Infant Behavior Questionnaire (Rothbart, 1981) has a subscale for "duration of orienting." Thus, sustained attention is considered an important aspect of temperament and of the quality of functioning. One advantage the temperament scales have over quantitative laboratory measures is that the judgments are based on the mother's extensive experience with her infant; the judgments, therefore, are likely to summarize the child's behavior over a wide variety of situations. Our understanding of individual differences in attention needs to make use of these more global ratings and to incorporate the relationship of attention to other temperamental characteristics.

One of the most interesting relationships is a link between expression of negative emotions and shorter durations of attention (Rothbart, in press a). This relationship is seen very early in development and in different contexts. Fagen, Ohr, Singer, and Fleckenstein (1987), for example, found that 3- to 4-month infants' crying and inability to complete an operant conditioning task were negatively related to mothers' ratings of duration of orienting on the Rothbart scale. Wachs and Smitherman (1985) found a positive relationship between fussiness and low adaptability and failure to complete an habituation task for girls from 2 to 6 months. In addition to these reports of concurrent relationships between lower attention and negative affect, there is some evidence of relationships across time. Riese (1987) found that newborn irritability was related to lower levels of attention at 2 years. We (Lawson & Ruff, 1988) found that negative reaction to a frustrating task at 1 year and negative emotionality as measured by the Colorado Children's Temperament Inventory (Rowe & Plomin, 1977) at 2 years were both related to lower durations of focused attention at 3.5 years.

It would be misleading, however, to state that these relationships represent a unique link between attention and negative affect. Negative emotionality appears to be embedded in a larger cluster of characteristics also involving adaptability and tendency to approach new objects. This larger cluster is seen most clearly, perhaps, in the research of Matheny and his colleagues. In factor analyses of the Carey Toddler Temperament Scale (TTS) and examiner ratings of behavior in the lab setting used with 12-, 18-, and 24-month-olds (Matheny, Wilson, & Nuss, 1984), attentiveness and emotional tone as rated by the laboratory staff were consistently related as were mood, adaptability, and approach as rated by the mother on the TTS. In our work with the small subgroups who were extremely and consistently attentive or inattentive (Ruff & Lawson, 1988), we found that the extremely inattentive children were rated at 1 year as less adaptable, less likely to approach new situations, and more negative in mood than either the extremely attentive children or the average group. They were also more negative and less soothable at 2 years (see Fig. 10.2).

These relationships suggest that the tendency to sustain attention to objects and events should not be considered in isolation. The fact that attention is related to affect, adaptability, and tendency to approach new situations suggests that attention is part of a style of coping with the environment. As Rothbart (in press

Comparison of Extreme Groups
Carey Toddler Temperament Scale

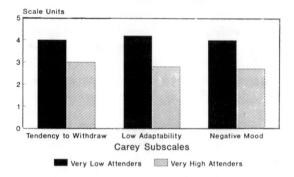

FIG. 10.2. Comparison of low attenders and high attenders on some dimensions of temperament as rated by their mothers on the Carey Toddler Temperament Scale.

a; Rothbart & Derryberry, 1981) emphasizes, attention is both the result of and a participant in the process of self-regulation. Understanding these processes with some precision may require that we differentiate between different sources of negative affect. Both understimulation as well as overstimulation might lead to irritability and distress. The child who cannot shift his attention to a more neutral part of the environment away from the source of distress or stimulation is more likely to become overaroused; for example, the important role of "gaze aversion" in the regulation of arousal in the early interactions between mother and child has been demonstrated in a number of investigations (e.g., Field, 1980). It is also possible, however, that children whose attention is not easily engaged by the objects and events around them will more often find themselves in boring circumstances and may be irritable for that reason.

In dealing with particular relationships, it is not always clear what part of the continuum is accounting for the correlation; it may be that the correlations are carried mainly by children who are extremely inattentive and that children of average or high attentiveness are not necessarily different from each other; our analysis (Ruff & Lawson, 1988) of extreme groups would support this. It is also possible that inattention is part of two or more quite different constellation of characteristics. With our extreme group of inattentive children, the evidence points to a lack of reactivity because, on the TTS, they were judged to be *less* distractible than normal, to have *higher* than average thresholds, and to be of average activity, certainly very different from the classic picture of the difficult child (Thomas, Chess, & Birch, 1969). In our extremely inattentive group, the negative mood and emotionality may be related to understimulation (Zentall & Zentall, 1983). Conversely, the lowering of positive affect may interfere in important ways with the child's engagement with the environment; that is, negative affect leads to withdrawal, and the apparent insensitivity seen in our low attenders may be further evidence of that withdrawal.

Other evidence, however, argues for a relationship between inattention, activity, and impulsivity (Campbell, 1985; Krakow, Kopp, & Vaughn, 1982). There may, therefore, be another constellation of behaviors that would characterize a different subgroup of inattentive children. In this case, attention would be linked more to behavioral inhibition (Rothbart, in press b); there is considerable theoretical background for hypothesizing that focused attention is related to inhibition of extraneous activity (Obrist, Howard, Sutterer, Hennis, & Murrell, 1973; Obrist, Webb, & Sutterer, 1969), and this relationship needs to be explored more extensively in the early years.

The Consequences of Attentiveness

With older children, attentiveness in the preschool years is positively related to later school achievement (Palisin, 1986), and signs of hyperactivity, also predictive of later performance, have been documented in the preschool years (Campbell, 1985). These data suggest that there may be important consequences of the child's tendency to sustain attention to age-appropriate objects and tasks for both cognition and behavioral pathology.

Kopp and Vaughn (1982) found that duration of sustained attention during active manipulation of objects at 8 months was a positive contributor to outcome on a developmental assessment at 2 years in a group of preterm infants; furthermore, it added significantly to the variance in 2-year outcome even when early developmental status was controlled. Ruff, McCarton, Kurtzberg, and Vaughn (1984) also found that a summary exploration score involving duration of fingering and rotating and frequency of transferring at 9 months of age was positively related ($r = .60$) to Bayley MDI at 2 years. Furthermore, when the videotapes of these same infants at 9 months were scored for focused attention, the duration of focused attention was positively related ($r = .55$) to Stanford–Binet IQs at 3 and 4 years of age (Ruff, 1988). Messer and colleagues (1986) found that duration of investigating toys at 6 months and persistence in solving problems at 12 months were predictive of later cognitive functioning as measured by the McCarthy scales. All these results suggest that sustaining of attention during interaction with objects is a positive characteristic and a potential contributor to cognitive development.

The infant who plays attentively with objects may be better able to generate activities that will lead to new information about the object; that is, the attentive infant may already be cognitively more advanced than the infant who does not readily initiate and maintain engagement. The tendency to pay attention, however, could stem more from a general style of interaction rather than from current cognitive level, but the outcome would still be that the infant who attends to objects and learns about their properties will have a better foundation for developing knowledge of the environment and for cognitive development, in general.

In this regard, it is of interest that the two extreme groups drawn from our longitudinal study (Ruff & Lawson, 1988) were equivalent on the Bayley MDI's at 1 and 2 years. By 3.5 years, however, the low attenders were significantly below average levels on the Stanford–Binet (L–M) Intelligence Scale, whereas the high attenders were within the average range (see Fig. 10.3). Because there were no obvious prior differences in cognition to account for the original differences in attentiveness, these data suggest that cognitive development was impeded by the lack of attentiveness in the low attenders. This possibility gains credence from the fact that the low attenders were not less cooperative during the 3.5-year assessment than the high attenders.

As before, we need to address the question of whether the later cognitive outcomes are directly affected by attention and what is learned during attending, or whether they are more generally affected by the constellation of temperamental variables of which attention is a part. The child who finds environmental stimulation to be aversive is not going to attend as readily but also will be affectively less invested in the environment. Perhaps it is this affective disengagement that underlies both poor attention and poor cognitive performance. The work reviewed by Bornstein and Sigman (1986) suggests that the response to novelty is an important factor in cognition, and again, it may be the pleasure that novelty arouses and the resulting greater attention that are related to later pleasure in solving problems and achieving. The mastery motivation literature emphasizes this motivational aspect of attending and acting.

Although most of the relevant data deal with the relationship of attention and

Comparison of Extreme Groups
Standardized Test Scores

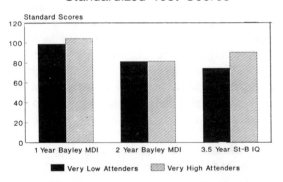

Standard Scores

1 Year Bayley MDI   2 Year Bayley MDI   3.5 Year St-B IQ

■ Very Low Attenders   ▨ Very High Attenders

FIG. 10.3.   The performance of low and high attenders on measures of cognitive status at three ages. MDI = Mental Development Index from the Bayley Scales of Infant Development; IQ = Intelligence Quotient from the Stanford–Binet (L–M).

measures of general cognitive status, we need to be mindful of the possibility of more subtle effects. The behavior of most children is adaptive, and though they may develop along somewhat different trajectories, the probability is high that they will be of at least average intelligence and capable of performing adequately in both social and educational settings. Within this range of normal, adaptive behavior, however, the propensity to maintain attention on objects, events, and tasks may still have consequences that would only be observed if searched for specifically. For example, the infant who prolongs his attention to and exploration of object properties may be learning, or overlearning, information about the less salient or less obvious aspects of the object. That infant may then be better able to make subtle discriminations among objects than the infant who attends only long enough to pick up the basic information and moves onto another object or another activity. If this difference were to extend over a long period of time, it could form the basis for later differences in cognitive and behavioral style.

There may also be social consequences of individual differences in attentiveness. In assessments of the interaction between mother and child, children who are typically inattentive elicit more directive and more negative responses from the mother (Campbell, 1985; Mash & Johnston, 1982). Hyperactive, inattentive children are also more likely to be aggressive and to have difficulty relating to peers (Campbell, 1985). Less is known about the social development of children who are unreactive but not necessarily active or aggressive. In either case, as Krakow et al. (1982) suggest, the attentive child may be more likely to pick up information about expectations for behavior than the inattentive child and therefore be somewhat advanced in general self-regulatory skills. Superior self-regulation is likely to make the child easier to have around for both adults and other children so that positive social experiences would then ensue.

The Origins of Individual Differences in Attention

The work that has been reviewed so far suggests that our understanding of attention is imperfect and that the nature of individual differences needs considerable further investigation. On the other hand, there is enough suggestive evidence for both short- and long-term stability that a preliminary conclusion in favor of stable individual differences in at least some aspects of sustained attention seems justified. Furthermore, these differences seem to be related to other temperamental characteristics and to a general approach to the environment that may have an important impact on a child's cognitive and social development.

Where do these differences come from? Most discussions of early individual differences assume either explicitly or implicitly that observed behavioral differences are based on biological differences or constitutional predispositions. Support for this assumption comes from studies of identical and fraternal twins (see Thompson's chapter in this volume). Task orientation as rated by several items on the Bayley Infant Behavior Record is consistently more highly correlated in identical twins than it is in same-sex fraternal twins (Matheny, 1980); and patterns of change over age in this factor are also more highly correlated in identical twins (Matheny, 1983). These findings suggest that there may be a genetic base for the degree of task orientation at different ages, and for the pattern of changes that occur in the first 2 years.

Other support for a biological basis of the tendency to sustain attention comes from psycho- and neurophysiological work that suggests a link between aspects of nervous system functioning and attention. Porges (1976), for example, discusses the importance of antagonistic excitatory and inhibitory systems that need to be balanced for proper control of attention; these systems involve neurotransmitters in brain stem, midbrain, and forebrain. He further suggests that hyperactive children have an imbalance toward greater excitatory processes and are therefore deficient in those processes that underlie attentional states. Using autonomic measures, Porges and Coles (1982) found evidence for stable individual differences in respiratory–heart period coupling for adults performing both reaction time and vigilance tasks. If deficits or pathology can be linked to the functioning of the autonomic nervous system or particular neurotransmitters in the central nervous system, then it seems reasonable that individual variability within the range of behavior considered normal would also be based on variations in these same systems. However, just as there may be different types of sustained attention, there may be more than one kind of physiological variation underlying individual differences in attention (Zametkin & Rapoport, 1987).

Let us assume, for the sake of this discussion, that the genetic and neural processes underlying sustained attention and various subtypes can be identified. Even if differences in these processes could be discerned very early, however, we could not assume that environmental factors would not act to change these processes or the balance between them. In recent years, a number of investigators have urged a systems approach to the study of infants and their development (e.g., Fogel & Thelen, 1987; Thelen, Kelso, & Fogel, 1987; Valsiner, 1987). A systems approach includes the principle of equifinality; that is, organisms that are developing toward the same endpoint may arrive there by quite different trajectories; also, differences at one point in development, even if stable over the short term, may not be predictive of outcome (von Bertalanffy, 1968). In some aspects of development, for example, behavioral style or personality, there may be somewhat different endpoints, but these also would be difficult to predict from the initial conditions. The difficulty stems from the fact that the developing organism, as an open system, is involved in a constant and changing interplay with its environment. We need, therefore, to know not only about constitutional predispositions that infant start with, but also about the influences of the larger environment, such as parents, as they take part in this dynamic interplay.

There are a number of studies that suggest that adult intervention or the interaction with adults will change an infant's immediate tendency to be attentive. Lawson, Parrinello, and Ruff (1989) found that mothers' behavior affected the degree to which their infants were attentive during a period of interaction even when the degree of independent attention to the same toys was controlled. Demonstrating the action of different objects and pausing to let the child act on the objects led to increases in attention, whereas changing the object of focus and physically restricting the child led to less focused attention and more passive attention. Belsky, Goode, and Most (1980) found that mothers who were made aware of the effects of their behavior engaged in more directing and stimulating behavior with their 1-year-old infants, which in turn affected exploratory competence. Adult behavior may influence attention by stimulating and arousing the infant; in contrast, the demonstration of attentive, engaged behavior on the part of the adult may be imitated by the infant (Meltzoff, 1988). In a study of older children, Johns and Endsley (1977) found that observation of mother's "curiosity" behavior led children to show more of the same behavior later when they played alone with the same objects; the same may be true of infants though their ability to imitate is still developing. In conjunction with a considerable body of data on the effects of adult behavior on children's behavior in other contexts, these data certainly suggest that consistent exposure over time to the parents' behavior will have some influence on children's propensity to sustain attention.

A systems approach to the problem dictates that the parental influence not be seen as unidirectional, but as part of a larger dynamic picture. Although it may be too simple a conceptualization for our eventual understanding of the infant, the notion of environmental factors interacting with individual predispositions is an important concept. At any one point in development, individual variation along the dimension of attentiveness will exist, and we can ask how that variation will interact with external factors to produce attention and behavior in a particular situation. Parrinello and Ruff (1988) found that 10-month-old infants who were low attenders as determined by a baseline procedure were more influenced by adult attempts to stimulate and encourage attention than were children who were high attenders to begin with. The adult intervention at moderate levels led the low attenders to attend to objects more frequently and to do so for longer periods, at least as measured by the longest single episode. The high attenders found the interaction with the adult more pleasant at moderate levels and more aversive at higher levels, but the amount of time they focused attention on the objects stayed the same across the different levels (see Fig. 10.4). The results were not a simple result of ceiling effects because even high attenders, as defined by a median split, spent only half the available time in focused attention to objects.

Similar results were found by Wenar (1976) in his study of low- and high-competence children between 1 and 2 years. The children who were highly competent at 1 year remained so over the next year even though their mothers varied widely in the way they interacted with their infants. In contrast, children who were low in competence at 1 year improved if their mothers were stimulating but not if they were restrictive. Gandour (1989) separated children along the

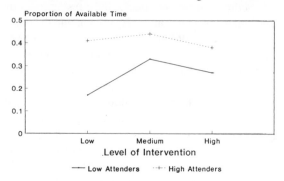

The Effect of Intervention on Attention
Comparison of Low and High Attenders

FIG. 10.4.   The effect of level of adult intervention on infants who
were low or high in spontaneous attention during independent play.
The figure is based on data reported in Parrinello and Ruff (1988).

dimension of activity level and found that high-intensity stimulation from mothers tended to increase exploratory competence in low-active children and to decrease exploratory competence in high-active children.

These results suggest that the trajectory of some children may be less influenced by environmental events than others, or that children with different predispositions will be influenced by different kinds of environmental influences (Wachs, 1987). The studies mentioned here clearly represent only a small part of the attempt to understand development of individual differences as the result of an organism/environment system, and much more work will be necessary to explicate the changes that could occur in the tendency to sustain attention even in such a short time as the first 2 years of life.

Future Directions

The preceding sections have embedded in them a number of suggestions for future investigation. Although there is clearly a gap in our knowledge of the extent and stability of individual differences in attention during the first 2 years, there are a number of issues that should be addressed prior to further investigation of individual differences as such. One of these issues involves the definition of attention. As the foregoing review emphasizes, attention has been measured in a number of different ways and in different situations, and we do not yet know to what degree measures of looking to static objects and events, focused attention to manipulable toys, and persistence in solving problems are governed by common processes and to what degree they are controlled by unique processes. What is needed, first of all, is a clearer definition of possible types of attention or possible processes underlying attention.

One such subcategorization of sustained attention was suggested earlier—attention maintained for the purpose of gathering and using information, and attention maintained while waiting to detect and respond to an expected event; these types may be controlled by quite different processes (Pribram & McGuiness, 1975). It is possible, however, that attention deployed while exploring and playing freely with objects should be separated from persistence of effort in solving a task, such as trying to obtain an object from behind a barrier. In the first case, attention may be governed more by the complexity and thoroughness of children's activity in relation to the objects, whereas the second may be governed more by the extent to which children can establish goals and the strength of their motivation to reach the goal. On the other hand, perhaps all three potential types of attention are governed, at least in part, by the extent to which the infant can be engaged or controlled by external stimulation.

The only way to explore and refine the definition of attention is to define one or more constructs, develop at least two measures of each construct, and test the same children on the different measures within the same time frame. Such designs allow for the determination of convergent and discriminant validity (Campbell & Fiske, 1959). An example of this kind of research was recently reported by Rothbart (Rothbart, Kenofer, & O'Curry, 1988). Experimental work will then be important to determine what factors affect different types of attention and how.

Research on the nature of attention and its underlying processes is necessary if we are going to conceptualize precisely how individuals vary. Once some firmer definitions are established and reliable, valid measures are developed, it makes sense to begin a very systematic search for individual differences. In this regard, it will be important to test the same subjects in different situations at several different times. Epstein (1980) has argued rather forcefully that stability of behavior within individuals is most likely to be found when values or scores over several measurements are aggregated. To some extent, this is the case because our measures are never perfectly reliable. It is also the case that individuals will fluctuate in their behavior, and we cannot know if they fluctuate around different means unless we sample the behavior, and therefore the construct, on more than one occasion. Epstein's empirical work with adults suggests that aggregating over 3 to 4 occasions may result in as much stability as aggregating over 10 occasions, but the situation could be somewhat different for children.

Even if we show that the tendency to sustain attention is stable in the short run, the individual variation observed could be due to a number of factors. One is differences in interest or responsiveness to the particular objects or events used. Sampling over different situations may reduce the effect of individual interests but probably would not eliminate it completely. Renninger's (1988) work with preschool children suggests that most children will sustain some activities when they are with the toys and in the situations that they are most interested in. Less is known about this factor in infancy, but it is very likely that we could establish individual preferences for different types of objects. Just as interest in particular objects is likely to influence the duration of attention in individual infants, it is reasonable to think that some children will be more attentive in the context of social interactions than with objects, or that some children will concentrate more on gross motor activities than either social- or object-oriented activities. In addition to the question of how long an infant will typically maintain attention, therefore, there is a question of individual differences in the particular situations that are most likely to elicit and maintain attention; that is, some infants may attend very little in any context at any time, and some infants may be very attentive in most contexts at most times, but we should expect the attention of the majority of infants to vary according to the context.

When considering a rapidly developing organism, it is very important to include the effect of differences in developmental status. For example, whether an infant is prelocomotor or has achieved independent locomotion may well affect how much an infant attends to particular aspects of the environment (Bertenthal et al., 1984). As mentioned earlier, it appears that infants who have been crawling or walking for a few weeks are more likely to keep their eyes on important spatial locations and to search effectively for hidden objects (Horobin & Acredolo, 1986). Although infants who are slow to locomote may be different for some time than locomotor infants, one would expect them to "catch up" once they have been locomoting for a while. On the other hand, it is possible that the infant who is slow to start crawling and walking may spend more time attending to graspable objects in the immediate vicinity and learn more about them than the crawler and walker. This could lead to a difference in experience that might have long-range effects on the development of attention.

There are many unanswered and exciting questions awaiting the researcher interested in individual differences in attention. I have tried to emphasize that there is a certain amount of background correlational and experimental work that needs to be done before we will be able to systematically investigate the nature of individual differences. With regard to the issue of sustained attention, in particular, we not only need to know what the infant's spontaneous "span" of attention is, but also if and how the infant responds to systematic manipulation of factors such as adult stimulation, object characteristics, and distractors, to name a few. In other words, the study of individual differences in attentiveness is likely not only to increase our knowledge of individuals but also our understanding of attention and the factors that affect it.

ACKNOWLEDGMENTS

The writing of this chapter was supported by Grants BNS 86-19487 from the National Science Foundation and by a Research Scientist Development Award from the National Institute of Mental Health (MH 00652). The research reported here was supported by the preceding grants and by Grants HD 11916, HD 01799, and MH 38227. I wish to thank Mary Capozzoli for her assistance in many phases of the work reported here. Special acknowledgment is due to Katharine Lawson whose collaboration on the longitudinal project and whose discussion with me on relevant issues has been invaluable. Requests for reprints should be addressed to Holly A. Ruff, Room 222, Rose F. Kennedy Center, Albert Einstein College of Medicine, 1300 Morris Park Road, Bronx, New York 10461.

REFERENCES

Acredolo, L. P., Adams, A., & Goodwyn, S. W. (1984). The role of self-produced movement and visual tracking in infant spatial orientation. *Journal of Experimental Child Psychology, 38,* 312–327.

Ainsworth, M. D. S. (1973). The development of infant–mother attachment. In B. M. Caldwell & H. N. Ricciuti (Eds.), *Review of child development research* (Vol. 3, pp. 1–94). Chicago: The University of Chicago Press.

Anderson, D. R., Choi, H. P., & Lorch, E. P. (1987). Attentional inertia reduces distractibility during young children's TV viewing. *Child Development, 58,* 798–806.

Belsky, J., Goode, M. K., & Most, R. K. (1980). Maternal stimulation and infant exploratory competence: Cross-sectional, correlational, and experimental analyses. *Child Development, 51,* 1168–1178.

Berlyne, D. E. (1970). Attention as a problem in behavior theory. In D. I. Mostofsky (Ed.), *Attention: Contemporary theory and analysis* (pp. 25–49). New York: Appleton-Century-Crofts.

Bertenthal, B. I., Campos, J. J., & Barrett, K. C. (1984). Self-produced locomotion: An organizer of emotional, cognitive, and social development in infancy. In R. N. Emde & R. J. Harmon (Eds.), *Continuities and discontinuities in development* (pp. 175–210). New York: Plenum Press.

Bornstein, M. H., & Sigman, M. D. (1986). Continuity in mental development from infancy. *Child Development, 57,* 251–274.

Campbell, D. T., & Fiske, D. W. (1959). Convergent and discriminant validation by the multitrait–multimethod matrix. *Psychological Bulletin, 56,* 81–105.

Campbell, S. B. (1985). Hyperactivity in preschoolers: Correlates and prognostic implications. *Clinical Psychology Review, 5,* 405–428.

Carey, W. B., & McDevitt, S. C. (1978). Revision of the Infant Temperament Questionnaire. *Pediatrics, 61,* 735–739.

Cohen, L. B., DeLoache, J. S., & Strauss, M. S. (1979). Infant visual perception. In J. D. Osofsky (Ed.), *Handbook of infant development* (pp. 393–438). New York: Wiley.

Cornell, E. H., & Heth, C. D. (1979). Response versus place learning by human infants. *Journal of Experimental Psychology: Human Learning and Memory, 5,* 188–196.

Cox, F. N., & Campbell, D. (1968). Young children in a new situation with and without their mothers. *Child Development, 39*(1), 123–131.

Davies, D. R., Jones, D. M., & Taylor, A. (1984). Selective- and sustained-attention tasks: Individual and group differences. In R. Parasuraman & D. R. Davies (Eds.), *Varieties of attention* (pp. 395–447). Orlando: Academic Press.

Donohue, R. L., & Berg, W. K. (1988, April). *7-month-old infants anticipate interesting events: Heart rate responses during a fixed foreperiod (S1-S2) paradigm.* Paper presented at the International Conference on Infant Studies, Washington, DC.

Elliot, R. (1970). Simple reaction time: Effects associated with age, preparatory interval, incentive-shift, and mode of presentation. *Journal of Experimental Child Psychology, 9,* 86–107.

Epstein, S. (1980). The stability of behavior. *American Psychologist, 35,* 790–806.

Fagen, J. W., Ohr, P. S., Singer, J. M., & Fleckenstein, L. K. (1987). Infant temperament and subject loss due to crying during operant conditioning. *Child Development, 58,* 497–504.

Field, T. M. (1980). Effects of early separation, interactive deficits and experimental manipulations on infant–mother face-to-face interaction. *Child Development, 48,* 763–771.

Fogel, A., & Thelen, E. (1987). Development of early expressive and communicative action: Reinterpreting the evidence from a dynamic systems perspective. *Developmental Psychology, 23,* 747–761.

Fullard, W., McDevitt, S. C., & Carey, W. B. (1979). *Toddler Temperament Scale.* Temple University, Philadelphia, PA, 19122.

Gandour, M. J. (1989). Activity level as a dimension of temperament in toddlers: Its relevance for the organismic specificity hypothesis. *Child Development, 60,* 1092–1098.

Gibson, E. J., & Rader, N. (1979). Attention: The perceiver as performer. In G. A. Hale & M. Lewis (Eds.), *Attention and cognitive development.* New York: Plenum Press.

Goldfield, E. C., & Dickerson, D. J. (1981). Keeping track of locations during movement in 8- to-10-month-old infants. *Journal of Experimental Child Psychology, 32,* 48–64.

Haith, M. M., Hazan, C., & Goodman, G. (1988). Expectation and anticipation of dynamic visual events by 3.5-month-old-babies. *Child Development, 59,* 467–479.

Heinicke, C. M., Diskin, S. D., Ramsey-Klee, D. M., & Oates, D. S. (1986). Pre- and postbirth antecedents of 2-year-old attention, capacity for relationships and verbal expressiveness. *Developmental Psychology, 22,* 777–787.

Horobin, K., & Acredolo, L. (1986). The role of attentiveness, mobility history, and separation of hiding sites on Stage IV search behavior. *Journal of Experimental Child Psychology, 41,* 114–127.

Jennings, K. D., Harmon, R. J., Morgan, G. A., Gaiter, J. L., & Yarrow, L. J. (1979). Exploratory play as an index of mastery motivation: Relationships to persistence, cognitive functioning, and environmental measures. *Developmental Psychology, 15,* 386–394.

Johns, C., & Endsley, R. C. (1977). The effects of a maternal model on young children's tactual curiosity. *Journal of Genetic Psychology, 131,* 21–28.

Kagan, J., McCall, R. B., Repucci, N. D., Jordan, J., Levine, J., & Minton, C. (1971). *Change and continuity in infancy.* New York: Wiley.

Kahneman, D. (1973). *Attention and effort.* Englewood Cliffs, NJ: Prentice-Hall.

Kopp, C. B., & Vaughn, B. E. (1982). Sustained attention during exploratory manipulation as a predictor of cognitive competence in preterm infants. *Child Development, 53,* 174–182.

Krakow, J. B., Kopp, C. B., & Vaughn, B. E. (1982). *Sustained attention during the second years: Age trends, individual differences and implications for development.* Unpublished manuscript.

Lawson, K. R., Parrinello, R. M., & Ruff, H. A. (1989). *The effect of maternal behavior on attention to objects.* Unpublished manuscript.

Lawson, K. R., & Ruff, H. A. (1988, April). *Negative emotionality and attention.* Poster presented at the International Conference on Infant Studies, Washington, DC.

Mash, E. J., & Johnston, C. (1982). A comparison of the mother–child interactions of younger and older hyperactive and normal children. *Child Development, 53,* 1371–1381.

Matheny, A. P. (1980). Bayley's Infant Behavior Record: Behavioral components and twin analyses. *Child Development, 51,* 1157–1167.

Matheny, A. P. (1983). A longitudinal twin study of stability of components from Bayley's Infant Behavior Record. *Child Development, 54,* 356–360.

Matheny, A. P., Wilson, R. S., & Nuss, S. M. (1984). Toddler temperament: Stability across settings and over ages. *Child Development, 55,* 1200–1211.

McCall, R. B. (1974). Exploratory manipulation and play in the human infant. *Monographs of the Society for Research in Child Development, 39,* Whole Serial 155.

McCune-Nicolich, L. (1981). Toward symbolic functioning: Structure of early pretend games and parallels with language. *Child Development, 52,* 785–797.

Meltzoff, A. N. (1988). Infant imitation and memory: Nine-month-olds in immediate and deferred tests. *Child Development, 59,* 217–225.

Messer, D. J., McCarthy, M. E., McQuiston, S., MacTurk, R. H., Yarrow, L. J., & Vietze, P. M. (1986). Relation between mastery behavior in infancy and competence in early childhood. *Developmental Psychology, 22*, 366–372.

Näätänen, R. (1982). Processing negativity: An evoked potential reflection of selective attention. *Psychological Bulletin, 92*, 605–640.

Obrist, P. A. Webb, R. A., & Sutterer, J. R. (1969). Heart rate and somatic changes during aversive conditioning and a simple reaction time task. *Psychophysiology, 5*, 696–723.

Obrist, P. A., Howard, J. L., Sutterer, J. R., Hennis, R. S., & Murrell, D. J. (1973). Cardiac-somatic changes during a simple reaction time task: A developmental study. *Journal of Experimental Child Psychology, 16*, 346–362.

Palisin, H. (1986). Preschool temperament and performance on achievement tests. *Developmental Psychology, 22*(6), 766–770.

Parrinello, R. M., & Ruff, H. A. (1988). The influence of adult intervention on infants' level of attention. *Child Development, 59*, 1125–1135.

Porges, S. W. (1972). Heart rate variability and deceleration as indexes of reaction time. *Journal of Experimental Psychology, 92*, 103–110.

Porges, S. W. (1976). Peripheral and neurochemical parallels of psychopathology: A psychophysiological model relating autonomic imbalance to hyperactivity, psychopathy, and autism. In H. W. Reese (Ed.), *Advances in child development and behavior* (Vol. 2, pp. 35–65). New York: Academic Press.

Porges, S. W., & Coles, M. G. H. (1982). Individual differences in respiratory–heart period coupling and heart period responses during two attention-demanding tasks. *Physiological Psychology, 10*, 215–220.

Posner, M. I. (1978). *Chronometric explorations of mind*. Hillsdale, NJ: Lawrence Erlbaum Associates.

Posner, M. I., & Boies, S. J. (1971). Components of attention. *Psychological Review, 78*, 391–408.

Power, T. G., Chapieski, L., & McGrath, M. P. (1985). Assessment of individual differences in infant exploration and play. *Developmental Psychology, 21*, 974–981.

Pribram, K. H., & McGuinness, D. (1975). Arousal, activation, and effort in the control of attention. *Psychological Review, 82*, 116–149.

Renninger, K. A. (1988, April). *Children's interests and task persistence*. Paper presented at the International Conference on Infant Studies, Washington, DC.

Richards, J. E. (1988). Heart rate responses and heart rate rhythms, and infant visual sustained attention. In P. K. Ackles, J. R. Jennings, & M. G. H. Coles (Eds.), *Advances in psychophysiology* (Vol. 3). Greenwich, CT: JAI Press.

Riese, M. L. (1987). Temperament stability between the neonatal period and 24 months. *Developmental Psychology, 23*(2), 216–222.

Rothbart, M. K. (1981). Measurement of temperament in infancy. *Child Development, 52*, 569–578.

Rothbart, M. K. (in press a). Temperament and development. In G. A. Kohnstam, J. Bates, & M. K. Rothbart (Eds.), *Handbook of temperament in childhood*. Sussex, England: Wiley.

Rothbart, M. K. (in press b). Behavioral approach and inhibition. In S. Resnick (Ed.), *Perspectives on behavioral inhibition*. Chicago: University of Chicago Press.

Rothbart, M. K., & Derryberry, D. (1981). Development of individual differences in temperament. In M. E. Lamb & A. L. Brown (Eds.), *Advances in developmental psychology* (pp. 37–86). NJ: Lawrence Erlbaum Associates.

Rothbart, M. K., Kenofer, B. P., & O'Curry, S. L. (1988, April). *Relevance of temperament to other constructs: Temperament and attention*. Paper presented at the International Conference on Infant Studies, Washington, DC.

Rowe, D. C., & Plomin, R. (1977). Temperament in early childhood. *Journal of Personality Assessment, 41*, 150–156.

Ruff, H. A. (1984). Infants' manipulative exploration of objects: Effects of age and object characteristics. *Developmental Psychology, 20,* 9–20.

Ruff, H. A. (1986). Components of attention during infants' manipulative exploration. *Child Development, 57,* 105–114.

Ruff, H. A. (1988). The measurement of attention in high risk infants. In P. Vietze & H. G. Vaughan (Eds.), *Early identification of infants with developmental disabilities* (pp. 282–296). Philadelphia, PA: Grune & Stratton.

Ruff, H. A. (1989). The infant's use of visual and haptic information in the perception and recognition of objects. *Canadian Journal of Psychology, 43,* 302–319.

Ruff, H. A., & Dubiner, K. (1986, April). *Infants' mouthing as active exploration.* Paper presented at the International Conference on Infant Studies, Los Angeles.

Ruff, H. A., & Dubiner, K. (1987). Stability of individual differences in infants' manipulation and exploration of objects. *Perceptual and Motor Skills, 64,* 1095–1101.

Ruff, H. A., Capozzoli, M., Dubiner, K., & Parrinello, R. (1990). A measure of vigilance in infancy. *Infant Behavior and Development, 13,* 1–19.

Ruff, H. A., & Lawson, K. R. (1988, April). *Development and individuality in sustained attention.* Paper presented at the International Conference on Infant Studies, Washington, DC.

Ruff, H. A., & Lawson, K. R. (1990). The development of sustained, focused attention during free play in young children. *Developmental Psychology, 26,* 85–93.

Ruff, H. A., Lawson, K. L., Parrinello, R., & Weissberg, R. (1990). Long-term stability of individual differences in sustained attention in the early years. *Child Development, 61.*

Ruff, H. A., McCarton, C., Kurtzberg, D., & Vaughan, H. G. (1984). Preterm infants' manipulative exploration of objects. *Child Development, 55,* 1166–1173.

Spitzer, H., Desimone, R., & Moran, J. (1988). Increased attention enhances both behavioral and neuronal performance. *Science, 240,* 338–340.

Thelen, E., Kelso, J. A. S., & Fogel, A. (1987). Self-organizing systems and infant motor development. *Developmental Review, 7,* 39–65.

Thomas, A., Chess, S., & Birch, H. G. (1969). *Temperament and behavior disorders in children.* New York: New York University Press.

Valsiner, J. (1987). *Culture and the development of children's action.* New York: Wiley.

von Bertalanffy, L. (1968). *General system theory.* New York: Braziller.

Wachs, T. D. (1987). Specificity of environmental action as manifest in environmental correlates of infant's mastery motivation. *Developmental Psychology, 23,* 782–790.

Wachs, T. D., & Smitherman, C. H. (1985). Infant temperament and subject loss in a habituation procedure. *Child Development, 56,* 861–867.

Wenar, C. (1976). Executive competence in toddlers: A prospective, observational study. *Genetic Psychology Monographs, 93,* 189–285.

Wenckstern, S., Weizman, F., & Leenaars, A. A. (1984). Temperament and tempo of play in eight-month-old infants. *Child Development, 55,* 1195–1199.

Yarrow, L. J., McQuiston, S., MacTurk, R. H., McCarthy, M. E., Klein, R. P., & Vietze, P. M. (1983). Assessment of mastery motivation during the first year of life: Contemporaneous and cross-age relationships. *Developmental Psychology 19*(2), 159–171.

Zametkin, A. J., & Rapoport, J. L. (1987). Neurobiology of attention deficit disorder with hyperactivity: Where have we come in 50 years? *Journal of the American Academy of Child and Adolescent Psychiatry, 26*(5), 676–686.

Zentall, S. S., & Zentall, T. R. (1983). Optimal stimulation: A model of disordered activity and performance in normal and deviant children. *Psychological Bulletin, 94,* 446–471.

11 The Study of Individual Differences in Infants: Auditory Processing Measures

Barbara A. Morrongiello
University of Western Ontario

INTRODUCTION

The use of auditory measures to index individual differences in infancy is well established in some professional domains and virtually untested in others. For example, there has been a burgeoning of research in the past 18 years to develop measures of auditory functioning in infants that can serve to identify those with hearing dysfunction. Similarly, professionals interested in the prediction from infancy to later speech and language skills have spent years on research to identify risk factors and auditory measures useful for this purpose. By contrast, professionals interested in establishing measures to index individual differences in infants' intellectual functioning have focused almost exclusively on measures of visual information processing. Despite the many analogous cognitive processes that occur in the visual and auditory domains (cf. Morrongiello, 1988), there is only one published report that has focused on auditory processing measures in studying individual differences in cognitive functioning in infancy (O'Connor, Cohen, & Parmelee, 1984). As discussed in this chapter, however, this is an area that seems to hold much promise for future research on individual differences in cognitive processes.

Three topics that involve auditory measures of individual differences are reviewed: the early screening and identification of infants with hearing problems, current approaches to identify infants at risk for, or having, speech and language problems, and the use of auditory measures to index individual differences in intellectual abilities and to identify infants at risk for later delay in cognitive functioning. For the most part, the literature review is selective rather than exhaustive in scope, and knowledge about structural and physiological aspects of the auditory system is assumed (for a discussion of these topics see, for example, Aslin, Pisoni, & Jusczyk, 1983; Martin, 1981).

SCREENING FOR HEARING
DYSFUNCTION IN INFANTS

Hearing plays an essential role in a child's development. The ability to hear facilitates learning about objects and events in the world, acquiring effective communication skills, and engaging in social exchanges. It has been estimated that approximately 12 in 10,000 babies are born deaf and 150 in 10,000 have some degree of hearing loss. Hearing impairment in newborns can occur for a variety of reasons (for further discussion see Gerkin, 1986), including maternal illness (e.g., diabetes mellitus) and infection during gestation (e.g., rubella, cytomegalovirus), faulty chromosomes (e.g., Treacher-Collins syndrome, Tri-somy-21), and problems encountered during the birth process (e.g., severe as-phyxia) or very soon thereafter (e.g., hyperbilirubinemia). Many more infants join this hearing-impaired population in the period following birth because of illness and the ototoxic nature of drugs prescribed to treat some illnesses (e.g., some antibiotics given to prematurely born infants with respiratory distress syndrome).

The heterogeneity in etiology is also reflected in significant variation in type of hearing loss (for further discussion see Schubert, 1980). Traditionally, hearing disorders are categorized according to the location and the nature of the problem. A *conductive* hearing loss typically reflects abnormal middle-ear functioning, such as fluid in the middle ear due to ear infection, or damage to middle-ear structures from accident or illness or congenital abnormality. In this case, sound waves are not carried properly from the outer ear through the middle ear into the cochlea. This condition may be temporary (e.g., ear infection) or permanent (e.g., damage to the ossicular chain of the middle ear). For permanent conduc-tive hearing loss, amplification of the acoustic signal, such as by a hearing aid, may suffice to ameliorate or minimize the problem. In this case, a primary goal in auditory testing is to determine the magnitude of hearing loss across frequen-cies in order that these may be amplified appropriately.

By contrast, a *sensorineural* hearing loss, which may be either acquired (e.g., following meningitis/encephalitis) or congenital (e.g., maternal rubella), is ir-reparable and may reflect damage at numerous sites in the auditory system including the receptor cells in the ear (e.g., due to noise exposure), the eighth nerve (e.g., due to multiple sclerosis), and/or brainstem structures (e.g., due to head trauma). Thus, for sensorineural loss, in addition to determining the magni-tude of hearing loss, a critical concern is to determine the site of the damage. As we see later, electrophysiological measures can be especially helpful in differ-entiating the site of a lesion. For purposes of determining the magnitude of hearing loss across frequencies, whether for conductive or sensorineural loss, both behavioral and electrophysiological measures have proven useful and are discussed later in this report.

Finally, hearing problems are identified as *central auditory processing disorders* if the auditory cortex is implicated in the problem. In this case, the person may hear words and sounds spoken normally but have difficulty recognizing these and assigning them meaning. Because this aspect of hearing is especially pertinent for speech and language functioning, screening for this type of hearing disorder typically does not occur until the child reaches at least 2 to 3 years of age and has an appreciation for the utility of speech and language in communication. As might be imagined, in most cases delayed language development provides the first indication that a central auditory-processing impairment may be present. Tests for central auditory-processing disorders are discussed under the Speech and Language section of this chapter.

Owing to the severe handicapping condition that hearing loss can have on child development (for review see, for example, Liben, 1978), it comes as no surprise that in the past 18 years there has been a tremendous effort to develop auditory screening tests in order to identify hearing problems as early as possible in infancy (see Swigart, 1986). In 1972 a joint meeting, composed of representatives of the Academy of Otolaryngology, the Academy of Pediatrics, and the American Speech and Hearing Association, was held to discuss the status of early infant screening (for further discussion see Gerber & Mencher, 1978). This Joint Committee on Infant Hearing Screening recommended the establishment of an "at risk" register, to identify infants in the newborn period who were at increased risk for hearing problems. Table 11.1 indicates several criteria, based on history and physical examination, that were to be used for this screening. At the time only the first five risk criteria were indicated, however, in 1982 two additional criteria were added by the Joint Committee. Because most data pertinent for the register were readily available in infant health records and no formal hearing testing was to be implemented during the newborn period, which elimi-

TABLE 11.1
ABCs of Risk Factors for Identifying Hearing Impairment
in Neonates and Young Infants

A. Asphyxia
B. Bacterial meningitis
C. Congenital or perinatal infections (CMV, herpes, maternal rubella, syphilis)
D. Defects of the ear, nose, or throat (e.g., cleft lip or palate, absent or low set pinna)
E. Elevated bilirubin concentration judged to be potentially toxic
F. Family history of hereditary childhood hearing impairment
G. Gram birthweight under 1,500

Note: Items A and B were added by the Joint Committee on Hearing Screening in 1983. The remaining items were recommended in 1972 (see Gerkin, 1986).

nated the need for specialized equipment and/or trained personnel, this represented a good alternative to proposed "mass screening" approaches in which large numbers of newborns were to be formally tested (for further discussion of the latter approach see Downs & Hemenway, 1969). Neonates on the register would then receive follow-up audiological testing within the first 6 months after birth, using behavioral and/or electrophysiological measures (for a more extensive review see Downs, 1986).

Since the time of this recommendation, many states have mandated by law the establishment of a High Risk Register for hearing screening and the development of procedures to insure appropriate follow-up testing of those identified to be at-risk infants (e.g., Massachusetts, New Jersey, Rhode Island). This approach to hearing screening has proven very successful for the *early* identification of infants with hearing problems. For example, the average age of onset of remediation has been estimated to be 3 months with the High Risk Register and follow-up electrophysiological testing (Gerkin, 1984). By contrast, prerisk register studies cited 27 months as the average age of onset of remediation, although parents of deaf children suspected the hearing loss and reported their concern to their pediatricians when their children were an average age of 11 months (Bergstrom, 1984; Bergstrom, Hemenway, & Downs, 1971).

The development of testing procedures for the study of individual differences in hearing loss has been a challenge because such tests must be both *sensitive* and *specific* to differentiate those few infants with hearing impairment from the general hearing population. A test is highly *sensitive* if those with hearing impairment fail rather than pass the test, in other words, the test has a high "hit" rate for detecting abnormality. A test has high *specificity* if those without hearing impairment pass rather than fail the test, in other words, the test has a low "false alarm" rate. In general, very few screening tests can boast both a high degree of sensitivity and specificity. Rather, most err toward having both a high hit *and* false alarm rate, in other words, failing many more observers than are impaired (see for example data cited in Table 5–4 in Mencher & Mencher, 1983b). Follow-up tests aimed at diagnosis then serve to confirm or disconfirm the results of the initial screening test.

In the field of hearing screening, unfortunately, very few studies provide data on the sensitivity and specificity of the test methods used. To do so would require a large number of neonates to be tested and followed throughout the language acquisition years, which is not economically feasible. Rather, most data on the topic come from follow-up testing of infants who are believed to have a hearing loss based on initial screening test results. Consequently, we know very little about the actual test–retest reliability and predictive validity of many clinical hearing tests used today. In large part, the psychometric characteristics of these tests are presumed to be good because, in laboratory settings in which these tests have been used to establish infant thresholds for hearing, there is fairly good agreement about the nature and magnitude of developmental change in frequency sensitivity in infancy and early childhood (see later). These are averaged data, however, and they are based on large numbers of infants. The performance of individual infants is seldom indicated. Although there are some recent trends toward validating hearing screening methods with select populations, such as graduates of the neonatal intensive care unit (Despland & Galambos, 1982) and developmentally handicapped children (Benham-Dunster & Dunster, 1985), considerably more research is needed in this area.

Behavioral Approaches

In the search for behavioral indices of infant hearing there have been several attempts in the past to utilize spontaneous behavioral responses to sound (e.g., startle response, cessation of activity, eye blink, head orientation to sound) in auditory screening. This approach, known as Behavioral Observation Audiometry, has sought to determine the normal developmental course of a variety of aspects of auditory responses and then to use these developmental milestones in drawing inferences about an individual child's level of auditory functioning (for further discussion see Wilson & Thompson, 1984). Examples illustrating this approach include determining the minimum sound intensity needed to elicit reliably a startle response in normally hearing infants (see Fig. 11.1); plotting the maturational course of auditory-orienting behaviors in infants, such as head orientation toward sound (see Fig. 11.2); and determining how response levels at an age vary with different auditory stimuli (see Table 11.2).

Whereas this approach is a reasonable one, these behavioral measures have unfortunately proven to have little predictive success, largely because intra and

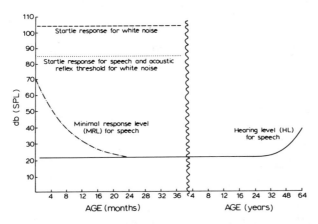

FIG. 11.1. Signal intensity needed to obtain: minimal response level (MRL) for speech, hearing level (HL) for speech, startle response for speech and acoustic reflex threshold for white noise, and startle response for white noise as a function of age (from Sweitzer, 1977).

FIG. 11.2. Development of an auditory orienting behavior, head turning to sound (from Northern & Downs, 1978).

intersubject response variability is high (Thompson & Weber, 1974), and there is rapid habituation of these responses to the repeated presentation of a sound (Moore, Thompson, & Thompson, 1975; Moore, Wilson, & Thompson, 1977). For example, Thompson and Weber (1974), using a complex noise signal, found intrasubject variability of more than 20 dB for three signal presentations for

TABLE 11.2
Response Levels as a Function of Signal and Age

Age (in Months)	Noisemakers (Approx. SPL)	Warbled Pure Tones (Re: Audiometric Zero)	Speech (Re: Audiometric Zero)
0 - 1.5	50 - 70 dB	78 dB (6 dB)	40 -60 dB
1.5 - 4	50 - 60 dB	70 dB (10 dB)	47 dB (2 dB)
4 - 7	40 - 50 dB	51 dB (9 dB)	21 dB (8 dB)
7 - 9	30 - 40 dB	45 dB (15 dB)	15 dB (7 dB)
9 - 13	25 - 35 dB	38 dB (8 dB)	8 dB (7 dB)
13 - 16	25 - 30 dB	32 dB (10 dB)	5 dB (5 dB)
16 - 21	25 dB	25 dB (10 dB)	5 dB (1 dB)
21 - 24	25 dB	26 dB (10 dB)	3 dB (2 dB)

Note: The values in parentheses are standard deviations. From Northern and Downs (1978).

infants between 3 and 60 months of age. Furthermore, in general, Trial 1 produced the best threshold, with successively poorer thresholds for Trials 2 and 3. The problem of response habituation over trials is an especially critical one for clinical testing because it reduces the number of trials available for threshold determination. This, coupled with large intrasubject variability in responding over trials, greatly reduces the sensitivity and specificity of the measures.

Early investigators provided data indicating some degree of effectiveness of these measures in infant screening (Ewing & Ewing, 1944; Hardy, Dougherty, & Hardy, 1959; Northern & Downs, 1978; Suzuki & Sato, 1961), but more systematic recent studies indicated that they are of little utility in detecting infants with mild hearing loss, although they may serve somewhat in identifying deaf infants. Furthermore, because these responses require the presentation of fairly loud sounds, they are ineffective for determining the absolute sensitivity with which infants hear different frequency sounds.

An example from the clinical audiology literature nicely illustrates this latter point. Considerable effort has been spent to develop and manufacture a device known as the Crib-o-gram to screen for hearing problems in newborn infants using measures of body activity level (for further discussion see Marcellino, 1986). This device eliminates the need for a highly trained observer and consists of a motion transducer that fits under the crib mattress. When the infant is still, a microprocessor triggers the presentation of a stimulus over a small loudspeaker in the crib. The transducer then records any changes in movement during the next 1½ seconds. About 30 trials are typically given, and the device then uses a statistical probability model to determine if the infant passed or failed. Although the concept of this device is a good one, in practice it suffers from several problems. The device is unable to determine whether the infant is awake during all stimulus presentations, or to assess whether response habituation is contributing to the infant's performance. As well, the sound must be fairly loud to elicit reliable behavioral responses (e.g., 90 dB SPL), so it is a very insensitive test for identifying those nondeaf infants with hearing loss. Not surprisingly, then, for these and other reasons (e.g., high breakdown rates), the Crib-o-gram has met with limited success as a hearing screening device in clinical settings. In fact, some studies indicate test–retest correlations of only .36 for preterms and .52 for full terms (Durieux-Smith, Picton, Edwards, Goodman, & MacMurray, 1985), coupled with high false–positive rates, indicating poor test sensitivity and specificity (Wright & Rabak, 1983).

At the present time, the most popular behavioral testing procedure to evaluate hearing functioning in infants 6 months and older is VRA or visual reinforcement audiometry (cf. Liden & Kankkunen, 1969); this procedure is based on earlier work that incorporated operant conditioning principles in testing hearing in infants 12 months and older (Suzuki & Ogibi, 1961). In VRA infants are taught to make a response, such as a directional head turn, when they detect the presentation of a sound. In most studies the sound is delivered over a loudspeaker, and it can occur either from the infant's right or left (e.g., Trehub, Schneider, & Bull, 1980); the procedure also works with earphone presentation (e.g., Berg & Smith, 1983), which is critical for screening for unilateral hearing loss. Chance level of responding to one side or the other is 50%. In other studies the sound occurs from only one loudspeaker but, in this case, there are an equal number of no-signal or control trials (e.g., Berg & Smith, 1983). Consequently, chance level of responding is still 50%. Over trials, the intensity level of the sound is varied to determine the listener's *threshold* for hearing, that is, the lowest intensity sound to which he or she responds significantly above chance. On each trial, two observers, each of which is unaware of trial condition, code the occurrence of head-turn responses independently. If they agree that the baby made a head-turn response on a signal trial, then the baby received visual reinforcement, such as the activation of a mechanical toy (see Fig. 11.3). In fact, this aspect of the

FIG. 11.3. Example of a mechanical toy reinforcer used in Visual Reinforcement Audiometry test procedures.

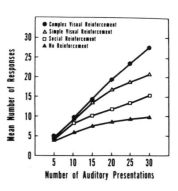

FIG. 11.4. Cumulative mean number of head-turn responses in Visual Reinforcement Audiometry procedures as a function of reinforcement condition, with N = 12 per condition (from Moore, Thompson, & Thompson, 1975).

procedure has proven to be particularly critical for its effectiveness (Moore et al., 1975; Moore et al., 1977; Trehub et al., 1980). Reinforcers serve to maintain the infant's interest and motivation in the task for long periods of time and have been shown to significantly impact on infants' performance (see Fig. 11.4). Reinforcement also allows for the completion of many testing trials (e.g., 25 to 40), which is essential for establishing reliable threshold estimates. For example, in numerous studies infants have been successfully tested repeatedly over several days to establish thresholds for a variety of frequencies (e.g., Sinnott, Pisoni, & Aslin, 1983).

Repeated testing on several frequencies allows one to construct an *audiogram*, which is essentially an indication of how threshold varies with sound frequency. The frequency characteristics of the hearing loss are important to know because each hearing loss pattern may differentially affect speech and language development. For example, a high-frequency loss (e.g., $>= 4000$ Hz) would not be expected to have as negative an impact on speech perception and language development as a low- to mid-frequency loss (e.g., 500 to 2,000 Hz).

Fig. 11.5 shows a compilation of data indicating developmental changes in infants' sensitivity to sound frequency. Notice that thresholds for hearing are closer to adult levels for high- than for low-frequency sounds, and this has been demonstrated in numerous labs and clinical settings using the VRA method. In fact, with increasing age there appears to be a steady improvement in low-frequency sensitivity and a steady decline in high-frequency sensitivity (for alternative interpretations see Olsho, Koch, Carter, Halpin, & Spetner, 1988; Wilson & Gerber, 1983). As well, although the range of thresholds cited varies somewhat across studies, within a study the range at a given age has been found to be fairly small (Wilson & Thompson, 1984), and to decrease with increasing age from 6 months (Olsho et al., 1988). Taken together, these results support the notion that these values can effectively serve as clinical norms. These normative data provide an important baseline against which to compare and judge the performance of individual infants who have been selected for follow-up testing based on the results of early screening tests like the High Risk Register. Further-

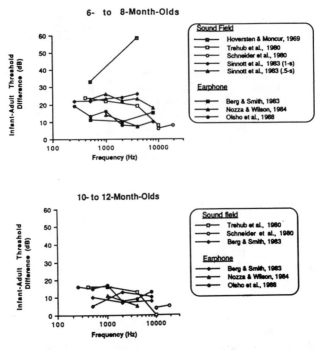

FIG. 11.5. Summary of data indicating infants' absolute thresholds, relative to adult values obtained in the same study, as a function of sound frequency (Hz). The top panel indicates data for 6- to 8-month-olds and the bottom panel indicates that for 10- to 12-month-olds (from Olsho et al., 1988).

more, most important for the study of individual differences, adaptation of these procedures for the determination of individual thresholds indicate good test–retest reliability across sessions (see Fig. 11.6).

In summary, VRA as a method for the study of individual differences in hearing sensitivity in infants has proven to be quite useful in the clinic and the laboratory setting. It is economical in time and applicable across a wide age range beginning at 6 months, it yields reliable threshold estimates, and it has produced useful clinical norms for infant hearing screening. On the latter point, it is worth noting that because differences in signal, sound-field environment, and the specifics of the VRA test protocol can have some influence on threshold estimates (e.g., although the pattern of performance across age is comparable across studies in Fig. 11.5, note there is some discrepancy in actual threshold values), it would seem best that individual clinics establish norms for their own test setting based on a small sample of normally developing infants.

Although VRA is effective for the study of individual differences in infant

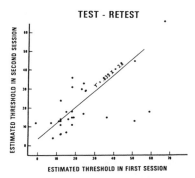

FIG. 11.6. Test–retest thresholds shown by 18-month-olds for a 4,000 Hz octave-band noise (from Schnieder & Trehub, 1983).

hearing, it does suffer one serious limitation—namely, it works only for infants 6 months and older (Moore & Wilson, 1978). Recently, Olsho and her colleagues have demonstrated success in estimating hearing thresholds in young infants using an observer-based testing procedure that shares some important features with VRA (Olsho et al., 1988). However, additional research is needed to establish psychometric properties of the method (e.g., test–retest reliability) before it can be applied to the study of individual differences in a clinical setting. At the present time, most clinical measures of hearing sensitivity in infants under 6 months of age involve electrophysiological indices of functioning, most notably, the auditory brainstem response (ABR). This measure has also proven useful for older infants in cases where behavioral testing is ill-advised (e.g., some multiply handicapped children) or behavioral results are unreliable. Also, many clinics utilize *both* behavioral testing *and* ABR testing in their evaluation process as a means of enhancing the validity of their measures of individual differences (e.g., Connelly & Oviatt, 1979).

Electrophysiological Approaches

The most popular electrophysiological measure used in clinical audiology today is the auditory brainstem response, which actually consists of a series of evoked potentials. Earlier investigators attempted to use heart rate change as an index of hearing in infants, but this research was largely unsuccessful (for a review see Eisenberg, 1976). The auditory brainstem response is particularly useful in clinical testing of infants because it is relatively independent of arousal state, attention, and sedation (Goff, Allison, Lyons, Fisher, & Conte, 1977; Picton & Hillyard, 1974). In addition, because stimuli are presented over earphones, ABR testing is especially valuable in documenting unilateral hearing impairment. Furthermore, because the components of the response correspond to different sites in the auditory system, ABR can significantly aid in determining the site of a lesion and separating the contribution of conductive, sensorineural, and neu-

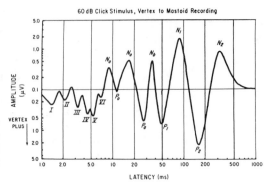

FIG. 11.7. Diagrammatic representation of the 15 waves comprising the auditory evoked potential response (from Picton et al., 1974).

ropathology components of hearing loss. For the latter reason, ABR is used with clients at all ages, not just in infancy. For example, it is especially useful in diagnosing eighth nerve tumors in adults (Jerger & Jerger, 1981).

Figure 11.7 shows a representation of the 15 waves that make up an auditory-evoked response. These waves can be divided into three categories. Waves I through VI comprise the brainstem potentials. These occur immediately following stimulus presentation and there is a good empirically based understanding of the site of each of these (see Table 11.3). The cortical-evoked potentials include two categories, the middle components, N_o through N_b, and the long latency components, waves P_1 through N_2. The middle components have received less empirical attention than the other potentials, and some debate exists as to the site of origin of these (Picton, Hillyard, & Krausz, 1974). The long latency components, unlike the ABR and middle components, are influenced by state and attentional factors (for review see Mendel, 1983). For these reasons, the auditory cortical responses have not proven as useful as the potentials of the brainstem response in clinical testing of young infants.

There are several parameters of the ABR that have clinical utility and for which age norms have been established for full-term infants. These parameter include *response latency*, which is the time period between stimulus onset and

TABLE 11.3
Site of Origin of the Six Evoked Potentials of the Brainstem Response

Wave	Site of Origin
I	Auditory nerve
II	Cochlear nucleus
III	Superior olivary complex
IV, V, VI	Rostral regions of the brainstem

Note. For further information on waves I, II, III see Jewett (1970) and Buchwald and Huang (1975).
    For further information on waves IV, V, VI see Starr and Hamilton (1976) and Stockard and Rossiter (1977).

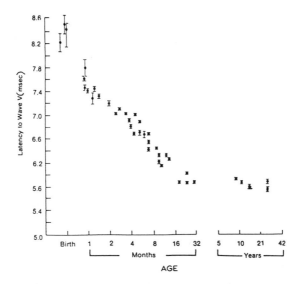

FIG. 11.8.   Latency of the wave V evoked potential response to a 60 dB
SL click as a function of age. Vertical bars enclose all measurements (at
least three) from a given subject (from Hecox & Galambos, 1974).

the peak of a component wave, most typically wave V, which is very stable
under a variety of test conditions (see Fig. 11.8); and *interpeak latencies,* most
notably, the time between wave I and V, which is presumed to indicate conduc-
tion time between the ear and brainstem nuclei (see Fig. 11.9). In addition,
response amplitude, which is often expressed as a ratio of amplitudes between
two waves, most typically wave I and V, also has been reported by some to be a
reliable predictor of longitudinal outcome in babies who suffered severe asphyxia
as newborns (Hecox & Cone, 1981), and to vary with age (see Fig. 11.10),
although age norms per se have not yet been established for this parameter.

In general, owing to the variability of amplitude measurements, clinical criteria for interpretation of ABR are usually based on latency rather than amplitude
measures, and these are very well articulated. For example, Fig. 11.11 shows
some typical ABR responses of infant patients. As can be seen, based on examination of the latencies of waves I and V and how these relate to one another, one
can identify infants with conductive hearing loss (i.e., prolonged wave I and V
latencies but normal I–V interpeak interval), cochlear based hearing loss (i.e.,
no wave I present, normal wave V at high-signal intensity but prolonged latency
with decreasing intensity), and neurological dysfunction (i.e., prolonged latency
for wave V with normal latency for wave I and prolonged I–V interpeak interval). Thus, ABR can serve as an important diagnostic tool in indicating the
nature and site of hearing dysfunction.

In addition to indicating the type of hearing problem and site of origin, ABR

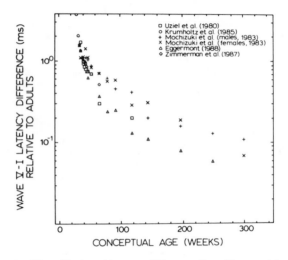

FIG. 11.9.   Wave V minus I latency difference (in milliseconds) relative
to adults as a function of conceptual age in weeks (from Eggermont,
1988).

also can be used to estimate the magnitude of hearing loss. ABR testing to
determine a threshold for hearing is common in clinical settings, although there
is debate on its usefulness in this regard owing to its lack of frequency specificity. The typical stimulus in ABR recording is a series of clicks, each of which
contains energy that spans many frequencies; a series of clicks is the preferred
stimulus because the near-instantaneous onset of a click initiates more syn-
chronized neural excitation and, consequently, a clearly defined ABR response.
Because ABR is relatively insensitive to pathology affecting the coding of very
low frequencies (i.e., < 500 Hz) or very high frequencies (i.e., > 8000 Hz), it
provides predominantly a test of mid- to high-frequency hearing. The use of
white noise maskers, tone pips, and filtered clicks have facilitated screening for
particular frequency selectivity problems. However, there have been few com-

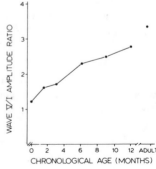

FIG. 11.10.   The   relation   between amplitude of wave V and
I as a function of age in months
(from Hecox & Burkard, 1982).

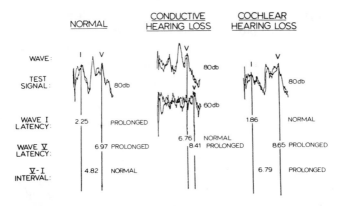

FIG. 11.11.   Prototypical ABR responses as a function of hearing status (from Worthington & Peters, 1984).

parative studies of the diagnostic utility of these different stimuli (for further discussion see Hecox & Burkard, 1982).

The general approach to establishing a threshold for hearing using ABR is to present stimuli, most typically a series of clicks, at a particular intensity over a calibrated earphone and to record changes in wave V latency in response to these; wave V is chosen because it is the most prominent and easily detectable at low-sensation levels. Decreasing signal intensity over trials allows one to determine a threshold for hearing. Plotting the latency of the response as a function of signal intensity indicates both the *slope* of the function and *absolute latency* values, and these then can be compared with clinical norms. For example, as can be seen in Fig. 11.12, elevated thresholds that reflect a conductive hearing loss often yield a function (solid line) that parallels but falls outside the normal range (dashed lines), whereas elevated thresholds that reflect a sensorineural loss often yield a function with an extremely steep slope (Picton et al., 1974). Thus, plotting ABR thresholds as a function of signal intensity and comparing both the slope and absolute values of these with clinical norms can provide important information

FIG. 11.12.   Diagrammatic representation of two types of abnormal latency-intensity functions for wave V (from Hecox, Gerber, & Mendel, 1983). The dashed lines designate a "normal" range of functioning. The solid line designates typical performance observed when a conductive or sensorineural (S–N) hearing loss is present.

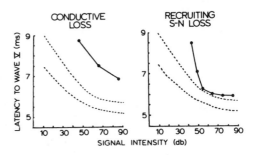

about the nature and extent of hearing loss in infants, although frequency specificity of the loss is not provided if click stimuli are used.

Although ABR measures were developed initially for use with healthy full-term infants, in fact, a major focus in current research is on extending its application to screen for hearing and/or neurologic dysfunction in preterms and infants in the neonatal intensive care unit (NICU). Because most premies and NICU babies will have at least one risk factor indicated on the High Risk Register (see Table 11.1), they, moreso than healthy full terms, are typically the focus of follow-up testing. Age norms based on full-term samples, however, are *not* really applicable to preterms, because gestational age directly impacts on the ABR. For example, the earlier the gestational age, the more prolonged the response latencies and the smaller the response amplitudes *independent* of hearing status (Despland & Galambos, 1980; Salamy, 1984; Salamy, Mendelson, Tooley, & Chaplin, 1980; Starr, Amlie, Martin, & Sanders, 1977). In fact, some investigators have argued that ABR is not effective for hearing screening in NICU infants, specifically because most failures are due to neurological immaturity and not necessarily to hearing problems (e.g, Roberts et al., 1982). Because of this confounding problem of gestational age, it is difficult to interpret many studies with preterms aimed at examining the validity of ABR measures in identifying hearing problems in at-risk infants. For example, in a recent review of research in which sensitivity of ABR as a screening device has been evaluated in longitudinal investigations of high-risk infants (i.e., preterms, full terms who were asphyxiated, suffered hyperbilirubinemia, or had neurologic abnormalities), it was reported that, of those high-risk infants who failed ABR screening as neonates (16.5% of all infants tested), only 1 in 3 (5.1% of the 16.5%) were found on follow-up to have a hearing impairment or other neurologic dysfunction (Murray, Javel, & Watson, 1985). Thus, the average confirmation rate across studies was only 31%. Whereas these findings would argue against ABR as a sensitive index of hearing dysfunction in infants, interpreting ABRs of preterms relative to full-term norms would likely have falsely elevated the number of preterm infants failing the initial screening test in some studies. Consequently, these confirmation rates must be cautiously interpreted. Furthermore, as can be seen for these data, which are given in Table 11.4, there also was considerable variation across studies in confirmation rates (4.8 to 100%). This variance illustrates two additional sources of problems in trying to validate ABR as a screening device—namely, the lack of consistency in pass/fail criteria and methods used in measuring ABR.

Some investigators, for example, define a fail by the absence of a wave. By contrast, others define a fail as one standard deviation on either side of the range designated as normal. Still others require a discrepancy of at least two standard deviations from the normal range. Obviously, how one defines a failure will directly impact on false alarm rate (for an excellent discussion see Murray et al., 1985). On the matter of methods used in measuring ABR, there is considerable

TABLE 11.4
Results from Clinical and Longitudinal Studies of High-Risk Infants
(From Murray et al., 1985, Table 3)

Study	# Screened	% Failed	# Followed	% Impaired	Hit Rate
Cox et al. (1982)	50	18.0%	50	6.0%	33.3%
Dennis et al. (1984)	200	11.5%	15	5.0%	43.5%
Galambos et al. (1984)	1613	16.0%	139	4.9%	30.5%
Hecox and Cone (1981)	126	16.7%	21	16.7%	100.0%
Hyde et al. (1984)	303	11.9%	197	1.0%	8.3%
Jacobsen and Morehouse (1984)	176	19.9%	33	4.0%	20.0%
Mencher and Mencher (1983a)	218	9.2%	13	5.0%	55.0%
Mjoen (1981)	81	25.9%	21	22.2%	85.7%
Roberts et al. (1982)	128	39.0%	24	2.3%	6.0%
Shannon et al. (1984)	168	12.5%	134	.6%	4.8%
Starr et al. (1977)	47	10.6%	3	4.2%	40.0%
Stein et al. (1983)	100	29.2%	8	6.0%	20.7%
Total or Average	3210	16.5%	658	5.1%	31.0%

Note. Hit rate indicates the number of repeat failures as a percentage of failures on the initial screening test.

research to indicate the effects on latency and amplitude parameters of variation in stimulus repetition rate, signal intensity, and even electrode placement (see Hecox & Jacobsen, 1984). Thus, standardization of pass/fail criteria and of recording and testing procedures are necessary to facilitate comparisons across ABR validation studies.

In addition, a recent study by Murray illustrates the utility of a multivariate approach to the problem of controlling for the effect on ABR of important variables like gestational age, pregnancy and delivery complications, and postnatal illness. Murray found that conceptual age was the strongest predictor of the I–V interwave latency in neonates, and that this ABR parameter had low but reliable correlations with measures of neurobehavioral functioning assessed by the Brazelton Neonatal Assessment Scale (Murray, 1988a). Furthermore, in a follow-up investigation she found that ABRs in the newborn period showed moderate predictive accuracy for sensorineural hearing impairment, and low to moderate prediction for deviant neurobehavioral development during the first year after birth (Murray, 1988b). These findings highlight the importance of considering gestational age when using ABR to screen for auditory and/or neurological dysfunction in at-risk infants, and they support other data with adults and infants that indicate the predictive validity of ABR measures for detecting impaired auditory and/or neurological functioning (e.g., Despland & Galambos, 1982).

In summary, ABR has proven a clinically useful tool for the study of individual differences in infant hearing. It provides information on the nature, site, and extent of hearing dysfunction, and can be reliably measured in infants, even in the newborn period. Although follow-up results of large infant population studies are still being gathered, several studies suggest that ABR has moderate predictive validity and that it provides a moderately sensitive index of auditory functioning, particularly when gestational age and developmental status are taken into account. Because ABR to broadband clicks provides limited information about frequency selectivity of hearing loss per se, behavioral audiometry may provide important information to supplement that from ABR testing, at least in infants 6 months and older. On this point, it goes without saying that a *comprehensive* approach to auditory testing will no doubt yield the most reliable and valid conclusions about individual differences in infant auditory functioning. When ABR is used in conjunction with behavioral measures and tests of middle-ear mechanical functioning (see Northern, 1981), one's conclusions and recommendations about intervention are greatly enriched. For example, middle-ear dysfunction is common in NICU infants and may be the cause of their failing an ABR screening test. Many of these types of problems are transient, however, and do not include permanent dysfunction. Examining the mechanical properties of the middle ear would likely indicate the temporary nature of the problem. Similarly, a middle-ear infection in an older infant may result in elevated behavioral thresholds, the cause of which would not be evident without middle-ear evaluation. On the other hand, elevated behavioral thresholds may result from problems at many levels in the auditory system, not just from middle-ear dysfunction. Supplementing these data with those from ABR testing then is likely to help to elucidate the site of the problem. Thus, it is unlikely that any single measure will prove sufficiently comprehensive to support the clinical study of individual differences in hearing throughout infancy. Instead, multiple measures of hearing functioning will be needed to capture both the scope and subtleties of individual differences in human auditory development.

PREDICTING SPEECH AND LANGUAGE PROBLEMS FROM INFANT MEASURES

Although infants at an early age are differentially responsive to speech as compared to nonspeech sounds (Butterfield & Siperstein, 1972; Molfese, 1977) and discriminate between numerous speech-sound contrasts (for a review see Aslin et al., 1983), it remains to be determined whether and how these capacities are predictive of later speech and language skills. Because infants' comprehension of the meaning of words does not emerge until about the first year after birth (Oviatt, 1981; Thomas, Campos, Shucard, Ramsay, & Shucard, 1981), it is not possible to assess directly their speech intelligibility and processing skills until after this time. In fact, because vocabulary development proceeds from 12 to 13 months, most tests aimed at screening for speech intelligibility or processing problems indicate 2 years as the youngest age at which they can be given. Consequently, any attempts to predict the later development of speech and language skills from infancy have proceeded largely by trying to identify "risk factors" that retrospective studies suggest may predispose infants toward problems in these areas.

Because a sound must be audible before it can be recognized, problems in detecting sounds are likely to impact on speech perception. For this reason, the same risk factors apply here as for hearing screening in general (see Table 11.1). In addition, there has been considerable debate about whether and to what extent temporary or fluctuating hearing loss may affect subsequent speech and language development. Research on chronic ear infections bears on this issue and is discussed later under Risk Factors. Note that the emphasis in this chapter is on the study of individual differences, particularly with respect to aberrant development. Consequently, research examining the impact of early language environments on an individual's acquisition of normal speech-perception skills is not considered (for further discussion on this topic see Werker, 1986; Werker & Tees, 1984).

Risk Factors

Numerous studies with nonhuman animals indicate the deleterious effect that early auditory deprivation, such as unilateral hearing loss, can have both on the structural and the functional aspects of the developing auditory system (Brugge, Feng, Reale, & Chan, 1983; Clements & Kelly, 1978; Coleman & O'Connor, 1979; Kitzes, 1984; Knudsen & Konishi, 1980; Webster, 1983). In humans, the auditory system is more structurally mature peripherally than centrally, and considerable development occurs postnatally (Hecox, 1975). Consequently, early auditory deprivation might be expected to have a significant impact on subsequent auditory development. For these reasons there has been considerable concern about the effect that recurrent ear infections in infancy may have on speech and language development, and whether this should be considered a risk factor.

Ear infection involving fluid in the middle-ear cavity, otherwise known as otitis media with effusion (OME), is one of the most infectious diseases in early childhood. It has been estimated that by age 3 approximately ⅓ of children will have experienced at least three episodes of OME (Teele, Klein, & Rosner, 1980). In general, with increasing age the frequency of OME decreases; however, some children suffer chronic OME attacks well beyond 2 to 3 years and eventually are labeled by physicians as "otitis prone." Mild to moderate conductive hearing loss due to fluid is the most common complication in this middle-ear disease, and fluid in the middle-ear space can persist for weeks or months after antibiotic drug therapy (Teele et al., 1980). For all these reasons, then, there have been numerous studies examining the long-term impact of recurrent auditory deprivation by OME on subsequent speech and language development (for a more extensive review see Kavanaugh, 1986; Webster, 1983).

Several studies indicate negative effects of early fluctuating hearing loss on the development of language comprehension and production skills, most notably, an increase in the incidence of articulation errors (Holm & Kunze, 1969; Needleman, 1977; Northern & Lemme, 1982). Other studies indicate significant developmental delay, though not deviance necessarily, in the acquisition of speech skills, such as sentence usage (Friel-Patti et al., 1982; Zinkus, Gottlieb, & Schapiro, 1978). There have also been numerous studies correlating early OME with later difficulties in school performance and other cognitive tasks (see Downs, 1983). A careful review of many of these studies, however, indicates significant methodological problems that constrain the interpretation and/or validity of the conclusions (for further discussion see Paradise, 1981; Ventry, 1980). For example, in many studies the incidence of OME is indicated by parental report based on memory, and no early measures are available on the degree of conductive loss actually experienced, there are no attempts to control for socioeconomic status, control groups are poorly matched with experimental, and a retrospective design is used with correlational rather than confirmatory analyses.

In summary, although it is apparent that early unilateral hearing loss can significantly impact on structural and functional postnatal development of the auditory system in many species, the extent to which recurrent OME in human infants produces similar effects and predicts later speech and language problems remains to be determined. Furthermore, demonstration of a correlation between early OME and later language problems at a particular age does not address the important question of whether such effects are reversible or permanent. Because language development results from an interactional process between the organism and its' language environment, one might hypothesize relatively short-term effects of temporally constrained abnormal auditory experiences. For example, examining the effect of three or fewer episodes of OME on 6- to 18-month-olds' binaural hearing, specifically, their accuracy in discriminating the direction of sound movement along the horizontal axis (Morrongiello, 1989), it was noted that accuracy was poor under certain conditions at the time of OME but was significantly improved in the same infants 2 weeks following the episode of OME (see Fig. 11.13). Although this study did not address the question of how chronic OME (i.e., > 3 episodes) affects sound localization performance, it does highlight the functional plasticity and potential for recovery of functioning following OME insult in the human auditory system. More carefully executed, prospective research should provide important information on the magnitude and persistence of speech and language problems in children that experience recurrent OME episodes during the formative language-learning years. Such data are needed before a conclusion can be made about whether OME should be considered a significant factor in the study of individual differences in speech and language development.

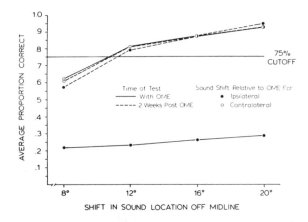

FIG. 11.13. Average proportion of correct head orientation toward lateralized sound as a function of the presence of otitis media with effusion (OME) and location of sound relative to OME ear (from Morrongiello, 1989).

Current Approaches

Speech audiometry functions not only in identifying the magnitude and nature of hearing loss with regard to speech, but also in screening for central auditory-processing problems, and evaluating hearing aid systems (see Konkle & Rintelman, 1983). At the present time, most clinical tests to evaluate speech and language processes are for children 2 years and older. Consequently, they serve largely diagnostic rather than prognostic functions. As is discussed later, however, based on the demonstrated success of VRA type procedures used for studying aspects of auditory development in experimental settings, the extension of some of these tests to young infants would seem worth pursuing.

Because many children referred for speech audiometry hear normally but do not understand speech, both threshold and suprathreshold recognition skills typically are evaluated. For threshold evaluation, the primary focus has been on estimating a *threshold for intelligibility*, that is, the lowest stimulus intensity at which the child correctly identifies at least 50% of the words spoken; in these tests, the words are presented either by earphone or sound-field presentation, and the child is expected either to repeat the spoken word or to point to pictures or objects represented by the word. This threshold has been shown to have a high correlation with that obtained for non-speech stimuli (Davis, 1970), and so it provides a good test of convergent validity. With young children, as well, several investigators report greater success in threshold testing for speech than nonspeech stimuli (e.g., Hodgson, 1972). Thus, speech reception threshold testing would seem invaluable in studying individual differences in hearing in young children. Of course, because familiarity with the spoken word is necessary in these tests, their applicability is limited to children who have a sufficiently large receptive vocabulary to allow enough trials to be presented so that a threshold can be estimated reliably. Studies that have examined the acquisition of word meanings in infancy indicate that by 13 months infants know a fair number of object names and will reliably select and fixate these objects when their names are presented (Oviatt, 1981; Thomas et al., 1981). These findings suggest that speech reception threshold measures might be possible to obtain in children younger than 2 to 3 years of age.

Speech discrimination is another facet of performance that is also considered when problems in speech and language development are suspected. Again, however, in the clinical setting the formalization of tests to evaluate this aspect of language functioning has been limited to children at least 2 to 3 years of age. This is quite surprising given the number of testing procedures that have been developed and proven successful for evaluating speech discrimination skills in laboratory settings for young infants (for review see Aslin et al., 1983). In fact, the most popular method currently used in the lab for this purpose is a conditioned head-turn procedure that is analogous in principle to the VRA procedure used by many clinicians to estimate nonspeech thresholds. Of course, owing to limitations in an infant's attention span and motivation, one cannot expect to examine his or her discrimination of many sound contrasts using these procedures. Nonetheless, in an infant identified at an early age to be at risk for hearing and/or speech and language problems, it would seem worthwhile to examine these skills, even in a limited way, as early and as often as possible in infancy.

For purposes of screening for central auditory disorders, both monaural and binaural processes are typically examined in the testing protocol (for a thorough discussion see Lasky & Katz, 1983). Most tests are concerned with evaluating three aspects of speech processing: (1) the child's ability to attend to one signal in the presence of competing signals, such as discriminating speech in noise or attending to the stimulus in one ear while ignoring that in the other ear; (2) the child's ability to recognize and discriminate speech when redundancy is reduced in the signal and, consequently, the central processing demands are increased. Time-altered or compressed speech introduces temporal distortion and eliminates bits of the speech signal, and filtered speech reduces the frequency redundancy in the signal. In both cases, the listener must fill in information for recognition; and (3) the child's ability to discriminate sequences of speech sounds, which involves both memory and sequencing skills.

In the case of central auditory disorders it is common to see normal pure-tone thresholds coupled with reduced speech discrimination scores in the ear contralateral to the damaged part of the brain, most notably when the speech is distorted in some way and redundancy is reduced or a dichotic presentation is used, such as with a competing signal presented to the opposite ear (e.g., Beasley, Maki, & Orchic, 1976; Willeford, 1976). Even nonspeech sounds (e.g., digits) are effective in dichotic listening tasks for indicating damage to the contralateral hemisphere (e.g., Kimura, 1961; Musiek & Sachs, 1980). In fact, some investigators argue against the use of speech in testing for central auditory disorders on the grounds that linguistic deficits rather than central auditory-processing problems could be responsible for poor performance on these tests (Ludlow, Cudahy, Bassich, & Brown, 1983). Consistent with this concern is evidence from adults indicating the independent nature of impairment in speech perception and auditory processing, depending on the location of brain lesions (Auerbach, Naeser, & Mazurski, 1981). Thus, although speech stimuli are typically used for central auditory testing, a good argument can be made for not limiting these tests to speech stimuli, particularly because the effects have been observed for non-speech stimuli as well. Other data from clinical studies also support this point.

Hochster and Kelly (1981) examined the effect of temporal lobe epilepsy on children's perception of an auditory illusion that functions in sound localization, the precedence effect (PE); the encoding of interaural timing differences is important for perception of the PE illusion and cortical processes have been implicated in numerous studies involving nonhuman animals (Cranford, Ravizza, Diamond, & Whitfield, 1971; Whitfield, Cranford, Ravizza, & Diamond, 1972) and human adults (Jerger, 1960; Sanchez-Longo & Forster, 1958). The findings of Hochster and Kelly were consistent with the notion that the PE taps temporal lobe functioning: These children were unable to perform above chance to PE sounds, although they had no difficulty with non-PE sounds. Because infants by 5 months experience the PE illusion (for a review of this developmental literature see Clifton, Morrongiello, Kulig, & Dowd, 1981a, 1981b; Morrongiello, Kulig, & Clifton, 1984), this phenomenon may hold promise in screening for central auditory disorders in prelinguistic infants.

In addition to the PE, tests that tap auditory pattern perception processes also might be useful in screening for central auditory disorders. Damage to the temporal lobe of lower order animals (Colavita, Szeligo, & Zimmer, 1974; Diamond & Neff, 1957; Heffner & Heffner, 1984; Kaas, Axelrod, & Diamond, 1967; Meyer & Woolsey, 1952) and human adults (Chedru, Bastard, & Efron, 1978; Edwards & Auger, 1965; Jerger, Weikers, Sharbrough, & Jerger, 1969; Lackner & Teuber, 1973) can result in a loss of the ability to discriminate between auditory sequences that involve the same components but in different temporal orders. Research examining such pattern discrimination skills in normally developing full-term infants indicates the presence of these capacities at an early age (for review see Morrongiello, 1988). Damage to the central auditory system, however, might be reflected in infancy in these auditory discrimination skills.

Tallal and her colleagues (Tallal & Newcombe, 1978; Tallal & Piercy, 1973), for example, found that some learning-disabled children had difficulty with the temporal patterning of conversational speech. When the speech sequence was presented at a slower rate of presentation, their performance significantly improved. In addition, Pinheiro (1976, 1977) reported that a pitch pattern test proved sensitive for identifying disruption of the interhemispheric auditory pathways in adults (see also Musiek, Pinheiro, & Wilson, 1980; Musiek & Sachs, 1980). Thus, auditory pattern perception tasks, which already have been successfully developed for testing infants, may be another means by which to identify central auditory disorders in the prelinguistic years.

In summary, for the most part, the identification of children with speech and language problems does not occur until 2 to 3 years of age when formal examination of these skills is possible using clinically standardized tests. As indicated before, however, data from experimental settings suggests several aspects of speech audiometry that may be applicable to infants, including estimating speech reception thresholds, examining speech sound discrimination skills, and screening for central auditory-processing disorders. Of course, it may be that scaling down clinical tests for older children for application to infants does not provide a sufficiently rich database on which to base a diagnosis (e.g., too few trials completed or test conditions sampled). Nonetheless, even examining the infant's individual performance curves over age would provide a greater wealth of information on which to draw clinical inferences about speech and language development than would examining skills at a single time between 2 and 3 years of age. This approach would seem to hold value too for the elucidation of risk factors that impact on speech and language development at an individual level (e.g., stability of functioning over time, recovery of functioning following an episode of OME).

PREDICTING INTELLECTUAL FUNCTIONING
FROM INFANT MEASURES

For years psychologists have been interested in establishing measures to index individual differences in infants' intellectual functioning. Early identification of mental deficiency would allow for early intervention, which would maximize the developmental potential of a child at risk. In the past decade, considerable advances have been made toward achieving this goal of early identification of infants at risk for mental handicaps, with the primary response measures being indices of visual information processing (see chapters in this volume by Colombo & Mitchell; Rose & Feldman). Nonetheless, this research has met with some criticism on grounds related to the reliability and validity of the measures (e.g., Malcuit, Pomerleau, & Lamarre, 1988; McCall, 1981). One approach to dealing with the important issue of validity is to look for converging evidence of the predictive validity of visual information-processing measures by examining other measures that tap analogous processes and determining their predictive value. In light of the many analogies that can be drawn between auditory and visual processes (cf. Morrongiello, 1988), the area of auditory information processing seems a likely candidate in this regard.

In this section the focus is on research on auditory information processing that highlights areas of investigation that may hold promise for the future study of individual differences in cognitive development. The section is divided into four major parts. The first presents a brief discussion of current approaches to measuring infant intelligence (for a more thorough review see other chapters in this volume). The second focuses on discussion of some visual information-processing measures that have been related to individual differences in cognitive functioning, specifically, tasks that tap memory, identification and discrimination, and abstraction and categorization processes. The third part reviews research findings in each of these domains within audition and includes literature examining the perception of speech as well as nonspeech sound patterns, with a predominant emphasis on the latter. Within the past few years there have been significant advances in our knowledge of infants' perception of auditory patterns, and this area seems to hold particular promise for the study of individual differences in cognitive functioning in infants. The final section suggests directions for future research using auditory measures of information processing and discusses the utility of multimodal measures to index individual differences in infancy and to predict later intellectual outcome in childhood.

Current Approaches

Since the early 1900s, child care professionals have been interested in the development of tests to index individual differences in mental functioning in young children (for review see Brooks & Weinraub, 1976). However, the motivation behind this interest, beliefs about the nature of intelligence, and the testing approaches taken have all changed considerably over the years. The early work emphasized identification of infants of subnormal intelligence (Binet & Simon, 1905), reflected beliefs in a fixed amount of intelligence (cf. Burt, Jones, Miller, & Moodie, 1934) coupled with the assumption of continuity in intellectual functioning (for review see Stott & Ball, 1965), and derived a global index of a child's developmental status based largely on items that sampled sensory and motor competencies (e.g., Bayley, 1969; Griffiths, 1954; Uzgiris & Hunt, 1966). By contrast, in more recent work the primary goal has been screening of infants to determine those *at risk* for future delays or intellectual handicap, the importance of environmental experiences in cognitive development has been recognized and often used as a basis of argument for early intervention programs, distinctions have been made between the question of stability of individual differences and that of continuity in mental functioning, and the primary emphasis has been on measures that index *information-processing* abilities as compared to sensory and motor skills.

In the past 10 years there has been considerable research aimed at determining processing measures that capture continuity in intellectual functioning at an individual level. The two measures that have received the most attention have been habituation of attention (i.e., a decrement in responding with the repeated presentation of a stimulus that is not due to sensory adaptation or fatigue) and recovery of attention or response to stimulus novelty (for a thorough discussion of these measures see other chapters in this volume). The underlying assumption in the use of these measures is that habituation reflects the infant's waning attention to the stimulus as its features are encoded and a mental representation is built up, and response to novelty indicates recognition by the infant that the new stimulus differs from the familiar one. Thus, both measures tap attention, recognition, and memory.

The use of attentional measures in infants as indices of cognitive functioning (cf. McCall, 1971) has met with fairly good success. Although tests of reliability and predictive validity are still underway, the data so far are encouraging. In an excellent review of several studies, Bornstein and Benasich (1986) report reasonable test–retest reliability coefficients for habituation (.44) as well as for response recovery (.46), and the results of more recent research are consistent with these conclusions (e.g., Colombo, Mitchell, O'Brien, & Horowitz, 1987). There also have been numerous demonstrations that these measures in infancy possess moderate predictive validity for intellectual functioning in childhood, as measured by verbal IQ tests (for reviews see Bornstein & Sigman, 1986; Fagan & Singer, 1983). Furthermore, although research has been limited, there is evidence indicating the inter-relatedness of these two measures as indicators of individual differences in infants, which provides support for the assumption that both are tapping related processes (Bornstein & Ruddy, 1984; O'Connor, Cohen, & Parmelee, 1984; Sigman, 1983). In summary, considerable data provide support for the notion of continuity in at least some aspects of mental functioning from infancy and suggest that measures of information processing in infancy reflect central cognitive capacities and predict select cognitive competencies in childhood. In the following section we consider some aspects of visual information processing that have been studied in the attempt to find measures of individual differences in cognitive functioning.

Visual Information-Processing Measures

There are several aspects of visual information processing in infancy that have been examined empirically and discussed in the context of individual differences in cognitive functioning, including rate of processing, memory and discrimination of novel from familiar stimuli, and abstraction and categorization.

Although there is general consensus that rate of visual information processing increases with age (e.g., Lasky & Spiro, 1980; Wickens, 1974; Zelazo & Kearsley, 1982) considerable argument and speculation exists as to whether this measure reflects stable individual differences. The most systematic research on the question attempted to utilize habituation as an index of information processing. Because the process of habituation is presumed to reflect an infant's waning attention to a stimulus as an internal representation is built up and the stimulus becomes increasingly familiar (e.g., Cohen & Gelber, 1975), one might expect that rate of habituation would prove a useful indicator of individual differences in rate or efficiency of information processing. Although some early results suggested promise in this regard (e.g., Lewis, 1971; Miller, Sinnott, Short, & Hains, 1976), the results of subsequent studies did not support the notion that fast habituators were necessarily quicker or more efficient in stimulus encoding than slow habituators (e.g., McCall, 1979). The discrepancy in results across studies probably relates to numerous methodological differences, including how investigators defined their criterion for habituation (e.g., proportional vs. fixed response decrement) and the basis on which they categorized infants into slow versus fast habituators. Suffice it to say that although it would seem reasonable to expect that rate of habituation should reflect rate of information processing and, consequently, index stable individual differences, this has not been unequivocably demonstrated.

In the study of infants' memory for a visual stimulus and their capacity to discriminate novel from familiar stimuli, two procedures have proven effective: the use of habituation followed by a test for response recovery to a novel stimulus, and the use of a paired-comparison preferential-looking task, which involves familiarizing infants with two stimuli and then presenting one of these paired with a novel stimulus and observing if infants look more to the familiar or novel stimulus (Fantz, 1956). In both cases responding to a change in stimulus, by response recovery or novelty preference, is presumed to index memory for the familiar stimulus and discrimination between stimulus conditions. Based on these discrimination procedures, there is considerable evidence that the magnitude of response recovery or novelty preference in early infancy reflects stable individual differences and predicts later intellectual functioning in early childhood (e.g., Caron, Caron, & Glass, 1983; Fagan, 1981; Fagan & McGrath, 1981; Fagan & Singer, 1983; Lewis & Brooks-Gunn, 1981). Moreover, this has been shown for preterm as well as full-term infants (e.g., Rose & Wallace, 1985). Thus, indices of memory and discrimination in infancy seem to reflect central cognitive capacities that remain fairly stable across age within individuals and are independent of test modality and infant health status.

In the area of visual abstraction and categorization, there is quite a tradition of research on inference abilities and concept learning with adults and children (see, for example, Rosch & Lloyd, 1978). However, examining these skills in infants has proceeded more slowly, primarily due to methodological limitations. Not surprisingly, it is difficult to devise tasks to allow nonverbal infants to indicate if they recognize similarity across stimuli that differ along some dimensions (i.e., categorization), and to determine if infants have developed the concept or theme that relates a group of stimuli (i.e., abstraction). Nonetheless, research examining abstraction and categorization abilities in the visual domain (e.g., Cohen & Strauss, 1979; Fagan, 1976; Younger & Cohen, 1983) reveals that by 6 to 7 months of age infants can abstract a prototype from exposure to various exemplars of a category, and they can subsequently categorize stimuli on the basis of similarity to a category prototype. The extent to which indices of abstraction and categorization predict later intellectual functioning remains to be determined empirically, but these skills play an important role in language acquisition (e.g., Newport & Bellugi, 1978) and learning about objects and events in the world (e.g., Rosch, Simpson, & Miller, 1976) and, consequently, would seem likely to hold promise for the study of individual differences in cognitive capacities in infancy.

Although the current emphasis on information-processing indices of individual differences in infancy has been primarily limited to measures of visual habituation and response recovery, there are neither theoretical nor practical reasons why this must be so. Traditional psychometric tests of intelligence in childhood (e.g., Wechsler Preschool and Primary Scale of Intelligence), as well as more recent tests (e.g., Kaufman Assessment Battery for Children, see Kaufman & Kaufman, 1983), tap numerous information-processing abilities, including memory, identification and discrimination, and abstraction and categorization. Furthermore, they include some items to sample similar abilities in both the visual and auditory modalities, for example, the child's ability to remember and correctly reproduce a sequence of several pictures and several numbers that were presented auditorily. In light of these observations and the success to date in using measures of information processing that tap attention, recognition, and discrimination to predict intelligence in childhood, it would seem a promising area of research to examine both the predictive utility of measures that tap other aspects of information processing in infancy and the convergent validity of measures that tap analogous processes in modalities other than vision. These two points are discussed further in the following section.

Pertinent Auditory-Processing Measures

Although there are numerous demonstrations of infants' abilities to discriminate basic features of simple auditory stimuli, such as a change in frequency, intensity, or temporal parameters (for a review see, for example, Aslin et al., 1983), the most likely area to hold promise for the study of individual differences is auditory pattern perception. A listener's ability to organize a sequence of discrete sounds into a unified event or ''pattern'' reflects numerous information-processing skills, including discrimination of and memory for the discrete units of the pattern, attention to and memory of the temporal ordering of these units, and the ability to abstract a "concept" regarding how these discrete events relate to one another, in other words, to recognize the "pattern." Furthermore, auditory patterns, like concepts, can be hierarchically organized. For example, with music a sequence of notes gives rise to a phrase pattern, and successive phrase patterns come to define the melody. In speech a sequence of phonemes forms a syllable and a sequence of syllables defines a word. Thus, systematic manipulation of the hierarchical structure of auditory sequences can provide a means by which to tap different levels of information processing.

Although the study of auditory pattern perception in infants has recruited wide attention only in the last decade (for a review see Morrongiello, 1988), numerous advances in our knowledge have been made. There is evidence that young infants group sounds subjectively on the basis of temporal proximity and the relative ordering of temporal intervals (e.g., Chang & Trehub, 1977a; Demany, McKenzie, & Vurpillot, 1977; Morrongiello, 1984). As well, infants' subjective grouping of sound sequences reflects sensitivity both to frequency differences and similarities among the component tones (e.g., Demany, 1982; Thorpe, Trehub, Morrongiello, & Bull, 1988). Furthermore, infants are sensitive to relational properties of sound sequences and discriminate changes in the frequency relations between successive tones in a sequence, such as when tones are reordered in a sequence (e.g., McCall, 1979; Morrongiello, 1986; Trehub, Thorpe, & Morrongiello, 1987).

In summary, because auditory pattern perception taps a variety of information-processing skills and numerous findings indicate that infants at an early age possess at least some rudimentary capacities in this regard, it seems an area that holds promise for the study of individual differences in infancy. In the following section developmental literature on auditory information processing is reviewed in greater detail, including literature on infants' memory for auditory events, their identification and discrimination of auditory events, and their ability to demonstrate abstraction and categorization for auditory material. A particular emphasis is on discussion of research that reveals performance differences between normal and at-risk infant populations, because such differences indicate the utility of the measures for the study of individual differences.

Memory for Auditory Events.   There has been very little systematic research on memory effects in infant audition, particularly as pertains to auditory pattern perception (for a review see Morrongiello, 1988). However, several studies reveal a decline in discrimination performance with increasing memory demands. Moreover, this decline in performance is particularly evident for discrimination of specific as contrasted with more general features of a pattern, suggesting that memory capacities differ as a function of level of featural analysis (cf. Craik & Lockhart, 1972). Finally, at least one study suggests differences between normal and at-risk infant populations in this aspect of information-processing capacity.

Leavitt and his colleagues examined infants' abilities to discriminate relatively simple auditory stimuli using two types of heart rate procedures, a discrete-trials procedure with intertrial intervals and a no-delay procedure that minimized the memory demands of the task by eliminating intertrial intervals. Infants 6 weeks of age reliably performed the discriminations, but only when the no-delay procedure was used (Leavitt, Brown, Morse, & Graham, 1976). In a subsequent study this research was extended to include infants who had experienced perinatal physiological stresses that might place them at risk for central nervous system dysfunction (e.g., Apgar less than 5, resuscitation with oxygen for longer than 3 minutes, low birthweight, under 37 weeks gestational age). Both normal and at-risk infants showed an inverse relation between the magnitude of discriminative responding and the duration of the interval between the last habituation trial and the introduction of the novel stimulus on the first test trial: Discriminative responding declined systematically with an increase in memory interval. However, some group differences in performance as a function of the duration of the stimulus suggests that the auditory short-term memory of at-risk infants may not be as robust as that of infants who have not experienced such perinatal trauma (Swoboda, Kass, Morse, & Leavitt, 1978).

Of particular relevance to the present topic is some research on infants' perception of music-like sequences that demonstrates an interaction of the memory demands of the task with infants' discrimination of hierarchically organized features of auditory patterns. When memory demands were minimal, infants readily discriminated both specific or "local" features such as the individual frequencies of the tones in the sequence, as well as more general or "global" pattern features such as the general melodic contour or pattern of rising and falling pitches (Trehub, Bull, & Thorpe, 1984). However, when the memory demands of the task were increased, by the introduction of a distractor sequence inserted between repetitions of the familiar sequence and between the familiar and novel test sequence, infants discriminated only more global pattern features (see also Morrongiello, 1984). Furthermore, research on preschool children's perception of musical sequences reveals a similar interaction of memory demands with discrimination of pattern features and indicates the generality of these effects across age. In this case, level of task difficulty was manipulated by varying the rate of presentation of the tones in the sequence (Morrongiello, Trehub, Thorpe, & Capodilupo, 1985). Slowing the rate of presentation of the tones causes a melody to lose coherence and increases the memory demands of the task. Under these circumstances, children had increasingly greater difficulty discriminating local pattern features (e.g., exact frequencies) in comparison to global features (e.g., melodic contour). By contrast, at faster presentation rates they performed both pattern discriminations at comparably high levels.

The results from these few studies reveal a trade-off between the level of task difficulty and the level of analysis of pattern features and suggest an interesting area for the study of individual differences in information processing. In this case, "difficulty level" is largely a relative parameter because it must, to some degree, be defined with respect to the individual listener because it depends directly on his or her memory capacities. For an infant with limited memory capacities it may take very little to tax her information-processing abilities, whereas an infant with greater capacity to remember events will have greater opportunity for featural analysis of these events and, consequently, may perform better on feature discrimination tasks. Consistent with this notion is the finding that preterm infants require longer exposure time to a stimulus to achieve comparable performance levels to full-term infants on a perception task (Rose, 1980, 1983). If preterm infants have poorer memory for events (see Gekoski, Fagen, & Pearlman, 1984; Rose, Feldman, McCarton, & Wolfson, 1988) and/or are slower at featural analysis, then the longer exposure time might enhance discrimination performance by allowing for greater analysis of distinguishing stimulus features.

Other research on infants' perception of auditory patterns also reveals effects on discrimination performance of factors that influence the memory demands of the task, specifically, the length of the auditory pattern and the redundancy of the units of the pattern. For example, Trehub (1973) reported that 4- to 17-week-old infants discriminated voicing contrasts in bisyllabic contexts but failed to do so when the pattern was increased to three syllables. Similarly, Morrongiello (1986) found that increasing the length and complexity of auditory patterns by defining patterns to comprise multiple groupings of elements negatively influenced 6-month-old infants' discrimination performance. Research examining 6½-month-old infants' discrimination of trisyllabic strings (Goodsitt, Morse, Ver Hoeve, & Cowan, 1984) indicates that reducing the memory demands by increasing pattern redundancy (e.g., /kobako/) results in significantly better discrimination performance than when redundancy is low and memory demands are greater (e.g., /kobati/).

In summary, there are several ways that memory demands have been manipulated in studying infants' information processing of auditory events, including varying the retention interval between exposure to the familiar and novel (i.e., test) event, the introduction of a "distractor" sequence between the familiar and novel event, varying the rate of presentation of the elements in an auditory sequence, varying the length of an auditory sequence, and varying the redundancy of the elements in an auditory sequence. All these manipulations indicate a systematic decline in performance as the memory demands of the task are increased. Furthermore, for auditory patterns, an increase in the memory demands of the task results in significantly poorer recognition of local pattern features in comparison to more general or global pattern features. Thus, systematic manipulation of the memory demands of a task may provide insights into individual differences in levels of information processing. To the extent that memory for events, in this case auditory sequences, is a central aspect of information-processing capacity, this is one area that may hold promise for the future study of individual differences in cognitive capacities in infants.

Auditory Identification and Discrimination.   Because the primary focus in the infant audition literature has been on examining discrimination abilities, the literature for this section is extensive. Consequently, this literature review is particularly selective, with an exclusive focus on research examining infants' discrimination of auditory patterns (for a more complete review of other auditory discrimination literature see Aslin et al., 1983; Kuhl, 1987). One study has examined the utility of measures of auditory pattern discrimination as an index of individual differences in infancy and a predictive measure for later mental outcome in childhood and obtained positive results (O'Connor et al., 1984).

Nonspeech Patterns.   With regard to the perception and recognition of nonspeech patterns, there are numerous demonstrations that infants readily discriminate a change in the order of tones in a sequence, which indicates that they encode and remember information about frequency relations in auditory sequences (e.g., Chang & Trehub, 1977b; Demany, 1982; Morrongiello, 1986). Moreover, discrimination performance is particularly high if the sequence change also produces a change in a global feature of the pattern, specifically, the frequency contour or sequence of rising and falling pitches. If the sequence change preserves the contour of the familiar pattern, infants do not discriminate the novel pattern as well (Trehub et al., 1984). And, in fact, if the memory demands of the task are sufficiently high, infants completely fail to perform the latter discrimination involving a local feature, although they continue to perform at high levels the former discrimination that involves a change in a more global feature of the pattern (Trehub et al., 1984, Experiment 2). These findings again highlight the utility of auditory patterns as a stimulus medium for the study of different levels of information processing and abstraction in infants (see also Morrongiello, 1984, 1986).

In research on auditory pattern perception in preterm infants (i.e., no more than 37 weeks gestational age, less than 2,500 grams at birth), O'Connor and her colleagues compared their cardiac discrimination performance with a group of full terms at 57 weeks postconception (O'Connor, 1980). Infants were habituated to a 12-sec sequence in which a 400 and 1000 Hz tone alternated in a contiguous fashion; each tone was 2 sec in duration. Following habituation to a criterion level, infants received a novel sequence in which the first tone of the standard stimulus sequence was replaced by a 700 Hz tone. Results indicated no group differences in prestimulus heart rate, responsiveness to the first presentation of the standard sequence, or magnitude and/or pattern of cardiac responding to the novel sequence. Both groups responded with a monophasic decelerative response on presentation of the novel sequence.

The same infants were subsequently given the Bayley Scales of Infant Development at 18 months of age. Although there were no group differences in performance on the mental or motor inventory, there were differences due to sex, with females scoring higher than males on the mental inventory. Using magnitude of cardiac change to the novel auditory sequence at 4 months as a predictor variable and Bayley mental and motor scores as outcome variables, the authors found some support for a relationship between these two measures; however, these effects were only significant for females. In particular, response to novelty on test trial 1 was positively correlated with Bayley mental score and that on test trial 2 was negatively correlated. Thus, females who recognized and responded to the novelty and then showed decreased responsiveness to novelty over trials had higher Bayley mental scores than those who did not respond as such to novelty; group differences as a function of risk factor did not reach significance.

Following up on a sample of these infants at 5 years of age (O'Connor et al., 1984), the authors found a significant positive correlation of .60 between response to novelty on test trial 1 at 4 months and the intelligence quotient on the Stanford–Binet ($r = .45$ for females and .54 for males). Moreover, dividing the sample into two groups based on whether or not they showed response to novelty at 4 months revealed significant differences: Those infants who had responded to novelty at 4 months scored significantly higher on the Stanford–Binet at 5 years than did the nonresponders. And, of those nonresponders, there was a significant positive correlation with gestational age, in other words, of infants who failed to respond to novelty at 4 months, the more premature they were, the poorer was their intellectual performance at 5 years. Finally, although there were no group differences on these measures as a function of risk status, it is of interest to note that of the 6 children who scores especially poorly (i.e., below 85) on the Stanford–Binet at 5 years, five of these infants had been in the premature or risk group and all had failed to respond to novelty at 4 months.

In summary, the results from these studies support the notion that auditory pattern perception taps central cognitive-processing abilities and can be useful for the study of individual differences in mental functioning in infancy. Whereas there is some suggestion that this measure may be more stable for females than for males when predicting from early infancy to 18 months, by 5 years of age there were no differences in predictability as a function of gender. Additional research on this topic is sorely needed to replicate these important findings and to examine systematically the utility of additional measures of auditory pattern processing for the study of individual differences in infancy.

Speech Patterns. With regard to infants' recognition of speech-sound sequences, there are numerous demonstrations of their ability to discriminate the introduction of a novel phoneme even when embedded within multisyllabic strings (for reviews see Kuhl, 1987; Morrongiello, 1988). Discrimination of the introduction of a new phoneme indicates that infants have internally represented and remembered the familiar phoneme, and that they distinguish the smallest meaningful units of the language. However, much more than this is essential for speech perception and production. Attention to the temporal order of phonemes and syllables and recognition of similarity across phonemes and syllable sequences and speakers are all important skills for word recognition. In this section research on temporal-order perception is reviewed; research on infants' perception of similarities in speech patterns is discussed in the next section on abstraction and categorization.

With regard to infants' perception of temporal-order information in speech, there has been surprisingly little research examining infants' abilities to discriminate a change in the relative order of syllables in multisyllabic sequences. In an early study, Trehub (1973) found that infants could discriminate a two-syllable contrast (i.e., /apa/ vs. /aba/) but had difficulty discriminating a change in temporal order for longer two-syllable strings (i.e., /pama/ vs. /mapa/). Miller and Eimas (1979) reported that 2- to 4-month-olds discriminated a recombination of familiar consonants and vowels that formed new syllables (e.g., /ba/ and /dae/ changed to form /bae/ and /da/), which suggests that sensitivity to relational properties in auditory sequences emerges fairly early in life.

In summary, for speech and nonspeech patterns alike young infants discriminate a change in the relative ordering of acoustic events. These findings indicate that they distinguish between the elements, encode relational information about the relative ordering of these elements, and remember these properties that define the "pattern" per se. Although there has not been any research on individual differences with speech as the stimulus, the one study on nonspeech patterns was successful in demonstrating the predictive utility of measures of auditory pattern discrimination in infancy for indexing mental functioning in early childhood (O'Connor, 1980; O'Connor et al., 1984).

Auditory Abstraction and Categorization.   Abstraction refers to the infant's ability to recognize a common theme or defining feature or property that unites a group of stimulus events. In more general terms, it is a process that facilitates the grouping and organization of stimulus events with respect to one another. Categorization refers to the infant's ability to treat as equivalent stimuli that are discriminably different, in other words, to respond to the similarity across stimulus events despite essential differences. Obviously, these two skills are interrelated and the capacity for abstraction is necessary for categorization (i.e., one must abstract the property of similarity for categorization). However, the reverse need not be true. It is possible that infants can abstract some global properties or features based on exposure to a group of stimuli before they are able to respond to similarity across stimuli and demonstrate categorization abilities per se. If abstraction is defined more generally in terms of organizational processes (e.g., abstraction of a "pattern" in a sound sequence), then "similarity" is but one basis along which stimulus events can be organized.

Research on infants' abilities to abstract information from sequences of sounds has primarily utilized nonspeech music-like sequences, and the focus has been on examining the level of abstraction of pattern features (e.g., local features like note frequencies vs. more abstract global features like frequency contour). By contrast, most research on categorization has utilized speech sounds, because recognition of phonetic similarity in the presence of acoustic differences is essential to the perception and production of language. Each of these related literatures provides important insights into infants' auditory information-processing abilities.

With regard to infants' perception of nonspeech music-like sequences, several studies reveal their processing of information at multiple levels of abstraction. Morrongiello (1986) examined 6- and 12-month-olds' sensitivity to numerous features, ranging from local to global pattern features, in auditory patterns that comprised multiple groups of elements. The test sequences introduced changes in (a) a very local feature, that is, the actual frequencies of the component tones; (b) the number of times a familiar frequency was presented (i.e., ratio of high (H) to low (L) frequencies); (c) the relations between successive tones in a group (i.e., reordered familiar tones); (d) the relations between successive groups (i.e., reordered familiar groups; and (e) a very global feature, that is, the frequency structure of a group (i.e., whether a group was homogeneous, LLL, or heterogeneous, LHL, in successive frequency relations) or the extended pattern (i.e., whether the pattern was homogeneous, LHL LHL LHL, or heterogeneous, LLL HHH LLL in successive group relations). At 12 months, infants reliably discriminated all frequency and pattern changes, demonstrating sensitivity to local as well as global pattern features of multiple-group patterns. However, at 6 months infants showed poorer discrimination of local than global pattern features. They reliably discriminated the introduction of a novel frequency, a change in the relative ratio of familiar frequency tones, and a change in the sequence of familiar tones in a group, but performance was strikingly poor *unless* there was also a concomitant change in a more global pattern feature such as a change in group or pattern structure, in which case they performed as well as the 12-month-olds. Thus, with multiple-group patterns the 6- and 12-month-olds were comparably good at discriminating global features of auditory patterns, but the younger infants were poorer than the older infants in abstracting and recognizing a change in local pattern features.

Although it is tempting to speculate about the possibility of increasing differentiation of pattern features with age (cf. Gibson, 1969), it seems unlikely that the noted developmental changes in performance reflect fundamental changes in auditory pattern perception skills per se. Younger infants have been shown to discriminate such local features in a variety of other test situations in which the information-processing demands of the task were less (e.g., Berg, 1972; Leavitt et al., 1976; Swoboda et al., 1978; Trehub et al., 1984). Furthermore, in several studies that tap a wide age range including infancy and the preschool years, there is evidence of a disproportionate decrease in discriminability of local features relative to global pattern features as the information-processing demands of the task are increased (aforementioned). Thus, these developmental changes probably reflect the fact that the lengthy stimulus sequences were more taxing on the information-processing capacities of the 6- than the 12-month-olds. In this context, the enhanced performance by the 12-month-olds most likely relates to improvements during the second half year of life in cognitive and memory capacities (Kagan, 1979; Rose, 1981), as opposed to necessarily indicating changes in pattern perception skills per se.

With regard to infant auditory categorization skills, the study of two phenomena in speech perception bear on this topic, namely, categorical perception and perceptual constancy (see Kuhl, 1984). Both phenomena involve the perceptual grouping of speech sounds on the basis of their assignment to phonetic categories, in other words, acoustic differences must be ignored and phonetic identity must be used as the basis for assignment of speech tokens to a category. The study of these phenomena in infants has recruited considerable attention because it bears on classic issues in the adult speech perception literature having to do with acoustic-cue invariance (Liberman, Cooper, Shankweiler, & Studdert-Kennedy, 1967) and acoustic-cue equivalence (Shankweiler, Strange, & Verbrugge, 1977). Although these phenomena have not been examined in the study of individual differences, they tap a number of cognitive processes (i.e., memory, identification, discrimination, and abstraction) and have been shown to emerge very early in life. Thus, measures of categorization skills may prove particularly useful indices of individual differences in cognitive-processing capacity in young infants.

On the topic of categorical speech perception in infancy, the goal of this research has been to determine if infants partition speech sounds that vary along a continuous acoustic dimension in ways that are consistent with adult phoneme categories. Under numerous test conditions and with a variety of response measures (e.g., heart rate, high-amplitude sucking, conditioned head turning) across a wide age range, infants have shown enhanced discriminability of speech sounds that come from different adult-defined phonetic categories, and failure to discriminate or, at the least, poor discriminability of speech sounds that are phonetically equivalent in that they come from within the same adult phoneme category (for reviews see Aslin et al., 1983; Kuhl, 1987). Thus, the data indicate that infants, like adults, perceive discontinuities (i.e., boundaries) between phonological categories. Moreover, infants have also shown some sensitivity to relational properties of speech sounds, in that they respond to context-dependent cues, not merely absolute cues, in speech perception. For example, there is evidence to suggest that infants consider rate of articulation when interpreting the durational properties of syllables (e.g., Eimas & Miller, 1980), and that they recognize that cues interact and "trading relations" exist between different acoustic cues that signal the identity of the same phoneme (e.g., Miller & Eimas, 1983; Morse, Eilers, & Gavin, 1982). Such sensitivity to the relational properties of speech are especially important, because phonetic segments are not related in a simple one-to-one fashion to acoustic segments in the sound sequence (Liberman et al., 1967).

The study of perceptual constancy for speech provides additional insights into infant's auditory information-processing skills. This research highlights the young infants' ability to ignore acoustically prominent but irrelevant features and to focus attention on select aspects of stimulus events. In this situation infants have been tested for their discrimination of speech tokens that vary along multiple dimensions (e.g., phoneme identity, speaker gender, intonation contour), rather than along a single dimension as in categorical perception. Using a transfer-of-learning paradigm, infants are initially trained to discriminate two stimuli that differ in phonetic identity and are then tested for their generalization to discriminably different novel stimuli representing the two phonetic categories. Generalization of discriminative responding is expected to occur to these novel instances of each category only if infants can ignore local variation along additional acoustic dimensions and still attend to the dimension of difference as represented by the original stimulus pair on which they were trained.

Results indicate that by 6 to 7 months infants recognize phonetic similarity despite prominent variation along several acoustic dimensions, such as fundamental frequency (low, high), speaker gender (male, female), intonation contour (rising, falling), and speaker age (child, adult) (e.g., Hillenbrand, 1983; Kuhl, 1979; Miller, 1983). Furthermore, they do so with respect to vowels as well as consonants (for reviews see Aslin et al., 1983; Kuhl, 1984, 1987); similar findings have been noted for nonspeech auditory categories (Clarkson & Clifton, 1985; Trehub, Thorpe, & Morrongiello, 1987). Thus, well before infants are fluent producers of language, they have the perceptual-organization skills to categorize speech sounds into adult-based phonological categories and to preserve the constancy of phoneme identity across different contexts and speakers.

The findings on infant abstraction and categorization indicate that young infants are fairly flexible in their processing of auditory information. When presented a sequence of auditory stimuli, they are sensitive to and manage to keep track of both differences and similarities between acoustic events. Moreover, they utilize this information in perceptually organizing these events, and similar organizational processes operate both for their perception of speech and nonspeech sounds.[1]

In summary, research on infants' information-processing skills with respect to auditory stimuli highlights their capacity to organize a sequence of auditory events, to remember the sequence, to recognize differences as well as similarities between the components in these sequences, and to learn to focus attention on a

---

[1]It should be apparent from the literature reviewed that infants' perceptual organization of both speech and nonspeech sounds is highly sophisticated very early in life. It remains to be determined whether or not common or separate mechanisms are involved in the processing of these sounds. The arguments on this point have been numerous (for review see Kuhl, 1987). At the least, however, the findings indicate that similar processes operate in the perception of both types of auditory patterns.

particular distinguishing dimension while ignoring other prominent acoustic dimensions. All these skills reflect fundamental aspects of information processing and are likely to be modality independent (see for example Fagan, 1984). Thus, measures of auditory information processing in infancy are likely to be useful indicators of individual differences in cognitive capacity and predictors to mental outcome in childhood.

Directions for Future Research

Although the measures currently recruiting the most empirical attention in the individual-differences literature are indices of visual information processing, it is assumed that the capacities tapped by these measures, namely, memory, recognition, discrimination, and abstraction, are not modality specific (e.g., Fagan, 1984). Indeed, in light of the predictive validity of these measures for later mental functioning in childhood, it seems that these tap quite central and stable cognitive processes. Thus, measures of information processing in other modalities that tap analogous processes should provide evidence for convergent validity and may also prove independently useful for the study of individual differences in infancy.

In this chapter, an attempt has been made to highlight aspects of auditory information processing that may hold promise for the study of individual differences. The literature reviewed emphasized research on infants' perceptual organization of sound sequences or ''patterns.'' Because auditory pattern perception requires that listeners identify and discriminate component elements, abstract relational features across elements, and remember the information that provides the basis for ''pattern'' recognition, it holds particular promise as a stimulus medium for the study of information-processing capacities in preverbal infants. In fact, the results from one study demonstrate its utility in this regard (O'Connor et al., 1984), although certainly additional research is needed.

Owing to the fact that auditory patterns can be hierarchically organized (cf. Morrongiello, 1986), systematic manipulation of pattern structure can provide numerous insights into processing capacities in preverbal infants. For example, manipulating the length and complexity of a pattern (e.g., number of groups in a pattern, degree of redundancy of elements and/or groups) may provide insights into individual differences in infants' capacity to process and recall information at numerous levels of abstraction. Systematic manipulation of task demands may yield information regarding individual differences in the capacity to remember sequences of events and abstract pattern features. Consistent with this is the finding noted in several studies that individual differences in discrimination performance become more pronounced with increasing task difficulty (Kuhl, 1980, 1983). The evaluation of infants' abilities to perform on categorization tasks may indicate individual differences in the capacity to ignore irrelevant information and focus attention on the key distinguishing features along which numerous stimulus events can be organized.

In summary, there are countless ways that auditory patterns can be used to provide insights into a variety of aspects of information-processing capacities in young infants. To the extent that these measures tap analogous processes to those visual measures currently in use in the area of individual differences, these measures can provide tests of convergent validity. Although one must necessarily be cautious in drawing conclusions about poor *capacities* based on failures on a *performance* measure, converging measures can increase one's confidence in judgments about prognosis. For example, an infant who performs poorly on response to novelty tasks in both the auditory *and* visual domains may be at greater developmental risk than an infant who performs well on these tasks in at least one of these modalities.

Measuring infant information-processing skills in the auditory as well as the visual modality may prove useful too in several other ways. Asynchronies in performance across modalities may provide information that is relevant to the early identification of infants at risk for learning disabilities that are modality specific. For example, several studies indicate that subgroups of learning-disabled children, particularly those with reading difficulties, often have problems specific to auditory information processing (e.g., Vellutino, 1977), such as limitations in rate of processing of sequential sounds (Tallal & Newcombe, 1978; Tallal & Piercy, 1973), or in detecting the invariant characteristics of words or sentences (e.g., Guthrie, 1973; Vogel, 1983). By contrast, visual coding problems are not evident in most learning-disabled readers (e.g., Swanson, 1978, 1986; Vellutino & Scanlon, 1982). Examining performance in infancy on information-processing tasks that tap analogous processes but via different modalities may facilitate the early identification of children likely to experience a disability in learning material presented via a particular modality.

Finally, measures that tap processing capacities using both the auditory and visual modalities provide for greater opportunity for the study of individual differences in infants with select perceptual deficits, such as blindness or deafness. Because most of these infants have experienced some type of prenatal insult resulting in their disability, one is always particularly concerned about whether there are accompanying compromises in developmental capacities, such as in mental functioning. Thus, the development of a test that comprises, at the least, measures of both visual and auditory information processing and reliably indexes individual differences in infants' mental capacities may serve several significant functions.

CONCLUSIONS

In identifying young infants at risk for or having hearing problems, both behavioral (VRA) and electrophysiological (ABR) measures have proven invaluable. Research indicates that these measures show good test–retest reliability and have moderately good predictive validity in identifying infants with hearing problems.

The current emphasis in research in this area is the study of high-risk populations, most notably, NICU graduates. Because as many as 14% are likely to experience significant hearing loss (Despland & Galambos, 1982), using these measures to study individual differences in this population is especially important. Furthermore, because these measures can provide convergent validity for some aspects of hearing (e.g., detection threshold), and they provide unique information on other aspects of hearing (e.g., ABR can indicate the site of origin of a particular problem, not just its presence), the greatest success in developing a clinical profile of an individual child's hearing will no doubt come from taking a *comprehensive* approach and using both measures, in addition to tympanometry, which provides unique information on middle-ear functioning. Such a comprehensive, multiple-measure approach is necessary to maximize drawing valid inferences about the nature, extent, and site of a hearing problem.

In the area of speech and language evaluation, unfortunately, most clinical tests are geared to children 2 to 3 years of age or older and, consequently, they are diagnostic rather than prognostic in purpose. Although skills relevant for language learning (e.g., pattern perception, sequence discrimination, speech discrimination) have been demonstrated in very young infants in laboratory settings, the application of these testing methods for clinical evaluation of hearing has not been forthcoming. This is an area in which research is sorely needed. For example, a variety of auditory-processing problems have been noted in many learning-disabled children. The development of *infant* tests for clinical evaluation of auditory-processing domains that have relevance for language learning might prove especially useful in the early identification of individuals at risk for learning disabilities and/or speech-processing problems.

Measures of auditory information processing in infants also may provide another avenue for the study of individual differences in cognitive functioning. In particular, measures of infants' perception and discrimination of auditory patterns should tap processes analogous to those visual measures that recently have proven successful in indexing individual differences in mental capacity. Perceiving an auditory "pattern" in a sound sequence depends on several information-processing skills, such as attention, memory, discrimination, and abstraction, and all these compromise the core of what one can more generally label as intellectual functioning. Thus, measures of auditory pattern perception would seem to hold particular promise for providing insights into individual differences. Future research should be aimed at providing data that speak to the value of auditory information-processing measures for the study of individual differences in infancy.

ACKNOWLEDGMENTS

While preparing this manuscript the author was supported by a University Research Fellowship award from the Natural Sciences and Engineering Research

Council of Canada. The author gratefully acknowledges Caroline Roes, for her assistance in library research, and Rick Robson, for his encouragement and careful editing of the manuscript.

REFERENCES

Aslin, R., Pisoni, D., & Jusczyk, P. (1983). Auditory development and speech perception in infancy (pp. 573–688). In P. Mussen (Ed.), *Handbook of child psychology: Infancy and developmental psychobiology* (Vol. 2). New York: Wiley.

Auerbach, S., Naeser, M., & Mazurski, P. (1981, October). *Primary auditory cortical function and auditory comprehension in aphasia.* Paper presented at the Academy of Aphasia, London, Ontario.

Bayley, N. (1969). *The Bayley scales of infant development.* New York: Psychological Corporation.

Beasley, D., Maki, J., & Orchic, D. (1976). Children's perception of time-compressed speech on two measures of speech discrimination. *Journal of Speech and Hearing Disorders, 41,* 216–225.

Benham-Dunster, R., & Dunster, J. (1985). Hearing loss in the developmentally handicapped: A comparison of three audiometric procedures. *Journal of Auditory Research, 25,* 175–190.

Berg, W. K. (1972). Habituation and dishabituation of cardiac responses in 4-month-old infants. *Journal of Experimental Child Psychology, 14,* 92–107.

Berg, K., & Smith, M. C. (1983). Behavioral thresholds for tones during infancy. *Journal of Experimental Child Psychology, 35,* 409–425.

Bergstrom, L. (1984, March). *Congenital deafness.* Paper presented at the Colorado Otology–Audiology Workshop, Aspen, CO.

Bergstrom, L., Hemenway, W., & Downs, M. (1971). A high risk registry to find congenital deafness. *Otolaryngology Clinics of North America, 4,* 369–399.

Binet, A., & Simon, T. (1905). Methodes nouvelles pour le diagnostic du niveau intellectuel des anormaux. *Annee Psychologie, 11,* 191–244.

Bornstein, M., & Benasich, A. (1986). Infant habituation: Assessment of short-term reliability and individual differences at 5 months. *Child Development, 57,* 87–99.

Bornstein, M., & Ruddy, M. (1984). Infant attention and maternal stimulation: Prediction of cognitive and linguistic development in singletons and twins (pp. 433–445). In H. Bouma & D. Bouwhuis (Eds.), *Attention and performance X: Control and language processes.* New York: Lawrence Erlbaum Associates.

Bornstein, M., & Sigman, M. (1986). Continuity in mental development from infancy. *Child Development, 57,* 251–274.

Brooks, J., & Weinraub, M. (1976). A history of infant intelligence testing (pp. 19–58). In M. Lewis (Ed.), *Origins of intelligence: Infancy and early childhood.* New York: Plenum Press.

Brugge, J., Feng, J., Reale, R., & Chan, J. (1983). Topographic distribution of primary auditory cortical field (AI) collosal neurons in cat reared with unilateral or bilateral cochlear destruction, *Society of Neuroscience Abstracts, 9,* 377.

Buchwald, J., & Huang, C. (1975). Far-field acoustic response: Origins in the cat. *Science, 189,* 382–384.

Burt, C., Jones, E., Miller, E., & Moodie, W. (1934). *How the mind works.* New York: Appleton-Century-Crofts.

Butterfield, E., & Siperstein, G. (1972). Influence of contingent auditory stimulation on non-nutritional suckle (pp. 29–52). In J. Bosma (Ed.), *Third symposium on oral sensation and perception: The mouth of the infant* (pp. 29–52). Springfield, IL: Charles Thomas.

Caron, A., Caron, R., & Glass, P. (1983). Responsiveness to relational information as a measure of cognitive functioning in nonsuspect infants (pp. 181–209). In T. Field & A. Sostek (Eds.),

Infants born at risk: Psychological, perceptual and cognitive processes. New York: Grune & Stratton.

Chang, H., & Trehub, S. E. (1977a). Auditory processing of relational information. *Journal of Experimental Child Psychology, 24,* 324–331.

Chang, H., & Trehub, S. E., (1977b). Infants' perception of temporal grouping in auditory patterns. *Child Development, 48,* 1660–1670.

Chedru, F., Bastard, V., & Efron, R. (1978). Auditory micropattern discrimination in brain damaged subjects. *Neuropsychologia, 16,* 141–149.

Clarkson, M., & Clifton, R. (1985). Infant pitch perception: Evidence for responding to pitch categories and the missing fundamental. *Journal of the Acoustical Society of America, 77,* 1521–1528.

Clements, M., & Kelly, J. (1978). Auditory spatial responses of young guinea pigs during and after ear blocking. *Journal of Comparative Physiological Psychology, 41,* 1–7.

Clifton, R., Morrongiello, B. A., Kulig, J., & Dowd, J. (1981a). Newborns' orientation toward sound: Possible implications for cortical processing. *Child Development, 52,* 833–838.

Clifton, R., Morrongiello, B. A., Kulig, J., & Dowd, J. (1981b). Developmental changes in auditory localization in infancy. In R. Aslin, J. Alberts, & M. Petersen (Eds.), *Development of perception: Psychobiological perspectives* (Vol. 1, pp. 141–160). New York: Academic Press.

Cohen, L. B., & Gelber, E. (1975). Infant visual memory. In L. Cohen & P. Salapatek (Eds.), *Infant perception: From sensation to cognition* (Vol. 1, pp. 347–403). New York: Academic Press.

Cohen, L. B., & Strauss, M. (1979). Concept acquisition in the human infant. *Child Development, 50,* 419–424.

Colavita, F., Szeligo, F., & Zimmer, S. (1974). Temporal pattern discrimination in cats with insular-temporal lesions. *Brain Research, 79,* 153–156.

Coleman, J., & O'Connor, P. (1979). Effects of monaural and binaural sound deprivation on cell development in the anteroventral cochlear nucleus of rats. *Experimental Neurology, 64,* 553–566.

Colombo, J., Mitchell, D., O'Brien, M. & Horowitz, F. (1987). The stability of visual habituation during the first year of life. *Child Development, 58,* 474–487.

Connelly, C., & Oviatt, D. (1979). Physiologic measures in pediatric audiology. *Human Communication,* Autumn, 299–305.

Cox, L., Hack, M., & Metz, D. (1982). Longitudinal ABR in the NICU infant. *International Journal of Pediatric Otorhinolaryngology, 4,* 225–231.

Craik, F., & Lockhart, R. (1972). Levels of processing: A framework for memory research. *Journal of Verbal Learning and Verbal Behavior, 11,* 671–684.

Cranford, J., Ravizza, R., Diamond, I., & Whitfield, I. (1971). Unilateral ablation of the auditory cortex in the cat impairs sound localization. *Science, 172,* 286–288.

Davis, H. (1970). Audiometry: Pure tones and simple speech tests. In H. Davis & S. Silverman (Eds.), *Hearing and deafness* (3rd ed., pp. 179–221). New York: Holt, Rinehart, & Winston.

Demany, L. (1982). Auditory stream segregation in infancy. *Infant Behavior and Development, 5,* 261–276.

Demany, L., McKenzie, B., & Vurpillot, E. (1977). Rhythm perception in early infancy. *Nature, 266,* 718–719.

Dennis, J., Shelton, R., & Toubas, P. (1984). *American Journal of Otolaryngology, 5,* 201–205.

Despland, P., & Galambos, R. (1980). The auditory brainstem response as a useful diagnostic tool in the intensive care nursery. *Pediatric Research, 14,* 154–158.

Despland, P., & Galambos, R. (1982). The brainstem auditory evoked potential is a useful diagnostic tool in evaluating risk factors for hearing loss in neonatology. In J. Courjon, F. Mavgviere, & M. Revol (Eds.), *Clinical applications of evoked potentials in neurology* (pp. 241–247). New York: Raven Press.

Diamond, I., & Neff, W. (1975). Ablation of temporal cortex and discrimination of auditory patterns. *Journal of Neurophysiology, 20,* 300–315.

Downs, M. (1983). Audiologist's overview of sequelae of early otitis media. *Pediatrics, 71,* 643–644.

Downs, M. (1986). The rationale for neonatal hearing screening. In E. Swigart (Ed.), *Neonatal hearing screening* (pp. 1–19). San Diego: College-Hill.

Downs, M., & Hemenway, W. (1969). Screening of 17,000 neonates. *International audiology, 8,* 72–76.

Durieux-Smith, A., Picton, T., Edwards, C., Goodman, T., & MacMurray, B. (1985). The crib-o-gram in the NICU: An evaluation based in brainstem electric response audiometry. *Ear and Hearing, 6,* 20–24.

Edwards, A,. & Auger, R. (1965). The effect of aphasia on the perception of precedence. *Proceedings of 73rd Annual Meeting of Eastern Psychological Association, 207*–208.

Eggermont, J. (1988). On the rate of maturation of sensory evoked potentials. *Electroencephalography & Clinical Neurophysiology, 70,* 293–305.

Eggermont, J. (1989). The onset and development of auditory function: Contributions of evoked potential studies. *Human Communication Canada.*

Eimas, P., & Miller, J. (1980). Contextual effects in infant speech perception. *Science, 209,* 1140–1141.

Eisenberg, R. (1976). *Auditory competence in early life.* Baltimore: University Park Press.

Ewing, I., & Ewing, A. (1944). The ascertainment of deafness in infancy and early childhood. *Journal of Laryngology and Otology, 59,* 309–333.

Fagan, J. F. (1981, April). *Infant memory and the prediction of later intelligence.* Paper presented at the meeting of the Society of Research in Child Development, Boston.

Fagan, J. F. (1976). Infants' recognition of invariant features of faces. *Child Development, 47,* 627–638.

Fagan, J. F. (1984). The intelligent infant: Theoretical implications. *Intelligence, 8,* 1–9.

Fagan, J. F., & McGrath, S. K. (1981). Infant recognition and later intelligence. *Intelligence, 5,* 121–130.

Fagan, J. F., & Singer, L. (1983). Infant recognition memory as a measure of intelligence. In L. Lipsitt (Ed.), *Advances in infancy research* (Vol. 2, pp. 31–78). Norwood, NJ: Ablex.

Fantz, R. (1956). A method for studying early visual development. *Perceptual and Motor Skills, 6,* 13–15.

Friel-Patti, S., Finitzo-Hieber, T., Conti, G., & Brown, K. (1982). Language delay in infants associated with middle ear disease and mild fluctuating hearing impairment. *Pediatric Infectious Disease, 1,* 104–109.

Galambos, R., Hicks, G., & Wilson, M. (1984). The ABR reliably predicts hearing loss in graduates of a tertiary cure nursery. *Ear & Hearing, 5,* 254–260.

Gekoski, M., Fagen, J., & Pearlman, M. (1984). Early learning and memory in the preterm infant. *Infant Behavior and Development, 7,* 267–276.

Gerber, S., & Mencher, G. (1978). *Early diagnosis of hearing loss.* New York: Grune & Stratton.

Gerkin, K. P. (1986). The development and outcome of the high risk register. In E. Swigart (Ed.), *Neonatal hearing screening* (pp. 31–46). San Diego: College-Hill.

Gibson, E. J. (1969). *Principles of perceptual learning and development.* New York: Appleton-Century-Crofts.

Goff, W., Allison, T., Lyons, W., Fisher, B., & Conte, R. (1977). Origins of short latency auditory evoked response components in man. In J. Desmedt (Ed.), *Auditory evoked potential* (pp. 30–43). New York: Basel Karger.

Goodsitt, J., Morse, P., Ver Hoeve, J., & Cowan, N. (1984). Infant speech recognition in multi-syllabic contexts. *Child Development, 55,* 903–910.

Griffiths, R. (1954). *The abilities of babies.* London: University of London Press.

Guthrie, J. (1973). Reading comprehension and syntactic responses in good and poor readers. *Journal of Educational Psychology, 65,* 294–299.

Hardy, J., Dougherty, A., & Hardy, W. (1959). Hearing responses and audiologic screening in infants. *Journal of Pediatrics, 55*, 382–390.

Hecox, K. (1975). Electrophysiological correlates of human auditory development. In L. Cohen & P. Salapatek (Eds.), *Infant perception* (Vol. 2, pp. 151–192). New York: Academic Press.

Hecox, K., & Burkard, R. (1982). Developmental dependencies of the human brainstem auditory evoked response. *Annals of New York Academy of Science, 388*, 538–556.

Hecox, K., & Cone, B. (1981). Prognostic importance of brainstem auditory evoked response after asphyxia. *Neurology, 31*, 1429–1439.

Hecox, K., & Galambos, R. (1974). Brainstem auditory evoked responses in human infants and adults. *Archives of Otolaryngology, 99*, 30–33.

Hecox, K., Gerber, S., & Mendel, M. (1983). Development of auditory brainstem responses. In S. Gerber & G. Mencer (Eds.), *The development of auditory behavior* (pp. 77–90). New York: Grune & Stratton.

Hecox, K., & Jacobsen, J. (1984). Auditory evoked potentials. In J. Northern (Ed.), *Hearing disorders* (pp. 57–73). Boston: Little, Brown.

Heffner, H., & Heffner, R. (1984). Temporal lobe lesions and perception of species specific vocalizations by macaques. *Science, 226*, 75–76.

Hillenbrand, J. (1983). Perceptual organization of speech sound by infants. *Journal of Speech and Hearing Research, 2*, 268–282.

Hochster, M., & Kelly, J. (1981). The precedence effect and sound localization by children with temporal lobe epilepsy. *Neuropsychologia, 19*, 49–55.

Hodgson, W. (1972). Filtered speech tests. In J. Katz (Ed.), *Handbook of clinical audiology* (pp. 313–324). Baltimore: Williams & Wilkins.

Holm, V., & Kunze, L. (1969). Effect of chronic otitis media on language and speech development. *Pediatrics, 43*, 833.

Hoversten, G., & Moncur, J. (1969). Stimuli and intensity factors in testing infants. *Journal of Speech and Hearing Research, 12*, 677–686.

Hyde, M., Rico, K., & Corbin, H. (1984). A neonatal hearing screening research program using brainstem electric response audiometry. *Journal of Otolaryngology, 13*, 49–54.

Jacobsen, J., & Morehouse, C. (1984). A comparison of auditory brainstem responses and behavioral screening in high-risk and normal newborn infants. *Ear & Hearing, 5*, 247–253.

Jerger, J. (1960). Observations on auditory behavior in lesions of the central auditory pathways. *Archives of Otolaryngology, 71*, 797–806.

Jerger, S., & Jerger, J. (1981). *Auditory disorders: A manual for clinical evaluation.* Boston: Little, Brown.

Jerger, J., Weikers, N., Sharbrough, R., & Jerger, S. (1969). Bilateral lesions of the temporal cortex. *Acta Otolaryngology*, Supp. *258*.

Jewett, D. (1970). Volume conducted potentials in response to auditory stimuli as detected by averaging in the cat. *Electroencephalography & Clinical Neurophysiology, 28*, 609–618.

Kaas, J. Axelrod, S., & Diamond, I. (1967). An ablation study of the auditory cortex in the cat using binaural tone patterns. *American Journal of Neuropsychologia, 30*, 716–724.

Kagan, J. (1979). Overview: Perspectives on human infancy. In J. D. Osofsky (Ed.), *Handbook of infant development* (pp. 1–25). New York: Wiley.

Kaufman, A., & Kaufman, N. (1983). *Kaufman assessment battery for children (K-ABC)*. Circle Pines, MN: American Guidance Service.

Kavanaugh, J. (1986). *Otitis media and child development.* Baltimore: University Park Press.

Kimura, D. (1961). Some effects of temporal lobe damage on auditory perception. *Canadian Journal of Psychology, 15*, 156–165.

Kitzes, L. (1984). Some physiological consequences of neonatal cochlear destruction in the inferior colliculus of the gerbil. *Brain Research, 36*, 171–178.

Knudsen, E., & Konishi, M. (1980). Monaural occlusion shifts receptive-field locations of auditory midbrain units in the owl. *Journal of Neurophysiology, 43*, 687–696.

Konkle, D., & Rintelman, W. (1983). *Principles of speech audiometry*. Baltimore: University Park Press.

Krumholtz, A., Felix, J., Goldstein, P., & McKenzie, E. (1985). Maturation of the brainstem auditory evoked potentials in preterm infants. *Electroencephalography & Clinical Neurophysiology, 62,* 124–134.

Kuhl, P. (1979). Speech perception in early infancy: Perceptual constancy for spectrally dissimilar vowel categories. *Journal of the Acoustical Society of America, 66,* 1668–1679.

Kuhl, P. (1980). Perceptual constancy for speech-sound categories in early infancy. In G. Yeni-Komshian, J. Davanaugh, & C. Ferguson (Eds.), *Child phonology: Vol. 2. Perception* (pp. 41–66). New York: Academic Press.

Kuhl, P. (1983). Perception of auditory equivalence classes for speech in early infancy. *Infant Behavior and Development, 6,* 263–285.

Kuhl, P. (1984). Categorization of speech by infants. In J. Mehler & R. Fox (Eds.), *Neonate cognition: Beyond the blooming buzzing confusion* (pp. 231–262). Hillsdale, NJ: Lawrence Erlbaum Associates.

Kuhl, P. (1987). Perception of speech and sound in early infancy. In P. Salapatek & L. Cohen (Eds.), *Handbook of infant perception, Volume 2: From perception to cognition* (pp. 275–382). New York: Academic Press.

Lackner, J., & Teuber, H. (1973). Alterations in auditory fusion thresholds after cerebral injury in man. *Neuropsychologia, 11,* 409–415.

Lasky, E., & Katz, J. (1983). *Central auditory processing disorders*. Baltimore: University Park Press.

Lasky, R., & Spiro, D. (1980). The processing of tachistoscopically presented visual stimuli by five-month-old infants. *Child Development, 51,* 1292–1294.

Leavitt, L. A., Brown, J., Morse, P., & Graham, F. (1976). Cardiac orienting and auditory discrimination in 6-week-old infants. *Developmental Psychology, 12,* 514–523.

Lewis, M. (1971). Individual differences in the measurement of early cognitive growth. In J. Hellmuth (Ed.), *Exceptional infant: Studies in abnormalities*. (Vol. 2, pp. 172–210). New York: Brunner/Mazel.

Lewis, M. & Brooks-Gunn, J. (1981). Visual attention at three months as a predictor of cognitive functioning at two years of age. *Intelligence, 5,* 131–140.

Liben, L. (1978). *Deaf children: Developmental perspectives*. New York: Academic Press.

Liberman, A. M., Cooper, F. S., Shankweiler, D., & Studdert-Kennedy, M. (1967). Perception of the speech code. *Psychological Review, 74,* 431–461.

Liden, G., & Kankkunen, A. (1969). Visual reinforcement audiometry. *Acta Oto-Laryngologica, 67,* 281–292.

Ludlow, C., Cudahy, E., Bassich, C., & Brown, G. (1983). Auditory processing skills of hyperactive, language impaired, and reading disabled boys. In E. Lasky & J. Katz (Eds.), *Central auditory processing disorders* (pp. 163–184). Baltimore: University Park Press.

Malcuit, G., Pomerleau, A., & Lamarre, G. (1988). Habituation, visual fixation and cognitive activity in infants: A critical analysis and attempt at a new formulation. *Cahiers de Psychologie Cognitive, 8,* 415–440.

Marcellino, G. (1986). The crib-o-gram in neonatal hearing screening. In E. Swigart (Ed.), *Neonatal hearing screening* (pp. 47–66). San Diego: College-Hill.

Martin, F. (1981). *Medical audiology*. Englewood Cliffs, NJ: Prentice-Hall.

McCall, R. (1971). Attention in the infant: Avenue to the study of cognitive development. In D. N. Walcher & D. L. Peters (Eds.), *Early childhood: The development of self-regulatory mechanisms* (pp. 107–137). New York: Academic Press.

McCall, R. (1979). Individual differences in the pattern of habituation at 5 and 10 months of age. *Developmental Psychology, 15,* 559–569.

McCall, R. (1981). Early predictors of later IQ: The search continues. *Intelligence, 5,* 141–147.

Mencher, G., & Mencher, L. (1983a). Infant hearing screening using auditory brainstem response. *Scandinavian Audiology, 17,* (supp), 102–106.

Mencher, G., & Mencher, L. (1983b). Clinical appraisal of auditory behavior in infancy. In S. Gerber & G. Mencher (Eds.), *The development of auditory behavior* (pp. 121–138). New York: Grune & Stratton.

Mendel, M. (1983). Development of primary cortical auditory responses. In S. Gerber & G. Mencher (Eds.), *The development of auditory behavior* (pp. 11–120). New York: Grune & Stratton.

Meyer, D., & Woolsey, C. (1952). Effects of localized cortical destruction on auditory discrimination conditioning in the cat. *Journal of Neurophysiology, 15,* 149–162.

Miller, C. (1983). Developmental change in male/female voice classification by infants. *Infant Behavior & Development, 6,* 313–330.

Miller, J., & Eimas, P. (1979). Organization in infant speech perception. *Canadian Journal of Psychology, 33,* 353–367.

Miller, J., & Eimas, P. (1983). Studies on the categorization of speech by infants. *Cognition, 13,* 135–165.

Miller, D., Sinnott, J., Short, E., & Hains, A. (1976). Individual differences in habituation rates and object concept performance. *Child Development, 47,* 528–531.

Mjoen, S. (1981). ABR in pediatric audiology. *Scandinavian Audiology, 13,* (supp), 141–146.

Mochizuki, Y., Go, T., Ohkubo, H., & Motomura, T. (1983). Development of human brainstem auditory evoked responses and gender differences from infants to young adults. *Progress in Neurobiology, 20,* 273–285.

Molfese, D. (1977). Infant cerebral asymmetry. In S. Segalowitz & F. Gruber (Eds.), *Language development and neurological theory* (pp. 1–24). New York: Academic Press.

Moore, J., Thompson, G., & Thompson, M. (1975). Auditory localization of infants as a function of reinforcement conditions. *Journal of Speech and Hearing Research, 40,* 29–34.

Moore, J., & Wilson, W. (1978). Visual reinforcement audiometry (VRA) with infants. In S. Gerber & G. Mencher (Eds.), *Early diagnosis of hearing loss* (pp. 177–213). New York: Grune & Stratton.

Moore, J., Wilson, W., & Thompson, G. (1977). Visual reinforcement of head turn response in infants under 12 months. *Journal of Speech and Hearing Disorders, 42,* 328–334.

Morrongiello, B. A. (1984). Auditory temporal pattern perception in 6- and 12-month-old infants. *Developmental Psychology, 20,* 441–448.

Morrongiello, B. A. (1986). Infants' perception of multiple-group auditory patterns. *Infant Behavior and Development, 9,* 307–320.

Morrongiello, B. A. (1988). The development of auditory pattern perception skills. In C. Rovee-Collier & L. Lipsitt (Eds.), *Advances in infancy research* (Vol. 5, pp. 137–173). Norwood, NJ: Ablex.

Morrongiello, B. A. (1989). Infants' monaural localization of sounds: Effects of unilateral ear infection. *Journal of Acoustical Society of America, 86,* 597–602.

Morrongiello, B. A., Kulig, J., & Clifton, R. (1984). Developmental changes in auditory temporal perception. *Child Development, 55,* 461–471.

Morrongiello, B. A., Trehub, S. E., Thorpe, L. A., & Capodilupo, S. (1985). Children's perception of melodies: The role of contour, frequency, and rate of presentation. *Journal of Experimental Child Psychology, 40,* 279–292.

Morse, P., Eilers, R., & Gavin, W. (1982). The perception of the sound of silence in early infancy. *Child Development, 53,* 189–195.

Murray, A. (1988a). Newborn auditory brainstem evoked responses (ABRs): Prenatal and contemporary correlates. *Child Development, 59,* 571–588.

Murray, A. (1988b). Newborn auditory brainstem evoked responses (ABRs): Longitudinal correlates in the first year. *Child Development, 59,* 1542–1554.

Murray, A., Javel, E., & Watson, C. (1985). Prognostic validity of auditory brainstem evoked response screening in newborn infants. *American Journal of Otolaryngology, 6,* 120–131.

Musiek, F., Pinheiro, M., & Wilson, D. (1980). Auditory pattern perception in "split brain" patients. *Archives Otolaryngology, 106*, 610–612.

Musiek, F., & Sachs, E. (1980). Reversible neuroaudiologic findings in a case of right frontal lobe abscess with recovery. *Archives Otolaryngology, 106*, 280–283.

Needleman, H. (1977). Effects of hearing loss from early recurrent otitis media on speech and language development. In B. Jaffe (Ed.), *Hearing loss in children* (pp. 640–649). Baltimore: University Park Press.

Newport, M., & Bellugi, U. (1978). Linguistic expression of category levels in a visual–gestural language: A flower is a flower is a flower. In E. Rosch & B. Lloyd (Eds.), *Cognition and categorization* (pp. 49–72). New York: Wiley.

Northern, J. (1981). Impedance measurements in infants. In G. Mencher & S. Gerber (Eds.), *Early management of hearing loss* (pp. 131–149). New York: Grune & Stratton.

Northern J., & Downs, M. (1978). *Hearing in children*. Baltimore: Williams & Wilkins.

Northern, J., & Lemme, J. (1982). Hearing and auditory disorders. In G. Shames & E. Wiig (Eds.), *Human communication disorders* (pp. 299–329). Columbus, OH: Charles Merril.

Nozza, R., & Wilson, W. (1984). Masked and unmasked pure-tone thresholds of infants and adults: Development of auditory frequency selectivity and sensitivity. *Journal of Speech and Hearing Research, 27*, 613–622.

O'Connor, M. (1980). A comparison of preterm and fullterm infants on auditory discrimination at four months and on Bayley scales of infant development at eighteen months. *Child Development, 51*, 81–88.

O'Connor, M., Cohen, S., & Parmelee, A. (1984). Infant auditory discrimination in preterm and fullterm infants as a predictor of 5 year intelligence. *Developmental Psychology, 20*, 159–165.

Olsho, L., Koch, E., Carter, E., Halpin, C., & Spetner, N. (1988). Pure tone sensitivity of human infants. *Journal of Acoustic Society in America, 84*, 1316–1324.

Oviatt, S. (1981). The emerging ability to comprehend language: An experimental approach. *Child Development, 51*, 97–106.

Paradise, J. (1981). Otitis media during early development: How hazardous to development? *Pediatrics, 68*, 869–873.

Picton, T., & Hillyard, S. (1974). Human auditory evoked potentials: Effects of attention. *Electroencephalography & Clinical Neurophysiology, 36*, 179–133.

Picton, T., Hillyard, S., & Krausz, H. (1974). Human auditory evoked potentials. *Electroencephalography & Clinical Neurophysiology, 36*, 184–190.

Pinheiro, M. (1976). Auditory pattern perception in patients with right and left hemisphere lesions. *Ohio Journal of Speech Research, 12*, 9–20.

Pinheiro, M. (1977). Tests of central auditory function in children with learning disabilities. In R. Keith (Ed.), *Central auditory dysfunction* (pp. 223–256). New York: Grune & Stratton.

Roberts, J., Davis, H., Phon, G., Reichert, T., Sturtevant, E., & Marshall, R. (1982). Auditory brainstem responses in preterm neonates: Maturation and follow-up. *Journal of Pediatrics, 101*, 257–263.

Rosch, E., & Lloyd, B. (1978). *Cognition and categorization*. New York: Wiley.

Rosch, E., Simpson, C., & Miller, R. S. (1976). Structural bases of typicality effects. *Journal of Experimental Psychology: Human Perception and Performance, 2*, 491–502.

Rose, S. (1980). Enhancing visual recognition memory in preterm infants. *Developmental Psychology, 16*, 85–92.

Rose, S. (1981). Developmental changes in infants' retention and visual stimuli. *Child Development, 52*, 227–233.

Rose, S. (1983). Differential rates of visual information processing in fullterm and preterm infants. *Child Development, 54*, 1189–1198.

Rose, G., Feldman, J., McCarton, C., & Wolfson, J. (1988). Information processing in seven-month-olds as a function of risk status. *Child Development, 59*, 589–603.

Salamy, A. (1984). Maturation of the auditory brainstem response from birth through early childhood. *Journal of Clinical Neuropsychology, 1,* 293–329.

Salamy, A., Mendelson, T., Tooley, W., & Chaplin, E. (1980). Contrasts in brainstem function between normal and high-risk infants in early postnatal life. *Early Human Development, 4,* 179–185.

Sanchez-Longo, L., & Forster, F. (1958). Clinical significance of impairment of sound localization. *Neurology, 8,* 119–125.

Schneider, B., & Trehub, S. (1983). Recent advances in the behavioral study of infant audition. In S. Gerber & G. Mencher (Eds.), *The development of auditory behavior* (pp. 167–186). New York: Grune & Stratton.

Schneider, B., Trehub, S., & Bull, D. (1980). High frequency sensitivity in infants. *Science, 207,* 1003–1004.

Schubert, E. D. (1980). *Hearing: Its function and dysfunction.* New York: Springer-Verlag.

Shankweiler, D., Strange, W., & Verbrugge, R. (1977). Speech and the problem of perceptual constancy. In R. Shaw & J. Bransford (Eds.), *Perceiving, acting, and knowing.* Hillsdale, NJ: Lawrence Erlbaum Associates.

Shannon, D., Felix, J., & Krumholtz, A. (1984). Hearing screening of high risk newborns with brainstem auditory evoked potentials: A follow-up study. *Pediatrics, 73,* 22–26.

Sigman, M. (1983). Individual differences in infant attention: Relations to birth status and intelligence at five years. In T. Field & A. Sostek (Eds.), *Infants born at risk: Physiological, perceptual, and cognitive processes* (pp. 271–293). New York: Grune & Stratton.

Sinnott, J., Pisoni, D., & Aslin, R. (1983). A comparison of pure tone auditory thresholds in human infants and adults. *Infant Behavior and Development, 6,* 3–17.

Starr, A., Amlie, R., Martin, W., & Sanders, S. (1977). Development of auditory function in newborn infants revealed by auditory brainstem potentials. *Pediatrics, 60,* 831–839.

Starr, A., & Hamilton, A. (1976). Correlation between confirmed sites of neurological lesions and abnormalities of far field brainstem responses. *Electroencephalography & Clinical Neurophysiology, 41,* 595–608.

Stein, L., Ozdamar, O., & Kraus, N. (1983). Follow-up of infants screened by ABR in the neonatal intensive care unit. *Journal of Pediatrics, 103,* 447–453.

Stockard, J., & Rossiter, V. (1987). Clinical and pathological correlates of brainstem auditory response abnormalities. *Neurology, 27,* 316–325.

Stott, L., & Ball, R. (1965). Evaluation of infant and preschool mental tests. *Monographs of the Society for Research in Child Development, 30*(3), Serial No. 101.

Suzuki, T., & Ogibi, Y. (1961). Conditioned orientation reflex audiometry. *Archives of Otolaryngology, 74,* 192–198.

Suzuki, T., & Sato, I. (1961). Free field startle response audiometry. *Annals of Otology, Rhinology & Laryngology, 70,* 998–1007.

Swanson, H. (1978). Verbal encoding effects on the visual short-term memory of learning disabled and normal readers. *Journal of Educational Psychology, 70,* 539–544.

Swanson, H. (1986). Multiple coding processes in learning disabled and skilled readers. In S. Ceci (Ed.), *Handbook of cognitive, social, and neuropsychological aspects of learning disability* (Vol. 1, pp. 21–40). New York: Lawrence Erlbaum Associates.

Sweitzer, R. (1977). Audiologic evaluation of the infant and young child. In B. Jaffe (Ed.), *Hearing loss in children* (pp. 101–131). Baltimore, MD: University Park Press.

Swigart, E. (1986). *Neonatal hearing screening.* San Diego: College-Hill.

Swoboda, P., Kaas, J., Morse, P., & Leavitt, L. A. (1978). Memory factors in infant vowel discrimination of normal and at-risk infants. *Child Development, 49,* 332–339.

Tallal, P., & Newcombe, N. (1978). Impairment of auditory perception and language comprehension in dysphasia. *Brain and Language, 5,* 13–24.

Tallal, P., & Piercy, M. (1973). Developmental aphasia: Impaired rate of non-verbal processing as a function of sensory modality. *Neuropsychologia, 11,* 389–398.

Teele, D., Klein, J., & Rosner, B. (1980). Epidemiology of otitis media in children. *Annals of Otology, Rhinology & Laryngology, 89,* (Suppl. 68), 5–6.

Thomas, D., Campos, J., Shucard, D., Ramsay, D., & Shucard, J. (1981). Semantic comprehension in infancy: A signal detection approach. *Child Development, 52,* 798–803.

Thompson, G., & Weber, B. (1974). Responses of infants and young children to behavior observation audiometry. *Journal of Speech and Hearing Disorders, 39,* 140–147.

Thorpe, L., Trehub, S., Morrongiello, B. A., & Bull, D. (1988). Perceptual grouping by infants and preschool children. *Developmental Psychology, 24,* 484–491.

Trehub, S. (1973). *Auditory linguistic sensitivity in infants.* Unpublished doctoral dissertation, McGill University, Montreal.

Trehub, S., Bull, D., & Thorpe, L. A. (1984). Infants' perception of melodies: The role of melodic contour. *Child Development, 55,* 821–830.

Trehub, S., Schneider, B., & Bull, D. (1980). Effect of reinforcement on infants' performance in an auditory detection task. *Developmental Psychology, 17,* 872–877.

Trehub, S., Thorpe, L., & Morrongiello, B. A. (1987b). Organizational processes in infants' perception of auditory patterns. *Child Development, 58,* 741–749.

Uzgiris, I., & Hunt, J. McV. (1966). *An instrument for assessing infant psychological development* (mimeographed paper). Psychological Development Laboratories, University of Illinois.

Uziel, A., Marot, M., & Germain, M. (1980). Les potentiels evoques du nerf auditef et du tronc cerebral chez le noeveau-ne et l'enfant. *Review Laryngology* (Bordeaux), *101,* 55–71.

Vellutino, F. (1977). Alternative conceptualizations of dyslexia. Evidence in support of a verbal-deficit hypothesis. *Harvard Educational Review, 47,* 334–345.

Vellutino, F., & Scanlon, D. (1982). Verbal processing in poor and normal readers. In C. Brainerd & M. Pressley (Eds.), *Verbal processes in children.* New York: Springer-Verlag.

Ventry, I. (1980). Effects of conductive hearing loss: Fact or fiction. *Journal of Speech and Hearing Disorders, 14,* 143–156.

Vogel, S. (1983). A qualitative analysis of morphological ability in learning disabled and achieving children. *Journal of Learning Disabilities, 16,* 416–420.

Webster, D. (1983). Effects of peripheral hearing losses on the auditory brainstem. In E. Lasky & J. Katz (Eds.), *Central auditory processing disorders* (pp. 185–202). Baltimore: University Park Press.

Werker, J. (1986). The effect of multilingualism on phonetic perceptual flexibility. *Applied Psycholinguistics, 7,* 141–156.

Werker, J., & Tees, R. (1984). Cross language speech perception: Evidence for perceptual reorganization during the first year of life. *Infant Behavior and Development, 7,* 49–63.

Whitfield, I., Cranford, J., Ravizza, R., & Diamond, I. (1972). Effects of unilateral ablation of auditory cortex in cat on complex sound localization. *Journal of Neurophysiology, 35,* 718–731.

Wickens, C. (1974). Temporal limits of human information processing: A developmental study. *Psychological Bulletin, 81,* 739–755.

Willeford, P. (1976). Central auditory function in children with learning disabilities. *Audiology and Hearing Education, 2,* 12–20.

Wilson, W., & Gerber, S. (1983). Auditory behavior in infancy. In S. Gerber & G. Mencher (Eds.), *The development of auditory behavior* (pp. 149–166). New York: Grune & Stratton.

Wilson, W., & Thompson, G. (1984). Behavior audiometry: Children. In J. Jerger (Ed.), *Pediatric audiology* (pp. 1–44). San Diego: College-Hill.

Worthington, D., & Peters, J. (1984). Electrophysiologic audiometry. In J. Jerger (Ed.), *Pediatric audiology* (pp. 95–124). San Diego: College-Hill.

Wright, L., & Rabak, L. (1983). Crib-o-gram and ABR: Effect of variables on test results. *Journal of Acoustical Society of America* (Suppl. 1), *74,* 540.

Younger, B., & Cohen, L. B. (1983). Infants' perception of correlations among attributes. *Child Development, 54,* 858–867.

Zelazo, P., & Kearsley, R. (1982, March). *Memory formation for visual sequences: Evidence for increased speed of processing with age.* Paper presented at the International Conference on Infant Studies, Austin, TX.

Zimmerman, M., Morgan, D., & Dubno, J. (1987). Auditory brainstem evoked response characteristics in developing infants. *Annals Otology, Rhinology & Laryngology, 96,* 291–299.

Zinkus, P., Gottlieb, M., & Schapiro, M. (1978). Developmental and psychoeducational sequelae of chronic otitis media. *American Journal of Diseases in Children, 132,* 1100–1104.

12 Individual Differences in Infant Spatial Cognition

Linda P. Acredolo
University of California, Davis

INTRODUCTION

People can be divided into groups on many dimensions. There are left-handers and right-handers, Democrats and Republicans, and those who shower in the morning and those who shower at night. Within the cognitive domain most people would agree that there are also those who get lost in the world and those who don't, those who can read a map from any perspective and those who must turn it upside down if they are going south, and those who can find their cars in mall parking lots and those who have, at least on occasion, reported their car stolen to mall police. The common denominator in this latter group of behaviors is the ability or inability to remain oriented in space, a capacity that relies heavily on spatial memories, symbolic representations, and the ability to integrate and manipulate both of these to solve the types of navigational problems with which people are faced on a daily basis.

The fact that striking individual differences exist among adults, in what I term *spatial cognition* or *cognitive mapping,* is based on more than anecdotal evidence. It is also the foundation of many "performance" measures on standard intelligence tasks, the idea being that the ability, for example, to look at a picture of an "unfolded" cube and mentally refold it is at lest related to the same abilities needed to mentally rotate a map and use it for navigation, or to relocate one's campsite in the trees when approaching the lake from a previously unexperienced direction. There is also experimental data gathered within the domain of spatial cognition itself that not only shows the existence of individual differences among adults, but also that adults know these things about themselves. In an intriguing study Kozlowski and Bryant (1977) simply asked adults to rate their sense of direction on a 7-point scale and then subjected them to a series of tasks: drawing maps of campus, pointing north and to unseen cities, traveling through an unfamiliar maze of underground tunnels and then pointing back to the starting place. Results showed definite advantages for those who rated their sense of direction more highly. Ratings were positively correlated with the accuracy of the maps and the ability to point to unseen cities, although not to pointing North. In addition, those reporting a better sense of direction benefited from repeat trips through the maze, whereas those reporting a poorer sense of direction did not. Thus, I think it is safe to say that individual differences among adults in the area of spatial cognition are a fact of life.

The goal of the developmental psychologist, of course, is to trace these differences back to their beginnings. Can we see them in adolescence? In child-hood? We certainly do see them in childhood, even as young as the nursery school period. Perhaps the example of individual differences best known to those researchers active in the field is that of "Buffy," a subject in an early study of cognitive mapping in children by Siegel and Schadler (1977) in which kindergar-teners were asked to reconstruct from memory a tabletop model of their class-room. The most interesting aspect of the results according to the investigators was, in fact, the extreme variability found among children of the same age with the same amount of exposure to the space. On the one hand, there were children with perfect scores on all measures of locational accuracy. On the other hand, there was Buffy—and others like her—for whom the task of modeling one space upon another seemed totally devoid of meaning, toy furniture arranged in a hodge-podge fashion in the middle of the toy room. Clearly some basic dif-ference in the understanding of spatial representation—where representation is used to indicate an external formulation—is in play here.

Reports of a similar nature come from studies of knowledge of maps, a domain in which the issue of external "representation" is also key. In a study from my own laboratory (Bluestein & Acredolo, 1979), we found that about half the 3-year-olds tested could easily relate to 2-dimensional line drawing of a simple square room to the real space as long as the map and room were aligned, whereas half could not. Such fairly narrow findings of individual differences in mapping skills have been lent additional support recently by the results of a uniquely thorough study of knowledge of maps undertaken by Liben and Downs (in press). Children from 3 to 6 years of age were interviewed for their impres-sions of a variety of place representations, including such things as aerial pho-tographs, road maps, tourist maps, etc., which varied on dimensions such as vantage point, color, and familiarity. Like Siegel and Schadler before them, they report that the most striking finding, apart from expected improvements with age, was the incredible range of performance within grade. Some children had clear, adult-like criteria for assigning a representation the label *map*, whereas others did not. Some were able to move back and forth between space and map, or between one map and another, whereas others were not. Although other examples could be garnered to support the case, I think the evidence is clear enough: Individual differences in abilities subsumed under the rubric "spatial cognition" are indeed present in childhood, and many of these involve representational skills.

As was the case with the adult data, we are left with the question, "From whence do they come?" Are these differences the result of differential progress toward representation that starts in childhood itself, or are these differences part of a system of behavior so basic to human existence—the ability to remember where one has been and where one should go—that we might expect to see signs of them as early as one has memories that guide behavior, that is, during infancy? The purpose of this chapter is to describe the little data that do exist on individual differences in this domain during infancy and to discuss what factors are probably contributing to the differences that are seen and those that would be seen if we were to really take a close look. Hidden in all of this will be specific "wish lists" for future research, strategies that—were they routinely included in infant work in this area—would yield much clearer answers to the developmental question posed previously.

EXTENT OF THE DATA

Alluded to before was the fact that there is comparatively little data that directly speak to the question of individual differences in spatial cognition during the infancy period. Perhaps one place to begin our discussion, then, is to ask why this is the case. Why have individual differences been ignored? The primary reason, it seems clear, stems from the fact that researchers have been struggling to paint an overall picture of the developmental changes one might expect in these spatial behaviors over the first year and a half of life. Just as Piaget's emphasis on a nomothetic approach is often excused on the basis of the need to first establish group trends, so the comparative newness of the study of spatial cognition in infants has meant that researchers have looked more at the behaviors that predominate among infants at a given age and less at those that diverge. This strategy has resulted in a heavy dependence on parametric analyses, full of means and standard deviations, rather than analyses focused on individual subjects. As a consequence, a search through the literature for evidence of individual differences is very frustrating: one knows that they must have been present in a particular study, but the authors provide no information that would allow their discovery by the reader.

Of course, once major trends have been described, then it is incumbent upon researchers to turn their attention to the outliers—to those who show differences in rate, order, or strategy of development—and determine the reasons underlying their divergence from the mean. Such a shift in direction obviously can feed back into the task of understanding development in general. If one finds, for example, that the infant outliers on a certain spatial task at a certain age are those who have had more locomotor experience, then one has a basis for pursuing the more general question of the role that locomotor experience plays for all infants as they conquer that particular spatial task. In other words, attention to individual differences should not be seen as a radical shift in the direction of research, but as a logical next step once basic developmental trends have been identified.

As a researcher who has been in this particular game from the beginning, it is clear to me that the time has come to take this next step. We do, in fact, now have a clear enough picture of development across the infant period in at least some important areas of spatial cognition to warrant a shift in attention away from group data to individual data. We need to take pride not only in discovering what's true for "most" children, but also in discovering what's true for individuals—and why. In fact, as I discuss in detail later, some researchers are already making important contributions in this regard. Specifically, the search for the nature of the relation between locomotor experience and spatial knowledge, pioneered by Joe Campos and Bennett Bertenthal with their colleagues, has started the ball rolling in a very rewarding and exciting direction. It's time for the rest of us to follow suit.

Kinds of Differences We Might Expect

Suppose that researchers in the area do now turn their full attention to the question of individual differences. Just what kinds of differences might we expect to find? It seems that there are three possibilities and that we shall probably find some evidence of each, although it will be exceedingly difficult to differentiate among them.

First, there is the possibility that we will see evidence of short-term differences in rate of development toward perfection on particular spatial tasks. As is true for every other realm of development, some children lag behind others even though they eventually achieve the same level of excellence. For example, although some children take longer to begin, all children eventually learn to walk and then to run, jump, skip, etc. This example is not a random one. If locomotor ability does in fact play a critical role in performance on a particular spatial task, then we should expect to see individual differences diminish as those children whose locomotor skills are developing more slowly catch up to their more precocious peers. Kopp (1979) points to this possibility in discussing why it may be that age of achievement of locomotor milestones has traditionally not been found to correlate with intelligence test scores later in childhood: The effect of locomotor skill may be transient. It is critical to keep in mind, however, that "transient" does not translate to "trivial." As was discussed earlier, information from these temporary correlations can provide a unique window into the mechanisms responsible for important change taking place within the infancy period itself.

A second possibility is that we may find changes that are still short-term in duration but different from those described earlier in being not simply reducible to differences in rate of development. In other words, we must be on the lookout for qualitative differences in the approach infants take to spatial problems, differences in strategies chosen or rules used. Such differences have been found in other areas of infant development, perhaps the most well-known example being the distinction made by language researchers between "Expressive" and "Referential" children (Nelson, 1981). Despite which strategy is chosen, each child eventually does conquer the language acquisition task, and differences between the groups fade. The same might be true within the spatial domain. Perhaps we will find infants who prefer to gather spatial information through active exploration and others who prefer to take in information from a single vantage point and mentally manipulate it. Perhaps we will find infants who will rely heavily on inference about where things should be, based on where they were in the past, and others who trust only what they are experiencing in the present. The possibilities are myriad; the evidence to support them is so far nonexistent.

A third possibility is that at least some of the differences we will find within the infant population will not be transient at all but will in fact contribute directly or indirectly to the differences we know exist among both children and adults. Long-term longitudinal data is obviously critical to testing this hypothesis, an approach that has not been used at all so far. It is not just the long-term nature of the search that makes this possibility a difficult one to assess. There is also the problem of distinguishing "direct" from "indirect" effects, parceling out all the other factors that may be contributing to any positive correlations that might be found. These difficulties must not, however, completely dissuade us from embarking on the venture.

General Trends Across Development

Before I turn to a description of the few data that do provide evidence of individual differences in the domain of spatial cognition, it is important to present an overview of development across the first year and a half of life so that those differences can be appreciated and evaluated. To do so, it is first necessary to define what is generally meant by the term *spatial cognition* as it is applied during the infancy period.

As is true for most phenomena, there are many ways one could operationalize *spatial cognition*. Behavior in this domain is multifaceted; a given task may differ from another in the degree to which direct perception versus memory is involved, in the amount of complexity in the spatial array to be remembered, in the specific behavior evoked from the infant (looking, reaching, crawling), or in the degree of familiarity of the environment or task to the child. Not all variations on these themes have been played out with infants. In fact, almost all the work done in the area can be subsumed under the familiar heading of object permanence, although with a set of variations greatly expanded from the Piagetian task familiar to us all. What makes the label *object permanence* appropriate is that in almost every study the task of the infant is to relocate an object or event hat was originally visible but has been hidden in one way or another. What happens in the time between hiding and recovery varies, as does the manner of occlusion, but the common denominator remains—the infant's notion of where things should be in space is assessed. Once assessed, however, interpretation is expanded from the traditional focus on the developing object concept to the development of concepts of space and movement as well.

One fairly representative example from my own laboratory clarifies the description just given and provides readers with a basic scheme to which subsequent paradigms can be related. The basis of much of my own work on infant spatial memory (e.g., Acredolo, 1978; Acredolo & Evans, 1980) is a task in which individual infants are seated in the middle of one wall of a 10 ft by 10 ft enclosure devoid of features except for two identical windows, one in the middle of the wall to the infant's right, the other in the middle of the wall to the infant's left. On each trial during training, a buzzer is sounded, after which there appears at one of the windows an interesting event. This pairing of buzzer and event at Window X occurs repeatedly until the infant has learned to anticipate the event, turning to Window X as soon as the buzzer is heard. Once this expectation is established, the infant is then smoothly rotated to the opposite side of the enclosure so that the window that had been to the infant's left is now to his or her right. The buzzer is sounded once again, and the experimenter simply watches to see toward which window the infant's gaze turns in anticipation of the event. If the infant takes his or her rotation into account and gazes back toward the original window (Window X), then the infant is said to be sensitive to an "objective" or "allocentric" frame of reference. However, if the infant turns instead to the window that maintains the left–right relation originally experienced (i.e., Window Y), then the infant's behavior is described as "egocentric."[1]

This distinction between egocentric and objective spatial responses plays a central role in most discussions of developmental changes during the infant period. What is at the heart of the matter is the ability of the infant to maintain his or her orientation to the objects and events in the external environment in the face of his or her own change in position. To do so, the infant must have a concept of the external world that includes permanency of objects, constancy of locations of

---

[1]Opinion varies as to the nature of such "egocentric" responses. Are they truly indicative of a particular "frame of reference" or are they a manifestation of a learned motor habit? Because the purpose of this chapter is to describe individual differences in response patterns, this interpretive issue is put aside and the term *egocentric* is used as shorthand for the behavioral response that indicates a failure to update, for whatever reason, one's relationship to objects after movement through space.

FIG. 12.1. Experimental space described in Acredolo, L. P. (1978), Development of spatial orientation in infancy, *Developmental Psychology*, 14, p. 226. Copyright 1978 by the American Psychological Association. Adapted with permission.

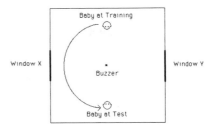

those objects, and a recognition that one's own relation to objects is not privileged but in fact must be updated after self- or object-movement.

Although there is some disagreement about terminology, the general consensus is that from 6 to 18 months we see increases in the tendency to behave "objectively" in paradigms such as the one I have just described. In other words, whereas the 6-month-old is extremely likely (90% of subjects or more) to look back at the window that maintains the left–right relation originally experienced (i.e., an egocentric response), by 18 months very few subjects are doing so. Up to this point, however, we have been talking about behavior in a space devoid of any distinguishing features. Environments in the real world, in contrast, are rich with such features and routinely provide individuals with "landmarks" that can be used to help one reorient after movement or, more simplistically, to mark a specific location that needs to be remembered in a straightforward paired-associate way. If we are truly to understand the infant's capacities, therefore, we need to factor in the effects of providing such environmental features. To this end, many of us have included "landmark" conditions of various types, all designed to assess the capacity of the infant to use such information to recover hidden objects or events. And in fact, the other major trend seen across infancy is an increase in the ease with which such information is used. At first the landmarks must be extremely salient and direct (i.e., in extremely close proximity; Acredolo, 1978; Acredolo & Evans, 1980), but as age increases the landmarks can be more subtle and more distanced from the target location. These changes in landmark usage, then, represent an extremely important component in the total picture of development trends within spatial cognition during infancy.

Individual Differences: Existing Data

If one reviews the studies contributing to the general picture just painted, one does find evidence of individual differences. The differences are predominantly in terms of rate of development with some infants at 9 months, for example, behaving more like 11-month-olds. Whether or not more qualitative differences (e.g., differences in strategy) underlie these differences in rate is completely unknown at this point but is certainly a possibility. Let me provide some concrete examples of the differences I'm talking about.

My own studies aforementioned (Acredolo, 1978; Acredolo & Evans, 1980) included 6-, 9-, 11-, and 16-month-old children. In general the 6-month-olds all behaved quite similarly. Unless a very salient landmark marked the target window (i.e., flashing lights around the window and stripes on the relevant wall), 90% or more of the infants responded egocentrically. It was only in the presence of the salient landmark that a few subjects diverged from the group. With the lights and stripes present, the majority of 6-month-olds (67%) looked at *both* windows, hedging their bets as to whether to trust the landmark or to trust the left–right relation they had learned. In contrast 17% used the landmark information to make an objective choice and 17% didn't use it at all, looking only at the window indicative of reliance on egocentric information. Thus, the individual differences seen here are in terms of sensitivity to landmark information.

The same underlying message comes from examination of the older age groups. At 9 months egocentric responding predominates (80%) with no landmark present but falls to 60% when a star is added around the target window, with the remaining 40% looking to both windows as the 6-month-olds had done with the more salient lights and stripes. Objective responding predominates among these slightly older infants in the lights and stripes condition (80%), but only as long as the lights and stripes mark the target window directly rather than indirectly. In this latter case (called the Indirect condition), the lights and stripes surround the nontarget window. In this condition at 9 months egocentric responding predominates (75%) with a subgroup of 25% responding with the more developmentally advanced behavior of checking out both windows. The message about individual differences at 9 months, then, is similar to the one characterizing the 6-month data: Some infants are more advanced than others in their sensitivity to landmark information.

Essentially the same conclusion can be drawn at 11 months. Whereas the extremely salient landmarks provided by the lights and stripes are effective for almost all the infants at this age (80%), even the addition of the simple star is effective for half (50%) the infants. Thus, progress over behavior at 9 months has been made for a significant subset of 11-month-olds. Evidence of individual differences at this age is also found in the Indirect condition in which the infant has to figure out that the event occurred at the *un*marked window. In this case over a third of the infants were able to use the indirect information (37%) whereas the others looked at both windows, unable to decide between them. The data at 16 months completes the picture of general developmental progress, objective responses predominating in the two conditions tested—no landmark and star.

Although the bottom line in all this is easy to draw—that individual differences in sensitivity to landmarks do exist between 6 and 11 months—it is not so easy from these data to understand why. Because the emphasis was on gathering information about general developmental trends, no information was gathered about the infants that might help us understand why some infants were more advanced than others. At the time I hazarded a guess that locomotor skills might be an important element, but I did so based totally on intuition rather than hard facts.

Additional evidence of individual differences comes from a study of 4-, 8-, and 12-month-olds by Cornell and Heth (1979). Although differing in some details, the basic goal was the same as in my own studies. In this case infants were seated between two screens upon which slides would appear. Across trials one of the screens would always show the same slide whereas the other would show a novel slide. It was presumed that the infant would try on a given trial to predict where the novel slide would be found. In Experiment 1 infants at each age were seated in the same position for 20 trials and then rotated 180° so that the relation of their bodies to the novel and familiar slides was reversed. Although egocentric responding predominated at 4 months, clear individual differences were seen at the two older ages. At 8 months the proportion of egocentric responders fell to 58% and at 12 months to 42%. Once again, then, we have evidence of differences but no information about the infants to help us understand them. What is also unfortunate is that a second experiment, which might have provided interesting additional evidence of individual differences in the capacity to *learn* when an objective response versus an egocentric response was appropriate, was never analyzed at the level of the individual subject.

One last study in this same vein deserves some mention for the individual differences it produced. Quite recently, Keating, McKenzie, and Day (1986) tested the ability of infants to relocate a target site when they had experienced it from *two* different locations, rather than from a single location, as was true in the studies described so far. Specifically, 8-month-old infants were seated in the center of a circular, waist-high display that itself was located within either a circular or a square enclosure. Around the waist-high enclosure were distributed eight identical balls, each of which marked the potential site of an event. However, only one of these balls was ever used as such, and this ball was marked with a landmark for half the subjects in the square room and for half the subjects in the circular room. All subjects in all conditions received three sets of training trials. In one set the infant's body was turned to face the ball 45° to the right of the ball where the event occurred. Soon the infant was anticipating the event's occurrence and turning 45° in expectation. At this point the second set of training trials was begun, this time conducted with the infant facing a ball 90° to the left of the target ball. Once the infant had learned to turn the 90° necessary to anticipate the event, a third set of training trials was begun in which the infant's position was alternated between the 45 and 90° positions previously experienced. The goal here was to create an opportunity for the infant to *abstract* the objective location of the target ball from the individual spatial relations experienced. To test this type of objective knowledge of the target site, a test trial was conducted in which the infant was turned 90° from the target ball—but in the direction opposite from the 90° perspective experienced before. Thus, the infant was seeing the target site from a vantage point not experienced at all during training. Were the infants able to relocate the target site despite the new vantage point? Were they successful in abstracting an objective location for the target site? Very simply, some did and some did not. In fact, the existence of striking individual differences is one of the major messages one can take from the study. Specifically, in the case of the Circular room *without* a landmark at the target site, getting through the training trials was so difficult that 30 infants had to be tested before 16 were found who could even learn to anticipate the event from the 45 and 90° training locations. (The difficulty of this condition is also indicated by the fact that only 2 of these 16 were able to correctly locate the target site on the test trial.) Additional evidence of individual differences was found in both the Circular room with a landmark and the square room without a landmark, 50 and 56% failing to relocate the target ball, respectively. Even in the easiest condition, the square room with a landmark, a full 25% still were unable to find the target site from the new perspective. Thus, across these four conditions we find evidence of individual differences among 8-month-old babies. Unfortunately, as was the case in the studies described earlier, no information is presented that might help us understand why some infants were more sophisticated in their ability to maintain their orientation than others.

The studies so far described have used looking as the index of the baby's belief as to the location of the hidden event and have used events in which the infants were not likely to be heavily invested. In an inventive study by Corter, Zucker, and Galligan (1980), 9-month-old infants watched as their mothers walked out of a room through one of two doors, one to the infant's right, the other to his or her left. The mothers then returned but left once again. On these subsequent trials the mothers left through the opposite door. Obviously of interest was the door toward which the babies crawled on these subsequent trials. Did they follow their mothers as they went through the new door, or did they perseverate as infants do in the classic Stage 4 object permanence problem and try the door through which the mother had previously disappeared? The vast

FIG. 12.2. Experimental space and procedures described in Keating, M. B., McKenzie, B. E., & Day, R. H. (1986), Spatial localization in infancy: Position constancy in a square and circular room with and without landmarks, *Child Development*, 57, p. 118. Copyright 1986 by the Society for Research in Child Development. Adapted with permission.

majority of the infants perseverated, whereas only a subset (26%) correctly followed the mother through the appropriate door. Thus, once again we have evidence of a significant group of infants capable of more sophisticated behavior. In this case, unlike the cases discussed previously, however, we do at least have some extra information in the form of records of the infant's visual activity during the trials. Those who resisted the temptation to perseverate tended to be those who spent more time looking at the correct door—holding on to it visually if you will. As discussed subsequently, this information is useful in the effort to form hypotheses about the source of the individual differences seen in all the studies described so far.

Contributing Factors

Having at least established that individual differences do exist among infants of the same age tested in spatial cognition tasks, the question then becomes how might we account for these differences? To what factors can we attribute one infant's propensity to hang on to egocentric information and another's propensity to rely on landmark information? As I've already indicated, definitive answers are not yet available. However, there does exist a growing body of evidence pointing to a number of factors that probably contribute directly or indirectly to the differences described earlier. These factors, as well as others fueled only by speculation, are discussed next.

Self-Produced Locomotion. Between 6 and 11 months of age most normally developing babies pass a milestone—the onset of self-produced locomotion in the form of crawling. The hypothesis that this developmental milestone might have implications for spatial behavior arose simultaneously with the initial uncovering of interesting shifts during these months from egocentric to nonegocentric spatial behavior (Acredolo, 1978; Bremner & Bryant, 1977). The hypothesis has intuitive appeal for many reasons. First, it would seem likely that the onset of the ability to move oneself from object to object would increase the child's *motivation* to keep track of the spatial location of those objects. When one is no longer helpless in maintaining proximity to mother, or recovering toys that have bounced away, then it would seem natural that enthusiasm for trying to remember locations would rise. And in fact, we do see, at least anecdotally (Ashmead & Perlmutter, 1980), evidence that the onset of crawling is linked with increased efforts to follow parents as they leave and to remember the spatial layout of the home environment.

So, we now have an infant who more than ever wants to remember locations, but how does he/she develop better skills at doing so? Self-produced locomotion contributes here as well. First, the ability to voluntarily change one's location means that the child can create for him or herself a multitude of minispatial problems that provide a great deal of *practice* in perfecting more sophisticated strategies. Indeed, a good proportion of the crawling child's waking hours are spent in just such practice: watching a toy roll behind a chair and trying to retrieve it, watching mother leave and trying to follow her, attempting to interact with sibs or pets as they move from place to place, or simply crawling to new rooms to see what's there and then crawling back (Ashmead & Perlmutter, 1980). In other words, the crawling infant has both the motivation and the opportunity to perfect spatial skills.

That is not all that he/she presumably has, however, If one examines at a more molecular level what data the infant is probably collecting during these new experiences in space, it is clear that the infant is being provided with overwhelming evidence that egocentric spatial relations (or motor habits, contingencies, or whatever you want to call them) are not very helpful in relocating objects once one is moving among those objects. Self-movement changes perspectives, and changing perspectives require that egocentric strategies be replaced. With what might they be replaced? One hypothesis, for which evidence is increasing, is that an attentional strategy develops: When in doubt, keep your eyes on the object you want to relocate. Thus, we see evidence accumulating that visual tracking rises as self-produced locomotion increases, and moreover, that it is this attentional behavior that most directly helps infants improve their performance on spatial cognition tasks of the type outlined earlier.

The picture just painted is a lovely, coherent one that should be true. But is it? Let us now briefly look at the growing body of data providing empirical support.

A recent study by Kermoian and Campos (1988) provides some of the best data yet in support of the hypothesis just outlined. The spatial memory task in this case involved a series of 7 to 9 object permanence tasks increasing in difficulty from uncovering an object half hidden under one cloth to solving the AB object permanence task with an object substituted for the one originally hidden. Subjects were all 8.5 months of age but differed in motor experiences in important ways. The major division was between those infants who could crawl by 8.5 months and those who could not. In addition, each of these two main groups were broken down into important subgroups. Half the noncrawling infants had managed to accumulate self-locomotor experience through the use of walkers; the other half had not. This division is an important one because comparison between these groups allows us to determine whether it is something about being too immature to crawl that inhibits spatial performance or whether it is the absence of the movement per se from place to place. An equally important distinction was made among the crawling infants based on the mode of crawling. Specifically, hands and knees crawlers were distinguished from belly crawlers who drag themselves from place to place. This latter group were judged in pretesting to be just as capable of moving across the laboratory; it was their manner of transit that differed.

Each infant was presented with the sequence of object permanence tasks and the most advanced task passed was noted. The results were very clear: The hands and knees crawlers and the prelocomotor, walker infants performed similarly and at a significantly more sophisticated level than the noncrawlers without walker experience and the belly crawlers. It is also important to note that these latter two groups did not differ. Additional analyses indicated that even among the non-belly movers (hands and knees plus walker group) performance improved with increasing weeks of movement experience (1–4 weeks versus 9+ weeks). The message seems to be, then, that self-locomoting does indeed facilitate spatial memory, but that the self-locomoting must be of a particular kind. Walker experience works, hand and knee crawling works, but crawling on one's belly does not. Why might that be? Kermoian and Campos seem to me to be right on target when they suggest that belly crawling involves both greater physical effort that may direct resources away from spatial problem solving and an inferior visual perspective on the environment through which one is moving. There is also the possibility I have heard them mention that belly crawling may result in an infant being distracted by items encountered along the way to the original goal, thus resulting in fewer goal-setting/goal-achievement experiences. These results obviously provide critical information for those interested in individual differences. Not only do they establish a relation between self-produced locomotion and spatial memory, but they even point to differences between types of crawlers. In fact, I think the identification of belly crawling as potentially a very different experience from hands and knees crawling provides one of the most intriguing clues to the puzzle of individual differences produced in the literature to date.

Admittedly, the tasks used by Kermoian and Campos differed from those used in the spatial orientation studies described in the main discussion of individual differences. Fortunately, we also have some data available from studies with tasks identical or analogous to those. For example, Bertenthal, Campos, and Barrett (1984) report the results of testing 8-month-old crawlers, noncrawlers with walker experience, and noncrawlers without walker experience on a task directly replicating the Direct Lights and Stripes condition devised for my own study (Acredolo & Evans, 1980). Analogous to the results of the Kermoian and Campos study, those groups with locomotor experience—regardless of whether gained through crawling or walker—showed significantly lower levels of egocentric behavior in comparison to those without such experience.[2]

Using the same spatial task, Campos and his colleagues also collected intrigu-

---

[2]One design feature of these studies by Campos and colleagues does mitigate to some extent the certainty we can feel about the conclusions being drawn. In none of the studies were prelocomotor infants randomly assigned to the walker, condition. Rather, the experimenters took advantage of the existence of a group of infants whose parents had decided on their own to provide such experience. Thus, the possibility remains that this decision by the parents was based on some subtle perception of maturity in their infants that they felt would make walker experience possible or valuable, and it may be this level of maturity that is responsible for the greater levels of spatial ability seen among the walker infants rather than the walker experience itself. Campos and Bertenthal and their colleagues are well aware of this design limitation and are in the process of collecting data not subject to this criticism.

ing evidence concerning the role of self-produced locomotion from an orthopedically handicapped infant (Bertenthal, Campos, & Barrett, 1984). The child had been born with two dislocated hips but no other physical or mental handicaps and was treated with a body cast for her first 7.5 months. At that point she was switched to a lighter cast and harness that still restricted movement. Finally, at 8.5 months she was given the freedom to begin to crawl, a skill she succeeded in mastering ghts and Stripes condition began at 6 months and continued on a monthly basis until 10 months of age. Consistent with the hypothesis that self-produced locomotion should facilitate the transition to landmark awareness, the proportion of egocentric responses she produced dropped sharply at the 9-month point, the first testing point following the onset of crawling.

In summary, evidence is accumulating that suggests that the onset of self-produced locomotion may be an important stimulus to improvements in spatial memory and, by implication, an important contributor to individual differences seen in spatial performance during infancy. As we now see, however, the research just described only paints a partial picture. Additional details are provided by studies in which the infant's visual behavior is monitored in addition to his/her locomotor experience. It is to these studies we now turn our own attention.

Visual Tracking. As Kermoian and Campos themselves point out, it is not the case that all nonlocomoting infants are poor at spatial memory tasks. In fact, in their own study, a few infants in their nonlocomoting group were equal to their locomotor peers in their ability to solve object permanence tasks. It is in part to account for such residual individual differences that we now turn to the issue of visual tracking and its role in spatial memory performance. After all, learning to move oneself through the environment need not be the only stimulus to increased perceptual vigilance. Perhaps smarter infants look harder and longer; perhaps more curious infants or less anxious infants do so—regardless of motor experience. Clearly, the role of visual attention itself is deserving of scrutiny.

Despite having just argued for the logical independence of self-produced locomotion and visual tracking, in truth most of the evidence demonstrating the importance of visual attention to spatial memory performance has occurred in studies assessing the impact of active movement through space. For example, in a study from my own laboratory (Acredolo, Adams, & Goodwyn, 1984) 12-month-old infants were trained to locate an object hidden repeatedly in one of two covered wells in a large, floor-level plexiglass box. Once they had found the object correctly four times, the object was hidden again, but with a plexiglass wall inserted so that they could not retrieve the toy. Instead, they were either allowed to crawl (active condition) or were carried under the arms (passive condition) around the enclosure to an opening in the other side. Of course, from this opening their view of the two wells was reversed, and correct search required them to compensate for this reversal by choosing the well that was in the opposite left–right relation to their body they had experienced during training. Thus, as in many spatial cognition studies, the infants could choose "egocentrically" or "objectively." The results were clear in showing a strong relation between active, self-controlled movement around the enclosure and correct, objective search. However, of even more interest was the data describing the infants' visual behavior en route. Those who moved themselves around the box were much more likely to keep their eyes on the inside of the box as they rounded each corner. As a result, once they reached into the box from the new side, they had information to guide their search. They had "hung on" to the correct location. In contrast, those who were carried essentially went into "visual idle," looking anywhere and everywhere. When these infants suddenly found themselves at the new opening, they had only egocentric information to guide them and as a consequence they made errors. In an effort to see if it was in fact the visual tracking that was helping infants in the active condition, a second group was tested. However, instead of plexiglass walls, the two side walls of the box were made opaque, thus blocking each infant's view into the box as he/she travelled from one side to the other. Performance in this case dropped to the level of the passive condition, thus providing strong evidence that it was the visual tracking, rather than the movement per se, that was facilitating performance. Interestingly, when subjects were brought back at 18 months and tested again, visual tracking had disappeared almost completely; infants in both the active and passive conditions at this age were capable of coordinating perspectives without heavy reliance on tracking. By this age they had apparently learned the lessons that visual tracking had been teaching them about spatial layouts and perspective change.

Visual tracking also emerged as a determinant of good spatial memory in a study of object permanence from my laboratory (Horobin & Acredolo, 1986). In this case 9-month-old infants were tested on versions of the traditional Stage 4, AB object permanence tasks in which a toy is repeatedly retrieved from under one of two cloths (A), following which it is hidden under the other (B). The results clearly showed better performance among infants who maintained attention to B during the interval before search was allowed on the critical test trial. Those who looked back to A during this period were much more likely to make the error of choosing A rather than B. The relation between visual tracking and locomotor experience gains support from our study as well. Comparison of the successful and unsuccessful subjects and the vigilant and nonvigilant subjects indicated significantly longer experience of mobility among the first group of subjects in each pair.

These results are very reminiscent of those described earlier from the study by Corter, Zucker, and Galligan (1980), in which infants saw their mothers exit through one of two doors and were allowed to follow. As was the case in the Horobin and Acredolo study, those infants who resisted the tendency to perseverate (i.e., repeat a previous response) were those who visually "held on" to the correct door. Thus, in all these studies we are seeing evidence that locomotion and visual tracking go together, and that it is the tracking that contributes most directly to improvements in performance in spatial memory tasks. Indeed the infants seem to be actively using the rule suggested earlier: "When in doubt, keep your eye on the target." The presence or absence of such a rule is probably an important contributor to individual differences in spatial behavior, at least up to the time when perspectives can be mentally manipulated.

Attachment.   In moving from the role of self-produced locomotion and visual attention to attachment as a contributor to individual differences, we are moving from direct to indirect evidence—and even to speculation. However, such speculation clearly can play an important role in guiding future research efforts.

First, let me outline the rationale for anticipating a role for attachment. Two possibilities come to mind. First, there is the argument that a strong attachment to one's mother (or other caretaker or sib) will increase one's motivation to keep track of that individual's location relative to oneself. Thus, more attention may be deployed and more active attempts to follow may occur, both of which could yield important gains in spatial knowledge. Second, there is the fact that a secure attachment yields lower anxiety about the surrounding environment and promotes exploration. Bowlby himself, in fact, talks about the infant's treatment of the mother as a "home base" from which the environment can comfortably be explored (Bowlby, 1969). Such exploration can yield lots of data for the child about spatial locations. The very task of venturing out, finding an object, and returning to show Mother involves the child in spatial reversals that conceivably promote coordination of perspectives.

Again, the picture is a pretty one, but do data exist to support it? The answer is yes, at least indirectly. Hazen and Durrent (1982) tested the spatial abilities of a group of 2.5-year-olds whose attachments had been assessed at 12 months in the traditional Strange Situation designed by Ainsworth (e.g., Ainsworth, Bell, & Stayton, 1973). Each child was allowed to explore with his/her mother a set of four interconnected rooms in a laboratory "playhouse." Assessments of the exploration as "active" (child moving alone or leading the mother) or "passive" (mother leading or carrying the child) were made. Following the exploration period, the mother was "hidden" in one of the rooms, and the experimenter helped the child learn the route to that room. Once the child could find the room without error, barriers to that particular route were added and a new starting point was used. The ability of the children to find their mothers despite these obstacles was assessed. Results of the study provide support for the role of attachment in the development of spatial competencies. Children whose attachment at 12 months has been assessed as "secure" were significantly more likely to engage in "active" exploration during initial exposure to the playhouse and were more efficient in dealing with the need for altered routes to the goal. Although these subjects were considerably older than those at issue in our main discussion, the finding of a relation between attachment and spatial capacities certainly holds tantalizing implications for individual differences in spatial development during infancy itself.

A second study bearing at least indirectly on the issue comes from my own laboratory (Acredolo, 1982). In an earlier study (Acredolo, 1979) I had demonstrated superior memory for object location when 9-month-old infants were tested in their homes compared to when tested in two laboratory environments. Various reasons for the home environment advantage existed, including greater familiarity with surrounding landmarks and greater attention to the task due to lowered anxiety. In an effort to differentiate among these two possibilities, I repeated the task in a laboratory setting devoid of landmarks but to which the infants were "adapted" by experiencing an extended period of play with mother and experimenter before the task materials were presented. The performance of the infants exposed to this situation matched that of the infants tested in their homes, thus indicating that the presence of landmarks was less critical than the presence or absence of something we might label *anxiety*. The conclusion I drew was that infant spatial performance is easily diminished when levels of anxiety are high, and that experiencing a novel environment without sufficient time to adapt can raise those levels. In terms of attachment, this message translates to a hypothesis that infants with secure attachments are less likely to suffer prolonged periods of heightened anxiety that might interfere with spatial performance.

These two studies provide hints of a relation between attachment and spatial abilities, but that is all. Clearly more direct evidence is necessary to provide definitive evidence in support of the hypothesis.

Pure Speculation.   In closing, let me speculate on three other variables that are deserving of attention as we attempt to explore individual differences in infant spatial memory. The first of these is the role that sex differences may play. Although much has been written about sex differences in spatial abilities among adolescents and adults, there is virtually no systematic evidence of such differences within the infancy literature. Of course, it is possible that the sample sizes in these studies have been too small to detect subtle differences that are there. It is also possible that the specific behaviors being tested in these studies are just so basic to the successful development of every individual child that systematic sex differences should not be expected. Future research specifically designed to reveal the correlates of individual differences in performance will help decide the issue.

A second area that I believe may be fertile ground for exploration is the role of "temperament" in accounting for individual differences in spatial memory. Temperament as an identifiable component of infant personality has received a good deal of attention over the past decade, stemming in large part from the classic attempts by Thomas and Chess (1977) to differentiate among babies very early in life. More recently Campos, Barrett, Lamb, Goldsmith, and Stenberg

(1983) have reviewed the evidence linking temperament to differences in cognitive development as broadly defined. The conclusions they reach support the hypothesis that we might well expect temperamental dimensions such as activity level, persistence, attentiveness, curiosity, and wariness to be linked to specific developments within the domain of spatial memory. Given the literature we have already discussed pertaining to the role of vigilance, anxiety, and active movement to performance on specific infant spatial tasks, this hypothesis is clearly one worth pursuing.

Finally, it seems logical to explore the possibility of a link between development of the "symbolic function" in an infant and his/her performance on spatial tasks that assess sensitivity to the role of landmarks in specifying location. In a recent article (Acredolo, in press) I develop the thesis that the infant who demonstrates an appreciation for the spatial-designation function of landmarks can be said to have achieved a "symbolic" notion of landmarks—that one object or feature can "stand-for" another in one's memory for spatial relations. In this regard it is interesting to note that appreciation of landmarks increases over the second half of the first year and at least through the first half of the second year—the same period during which important strides in symbolic play and symbolic language are occurring. Given this possible commonality, it is ironic that we so often treat spatial skills and verbal skills as diametrically opposed domains. During this period of infancy they may have more in common than we have hitherto believed. Once again, research specifically designed to assess the correlates of good spatial performance is needed to clarify the issue. Such work will have the added benefit of helping solve the debate as to the existence or nonexistence of a common mechanism underlying the development of symbols in multiple domains.

Summary

The main purpose of all the preceding discussion has been to generate enthusiasm for the idea that it is time to look more closely at individual differences in spatial memory during infancy. Even though there have been no efforts specifically directed to this question as there have been in other areas of infant development, the literature already contains intriguing hints that important differences exist. Many of these pertain to sensitivity to landmark information, but whether such differences represent differences in rate of development, differences in strategies, transient differences, or long-term differences all remains to be determined. Possible contributions by locomotor experience, visual attention, attachment, sex, temperament, and knowledge of symbols have all been suggested. Once the role of these and other as yet unspecified factors are understood, there is no doubt that our understanding of the dynamics of infant development in general will be enhanced.

REFERENCES

Acredolo, L. P. (1978). Development of spatial orientation in infancy. *Developmental Psychology, 14*, 224–234.

Acredolo, L. P. (1979). Laboratory versus home: The effect of environment on the nine-month-old infant's choice of spatial reference system. *Developmental Psychology, 15*, 666–667.

Acredolo, L. P. (1982). The familiarity factor in spatial research. In R. Cohen (Ed.), *Children's conceptions of spatial relationships* (pp. 19–30). San Francisco: Jossey-Bass.

Acredolo, L. P. (in press). From signal to "symbol" the Development of landmark knowledge from 9 to 13 months. *British Journal of Developmental Psychology.*

Acredolo, L. P., Adams, A., & Goodwyn, S. W. (1984). The role of self-produced movement and visual tracking in infant spatial orientation. *Journal of Experimental Child Psychology, 38*, 312–327.

Acredolo, L. P., & Evans, D. (1980). Developmental changes in the effects of landmarks on infant spatial behavior. *Developmental Psychology, 16*, 312–318.

Ainsworth, M. D. S., Bell, S. N. U., & Stayton, D. J. (1973). Individual differences in the strange-situation behavior of one-year-olds. In L. S. Stone, H. T. Smith, & L. B. Murphy (Eds.), *The competent infant* (pp. 1150–1160). New York: Basic Books.

Ashmead, D., & Perlmutter, M. (1980). Infant memory in everyday life. In M. Perlmutter (Ed.), *Children's memory* (pp. 1–16). San Francisco: Jossey-Bass.

Bertenthal, B., Campos, J., & Barrett, K. (1984). Self-produced locomotion: An organizer of emotional, cognitive, and social developments in infancy. In R. Emde & R. Harmon (Eds.), *Continuities and discontinuities in development* (pp. 175–210). New York: Plenum Press.

Bluestein, N., & Acredolo, L. P. (1979). Developmental changes in map-reading skills. *Child Development, 50*, 691–697.

Bowlby, J. (1969). *Attachment and Loss (Vol. 1, Attachment).* New York: Basic Books.

Bremner, J. G., & Bryant, P. E. (1977). Place versus response as the basis of spatial errors made by young infants. *Journal of Experimental Child Psychology, 23*, 162–171.

Campos, J., Barrett, K., Lamb, M., Goldsmith, H. H., & Stenberg, C. (1983). Socioemotional development. In M. Haith & J. Campos (Eds.), *Infancy and developmental psychobiology* (Vol. 2, pp. 783–916), P. Mussen (Series Ed.), *Handbook of child psychology.* New York: Wiley.

Cornell, E. H., & Heth, C. D. (1979). Response versus place learning by human infants. *Journal of Experimental Psychology: Human Learning and Memory, 5*, 188–196.

Corter, C. M., Zucker, K. J., & Galligan, R. F. (1980). Patterns in the infant's search for mother during brief separation. *Developmental Psychology, 16*, 62–69.

Hazen, N., & Durrett, M. E. (1982). Relationship of security of attachment to exploration and cognitive mapping abilities in 2-year-olds. *Developmental Psychology, 18*, 751–759.

Horobin, K., & Acredolo, L. P. (1986). The role of attentiveness, mobility history, and separation of hiding sites on Stage IV search behavior. *Journal of Experimental Child Psychology, 41*, 114–127.

Keating, M. B., McKenzie, B. E., & Day, R. H. (1986). Spatial localization in infancy: Position constancy in a square and circular room with and without a landmark. *Child Development, 57*, 115–124.

Kermoian, R., & Campos, J. (1988). Locomotor experience: A facilitator of spatial cognitive development. *Child Development, 59*, 908–917.

Kopp, C. B. (1979). Perspectives on infant motor system development. In M. Bornstein & W. Kessen (Eds.), *Psychological development from infancy: Image to intention* (pp. 9–35). New York: Wiley.

Kozlowski, L. T., & Bryant, K. J. (1977). Sense of direction, spatial orientation, and cognitive maps. *Journal of Experimental Psychology: Human Perception and Performance, 3*, 590–598.

Liben, L. S., & Downs, R. M. (in press). Understanding maps as symbols: The development of map concepts in children. In H. W. Reese (Ed.), *Advances in child development and behavior.* New York: Academic Press.

Nelson, K. (1981). Individual differences in language development: Implications for development and language. *Developmental Psychology, 17,* 170–187.

Siegel, A. W., & Schadler, M. (1977). Young children's cognitive maps of their classroom. *Child Development, 48,* 388–394.

Thomas, A., & Chess, S. (1977). *Temperament and development.* New York: Brunner/Mazel.

13

The Process of Developmental Change in Infant Communicative Action: Using Dynamic Systems Theory to Study Individual Ontogenies

Alan Fogel
Department of Psychology University of Utah

". . . life is process, not substance."

-Paul Weiss, 1969, p. 8

In this excerpt, the biologist Paul Weiss contrasts process and substance. His point is that living beings are not static but dynamic, and therefore the units of their description must be in terms of interactive processes that unfold over time. Weiss (1969) stated:

> A living system is no more adequately characterized by an inventory of its material constituents, such as molecules, than the life of a city is described by the list of names and numbers in a telephone book. Only by virtue of their ordered interactions do molecules become partners in the living process: in other words through their behavior. (p. 8)

Living systems are constituted by the dynamic partnership between their components acting together in a context. Patterned regularities emerge in this dynamic process, not because there is some higher order control center, but, according to Weiss (1969), because the component parts "submit to the ordering restraints exerted upon them by the intergral activity of the 'whole' in its patterned systems dynamics" (p. 9). There are two essential points here. One is that living systems acting in a context are *dynamically self-organizing,* and the other is that dynamic self-organization creates regularities or *patterns* rather than random associations.

341

PROCESS-ORIENTED DEVELOPMENTAL RESEARCH
ON COMMUNICATION

In the literature on early communicative development one can find a number of examples of process-oriented research, because communicative action, by definition, must be understood in a social context and must reflect the continually changing status of the subjects' intent. It would make little sense in the study of individual differences in language usage, for example, to correlate across subjects the frequency on noun usage with the frequency of verb usage. One is more interested in the specific sequences of communicative action—including words and gestures—in the context of a social interaction.

Because it is labor intensive this work has usually been done on small samples of infants. In early infancy, my own studies of the ontogeny of mother–infant face-to-face interaction in individual parent–infant dyads observed weekly can be cited as an example (Fogel, 1977, 1981, 1982, 1985). This work reveals both gains and losses of communicative actions over developmental time, changes in the temporal organization of the mother-infant interaction, as well as between-dyad variability in the developmental process. Similar approaches to the early face-to-face interaction have been taken by Papousek and Papousek (1984), Tronick, Als, and Brazelton (1980), Trevarthen (1977), and van Wulfften Palthe and Hopkins (1984). A large number of studies of one-word and gestural communication take a process approach in which individual dyads are studied intensively and longitudinally (Bates, 1979; Bruner, 1983; Zukow, Reilly, & Greenfield, 1982). Most research on language development in the second and third years is typified by a process-oriented methodology.

These investigators do not believe that the universe of human possibility is revealed in the intensive study of a few cases, and developmental psychologists correctly are skeptical about the generality of inferring to the population from single-subject (or single-dyad) research designs, as shown by the preference for nomothetic over idiographic approaches.

By advocating a within-dyad longitudinal process methodology, I am not eschewing the search for nomothetic laws, the general principles regulating the formation of individual differences. On the contrary, I agree with Thorngate's (1987) assessment that nomothetic laws cannot be derived from group statistics:

> It is tempting to equate the nomothetic approach with the analysis of averages. To do so is to equate statistical models of experiments with models of people . . . To find out what people do in general, we must first discover what each person does in particular, then determine what, if anything, these particulars have in common. This implies that we pay more attention to case histories, find or develop models sufficient to account for each, then examine the models for common themes or elements. (p. 75)

Case study approaches are recognized as a means for exploratory work, and for gaining post-hoc insight into processes revealed by correlational approaches on larger samples. But that is not all that case histories can contribute. Given large samples, repeated observations on the same subjects, and contextually appropriate measures, analytic approaches can be applied that preserve the integrity of the individual's life history in order to construct generalities of developmental change. *It is only when a sufficiently large sample of individual case histories are collected that longitudual process research can be generalized to the population.*

The difficulty in using case histories to generate general laws of development is to construct those histories in a way that they can be compared. We require a theoretical and methodological foundation for this work, one that gives some clues about what to focus on for comparison across individuals, and clues about what to ignore. How can we look at idiosyncratic sequences of action in time and recognize patterns that are potentially of developmental interest?

To cope analytically with case history data, it will be necessary to shift our data-reduction strategies. *Rather than refining multivariate statistical strategies to detect patterns in correlation matrices, developmentalists should be inventing means to seek patterns in sequences of action in a context, in both real-time and developmental-time scales.* In examining a matrix of multiple correlations, we trust that significant relationships will fall into some interpretable pattern. A similar logic applies to the examination of action sequences within individuals: out of all the possible arrangements of behavior in time, only a small number of systematic patterns actually occurs. For example, some investigators have used principles of ethnography to find patterns in complex sequential data (Rogoff & Gauvain, 1986; Zukow, Reilly, & Greenfield, 1982), others apply contextualism (DeLemos, 1981), whereas others appeal to general systems theory (Horowitz, 1987; Sameroff, 1984), a view of the whole organism in its interaction with the context.

Similarly, in my own work I have been using a dynamic systems approach (Fogel & Thelen, 1987; Thelen & Fogel, 1989; Thelen, Kelso, & Fogel, 1987) as a guide to the study of the processes of communicative development within individual dyads. I believe that a dynamic systems approach offers concrete suggestions for the study of developmental change in context. In the remainder of this chapter, the implications of dynamic systems thinking for the study of the development of interindividual and interdyad differences are discussed.

This chapter addresses the following issues: (a) the relationship between the context (in this case the communicative partner) and the individual; (b) an illustration of how dynamic processes can be seen in the sequential interweave of actions in a social context; and (c) suggestions for how to use longitudinal case histories of such processes to understand infant developmental change.

A Dynamic Conceptualization of the Infant-Context Relationship

Although investigators may believe otherwise, typical developmental methodologies that seek independent measures of mother and infant assume that a rather sharp line can be defined between the individual and the social environment. Environmental influences on the formation of individual variation are assumed to exist, and it is left to the skill of the methodologist to measure those influences in reliable and valid ways. Standardized measures of individual functioning are no less avidly sought. Such measures and premises shape the research in fields as widely different as behavioral genetics and education, mental health, and behavioral ecology (Bronfenbrenner, 1979; Plomin, Loehlin, & DeFries, 1985; Scarr & McCartney, 1983).

As long as one's goal is predicting the variance in some outcome measure, this measurement and analysis strategy is appropriate. The error comes in the post-hoc interpretation of the resultant patterns of statistical significance. Do these measures and statistics have any psychological reality in the life of the individual? Do the variables so measured reflect actual processes that shape the child?

Just because we can predict an outcome does not mean that we understand its origins. Before Copernicus, astronomers recognized the regularities in planetary motion and could predict with some accuracy the seasons, the moon's phases, and the eclipses. Their interpretation of the data, however, was phrased in terms of supernatural forces and a geocentric universe. To borrow (and twist) a metaphor from developmental psycholinguistics, prediction often precedes comprehension.

When investigators reify the boundary between organism and environment, they mask the dynamic processes of self-organization that constitute developmental change. *When organism and environment are conceptualized as distinct for the purpose of measurement, one cannot reconstruct from those measures alone the dynamics of the developmental process.* Organisms possess real, physical boundaries—skin, hair, and membranes—by which they maintain homeostasis as living systems (Sameroff, 1984). Other persons, tools, surfaces, and even parts of the child's own body may support or interfere with individual action and must be conceptualized in their dynamic and changing relationship to the child's task orientations. Examples of this dynamic interface between individual and environment follow.

The Child's Body Can Be Part of the Context or Task.   Early studies of the development of reaching between 2 and 4 months (Piaget, 1954; White, Castle, & Held, 1964) suggested that the visual identification of the infant's own hand may be part of the process. These authors explained the development of reaching in terms of cognitive–perceptual advances: understanding the relationship between self, hand, and object.

More recent work (Bushnell, 1985; Butterworth, 1981; Von Hofsten, 1979) shows that even newborns possess the ability to reach toward an object. The newborn reach is rarely successful and often consists in little more than a stirring of the infant's upper body or a gross swiping movement at the sight of the object. Because newborns demonstrate even crude reaching it suggests, contrary to the earlier view, that a synergetic link between action and perception is present at birth.

So what accounts for the developmental shift in reaching between 2 and 4 months? According to research by Von Hofsten (1979), infants do not look at their hands at any point during a reach at any age: They always look at the object. The improvement comes in the infant's ability to counterbalance the inertial forces generated by the moving arm against the effects of gravity. At first, reaching movements are ballistic and poorly adjusted to the target. Later, the arm comes closer to the target but in a series of zig-zags that may overshoot or fall short of the goal. Finally, consistently successful reaches occur when the arm transport becomes smooth and stable.

This research suggests that the perceptual-motor links are present early in life, but the motor control over the arm and hand is relatively immature. Thus, reaching arises as infants develop mastery over an initially recalcitrant part of their bodies. Once that part of the body comes under voluntary control, it is free to interact with perceptual, motivational, and contextual factors to create an emergent reaching skill through dynamic self-organization.

The body's influence is no less important for social and communicative action than it is for motor skills like reaching. My own work (Fogel, 1985) on the development of emotion expression in infants is an example of the role played by the body. From birth there is a synergy between sucking and calming (Kessen, Haith, & Salapatek, 1970). In early infancy the synergy is used to advantage by adults. Nipples or fingers inserted into a fussy baby's mouth afford almost guaranteed cessation of crying. We have observed that if no adult assistance is available, upset infants either turn their heads and root (as if to search for something on which to suck) or bring their arms and hands up to the facial region (see Fig. 13.1). Young infants are rarely successful at getting the hand into the mouth to calm themselves for the same reasons that prevent them from reaching: poor control over arm and hand movements. If the infant's hand is stabilized by some contextual support (see Fig. 13.2), the hand will be maintained in the mouth and self-calming will occur.

It is not until 4–5 months of age that infants can independently control their arms well enough to bring the hands to the midline of the body and up to the mouth. When this happens, infants can readily calm themselves without displaying prolonged expressions of distress (Fogel, 1985; see Fig. 13.3). It is not the

FIG. 13.1.   At 2 months of age fussing infants root and attempt to bring their hands up toward their mouths. These efforts are rarely successful, typically resulting in touching the face or head and continued fussiness.

ability to regulate distress by sucking that develops. It is mastery over arm movement that develops and becomes available to be recruited by the infant into that existing suck–calm synergy for the task of self-calming.

The Context or Task Can Be Intergal to the Child's Competence.   Just as the child's body can at times be experienced as a feature of the context or the task to be mastered, components from the context may be experienced by the child as inseparable from the performance. For example, adults can provide supports that enhance a child's skill beyond that which the child alone or in another context could produce. This phenomenon has been described using terms like framing (Fogel, 1977; Kaye, 1982) scaffolding (Bruner, 1983), and the zone of proximal development (Vygotsky, 1978).

The result is that the infant's action is an emergent product of the dynamic interaction of infant and context, even when the context is another individual (Fentress, 1978). Even highly ritualized social sequences in nonhuman species can be explained as emergent social products. For example, play fighting in wolf pups is organized into highly stable social states and transitions between states, as when pups who have been repeatedly circling around each other establish contact with a thrust of their heads (Moran, Fentress, & Golani, 1981). These rituals are not the result of some innate template for social behavior; rather they

FIG. 13.2.   At 2 months, the hand can be maintained in the mouth only if the arm is supported by the context. As in the case shown here, the support is accidental. The infant's arm is caught against the mother's body and the infant uses the opportunity to best advantage. In this case, aspects of the context become incorporated spontaneously into the suck–calm synergy to create an emergent ability for self-calming.

FIG. 13.3. At 8 months the infant becomes fussy while sitting and lowers the head while at the same time raising the hand toward the mouth (left). The hand can be maintained in the mouth as the infant returns to exploratory play (right). In this case, the suck–calm synergy available since birth is combined with the newly acquired motor skill of bringing one hand to midline, while using the other hand to manipulate objects.

are established and maintained via the constant mutual monitoring of the animals in relation to subtle and changing postural and movement cues.

Human infants depend on such joint regulations to complete even simple sensorimotor tasks. When mothers of toddlers are asked to experimentally withhold support during social exploratory play, the toddlers request assistance (Ross & Lollis, 1987), and if none is forthcoming the complexity of the infant's actions on objects declines (Slade, 1987). Mother's spontaneous actions during this period are not simple or constant. Mothers constantly adjust their level of participation and support to the infant. On the one hand the parent's action is suited to best assist the child. On the other, parents gradually withdraw support as their toddler's competence changes on particular tasks, becoming less explicit, less concrete, and more verbal in their instructions (Heckhausen, 1987).

One need not speak of the infant's skills as if they belonged to the infant organism as a trait. Nor would it be correct to say that the infant's behavior is due to parental competence. Rather, these skills are assembled dynamically in the context of the adult–child social interaction (Fogel & Thelen, 1987). From this perspective, there is little doubt that a baby using only single-word utterances can communicate complex intentions, that a person with crutches can walk, or that a scientist with good equipment and helpful colleagues can discover new knowledge. These achievements are no less profound, no less part of the individual's competence, for having incorporated aspects of the surround.

Summary.   The dynamic systems approach does not deny the existence of physical boundaries between self and other. Rather, the boundaries need to be construed from the perspective of the individual's task orientation. As the examples in this section show, the psychological boundaries are dynamic and fluid. Although one component of the body is experienced as part of a task to be mastered at one point in time, that same component may be experienced as integrated with other aspects of the self once mastery is achieved. In addition, aspects of the context that are at one time experienced as integral with the self may be later perceived as differentiated. Individual and context do not exist as ideal categories but as part of a dynamically changing perception–action system for the individual. The goal is not to disentangle the individual from the context—a goal that rests on an illegitimate dichotomy—but rather to examine carefully subtle changes in the ways in which individuals use and are supported by their environment.

Sequences of Action in a Social Context Are Dynamically Self-Organized Patterns

In the previous section I argued that the boundary between the individual and the context is defined in the dynamic interaction of the two. In this section I extend this notion by giving examples of such dynamic interactions. In so doing the definition of a dynamic process as applied to social communication should become more clear.

If one were to count all the possible forms of movement of each of the components involved in a complex communicative action—a smile or a sentence—and then calculate all the possible combinations of those elements, an extremely large number of possible actions could be produced. In spite of this potential complexity, action is produced in a relatively small number of distinct patterns. For example, all the muscles of the face, if allowed to move independently, could generate tens of thousands of different facial expressions. In fact, only small proportion of all the potential patterns of facial muscle configurations actually occur, those that correspond to the repertoire of discrete human facial expressions (Izard, 1977).

A dynamic account of how this happens suggests that in the process of interacting, components of the individual-context system—some of which may be neurological, others muscular, and others found outside the body—constrain each other's behavior. In this view, patterned actions emerge in the process of behaving, as components interact with each other. The muscles at the periphery of the body and the social context in which the expression occurs are *sources of order* rather than mere recipients of instructions from a neurologically encoded scheme or internal organizer (Thelen, Kelso, & Fogel, 1987).

Muscles—able only to flex and extend—interact with each other in terms of their local linkages across bones and joints. Muscles are subject to biomechanical forces such as stretch, torque, and gravity. The facial muscles do less work against gravity than the legs or arms. Nevertheless, the action of one facial muscle is contrained by the ways in which it is connected to bone and other muscles (Fogel & Reimers, 1989).

The point of this is to suggest that one cannot read backward from the face into some specific brain state. There may be a number of states that would produce a general tensor tone. Signals from the brain become embodied as movements as they interact with the biomechanical constrains of tissues. These constraints will change as a function of positional orientation, posture, and social context. This model predicts a rather fluid linkage between internal state and expression such that, if the preferred facial pathway is not available to the infant because of current goals or the context, alternative pathways for expression will arise. Distress may be expressed by crying (Wolff, 1967), turning away of the head or body (Stern, 1984), bringing the hands to the mouth (Fogel, 1985), or lowering the eyes, clenching the hands, and kicking (Papousek & Papousek, 1984; Tronick et al., 1980).

These behaviors are more than a curious catalogue of baby idiosyncrasies. If these examples are taken seriously as evidence of the dynamic organization of expressive action, they can lead us to a conceptualization of the process of formation of individual differences that is free of simple monadic notions of nature and nurture. Individual patterns of action can be understood as an emergent product of all the components and linkages acting together in a context, and not the mere result of genetic instructions nor environmental shaping.

Even ordinary adult—infant social encounters, when examined as dynamic systems, are not as stimulus bound as they first appear. For example, the metaphor of "scaffolding" or "framing" alluded to in the last section implies a rigid structure that supports infant action. However, consider this description from Clark (1978) of an interaction in which a mother helps to pull her baby into a sitting position: "the child is on his back on the floor and the mother takes hold of his hands, pulling gently. She pauses expectantly and the child strenuously pulls himself upward against the hands, using his arms and legs to effect this. The mother then completes the infant's actions and pulls him to a sitting position" (p. 246).

In this example we can see that the mother is not a rigid mechanical pulley exerting constant force on the baby's limbs. On the contrary, there seems to be a dynamic shifting of exertion between mother and infant as mother pauses to assess the child's effort and resumes her pulling only as the child's ability wanes.

How do these examples of dynamic processes affect the study of individual differences? One cannot assume that a particular constellation of action tendencies (e.g., a baby who is relatively irritable and tense vs. one who is more alert and relaxed) reflects a prewired trait. These characteristic constellations may be a reflection of the way a particular infant's actions become organized in a particular social context. Environmental inputs, internal wirings, and genetic potentials simply do not carry enough information to specify complex actions in a context. There is, in a word, a *nondeterminism* at work here (cf. Thelen, this volume). Individual differences are created as action in a context that is assembled at the periphery of the body. If one or more peripheral or contextual features change, radically different patterns may emerge, even if their neurologies are generating the same sets of signals. Thus, even a small shift in the balance of exertion in the pull-to-sit example will lead to the experience of failure to achieve sitting, to a sense of mastery, or to the experience of being the passive recipient of external control.

How does one approach these dynamic processes analytically? The answer is not clearly articulated, because the dynamic systems approach is a relative newcomer to the sciences. In the physical and biological sciences one can measure continuous variations in system components, and their behavior can be described with a set of differential equations (equations that embody a description of the course of change over time; cf. Haken, 1983; Nicolis & Prigogine, 1977; Schoner & Kelso, 1988). When the appropriate mathematical linkages are imposed to mutually constrain the sets of equations, the system's future behavior can be simulated.

It is worth noting that a successful simulation based on such mathematical models does not necessarily lead to accurate predictions of the future behavior of the system. There are a class of simple dynamical systems whose behavior can be modeled based on a knowledge of all the dynamics whose future behavior cannot be precisely known. So-called *chaotic* systems display some regularity, but their exact future is highly sensitive to variations in the conditions in the system at an earlier point in time, a property known as sensitivity to initial conditions. As Thelen (this volume) suggests, certain neurological and behavioral systems appear to share these properties. Yet until precise mathematical modeling can be done to compare prediction and experiment, behavioral scientists need to proceed with caution in using chaos as a metaphor for behavior and development.

Most social and communication processes of interest to human developmentalists are not so easily defined and measured. In spite of persistent attempts to derive continuous variables that capture the dynamic interplay between parents and infants (Tronick et al., 1980), these measures are still burdened with serious validity problems (Fogel, 1988). It would indeed be difficult to measure the balances of forces in even the simple pull-to-sit example. One promising approach is the conceptualization of intensity contours in verbal and nonverbal expressive actions, the so-called "vitality" affects (Stern, 1984). Although seemingly amenable to qualitative categorization, intensity contours have yet to yield to a quantitative measurement. Aside from not knowing the true metric of the process, one has to sample at intervals considerably smaller than the period of time it takes the system to make a measurable change, which in social processes seem to be on the order of microseconds.

In my current work my students and I are using a combination of verbal description and visual representation of sequences derived from videotaped records. We are also restricting our efforts to sequences of action in which most of the relevant components can be seen clearly: those involving displacement of objects and bodies in space and time.

For example, we are examining postural-vestibular interactions between mothers and young infants. When interacting with infants on their laps, mothers move the babies' bodies several times a minute. On the one hand these movements have the resultant effect of changing the infant's state or gaze direction (Kaye & Fogel, 1980). When looked at more closely—that is, the infant's instantaneous responses to being moved—we are beginning to observe remarkably flexible dynamic adjustments much like the ones described for pull-to-sit. During a move infant's heads, bodies, and limbs swing and bend, facial expressions and eye movements change rapidly.

We think that the mother's compensatory dynamic adjustments to these subtle changes are in fact the real process out of which the infant's resultant state, and speculatively developmental progress, is being built. Because of a possible sensitivity to initial conditions, extremely small shifts in the mother's control over the infant's momentum may differentiate between infant experiences such as feeling passively jerked around (out of control), trapped and confined, or relieved and attentive.

Another area in which we are working is the transfer of objects between mothers and toddlers. Aside from being easy to observe and measure displacements, velocities, and object locations vis-a-vis the mutual postural orientations of the interactants, object transfers are important in the development of referential and linguistic communication. We think that the emergence of true referential offers from these initial object transfers is due to changes in the dynamic balances between holding and letting go, moving and pausing, all in the context of jointly coordinating attention and goals.

Summary. Dynamic processes in interactions involve the joint construction of actions assembled in time. The description of these processes warrants measures that are free to vary continuously as a function of time. Social routines can thus be studied as emergent products of dynamic mutual adjustments in a context. The current work, my own especially, is limited to those situations in which such measurements can be made. From this basic research program we hope to generate both the measurement tools and strategies that might apply to a wider variety of developmental phenomena. In the next section I discuss how developmental change might be the result of dynamic emergent processes.

Using Dynamic Systems Approaches to Study Developmental Change and Outcome

All the preceding examples apply to a baby at one point in time. The story gets more interesting by placing the infant in the context of his or her own ontogeny. All the infant's action systems, neuromotor processes, and social contextual components are dynamically changing as they interact with each other. One need not assume that there is one developmental story to be told. There are many subplots in which the characters in the play have multiple and entangling alliances.

To find the antecedents of variations in distress regulation at 1 year, for example, one might naturally look at the dynamics of crying–calming sequences early in infancy. Crying–calming may bear some relationship to later development of the cry system, but it is not the whole story. As we saw in the last section, motor factors, social skills, postural change and co-orientation, and a variety of other peripheral factors serve to sustain and organize a behavior such as calming.

In the subplot metaphor, to understand the origins of individual differences in distress regulation we must focus attention on the other components involved in self-regulation, and not simply on antecedent instances in which distress and calming occurred. We need to look, for example, at contexts in which upper body control is developed (such as gross motor exercise and exploratory play), and at how social initiatives and turn-taking have evolved (such as during caregiving routines and mother–infant play). These postural and social skills may be used by an infant to elicit an adult's assistance in the service of calming.

As applied to developmental sequences, therefore, a dynamic systems approach suggests analyzing the outcome behavior into its component features, and looking earlier in time for the possible origins of those components. One critique that may be leveled at a dynamic systems approach is that, to study the developmental origins of a single outcome, the investigator might have to examine everything that happened to the baby prior to that point in time. How does one know what to measure and when to stop?

The particular outcome behavior one is interested in predicting should, once examined dynamically as explained in the previous section, give ample clues for how to focus one's efforts. An exploratory observational study of the outcome behavior on a representative sample of subjects at a given age should suggest the usual contexts in which the behavior appears, the social processes likely to be involved, and the component cognitive, affective, motoric, and postural elements specific to that outcome. Each of these factors becomes implicated in a follow-up study to determine how those factors dynamically interact to constrain each other within the individual over developmental time.

Due to the mutual constraints exerted by one component dynamically interacting with others, only a relatively small number of ontogenetic sequential patterns is likely to emerge. In examining an ontogeny that is ordered and patterned, one need not assume that it is predetermined by information encoded in the genes or by the concerted shaping of the environment. The dynamic systems perspective suggests that outcomes are emergent products of all the components acting in concert.

In the analysis of a systems' components, care must be taken not to dichotomize the organism and environment. If a particular ontogeny is described as pathological, and children with such ontogenies have mothers who failed to respond, say, to their bids for attention, I need not conclude that the mother as an environmental factor caused the developmental pathology of the child. Responsiveness to bids for attention is a component in the system and nothing more or less. Understanding developmental outcome arises—not by passing responsibility to the mother—but by examining how the lack of that particular component affected the ongoing organization of the existing components, including the behavior of both mother and infant.

Because dynamic systems are extremely sensitive to changes in the local conditions, it is often alterations of only a small number of components or extremely small changes in even one component that creates the conditions under which different or pathological ontogenies might arise. If we knew more about the way developing systems are dynamically organized before, during, and after developmental transitions, our interventions might be more informed, precise, and economical. Once those critical components are supplied or changed through intervention, assuming all the others are intact and available, the system may be able to reorganize itself spontaneously. Such self-righting phenomena are common in development (Sameroff, 1984), and dynamic systems theory helps to illuminate the process by which self-righting may occur.

How do we study developing systems as dynamic systems? By analogy from our discussion of methodological approaches to real-time dynamic processes, we can intuit several potential directions for research in this area. First of all we need a continuous metric for each of the components of the system. This puts constraints on what can be studied using currently available technology. For my own work I find social systems especially easy to study because many of the components of the system are actions and hence observable. My students and I are following the developmental course of postural interactions in early infancy and object transfer interactions in the second year, because we can use the same measures for each observation of the same mother–infant pair.

It is essential to study the same social system over time, because the outcome is a product of their joint evolution as a couple, hence the need for case history approaches. The problem of how one compares the results of one case history to others—raised in the early part of this chapter—remains. However, given an appropriate metric and a means of describing dynamic processes, individual differences should arise as a result of differences in some of the ways in which mothers and infants strike a dynamic partnership. I hypothesize that if we can solve the measurement problems, variables representing the abstract features of the dynamic flow of control between mother and infant will be considerably better predictors of infant outcomes than infant temperament, maternal sensitivity, infant attachment, infant attention, or other such measures that derive from an artificially static conception of the infant-environment interface.

Next we need to measure the system at sampling intervals that are considerably shorter than the period of time over which developmental change takes place. *To study development as a dynamic phenomenon, we must observe the system in the process of changing,* and not simply before and after the change takes place. If a developmental change takes place over several months time, then we should be observing the infant weekly or even more frequently (Fogel, 1982, 1985).

One of the predictions of such an approach is that new skills cannot emerge until all the necessary components are present. One can examine within dyads how new social actions emerge in relation to the availability of components (from infant, mother, and context). In this endeavor the instances in which the skill is not displayed are just as important as those instances in which it is displayed. The former situations should be lacking in one or more of the hypothesized components that support the action. Individual differences in the age of emergence and the level of skills may result from small differences in the availability of particular components rather than to the direct effects of the genes or the environment.

Thus, Eckerman, Davis, and Didow (1989) found that turn-taking in complementary peer play emerged only after each child was capable of imitating the other. Although the children had a variety of social and communicative skills, they were not able to be organized in relation to another child until each child had the experience being imitated. Thus, when all the other components for complementary play were available, the missing component, or control parameter (Fogel & Thelen, 1987), precluded the emergence of bouts of turn-taking. One can only discover this by following the same pairs of children over time with sufficiently frequent sampling of all the components.

I have already reported the emergence of hand-to-mouth distress regulation based on weekly observations of mother–infant dyads over the first year (Fogel, 1985). I have also looked at the changing dynamics of face-to-face interaction between 2 and 6 months using a similar observational methodology (Fogel, 1982). In that work I showed how patterns of repeated smiles and laughs during face-to-face play emerge at 3 months as a result of dynamic social processes that help infants regulate their internal levels of activation. Only in current work in progress, however, have I begun to explore the implications of a dynamic systems approach in both real-time and developmental-time frames.

Using weekly observations of free play in 7 mother–infant dyads between 4 and 52 weeks, we coded games and turns within games (Nwokah & Fogel, 1988) to discover the conditions most likely to elicit maternal laughter. We found that a variety of components contributed to maternal laughter occurrences versus nonoccurrences. Infants were likely to be smiling and gazing at the mother, and there was a prior increase in the mother's intensity of smiling. None of these factors was obligatory, however, and all were embedded into the dynamics of the game. Sometimes mothers laughed at their own exagerrated behavior in the absence of infant smiling. Some laughed when it would have been socially appropriate if interacting with an older child, as at the climax of "eency weency spider." In other cases, mothers seem to complete the laughter that the infant almost, but not quite, produced. For example, one mother laughed after tickling her son under the chin until he produced a wide, open-mouthed active smile, but he did not himself laugh. In yet other cases if the mother had an active open smile and the baby looked at her, she stated to laugh.

Although our interpretations are tentative about this research, it seems that some expected, experienced, or intended level of positive affect was the control parameter for the onset of maternal laughter. In other words, if laughter seemed conventionally appropriate, if the mother herself was at the point of laughter, or if by her play she intended her baby to be there, she herself laughed. The mothers laughed more during games after 6 months than before because the baby was capable of participating in the game by initiating looks and smiles. Thus, laughter did not appear unless all its constituent components were available.

There are unfortunately few examples of this kind of work in the literature on human infant communication. Even when infants and dyads are sampled frequently, investigators have assumed that development is spurred by maturation, or by some underlying cognitive or affective organizer (cf. Fogel & Thelen, 1987). Thus, their measures have not allowed the detection of emergent processes.

One must ask questions about individuals and differences between them in ways that do justice to life's inherent dynamic. This calls for no less than a fundamental re-evaluation of the theories and approaches of developmental psychology (Oyama, 1985). We are not simply talking about getting more valid measures, or more encompassing statistics. We must define our science in terms of the individuals it purports to understand. According to Oyama (1985), rather than measuring and ranking, correlating and predicting, research should:

> show us about the timing of events, the susceptibility of processes to various kinds of perturbation and the manner in which regulation is achieved, if it is achieved . . . what is needed to enable a particular developmental sequence to proceed, what will induce, facilitate or maintain such a sequence, how does sensitivity to these factors change with developmental state, what degree of specificity is evident in these interactions, what is the relationship among events at various levels of analysis? (pp. 160–161)

The best model that I have found for this type of work is neural and behavioral embryology (Prechtl, 1981; Provine, 1984). Embryologists have the opportunity to observe a number of different component systems as they unfold at different rates and with different onset times. In addition to being able to see how each component interacts with and constrains the others in the natural course of events, embryologists can also perform experiments that alter initial conditions in order to observe the consequences of the resulting developmental process. It is not the ability to predict a particular deformity as the result of a specific early insult that concerns these developmental biologists. Rather, they wish to know how the insult affects all the subsequent processes of interactions between the component subsystems of the embryo.

Summary. Dynamic systems theory suggests that the sources of individual differences in developmental outcomes are never domain specific. The origins of individual variation can be found in the dynamic interplay between all the relevant components that constitute the mature outcome. These components may come from diverse domains such as physiological, neuromotor, social, affective, and cognitive. Without the cooperation of muscles, joints, stances, and postures, communicative intentions could never be realized. Variations in the age and level of the outcome measure may often depend on the ontogeny of components that may seem to play only minor roles in the outcome dynamics. Finally, developmental research on dynamic processes must sample behavior in such a way as to observe the system during the process of change, and not just before and after the change.

These approaches to the study of development are clearly within the grasp of developmentalists. It appears, however, that those committed to process research will have to settle in the short term for the study of relatively simple systems that can be observed sufficiently frequently and measured in sufficient detail to permit a systems analysis. The developmental processes discovered in these more tractable developmental problems may later generalize to the development of humans in more ecologically relevant situations.

ACKNOWLEDGMENTS

The work reported in this chapter was supported in part by a grant from the National Institute of Health (HD21036), and from the National Science Foundation (BNS-77-14525). I am grateful to the following individuals for their comments on earlier drafts of this chapter: John Colombo, Carol Eckerman, Jeff Fagen, Tom Hannan, Daniel Messinger, Eva Nwokah, Mark Reimers, Barbara Rogoff, Esther Thelen, and Heather Walker.

REFERENCES

Bates, E. (1979). *The emergence of symbols: Cognition and communication in infancy.* New York: Academic Press.
Bronfenbrenner, U. (1979). *The ecology of human development: Experiments by nature and design.* Cambridge, MA: Harvard University Press.
Bruner, J. (1983). *Child's talk: Learning to use language.* New York: Norton.
Bushnell, E. W. (1985). The decline of visually guided reaching during infancy. *Infant Behavior and Development, 8,* 139–155.
Butterworth, G. (1981). The origins of auditory–visual perception and visual proprioception in

human development. In R. D. Walk & H. L. Pick (Eds.), *Intersensory perception and sensory integration* (pp. 37–69). New York: Plenum Press.

Clark, R. A. (1978). The transition from action to gesture. In A. Lock (Ed.), *Action, gesture and symbol: The emergence of language* (pp. 231–257). New York: Academic Press.

DeLemos, C. T. G. (1981). Interactional process and the child's construction of language. In W. Deutsch (Ed.), *The child's construction of language*. London: Academic Press.

Eckerman, C. O., Davis, C. C., & Didow, S. M. (1989). Toddlers' emerging ways of achieving social coordination with a peer. *Child Development, 60,* 440–453.

Fentress, J. C. (1978). Mus musicus. The developmental orchestration of selected movement patterns in mice. In G. M. Burghardt & M. Beckoff (Eds.), *The development of behavior* (pp. 321–342). New York: Garland.

Fogel, A. (1977). Temporal organization in mother–infant face-to-face interaction. In H. R. Schaffer (Ed.), *Studies in mother-infant interaction* (pp. 119–152). New York: Academic Press.

Fogel, A. (1981). The ontogeny of gestural communication: The first six months. In R. Stark (Ed.), *Language behavior in infancy and early childhood* (pp. 17–44). New York: Elsevier.

Fogel, A. (1982). Affect dynamics in early infancy: Affective tolerance. In T. Field & A. Fogel (Eds.), *Emotion and early interaction* (pp. 15–56). Hillsdale, NJ: Lawrence Erlbaum Associates.

Fogel, A. (1985). Coordinate structures in the development of expressive behavior in early infancy. In G. Zivin (Ed.), *The development of expressive behavior: Biology–environment interactions* (pp. 249–267). New York: Academic Press.

Fogel, A. (1988). Cyclicity and stability in mother–infant face-to-face interaction: A comment on Cohn and Tronick (1988). *Developmental Psychology, 24,* 393–395.

Fogel, A., & Reimers, M. (1989). On the psychobiology of emotions and their development. *Monographs of the Society for Research in Child Development, 54,* (Serial no. 219), 105–113.

Fogel, A., & Thelen, E. (1987). The development of early expressive and communicative action: Re-interpreting the evidence from a dynamic systems perspective. *Developmental Psychology, 23,* 747–761.

Haken, H. (1983). *Synergetics—an introduction* (3rd ed.). Springer–Verlag: New York.

Heckhausen, J. (1987). Balancing for weaknesses and challenging developmental potential: A longitudinal study of mother–infant dyads in appreticeship interactions. *Developmental Psychology, 23,* 762–770.

Horowitz, F. D. (1987). *Exploring developmental theories: Toward a structural/behavioral model of development.* Hillsdale, NJ: Lawrence Erlbaum Associates.

Izard, C. E. (1977). *Human emotions.* New York: Plenum Press.

Kaye, K. (1982). *The mental and social life of babies.* Chicago: University of Chicago Press.

Kaye, K., & Fogel, A. (1980). The temporal structure of face-to-face communication between mothers and infants. *Developmental Psychology, 16,* 454–464.

Kessen, W., Haith, M., & Salapatek, P. (1970). Human infancy: A bibliography and guide. In P. H. Mussen (Ed.), *Charmichael's manual of child psychology* (pp. 287–445). New York: Wiley.

Moran, G., Fentress, J. C., & Golani, I. (1981). A description of relational patterns of movement during ritualized fighting in wolves. *Animal Behavior, 29,* 1146–1165.

Nicolis, G., & Prigogine, I. (1977). *Self-organization in nonequilibrium systems.* New York: Wiley.

Nwokah, E., & Fogel, A. (1988). *The role of laughter in communication during mother–infant games.* Paper presented at Developmental Psychology Annual Conference of the British Psychological Society, University of Exeter.

Oyama, S. (1985). *The ontogeny of information: Developmental systems and evolution.* Cambridge, England: Cambridge University Press.

Papousek, H., & Papousek, M. (1984). Qualitative transitions in integrative processes during the first trimester of human postpartum life. In H. F. R. Prechtl (Ed.), *Continuity of neutral functions from prenatal to postnatal life* (pp. 220–241). Oxford: Blackwell.

Piaget, J. (1954). *The construction of reality in the child.* New York: Ballantine Books.

Plomin, R., Loehlin, J. C., & DeFries, J. C. (1985). Genetic and environmental components of "environmental" influences. *Developmental Psychology, 21,* 391–402.

Prechtl, H. F. R. (1981). The study of neural development as a perspective on clinical problems. In K. J. Connolly & H. F. R. Prechtl (Eds.), *Maturation and development: Biological and psychological perspectives.* Philadelphia: Lippincott.

Provine, R. (1984). Wing-flapping during development and evolution. *American Scientist, 72,* 448–455.

Rogoff, B., & Gauvain, M. (1986). The analysis of functional patterns in mother–child instructional interaction. In J. Valsiner (Ed.), *The role of the individual subject in scientific psychology.* New York: Plenum Press.

Ross, H. S., & Lollis, S. P. (1987). Communication within infant social games. *Developmental Psychology, 23,* 241–248.

Sameroff, A. J. (1984). Developmental systems: Contexts and evolution. In P. H. Mussen (Series Ed.) & W. Kessen (Vol. Ed.), *Handbook of child psychology: Vol 1, History, theory, and methods* (4th ed., pp. 237–294). New York: Wiley.

Scarr, S., & McCartney, K. (1983). How people make their own environments: A theory of genotype–environment effects. *Child Development, 21,* 391–402.

Schoner, G., & Kelso, J. A. S. (1988). Dynamic patterns in behavioral and neural systems. *Science, 239,* 1513–1520.

Slade, A. (1987). A longitudinal study of maternal involvement and symbolic play during the toddler period. *Child Development, 58,* 367–375.

Stern, D. N. (1984). *The interpersonal world of the infant.* New York: Basic Books.

Thelen, E., & Fogel, A. (1989). Toward an action-based theory of infant development. In J. Lockman & N. Hazen (Eds.), *Action in social context: Perspectives on early development.* New York: Plenum Press.

Thelen, E., Kelso, J. A. S., & Fogel, A. (1987). Self-organizing systems and infant motor development. *Developmental Review, 7,* 39–65.

Thorngate, W. (1987). The production, detection, and explanation of behavior patterns. In J. Valsiner (Ed.), *The individual subject and scientific psychology* (pp. 71–93). New York: Plenum Press.

Trevarthen, C. (1977). Descriptive analysis of infant communicative behavior. In H. R. Schaffer (Ed.), *Studies in mother–infant interaction* (pp. 227–270). London: Academic Press.

Tronick, E., Als, H., & Brazelton, T. B. (1980). Monadic phases: A structural descriptive analysis of infant–mother face-to-face interaction. *Merrill-Palmer Quarterly, 26,* 3–24.

Van Wulfften Palthe, T., & Hopkins, B. (1984). Development of the infant's social competence during face-to-face interaction: A longitudinal study. In H. F. R. Prechtl (Ed.), *Continuity in neural functions from prenatal to postnatal life* (pp. 198–219). Oxford: Blackwell.

Von Hofsten, C. (1979). Development of visually directed reaching the approach phase. *Journal of Human Movement Studies, 5,* 160–178.

Vygotsky, L. S. (1978). *Mind in society.* Cambridge, MA: Harvard University Press.

Weiss, P. A. (1969). The living-system: Determinism stratified. In A. Koestler & J. R. Smythies (Eds.), *Beyond reductionism: New perspectives in the life sciences* (pp. 3–55). Boston: Beacon Press.

White, B. L., Castle, P., & Held, R. (1964). Observations on the development of visually-directed reaching. *Child Development, 35,* 349–364.

Wolff, P. H. (1967). The role of biological rhythms in early psychological development. *Bulletin of the Menninger Clinic, 31,* 197–218.

Zukow, P. G., Reilly, J., & Greenfield, P. M. (1982). Making the absent present: Facilitating the transition from sensorimotor to linguistic communication. In K. E. Nelson (Ed.), *Children's language* (Vol. 3, pp. 1–90). Hillsdale, NJ: Lawrence Erlbaum Associates.

14 Continuity and Variation in Early Language Development

Donna Thal
Elizabeth Bates
University of California, San Diego

INTRODUCTION

The study of language acquisition in normal children began in earnest in the 1960s.[1] Linguists and psycholinguists committed to this new enterprise set out in search of orderly sequences or stages through which normal children pass enroute to adult language. A major goal was to identify universals that would characterize the language acquisition process for all children and all languages. In the last 20 years studies have successfully documented some regularity in development of phonology, morphology, syntax, and semantics. However, substantial diversity has also been found. Some of this variation appears to be a product of the structural differences among natural languages (e.g., English children acquire word-order regularities before they acquire grammatical morphology, whereas Turkish children show the opposite pattern; see Bates & Marchman, 1987; Slobin, 1985). But differences among individual children from the same language group have also become increasingly apparent, and these pose a substantial challenge to models of language acquisition that grew out of the search for universals. The most important challenges come under three headings: innateness, domain specificity, and normality.

Innateness. The discovery of variation in language development does not constitute, ipso facto, evidence against a biological view—a point that is badly

---

[1]In this chapter we focus on the group studies that were carried out after 1960. A history of diary and count studies prior to that date exists, however. The interested reader is referred to Bar-Adon, A. and Leopold, N. (1971), Child Language: A Book of Readings, Englewood Cliffs, NJ: Prentice Hall, for examples.

misunderstood by many linguists and psycholinguists interested in the biology of language (e.g., Bickerton, 1984; Chomsky, 1980). Variation is endemic in nature, within and across species; if language acquisition showed no such variation, we would have to be suspicious of the argument that it has a strong genetic base! On the other hand, some patterns of variation may call into question the claim that there is only one, unitary Language Acquisition Device (McNeill, 1970), and/or the belief that this device unfolds in accord with a universal bioprogram (Bickerton, 1984; Lenneberg, 1967). If there are individual differences in the rate at which subcomponents of language ability develop, we must conclude that "the" language processor involves a number of different component processes, some of which can apparently develop out of synchrony with the others.

Domain Specificity.   A number of linguists have argued that language constitutes a kind of "mental organ" (Chomsky, 1980), a biological system that is developmentally and neurologically autonomous from the rest of cognition. This view is contradicted by a large psychometric literature showing that various language measures are reliably associated with general and specific aspects of nonlinguistic cognition. It is also contradicted by a substantial literature on early language and cognitive development in normal and abnormal populations (for reviews see Bates & Snyder, 1987; Bates, O'Connell, & Shore, 1987; Johnston, 1985; Shore, O'Connell, & Bates, 1984). To be sure, some aspects of nonlinguistic cognition are clearly dissociable from progress in language (e.g., developments in spatial cognition). But there are also a number of specific cognitive skills that are reliably associated with specific changes in language ability (e.g., aspects of communicative gesture, combinatorial play, symbolic play, and object categorization). These nonverbal correlates may reflect the development of general information-processing mechanisms that are essential for language acquisition to take place—skills that have been referred to elsewhere as *cognitive infrastructures.*

Normality.   Yet another difficulty posed by the discovery of variability in language acquisition lies in the definition of normality. If sequences of "normal" development can be identified, then it should also be possible to identify and (perhaps) to predict patterns of abnormal development—a critical concern for the applied areas of psychology, linguistics, and speech–language pathology. However, accurate diagnosis and prediction both depend on consistency and continuity in baseline developmental patterns. If there is more than one way to acquire a language "normally," then our definition of deviance has to change accordingly.

In this chapter we review the growing literature on individual differences in rate and style of early language development. We describe evidence for continuity in the patterns observed to date and discuss correlations with other aspects of cognitive development. Then we describe behaviors, linguistic and non-linguistic, which may serve as potential predictors of later language skill.

QUANTITATIVE DIFFERENCES

The major milestones of early language development usually occur in the following order, within and across natural languages:

Canonical babbling and evidence for word comprehension begin in the second half of the first year.

Productive use of single words begins around the first birthday, with the pace of vocabulary development quickening across the next few weeks or months.

Novel combinations of two or more words come in late in the second year.

Depending on the child's target language, the appearance of word combinations is usually followed by a sharp acceleration in the development of grammatical inflections and function words.

However, there is substantial variation within any given language in the timing and rate of development around these milestones, as follows.

Babbling.   The noted linguist Roman Jakobson (1942) proposed a theory of universals in phonological development based on the concept of "markedness." Specifically, he proposed that all children will begin to babble at approximately the same age, starting with a set of "unmarked" phonetic contrasts that are present in every natural language (i.e., sound patterns based on only a few relatively easy phonetic features). Each successive stage of phonological development will follow a universal markedness hierarchy, with the most complex sounds (which are relatively rare across natural languages) coming in last. Alas, there is relatively little evidence in favor of this elegant theory; instead, individual children vary markedly in the content and timing of their prespeech babble (Ferguson, 1984; Locke, 1988, 1983; Vihman & Carpenter, 1984; Vihman, Ferguson, & Elbert, 1986; Vihman & Greenlee, 1987). Normal children typically begin to produce canonical babble (i.e., meaningless consonant–vowel strings) somewhere between 6 and 10 months—a substantial range of variation, considering how many changes occur in the first year of life. There is also considerable variability in the course of phonological development after this point. Some children stick with a very small set of phonetic contrasts for many weeks or month; other children bravely attempt a much larger array of sounds from the very beginning. Some consonants are indeed more common than others in babbling and in early speech (velars like "ga" and dentals like "da"); however, some children show a clear preference from the beginning for sound patterns that are far down Jakobson's markedness hierarchy (e.g., fricatives like "fa"). The long-range implications of all this diversity are still not clear (see qualitative differences, following), but the findings are systematic enough that they warrant further investigation.

Word Comprehension.   There is very little systematic evidence for word comprehension under 9 months of age (Oviatt, 1979), but there is enormous variability after this point in the rate at which receptive vocabulary expands (Bates, Bretherton, Snyder, 1988; Benedict, 1979; Fenson, Vella, Flynn, & Thal, 1988; Reznick, 1988). Because laboratory measures of word comprehension necessarily focus on only a small, well-controlled subset of the words children might know (Reznick, 1988), the best estimates of receptive vocabulary in this age range necessarily come from parental report (based on diaries and/or response to a standardized checklist). According to Bates et al. (1988), parents of middle-class infants report a mean of 17.9 words comprehended at 10 months (with a range from 6 to 35). Estimates have gone up markedly by 13 months, with a mean of 48.25 words, ranging from 17 to 97. More recently, we have collected new estimates of word comprehension from parents of 194 children, using a standard checklist of 325 words that are commonly found in the receptive and/or expressive vocabularies of children in the second year (Fenson et al., 1988). By 12 months of age, estimates ranged from 9 to 229, with a mean of 84.5; by 16 months of age, the mean has expanded to 164.8, with a range from 27 to 295. Although we have no way of determining whether these absolute numbers are correct, several studies have at least demonstrated that parental estimates of word comprehension are significantly correlated with children's performance on laboratory tests of word comprehension (Bates, Bretherton, & Snyder, 1988; Bates, Thal, Whitesell, Fenson, & Oakes, 1988; Reznick, 1988; Thal & Bates, 1988). So we think it fair to conclude that there is extraordinary variation in comprehension vocabulary between the ages of 9 and 16 months.

Word Production.   There is also a great deal of variation in the onset and time course of early expressive vocabulary. According to Bates et al. (1988), parents of middle-class infants report a mean of 5.7 words produced at 10 months (with a range from 1 to 13). More recently, the 194 parents who were asked about comprehension (see earlier) reported that their 12-month-old children produced an average of 13.1 words, with a range of 0 to 83. At 16 months an average of 62.5 words was reported, with a range of 2 to 231. In a similar sample of 191 parents who filled out a checklist of 656 words, 24-month-olds were reported to use a mean of 332 words with a range of 28 to 628. These new data are similar to those reported by others who have used similar parental report instruments (Nelson, 1973; Rescorla, 1989; Rescorla & Schwartz, 1988) and add support for the validity of such instruments in this age range.

   Many children reportedly show a clear "burst" in rate of vocabulary development that begins some time after the 50-word point is reached. However, in a longitudinal study of vocabulary development in the second year, Goldfield, Reznick and Johns (1988) report that there are also individual differences in the shape of vocabulary change over time. Some of their children did indeed show the canonical quadratic function: a slow rate of development up to 20–30 words, with a sharp increase in rate of change after that point. Other children showed a more even rate of change at every point (with slower development overall). Yet another subgroup seemed to develop in a series of small bursts, each followed by a brief plateau. The correlates and consequences of these different developmental profiles are still unknown.

Comprehension/Production Disparities.   One of the most striking findings in the second year is the sharp disparity that can be observed between comprehension and production. To be sure, comprehension does seem to place an upper limit on the number of words a child can produce (see Fig. 14.1). Our own data (Bates et al., 1979; Bates, Thal, Whitesell, Fenson & Oakes, 1989; Fenson et al., 1988) suggest that children with receptive vocabularies under 50 words rarely produce more than 10 words, and many produce no words at all. Children with receptive vocabularies under 100 words generally have expressive vocabularies in the 0–50 word range. Very large expressive vocabularies are usually not encountered before the point at which comprehension exceeds 150 reported words. However, at every point across a comprehension range from 0–200 words, we have found at least a few children who produce little or no meaningful speech. It seems fair to conclude that receptive vocabulary is a necessary but not

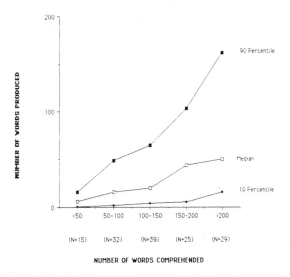

FIG. 14.1.   The relationship between number of words comprehended and number of words produced in 12- to 18-month-old infants.

sufficient condition for the development of expressive language. These comprehension/production profiles are also associated with some qualitative differences in style of language development, discussed later.

Word Combination.   Although 20 months is the mean age for production of novel word combinations, the range of normal variation for this milestone is very wide. Novel combinations (as opposed to memorized formulae) have been reported as early as 14 months of age (Bates et al., 1988); at the other end of the scale, many normal children do not begin to produce sentences of any kind before 24 months of age. The one-word stage can last as long as a year (e.g., from 10 to 24 months).

Early Grammar.   There is typically a burst in grammatical development after the so-called telegraphic stage (but see later). However, this is another phenomenon that is subject to marked variation within and across languages. In richly inflected languages like Italian or Turkish, some children actually begin to produce correct noun and verb inflections in the one-word stage! In these languages, there is also no "telegraphic stage," in which the children produce combinations of content words with no inflections at all.

Even within English, there is marked variation in the nature and pace of grammatical development. A typical index of development in English is Mean Length of Utterance in Morphemes (a count that includes content words, function words, as well as inflections like the plural "-s" or the past tense "-ed"). In his classic longitudinal study of early grammar, Brown (1973) used the MLU measure to break development down into epochs: MLU ranges from 1.05–1.50 in Early Stage I (from single words to first word combinations), from 1.50–2.00 in Late Stage I (the very first inflections appear), from 2.00–2.50 in Stage II (productive control over grammar begins), 2.50–3.00 in Stage III (grammatical development is well underway, though children typically use only simple sentences), from 3.00–3.50 in Stage IV (complex sentences start to come in), and so on. Miller and Chapman (1981) have provided a set of norms for healthy middle-class children, using the Brown stages: 19.1–23 months is the average range for Early Stage I, 23.8–26.9 months for Late Stage I, 27.7–30.8 for Stage II, 31.6–34.8 for Stage III, and 35.6–38.7 for Stage IV. However, in observational data from videotaped laboratory sessions, Bates et al. (1988) found cases across the full range from Stages I through IV in a sample of 27 healthy middle-class children at 28 months of age. So the quantitative variation in grammatical development is substantial; qualitative differences are discussed later.

Early and Late Talkers.   Even more interesting information comes from the extremes of language development in the second year (i.e., from normal children in the top and bottom 10th percentile in lexical and/or grammatical development, (where "normal" means that there are no known medical or socioeconomic risk factors that could account for a child's position at the far end of the spectrum). Thal and Bates (1988) have described the language and symbolic gesture relationships in a group of children who were between 18 and 32 months of age and still in the single-word stage of language production. Within that group some individuals demonstrated an unusually long period between onset of vocabulary development and the passage into multiword speech, and they tended to continue developing vocabulary well beyond 50 words without combining any of those words. One single-word late talker, for example, had a vocabulary of 235 words. This does not appear to be the product of delayed language, or the longer time spent in the single-word stage, however, because more extreme gaps were found in linguistically precocious children. Two children from that group provide an interesting and contrastive example. One was 17 months old, had a production vocabulary of 596 words, and an MLU equivalent to a 30-month-old child. The other was 21 months old, had a production vocabulary of 627 words, and an MLU equivalent to that of a 20-month-old child. These data are compatible with those reported by Dale and Robinson (1988) for a similar group of precocious toddlers. Later on, we describe the interesting profiles of language and cognition that we have observed in these same children.

QUALITATIVE DIFFERENCES

There is now solid evidence that language learning is approached in at least two different ways. Evidence for stylistic differences has been identified in children as young as 10–13 months, and at least some of these differences seem to be related to dimensions of variation that are also seen in adults. Our brief review is organized around these linguistic categories, describing differences in lexical development (i.e., vocabulary), grammatical development, phonology, and pragmatics. Table 14.1 presents an outline of these data. A short description of stylistic differences in older children and nonlinguistic correlates of stylistic differences completes this section.

Lexical Development

Qualitative differences in early vocabulary development were first described by Katherine Nelson (1973) in a study of the first 50 words of 18 children (7 boys and 11 girls). Data were gathered through maternal report of words used by the children. Based on a median split of the number of general nominals used by each child, Nelson divided them into two groups that she called "referential style" and "expressive style" children. Referential children used a high proportion of common nouns, primarily to label objects. They also had larger vocabularies and appeared to acquire words at a faster rate, but their speech was nevertheless restricted to single words for many weeks or months. Expressive

TABLE 14.1
Individual Differences in Early Language Development:
Summary of Claims in the Literature

Referential/Nominal	Expressive/Pronominal
Semantics	
High proportion of nouns in first 50 words	Low proportion of nouns in first 50 words
Single words in early speech	Formulae in early speech
Imitates object names	Unselective imitation
Greater variety within lexical categories	Less variety within lexical categories
Meaningful elements only	Use of "dummy" words
High adjective use	Low adjective use
Context-flexible use of names	Context-bound use of names
Rapid vocabulary growth	Slower vocabulary growth
Grammar	
Telegraphic in Stage I	Inflections and function words in Stage I
Refers to self and others by name in Stage I	Refers to self and others by pronoun in Stage I
Noun-phrase expansion	Verb-phrase expansion
Morphological overgeneralization	Morphological undergeneralization
Consistent application of rules	Inconsistent application of rules
Novel combinations	Frozen forms
Imitation is behind spontaneous speech	Imitation is ahead of spontaneous speech
Fast learner	Slow learner
Phonology	
Word oriented	Intonation oriented
High intelligibility	Low intelligibility
Segmental emphasis	Suprasegmental emphasis
Consistent pronunciation across word tokens	Variable pronunciation across word tokens
Pragmatics	
Object oriented	Person oriented
Declarative	Imperative
Low variety in speech acts	High variety in speech acts
Demographic Variables	
Female	Male
First born	Later born
Higher SES	Lower SES

Note: Adapted from Bates, Bretherton, and Snyder (1988). *From first words to grammar: Individual differences and dissociable mechanisms.* New York: Cambridge University Press.

children had much more heterogeneous vocabularies: fewer object labels, with more pronouns, quantifiers, and other non-nominals (e.g., "more," "all-gone"). They also produced some phrases, such as "I want it" or "don't do that," which served a specifically social–personal rather than a labeling function. The existence of some frozen phrases in the so-called one-word stage can give a rather sophisticated look to the early speech of expressive style children. However, children at this extreme tend to be somewhat slower in their overall rate of vocabulary development.

The distinction between these two groups appears to reflect an object-centered versus a function-oriented approach to learning about and interacting with the world. This distinction has been replicated and extended many times, with various terminologies used to describe it. The terms are usually expressed as polarities and include referential/expressive, nominal/pronominal, cognitive/pragmatic, analytic/gestalt, analytic/holistic, noun lovers/noun leavers, and code-oriented/message-oriented. The same polarities have been described at various levels of language development. For example, in her own follow-up study, Nelson (1975) reported that the styles persisted to at least 30 months of age. Starr (1975) replicated Nelson's findings, showing continuity from single-word speech through two-word combinations. Similar differences were found by Bloom (1973) in four children, Ramer (1976) for 7 children, and Horgan (1978, 1979) for 30 children. Furthermore, versions of the dichotomy have also been identified in the transition from babbling to first words (Dore, 1974).

At the lexical level, the referential/expressive distinction is not restricted to "nouniness." Among the correlates of referential style, researchers have reported a greater variety of words within lexical categories (Lieven, 1980), higher numbers of adjectives (Horgan, 1981), faster rate of lexical development (Horgan, 1978, 1979; Nelson, 1973; Ramer, 1976), more flexible and general use of object names across different contexts (Snyder, Bates, & Bretherton, 1981), less imitation overall (Bloom, Hood, & Lightbown, 1974; Clark, 1974; Nelson, 1973), but higher rates of imitation when presented with the names of novel objects (Leonard, Schwartz, Folger, Newhoff, & Wilcox, 1979). Expressive style, on the other hand, correlates with the use of formulae (as opposed to single words) in early speech (Clark, 1974; Nelson, 1973; Peters, 1983), more immediate imitation of phrases and words (Bloom et al., 1975; Clark, 1974; Nelson, 1973), slower rate of language development (Nelson, 1973; Ramer, 1976; Snyder et al., 1981), use of "dummy forms" (Ramer, 1976), and a tendency to use of object names only with a restricted set of referents or contexts (Snyder et al., 1981). Snyder et al. (1981) report that stylistic differences along these lines exist in both comprehension and production and can be found as early as 12–13 months of age. Bates et al. (1988) also provide evidence to suggest that children with comprehension vocabularies well in advance of their expressive language are more likely to demonstrate a referential style—pointing us toward some possible explanations for the comprehension/production disparities that we discussed earlier (more on this later).

Grammatical Development

Bloom, Lightbown, and Hood (1975) were the first to identify individual differences in early grammar. In a longitudinal study of four children, two appeared to approach grammar with a nominal strategy: Multiword constructions were composed mostly of nouns and other content words, and they tended to refer to themselves and the listener by name (e.g., saying "Adam truck" rather than "my truck"). The other two used a pronominal strategy: Their multiword constructions conveyed the same meanings that appear in nominal-style speech, but these meanings were expressed through nonspecific pronominal forms combined with content words (e.g., "my truck" or "Do dat" instead of "Adam truck" or "Mommy cut"). Although the specific contrast between nouns and pronouns seems to disappear when MLU reaches approximately 2.5, the finding is solid. It has been demonstrated in a number of other studies (Branigan, 1977; Goldfield, 1982; Peters, 1977), and in Nelson's follow-up of her original referential/ expressive sample (Nelson, 1975, 1981). Nelson (1975) also found other grammatical characteristics associated with the pronominal or expressive style in the follow-up of her original study. Among these were the continuation of formulaic expressions into the early stages of grammar (see also Branigan, 1977; Clark, 1974; Goldfield, 1982; Lieven, 1980; Ramer, 1976), and the use of "dummy terms" that have the effect of increasing sentence length and giving the utterances a more adult shape. A classic example of the latter phenomenon comes from Bloom's daughter Allison (Bloom, 1973), who used a dummy word "wida" in many of her utterances late in the one-word stage, giving her single-word utterances a "sentence-like look" without (as far as the observer could tell) any additional meaning at all—a kind of "oral scribbling" (see also Branigan, 1979; Horgan, 1978; Leonard et al., 1979; Peters, 1977; Ramer, 1976). Finally, the greater tendency for expressive children to imitate adult speech occurs in multiword as well as single-word utterances.

Bates et al. (1988) report that expressive/pronominal style is associated with precocious use of grammatical inflections and function words at 20 months of age. However, this early use of grammatical forms is misleading, because it is in fact negatively correlated with productive control over the same grammatical forms many months later! Bates et al. interpret this surprising finding as follows. First, they suggest that the telegraphic utterances of referential/nominal speech reflect an analytic strategy; that is, the child analyzes her input carefully to determine which elements she does and does not understand. Because inflections and function words have meanings that are relatively opaque to a 20-month-old child, these forms are (temporarily) left out of the child's own speech. By contrast, Bates et al. suggest that expressive/pronominal speech reflects a formulaic strategy (i.e., a tendency to "get the tune before the words"). These children try to reproduce their input and "sound like other people," without worrying about which elements they do and do not understand. Thus, ironically, their precocious use of pronouns and other grammatical elements actually reflects less analysis of the sound stream! As a result, it takes these children longer to acquire productive use of the grammar. However, Bates et al. stress that the fastest rates of development overall are found in children who makes extensive use of both strategies, producing a combination of telegraphic utterances and formulaic expressions. So we should not conclude that formulaic style is a reflection of a "bad" language-learning strategy. Rather, it reflects a "tool" that is not strong enough by itself for acquisition of productive control over grammar.

As we have described them so far, there seems to be an obvious parallel between the referential/expressive and nominal/pronominal dichotomies. As we see later, similar dichotomies can also be found in other aspects of language (e.g., phonology and pragmatics) and may extend even into adulthood. However, more recent research (Bates, Bretherton, & Snyder, 1988; Bretherton, McNew, Snyder, & Bates, 1983) has shown that the two-style picture of language acquisition is probably too simple. The two clusters that we have described so far do indeed emerge in all their analyses, at different stages of development. But the internal composition of these clusters changes from one stage to another. And additional factors or clusters also appear at certain points in development. For example, at 10–13 months the "two strands" are defined primarily by a split between comprehension (which loads highly on the referential strand) and production (which loads primarily on the expressive strand). At 20 months, the variance has now split into three distinct factors: comprehension, analyzed/referential production, and rote production. At 28 months, the rote factor has all but disappeared. However, a dissociation between comprehension and production still remains.

From a somewhat different point of view, Bretherton et al. used cluster analysis rather than factor analysis to examine both parental report and observational data at 20 months of age in the same sample of children. Again, they did find the expected nominal/pronominal split. However, an additional cluster also emerged in both the reported and observed language data, defined by high rates of question answering in dialogue, and by a propensity to engage in high rates of both imitation and object labelling (i.e., behaviors that were supposedly associated with separate factors). They termed this the *dialogue cluster,* a dimension of variation that is at least partially dissociable from either nominal or pronominal style. Clearly, the two-strand characterization of early language development is much too simple—a finding that will come as no surprise to readers who are familiar with the adult psychometric literature.

Phonology

Only a small number of studies have examined phonological development with an eye to individual stylistic differences. Several of the studies cited thus far have pointed out that pronominal/expressive children tend to be very difficult to understand and transcribe (Branigan, 1977; Horgan, 1979, 1981; Leonard, Newhoff, & Masalem, 1980; Nelson, 1981; Peters, 1977). Ferguson (1984) noted that children may take different paths in the acquisition of the sound system of their language. Some he described as cautious system builders who fit each new sound into a carefully analyzed existing system (i.e., referential–analytic). Others called imitative experimenters, took a more holistic and carefree approach (i.e., expressive). More evidence for clear articulation occurring within a referential–analytic style and poor intelligibility occurring within the expressive–holistic style comes from researchers in the Stanford Child Phonology Project. Vihman (1981) reports that, in the one-word stage, subjective intelligibility ratings are highly correlated with the number and variety of consonants that a child uses. The less intelligible child uses a homonym strategy that possibly reflects a desire to achieve proficiency in performance instead of clarity. Their goal seems to be to produce the largest number of words with a minimum repertoire of sounds. In addition, some children are more inconsistent in their pronunciation of words. The phonological inconsistency in such children is reliable and continuous from the one-word stage through 3 years of age, and at 3 years of age phonological inconsistency is associated with greater inconsistency in grammatical use of grammatical rules (Vihman & Carpenter, 1984).

Closer study of the children with "poor" phonological development revealed concentration on a different aspect of the system rather than failure to learn the system as well as referential–analytic children. Expressive–holistic children seem to focus on prosody or intonation instead of individual units at both the word and the sentence level. Thus, expressive children again are shown to focus on whole forms whereas referential children focus on the individual units. Vihman and Greenlee (1987) found variation in the general approach to learning the sound system among their subjects with some (analytic children) focusing on specific segments and others (holistic children) focusing on whole-word processes.

Pragmatics

Pragmatics is defined as the study of how language is used in context (Bates, 1976). The small amount of evidence on individual differences in pragmatic development is focused primarily on variation in communicative goals (as opposed to variation in the forms of language, i.e., grammar, words, and sound). In her original study Nelson pointed out that referential children engaged in more object play and were involved in the labeling functions of language, whereas expressive children generally spent more time involved with other human beings and made greater use of social–regulatory expressions like "stop it." Similarly, Furrow (1980) found that nominal (referential) children engaged in more referential (i.e., object–related) speech, whereas pronominal (expressive) children used more personal functions. Lieven (1980) noted that expressive–pronominal speech consisted of more comments about existence and recurrence, more bids for attention, and a greater tendency to make comments that are irrelevant to the conversation. Dore (1974), Starr (1975), Branigan (1977), and Nelson (1985) have also provided related evidence. What seems clear then is that referential and expressive children differ from each other in two aspects of pragmatic development. Expressive children produce a greater variety of speech act forms, and they spend more time engaged in social interaction that does not involve objects.

As Bates et al. (1988) point out, these differences could be explained in a variety of ways. For example, expressive–style children may produce a greater variety of speech acts not because they have a larger social repertoire (i.e., more communicative goals), but because they are imitating a larger array of sentence types without regard to their meaning or function. In the same vein, referential-style children may spend more time in play with objects not because they are inherently asocial, but because they have a somewhat longer attention span while they are involved in object play. In fact, Goldfield (1985) has shown that referential children use objects more often as a means of communication (i.e., through pointing and labeling). There is a small amount of evidence to suggest that expressive-style children rank higher on the sociability scale of the Rowe and Plomin Temperament Scale (Rowe & Plomin, 1977; cited in Bates et al., 1988), so they may be more gregarious overall. However, given the Goldfield findings, we should probably not conclude that referential children are less person oriented. Rather, they differ from expressive-style children in the means they choose for communicating with others.

Demographics

Nelson (1973) also reported that referential children were more likely to be firstborns, from families with higher levels of education. Ramer (1976) found that females were more likely to be referential whereas males tended to be expressive. Expressive children are also more likely to be later born children of families with lower levels of education (Nelson, 1973). Although these demographic differences are interesting (and quite familiar to psychometricians), it is important to note that they do not replicate in every study of individual differences in early language (e.g., Bates et al., 1988).

Later Differences

In contrast with the burgeoning literature on individual differences in early language development, there is relatively little known about variations in style after 3 years of age. In part, this situation reflects the field at large: Most research on language acquisition concentrates on developments under 3, because this is the era in which the most obvious developments take place. Indeed, many investigators maintain that language development is essentially over at that point. Vocabulary will continue to increase throughout life, and children may become more fluent in their use of grammatical knowledge (particularly in literate cultures), but little of theoretical interest takes place beyond the preschool years (or so the story goes).

In the last few years, psycholinguists have begun to question this traditional belief. New evidence has accumulated to suggest that there is a "second wave" of language development after the age of 5, as semantic and grammatical knowledge is reorganized in the service of complex discourse functions (i.e., storytelling, conversation). (For examples, see Bowerman, 1982; Karmiloff-Smith, 1979; Marchman, Bates, Good, and Burkhardt, 1988).[2] In view of these findings, we may well suspect that individual differences will be found around these late milestones as well. For the moment, however, we must be satisfied with a few promising findings.

Horgan (1981) compared aspects of grammatical structure in the speech of "early talkers" and "late talkers," at Brown Stage III and beyond. She notes that these children vary substantially in the extent to which noun phrases are elaborated in their speech. Some children, called *noun lovers*, produce a large number of noun phrases with simple and complex modifiers; these include adjectives ("the red car"), prepositional phrases ("the car in the driveway"), and relative clauses ("the car that just drove in"). Other children, called *noun leavers*, tend to use a high proportion of pronominal forms to refer to concrete objects and events. Children in the latter group tend to "earn" their syntactic complexity scores by elaborating aspects of the verb phrase ("was driving," "is going to drive," "wanted to drive"). Johnston and Kamhi (1980) have reported similar results in their comparison of late talkers and age-matched controls. The "noun lover/noun leaver" dichotomy sounds strikingly similar to nominal–pronominal style, but there is to date no longitudinal evidence connecting the two.

Hass and Wepman (1974) have provided more extensive information about stylistic variation in a sample of 180 children between 5 and 10 years of age, describing the same set of complex picture stimuli (taken from the Thematic Apperception Test; Murray, 1943). The children's story protocols were computerized and analyzed with a series of text-scanning programs supplemented by hand-executed coding. Fifty-seven variables were extracted, including part-of-speech frequencies and proportions, indices of syntactic elaboration, and measures of constructional variety. Principal component factor analyses were performed for each age group, and for the sample as a whole (with age entered as an additional variable). Results at every age level were strikingly similar to results for the group as a whole. Five different factors were identified. Only one of these was strongly associated with age: an embeddedness factor, reflecting developmental changes in sentence complexity. The other four factors were all stylistic and were described as follows:

General fluency, defined by its extremely high positive loading on total words and most of the part-of-speech frequencies.

---

[2]These linguistic changes may or may not have a cognitive base. See Karmiloff-Smith (1979) and Beilin (1975) for discussions of this topic.

Finite verb structure, with positive loadings on the proportion of verbs and pronouns, and negative loadings on the proportion of nouns, adjectives, and articles.

Noun phrase structure, a factor defined primarily by negative loadings from pronouns, adjectives, relative clauses, and articles, with positive loadings from several function word categories.

Qualified speech, a small factor that was defined primarily by adverbs, conjunctions, interjections, and adverbial modifiers—perhaps reflecting a tendency for the speaker to interrupt the story with digressions and qualifying materials.

Notice that two of the age-independent factors (finite verbs and noun phrase structure) seem to reflect a now-familiar opposition between nouns and non-nominal forms, similar to "nominal style" and "pronominal style" in children under 3 years of age, and to the distinction *noun lovers* and *noun leavers* that Horgan describes for somewhat older children.

Parallels to the variation observed in first-language acquisition have recently been pointed out for children and adults who are acquiring a second language. Hatch (1974) described second-language learners as rule learners versus data gatherers. Fillmore (1979) described children learning a second language as slow, cautious learners versus quick, formulaic, and error-filled learners. Finally, there are some similarities between the dimensions of variation in spoken language described here, and individual differences in the acquisition of reading skills (i.e., "phonic" versus "whole-word" styles). However, we must emphasize that all these parallels are still purely speculative; longitudinal research is needed to determine whether or not the "same" mechanisms are responsible for these apparent similarities in language style, from early language development through the acquisition of literacy and/or second-language skills.

PREDICTION

Very little in the literature exists that is directly concerned with prediction of later language from measures performed in infancy. The largest body of data is concerned with continuity within language itself, that is, correlations between specific prelinguistic and early language skills and later specific language skills. There are also data that describe between-domain predictions, specifically, relations between language and other aspects of cognition. An even smaller literature describes evidence for predictive relations between early nonlanguage-related skills and later general language ability. It includes studies that use habituation as the early measure and those that use family or maternal factors as indicators of later behavior. Each of these is described below.

Evidence for Continuity Within Language

The strongest evidence for continuity comes from within the language modality itself. For example, McCall, Eichorn, & Hogarty, (1977) have reanalyzed the original longitudinal studies using the Bayley scales, extracting first principal components at each age and correlating these components over time. The same children were followed through 5 years of age, using a variety of tests appropriate to the children's age at time of testing. They obtain two findings that are important for our purposes here: (1) although total scores in first year are poor predictors of later performance, first principal components are correlated significantly over age; (2) from 12 months of age onward, the first principal components of the Bayley scale are loaded more and more heavily on language and language-related measures. These findings suggest that there is indeed substantial continuity in language skills over the age range studied (i.e., from infancy to at least 5 years of age).

The early stages of language acquisition were the focus of a longitudinal study conducted by Bates et al. (1988). They followed 27 infants from 10 months of age through 28 months of age, examining communicative development from early word comprehension through early production of grammar. They found a sharp dissociation between comprehension and production, in the lexicon at 13 and 20 months, and within the domain of grammar at 28 months. However, the dissociation is not absolute. Instead, there appear to be two aspects of production: rote or holistic production and analyzed production. The dissociation between comprehension and production comes entirely from rote production. Using a factor analysis, Bates et al. (1988) found one continuous pathway from comprehension and analyzed production at 13 months, through isolated analyzed production at 20 months to both general comprehension and general production at 28 months. They note that this appears to be the major route from first words to grammar, but that two smaller pathways play a part as well. They include a rote production factor that appears at both 13 and 20 months, and a pure comprehension factor that is linked between 20 and 28 months. These associations or predictors are seen in specific aspects of language at each age studied. In particular, Bates et al. (1988) found the following: (a) flexible use of names for objects (analytic production) from 10 to 13 months correlated with comprehension; (b) variation in MLU at 20 months was due largely to rote or unanalyzed use of closed-class morphemes (bound inflections and grammatical function words) and that grew out of pure rote or lexical production at 13-months; (c) flexible (analyzed) use of object names at 13 months predicted productivity in the use of grammatical morphemes at 28 months; (d) grammatical comprehension was predicted by lexical comprehension, from 10 through 28 months.

Thus, considerable stability exists in the early stages of language development, in both rate and style. This finding may come as no surprise to psychometricians, who have long noted the reliability and stability of verbal IQ after the age of 5. The internal coherence and stability of language measures may reflect the psychological and neurological integrity of this "special" domain. Alternatively, insofar as language constitutes the only truly public form of thinking and reasoning, the long-term stability of language variance may simply mean that we know what to measure at each stage of development. This brings us to the next point.

Evidence for Concurrent Relations Between Language and Cognition

In the 1970s, studies began to report correlations between specific developments in language and other cognitive domains. For example, symbolic play, imitation, and some limited aspects of tool use in problem solving were shown to correlate reliably with the emergence of meaningful speech (Bates et al., 1979; Harding & Golinkoff, 1978). However, several other domains of development do not seem to correlate with language at all—at least not in the earliest stages of one-word speech. These include spatial relations (Bates et al., 1979) and object permanence (Bates et al., 1979; Corrigan, 1978; Snyder, 1978; for some late-emerging relations between language and object permanence, see Corrigan 1978; Gopnik & Meltzoff, 1987).

In the area of symbolic play, symbolic gestures seem to be most closely related to language. Specific language and gesture associations have been demonstrated from prelinguistic to combinatorial stages of language development, in normal infants (Bates et al., 1977; Bates, Benigni, Bretherton, Camaioni, & Volterra, 1979), and in several different populations of impaired children (Beeghly & Cicchetti, 1987; Sigman & Mundy, 1987; Thal & Bates, 1988). The following is a short summary of those findings.

Symbols. Between 13 and 20 months first words emerge vocally and a parallel shift is seen in the gestural modality. In this stage children use conventional gestures associated with objects, such as drinking from a toy cup or sniffing a flower, to recognize or classify members of that object class (Bates et al., 1979; Escalona, 1973; Werner & Kaplan, 1963). In other words, both words and object-associated or "recognitory" gestures appear to serve the function of naming. In this sense, it has been suggested that recognitory gestures are the gestural analogue of lexical production in language (Bates et al., 1979; Thal & Bates, 1988).

During this period we find common onset times for words and recognitory gestures (Bates et al., 1979; Bates et al., 1988), positive correlations between the number of recognitory gestures and the number of names for objects in a given child's vocabulary (Bates et al., 1979; Volterra & Caselli, 1983), the same basic "vocabulary" in both modalities (Bates et al., 1979), and a similar course of development from context bound to generalized use (Acredolo & Goodwyn,

1985, 1988; Bates et al., 1979; McCune-Nicolich, 1981; McCune-Nicolich & Bruskin, 1982; Volterra & Caselli, 1983).

Symbol Combinations. Between 20 and 24 months children begin to combine words into phrases and sentences, and to combine single gestural schemes into multischeme combinations (e.g., pouring in a cup and then pretending to drink in a single, smooth action plan). At this stage we find similarities in onset time (Fenson & Ramsay, 1981; McCune-Nicolich, 1981; McCune-Nicolich, & Bruskin, 1982), average length of sequence, and the longest chain of different elements that the children produce in a single plan (Shore, O'Connell, & Bates, 1984). Combinations of content words and combinations of gestures correlate, even when size of vocabulary in either modality is partialled out, indicating that the common combinatorial ability was not just a by-product of the earlier linkage between vocabulary in the two modalities (Shore et al., 1984). Also, individual styles (nominal or referential) are consistent across modalities (Bauer, 1985; Shore & Bauer, 1983). Correlations in this age range among language, object/manipulative play, pretense play, social play, motor play and peer interaction have also been described by Brownell (1988).

Symbol Sequencing. By 28 months grammaticization in language begins; that is, children begin learning the rules for morphology and syntax. Symbolic play has no counterpart to the morphological component of grammar, but it does to the ordering principles of syntax. During the period between 20–30 months the ability to produce symbolic gestures in a conventional sequence increases dramatically and corresponds to greater linguistic sophistication (Brownell, 1988; McCune-Nicolich, 1981; McCune-Nicolich & Bruskin, 1982; O'Connell & Gerard, 1985; Shore et al., 1984). Thus, it has been suggested that conventional sequencing of symbolic gestures is the gestural equivalent of syntactic structure in language (Shore et al., 1984; Thal & Bates, 1988).

There is now a large literature demonstrating an empirical link between recognitory gestures and language at one or more of these levels, in normal infants and in several different populations of retarded and/or language impaired children. These include links in time of onset, function, frequency of use, size of repertoire, content, rates of "decontextualization," individual differences in "style," and some neuropsychological evidence suggesting that language and symbolic/recognitory gestures share aspects of left hemisphere control (Bates et al., 1977; Bates, et al., 1979; Bates, Bretherton, Snyder, Shore, & Volterra, 1980; Bates & Volterra, 1984; Bauer & Shore, 1986; Brownell, 1988; Curcio, 1977; Elder & Pederson, 1978; Golden-Meadow & Mylander, 1984; Gopnik & Meltzoff, 1986, 1987; Killen & Uzgiris, 1981; Lezine, 1978; Nicolich, 1977; Overton & Jackson, 1973; Roth & Clark, 1987; Snyder, Bates, & Bretherton, 1981; Volterra, Bates, Benigni, Bretherton, & Camaioni, 1979; Wolf & Gardner, 1979; for reviews see Bates & Snyder, 1987; Harris, 1983; Johnston,

1985). Similar links have also been demonstrated for a number of clinical populations. For example, Beeghly and Cicchetti (1987) have reported that children with Down syndrome demonstrate the same relationships between language and gesture as those reported previously for normal children. •

However, this lockstep story is (as we might expect) much too simple. We noted earlier that language production and language comprehension can be dissociated to a remarkable degree in normal children. It should come as no surprise, then, that some nonlinguistic measures are correlated with comprehension but not production, whereas others show the opposite pattern. For example, when symbolic play is measured in a free-play setting (with accompanying narrative from the adult), then correlations are higher with measures of language comprehension (Bates et al., 1980; Bates, Thal, Whitesell, Fenson, & Oakes, 1989). However, when the same gestures are elicited out of context, with little or no verbal support (and with substitute objects), gestural production is instead correlated with measures of expressive language (Bates et al., 1980; Bates et al., 1989). Thal and Bates (1988) report similar findings for children who are late in expressive language despite scores within the normal range in language comprehension.

We also noted earlier that vocabulary development can be dissociated from the onset of first-word combinations. This dissociation is also reflected in language/gesture correlations. Thal and Bates (1988) report that their late talkers (still in the one-word stage) are nevertheless able to combine and sequence gestures at a level commensurate with their language comprehension abilities. It is as though their combinatorial abilities were developing "underground." If this is true, it may account for anecdotal reports of late talkers who suddenly begin to talk in complete sentences—drawing on abilities to combine and sequence symbols that have been there for some time, masked by a roadblock to expressive language that still has no explanation. At the very least, we must conclude that the relationships observed to date between language and cognitive development are not "one to one" but "many to many," reflecting the emergence of a number of different skills or mechanisms that sometimes come apart.

Evidence for Predictive Relations Between Prelinguistic, Nonlanguage-Related Skills, and Later General Language Skills

In keeping with the conclusion originally reached by Bayley (1969), in a large study of 193 infants Bee et al. (1982) report that standardized tests were of little value in long-term prediction prior to 24 months of age. Measures of perinatal functioning were also not helpful in predicting later child functioning. However, a cluster of factors taken in the first year (termed *family ecology*) predicted later IQ and language better than any of their other variables, and as well as 24-month measures. Among those, social support of the mother during pregnancy, birth, and the first year, and the mothers level of education were the strongest predictors. Olson, Bates, and Bayles (1984) also found that mother–infant interaction at 13 months was the best predictor of a composite factor consisting of cognitive and language measures at 24 months.

However, as investigators have documented throughout this volume, at least some aspects of preverbal cognition are significantly correlated with performance on traditional intelligence tests in early and middle childhood. There are also some that correlate specifically with later language development. For example, Bornstein and Sigman (1986) have reported that infants who code visual stimuli more efficiently, or who recollect visual or auditory stimuli more efficiently (as measured by habituation), tend to be more proficient on traditional psychometric tests of intelligence and language in childhood. In this regard, Tamis-LeMonda and Bornstein (1989) have evaluated the predictive value of infant habituation and maternal encouraging attention at 5 months for language comprehension and production and pretense play at 13 months. They found that more mature habituation (as shown by shorter baselines, shallower slopes, and lower decrement scores) predicted (a) a greater number of flexible common nouns and non-nouns in comprehension, (b) a higher proportion of flexible comprehension of words, and (c) a higher proportion of symbolic play. Habituation was not associated with variance in word production at this age level. Maternal-encouraging attention predicted comprehension but not production or symbolic play.

Molfese and Molfese (1985) have studied hemispheric differences in auditory-evoked potentials, using a combination of verbal and nonverbal stimuli. Presence or absence of a hemispheric difference in the evoked potentials discriminated between those children who, at 3 years of age, had high versus low levels of language skills as tested by the McCarthy Scales.

CONCLUSION

We began this chapter by noting that the existence of individual differences within languages posed a significant challenge to models of language acquisition that grew out of a search for universals—with specific important challenges in claims of innateness, domain specificity, and normality in language development. The research reviewed in this chapter clearly demonstrates that individual differences in language development are stable, reliable, and relatively easy to measure. However, much of that literature has also demonstrated that many individual differences are related across different cognitive domains. If language were an isolated domain, a "mental organ" unrelated to the rest of mind, then the stability and reliability of individual differences would be of interest primarily to psycholinguists; it would have few implications for a general theory of cognitive development, and fewer still for practitioners interested in the early diagnosis of children who are at risk for learning disabilities. We think, however, that the evidence in favor of linguistic autonomy is slim at best. Language is better viewed as a window on the mind, a domain in which we can observe with exceptional clarity the universal mechanisms and processes that underlie individual differences in mental development; a domain of particular importance for psychological research.

REFERENCES

Acredolo, L., & Goodwyn, S. (1985). Symbolic gesturing in language development. *Human Development, 28,* 40–49.

Acredolo, L., & Goodwyn, S. (1988). Symbolic gesturing in normal infants. *Child Development, 59,* 450–466.

Bar-Adon, A. & Leopold, N. (1971). *Child language: A book of readings.* Englewood Cliffs, NJ: Prentice Hall.

Bates, E. (1976). *Language and context: The acquisition of pragmatics.* New York: Academic Press.

Bates, E., Benigni, L., Bretherton, I., Camaioni, L., & Volterra, V. (1977). From gesture to the first word. In I. M. Lewis & L. Rosenblum (Eds.), *Interaction, conversation and the development of language.* New York: Wiley.

Bates, E., Benigni, L., Bretherton, I., Camaioni, L., & Volterra, V. (1979). *The emergence of symbols: Cognition and communication in infancy.* New York: Academic Press.

Bates, E., Bretherton, I., Snyder, L. (1988). *From first words to grammar: Individual differences and dissociable mechanisms.* New York: Cambridge University Press.

Bates, E., Bretherton, I., Snyder, L., Shore, C., & Volterra, V. (1980). Gestural and vocal symbols at 13 months. *Merrill-Palmer Quarterly, 26,* 407–423.

Bates, E., & Marchman, V. (1987). What is and what is not universal in language acquisition. In F. Plum (Ed.), *Language, communication, and the brain.* New York: Raven Press.

Bates, E., O'Connell, B., & Shore, C. (1987). Language and communication in infancy. In J. Osofsky (Ed.), *Handbook of infant competence (2nd ed.).* New York: Wiley.

Bates, E., & Snyder, L. (1987). The cognitive hypothesis in language development. In I. Uzgiris & J McV. Hunt (Eds.), *Research with scales of psychological development in infancy.* Champaign-Urbana: University of Illinois Press.

Bates, E., Thal, D., Whitesell, K., Fenson, L., & Oakes, L. (1989). Integrating language and gesture in infancy. *Development Psychology, 25,* 1004–1019.

Bates, E., & Volterra, V. (1984). On the invention of language: An alternative view. Commentary on S. Golden-Meadow & C. Mylander. Gestural communication in deaf children: The effects and non-effects of parental input on early language development. *Monographs of the Society for Research in Child Development, Serial #207, Vol. 49, #s 3–4.*

Bauer, P. (1985). *Referential and expressive styles in linguistic and non-linguistic domains.* Unpublished doctoral dissertation, Miami University of Ohio, Oxford.

Bauer, P., & Shore, C. (1986). *Nonlinguistic concomitants of stylistic differences in early multi-word speech.* Unpublished manuscript.

Bayley, N. (1969). *Bayley Scales of Infant Development.* The Psychological Corporation, New York.

Bee, H., Barnard, K., Eyres, S., Gray, C., Hammond, M., Spietz, A., Snyder, C., & Clark, B. (1982). Prediction of IQ and language skill from perinatal status, child performance, family characteristics, and mother–infant interaction. *Child Development, 53,* 1134–1156.

Beeghly, M., & Cicchetti, D. (1987). An organizational approach to symbolic development in children with Down syndrome. In D. Cicchetti & M. Beeghly (Eds.), *Atypical symbolic development*. San Francisco: Jossey-Bass.

Beilin, H. (1975). *Studies in the cognitive bases of language development*. New York: Academic Press.

Benedict, H. (1979). Early lexical development: Comprehension and production. *Journal of Child Language, 6,* 183–200.

Bickerton, D. (1984). The language bioprogram hypothesis. *The Behavioral and Brain Sciences, 7,* 173–187.

Bloom, L. (1973). *One word at a time: The use of single word utterances before syntax*. Cambridge, MIT Press.

Bloom, L., Hood, L., & Lightbown, P. (1974). Imitation in language development: If, when and why. *Cognitive Psychology, 6,* 380–420.

Bloom, L., Lightbown, P., & Hood, L. (1975). Structure and variation in child language. *Monographs for The Society for Research in Child Development, 40(Serial #160).*

Bornstein, M., & Sigman, M. (1986). Continuity in mental development from infancy. *Child Development, 57,* 87–99.

Bowerman, M. (1982). Reorganization processes in lexical and semantic development. In E. Wanner & L. Gleitman (Eds.), *Language acquisition: The state of the art*. New York: Cambridge University Press.

Branigan, G. (1977, September). *If this kid is in the one word stage, so how come he's saying whole sentences?* Paper presented at the Second Annual Boston University Conference on Language Development, Boston.

Bretherton, I., McNew, S., Snyder, L., & Bates, E. (1983). Individual differences at 20 months-analytic and holistic strategies in language acquisition. *Journal of Child Language, 10,* 293–320.

Brown, R. (1973). *A first language: The early stages*. Cambridge, MA: Harvard University Press.

Brownell, C. (1988). Combinatorial skills: Converging developments over the second year. *Child Development, 59,* 675–685.

Chomsky, N. (1980). *Rules & representations*. New York: Columbia University Press.

Clark, R. (1974). Performing without competence. *Journal of Child Language, 4,* 341–358.

Corrigan, R. (1978). Language development as related to stage 6 object permanence development. *Journal of Child Language, 5,* 173–189.

Curcio, F. (1977). *A study of sensorimotor functioning and communication in mute autistic children*. Paper presented to the Boston Child Language Forum, Boston.

Dale, P., & Robinson, N. (1988, April). *Linguistic precocity, cognition, and development*. Paper presented at the Sixth International Conference on Infant Studies, Washington, DC.

Dore, J. (1974). A pragmatic description of early language development. *Journal of Psycholinguistic Research, 4,* 423–430.

Elder, J., & Pederson, D. (1978). Preschool children's use of objects in symbolic play. *Child Development, 42,* 500–505.

Escalona, S. (1973). Basic modes of social interaction: Their emergence and patterning during the first two years of life. *Merrill-Palmer Quarterly, 19,* 205–232.

Fenson, L., & Ramsay, D. (1981). Effects of modelling action sequences on the play of twelve, fifteen, and nineteen month old children, *Child Development, 32,* 1028–1036.

Fenson, L., Vella, D., Flynn, D., & Thal, D. (1988). *Developmental norms for 4 parental inventory reports of language acquisition and communication between 9 and 28 months*. Unpublished manuscript, San Diego State University and University of California, San Diego.

Ferguson, C. (1984, April). *From babbling to speech*. Invited Address to the International Conference on Infant Studies, New York.

Fillmore, L. (1979). Individual differences in second language acquisition. In C. Fillmore, D.

Kempler, & W. Wang (Eds.), *Individual differences in language ability and language behavior.* New York: Academic Press.

Furrow, D. (1980). *Social and asocial uses of language in young children.* Unpublished doctoral dissertation, Yale University, New Haven, CT.

Golden-Meadow, S., & Mylander, C. (1984). Gestural communication in deaf children: The effects and non-effects of parental input on early language development. *Monograph of the Society for research in Child Development* (Serial #207)

Goldfield, B. (1982, October). *Intra-individual variation: Patterns of nominal and pronominal combinations.* Paper presented at the Seventh Annual Boston University Conference on Language Development.

Goldfield, B. (1985). *The contribution of child and caregiver to referential and expressive language.* Unpublished doctoral dissertation, Harvard University, Cambridge, MA.

Goldfield, B., Reznick, J. S., & Johns, T. B. (1988). *Early Lexical Acquisition: Rate, content and the vocabulary spurt.* Abstracts of the papers presented at the Sixth International Conference on Infant Studies, Norwood, NJ: Ablex.

Gopnik, A., & Meltzoff, A. (1986). Relations between semantic and cognitive development in the one word stage: The specificity hypothesis. *Child Development, 57,* 1040–1053.

Gopnik, A., & Meltzoff, A. (1987). The development of categorization in the second year and its relation to other cognitive and linguistic developments. *Child Development, 58,* December Issue.

Harding, C., & Golinkoff, R. (1978). The origins of intentional vocalizations in prelinguistic infants. *Child Development, 49,* 33–40.

Harris, P. (1983). Infant cognition. In J. Campos & M. Haith (Eds.), *Handbook of child psychology, (Vol. 2).* New York: Wiley.

Hass, W., & Wepman, J. (1974). Dimensions of individual difference in the spoken syntax of school children. *Journal of Speech and Hearing Research, 17,* 455–469.

Hatch, E. (1974). Second language learning-universals? *Working Papers on Bilingualism, 3,* 1–8.

Horgan, D. (1978). How to answer questions when you've got nothing to say. *Journal of Child Language, 5,* 159–165.

Horgan, D. (1979, May). *Nouns: Love 'em or leave 'em.* Address to the New York Academy of Sciences.

Horgan, D. (1981). Rate of language acquisition and noun emphasis. *Journal of Psycholinguistic Research, 10,* 629–640.

Jakobson, R. (1942). Kindersprache. Aphasie und Allgemaine Lautgesetz. *Uppsala Universitets Arsskrift,* 1–83.

Johnston, J. (1985). Cognitive prerequisites: The evidence for children learning english. In D. Slobin (Ed.), *The cross-linguistic study of language acquisition.* Hillsdale, NJ: Erlbaum Associates.

Johnston, J., & Kamhi, A. (1980). *The same can be less: Syntactic and semantic aspects of the utterances of language impaired children.* Paper presented to the Symposium on Research in Child Language Disorders. University of Wisconsin, Madison. (Rev. version to appear in *Merrill-Palmer Quarterly.*)

Karmiloff-Smith, A. (1979). *A functional approach to child language.* Cambridge, MA: Cambridge University Press.

Killen, M., & Uzgiris, I. (1981). Imitation of actions with objects: The role of social meaning. *Journal of Genetic Psychology, 138,* 219–229.

Lenneberg, E. (1967). *The biological foundations of language.* New York: Wiley.

Leonard, L., Newhoff, M., & Masalem, L. (1980). Individual differences in early childhood phonology. *Applied Psycholinguistics, 1,* 7–30.

Leonard, L., Schwartz, R., Folger, M., Newhoff, M., & Wilcox, J. (1979). Children's imitations of lexical items. *Child Development, 59,* 19–27.

Lezine, I. (1978). The transition from sensorimotor to earliest symbolic function. *Early Development, 51,* Research Publication of A.R.N.M.D., 22–232.

Lieven, E. (1980). Conversations between mothers and young children: Individual differences and their possible implications for the study of language learning. In N. Waterson & C. Snow (Eds.), *The development of communication: Social and pragmatic factors in language acquisition.* New York: Wiley.

Locke, J. (1983). *Phonological acquisition and change.* New York: Academic Press.

Locke, J. (1988). The sound shape of early lexical representations. In M. Smith & J. Locke (Eds.), *The emergent lexicon.* New York: Academic Press.

Marchman, V., Bates, E., Good, A., & Burkhardt, K. (1988, October). *Functional constraints on the acquisition of the passive: Toward a model of the competence to perform.* Paper presented at the Boston University Conference on Language Development, Boston.

McCall, R., Eichorn, D., & Hogarty, P. (1977). Transitions in early mental development. *Monographs for the Society for research in Child Development, Serial #171.*

McCune-Nicolich, L. (1981). Toward symbolic functioning: Structure of early pretend games and potential parallels with language. *Child Development, 52,* 785–797.

McCune-Nicolich, L., & Bruskin, C. (1982). Combinatorial competency in play and language. In K. Rubin & D. Pepler (Eds.), *The play of children: Current theory and research* (pp. 30–40). New York: Karger.

McNeill, D. (1970). *The acquisition of language.* New York: Harper & Rowe.

Miller, J., & Chapman, R. (1981). Procedures for analyzing free-speech samples: Syntax and semantics. In J. Miller (Ed.), *Assessing language production in children.* Baltimore: University Park Press.

Molfese, D., & Molfese, V. (1985). Electrophysiological indices of auditory discrimination in newborn infants: The bases for predicting later language development? *Infant Behavior and Development, 8,* 197–211.

Murray, H. (1943). *Thematic Apperception Test.* Cambridge, MA: Harvard University Press.

Nelson, K. (1973). Structure and strategy in learning to talk. *Monograph of the Society for Research in Child Development, 38,* (1 & 2, Serial #49).

Nelson, K. (1975). The nominal shift in semantic-syntactic development. *Cognitive Psychology, 7,* 461–479.

Nelson, K. (1981). Individual differences in language development: Implications for development and language. *Developmental Psychology, 17,* 170–187.

Nelson, K. (1985). *Making sense: The acquisition of shared meaning.* New York: Academic Press.

Nicolich, L. (1977). Beyond sensorimotor intelligence: Assessment of symbolic maturity through analysis of pretend play. *Merrill-Palmer Quarterly, 23,* 89–99.

O'Connell, B., & Gerard, A. (1985). Scripts and scraps: The development of sequential understanding. *Child Development, 56,* 671–681.

Olson, S., Bates, J., & Bayles, K. (1984). Mother–infant interaction and the development of individual differences in children's cognitive competence. *Developmental Psychology, 20,* 166–179.

Overton, W., & Jackson, J. (1973). *The representation of imagined objects in action sequences: A developmental study.*

Oviatt, S. (1979, April). *The developing awareness of linguistic generality in 9- to 17-month-old infants.* Paper presented to the Society for Research in Child Development, New Orleans.

Peters, A. (1977). Language learning strategies: Does the whole equal the sum of the parts? *Language, 53,* 560–573.

Peters, A. (1983). *The units of language acquisition.* Cambridge: Cambridge University Press.

Ramer, A. (1976). Syntactic styles in emerging language. *Journal of Child Language, 3,* 49–62.

Rescorla, L. (1989). The language development survey: A screening tool for delayed language in toddlers. *Journal of Speech and Hearing Disorders, 54,* 587–599.

Rescorla, L., & Schwartz, E. (1988, April). *Outcome of specific expressive language delay (SELD)*. Poster presented at the Sixth International Conference on Infant Studies, Washington, DC.

Reznick, J. S. (1988). *Visual preference as a test of infant word comprehension*. Unpublished manuscript, Yale University, Department of Psychology.

Roth, F., & Clark, D. (1987). Symbolic play and social participation abilities of language-impaired and normally developing children. *Journal of Speech and Hearing Disorders, 48*, 347–359.

Shore, C. (1986). Combinatorial play: Conceptual development and early multiword speech. *Developmental Psychology, 22*, 184–190.

Shore, C., & Bauer, P. (1983). *Individual styles in language and symbolic play*. Paper presented at the annual meeting of the American Psychological Association, Anaheim, CA.

Shore, C., O'Connell, B., & Bates, E. (1984). First sentences in language and symbolic play. *Developmental Psychology, 20*, 872–880.

Sigman, M., & Mundy, P. (1987). Symbolic processes in young children. In D. Cicchetti & M. Beeghly (Eds.), *Symbolic development in atypical children*. San Francisco: Jossey-Bass.

Slobin, D. (1985). *The cross-linguistic study of language acquisition*. Hillsdale, NJ: Lawrence Erlbaum Associates.

Snyder, L. (1978). Communicative and cognitive abilities in the sensorimotor period. *Merrill-Palmer Quarterly, 24*, 161–180.

Snyder, L., Bates, E., & Bretherton, I. (1981). Content and context in early lexical development. *Journal of Child Language, 8*, 565–582.

Starr, S. (1975). The relationship of single words to two-word sentences. *Child Development, 46*, 701–708.

Tamis-LeMonda, C., & Bornstein, M. (1989). Habituation and maternal encouragement of attention in infancy as predictors of toddler language, play, and representational competence. *Child Development, 60*, 738–751.

Thal, D., & Bates, E. (1988). Language and gesture in late talkers. *Journal of Speech and Hearing Research, 31*, 115–123.

Vihman, M. (1981). Phonology and the development of the lexicon: Evidence from children's errors. *Journal of Child Language, 8*, 239–264.

Vihman, M. (1985). Individual differences in babbling and early speech: Predicting to age three. In B. Lindblom & R. Zetterstrom (Eds.), *Precursors of early speech*. Baskingstroke, Hampshire: MacMillan.

Vihman, M., & Carpenter, K. (1984). Linguistic advance and cognitive style in language acquisition. In C. Brugman & M. Macaulay (Eds.), *Proceedings of the Tenth Annual Meeting of the Berkely Linguistic Society*.

Vihman, M., Ferguson, C., & Elbert, M. (1986). Phonological development from babbling to speech: Common tendencies and individual differences. *Applied Psycholinguistics, 7*, 3–40.

Vihman, M., & Greenlee, M. (1987). Individual differences in phonological development: Ages one to three years. *Journal of Speech and Hearing Research, 30*, 503–521.

Volterra, V., Bates, E., Benigni, L., Bretherton, I., & Camaioni, L. (1979). First words in language and action: A qualitative look. In E. Bates, L. Benigni, I. Bretherton, L. Camaioni, & V. Volterra (Eds.), *The emergence of symbols: Cognition and communication in infancy*. New York: Academic Press.

Volterra, V., & Caselli, M. (1983). From gestures and vocalizations to signs and words. In W. Stokes & V. Volterra (Eds.), *Proceedings of the III International Symposium in Sign Language Research*, Rome, Italy.

Werner, L., & Kaplan, B. (1963). *Symbol formation: An organismic- developmental approach to language and expression of thought*, New York: Wiley.

Wolf, D., & Gardner, H. (1979). Style and sequence in symbolic play. In M. Franklin & N. Smith (Eds.), *Early symbolization*. Hillsdale, NJ: Lawrence Erlbaum Associates.

IV TEMPERAMENT AND SOCIOEMOTIONAL DEVELOPMENT

15

The Psychobiology of Infant Temperament

Megan R. Gunnar
University of Minnesota

Historically, the concept of temperament has its roots in age-old attempts to relate individual differences in behavioral styles to differences in physiology (Rothbart, in press). Such attempts to relate behavior to physiology have often resulted in placement of the temperament construct on the nature side of nature–nurture equations. In this chapter, recent work on the physiological correlates of infant emotional temperament is reviewed. However, rather than adopting the view that emotional temperament is constrained or directed by inborn physiological characteristics and thus that the causal arrow runs from physiology to behavior, in what follows a psychobiological orientation is maintained. Psychobiology is closely aligned with systems theory (Cairns, 1979). Accordingly, the psychobiologist attempts to understand the organism as a whole and not as a functioning gene machine nor as an entity shaped by external forces. Physiological, behavioral, and social systems are viewed as open systems that interact dynamically in the process of maintaining the integrity of the organism. From this perspective, the study of physiology–temperament relations is the study of dynamic interactions among systems.

Admittedly, a psychobiological orientation to the study of temperament is difficult to maintain. Most of the theorizing in this area (see Gray, 1979, 1987 or Kagan, Reznick, & Snidman, 1987 for example) clearly identifies physiological differences as the causal bases for differences in temperament. One approach, however, points the way to a more system-oriented, psychobiological perspective. In their theory of temperament, Rothbart and Derryberry (1981) define temperament as individual differences in reactivity and self-regulation that are assumed to have a constitutional basis. Reactivity and self-regulation are general properties of biological systems and, as such, can be used in the analysis of both behavior and physiology. Given the open nature of biological systems, reactivity and regulation within one system may be expected to influence reactivity and regulation in other related systems. However, no strong linear assumptions are made, and behavioral reactivity is not reduced to hypothesized differences in physiological reactivity. Furthermore, constitution is defined as relatively enduring aspects of the organism's physiological makeup influenced over time by heredity, maturation, *and* experience. Thus, Rothbart and Derryberry (1981) explicitly note the plasticity of physiological as well as behavioral systems.

EMOTIONAL TEMPERAMENT

The focus of this review is on the physiological correlates of emotional temperament; in particular, negative emotionality. Emotionality was chosen for several reasons. First, despite differences among temperament theories, all identify emotionality as a component of temperament (Goldsmith, Buss, Plomin, Rothbart, Thomas, Chess, Hinde, & McCall, 1987). Second, most physiological theories of temperament focus on associations between physiological activity and aspects of emotionality (see Rothbart, in press). And third, as noted by Bates (1986), negative emotionality forms the core of the difficult temperament construct that has motivated so much of the research on infant temperament.

The construct of emotional temperament, however, does not have a unitary referent. For theorists like Buss and Plomin (1975), the emotionality dimension of temperament refers only to emotional states associated with high autonomic arousal. For young children they include only negative emotions such as distress (early infancy), and fear and anger (emerging later in the first year). In contrast, for theorists like Rothbart (in Goldsmith et al., 1987), emotionality includes both positive affectivity (smile/laugh) and negative affectivity (distress to limitations and fear). Furthermore, some theorists emphasize emotional state as indicated previously, whereas others emphasize the behavioral regulatory response to emotion, including the balance between approach and withdrawal tendencies (Thomas & Chess, 1977) or behavioral inhibition versus boldness (e.g., Kagan et al., 1987). Still other theorists emphasize the effects that the child's emotional reactions have on others, especially with regard to the ease or difficulty of caretaking (e.g., Bates, 1986).

For someone new to the area, this lack of agreement can be very disconcerting. Fortunately, there appears to be more unity in the data than is reflected among the theories. This unity is especially apparent for aspects of negative emotional temperament. For example, temperament questionnaires based on the New York Longitudinal Study (e.g., Thomas & Chess, 1977) typically assess three dimensions of negative affectivity: withdrawal to novel stimuli, adaptability, and negative mood. Across various questionnaires and various samples, in factor analyses these three dimensions consistently load on the same factor

(Bates, 1986). Similarly, in their multimeasure study of temperament among twins, Wilson and Matheny (1986) attempted to assess several dimensions of temperament, including emotional tone, activity level, persistence, and social orientation. However, by 9 months their observational measures consistently loaded on one dimension that could be described as emotionality. In addition, Rothbart (1986) recently noted that both home observations and parental reports of various dimensions of temperament yielded one primary dimension during early infancy, that of positive–negative affect.

Because the data on emotional temperament during infancy appears to be adequately characterized along a single positive–negative dimension does not mean that emotionality exists as a unitary dimension within the infant or young child. Although this could be the case, it might also be that the structure of the data reflect the structure of the situations used to assess emotionality or, given the emphasis on parental reports, the structure of adult perceptions of infant emotionality. Regardless of the reasons for this unitary structure, from the standpoint of this review one problem is solved. At this stage it makes little sense to agonize over how best to organize the data to accurately reflect what we know. It seems likely that, empirically, studies of the relations between physiological activity and behavioral inhibition overlap, for example, with studies of physiological activity and emotional tone, fearfulness, and adaptability. Given the paucity of the data, this assumption is acted on in the following review. I hope, however, that this decision will not obscure important differences in the psychobiological processes involved in different aspects of infant emotionality.

STABILITY

Before examining physiological models and correlates of emotionality, it is important to consider issues of stability and change in emotionality during the first years of life. The infancy period involves tremendous developmental changes in the child's capacity to experience and express emotion (see Sroufe, 1979 for review). Briefly, during the first days and weeks following birth, affective life appears to be characterized largely by states of distress versus nondistress. (Although see Izard, 1985 for evidence of greater early differentiation of affect based on facial expressions.) Clear expressions of positive emotion begin to appear during the second month, and over the first year there is a gradual decrease in the amount of time the infant spends in negative affect states and a corresponding increase in the time spent expressing positive affect (Rothbart, in press). In addition, during these early months, some infants develop colic resulting in a tremendous increase in their expressions of distress that is not predictive of their later emotional character (however, see Kagan et al., 1987 for an alternative view). Although general distress declines, the second part of the first year sees an increase in the frequency and organization of specific negative affects including wariness, fear, and anger (Sroufe, 1979). Distress during the latter part of the first year is also increasingly a response to separation. Furthermore, whereas separation appears to enhance negative responses to strangers and strange places, the developmental course of separation distress and stranger fear do not coincide (Emde, Gaensbauer, & Harmon, 1976). During the second year, emotions continue to become more highly differentiated. One transient aspect of negative emotionality at this time is the emergence of tantrum behavior. Tantruming is highly sensitive to environmental contingencies. Thus, how long toddlers persist in throwing tantrums as well as their intensity varies with caregiver experience and expertise, in addition, perhaps, to the toddlers' emotional temperament (Williams, 1959).

Given the dramatic changes in emotional behavior during infancy and the appearance of transient conditions such as colic and later tantruming, it would be surprising to find that emotionality is a highly stable characteristic during this developmental period. The evidence indicates, however, that there is modest stability in emotionality and that this stability increases over the course of the first 2 years. For example, Rothbart (1986) examined the stability of both parental report and home observation measures of emotional temperament at 3, 6, and 9 months. Both positive and negative emotionality were moderately stable between 3 and 6, and 6 and 9 months when measured by parental report (r's = 0.60, approximately). However, less stability was apparent especially for negative emotionality when 3-month measures were used to predict 9-month measures. Longer term stability begins to be apparent sometime between 6 and 9 months. Bates (1986), for example, has reported that measures of difficult temperament obtained at 6 months predict difficultness at 24 months. Likewise, by about 9 months, brief laboratory assessments of temperament (e.g., the Louisville Temperament Assessment), which at earlier ages did not yield stability, begin to be predictive of later laboratory assessments. The magnitude of the stability coefficients for such laboratory assessments increases from around 0.3 to 0.4 for measures at 9 months predicting to 12 months, to around 0.6 to 0.7 for measures at 18 months predicting to 24 months (Wilson & Matheny, 1986).

Despite increasing stability over the first 2 years of life, emotional temperament during infancy is not very predictive of emotionality later in development. In a recent report from the New York Longitudinal Study, Thomas and Chess (1986) described stability on their dimensions of approach/ withdrawal, adaptability, and mood over the first 5 years, and the links between these early childhood measures and adult temperament. There was modest year-to-year stability for measures of all three dimensions with the exception of approach/withdrawal, which did not show year-to-year stability until age 3. Scores on these dimensions during the first 2 years, however, did not predict to the preschool years. Furthermore, whereas scores obtained during years 3 and 4 modestly predicted adult behavior, those obtained during years 1 and 2 did not. A similar pattern was obtained for summary scores of difficult temperament that included these and other dimensions. The correlations with adult scores were 0.17 and 0.09 for years 1 and 2, respectively; they were 0.31 and 0.37 for years 3 and 4. Thus although stability increases over the infancy period, there does appear to be a discontinuity between infant emotional temperament and emotional temperament later in life. Whereas this discontinuity may merely reflect properties of the measures used at different points in development, it may also reflect true developmental reorganization. This reorganization could result from the emergence of processes such as symbolic thought and language that dramatically reorganize the individual's characteristic emotional moods and responses. Alternatively or in addition, it may reflect discontinuities in eliciting conditions as the social world of the infant expands into the social world of the preschool child. Regardless, these patterns of stability and change in emotionality during the early years of life are important to keep in mind as we begin to examine the role of physiological processes in the development of emotional temperament.

HERITABILITY

Although from a psychobiological perspective we would not expect to reduce emotional temperament to the running off of a genetic program, an understanding of the heritability of emotionality is one aspect of the psychobiological study of temperament (see also Thompson, this volume). As noted by Goldsmith (1983), behavior genetics work on temperament in infancy is dominated by twin designs. Unfortunately, the small size of the samples employed in most of this work have resulted in unreliable h^2 estimates (Goldsmith, 1983). However, if only those studies with sufficient sample sizes are considered, the data on the heritability of emotionality rather clearly parallel the data on stability. Generally speaking, there is little or weak evidence of heritability during the first year and increasing evidence of heritability during the second year of life (Wilson & Matheny, 1986). Thus, Torgersen and Kringlen (1978), using the Thomas and Chess (1977) temperament dimensions, reported that at 2 months none of the emotionality dimensions (e.g., mood, adaptability, approach/withdrawal) showed evidence of greater MZ than DZ similarity, whereas by 9 months this was the case for all three dimensions. The researchers hypothesized that the pattern of results at 2 months reflected the continued influence of pregnancy and birth factors, variables that ceased to have much influence by 9 months. It is doubtful, however, that this is the whole story. Using observational and questionnaire measures of emotional tone, Wilson and Matheny (1986) failed to find evidence of heritability at 9 months, but their laboratory measure of emotional tone began to exhibit significantly greater MZ than DZ correlations by 18 months. Recently (Matheny, 1988, in press), this research group has reported that when their laboratory measure of emotional tone is combined with scores on fearfulness from the Bayley Infant Behavior Record and parental reports on the approach/withdrawal dimension of the Toddler Temperament Scale, then MZ correlations are significantly greater than DZ correlations by 12 months, and these differences are preserved over the second and third year. Finally, they report impressive evidence that variations in emotional reactions both across situations and across time are significantly more similar in MZ than in DZ twin pairs by the second year of life.

These results, in part, correspond to findings from studies using smaller sample sizes. As reviewed by Goldsmith (1983), when studies with both adequate and inadequate sample sizes are considered as a whole, there appears to be a general tendency for shared environmental factors to be more important than shared genetic factors in mathematically modeling emotional temperament during the first year. The reverse is the case beginning in the second year. The reason or reasons for this changing pattern are not known; however, it seems likely that normative changes in emotional processes play a role. Perhaps the greatest normative change over this period is the shift from stimulation to appraisal (Sroufe, 1979). Increasingly over the first year stimulus properties such as intensity, rate of onset, and so on play less of a role, and the meaning the infant imposes on the stimulus plays more of a role in determining the affective response. A second change less frequently discussed is the transition from reactivity to regulation (Rothbart, in press). There is a dramatic increase in the infant's ability to regulate stimulation over the course of the first 2 years. The second half of the first year sees improvements in the infant's ability to not only avoid aversive events (e.g., crawl away), but also to inhibit approach to uncertain events (Rothbart, in press). Coping abilities continue to improve in both flexibility and complexity during the second year, with one major change being the emergence of attempts to directly control and alter unacceptable circumstances (Hornik & Gunnar, 1987). The result of this change is a transition from primarily emotion-focused coping to the emergence of problem-focused coping (Lazarus & Folkman, 1984). Taken together, these normative changes describe a shift from more external to more internal control of emotion. Because internal factors are more likely to be heritable than external or environmental factors, this shift in regulatory controls may support the emergence of statistically significant heritability estimates for emotional temperament.

The increasing importance of heritable factors undoubtably has some consequences for our understanding of the role of physiological processes in temperament. However, the absence of strong evidence of heritability does not imply that physiological processes are unimportant in emotionality during the early months of life. Nor does it imply that the physiological processes involved in early emotionality are not heritable. From a psychobiological or systems perspective, it is likely that numerous processes play a role in determining the individual's emotional temperament. At any given point in development the individual, in a sense, assembles these processes with the result being the observed or phenotypic temperament. The increasing evidence of heritability only implies that either more of the processes involved in constructing emotional temperament reflect genetic differences, or that the weighting of processes involved in the construction of temperament shifts towards those reflecting genetic differences.

PHYSIOLOGICAL PERSPECTIVES ON TEMPERAMENT

Despite the focus in this chapter on the role of physiology in emotional temperament, little space is given to a review of physiological theories of temperament. This is because Rothbart (in press) has recently completed a thorough review of this area. The interested reader is directed to her paper. In this section we briefly overview the major points to be gleaned from general theoretical models relying heavily on Rothbart's review. Then the models guiding current work with human infants are described.

Since earliest attempts to relate bodily humors to different characteristic emotional styles, there have been numerous theories linking temperament to physiology. Modern attempts share several common assumptions. First, they share the assumption that temperament variation is regulated by the central nervous system. Thus differences in the brain serve as the basis for differences in emotional temperament. Second, they share the assumption that measures of peripheral systems inform us about the physiological bases of temperament because peripheral activity is regulated centrally. This assumption, of course, is crucial to research on human infants because most direct measures of brain function are invasive. Third, they share the assumption that fundamental temperament and emotional processes reflect a common mammalian heritage (Panskepp, 1982). This assumption is crucial because the invasive nature of brain research requires that nonhuman mammals be used in most studies of brain-temperament relations. Fourth, they share the assumption that the aspects of central functioning related to temperament variation are those linked to broad or general behavioral tendencies rather than to specific affects or motor acts. This last assumption helps to distinguish research on the neural basis of temperament from research on the neural bases of emotions, although of course, the two areas of work are closely related. Finally, as reflected in Rothbart and Derryberry's (1981) theory, concepts such as reactivity or arousal and self-regulation or inhibition are central to most physiological theories of temperament.

Three interrelated aspects of brain functioning have received the greatest attention by temperament theorist. They include the brain circuits potentially linked to emotional temperament, the role of regulatory biogenic amines in temperament, and the relations between brain laterality and temperament (see Rothbart, in press for a more thorough review). Many current physiological theories of temperament draw on all three of these factors (e.g., Gray, 1979, 1987). With regard to brain circuits, the greatest attention has been paid to circuits involving the limbic system, hypothalamus, and brainstem. This is not surprising given the historic link between the limbic system and emotions (e.g., Arnold, 1960). Within these areas of the brain, however, there is little concensus on which structures are related to which aspects of emotionality. Gray (1979, 1987), for example, considers fear and behavioral inhibition to be regulated by septal-hippocampal circuits in the limbic system. Panskepp (1982) argues that these aspects of emotionality have their command centers in the hypothalamus. Recently, as described more fully later, Kagan (Kagan et al., 1987) has argued that extreme fearfulness and inhibition in childhood results from greater tonic arousal and reactivity of the amygdala, a limbic system structure.

Despite their differences, the consequences of activation of all the neural pathways can be traced through hypothalamic areas important in the regulation of (a) sympathetic arm of the autonomic nervous system and (b) the pituitary–adrenocortical system. Taken together, these two systems form the major peripheral arms of the mammalian stress–response system (Borysenko, 1984). Research on the psychobiology of emotional temperament, thus, overlaps extensively with research on the psychobiology of stress and coping (see Gunnar, 1986).

As noted by Rothbart (in press), the study of neuroregulatory amines also holds great promise for our understanding of physiological processes in temperament. Although many different neurotransmitter substances ultimately may be found to play a role in temperament, two have received the most attention to date. They are norepinephrine and serotonin. These biogenic amines are typically viewed as playing opposite, yet complimentary, roles in maintaining a balance between arousal or reactivity (norepinephrine) and inhibition or regulation (serotonin).

Norepinephrine pathways arising from the locus coeruleus project broadly throughout the brain to areas in the neocortex, limbic system, and hypothalamus. Increased activity of the locus coeruleus is associated with increased behavioral and emotional arousal. Cells in the locus coeruleus appear especially sensitive to intense and novel input. In addition, norepinephrine operates centrally to increase attention to novel elements of the surround. Norepinephrine activity is thus viewed in many temperament accounts as modulating the arousal component of emotion, in particular, emotional reactivity to novel, strange, or intense experiences (see Rothbart, in press). Serotonin activity in the brain is distributed in areas roughly paralleling those of norepinephrine. Consistent with hypothesized complementary roles, increased serotonin activity is associated with behavioral and emotional inhibition (Panskepp, 1982).

Although there is some agreement about the central effects of norepinephrine and serotonin, how these biogenic amines are linked theoretically to positive and negative emotionality depends on the extent to which the concept of overarousal is invoked. Typically, when negative emotionality and behavioral inhibition are viewed as resulting from overarousal, then it is norepinephrine that is seen as playing the predominant role (e.g., Kagan et al., 1987; Zuckerman, Ballenger, & Post, 1984). When these facets of emotionality are viewed as being a function of overinhibition, then serotonin is causally linked to negative emotional temperament and epinephrine is linked to positive emotionality and approach (e.g., Cloninger, 1986; Gray, 1987).

The idea that emotional temperament is the result of the balance between opposing, yet complimentary, approach–withdrawal tendencies linked to positive–negative emotional reactivity can be traced through all physiological theories of temperament (see Rothbart, in press). This can be clearly seen in brain laterality theories. Thus, as reviewed by Rothbart (in press), there is increasing evidence that the left and right hemispheres of the brain are differentially organized for the processing of affective information and reactions. According to several theories, activity in the left hemisphere is associated with positive responses and behavioral activation, whereas activity of the right hemisphere is associated with negative reactions and behavioral inhibition (e.g., Kinsbourne & Bemporad, 1984; Fox & Davidson, 1983; see, however, Tucker & Williamson, 1984 for the opposite conclusion). Responses at any given moment are viewed as resulting from the balance of activation and reciprocal inhibition, which is in turn a function of the organism's prior state and the current demands of the situation. However, the typical balance between activity of the two hemispheres is seen as playing a role in the general or temperamental orientation of the individual. For example, individuals with greater right hemisphere dominance of emotional responses are expected to exhibit more negative emotionality, and those with greater left hemisphere dominance more positive emotionality across situations.

PHYSIOLOGICAL THEORIES OF EMOTIONALITY IN EARLY CHILDHOOD

Although many physiological theories of temperament hold promise for developmental analyses of temperament, few have specifically focused on emotionality during early human development. Three theories with direct links to research on human infants and children are outlined briefly next.

Kagan's Theory of Behavioral Inhibition.   Over the past decade, Kagan and his colleagues (Garcia-Coll, Kagan, & Reznick, 1984; Kagan, Reznick, Clarke, Snidman, & Garcia-Coll, 1984; Kagan et al., 1987) have developed a theory about the physiological basis of intense behavioral inhibition in young children. According to their theory, behavioral inhibition is triggered in young children in reaction to uncertainty. This uncertainty may be generated by unfamiliar events, unfamiliar people, or uncertain problem-solving situations. They have argued that both behavioral inhibition and its hormonal–visceral correlates are regulated by the amygdala and areas of the hypothalamus controlling sympathetic and pituitary–adrenocortical activity. Accordingly, behaviorally inhibited children are expected to have tonically lower thresholds for arousal in the amygdala and hypothalamus that peripherally should be associated with increased muscle tension, a rise and stabilization of heart rate, and increased cortisol levels to minimally uncertain situations (Kagan et al., 1987). They have tentatively traced the lower threshold for reactivity to high levels of central norepinephrine, as they note that this neurotransmitter appears to amplify the brain's reaction to novelty. Greater levels of central norepinephrine are further traced, albeit tentatively, to greater activity of the locus coeruleus. Thus, ultimately, in their theory, differences in behavioral inhibition in response to uncertainty are traced to tonically higher central concentrations of norepinephrine due to enhanced reactivity of the locus coeruleus. In infancy, prior to the development of reactivity to novelty and strangeness, Kagan and his colleagues expect that the physiological basis of later behavioral inhibition will be reflected in higher cortisol levels, higher and more stable heart rate responses, and infant symptoms of greater sympathetic activity including colic, allergies, and constipation.

Porges' Vagal Tone Theory.   Another theoretical perspective currently generating a considerable amount of data on human infants and young children is Porges' Vagal Tone model of attention and attention regulation. This theory continues a long line of work on autonomic balance and its relation to personality and temperament (e.g., Wenger, 1941). With regard to peripheral systems, activity of the sympathetic arm of the autonomic nervous system (ANS) is balanced by antagonistic effects produced by the parasympathetic arm of the ANS. Whereas sympathetic activity increases heart rate, parasympathetic activity serves to decrease heart rate. Although the theory deals with peripheral activity, as Porges and Smith (1980) note, the interest is really in activity of the central nervous system. Peripheral measures are used only because it is expected that there is continuity with central processes. Thus the balance between the sympathetic and parasympathetic nervous system is expected to reflect the central integrity of systems regulating the balance between arousal and inhibition.

Porges measures parasympathetic activity through isolating the component of heart rate associated with respiratory sinus arrhythmia. He has labeled his measure vagal tone. Increased vagal tone is viewed as reflecting greater maturity and organization of brainstem areas controlling the parasympathetic nervous system. Other measures of cardiac function, such as heart period and heart rate variability, should also reflect the balancing of sympathetic and parasympathetic activity and are also the focus of current research studies (see Fox, 1988, in press, for discussion). Empirically and theoretically, Porges and his colleagues (1982) have focused most of their work on the relations between vagal tone and attention. They have shown that individuals with poor or low vagal tone have difficulty sustaining attention and using attentional strategies to regulate behavior, whereas those with good vagal tone do not have these difficulties. As Fox (in press) notes, attentional strategies are key components of self-regulation in Rothbart's (Rothbart & Posner, 1985) theory of temperament. Thus the relations between vagal tone and emotional temperament are, for the most part, traced through attention regulation. Children with poor or low vagal tone are expected to exhibit poor attention-regulation capacities, which in turn should result in less ability to regulate emotional arousal resulting in more instances of overarousal and negative emotional responses. Developmentally, improvements in vagal tone over the first year should be related to the development of attention-regulation strategies and increasing control over emotional reactions. This, in turn, should be linked to a gradual decrease in negative emotionality.

Because both Kagan and Porges use cardiac activity as a dependent measure in their research, these two perspectives on temperament are often confused. They are, however, quite different. First, both theoretically and empirically, Kagan and his colleagues focus on reactivity. Their concern is with the sympathetic nervous system as a reflection of central arousal or overarousal. Heart rate variability is examined primarily as a reflection of the extent to which sympathetic activation overrides parasympathetic control. In contrast, Porges and his colleagues focus theoretically and empirically on regulation. Increases and decreases in heart rate (reactivity) in response to stimulation are not of concern. Predictions based on vagal tone are made independent of tonic heart rate and heart rate reactivity (see Fox, 1988, in press). A second major difference concerns the scope of the theory. Kagan's Behavioral Inhibition theory is focused on extreme cases and Kagan (Kagan, Reznick, & Snidman, 1988) has recently raised the possibility that extremely inhibited children differ qualitatively, not just quantitatively, in their physiological and behavioral organization. Porges' Vagal Tone model, however, is described as applying to all individuals.

Fox and Davidson's Laterality Theory. The third and final physiological theory generating infancy data currently is the model of brain laterality proposed by Fox and Davidson (1983). Along with others (see Rothbart, in press for review), they have proposed that the left hemisphere is specialized for the processing and expression of positive affect and approach, whereas the right hemisphere is specialized for negative affect and avoidance. Differential EEG activity over the frontal lobes is used as the measure of hemispheric dominance for positive (left) and negative (right) emotionality. Although such differences can be detected in the earliest days of life (Fox & Davidson, in press), ontogenetic changes are expected when, near the end of the first year, the development of commissural transfer permits left hemisphere inhibition of right hemisphere function leading to an attenuation of the expression of negative affect and greater behavioral alteration between approach and avoidance. According to this theory, negative emotional temperament should be associated with more or less chronic right hemisphere dominance. Increasingly over the latter part of the first year, it should also be associated with weaker left hemisphere inhibition of right hemisphere function.

PHYSIOLOGY–TEMPERAMENT RESEARCH ON YOUNG CHILDREN

The theories just outlined specify a number of relatively noninvasive physiological measures relevant to the study of emotional temperament. The studies reviewed next include those using the following measures: cardiac measures of heart rate, heart period variability and vagal tone; salivary measures of cortisol, an index of adrenocortical activity; and EEG measures of activity over the left and right frontal lobes. Other measures potentially might be important to our understanding of physiological correlates of emotionality, including measures of other neuroendocrine systems (e.g., urinary measures of catecholamine metabolites reflecting adrenomedullary activity) and other measures of brain activity (e.g., evoked potentials). Research involving these and other measures with young children, however, is too limited at this point to include in the present review. In addition, it is important to note that research on physiology–temperament relations in human infants is in its own infancy. There are only a handful of studies relating the preceding measures to emotional temperament; far too few to serve as "tests" of the different approaches outlined previously. At best, what can be done is to point out where results are consistent with theory, and where results, if replicable, will require a reappraisal of current theory.

Vagal Tone and Heart Period Variability. There is now good evidence that noxious, painful stimulation associated with behavioral distress produces decreases in vagal tone both among normal newborns (Porter, Porges, & Marshall, 1988) and among preterm neonates (Porter & Porges, 1988). There is also evidence that the law of initial values (Wilder, 1956) applies to changes in vagal tone. Thus, the largest decreases in vagal tone in response to noxious events are seen for infants with the highest prestress tone (DiPietro & Porges, 1988; Porter et al., 1988). It also appears that, normatively, decreases in vagal tone during stress are associated with periods of heightened negative emotionality or crying. Thus, in prematures DiPietro and Porges (1988) found that babies who fussed and cried more during gavage feedings exhibited smaller increases in vagal tone to the feedings. Likewise, Porter and colleagues (1988) noted that increases in the fundamental frequency of crying during circumcision corresponded to periods of greatest decrease in vagal tone. Although these data are clear, the link between prestress vagal tone and negative emotional reactions to stressors is less clear in the neonatal period. DiPietro and Porges (1988) found that pregavage vagal tone was associated with greater negative behavioral reactions to gavage feedings, a finding that seems consistent with these infants' smaller increases in vagal tone during the event. In contrast, Porter and colleagues noted that among full-term infants undergoing circumcision, low precircumcision vagal tone was associated with higher fundamental frequencies in crying during circumcision, a finding that seems inconsistent with the smaller decrease in vagal tone to circumcision among these infants. Clearly, the linkages between prestimulation vagal tone and behavioral reactions to aversive events needs further empirical investigation during the newborn period.

The pattern of relations between either vagal tone or heart rate variability and behavioral responses to stressors is not much clearer later in infancy. Thus, Kagan and his colleagues (1978) reported few heart rate variability relations with behavior among Chinese and Caucasian infants tested repeatedly from 3 to 29 months. Furthermore, they reported little evidence of stability in heart rate variability among Caucasian infants, although there was strong evidence of stability in their Chinese sample. In contrast, DiBiase (1988) recently noted stability in heart rate variability among Caucasian infants between 5 and 13 months, but no stability when either the 5- or the 13-month measures were used to predict to measures of heart rate variability obtained at 24 months. Finally, DiBiase reported that infants with higher heart rate variability exhibited greater subsequent emotionality, both positive and negative in the laboratory; she, however, found few concurrent relations with parental reports of temperament using the Toddler Temperament Scale.

Additional evidence that both positive and negative emotionality may be linked with either higher vagal tone or heart rate variability comes from a longitudinal investigation conducted by Fox and his co-workers (Fox, 1988, in press, Stifter & Fox, 1988 as cited in Fox, 1989, in press). Briefly, they found that baseline vagal tone among healthy newborns was not related significantly to behavioral distress to pacifier removal during the neonatal period and further showed little stability with vagal tone measured later in infancy. By 5 months, however, baseline vagal tone was positively related to behavioral distress in response to limb restraint. These findings are similar to DiPietro and Porges' (1988) results with prematures. Unfortunately, Fox and his colleagues did not report the effect of limb restraint on vagal tone; thus we do not know whether baseline vagal tone predicted cardiac reactions to this stimulus or how changes in vagal tone during limb restraint were related to behavioral reactions to this procedure. Finally, at 13 months, they found that baseline vagal tone was significantly correlated with the 5- month baseline measures. Similar to the 5-month results, there was also evidence at 13 months that high vagal tone was associated with more rapid and intense negative emotional reactions to an aversive event, the departure of the mother. Taken together, in contrast to the general tone of the theories, these data suggest that high vagal tone may be related to greater negative emotionality during infancy. However, at 13 months Fox and his co-workers also found that high vagal tone was associated with more rapid approach to a strange adult experimenter. This last result is in line with the expectation that behavioral inhibition is associated with low vagal tone or an imbalance of arousal in the autonomic nervous system (Kagan et al., 1987).

Whereas seemingly disparate, the pattern of results just outlined may indicate that infants with higher baseline vagal tone or heart rate variability exhibit more appropriate behavioral organization: They express more intense and immediate behavioral distress to noxious events (e.g., limb restraint and maternal separation) and more immediate and positive reactions to potentially pleasant events (e.g., play invitations by a friendly adult in mother's presence). If self-regulation is construed broadly to include the infant's use of emotional expressions to regulate relations with the surround, then as a whole these findings would support linking high vagal tone with better regulatory abilities. This interpretation, however, would require a more systems-oriented approach to the psychobiology of emotional temperament; that is, it requires that we appraise the function of emotionality in maintaining the integrity of the infant organism.

There have been several studies of the relations between temperament and vagal tone and/or heart rate variability with young children postinfancy that are also pertinent to this review. Fox and his colleagues (1987) recently analyzed baseline vagal tone in 30 children entering nursery school. They found that children with higher baseline vagal tone increased in play more over the first 6 weeks of nursery school and were reported by their mothers to have less difficult temperaments on the Dimensions of Temperament Scale (DOTS). The relations with the DOTS measure was preserved when the children were retested 6 months later as was the rank ordering of vagal tone scores.

These data are consistent with data on two cohorts of preschool children studied by Kagan and his co-workers (1987). These researchers observed infants interacting with mother and stranger at 21 months and selected groups extreme on boldness and inhibition defined behaviorally. They then followed these children and a second cohort examined similarly over the preschool years. With regard to heart rate variability, Kagan and his co-workers have reported that within and across age extremely bold children exhibit greater variability than extremely inhibited children. Indeed, the cross-age correlations have been quite striking, suggesting substantial stability linked to physiological differences for these extreme groups of children. Unfortunately, this research group has relied on Pearson product moment correlations to assess relations between physiological measures and behavioral inhibition. These coefficients, of course, are inflated because of the use of extreme groups. This makes it difficult to appraise the true degree of association both within and across age. Indeed, this is exemplified by the fact that, whereas the early measures of behavioral inhibition used to select the extreme groups do predict later heart rate variability (e.g., 21-month behavioral inhibition predicting to heart rate variability at 4 years, $r = 0.49$, and 5.5 years, $r = -0.39$), early measures of heart rate variability that were not selected for extremes do not predict later measures of behavioral inhibition (e.g.,

21-month heart rate variability to behavioral inhibition at 4 years, $r = -0.15$, and 5.5 years, -0.06).

However, even given concerns regarding the statistics, the pattern of associations appears consistent especially when considered in light of the Fox et al. findings that did not rely on extreme groups. In addition, although the Fox et al. (1987) data are based on correlations with measures of difficult temperament, it is noteworthy that when temperament measures were obtained by Kagan and his co-workers (Kagan et al., 1984), the extreme groups differed on three of the key indices of difficult temperament. Thus, extremely inhibited children relative to extremely bold children were described by their parents as less approaching, less adaptable, and more negative in mood. In all, during the preschool years it does appear that higher vagal tone and greater heart rate variability are associated with less difficult, fearful, or negative emotional temperament. In contrast, during the infancy period it is not as clear that vagal tone is linked to negative emotionality. Instead, high vagal tone appears to be associated with greater expressions of both negative and positive emotions. Given the relatively low correlations between infant and preschool emotional temperament, it is perhaps not surprising to find varying patterns of physiology-behavior relations across this transition in development. What is needed, of course, are studies examining these cardiac measures and temperament from early infancy through the transition into the preschool years.

Adrenocortical Activity. Currently, considerable debate exists over the role of negative emotional states in activating the stress response of the adrenocortical system. Although a number of researchers believe that the psychological regulation of the adrenocortical stress response is primarily determined by the individual's emotional state, others believe that novelty and uncertainty serve as the primary psychological triggers of this system (see review by Gunnar, Marvinney, Isensee, & Fisch, in press). Because negative emotional responses are frequently seen in response to novel or uncertain events, these positions often lead to the same prediction (i.e., elevations in cortisol should be associated with negative, distressed behavior). However, according to the latter position there should be instances in which novel stimulation produces elevations in cortisol in the presence of neutral or positive affect. In addition, the latter position would predict that with repeated or prolonged exposure, elevations in cortisol would decline even under conditions associated with continued, intense negative emotions. Increasingly, data are accumulating supporting the latter view. Thus, for example, in healthy human newborns, elevations in cortisol have been associated with a number of events that produce behavioral distress. These include such noxious events as circumcision and blood sampling, and seemly less noxious events such as weighing and measuring and neonatal behavioral exams (Gunnar, Connors, Isensee, & Wall, 1988). However, at least when the seemingly less noxious events are repeated on two consecutive days, the adrenocortical system of the healthy newborn ceases to respond to the stimulation, even though the newborns continue to exhibit a similar degree of behavioral distress (Gunnar, Connors, & Isensee, 1989). Likewise, we (Gunnar et al., 1989) have found that among 3- and 4-year-olds with PKU, clinic visits involving blood sampling are associated with sometimes extreme behavioral distress; however, these children who have been attending the same clinic since infancy do not exhibit elevations in cortisol to clinic visits. Rose (1980) also noted in a review of the adult literature that one of the striking characteristics of the human adrenocortical system is its sensitivity to novelty and the rapidity with which it adapts with repeated or prolonged exposure. Finally, the data on nonhuman primates are similar. Indeed, Levine (1985) has recently concluded that for mammals, in general, uncertainty or novelty is the primary psychological trigger of the adrenocortical system.

Given this, one would expect that linkages with emotional temperament would be found primarily in uncertain or strange situations. Unfortunately, to date there have been so few studies with normal infants that overall patterns of association are difficult to discern. With newborns, both positive and negative correlations have been obtained between crying and measures of adrenocortical response to stimulation. Positive correlations have been noted primarily when events are noxious, for example blood sampling and circumcision, or when newborns with slight perinatal complications are tested. In contrast, negative correlations between cortisol increases and crying have been found when the newborns are extremely healthy and the stimulus events are closer to normal handling (e.g., the Brazelton Neonatal Assessment Exam; (Gunnar, Isensee, & Fust, 1987). These associations, however, may be somewhat artificial as they reflect responses of the adrenocortical system imposed on highly controlled and low baselines.

Spangler and his colleagues (1988) have obtained slightly different results using baseline estimates consisting of daily averages of cortisol produced under less controlled conditions. This research group found daily average cortisol concentrations were highly stable from day to day during the neonatal period and were also highly correlated with maternal daily cortisol concentrations. Furthermore, they found that newborns with higher daily average cortisol showed less of an adrenocortical response to the Brazelton exam, were less irritable in the hospital nursery, and were also less irritable and more organized according to the Brazelton measures. Thus whereas both research groups have found that higher cortisol levels are associated with less irritability in healthy newborns, in the Gunnar et al. work this was reflected in relations between distress and elevations in cortisol to the Brazelton exam, whereas in the Spangler et al. work the association was with baseline cortisol.

The pattern of relations with cortisol may well depend on whether baseline or response measures are being examined. In a short-term longitudinal study of healthy infants, we (Gunnar, Mangelsdorf, Larson, & Hertsgaard, 1989) found that at 9 months and again at 13 months negative emotional temperament was positively correlated with elevations in cortisol during maternal separation. At 13 months, however, we also noted a negative correlation with baseline cortisol such that infants with negative emotional temperaments exhibited lower baseline concentrations. Whereas these latter results are consistent with Spangler et al.'s newborn data, they are inconsistent with results recently reported by Kagan and his colleagues (1987). They found that at 5.5 years their extremely inhibited children had higher cortisol concentrations at home (baseline) and in the laboratory when compared to concentrations observed in their extremely bold children. In addition, they noted that adrenocortical activity was more closely associated with behavioral inhibition in their preschoolers than were measures of cardiac activity. As in the work on vagal tone, these data may indicate a reorganization of the relations between physiology and emotional temperament with the transition from infancy to the preschool years. However, with so few studies to draw on, it is too early to speculate.

Returning to the issue of baseline versus response activity of the adrenocortical system, in line with the law of initial values, changes in cortisol concentrations in response to stimulation do appear to be partly a function of prestimulation cortisol levels (Lewis & Thomas, 1988). When cortisol baselines are allowed to vary, infants with higher baselines exhibit less of an increase in cortisol to a stressor than do infants with lower baselines (Gunnar et al., 1989). Indeed, when prestimulation concentrations are quite high, large declines in cortisol during stimulation have been noted (Lewis & Thomas, 1988). Although there are clearly statistical implications of these findings, there also may be theoretical implications. Specifically, infants who have higher baseline cortisol concentrations in the normal range may be more prepared to cope with novel, uncertain stimulation than infants with lower baseline concentrations. These infants may experience these situations as less physically demanding and this, in turn, may result in less behavioral distress. Although this interpretation links emotional temperament to adrenocortical reactivity, it is consistent with a more systems-oriented approach; that is, instead of linking emotional temperament directly to higher tonic physiological arousal, the linkages in the present analysis result from an interaction between organism characteristics and situational demands.

Finally, it is important to note that the correlations reported to date, although significant, have been relatively small in magnitude. This is especially the case for relations between elevations in cortisol and postnatal emotional temperament. The small magnitude of the correlations is consistent with the fact that it has been difficult to find situations that produce large increments in cortisol and that are ethical to impose on normal infants. Maternal separation, a classic infant stressor, has been found to either produce no increase in cortisol or only very modest increases (Gunnar et al., 1989; Tennes, Downey, & Vernadakis, 1977). This may be because it has been necessary to terminate experimental separation early for infants who become highly distressed. Alternately, it may reflect the human infant's familiarity with separation by the end of the first year. With regard to familiarity, it is interesting to note that Lewis and Thomas (1988), in their examination of infant responses to inoculations, noted significant and large elevations in cortisol among 2-month-olds receiving their first inoculations, and nonsignificant increases in cortisol among 4- and 6-month-olds receiving their second and third inoculations, respectively. Consistent with the hypothesis that the correlations with emotional temperament may reflect the magnitude of the adrenocortical response, these researchers found significant associations with behavioral distress among their 2-month-olds, but nonsignificant correlations among their 4- and 6-month-olds.

To summarize, it is far too early to draw conclusions regarding the relations between adrenocortical activity and emotional temperament in human infants. This is partly because this is a relatively new area of research and too few data exist on which to base conclusions. However, this is also partly because there appears to be no simple linkages between cortisol and temperament. Patterns of relations appear to depend on whether baseline or response activity is being measured, and on whether the events under study are capable of triggering significant and large elevations in cortisol.

Laterality and Temperament.   To date, there is only one published study relating EEG asymetry to emotional temperament in human infants. Accordingly, Fox and Davidson (1988) examined 10-month-old's reactions to a stranger and maternal separation. EEG measures were obtained prior to and during these stressors and the analysis was based on changes in hemispheric EEG activity to stimulation. Furthermore, the focus of the analysis was on a post hoc grouping of the subjects into those who did and those who did not cry during maternal separation. Artifact-free data were available on only a few subjects (i.e., 5 to 6) in each of these two groups. However, the results were fairly clear in showing that infants who cried exhibited more frontal lobe activity during these stressors than did infants who did not cry. Criers also showed more left frontal activation during a maternal approach segment; whereas they showed more right frontal activation (indicative of negative affect) than did noncriers during maternal separation. Although consistent with their theory of hemispheric relations with emotions, these data are also reminiscent of the vagal tone data described earlier. Specifically, when developmentally appropriate psychological stressors are used, infants who are more emotionally reactive appear better organized physiologically to exhibit and experience both positive and negative emotions depending on the context.

CONCLUSIONS AND SPECULATIONS

The data reviewed in this chapter clearly indicate that potentially important relations exist between physiological activity and emotional temperament to be explored during infancy and early childhood. The results with infants, however, are somewhat inconsistent with the physiology–temperament perspectives outlined earlier. Specifically, neither poor baseline vagal tone, high baseline cortisol, nor right hemisphere dominance have been found to be clearly associated with greater negative emotional temperament during infancy. As noted, for vagal tone and hemispheric dominance, the results tend to suggest a relationship with emotion organization. Thus, infants with high vagal tone or heart rate variability and those with right hemispheric dominance during stressful events tend to be infants who exhibit both more negative and more positive emotional responses, and who exhibit these reactions in an organized fashion as a function of the demands of the situation. Similarly, with regard to adrenocortical activity, whereas stressful events appear to produce elevations in cortisol to some degree, infants with higher baseline concentrations (higher tonic arousal of the hypothalamic–pituitary–adrenocortical axis), if anything, appear to be less irritable and less easily distressed by psychosocial stressors. If these patterns hold, they would require substantial revision of the physiology–temperament theories outlined earlier as applied to the infancy period. Interestingly however, when data on older children (preschoolers) are considered, the match with theory is much closer. In line with theory, among preschoolers higher vagal tone (and/or heart rate variability) and lower baseline cortisol have been found to correlate with less difficult temperament, more rapid adaptation to new situations, and less behavioral inhibition.

The possibility that there is a major reorganization of physiology–temperament relations during the transition from infancy to early childhood is certainly intriguing. It is especially intriguing when considered in light of the low correlations between infant and preschool emotional temperament and the increase in heritability estimates of temperament with the transition to the toddler period. However, the caveat that there are too few data to draw firm conclusions at this point in time remains. Thus the possibility that such a reorganization occurs across this developmental transition is presented only as a very tenuous speculation. It is a speculation, however, that may serve as a guide to future research.

Several other guides to future work can also be discerned from this review. First, although not clearly specified by theory, baseline and response activity of the physiological systems reviewed here often appear to bear different relations with emotional temperament. Furthermore, for both cardiac and endocrine measures, prestimulation activity (which may or may not constitute estimates of nonstressed baseline) appear to exert effects on changes in activity in response to stimulation. For the most part, these effects appear to follow the law of initial values. Taken together, this pattern of results strongly argues that an adequate understanding of physiology–temperament relations will require that we obtain good baseline as well as good response measures.

Second, with rare exception (see Kagan et al., 1987), the studies that I reviewed involved the examination of only one type of physiological measure.

Thus, studies of cardiac activity typically have not also included measures of hemispheric laterality or neuroendocrine activity and vice versa. Although this is often the case in research on physiology–behavior relations, it does make it difficult to compare results across measures. When this problem is noted in reviews, the reviewers typically argue for the incorporation of multiple physiological measures within the same research design. This, however, may not be the answer and may be especially problematic in research on human infants. Because different physiological systems operate on their own time course (e.g., heart rate responds very quickly whereas the adrenocortical system responds slowly), obtaining accurate indices of system activity requires attention to the dynamics of each system under study. Research designs that may be adequate for the assessment of one system may violate the requirements for accurate assessment of other relevant systems. The results of multiple physiological assessment research, thus, can easily be very muddy and muddled. Furthermore, the manipulations necessary to obtain measures of multiple systems can overburden the subject, a problem of particular concern in research with infants. When multiple systems can be measured adequately in the same study, this should be done. In lieu of attempting to measure multiple systems, however, what we may need in the infant physiology–temperament area is an agreement on common measures of emotional temperament. At least it would be helpful to have a common reference point in each study, even if this only meant the inclusion of a common temperament questionnaire. This would not only help with the problem of relating findings across studies and physiological systems, but it would also help with the problem of determining the aspect of emotional temperament under study. As noted earlier, whether the dimension is labeled inhibition, difficult temperament, or fearfulness makes a difference in how we theorize about relations with physiological activity. However, given the state of our measurement art, it is not clear that these different labels reflect different aspects of infant behavior.

Finally, as noted, studies of the psychobiology of emotional temperament overlap with studies of normative emotional development. Yet surprisingly, only a very modest degree of attention has been paid to the relations between normative changes and individual differences in this area. This would seem important not only because of the rapid and significant normative changes in emotional behavior during infancy, but also because the maturation of physiological systems over the first 2 years of life may contribute both to the normative development of emotions and to the emergence of individual differences in temperament (see Rothbart, in press). Indeed, it may be that the most crucial area for research in physiology–temperament relations lies at this intersection between concerns with normative change and individual variation.

ACKNOWLEDGMENTS

The writing of this manuscript was supported by an NIH Research Center Development Award, HD00712, to Megan R. Gunnar.

REFERENCES

Arnold, M.B. (1960). *Emotion and personality.* New York: Columbia University Press.

Bates, J. E. (1986). The measurement of temperament. In R. Plomin & J. Dunn (Eds.), *The study of temperament changes, continuities and challenges* (pp. 1–12). Hillsdale, NJ: Lawrence Erlbaum Associates.

Borysenko, J. (1984). Stress and coping, and the immune system. In J. D. Matarazzo, S. M. Weiss, J. A. Herd, N. E. Miller, & S. M. Weiss (Eds.), *Behavioral health* (pp. 248–260). New York: Wiley.

Buss, A. H., & Plomin, R. (1975). *A temperament theory of personality development.* New York: Wiley–Interscience.

Cairns, R. B. (1979). *Social development: The origins and plasticity of interchanges.* San Francisco, Freeman.

Cloninger, C. R. (1986). A unified biosocial theory of personality and its role in the development of anxiety states. *Psychiatric Developments, 3,* 167–226.

DiBiase, R. (1988). Heart rate variability and parental reports of temperament as predictors of emotional expression in infancy. *Infant behavior and development, 11,* (Special ICIS Issue), 70.

DiPietro, J. A., & Porges, S. W. (1988). Reactivity of preterms to gavage feeding. *Infant behavior and development, 11,* (Special ICIS Issue), 73.

Emde, R., Gaensbauer, T., & Harmon, R. (1976). Emotional expression in infancy: Biobehavioral study. *Psychological Issues Monographs, #37.* New York: International University Press.

Fox, N. A. (1988, in press). Heart rate variability and self-regulation: Individual differences in autonomic patterning and their relation to infant and child temperament. In S. Reznick & J. Kagan (Eds.), *Perspectives on behavioral inhibition.* Chicago: University of Chicago Press.

Fox, N. A. (1989, in press). Psychophysiological correlates of emotional reactivity during the first year of life. *Developmental Psychology.*

Fox, N. A., & Davidson, R. J. (1983). Hemispheric substrates of affect: A developmental model. In N. A. Fox & R. J. Davidson (Eds.), *The psychology of affective development* (pp. 353–382). Hillsdale, NJ: Lawrence Erlbaum Associates.

Fox, N. A., & Davidson, R. J. (1988). Patterns of brain electrical activity during facial signs of emotion in 10-month-old infants. *Developmental Psychology, 24,* 230–236.

Fox, N. A., Field, T., Porges, S. W., & Luebering, A. (1987). *Individual differences in heart period patterning and their relation to temperament behaviors in preschool children.* Unpublished manuscript cited in Fox (1988, in press).

Garcia-Coll, C., Kagan, J., & Reznick, J. S. (1984). Behavioral inhibition in young children. *Child Development, 55,* 1005–1019.

Goldsmith, H. H. (1983). Genetic influence on personality from infancy to adulthood. *Child Development, 54,* 331–355.

Goldsmith, H. H., Buss, A. H., Plomin, R., Rothbart, M. K., Thomas, A., Chess, S., Hinde, R. A., McCall, R. B. (1987). Round table: What is temperament? Four approaches. *Child Development, 58,* 505–529.

Gray, J. A. (1979). A neuropsychological theory of anxiety. In C. E. Izard (Ed.), *Emotions in personality and psychopathology.* New York: Plenum Press.

Gray, J. A. (1987). *The psychology of fear and stress* (2nd ed.). New York: Cambridge University Press.

Gunnar, M. (1986). Human developmental psychoendocrinology: A review of research on neuroendocrine responses to challenge and threat in infancy and childhood. In M. Lamb, A. Brown, & B. Rogoff (Eds.), *Advances in developmental psychology* (Vol. 4, pp. 51–103). Hillsdale, NJ: Lawrence Erlbaum Associates.

Gunnar, M. R., Connors, J., Isensee, J., & Wall, L. (1988). Adrenocortical activity and behavioral distress in newborns. *Developmental Psychobiology, 21,* 279–310.

Gunnar, M. R., Connors, J., & Isensee, J. (1989). Lack of stability in neonatal adrenocortical reactivity because of rapid habituation of the adrenocortical response. *Developmental Psychobiology.*

Gunnar, M. R., Isensee, J., & Fust, L. S. (1987). Adrenocortical activity and the Brazelton Neonatal Assessment Scale: Moderating effects of the newborn's biomedical status. *Child Development, 58,* 1448–1458.

Gunnar, M. R., Mangelsdorf, S., Larson, M., & Hertsgaard, L. (1989). Attachment, temperament, and adrenocortical activity in infancy: A study of psychoendocrine regulation. *Developmental Psychology, 25,* 355–363.

Gunnar, M. R., Marvinney, D., Isensee, J., & Fisch, R. P. (1989). Coping with uncertainty: New models of the relations between hormonal, behavioral and cognitive processes. In D. Palermo (Ed.), *Coping with uncertainty: Biological, behavioral, and developmental perspectives.* Hillsdale, NJ: Lawrence Erlbaum Associates.

Hornik, R., & Gunnar, M. (1987, April). Towards a taxonomy of infant coping strategies. Paper presented at meetings of the *Society for Research in Child Development,* Baltimore.

Izard, C. E. (1985). Measuring emotion expression and their significance in early development. In J. T. Spence & C. E. Izard (Eds.), *Motivation, emotion and personality* (pp. 297–304). North Holland: Elsevier.

Kagan, J., Kearsley, R. B., & Zelazo, P. R. (1978). *Infancy: Its place in human development.* Cambridge, MA: Harvard University Press.

Kagan, J., Reznick, S., & Snidman, N. (1987). The physiology and psychology of behavioral inhibition. *Child Development, 58,* (6), 1459–1473.

Kagan, J., Reznick, S., & Snidman, N. (1988). Cortisol and behavioral inhibition. *Infant Behavior and Development, 11* (Special ICIS Issue), 459.

Kagan, J., Reznick, J. S., Clarke, C., Snidman, N., & Garcia-Coll, C. (1984). Behavioral inhibition to the unfamiliar. *Child Development, 55,* 2212–2225.

Kinsbourne, M., & Bemporad, B. (1984). Lateralization of emotion: A model of the evidence. In N. A. Fox & R. J. Davidson (Eds.), *The psychology of affective development* (pp. 259–292). Hillsdale, NJ: Lawrence Erlbaum Associates.

Lazarus, R. S., & Folkman, S. (1984). *Stress, appraisal and coping.* New York: Springer.

Levine, S. (1985). A definition of stress? In G. P. Moberg (Ed.), *Animal stress* (pp. 51–69). Bethesda, MD: American Physiological Society.

Lewis, M., & Thomas, D. (1988, under editorial review). *Cortisol release in infants in response to inoculation.*

Matheny, A. P. (in press). Children's behavioral inhibition over age and across situations: Genetic similarity for a trait during change. *Journal of Personality.*

Panskepp, J. (1982). Toward a general psychobiological theory of emotions. *Behavioral and Brain Sciences, 5,* 407–467.

Porges, S. W., McCabe, P. M., & Yongue, B. G. (1982). Respiratory-heart rate interactions: Physiological implications for pathophysiology and behavior. In J. Cacioppo & R. Petty (Eds.), *Perspectives in cardiovascular psychophysiology* (pp. 223–264). New York: Guilford Press.

Porges, S. W., & Smith, K. M. (1980). Defining hyperactivity: Psychophysiological and behavioral strategies. In C. K. Whalen & B. Henker (Eds.), *Hyperactive children: The social ecology of identification and treatment.* New York: Academic Press.

Porter, F., & Porges, S. (1988). Neonatal cardiac responses to lumbar punctures. *Infant behavior and development, 11* (Special ICIS Issue), 261.

Porter, F. L., Porges, S. W., & Marshall, R. E. (1988). Newborn pain cries and vagal tone: Parallel changes in response to circumcision. *Child Development, 59,* 495–505.

Rose, R. M. (1980). Endocrine responses to stressful psychological events. Advances in psychoneuroendocrinolohy. *Psychiatric Clinics of North America, Vol. 3*(2), 251–276.

Rothbart, M. K. (1986). Longitudinal observation of infant temperament. *Developmental Psychology, 22,* 356–365.

Rothbart, M. K. (in press). Biological processes in temperament. In G. A. Kohnstamm, J. Bates, & M. K. Rothbart (Eds.), *Handbook of temperament in childhood.* Sussex, England: Wiley.

Rothbart, M. K., & Derryberry, D. (1981). Temperament and the development of self-regulation. In L. C. Hartlage & Telzrow (Eds.), *The neuropsychology of individual differences: A developmental perspective.* New York: Plenum Press.

Rothbart, M. K., & Posner, M. I. (1985). Temperament and the development of self-regulation. In H. Hartlage & C. G. Telzrow (Eds.), *Neuropsychology of individual differences: A developmental perspective* (pp. 93–123). New York: Plenum Press.

Spangler, G., Meindl, E., & Grossman, K. (1988, April). Behavioral organization and adrenocortical activity in newborns. *Infant behavior and development, 11,* (Special ICIS Issue), 295.

Sroufe, L. A. (1979). Socioemotional development. In J. Osofsky (Ed.), *Handbook of infant development* (pp. 462–516). New York: Wiley.

Tennes, K., Downey, K., & Vernadakis, A. (1977). Urinary cortisol excretion rates and anxiety in normal one-year-old infants. *Psychosomatic Medicine, 39,* 175–179.

Thomas, A., & Chess, S. (1977). *Temperament and development.* New York: Brunner/Mazel.

Thomas, A., & Chess, S. (1986). The New York longitudinal study: From infancy to early adult life. In R. Plomin & J. Dunn (Eds.), *The study of temperament: Changes, continuities and challenges* (pp. 39–52). Hillsdale, NJ: Lawrence Erlbaum Associates.

Torgersen, A. M., & Kringlen, E. (1978). Genetic aspects of temperamental differences in twins. *Journal of the American Academy of Child Psychiatry, 17,* 433–444.

Tucker, D. M., & Williamson, P. A. (1984). Asymmetric neural control systems in human self-regulation. *Psychological Review, 91,* 185–215.

Wenger, M. A. (1941). The measurement of individual differences in autonomic balance. *Psychosomatic Medicine, 3,* 427–434.

Wilder, J. (1956). The law of initial values in neurology and psychiatry. *Journal of Nervous and Mental Disorders, 125,* 73–86.

Williams, C. (1959). The elimination of tantrum behavior by extinction procedures. *Journal of Abnormal and Social Psychology.*

Wilson, R. S., & Matheny, A. P. (1986). Behavior-genetics research in infant temperament: The Louisville twin study. In R. Plomin & J. Dunn (Eds.), *The study of temperament: Changes, continuities and challenges* (pp. 81–98). Hillsdale, NJ: Lawrence Erlbaum Associates.

Zuckerman, M., Ballenger, J. C., & Post, R. M. (1984). The neurobiology of some dimensions of personality. *International Review of Neurobiology, 25,* 391–436.

16 Questionnaire Approaches to the Study of Infant Temperament

Mary K. Rothbart
Jennifer Alansky Mauro
University of Oregon

INTRODUCTION

The past decade has seen rapid development of the study of temperament. Although temperament is defined somewhat differently from one theoretical position to another (for a discussion of these positions, see Goldsmith et al., 1987), the temperament domain at its most inclusive can be seen to contain individual differences in emotionality, activity, and attention (Rothbart, 1989). As interest in temperament grows, assessment instruments are increasingly sought, both for investigations within the domain of temperament, and for studies relating temperament to variables in other domains such as cognition or personality. The choice of appropriate measures for this work depends on the dimension or dimensions of individual differences the investigator wishes to measure, and on the psychometric properties of the instrument(s) available.

To date, temperament has been assessed chiefly through three techniques: parent-report questionnaires, home observations, and laboratory observations (Rothbart & Goldsmith, 1985). By far the most frequently used method has been the parent-report questionnaire, in large part because of its ease of use and the low cost of implementing the measure. This chapter reviews the content, reliability, and stability of some of the most frequently used infant temperament questionnaires. For additional information on temperament assessment in infancy, the reader can also consult reviews by Bates (1987); Bornstein, Gaughran, and Homel (1986); Goldsmith and Rieser-Danner (in press); Hubert, Wachs, Peters-Martin, and Gandor (1982); Rothbart and Goldsmith (1985); and Windle (1988).

Before beginning this review, however, we should consider some general methodological concerns for the researcher who chooses to rely on caregiver

411

report for information about infant temperament. Rothbart and Goldsmith (1985) have reviewed potential sources of variability other than the actual behavior of the infant that may influence the infant's score on a temperament questionnaire. We identified characteristics of the informant (the caregiver) that could influence the measure as including: the caregiver's degree of comprehension of instructions, items and response options; the caregiver's actual knowledge of the infant's behavior; inaccurate memory, which may lead to biased recall; the caregiver's state when filling out the questionnaire; caregiver's response sets, including social desirability and acquiescence biases; and knowledge of implicit reference groups for ratings. Biases that could result as a function of rater–infant interaction included infant behaviors occurring in response to the caregiver's behavior, and biases in parental interpretation related to characteristics of the caregiver. Finally, method factors relatively independent of characteristics of infant and caregiver included the adequacy of selection of items, wording of items, and choice of response options in the questionnaire.

Although these sources of influence are important to consider in the use of temperament questionnaires, the questionnaire developer and user can attempt to minimize some of them. Strategies include careful item construction, asking the caregiver to respond concerning relatively recent events, wording some of the items in the opposite direction, and avoiding the use of highly global ratings (e.g., items like, ''My child is very active''), that might require the caregiver to consult implicit reference groups (some parents have little knowledge of other infants for comparison). The influence of the caregiver on the infant's behavior is a more difficult source of variability to deal with; we discuss this problem in more detail in the Stability section of the chapter. Biases in caregiver interpretation related to characteristics of the caregiver are the subject of research projects currently under way (e.g., Bates & Bayles, 1984; Goldsmith, Rieser-Danner, & Pomeranz, 1983; Lyon & Plomin, 1981; Matheny, Wilson, & Thoben, 1987). Although it is likely that these studies will provide further evidence for Bates and Bayles' (1984) conclusion that mothers' reports contain both objective and subjective components, it is important that such relationships be identified for each assessment instrument.

In spite of these biases and sources of error in caregiver report, there are several important advantages associated with use of questionnaires in addition to their ease of administration. Parents as informants are relying on an informational base that is both broad and deep. By sampling across the domain of the caregiver's experience, we can thereby develop questionnaire scales with high internal reliability. In addition, the observations reported to us by caregivers are made under normal circumstances, telling us what the child is usually like. Finally, validational studies have indicated enough correspondence between caregiver report and laboratory and home observations to give us some confidence that caregivers are describing characteristics of their children to us (see review by Bates, 1987).

The researcher using a caregiver-report questionnaire for temperament assessment can also consider the utility of employing multiple assessments of temperament. Although home observations are expensive and require multiple observations to achieve high reliability, laboratory assessments of temperament using standardized episodes designed to elicit temperament-related reactions are now being developed (Goldsmith & Rothbart, 1988; Matheny & Wilson, 1981), and these can be employed in tandem with caregiver-report questionnaires.

In this review of temperament questionnaire research, we define infancy narrowly to include only the first year of life, although we include information about longitudinal stability of questionnaire scale scores that involves the use of temperament questionnaires for toddlers and older children. The review first considers questionnaires following in the conceptual tradition of Thomas and Chess (1977) and the New York Longitudinal Study (NYLS). These questionnaires have been developed using both rational (Carey & McDevitt, 1978; Fullard, McDevitt, & Carey, 1984) and factor analytic methods (Bates, Freeland, & Lounsbury, 1979; Bohlin, Hageküll, & Lindhagen, 1981; Persson-Blennow & McNeil, 1979; Sanson, Prior, Garino, Oberklaid, & Sewell, 1987). We then review questionnaires developed by Buss and Plomin (1975) and Rothbart (1981), following from differing theoretical frameworks than the NYLS. We first present a brief conceptual analysis of each of the scales, then give information on the internal reliability and/or factor analysis of the scales as provided by their authors, and finally consider information about longitudinal stability of the measures. In the concluding section, we discuss the kind of further research we think would be helpful in improving measurement in this area.

The NYLS Approach

Let us begin with the nine dimensions of temperament employed by Alexander Thomas and Stella Chess and their co-workers. These dimensions were originally derived from a content analysis of the first 22 interview protocols from parents of young infants who were enrolled in the New York Longitudinal Study sample (Thomas, Chess, Birch, Hertzig, & Korn, 1963). The operational definitions for each of these nine dimensions, as reported by Thomas and Chess (1977, pp. 21–22), are as follows:

1. *Activity Level:* the motor component present in a given child's functioning and the diurnal proportion of active and inactive periods. Protocol data on motility during bathing, eating, playing, dressing, and handling, as well as information concerning the sleep–wake cycle, reaching, crawling, and walking are used in scoring this category.

2. *Rhythmicity* (Regularity): the predictability and/or unpredictability in time of any function. It can be analyzed in relation to the sleep–wake cycle, hunger, feeding pattern, and elimination schedule.

3. *Approach or Withdrawal:* the nature of the initial response to a new stimulus, be it a new food, new toy, or new person. Approach responses are positive, whether displayed by mood expression (smiling, verbalizations, etc.) or motor activity (swallowing a new food, reaching for a new toy, active play, etc.) Withdrawal reactions are negative, whether displayed by mood expression (crying, fussing, grimacing, verbalizations, etc.) or motor activity (moving away, spitting new food out, pushing new toy away, etc.)

4. *Adaptability:* responses to new or altered situations. One is not concerned with the nature of the initial responses, but with the ease with which they are modified in desired directions.

5. *Threshold of Responsiveness:* the intensity level of stimulation that is necessary to evoke a discernible response, irrespective of the specific form that the response may take, or the sensory modality affected. The behaviors utilized are those concerning reactions to sensory stimuli, environmental objects, and social contacts.

6. *Intensity of Reaction:* the energy level of response, irrespective of its quality or direction.

7. *Quality of Mood:* the amount of pleasant, joyful, and friendly behavior, as contrasted with unpleasant, crying, and unfriendly behavior.

8. *Distractibility:* the effectiveness of extraneous environmental stimuli in interfering with or in altering the direction of the ongoing behavior.

9. *Attention Span and Persistence:* two categories that are related. Attention span concerns the length of time a particular activity is pursued by the child. Persistence refers to the continuation of an activity in the face of obstacles to the maintenance of the activity direction.

Note that Thomas and Chess did not attempt to maintain conceptual independence across these dimensions. Thus their definition of Quality of Mood clearly overlaps with Approach, and Distractibility overlaps with Attention Span and Persistence. This conceptual nonindependence of scales is in turn reflected in rationally derived measures based on the NYLS dimensions, such as the Infant Temperament Questionnaire, or ITQ, developed by Carey in 1970 and the later Revised Infant Temperament Questionnaire, or RITQ, developed by Carey and McDevitt (1978).

The RITQ (Carey & McDevitt, 1978) is probably the most widely used questionnaire assessment of infant temperament. In addition to yielding measures for each of the nine NYLS dimensions, it also allows assignment of infants to the clinical diagnostic categories of difficult, slow-to-warm-up, intermediate high (difficult), intermediate low (easy), and easy children. Assignment of children to these diagnostic categories is based on the number of scale scores for a given infant that are one standard deviation above or below the mean of Carey and McDevitt's (1978) standardization sample. Six of the nine scales of the instrument are employed in the difficulty analysis: Activity, Rhythmicity, Approach, Adaptability, Intensity, and Mood.

As suggested by the overlap of conceptual definitions for the nine NYLS dimensions, there is also item overlap across some of the scales in the RITQ. Thus, the Mood Scale includes the item: "The infant is pleasant (smiles, laughs) when first arriving in unfamiliar places (friend's house, store)." This item would also conceptually belong on the Approach scale, defined as the child's initial response (positive versus negative) to a new stimulus, as well as on the Mood scale, defined as the amount of "pleasant, joyful, and friendly behavior" (Thomas & Chess, 1977, p. 22). Similarly, the Adaptability scale includes the item, "The infant adjusts within 10 min. to new surroundings (home, store, play area)," overlapping with both the Approach scale (which includes the item, "For the first few minutes in a new place or situation (new store or home) the infant is fretful," and the Mood scale. The Distractibility scale in turn demonstrates overlap with the Adaptability scale with items like, "The infant continues to reject disliked food or medicine in spite of parents' efforts to distract with games and tricks." In fact, in terms of content, most of the items on the Distractibility scale are actually soothability items, and these items would thus fit with the Adaptability definition, that is, the ease with which infants' responses are modified in a direction desired by the caregiver.

This conceptual overlap of items suggests that the scale scores of the RITQ would be empirically highly intercorrelated, and this proved to be the case in research performed by Sanson and her associates (Sanson, Prior, & Oberklaid, 1985; Sanson, Prior, Garino, Oberklaid, & Sewell, 1987) with a sample of 2,443 Australian 4–8 month infants (where item language of the RITQ was changed slightly to conform to Australian usage). The nine subscales showed substantial intercorrelation, particularly the Approach, Mood, and Adaptability scales, where correlations ranged between .52 and .67. Such high degrees of intercorrelation suggest that some of the scales are measuring close to the same, if not the same, construct. They have also led Sanson et al. (1987) and Hageküll (1982) and her associates in Sweden (Bohlin et al., 1981) to carry out item-level factor analyses in the attempt to empirically purify the scales.

A second concern about the conceptual content of the RITQ scales has to do with the extent to which the scales themselves are internally consistent. Thus one question important both conceptually and methodologically is whether threshold and intensity are individual differences that generalize across both response classes and stimulus sensory modalities. If this proved to be the case, the finding would be an exciting one. An empirical argument against their generality, however, is temperament work done in Soviet and Eastern European laboratories as reviewed by Strelau (1983). Results of these laboratory studies suggest that, at least for adults, there is not good generalizability across different response classes and sensory modalities in temperament measures. In addition, attempts by other researchers to develop Threshold and Intensity caregiver-report scales of temperament for infants and children have proved unsuccessful due to inadequate internal reliability of the scales (Martin, 1988; Rothbart, 1981). It should be noted in this regard that the internal consistency of these scales within the RITQ is not high, with internal consistencies (statistic unspecified) of .56 for Intensity and .57 for Threshold (Carey & McDevitt, 1978). Sanson et al. (1987) also found very low alpha coefficients for these two scales: .43 for Intensity and .42 for Threshold.

Another scale that raises concerns about internal reliability is Distractibility, with an initial internal consistency reported by Carey and McDevitt (1978) of .49. This concern has to do with the mix on the scale of mainly soothability items, with a few additional items assessing the infant's likelihood of noticing stimulus change. If perceptual sensitivity and soothability to distraction are highly correlated, this is of both theoretical and methodological interest. On the other hand, the relatively low internal consistency statistic leads us to worry about whether items from these two domains do vary consistently. In the factor analysis performed by Sanson et al. (1987), items from the Distractibility scale separated into those referring to perceptual sensitivity and those referring to soothability, with each subset loading on a different factor. Note, however, that Hageküll's (1982; Bohlin et al., 1981) factor analysis of ITQ items (with several additional items; we must of course remember that the factors derived from a factor analysis are dependent on the items included in the scale) yielded a small factor called Sensory Sensitivity, assessing intensity of infants' reactions to rapid movements, strong sounds, and sharp light. Although this scale is not a direct measure of either intensity or threshold, it measures an important aspect of reactivity and may prove to be an important dimension for further study.

Although some American studies have had trouble finding an internally consistent rhythmicity scale (Martin, 1988; Rothbart, 1981), both the Australian (Sanson et al., 1987) and the Swedish samples' (Hageküll, 1982) factor analyses have yielded a rhythmicity or regularity factor, and the RITQ internal consistency coefficient is a more acceptable .65 (Carey & McDevitt, 1978).

Given the questions raised about possible lack of discriminant validity for some scales (Approach, Adaptability, Mood) and lack of internal reliability for other scales (Threshold, Intensity, Distractibility), what *do* factor analyses of the RITQ at the item level suggest about the structure of this item set? Using their very large infant sample in the same age range (4–8 months) as Carey and McDevitt's (1978) standardization sample, Sanson et al. (1987) performed an orthogonal factor analysis yielding nine factors. Only two of these factors, however, proved to be relatively pure representations of the original RITQ dimensions; these were *Persistence* and *Rhythmicity*. No distinction was found between the Approach and Adaptability scales, with items from both scales loading on Factor 1, which Sanson et al. labeled *Approach*. Activity and Intensity items fell into two factors, one labeled *Activity/Reactivity*, which included the perceptual sensitivity items from the Distractibility scale, and the other *Placidity,* which included items like "Lies quietly in bath (from Activity) and "Plays quietly with toys" (Intensity).

Mood separated into items relating to new situations, which loaded on the *Approach* factor, and items related to caretaking procedures, which loaded on two additional factors: *Cooperation–Manageability,* which included chiefly measures of positive affect (e.g., "happy sounds during changing") and *Irritability,* which included chiefly measures of negative affect (e.g., "cries when left alone to play"). To the extent that Threshold appeared in the results of the analysis, it was weak and situation specific, with one cluster of Food Fussiness items and a two-item cluster on reactivity to soiled nappies (diapers). Based on their factor-analytic work, Sanson et al. (1985) developed a short-form temperament scale assessing Approach, Rhythmicity, Cooperation–Manageability, Activity–Reactivity, and Irritability, the most robust of their factors. These scales have demonstrated good internal reliability and test–retest reliability for the Australian sample, and they are very promising for use in English-speaking countries.

We can now consider briefly the factor analyses done by Hageküll (1982; Bohlin et al., 1981) on questionnaires filled out for 381 3–6-month infants and 410 6–10-month-old Swedish infants. Items from the ITQ and additional items yielded a 7-factor orthogonal solution for the younger group and an 8-factor orthogonal solution for the older group. Later combined analysis (N = 791) led to another 7-factor solution, with several of these factors showing similarity to those identified by Sanson et al. (1987): *Intensity/Activity,* similar to *Activity/Reactivity* aforementioned, *Regularity,* similar to *Rhythmicity,* and *Approach-Withdrawal,* similar to *Approach.* Although Hageküll's *Manageability* factor has a name similar to Sanson et al.'s *Cooperation–Manageability,* it is not so clearly an assessment of positive affect as is the Sanson et al. scale, and it also includes some activity and adaptability items. The BBQ was administered to a sample of 3- to 10-month-old infants and analyses of internal consistency were performed. Estimates of internal consistency alphas ranged from .51 to .77 (Bohlin et al., 1981).

One methodology combining both the NYLS and Carey approaches is the Swedish Temperament Questionnaire developed by Persson-Blennow and McNeil (1979). The STQ is comprised of 44 multiple-choice items similar in format to the ITQ and the NYLS interviews. Believing the ITQ and NYLS interviews to be costly in terms of scoring and administration time, the STQ was designed to alleviate this burden. The STQ was standardized on a sample of 160 Swedish infants ranging in age from 5 to 8 months. Item analysis eliminated items if they were endorsed by more than 80% or fewer than 5% of the sample, or if they failed to discriminate between high- and low-scoring individuals. A subsample of 14 infants was then retested 3 weeks later in an attempt to assess the reliability of the STQ. Analyses of 8 of the 9 dimensions showed moderate to strong test–retest figures (.53 to .86) with the attention–persistence dimension being the weakest (.40). However, estimates of the STQ's reliability based on these figures should be made cautiously, given the small sample size and time between testings.

Another important measure, developed with the purpose of assessing infant difficulty as perceived by the parent, is the Infant Characteristics Questionnaire, or ICQ, developed by Bates and his associates (Bates, Freeland, & Lounsbury, 1979). Content of items on this questionnaire included items assessing NYLS dimensions, items assessing changeability and soothability derived from Prechtl (1963), and fussiness and sociability items from Robson and Moss (1970). The ICQ was developed with a sample of 322 parents of infants age 4 to 6 months. A principal-axes factor analysis with varimax rotation was employed by Bates et al. (1979), yielding four factors: *Fussy–difficult, Unadaptable* (to new events, things and people), *Dull* (items assessing social responsiveness), and *Unpredictable* (ease of predicting the infant's needs).

Three types of reliability analyses were performed on a second sample of 196 subjects. Internal consistency alphas were highest for the fussy–difficult (.79) and unadaptable (.75) factors, with lower values for the dull and unpredictable factors. The reliability of the fussy–difficult dimension remained strong when agreement between maternal and paternal report were analyzed, as well as test–retest results over a 1-month period (.70 and .61) with the other factors showing moderate reliability (range .38 to .57). It should be noted that Bates et al. (1979) were not attempting to sample from the entire domain of temperament but were specifically trying to assess infant difficultness, so they employed a number of negative affect items. An important result of their work was thus the distinction between two kinds of distress proneness items: those involved in reaction to new events, things, and people (the *Unadaptable* factor), and other distress proneness or susceptibility (the *Fussy–difficult* factor).

An alternative to traditional parent report questionnaires based on the NYLS dimensions is the Perception of Baby Temperament (PBT), developed by Pedersen, Anderson, and Cain (1976). The PBT consists of 54 items that can be sorted in a Q-sort format by either parent. In an attempt to establish reliability of the PBT, mothers and fathers of 26 infants aged 5 months completed the instrument. Reliability was assessed by a split-half technique and examination of the correlation between maternal and paternal report. Results of split half analyses were as follows: Activity = .69, Rhythmicity = .65, Adaptability = .60, Approach = .58, Positive Mood = .54, Threshold = .48, Persistence = .42, Distractibility = .38, and Intensity = .31. Correlations between 26 pairs of parents within the same family ranged from .57 (Positive Mood) to .08 (Distractibility). Intercorrelations among the nine scales are in the low to moderate range (-.38 to .40) with a median correlation of .13 (Pedersen, Anderson, & Cain, 1976).

Other Approaches

Buss and Plomin (1975, 1984) have put forward a conceptualization of temperament represented by the acronym that also serves as the name of their assessment instrument: EASI. In their initial factor-analytic work on the EASI–I they attempted to develop scales assessing Emotionality (negative emotions only), Activity, Sociability, and Impulsivity. A sample of 139 parents of twins aged 1 to 9 years yielded questionnaire data that was factor analyzed and rotated with a Varimax solution. Although the four factors identified agreed with the four dimensions sought, there were relatively high factor correlations between Impulsivity and the other factor scores, which EASI–II was created to eliminate. EASI–II was administered to adults only, however (Buss & Plomin, 1975).

In their most recent book, Buss and Plomin (1984) have concluded that Impulsivity is not established as a dimension of temperament, so presumably the EASI would now be used to assess Emotionality (negative), Sociability, and Activity. One concern with using the EASI with subjects as young as 12 months, or especially as young as 5 months as in the study by Rowe and Plomin (1977) described below is that some of the items do not seem appropriate for infants (e.g., "Child is off and running as soon as he wakes up in the morning," "Child prefers quiet games such as coloring or block play to more active games," and "Child makes friends easily").

Another study with a separate sample reported a factor analysis of the EASI–I (20 items) combined with 54 items assessing the NYLS dimensions of Thomas and Chess (Rowe & Plomin, 1977). A sample of 91 mothers of children aged 5 months to 9 years filled out the questionnaire, with a mean child's age of 3.6 years. The analysis with Varimax rotation resulted in factors of Sociability, Activity, Emotionality, Attention span/persistence, Reaction to food and Soothability. As would be expected, most of the EASI items were included in the first three factors; NYLS items in the latter three factors. Given the wide range of age of subjects in this study, however, we would be hesitant to conclude that these factors apply to variability of temperament in infants until additional research is done.

A second questionnaire influenced by a search for dimensions going beyond those of the NYLS study is the Infant Behavior Questionnaire (IBQ), developed by the first author of this chapter (Rothbart, 1981). Choice of dimensions for the IBQ was influenced by the NYLS study, the work of Shirley (1933), Escalona (1968), reviews of longitudinal studies of stability of personality, and the review of studies of behavioral genetics and temperament by Diamond (1957), which also influenced the Buss and Plomin (1975) research. In the original IBQ, items were written to assess four general characteristics of response (across differing sensory receptors and response channels): Threshold, Intensity and Adaptability (including soothability) of response, and Rhythmicity. Seven scales were also written to assess reactivity of more specific motor and emotional responses:

Activity level, Fear, Distress to Limitations (Frustration), Overall Negative Emotionality, Smiling and Laughter, Persistence or Duration of Orienting, and Distractibility.

We performed two kinds of analyses: conceptual and item analyses. This would be considered a rational method of scale construction, in contrast with scales such as those developed by Bates et al. (1979) and Buss and Plomin (1975, which were factor-analytic strategies. In the conceptual analysis, we eliminated all scales whose operational definitions overlapped with those of other scales. Scales discarded were Negative Emotionality (overlap with Fear and Distress to Limitations), and Distractibility (overlap with Duration of Orienting). Our item analysis was based on the responses of 463 parents of 3-, 6-, 9-, and 12-month-old infants. Three scales were eliminated due to unsatisfactory item characteristics and internal reliability: Threshold, Rhythmicity, and Intensity. In addition, only the soothability items of the original Adaptability scale had satisfactory interitem correlations, and they were extracted to form a Soothability scale.

Our final six scales thus assessed Activity Level, Smiling and Laughter, Fear, Distress to Limitations, Duration of Orienting, and Soothability. Coefficient alphas were computed for each age (3-, 6-, 9-, and 12 months). Average alphas for dimensions were: Activity Level, .79, Smiling and Laughter, .79, Fear, .81, Distress to Limitations, .79, Duration of Orienting, .71; and Soothability $= .78$. Interscale correlations were also reported for the 6- and 12-month ages. Four of these 15 correlations were significant, with positive correlations for Fear and Distress to limitations (r's $= .36$ and $.29$ at 6 and 12 months, respectively), Activity Level and Distress to Limitations ($r = .28$ and $.33$ at 6 and 12 months, respectively), negative correlations for Smiling and Laughter and Fear (r's $= -.22$ and $-.34$ at 6 and 12 months, respectively), and a negative correlation for Smiling and Laughter and Distress to Limitations at 12 months ($r = -.30$). Positive correlations were found for all scales between reports of the mother and another adult who spent considerable time caring for the infant (household reliability).

Measures Common to Different Temperament Questionnaires

On the basis of our conceptual analysis of temperament scale content briefly described earlier, we have identified and listed in Table 16.1 six dimensions that are currently assessed by at least four infant temperament questionnaires. Each of these dimensions also represents a factor that has emerged from at least one of the item-based factor-analytic studies. The first of these dimensions assesses *reaction to novelty*. This variable is most commonly labeled Approach, although scales in this list are also labeled Fear and Unadaptable. In factorially developed scales, this scale includes adaptability (how long it takes the child to adjust to a new situation) as well as approach, withdrawal, and distress items to new situations.

A second distress-related variable assesses *distress proneness in situations that do not involve novelty:* This scale is labeled variously Irritability, Fussy–Difficult, Distress to Limitations, and Mood. Note that the mood variable differs from the first three scales, however, in that it assesses positive as well as negative affect. A third dimension assesses the child's *susceptibility to positive affect* and includes the measures Smiling and Laughter, Dull, Cooperation–Manageability, and again Mood, which as noted before, includes negative as well as positive reactions.

Activity level is frequently measured in infant temperament questionnaires, although it is interesting to note that in the factor-analytic studies by Hageküll (1982) and Sanson et al. (1987) this scale also includes other items: intensity and persistence items in the Hageküll study and reactivity items (including intensity) on the Sanson et al. scale. Part of the reason for the association between activity and intensity may be that parents' general assessments of the intensity of the child's reaction (e.g., during diaper changing or bath) include judgments of the infants' activity.

Rhythmicity emerges in both of the factor analytic studies and is labeled variously Rhythmicity and Regularity. With the exception of items assessing regularity in the amount of food intake, another way of looking at this scale is that it assesses the extent to which the infant is on a schedule, and we would expect parents to make a strong contribution to the child's position on this variable. Finally, an *Attention span/Persistence* factor has also emerged from both of the item factor-analytic studies, although Sanson et al. have not included it on their short-form questionnaire, and the Hageküll factor includes also a mood item, activity, and adaptability items. Although one might be tempted on the basis of the name of Hageküll's Attentiveness scale to include it as Attention span/Persistence scale, the Attentiveness scale actually includes distractibility, activity, and approach items, and we have therefore included it on Table 16.2 with other dimensions rather than on Table 16.1 with the attention span/persistence measures. It is possible that this mix of items is related to the tendency of infants who shift focus of attention frequently to also move more frequently from one location to another (Rothbart, 1988).

Our assignment of scales to columns in Tables 16.1 and 16.2 was done conceptually; is there any empirical evidence that the scales thus identified are actually measuring similar constructs? In a study of Goldsmith and Rieser-Danner (1986), mothers and day-care teachers of 35 infants age 4–8 months filled out the Revised Infant Temperament Questionnaire (RITQ; Carey & McDevitt, 1978), the Infant Characteristics Questionnaire (ICQ; Bates et al., 1979), and the Infant Behavior Questionnaire (IBQ; Rothbart, 1981). The first dimension on Table 16.1 assessed by all three of these instruments is the reaction to novelty dimension; it is assessed in IBQ Fear, ICQ Unadaptable, and ITQ

TABLE 16.1

Dimensions Assessed in Four or More Infant Temperament Questionnaires

Scale	Reaction to Novelty	Other Distress Proneness	Positive Affect
Carey and McDevitt	Approach/Withdrawal	Mood (also includes positive affect)	Mood (also includes negative affect)
Sanson et al.	Approach	Irritability	Cooperation/ Manageability
Hagekull	Approach/Withdrawal Unadaptable	Fussy/difficult	Dull
Bates			
Buss and Plomin	Emotionality ——————→	←——————— Emotionality	
Rothbart	Fear	Distress to Limitations	Smiling and Laughter
Carey and McDevitt	Activity	Rhythmicity	Attention Span
Sanson et al.	Activity/Reactivity	Rhythmicity	Attention Span/ Persistence
Hagekull	Intensity/Activity	Regularity	Persistence (not included on short form)
Bates	Activity	Unpredictable	Manageability
Buss and Plomin	Activity Level		
Rothbart			Duration of Orienting

TABLE 16.2
Other Dimensions Assessed for the Period of Infancy

Carey and McDevitt	Distractibility, Intensity, Threshold, Adaptability
Hagekull	Sensory Sensitivity, Attentiveness
Buss and Plomin	Sociability
Rothbart	Sociability

Approach–Withdrawal scales. The intercorrelations across these scales were high. For mothers, they ranged from .60–.69, with the average $r = .64$; for day-care teachers, the intercorrelations ranged from .51–.73, with the average $r = .63$ (Goldsmith & Rieser-Danner, 1986).

The second dimension from Table 16.1 includes (non-novelty induced) distress proneness or irritability, assessed by the IBQ Distress to Limitations, RITQ Negative Mood, and ICQ Fussy/Difficult scales. The intercorrelations among these scales for mothers ranged from .44–.63, with an average of .54; for day-care teachers from .66–.74, with an average of .71. The third dimension from Table 16.1 is Activity Level, assessed only on the RITQ and IBQ Activity Level scales. The correlation across these two scales for mothers was .65, and for day-care teachers also .65. Thus the conceptual overlap we have identified in Table 16.1 is also supported empirically, at least for these three questionnaires. Additional empirical work will be helpful in further identifying similarities and differences across the temperament questionnaires.

Stability

What kinds of stability across age have been found for caregiver report measures of temperament in infancy? For the RITQ, correlations have not been reported separately for all scales, but McDevitt and Carey (1981) did report that they have found general stability on the RITQ from infancy to 1 to 3 years. The RITQ was administered to mothers of 115 infants between 4 and 8 months, and these mothers later filled out the Toddler Temperament Scale (TTS; Fullard, McDevitt, & Carey, 1984). Both instruments are designed to assess the nine NYLS temperament dimensions. The average age for the first assessment was 5.6 months; for the second assessment, 23.4 months. McDevitt and Carey (1981) reported they found significant stability correlations for all scales, ranging from .24 to .58, with a median of .38. It is interesting to note further that all the scales with stabilities above their median stability value also appear on Table 16.1 (Activity Level, Rhythmicity, Mood, Persistence, and Approach–Withdrawal); those appearing on Table 16.2 all showed stabilities below the median (Threshold, Distractibility, Intensity, and Adaptability). Reasons have been given earlier as to why these latter scales would be expected to be less reliable, and hence less capable of demonstrating stability across age.

Again using the RITQ to assess temperament during infancy and the TTQ when subjects were reassessed at a later age, Peters-Martin and Wachs (1984) investigated correlations between mother reports of temperament at 6 and 12 months of age. Data for 30 infants were collected at both ages. For the variables in Table 16.1, stability correlations were .49 for Activity, .38 for Rhythmicity, .32 for Approach–Withdrawal, .46 for Mood, and .16 for Persistence. All correlations except Persistence were significant at the .05 level or above. For the variables in Table 16.2, the correlations were .04 for Intensity, .27 for Threshold, .14 for Distractibility, and .57 for Adaptability. Only the Adaptability correlation was significant in this group.

Wilson and Matheny (1986) in the Louisville Twin Study report correlations from 9 months with the Revised Infant Temperament Questionnaire (RITQ) to 12 months using the Toddler Temperament Questionnaire (TTQ), with samples of twins ranging in size from 86 to 102. Stability correlations for Table 16.1 variables were .46 for Activity, .54 for Rhythmicity, .21 for Approach–Withdrawal, .29 for Mood, and .44 for Persistence. For the variables in Table 16.2, the correlations were .54 for Intensity, .34 for Threshold, -.07 for Distractibility, and .13 for Adaptability. Wilson and Matheny (1986) continued to use the Toddler Temperament Questionnaire for older age groups (12 to 18 months and 24 months) and reported that stability correlations increased as the infants became older, especially for Approach, Mood, Distractibility, and Adaptability scales.

Hageküll and Bohlin (1981) have reported stability estimates for a large group of subjects assessed at 4 and again at 13 months of age using the Baby Behavior Questionnaire for the 4-month assessment (BBQ; Bohlin et al., 1981) and the Toddler Behavior Questionnaire (TBQ: Hageküll, Lindhagen, & Bohlin, 1980) for the 13-month assessment. The correlations across this 9-month period for Table 16.1 variables were .50 for Intensity/Activity, .33 for Regularity, .24 for Approach–Withdrawal, and .30 for Attentiveness. For Table 16.2 variables, they reported a stability correlation of .20 for Manageability.

Using the Infant Characteristic Questionnaire (ICQ; Bates et al., 1979), a study by Lee and Bates (1985) reported correlations for 111 infants from 6 to 13 months, and from both these ages to 24 months on the Child Characteristics Questionnaire. Correlations were not reported for the Unadaptable factor, but for a Difficulty measure (using presumably the Fussy/Difficult measure at the earlier ages), correlations were .57 (N = 127) from 6 to 24 months and .71 (N = 122) from 13 to 24 months. We do not know to what degree these stability correlations are influenced by an item included at all ages assessing the mother's subjective rating of the difficultness of her child, but these stability correlations are very impressive.

Based on the short form of the infant questionnaire and a short form of the toddler temperament scale, Sanson, Prior, and Oberklaid (1986) have extracted two measures of easy–difficult temperament, the Easy–Difficult Scale or EDS.

For the infant version, the score is composed of the mean for items in the Approach, Cooperation–Manageability, and Irritability scales; for the toddler version, the mean of items in the Approach, Cooperation–Manageability, Intensity/Activity, and Irritability scales. Correlations for over 1,000 infants (exact *N*s for each correlation were not given in this preliminary report) using the EDS at three age levels were as follows: between Time 1 (4–8 months) and Time 2 (18–24 months), $r = .43$; between Time 2 and Time 3 (32–36 months), $r = .69$; between Time 1 and Time 3, $r = .37$. Sanson et al. also report more stability across time for children at the extremes and greater stability of the measure for girls than for boys across this period.

Research using the Infant Behavior Questionnaire (IBQ; Rothbart, 1981) has chiefly reported stability assessment across the first year of life. In this work, Worobey and Blajda's (1989) adaptation of the IBQ to ages 2 weeks and 2 months provides estimates on stability for a longer age range than those reported by Rothbart (1981, 1986). Worobey and Blajda found average split-half stability for IBQ scales to be $r = .70$ for 2 weeks and $r = .79$ for 2 months. For 36 infants, correlations from 2 weeks to 2 months were .62 for Activity Level, .52 for Fear, .65 for Distress to Limitations, .33 for Soothability, .39 for Smiling and Laughter, and .40 for Duration of Orienting. Between 2 months to 12 months the correlations were .40 for Activity Level, .33 for Fear, .20 for Distress to Limitations, .50 for Soothability, .36 for Smiling and Laughter, and .44 for Duration of Orienting. All these correlations were statistically significant except the stability correlation for Distress to Limitations from 2 to 12 months. In assessment of stability from 2 weeks to 12 months, only Soothability showed a significant correlation across age ($r = .42$).

Rothbart (1981) reported across age stability correlations for the IBQ in infants assessed at 3, 6, 9, and 12 months (Cohort, 1, $n = 36$), 6, 9, and 12 months (Cohort 2, $n = 34$), and 9 and 12 months (Cohort 3, $n = 36$). She did not find stability for distress measures from 3 to 6 months, but average 3-month interval correlations from 6–9 and 9–12 months were .60 for Fear and .61 for Distress to Limitations. Across the 6-month period 6–12 months, average correlations were .37 for Fear and .61 for Distress to Limitations. For the other four variables, stability was found from the earliest period tested, with average correlations across 3-month, 6-month, and 9-month periods for Activity Level, .62, .60, and .48; for Smiling and Laughter, .86, .69, and .57; for Duration of Orienting, .59, .34 and .11 (ns), and for Soothability, .36, .38, and .41. With the exception of the soothability scale, correlations across age were higher as the children grew older, and larger when the age intervals were smaller. Similar stability correlations were found for the IBQ in Rothbart's 1986 longitudinal study where 46 subjects were assessed at 3, 6, and 9 months, with the exception that significant correlations were also found from 3 to 6 months for the Fear and Distress to Limitations measures (r's $= .44$ and .46, respectively.

The most notable differences between Rothbart's (1981, 1986) and Worobey and Blajda's (1989) stability findings have to do with the Smiling and Laughter scale. Stability between 2 weeks and 2 months in Worobey and Blajda's study was relatively low ($r = .39$), whereas the correlations from 3 months onward in the Rothbart study were relatively high (average $r = .86$ across 3-month periods). Although more research will be necessary to substantiate this finding, it may be the case that infant's positive reactivity is not sufficiently matured at the lower ages to show high stability (see review by Rothbart, 1989). Worobey and Blajda's general failure to find stability from 2 weeks to 12 months may also suggest that the temperamental response systems assessed (with the possible exception of soothability) are not sufficiently matured to demonstrate stability from 2 weeks of age.

We must consider some caveats before concluding this section on stability. One concerns the fact that these studies typically employ the same informants at two ages: Caregiver response biases consistent across these ages may contribute to the size of the correlations. We do know, however, on the basis of studies on questionnaire validity (see review by Bates, 1987) that caregiver reports show enough agreement with observer assessments for us to know that stability estimates are, at least to a degree, objective measures. Nevertheless, even assuming that caregiver reports provide good estimates of children's temperament-related behavior in the home, stability of the child's behavior may be strongly influenced by the caregiver and by context in which it is observed.

In the home the child is observed with the caregiver, and behavior by the caregiver is likely to be modulating the reactions of the child. For example, one commonly used item on temperament questionnaires inquires about the infant's reactions to the bath. While making systematic home observations (Rothbart, 1986) we were also able to take note of differences across households in the bathing situation, not reported in the published article. In some homes baths were very carefully prepared, with a check on water temperature, and with the infant eased into the water by gradual degrees. In other homes, bath water temperature was not carefully checked, infants were quickly lowered into the bath, and in one home the water was poured in large quantities over the infant's head from another container. Thus, differences in infant reactions across homes that show stability over time may reflect differences in the intensity of the stimulation they experience as well as temperamental individual differences among children. It may also be the case that some parents value smiling and positive affect in their infants more than other; these parents may attempt to turn every caregiving situation into one with positively toned interaction with the infant. Here, a positive reaction to the bath that shows stability across time may chiefly reflect a child's reactions to the social stimulation of the parents, which just happens to coincide with the bathing and other caregiving situations.

For estimates of longitudinal stability that avoid these interpretive problems, it is necessary to examine stability of infant reactions to episodes with intensity of eliciting stimulation controlled, and this is typically done in a laboratory situation. One of us has reviewed these studies in another chapter (Rothbart,

1989). Stability correlations for laboratory observations tend to be lower than those for caregiver reports, but the reliability of the laboratory measures also tends to be lower because they are based on fewer behavioral instances and fewer occasions. In general, stability correlations are improved with greater aggregation across temperament dimensions, as has been reported in the laboratory work of the Louisville Twin Study (Matheny et al., 1987; Wilson & Matheny, 1986).

CONCLUSIONS

We have reviewed temperament questionnaires according to their content, reliability, and stability over time. On the basis of our conceptual analysis we have identified six temperament dimensions that can be assessed via multiple questionnaire measures and that have also emerged from at least one item-level factor analysis. These include two measures of negative affect, one related to reactions to novelty and the other to more general distress proneness, one measure of positive affect, an activity level dimension, rhythmicity, and attention span–persistence variables. Initial work by Goldsmith and Rieser-Danner (1986) suggests that different questionnaire measures of these variables may be highly correlated.

We suggest that investigators looking for temperament scales should consider these six dimensions carefully, being more wary of the Threshold and Intensity scales, remembering that Adaptability and Approach–Withdrawal scales have strong overlap, and that the Distractibility scale on the RITQ includes many soothability items. Other scales from Table 16.2, especially those from item-level factor-analytic studies, may be worthy of further study, but it should also be remembered that the factor analytically derived scales often include a conceptual mix of items that may not be appropriate for the investigator's specific research questions.

Would more psychometric work be helpful with caregiver report measures of temperament? We say yes, in agreement with the judgment by Goldsmith and Rieser-Danner (in press) and Windle (1988), and we suggest that researchers investigate the applicability of the Australian short form of the ITQ and the Swedish questionnaires developed by Hageküll and her colleagues (the latter would require translation into English) to other samples of subjects. We were positively surprised in writing this review at the extent of conceptual and empirical overlap across temperament scales, but we are convinced that more careful psychometric work will continue to improve this area.

REFERENCES

Bates, J. E. (1987). Temperament in infancy. In J. D. Osofsky (Ed.), *Handbook of infant development* (pp. 1101–1149). New York: Wiley.

Bates, J. E., & Bayles, K. (1984). Objective and subjective components in mothers' perceptions of their children from age 6 months to 3 years. *Merrill–Palmer Quarterly, 30*(2), 111–130.

Bates, J. E., Freeland, C. A. B., & Lounsbury, M. L. (1979). Measurement of infant difficultness. *Child Development, 50,* 794–803.

Bohlin, G., Hageküll, B., & Lindhagen, K. (1981). Dimensions of infant behavior. *Infant Behavior and Development, 4,* 83–96.

Bornstein, M. H., Gaughran, J. M., & Homel, P. (1986). Infant temperament: Theory, tradition, critique and new assessments. In C. E. Izard & P. B. Read (Eds.), *Measuring emotions in infants and young children* (Vol. 2, pp. 172–202). Cambridge: *Cambridge University Press Bulletin, 56,* 81–105.

Buss, A. H., & Plomin, R. (1975). *A temperament theory of personality development.* New York: Wiley.

Buss, A. H., & Plomin, R. (1984). *Temperament: Early developing personality traits.* Hillsdale, NJ: Lawrence Erlbaum Associates.

Carey, W. B. (1970). A simplified method for measuring infant temperament. *Journal of Pediatrics, 77,* 188–194.

Carey, W. B., & McDevitt, S. C. (1978). Revision of the infant temperament questionnaire. *Pediatrics, 61,* 735–739.

Diamond, S. (1957). *Personality and temperament.* New York: Harper.

Escalona, S. K. (1968). *The roots of individuality: Normal patterns of development in infancy.* Chicago: Aldine.

Fullard, W., McDevitt, S. C., & Carey, W. B. (1984). Assessing temperament in one- to three-year-old children. *Journal of Pediatric Psychology, 9,* 205–217.

Goldsmith, H. H., Buss, A. H., Plomin, R., Rothbart, M. K., Thomas, A., Chess, S., Hinde, R. A., & McCall, R. B. (1987). Roundtable: What is temperament: Four approaches. *Child Development, 58,* 505–529.

Goldsmith, H. H., & Rieser-Danner, L. A. (1986). Variation among temperament theories and validation studies of temperament assessment. In G. A. Kohnstamm (Ed.), *Temperament discussed* (pp. 1–10). Lisse, The Netherlands: Swets & Zeitlinger.

Goldsmith, H. H., & Rieser-Danner, L. (in press). Assessing early temperament. In C. R. Reynolds & R. Kamphous (Eds.), *Handbook of psychological and educational assessment of children (Vol. 2): Personality, behavior, and context.* New York: Guilford Press.

Goldsmith, H. H., Rieser-Danner, L. A., & Pomeranz, S. (1983, April). *Maternal attitudinal structure as a correlate of perceived infant temperament.* Southwestern Psychological Association meeting, San Antonio, TX.

Goldsmith, H. H., & Rothbart, M. K. (1988). *The Laboratory Temperament Assessment Battery (LAB-TAB): Locomotor version, Edition 1.2.* Oregon Center for the Study of Emotion Technical Report #88-01.

Hageküll, B. (1982). Measurement of behavioral differences in infancy. *Acta University Uppsala: Abstracts of Uppsala dissertations from the Faculty of Social Sciences, 26.* Stockholm: Almquist & Wiksell International.

Hageküll, B., & Bohlin, G. (1981). Individual stability in dimensions of infant behavior. *Infant Behavior and Development, 4,* 97–108.

Hageküll, B., Lindhagen, K., & Bohlin, G. (1980). Behavioral dimensions in one year olds and dimensional stability in infancy. *International Journal of Behavioral Development, 3,* 351–364.

Hubert, N. C., Wachs, T. D., Peters-Martin, P., & Gandor, M. J. (1982). The study of early temperament: Measurement and conceptual issues. *Child Development, 53,* 571–600.

Lee, C., & Bates, J. (1985). Mother–child interaction at age two years and perceived difficult temperament. *Child Development, 56,* 1314–1326.

Lyon, M. E., & Plomin, R. (1981). The measurement of temperament using parental ratings. *Journal of Child Psychology and Psychiatry, 22,* 47–53.

Martin, R. P. (1988). *The temperament assessment battery for children.* Brandon, VT: Clinical Psychology Publishing Co.

Matheny, A. P., & Wilson, R. S. (1981). Developmental tasks and rating scales for the laboratory assessment of infant temperament. *JSAS Catalog of Selected Documents in Psychology, 11*, 81–82 (Ms. No. 2367).

Matheny, A. P., Wilson, R. S., & Thoben, A. (1987). Home and mother: Relations with infant temperament. *Developmental Psychology, 23*, 323–331.

McDevitt, S. C., & Carey, W. B. (1981). Stability of ratings versus perceptions of temperament from early infancy to 1–3 years. *American Journal of Orthopsychiatry, 11*, 342–345.

Pedersen, F. A., Anderson, B. J., & Cain, R. L. (1976). *A methodology for assessing parental perception of infant temperament.* Paper presented at Fourth Biennial Southeastern Conference of Human Development, Children's Hospital, Pittsburgh.

Persson-Blennow, I., & McNeil, T. F. (1979). A questionnaire for measurement of temperament in six-month-old infants: Development and standardization. *Journal of Child Psychology and Psychiatry, 20*, 1–13.

Peters-Martin, P., & Wachs, T. D. (1984). A longitudinal study of temperament and its correlates in the first 12 months. *Infant Behavior and Development, 7*, 285–298.

Prechtl, H. F. R. (1963). The mother–child interaction in babies with minimal brain damage (a follow-up study). In B. M. Foss (Ed.), *Determinants of infant behavior* (Vol. 2). New York: Wiley.

Robson, K. S., & Moss, H. A. (1970). Patterns and determinants of maternal attachment. *Journal of Pediatrics, 77*, 976–985.

Rothbart, M. K. (1981). Measurement of temperament in infancy. *Child Development, 52*, 569–578.

Rothbart, M. K. (1986). Longitudinal observation of infant temperament. *Developmental Psychology, 22*, 356–365.

Rothbart, M. K. (1988). *Attention and emotion in the development of temperament* (Tech. Rep. No. 88-3). Eugene: University of Oregon, Center for the Study of Emotion. M. I. Posner (organizer).

Rothbart, M. K. (1989). Temperament and development. In G. A. Kohnstamm, J. Bates, & M. K. Rothbart (Eds.), *Handbook of temperament in childhood* (pp. 187–247). Sussex, England: Wiley.

Rothbart, M. K., & Goldsmith, H. H. (1985). Three approaches to the study of infant temperament. *Developmental Review, 5*, 237–260.

Rowe, D. C., & Plomin, R. (1977). Temperament in early childhood. *Journal of Personality Assessment, 41*, 150–156.

Sanson, A. V., Prior, M., Garino, E., Oberklaid, F., & Sewell, J. (1987). The structure of infant temperament: Factor analysis of the Revised Infant Temperament Questionnaire. *Infant Behavior and Development, 10*, 97–104.

Sanson, A. V., Prior, M., & Oberklaid, F. (1985). Normative data on temperament in Australian infants. *Australian Journal of Psychology, 37*, 185–195.

Sanson, A. V., Prior, M., & Oberklaid, F. (1986, August). *The stability of temperament over the first three years of life.* Paper presented at meetings of the Australian Psychological Society, Townsville.

Shirley, M. M. (1933). *The first two years: A study of 25 babies.* Minneapolis: University of Minnesota Press.

Strelau, J. (1983). *Temperament personality activity.* New York: Academic Press.

Thomas, A., & Chess, S. (1977). *Temperament and development.* New York: Brunner/Mazel.

Thomas, A., Chess, S., Birch, H. G., Hertzig, M. E., & Korn, S. (1963). *Behavioral individuality in early childhood.* New York: New York University Press.

Wilson, R. S., & Matheny, A. P., Jr. (1986). Behavior–genetic research in infant temperament: The Louisville Twin Study. In R. Plomin & J. Dunn (Eds.), *The study of temperament: Changes, continuities and challenges* (pp. 81–97). Hillsdale, NJ: Lawrence Erlbaum Associates.

Windle, M. (1988). Psychometric strategies of measures of temperament: A methodological critique. *International Journal of Behavioral Development, 11*, 171–201.

Worobey, J., & Blajda, V. M. (1989). Temperament ratings at 2 weeks, 2 months, and 1 year: Differential stability of activity and emotionality. *Developmental Psychology*, 257–263.

17

Individual Differences During the Second Year of Life: The MacArthur Longitudinal Twin Study

Robert Plomin
Joseph Campos
Robin Corley
Robert N. Emde
David W. Fulker

Jerome Kagan
J. Steven Reznick
Joann Robinson
Carolyn Zahn-Waxler
J. C. DeFries

Surprisingly little is known about individual differences in change and continuity during the second year of life, a dramatic developmental turning point that marks the transition from infancy to early childhood (Kagan, 1981). In addition to major cognitive advances such as symbolic representation and language acquisition, new qualities emerge in the area of emotion such as increasingly sophisticated emotional communication and the first signs of empathy (Campos, Barrett, Lamb, Goldsmith, & Stenberg, 1983). Cognitive and emotional changes during the second year of life are also likely to play a role in developmental changes in temperament (Plomin & Dunn, 1986). The neglect of individual differences in research during infancy, and the need to go beyond analyses of central tendencies to describe, predict, and explain individual differences has recently been discussed (Plomin, DeFries, & Fulker, 1988). Although our special collaborative interest is in behavioral genetic explanations of individual differences, this chapter focuses on the prior issues of description and prediction of individual differences.

Descriptive research on individual differences in infancy has typically focused on homotypic change and continuity for a single trait or single domain, most notably mental development. A multivariate perspective adds synergistically to such research in that heterotypic as well as homotypic links can be identified between different behaviors across ages (Kagan, 1971). In addition, a multivariate approach makes it possible to address a key issue in developmental analyses of individual differences: Change and continuity in covariance structure, the interrelationship among variables.

Werner's (1948) orthogenetic principle, for example, suggests that development is marked by differentiation. Although the orthogenetic principle is phrased in terms of normative development, from an individual-differences perspective, differentiation can be seen as a decline in the magnitude of intercorrelations among measures, assuming that variability between individuals exists for these measures. For instance, the correlation between mental and motor development as measured by the Bayley tests declines from about .40 at 1 year of age to about .20 at 2 years (Plomin et al., 1988). Differentiation, however, is not the only pattern of developmental change in covariance structure that may occur. For some domains, especially temperament, covariance structure appears to be stable throughout infancy (Matheny, 1980). Contrary to the differentiation hypothesis, intercorrelations among measures of mental development, as seen in a general g factor (an unrotated first principal component), increase during infancy and early childhood (Plomin et al., 1988).

In 1982, as part of the MacArthur Network on the Transition from Infancy to Early Childhood, we began to plan a collaborative research project that would integrate our interests in individual differences in change and continuity during the second year of life in the domains of temperament, emotion, and cognition. The approach was to be multivariate, emphasizing relationships within and among domains, and multimethod in that the research would employ assessments in both the home and laboratory and include standard tests, eliciting situations, videotaped observations, and ratings by observers and by parents. After considerable discussion, review, and reformulation, we eventually designed a longitudinal twin study of more than 300 same-sex pairs of twins tested at 14, 20, 24, and 36 months of age. The longitudinal component was deemed critical for the analysis of individual differences in change and continuity. The ages were chosen to bracket the major transition period from 20 to 24 months, an age that encompasses language spurts such as the use of two-word phrases, growth of a sense of self, and development of appreciation of standards. This period of change is bracketed by assessments during periods of relative quiescence at 14 and 36 months. The twin design will permit analyses of genetic and environmental contributions to change and continuity, as discussed in this volume in the chapter by Thompson.

The MacArthur Longitudinal Twin Study was launched in 1986. This first report of the 7-year project describes its sample, procedures, measures, and some preliminary findings in relation to individual differences for 200 infants at 14 months and for 60 of these children tested again at 20 months. The sample is not yet large enough for analyses at 24 and 36 months or for analyses of identical and fraternal twins. In this preliminary report, we examine the covariance among selected variables at 14 months to illustrate the value of a multivariate approach to the study of individual differences during infancy. We also explore heterotypic as well as homotypic associations among variables from 14 to 20 months.

METHOD

Sample

On a monthly basis, the Division of Vital Statistics of the Colorado Department of Health provides the names and addresses of the parents of twin births (screened for infant mortality), as well as perinatal information recorded on the birth certificate. Twins are selected preferentially for normal gestational age and birth weights appropriate for gestation age. No twins with birth weights less than 1,750 grams or with gestational ages less than 34 weeks are selected—60% of twins meet these criteria. Only one twin in this sample had a birth weight less than 2,000 grams, one-third of the twins have birth weights between 2,000 to 2,500 grams, and the rest have birth weights greater than 2,500.

Parents are informed about the project and asked to participate—the response rate has exceeded 50%. Over 90% of the sample is Caucasian; the other participating parents are primarily hispanic and 1% are black. The mean ages of mothers and fathers are 29.2 and 31.3. Mean educational level of mothers is 14.5 years with a range of 11 to 18; the mean for fathers is also 14.5 with a range of 12 to 18. In terms of age and educational level, these parents are somewhat better educated and slightly older than the average of all parents of newborns in Colorado. From birth certificate information for almost 50,000 infants born in 1985 in Colorado to married couples, the average age was 27 for mothers and 29 for fathers, respectively. Average education in the population was 12.2 years for mothers and 12.5 for fathers.

Attrition in MALTS has been low. Of the families tested at 14 months whose infants have reached 20 months of age, 93% have been tested at 20 months. Zygosity of the twins is assessed using physical similarity criteria at both the home and laboratory test sessions at 14 and 24 months. For twins whose diagnosis of zygosity remains uncertain using physical similarity criteria (approximately 5%), similarity is assessed again at 36 months, and, if necessary, blood typing is conducted.

Procedure

At 14 and 20 months, the twins and their mother are visited in their home by two female examiners, and about 2 weeks later, the mother brings her two children to the laboratory at the Institute for Behavioral Genetics. Visits are scheduled at a time when the children are likely to be at their best, usually following naps or meals. Each visit is completed in less than 3 hours. Questionnaires are given to parents at the home visit and collected at the laboratory visit. Table 17.1 provides an overview of the procedures and measures.

TABLE 17.1

Summary of Procedures and Measures at 14 Months

Procedure	Measure
Home Visit	
Entry	Shyness
Collection of saliva	Cortisol
Prone length	Length
Restraint	Reactivity to restraint
Toy removal	Anger
Prohibition	Evaluation of standards
Bayley mental scales	Mental Development Index
	Hedonic tone
Bayley Infant Behavior Record	Behavioral ratings
Sequenced Inventory of Communication Development	Receptive and productive language
Empathy probe with examiner	Empathy
Teaching task	Nonshared environment
Empathy probe with mother	Empathy
Free play	Hedonic tone and mood
	Twins' interactions
Flawed and unflawed toys	Evaluation of standards
Laboratory Visit	
Entry	Shyness
Toy removal	Anger
Cognitive testing room	
Pre and post heart rate	Heart rate and variability
Word comprehension	Word comprehension
Categorization	Categorization
Memory for locations	Memory for locations
Weight	Weight
Play room	
Flawed and unflawed toys	Evaluation of standards
Free play	Behavioral inhibition
Baby cry empathy stimulus	Empathy
Empathy probe with mother	Empathy
Stranger entry	Behavioral inhibition
Empathy probe with examiner	Empathy
Discrepant object	Behavioral inhibition
Prohibition	Evaluation of standards
Other	
Questionnaires	Parental ratings of temperament
	Maternal ratings of discrete emotions
	Dyadic Adjustment Scale
	Family Environment Scales
	Eysenck Personality Inventory
Birth certificates	Perinatal information
Maternal interview	Pregnancy and delivery
	Children's health
	Nonshared environment
	Twins' interactions

Home Visit.   The home visit begins with one examiner using a portable color videotape camera to record the children's reactions during the examiners' first 5 minutes in the home. During the first 2 minutes, the other examiner describes the visit and obtains informed consent. Following this, the examiner attempts to engage the twins in play using a standardized format similar to that used by Plomin and Rowe (1979) to assess shyness. The children continue to be videotaped as vests of different color are put on each child. Examiners then demonstrate to the mother the procedure for collecting saliva that is used for cortisol assays. A cotton dental swab is lightly coated with a flavored sugar candy and placed in the child's mouth. The child sucks on the swab, soaking it with saliva. The swab is then placed in an oral syringe and, as the syringe is plunged, the saliva is expelled into a test tube. Each mother is requested to take two additional samples in a similar manner before 10 o'clock on two mornings prior to her laboratory visit.

A brief frustration episode involving restraint is employed for one child, then the other. Each child is videotaped in a prone position with mother seated at the child's head while the examiner measures the child's length. The examiner firmly tells the child to lie still as the examiner applies moderate pressure to the child's abdomen in order to restrain the child. The child is restrained for 3 minutes or until a vocal or physical protest is made. The restraint episode lasts about 4 minutes for each child.

The next episode was also designed to elicit anger, again administered to one child, then the other. An attractive toy is presented to the child. If after 30 seconds the child has not approached the toy, the examiner entices the child to play with it. At the point of peak engagement with the toy, the examiner abruptly picks up the toy and puts it away, saying "I have to put it away now." The examiner then places the toy in a zippered bag placed several feet from the child and the examiner retreats. The child's reaction is filmed for another 2 minutes. For each child, 4 minutes are spent on this toy-removal episode. The children then play freely and the mother and examiner discuss the upcoming procedures in detail while two videocameras are set up on tripods for filming the administration of the Bayley Mental Scales.

The children are seated in high chairs in different rooms for administration of the Bayley Mental Scales (Bayley, 1969) and the Sequenced Inventory of Communication Development (Hedrick, Prather, & Tobin, 1975), which require 40 minutes. A brief prohibition episode (1 minute) is administered at the beginning of the Bayley testing. An attractive toy (a 4-inch glitter wand) is placed in front of the child in the high chair. The examiner manipulates the wand causing the glitter to move for about 15 seconds. She makes eye contact with the child and then places the wand on the tray in front of the child saying sternly, "(child's name), don't touch." After 30 seconds, the examiner removes the prohibition saying kindly, "It's OK, you can touch it now." If the child has not yet touched the wand, the examiner continues to encourage the child to do so until the child explores it freely.

Immediately following these tests (approximately 90 minutes into the visit) and while the children are still seated in high chairs, an empathy probe occurs in which the examiner feigns injuring her finger while closing the testing case. Moderate distress is expressed by the examiner for 30 seconds, followed by 30 seconds of recovery and reassurance to the child. This empathy episode requires 1 minute.

The children are then taken out of the high chairs and given a break with a snack. A 7-minute session ensues in which the mother attempts to teach a difficult task (a form board) to both twins simultaneously. Each twin has a separate form board. The procedure for this task follows the work of Scarr (1985). During the next 2 minutes, a second empathy probe is administered by the mother to each child separately. Mother mimicks the same sequence as in the previous empathy episode involving the examiner, but the mother feigns injury of her knee. In the final 15-minute segment, the twins are videotaped as they play freely with six flawed and six unflawed toys arrayed on the floor.

At 20 months, free play is followed by a cooperation/competition situation. A single toy (Sit 'n Spin) is made available for 10 minutes for exploration and joint play. Mother demonstrates its use and encourages cooperation after several minutes of exploration. Videotapes of the free play and the cooperation/competition episodes permit ratings of the twins' social interaction including dominance, aggression, and prosocial behavior.

Laboratory Visit.   The laboratory visit begins in the same manner as the home visit, with an assessment of the children's shyness as they enter the reception room, the first of three rooms used as part of the laboratory protocol. During a 5-minute warm-up period, the children are videotaped as they venture forth from their mother to explore the new environment. During this time, the examiners discuss procedures with the mother and obtain informed consent. About 10–15 minutes after arrival, three electrodes are placed on the abdomen of one of the twins and that child and mother are escorted to the cognitive testing room. The other twin remains in the reception room with the second examiner while the co-twin participates in the cognitive testing. In the reception room, the twin plays freely with toys, in a situation designed to be soothing during mother's absence. However, at 14 months, a brief anger episode (toy removal) occurs during this time. At 20 months, two other tasks are employed: a self-recognition task involving a mirror, which is administered as in the work of Lewis and Brooks-Gunn (1979), and role-play. The role-play episode is based on the work of Watson and Fischer (1977, 1980). The child is seated facing the examiner who presents a stuffed bunny, saying "The bunny is sleeping." The examiner then pretends to wake the toy and begins a sequence in which the child is asked to imitate the examiner's actions. The examiner makes the toy hop, feeds it a carrot, and has it feed itself a carrot. Each time, the examiner says to the child, "Now you do it." Several additional props are placed on the table and then the examiner pretends that the toy has hurt itself. The examiner says to the child, "Oh, look, the bunny has hurt her hand. What would mommy do to make it better?" Following the child's response, the examiner hops and invites the child to "be a bunny, too."

In the cognitive testing room, the infant is seated in a high chair facing a testing apparatus that holds two rear-projection screens—used to present slide stimuli—and a videocamera for taping the session. The mother is seated in a chair next to the child. After the electrodes are connected to a heart rate pre-amplifier, six pairs of slides are presented to the child for 15 seconds each to obtain a baseline heart rate. The preamplifier is connected directly to a Zenith model 158–43 personal computer that times and records the length of the inter-beat intervals. A word comprehension task is administered next through the repeated presentation of paired slides (Reznick, 1989). The child sees two slides for 8 seconds, is prompted by the examiner with the name of one of the slides, and continues looking at the slides for 8 more seconds. The examiner records visual fixation during both intervals. Comprehension is inferred if fixation to the named slide increases after the prompt. The word comprehension task requires 5 minutes. A sorting test is used to provide a break from the focused attention of the word comprehension task (Reznick & Snedley, 1987). The child is offered a tray of objects of two types, people versus animals and, on a second trial, cars versus trucks. The child's manipulation of the objects is recorded for later coding of sequential touching of objects from the same category. After the 5 minutes required for the categorization tasks, the child returns to the word comprehension task for a total of 15 trials.

Next, memory for locations is assessed using a variant of the shell game. A toy is hidden under one of 2, 4, or 6 cups. A barrier is used to delay responding for 1, 5, or 10 seconds before the child is asked to find the hidden toy. Memory for locations requires 6 minutes. Finally, posttest heart rate is recorded during 2 minutes of paired slide presentations. Finally, the child is weighed on a digital scale.

Mother, child, and examiner return to the reception room. Electrodes are placed on the second twin and the same cognitive procedure is administered to the second twin while the first twin remains in the reception room with an examiner. Following cognitive testing for the second twin, the mother accompanies the first twin to a play room with six flawed and six unflawed toys arrayed on the floor. The mother sits on a sofa against a wall and completes two questionnaires while the child plays freely for 12 minutes. The only other furniture in the room is a closed cabinet that is described next. Two videocameras are used to film the procedures. One remote-controlled camera is mounted near the ceiling on the wall opposite the mother, and a second camera is operated from behind a one-way mirror in the wall behind the mother.

The initial 12 minutes of free play represent the first of three inhibition episodes. The free-play session provides an opportunity to observe the child's willingness to explore an unfamiliar room, as indexed, for example, by latency to leave mother and latency to approach novel toys. After approximately 3 minutes, the first of three empathy stimuli occurs: The sound of a baby crying is broadcast into the room from a speaker for approximately 30 seconds. The mother is instructed to respond to the child's bids for attention or reassurance but otherwise to continue filling out the questionnaires. About 5 minutes later, at a time when the child is away from mother's side, the second empathy probe is administered. The mother is signaled to act as if her finger has been injured on the clipboard in her lap. The same injury/recovery sequence was followed as in the home visit.

After a total of 12 minutes, the second inhibition probe is administered. A female stranger holding a high-interest toy enters the room. She maintains a downcast gaze as she sits on the floor several feet from the child. At 1-minute intervals, she increases her activity with the toy until 4 minutes has elapsed. If the child has not approached the stranger after 4 minutes, the stranger raises her gaze and verbally invites the child to play. The stranger leaves after engaging in play with the child for 2 minutes. Following this, the third and final empathy probe begins. The examiner returns to the room and feigns injury of her foot as she repositions a chair. After recovering, the examiner opens the cabinet, which houses a large discrepant object (a furry monster at 14 months and a tin can robot at 20 months). Presentation of the discrepant object is the third inhibition episode. The child is invited to approach and explore the object. If the child approaches or after 2 minutes of encouragement, a voice is projected through a speaker in the cabinet. This discrepant object episode requires 3 minutes. The final 1-minute procedure involves another prohibition. A basket of colorful balls is placed in front of the child who is told firmly, "Now don't touch!" After a brief period of recovery from the prohibition, mother and child return to the reception room and the second twin then accompanies the mother to the play-room.

Measures

The major domains assessed in MALTS include temperamental, emotional, and cognitive processes. In this section, measures within each domain are described to provide an overview of the project, even though only a few composite measures are included in our preliminary analyses. The measures are similar at 14 and 20 months.

Temperament

Measures of temperament include observational measures of behavioral inhibition to unfamiliar events and of shyness to unfamiliar people, parental ratings of temperament, and tester ratings on the Infant Behavior Record.

Behavioral Inhibition.   Inhibited and uninhibited behavior to the unfamiliar are assessed by behavioral reactions to unfamiliar events in a playroom and at home and, in addition, by measures of heart rate and heart rate variability during the cognitive procedures. The rationale for these measures comes from previous research by Kagan, Reznick, Snidman, and their colleagues (Garcia-Coll, Kagan, & Reznick, 1984; Kagan, 1989; Kagan, Reznick, Clarke, Snidman, & Garcia-Coll, 1984; Kagan, Reznick, & Snidman, 1987, 1988; Kagan, Reznick, Snidman, Gibbons, & Johnson, 1988). Unfamiliar events in the laboratory include a female stranger and discrepant objects. The videotapes are coded for variables like latency to approach an unfamiliar object or person, withdrawal and duration of proximity to the mother, and staring. A high and stable heart rate during the cognitive testing is also associated with behavioral inhibition. At the laboratory visits at 24 and 36 months, peer play is added as an additional situation to assess inhibition. Two families are scheduled to overlap so that the four children and their mothers are together during a play session. In addition, at 14, 24, and 36 months, salivary cortisol is obtained as another indicant of behavioral inhibition.

Shyness.   Although a measure of shyness is included as part of the protocol for behavioral inhibition (i.e., stranger entry towards the end of the laboratory session), independent measures of shyness are obtained based on the children's initial reactions to the examiners' arrival in the home and to the children's entry into the laboratory. Discrete behaviors are recorded such as reaction to approach of the examiner, the children's latency to approach a proffered toy, and the frequency of vocalization. In addition, global ratings of shyness and hesitation are completed by videoraters for each minute of the 5-minute entry episodes. Measures are averaged across each minute and then across the 5-minute episodes in the home and laboratory. An unrotated first principal component score (described later) was used as a composite measure of shyness. Mothers are also interviewed concerning the twins' shyness.

Colorado Childhood Temperament Inventory (CCTI).   At 14 and 20 months, both parents rate each child using the CCTI (Rowe & Plomin, 1977). A new scale assesses shyness as distinct from sociability and the sociability scale has been modified to attenuate its overlap with shyness (Buss & Plomin, 1984). Scores were averaged across mothers and fathers. CCTI activity and sociability scales were used in our preliminary analyses.

Toddler Temperament Survey (Fullard, McDevitt, & Carey, 1984).   Both parents also complete the Toddler Temperament Survey, which assesses the nine dimensions studied by Thomas and Chess in their New York Longitudinal Study (Chess & Thomas, 1984).

Bayley's Infant Behavior Record (IBR). Examiners use the IBR (Bayley, 1969) to rate each child's behavior while the Bayley mental scales are administered and again during the non-Bayley portion of the home visit. IBR items are scored on three scales—Affect–Extraversion, Activity, and Task Orientation—as suggested by Matheny (1980).

Emotion

Measures of emotion include time-sampled observations of hedonic tone and mood from the videotapes, videotape ratings of reactivity in response to the restraint and toy removal episodes, videotape ratings of empathy in response to the empathy episodes, and ratings of discrete emotions by mothers.

Hedonic Tone and Overall Mood (Easterbrooks & Emde, 1983). Ratings of the child's strongest positive and negative affect are made from each 5-minute period of the videotape recordings of the children during administration of the Bayley test and during free play. A measure of lability of hedonic tone is also obtained by calculating each child's variance across the 5-minute time samples.

Reactivity to Restraint and Toy Removal. The child's responses to the restraint and toy-removal episodes are rated from videotapes. Five-point global ratings of the child's expressivity, protest strength, and distress level are completed for each episode. In addition, the duration of the restraint and the child's predominant state during the restraint are scored. The latter is a 7-point scale that assesses the child's state, from a low of sleeping to a high of crying. Ratings are made every 10 seconds during the restraint. As described in the results section, an unrotated first principal component based on these measures was used as a composite measure of anger.

Empathy. Empathy probes were coded based on a modification of a scheme by Zahn-Waxler and her colleagues (Radke-Yarrow & Zahn-Waxler, 1973; Zahn-Waxler, Radke-Yarrow, & King, 1979) for rating empathic responses of 1- and 2-year-old children. Independent observers rated the videotapes of one child in each twin pair, minimizing within-pair rating bias. Ratings included approach, complexity of hypothesis testing, strength of concern as expressed in the child's face, level of emotional arousal as expressed in the child's body tension, presence or absence of prosocial intervention by the child (e.g., comforting by patting the victim's knee or bringing the victim a toy), and a global rating of overall empathic involvement with the victim. These ratings were averaged across the five empathy probes administered at home and in the laboratory. Interobserver agreement for these scales exceeds 80%. For this preliminary report, a composite was formed from an unrotated first principal component of these measures, as described next. Mothers are also interviewed concerning their children's empathic responses.

Discrete Emotions. Expression of discrete emotions is rated by mother using the Differential Emotions Scale (DES; Izard, 1972) as modified by Emde and colleagues (Fuenzalida, Emde, Pannabecker, & Stenberg, 1981; Johnson, Emde, Pannabecker, Stenberg, & Davis, 1982). The DES yields 10 scores assessing such differential emotions as joy, fear, and surprise.

Cognition and Language

The development of temperament and emotion during the transition must be studied in the context of the dramatic emergence of new cognitive functions, both linguistic and nonlinguistic. In addition to standard tests in these domains, experimental tests of word comprehension, memory for locations, and categorization tasks are employed.

The Bayley Mental Scale from the Bayley Scales of Infant Development (Bayley, 1969) is administered and the Mental Development Index (MDI) is derived. Number of items passed on the Sequenced Inventory of Communication Development (SICD; Hedrick, Prather, & Tobin, 1975) is used to assess receptive and productive language.

A measure of word comprehension is based on visual fixation to paired slides. Greater fixation to the picture representing the target word is considered evidence for comprehension of that word. Each child receives 15 word tests representing 5 easy words, 5 moderate words, and 5 difficult words. The word comprehension score is the number of words comprehended weighted by the level of word difficulty.

Two other experimental cognitive measures are derived from the memory for locations and the categorization tasks. The main measure of memory for locations is highest level of the child's performance through the progression of increasingly difficult conditions. The child's manipulation of objects is coded for presence of sequential touching or stacking of objects from the same category.

Evaluation of standards is a dimension relevant to cognition that appears to emerge during the second year (Kagan, 1981). The presence of such standards can be assessed from reactions to prohibition and to flawed objects. For our preliminary analyses, videotapes of the prohibition episodes were used to code the child's affect, latency to touch, hesitation, and compliance. As described later, an unrotated first principal component score from these measure was used to represent evaluation of standards. In future analyses, the difference in latency to touch flawed and unflawed objects will be added to this measure.

Other Infant Measures

Cortisol from saliva samples taken on three mornings with the same hour is analyzed using standard radioimmunoassays (Walker, Riad-Fahmy, & Read, 1978). Height and weight are measured to compare results for these physical variables to those for the behavioral measures. Perinatal information is obtained from birth certificates, and mothers are also interviewed about their pregnancy and delivery and the twins' health.

Nonshared Environment

Identical twins provide a unique opportunity to isolate aspects of nonshared environment that is of crucial importance in the development of individual differences in personality (Plomin & Daniels, 1987). Because members of identical twin pairs are identically genetically, differences within pairs can be due only to nongenetic factors. For this reason, measures of mothers' differential interactions with her twins and the twins' social interactions with each other are assessed. These measures are obtained for fraternal as well as identical twins because the fraternal-twin comparison permits exploration of genetic involvement in associations between nonshared environmental factors and twin differences in behavior.

The major source of information about mothers' differential interaction with the twins comes from the teaching task. The videotapes are used to code maternal behavior specific to each child. Measures include number of times mother attends to each twin, number of times mother initiates attention, percentage of time attending to each twin, mother's affective quality, number of times mother orients child to task, number of times mother helps twin to perform task, and number of times mother praises child.

A second source of differential maternal treatment is the examiner's ratings of mother's controlling behavior, warmth, responsiveness, tolerance, and interest toward each child. Mothers are also interviewed concerning differential discipline, affection, and attention toward their twins.

Another facet of nonshared environment is the co-twin's behavior toward the twin. From videotapes during 15 minutes of free play, aggression, dominance, and prosocial behavior of each twin toward the co-twin are rated based on an adaptation of a scheme developed by Cummings, Hollenbeck, Iannotti, Radke-Yarrow, and Zahn-Waxler (1986). Mothers are also interviewed about the twins' affection, helping, sharing, jealousy, competition, quarrels, and physical fights with their co-twin.

Other Environmental and Parental Measures

Two other measures of the family environment are obtained at 14 months: Spanier's Dyadic Adjustment Scale (Spanier, 1976), which assesses marital adjustment, and an abbreviated form of the Family Environment Scales (Moos & Moos, 1981), which assesses parental perceptions of the general atmosphere of the family such as its cohesiveness and freedom to express emotions. Education and socioeconomic status are employed as demographic descriptors of the sample.

A few measures are obtained about the parents to incorporate parental variables into analyses of children's temperament, emotion, and cognition. Mother's WAIS vocabulary is assessed during a telephone interview at the time of the 14-month visit. A short form of the Eysenck Personality Inventory (Floderus, 1974), which assesses extraversion and neuroticism, is administered to both parents when the children are 14 months of age.

RESULTS

In deference to sample-size considerations at this early stage of the study, a few composite variables from each domain of temperament, emotion, and cognition were selected to represent its multivariate diversity. Temperament measures included a shyness composite (based on initial reactions to the stranger's entry to the home and to the child's entry to the laboratory), and CCTI parental ratings of activity and sociability. Measures of emotion included positive and negative hedonic tone and composite measures of reactivity to restraint, and empathy. Measures representing the cognitive domain are the Bayley Mental Development Index, SICD receptive and productive scales, and a composite measure assessing evaluation of standards.

Our preliminary analyses focus on dimensional analyses of covariance among these variables at 14 months rather than categorical analyses of types of children at the extremes of these distributions. Homotypic and heterotypic correlations from 14 months to 20 months are also considered. We begin with results of principal component analyses that led to construction of composite scores.

Principal Component Analyses

Although analyses will be conducted at the level of individual variables, this preliminary report focuses on a few composite measures within each domain. For the CCTI scales, Bayley MDI, and SICD receptive and productive scales, composite scores were obtained according to established procedures. Global measures of positive and negative hedonic tone were created by averaging time-sampled ratings from videotapes of the Bayley test session and during free play. At 14 months, positive hedonic tone correlated .33 during the Bayley and free-play sessions; the correlation for negative hedonic tone across the two sessions was .32.

Composite scores representing shyness, reactivity to restraint, empathy, and evaluation of standards were constructed as unrotated first principal component scores derived from the individual measures described earlier. Table 17.2 lists the results of separate factor analyses for each of these four sets of variables. As shown in Table 17.2, component loadings and the percentage variance accounted

TABLE 17.2
Four Principal Component Analyses

Dimensions and Measures	Loading on First Principal Component
Shyness (34%)	
Latency to approach	.81
Hesitation	.78
Reaction to Stranger	-.43
Overall shyness rating	.90
Sum proximity to stranger	-.63
Sum play with toy	-.80
Sum proximity to mother	.47
Sum touch mother	.54
Sum cling to mother	.54
Sum play with own toys	-.07
Sum self-soothing actions	.09
Sum positive vocalizations	-.33
Sum crying	.36
Reactivity to Restraint (67%)	
Duration of restraint	-.88
Predominant state during restraint	.89
Expressivity	.86
Protest strength	.51
Distress strength	.89
Empathy (61%)	
Approach	.82
Hypothesis testing	.84
Facial display of concern	.92
Emotional arousal	.50
Prosocial intervention	.59
Global rating	.91
Evaluation of Standards (61%)	
Child attention to prohibition	-.79
Child touches prohibited object	.85
Rated arousal level during prohibition	.73
Latency to touch prohibited object	.89
References to mother or examiner during prohibition	.35
Overall rating of response to prohibition	.94

Note. Each of the four sets of items were analyzed separately. Percentage of variance accounted for by the first unrotated principal component for each analysis is shown in parentheses. Because listwise deletion was employed for missing data, N is from 181 to 200.

for by the principal component indicate that in each case the unrotated first principal component adequately represents a composite of the individual measures.

Shyness variables were coded each minute from videotapes of the first 5 minutes in the home and in the laboratory and averaged across 5 minutes in the home and in the laboratory. As shown in Table 17.2, a shyness component emerged that accounted for 34% of the variance. The highest loading item was the average rating of shyness. Of the 13 variables, only two loaded less than .30 on the principal component.

A composite representing reactivity to restraint was derived from duration, predominant state, expressivity, protest strength, and distress level during the restraint episode. All five variables loaded highly on the first unrotated principal component, which accounted for 67% of the variance.

Responses to the empathy probes are well represented by the first unrotated principal component, which accounts for 61% of the variance. All six variables (z-scored and averaged across the empathy probes) load highly on the factor, although ratings of emotional arousal and counts of prosocial interventions load less highly than the other variables.

A composite representing evaluation of standards was obtained from a first principal component analysis of six variables (listed in Table 17.2) from the episodes involving prohibition. The first principal component accounted for 61% of the variance. The highest loading item was an overall rating of the child's response to the prohibition, followed by latency to touch the prohibited object.

On the basis of these results, standardized component scores were constructed for shyness, reactivity to restraint, empathy, and evaluation of standards at 14 months. The weights used to create component scores at 14 months were also applied to z-scored data at 20 months because the sample size at 20 months is not yet large enough to yield reliable estimates of the covariance structure at the later stage.

Average Differences

Between normative research and individual-differences research lies the study of average group differences. The most frequently reported group differences in infancy are average differences between boys and girls and average differences between ages. Table 17.3 lists means and standard deviations for boys and girls at 14 months and for the longitudinal sample at 14 and 20 months. (The sample at 20 months is too small to present results separately by gender.)

At 14 months, the only significant differences between boys and girls are seen for the shyness principal component, the positive hedonic tone measure, and for the SICD receptive language score. However, the effect size is small: These gender differences account for only about one-third of a standard deviation. Other analytic approaches may show greater gender differences. For example, gender differences favoring girls were found for five of the six components of the empathy dimension (Robinson, 1989).

Although the sample size is still relatively small at 20 months, some significant mean differences emerge from 14 to 20 months. Paired t-tests showed significant increases from 14 to 20 months for the SICD scales and for positive hedonic tone. Because the principal component weights at 14 months were applied to scores at 20 months, the principal component scores can be compared at 14 and 20 months. No significant age differences emerged, however, for these principal component scores.

TABLE 17.3
Means and Standard Deviations for Boys and Girls at 14 Months
and for Total Sample at 14 and 20 Months

| | 14 Months | | | | Longitudinal Sample | | | |
| | Girls | | Boys | | 14 Months | | 20 Months | |
Measure	Mean	SD	Mean	SD	Mean	SD	Mean	SD
Temperament								
Shyness PC	0.13	1.0	-0.20*	1.0	-0.18	1.0	0.02	1.0
CCTI Activity	19.9	3.3	20.6	2.8	21.1	2.6	21.0	3.1
CCTI Sociability	18.0	2.9	17.8	2.7	18.4	2.3	18.5	2.8
Emotion								
Pos. Hedonic Tone	2.4	0.3	2.3*	0.3	2.4	0.3	2.5*	0.2
Neg. Hedonic Tone	1.4	0.3	1.4	0.3	1.4	0.3	1.2	0.2
Reactivity PC	0.01	1.0	-0.01	1.0	-0.08	0.9	0.02	1.0
Empathy PC	0.04	1.2	-0.06	0.7	-0.02	1.2	0.00	0.8
Cognition								
Bayley MDI	103.0	14.3	99.9	14.5	101.3	15.3	102.6	17.1
SICD Receptive	16.3	5.3	14.2*	4.2	15.0	5.2	31.9*	7.0
SICD Productive	20.7	4.2	19.7	3.3	19.6	3.5	29.2*	5.6
Eval. Standards	0.04	1.1	-0.05	0.9	0.01	1.0	0.01	0.9

*$p < 0.05$ for boys vs. girls or 14 vs. 20 months.

Note. N = from 104 to 114 girls and from 76 to 84 boys at 14 months. N = from 51 to 60 at 20 months except for the CCTI scales for which N = 44. The longitudinal sample at 14 months includes only the children for whom data are available at 20 months. Principal components (PC) are standardized within age. The 14-month means and standard deviations deviate from 0.0 and 1.0, respectively, in the longitudinal sample because only those 14-month-olds are included who have also been tested at 20 months. The 20-month means and standard deviations deviate from 0.0 and 1.0 because 14-month PC weights were applied to the z-scored 20-month data.

The means and standard deviations for the Bayley Mental Development Index at 14 and 20 months indicate the representativeness of the present sample.

Covariance Among Measures at 14 Months

It is important to distinguish average differences between groups and individual differences because description and explanation of differences between groups are not necessarily related to those within groups (e.g., Plomin et al., 1988). Moreover, average differences between groups usually account for only a small portion of individual differences within groups. The standard deviations listed in Table 17.3 indicate the wide range of variability among infants in these temperamental, emotional, and cognitive measures.

A fundamental set of questions concerning individual differences in infancy involves covariance within and between the domains of temperament, emotion, and cognition at each age and across ages.

Correlations Within Domains

Table 17.4 lists correlations among the measures at 14 months. We begin with a discussion of correlations within the domains of temperament, emotion, and

TABLE 17.4
Correlations (X 100) Among Measures at 14 Months

Measures	Shy	Act	Soc	P-HT	N-HT	Reac	Emp	MDI	SI-R	SI-P	ES
Temperament											
Shyness PC	100	-11	-07	-06	-02	09	07	07	07	-08	09
CCTI Activity		100	25*	06	-09	01	04	-02	02	09	-05
CCTI Sociability			100	01	-10	-07	03	-04	-01	09	-09
Emotion											
Pos. Hedonic Tone				100	-20*	-14	-01	25*	16*	18*	07
Neg. Hedonic Tone					100	25*	01	-24*	-08	-15*	08
Reactivity PC						100	07	01	01	-09	-09
Empathy PC							100	07	17*	06	-01
Cognition											
Bayley MDI								100	45*	42*	10
SICD Receptive									100	46*	19*
SICD Productive										100	07
Eval. Standards PC											100

*p < .05.   Note.   N = from 170 to 199.

cognition and then we consider cross-domain correlations. Overall, the correlations within and across domains are low, indicating the multivariate nature of individual differences in infancy.

Within the domain of temperament, the only significant overlap emerges for parental ratings of activity and sociability. This significant but small correlation between activity and sociability has been found in other studies as well (Buss & Plomin, 1984). The observational measure of shyness is independent of the other temperament measures. The negligible correlation between shyness and sociability might seem surprising given the common assumption that shyness is synonymous with low sociability. Sociability is the tendency to affiliate with others and to prefer being with others rather than being alone. Shyness, on the other hand, refers to reactions to strangers. When measured independently, shyness and sociability are only modestly correlated in adults ($r = -.30$; Buss & Plomin, 1984), and the present report suggests that the two traits are independent in infancy. However, the lack of association could be a function of the use of different procedures: The measure of shyness is based on observations whereas the index of activity is a parental rating measure.

A similar picture of multivariate diversity emerges in the emotion domain. Most notable is the low correlation ($-.20$) between positive and negative hedonic tone. This supports the emerging consensus (Emde, 1988) that positive and negative aspects of emotional expressiveness are not merely opposite ends of a single continuum. Although reactivity to restraint correlates significantly (.25) with negative hedonic tone, the magnitude of the association suggests, not surprisingly, that these two dimensions are not isomorphic. Because empathy has not been studied previously in a multivariate context, it is interesting to note that empathy is not significantly correlated with hedonic tone or reactivity to restraint. This finding implies that empathy is an independent dimension within the emotion domain. As in the case of temperament, the domain of emotion appears to be multifaceted.

Correlations between the Bayley MDI and the SICD receptive and productive scales indicate substantial overlap between individual differences in cognitive and language development. The two dimensions of communication development correlate .46. Our experimental measure of evaluation of standards appears to be relatively independent of mental development as assessed by the Bayley MDI. The only significant correlation with the evaluation of standards measure is the correlation of .19 with the receptive communication score of the SICD. It would be reasonable to hypothesize that this association with receptive but not productive communication might arise because the prohibition involves a verbal command ("don't touch"). However, as we see later, 14-month evaluation of standards correlates significantly with both receptive and productive communication as well as Bayley MDI at 20 months. This suggests that reactions to prohibition at 14 months involve, among other factors, emerging properties of cognition, as implied by our use of the phrase "evaluation of standards."

Correlations Across Domains

Do the relatively independent dimensions within each domain correlate with measures in other domains? The temperament domain shows no associations with the emotion and cognition domains. The emotion domain, however, yields significant correlations with measures in the cognitive domain. Most notably, both positive and negative hedonic tone are correlated with MDI and SICD scores. Although it is possible that brighter infants are for some reason more positive and less negative, a more interesting possibility is that positive hedonic tone and lack of negative hedonic tone promote test-taking behavior. For example, positive affectivity can engage the examiner's attention and result in better scaffolding during testing. Other ways in which hedonic tone could interact with test-taking behavior include the possibility that fussier children may refuse more items and thereby receive lower scores, or brighter infants may be more positive and less negative because they perform better on the tests. A potential bias in the current study is that hedonic tone is assessed from videotapes obtained during the Bayley/SICD testing as well as during free play. To explore the hypothesis that our hedonic tone measures merely assess affect expressed as a result of performance on the tests, we obtained separate measures of hedonic tone during the testing and during free play. If the hypothesis were correct, one would predict that hedonic tone assessed during testing would relate more strongly to cognitive test scores than would the free-play hedonic tone measures. To the contrary, the correlations with the Bayley MDI are on average slightly greater for the free-play measure of hedonic tone (.29 for positive hedonic tone and -.17 for negative hedonic tone) than for the hedonic tone measures obtained during testing (.13 for positive and $-.22$ for negative hedonic tone). Thus, the association between hedonic tone and cognitive development does not appear to be merely a methodological artifact.

No significant correlations emerged between reactivity to restraint and any measures of temperament or cognition. For the empathy measure, the only significant correlation across domains involves the receptive scale of the SICD. One possible interpretation of this association is that receptive language skills are needed for empathy as assessed in our study. However, the empathy episodes are much more affective than linguistic; moreover, our measure of empathy primarily involves videotaping coding of nonverbal reactions to the empathy probes. This suggests that the empathy measure does not depend on language skills. Another possibility is that empathy might contribute to the development of language skills. Possibly, children who are more empathic may be more imitative of others both in terms of emotion and language (Harris, 1989). The fact that empathy is uncorrelated with the other measures of temperament and emotion suggests that empathy largely represents an independent dimension of individual differences in infancy.

Correlations from 14 to 20 Months

Data for 60 children tested at both 14 and 20 months are currently available to explore homotypic and heterotypic change and continuity from 14 to 20 months (see Table 17.5). It should be emphasized that these are preliminary analyses that will be on much firmer ground when the full sample, which will be 10 times larger, is available. With a sample size of 60, correlations are statistically significant ($p < .05$, one-tailed) only if they exceed .21 and differences between correlations are statistically significant ($p < .05$, two-tailed) only when correlations are as different as .00 versus .37. Furthermore, error of measurement will

TABLE 17.5

Correlations (X 100) from 14 to 20 Months

14 Months	20 Months										
	Shy	Act	Soc	P-HT	N-HT	Reac	Emp	MDI	SI-R	SI-P	E S
Temperament											
Shyness PC	37*	-24	-13	17	-08	14	-11	-02	-25*	-19	-29*
CCTI Activity	09	41*	10	-16	22	-11	15	16	22	05	03
CCTI Sociability	15	18	40*	-01	-04	-13	16	12	08	-08	-20
Emotion											
Pos. Hedonic Tone	-01	37*	-37*	21	07	-05	27*	43*	35*	24*	41*
Neg. Hedonic Tone	-02	03	15	-15	01	-11	09	-06	-03	-24*	-04
Reactivity PC	11	24	00	-12	-01	18	18	12	18	-04	18
Empathy PC	40*	10	-07	-01	-01	06	19	18	17	12	-12
Cognition											
Bayley MDI	-18	26*	-17	09	-04	07	17	47*	41*	43*	17
SICD Receptive	15	07	-40*	-11	-10	24*	06	58*	53*	46*	13
SICD Productive	02	08	-16	-07	05	-06	12	51*	47*	38*	18
Eval. Standards PC	06	20	06	03	02	-03	18	38*	24*	37*	06

*$p < .05$.
Note: N = from 41 to 60.

attenuate such correlations. Estimates of reliability will be available in the future and will be incorporated in analyses of change and continuity.

Homotypic correlations in the diagonal of Table 17.5 indicate some continuity in the face of considerable change in the rank order of individuals from 14 to 20 months. Significant continuity from 14 to 20 months was found for all variables except hedonic tone, reactivity to restraint, empathy, and evaluation of standards. The emotion variables clearly show less stability than the temperament or cognition variables.

Heterotypic associations between 14 and 20 months are listed in Table 17.5 above the diagonal for 14 versus 20 months comparisons and below the diagonal for 20 versus 14 months. Differences between cross-lag comparisons (14 to 20 months vs. 20 to 14 months) provide hints of causal directions in heterotypic associations across ages. For example, 14-month MDI correlates .41 with 20-month receptive SICD and the correlation between 14-month receptive SICD and 20-month MDI is .58. Although the difference in cross-lag correlations between the MDI and receptive SICD is not statistically significantly, these results suggest that receptive communication skill at 14 months leads to better performance on the MDI at 20 months. It is noteworthy that the correlations between the 14-month MDI and the other cognitive measures at 20 months are also lower than the correlations between the 20-month MDI and these cognitive measures at 14 months.

Indeed, 14-month SICD appears to predict 20-month MDI better than the 14-month MDI itself, although the correlations of .58 and .47 are not significantly different with the current sample size. A composite of the two SICD measures and the evaluation of standards measure at 14 months is likely to predict 20-month MDI far better than the 14-month MDI. Multivariate analyses of this type are the target of future analyses from this project. Another example of heterotypic associations from 14 to 20 months within the cognitive domain was mentioned earlier: 14-month evaluation of standards correlates more highly with cognitive measures at 20 months than at 14 months.

The strongest heterotypic links across domains involve positive hedonic tone at 14 months and cognitive measures at 20 months. These correlations between 14 and 20 months are even stronger than the correlations between hedonic tone and cognition at 14 months (Table 17.4). The finding that 20-month hedonic tone does not correlate with 14-month cognitive measures suggests that the association might be causal in the sense that positive affectivity at 14 months is associated with better performance on cognitive measures at 20 months. As mentioned earlier in relation to Table 17.4, it will be useful to reanalyze these associations separately for hedonic tone as assessed during the administration of the Bayley test and as assessed during free play. Finally, it should be noted that the prediction of 20-month cognitive measures primarily involves positive rather than negative hedonic tone.

One of the few significant differences in cross-lag correlations for this small sample involves shyness and empathy. As seen in Table 17.4, empathy and shyness do not correlate at 14 months. However, empathy at 14 months correlates significantly with shyness at 20 months, but shyness at 14 months does not correlate with empathy at 20 months. The significant difference in these cross-lag correlations suggests the possibility that empathy at 14 months may be related to shyness at 20 months. An explanation for this association is not readily apparent. Future analyses will attempt to clarify the association by comparing empathy episodes involving the mother and those involving the examiner on the hunch that shyness relates more strongly to empathic responses toward a stranger than toward the mother.

Several of the other heterotypic links between 14 and 20 months are even more puzzling. For example, shyness at 14 months correlates negatively with 20-month receptive SICD and evaluation of standards. One possibility is that shyness at 14 months leads to poorer performance on these highly social tests at 20 months. Another example of unexpected heterotypic links involves positive hedonic tone at 14 months and parental ratings of activity and sociability at 20 months.

It is noteworthy that even when variables show no homotypic continuity, interesting heterotypic relationships can emerge. The most striking example in Table 17.5 involves evaluation of standards (ES). Although ES shows no homotypic continuity from 14 to 20 months, 14-month ES significantly predicts MDI and SICD scores at 20 months. Such unexpected results must await replication with our tenfold larger sample. Nonetheless, as they stand, these results suggest that reactions to prohibitions at 14 months involve, among other factors, emerging properties of cognition.

DISCUSSION

This chapter describes the MacArthur Longitudinal Twin Study, a multivariate, longitudinal twin study that focuses on individual differences during the transition from infancy to early childhood. The sample will eventually include over 600 individuals, members of over 300 twin pairs, studied in both the home and laboratory at 14, 20, 24, and 36 months of age. The design is multivariate and multimethod, employing standard tests, eliciting situations, videotaped observations, and ratings by observers and by parents in order to assess major dimensions of temperament, emotion, and cognition. Temperament variables include observational measures of behavioral inhibition and of shyness, tester ratings on the Infant Behavior Record, and parental ratings of numerous temperament dimensions. Emotion measures include observations of positive and negative hedonic tone, mood, anger, empathy, and maternal ratings of these behaviors as well as discrete emotions. Cognition variables used were the Bayley Mental Scale, the receptive and productive scales of the Sequenced Inventory of Communication Development, word comprehension, memory for locations, categorization, and evaluation of standards. Nonshared environment, family background, and parental characteristics are also assessed.

For this preliminary report of the ongoing project, measures were selected within each of the three domains to illustrate the multivariate nature of individual differences during the second year of life for a sample of 200 children studied at 14 months and for 60 of these children tested again at 20 months. Our assignment of measures to temperament, emotion, and cognition domains is not meant to imply that the variables are pure measures of a single domain or that these variables exhaust the multivariate diversity within each of the domains. Within the temperament domain, results confirmed in infancy the emerging finding for adults that shyness and sociability are relatively independent. The multivariate nature of temperament no doubt extends far beyond these two dimensions and activity level. Future research will relate these components of temperament to behavioral inhibition.

Within the domain of emotion, the most interesting finding was that positive and negative hedonic tone are relatively independent dimensions of emotion, as are reactivity to distress and empathy. In contrast, the domain of cognition indicated moderate overlap between mental development as assessed by the Bayley Mental Scales and language development as measured by the receptive and productive scales of the Sequenced Inventory of Communication Development. Evaluation of standards, based on responses to prohibitions, is relatively independent of these other measures of cognition development at 14 months, although this dimension at 14 months predicts all cognition measures at 20 months.

Across domains, measures of temperament showed no significant associations with measures of emotion or cognition at 14 months. The most interesting link across domains at 14 months involves hedonic tone and cognition.

Homotypic and heterotypic change and continuity was explored for these measures from 14 to 20 months, although the sample at 20 months is as yet too small to view these analyses as anything more than preliminary. Homotypic correlations indicate significant continuity for the temperament and cognition measures but not for the emotion measures. Some heterotypic continuity also emerged. For example, 14-month receptive SICD predicts 20-month MDI better than does the 14-month MDI itself. Even though evaluation of standards shows no homotypic continuity from 14 to 20 months, 14-month evaluation of standards significantly predicts all other cognitive measures at 20 months. Another example of heterotypic continuity is that positive (but not negative) hedonic tone at 14 months predicts cognitive and language development at 20 months.

As the sample size increases at 14, 20, 24, and 36 months, MALTS will be able to compare covariance structures, both within and between domains, across the four ages. However, the special feature of MALTS is its longitudinal twin design that facilitates analyses of the etiology of individual differences in infancy. Descriptive analyses of individual differences involve variance, covariance structure within an age, and age-to-age covariance. Developmentalists are interested in developmental change and continuity for these phenomena. Behavioral genetic designs such as the comparison of identical and fraternal twin pairs can explore the relative contribution of genetic and environmental factors to variance, covariance structure within ages, and age-to-age covariance. Developmental behavioral genetics focuses on change and continuity for each of these issues. For example, does heritability change during infancy? The scanty evidence to date suggests that, when heritability changes during infancy, it increases (Plomin, 1986). Does the genetic and environmental architecture underlying covariance among measures at each age change during infancy? Multivariate genetic–environmental analyses have scarcely been applied in infancy; developmental comparisons of genetic and environmental architecture during the transition from infancy to early childhood are nonexistent. The key question of developmental behavioral genetics is genetic and environmental mediation of age-to-age change as well as continuity. These are questions that will be addressed in MALTS as more twins are tested at each age.

ACKNOWLEDGMENTS

The MacArthur Longitudinal Twin Study is supported by the John D. and Catherine T. MacArthur Foundation from a grant that emanated from the MacArthur Foundation's Research Network on the Transition from Infancy to Early Childhood. We are grateful to the participating families of the MacArthur Longitudinal Twin Study who have so generously contributed their time and effort, and to the Health Statistics Section of the Colorado Department of Health for assistance in family recruitment.

REFERENCES

Bayley, N. (1969). *Manual for the Bayley Scales of Infant Development.* New York: Psychological Corporation.
Buss, A. H., & Plomin, R. (1984). *Temperament: Early developing personality traits.* Hillsdale, NJ: Lawrence Erlbaum Associates.
Campos, J., Barrett, K., Lamb, M., Goldsmith, H., & Stenberg, C. (1983). Socioemotional development in infancy. In M. Haith & J. Campos (Eds.), *Infancy and developmental psychobiology* (Vol. II of *Mussen's manual of child psychology,* 4th ed., pp. 783–916). New York: Wiley.
Chess, S., & Thomas, A. (1984). *Origins and evolution of behavior disorders: Infancy to early adult life.* New York: Brunner/Mazel.
Cummings, M., Hollenbeck, B., Iannotti, R., Radke-Yarrow, M., & Zahn-Waxler, C. (1986). Early organization of altruism and aggression: Developmental patterns and individual differences. In C. Zahn-Waxler, M. Cummings, & R. Iannotti (Eds.), *Altruism and aggression* (pp. 165–188). Cambridge: Cambridge University Press.

Easterbrooks, A., & Emde, R. N. (1983). *Hedonic tone and overall mood scales.* Unpublished manuscript.

Emde, R. N. (1988). Development terminable and interminable: I. Innate and motivational factors from infancy. *International Journal of Psycho-Analysis, 69,* 23–42.

Floderus, B. (1974). Psycho-social factors in relation to coronary heart disease and associated risk factors. *Nordisk Hygienisk Tidskrift* (Monograph Supplement 6), 1–148.

Fuenzalida, C., Emde, R. N., Pannabecker, B. J., & Stenberg, C. (1981). Validation of the Differential Emotions Scale in 613 mothers. *Motivation and Emotion, 5,* 37–45.

Fullard, W., McDevitt, S. C., & Carey, W. B. (1984). Assessing temperament in 1 to 3-year-old children. *Journal of Pediatric Psychology, 9,* 205–217.

Garcia-Coll, C., Kagan, J., & Reznick, J. S. (1984). Behavioral inhibition in young children. *Child Development, 55,* 1005–1019.

Harris, P. (1989). *Children and emotion.* London: Blackwell.

Hedrick, D. L., Prather, E. M., & Tobin, A. R. (1975). *Sequenced Inventory of Communication Development.* Seattle: University of Washington Press.

Izard, C. (1972). *Patterns of emotion: A new analysis of anxiety and depression.* New York: Academic Press.

Johnson, W. F., Emde, R. N., Pannabecker, B. J., Stenberg, C., & Davis, M. (1982). Maternal perception of infant emotion from birth through 18 months. *Infant Behavior and Development, 5,* 313–322.

Kagan, J. (1971). *Change and continuity in infancy.* New York: Wiley.

Kagan, J. (1981). *The second year.* Cambridge: Harvard University Press.

Kagan, J. (1989). Temperamental contributions to social behavior. *American Psychologist, 44,* 668–674.

Kagan, J., Reznick, J. S., Clarke, C., Snidman, N., & Garcia-Coll, C. (1984). Behavioral inhibition to the unfamiliar. *Child Development, 55,* 2212–2225.

Kagan, J., Reznick, J. S., & Snidman, N. (1987). The physiology and psychology of behavioral inhibition. *Child Development, 58,* 1459–1473.

Kagan, J., Reznick, J. S., & Snidman, N. (1988). Biological bases of childhood shyness. *Science, 140,* 167–171.

Kagan, J., Reznick, J. S., Snidman, N., Gibbons, J., & Johnson, M. O. (1988). Childhood derivatives of inhibition and lack of inhibition to the unfamiliar. *Child Development, 59,* 1580–1589.

Lewis, M., & Brooks-Gunn, J. (1979). *Social cognition and the acquisition of self.* New York: Plenum Press.

Matheny, A. P., Jr. (1980). Bayley's Infant Behavior Record: Behavioral components and twin analyses. *Child Development, 51,* 1157–1167.

Moos, R. H., & Moos, B. S. (1981). *Family Environmental Scale manual.* Palo Alto, CA: Consulting Psychologists Press.

Plomin, R. (1986). *Development, genetics, and psychology.* Hillsdale, NJ: Lawrence Erlbaum Associates.

Plomin, R., & Daniels, D. (1987). Why are children in the same family so different from each other? *The Behavioral and Brain Sciences, 10,* 1–16.

Plomin, R., DeFries, J. C., & Fulker, D. W. (1988). *Nature and nurture during infancy and early childhood.* New York: Cambridge University Press.

Plomin, R., & Dunn, J. (1986). *The study of temperament: Changes, continuities, and challenges.* Hillsdale, NJ: Lawrence Erlbaum Associates.

Plomin, R., & Rowe, D. C. (1979). Genetic and environmental etiology of social behavior in infancy. *Developmental Psychology, 15,* 62–72.

Radke-Yarrow, M., & Zahn-Waxler, C. (1973). *Developmental studies of altruism.* NIMH Protocol 73-M-02.

Reznick, J. S. (1989). *Visual preference as a test of infant word comprehension.* Manuscript submitted for publication.

Reznick, J. S., & Snedley, B. (1987, April). *Individual differences in categorization.* Paper presented at the Biennial Meeting of the Society for Research in Child Development, Baltimore.

Robinson, J. L. (1989, April). *Sex differences in the development of empathy during late infancy: Findings from the MacArthur Longitudinal Twin Study.* Poster presented at the Biennial Meeting of the Society for Research in Child Development, Kansas City.

Rowe, D. C., & Plomin, R. (1977). Temperament in early childhood. *Journal of Personality Assessment, 41,* 150–156.

Scarr, S. (1985). Constructing psychology: Making facts and fables for our times. *American Psychologist, 40,* 499–512.

Spanier, G. (1976). Measuring dyadic adjustment: New scales for assessing the quality of marriage and similar dyads. *Journal of Marriage and the Family, 38,* 15–38.

Walker, R. F., Riad-Fahmy, D., & Read, G. F. (1978). Adrenal status assayed by direct radioimmune assay of cortisol in whole saliva or parotid saliva. *Clinical Chemistry, 24,* 1460–1463.

Watson, M. W., & Fischer, K. W. (1977). A developmental sequence of agent use in late infancy. *Child Development, 48,* 828–836.

Watson, M. W., & Fischer, K. W. (1980). Development of social roles in elicited and spontaneous behavior during the preschool years. *Developmental Psychology, 16,* 483–494.

Werner, H. (1948). *Comparative psychology of mental development.* New York: International Universities Press.

Zahn-Waxler, C., Radke-Yarrow, M., & King, R. A. (1979). Child-rearing and children's prosocial initiations toward victims of distress. *Child Development, 50,* 319–330.

Author Index

Page numbers for complete references are printed in italics.

A

Abeles, R. P., 92, *108*
Abelson, R. P., 220, *221*
Aberger, E., 211, 214, *225*
Acebo, C., 117, 124, 125, 127, *132, 133*
Acredolo, C., 142, *151*
Acredolo, L. P., 244, 248, 254, 266, *267, 268,* 322, 326, 327, 328, 331, 333, 334, 335, 337, 338, *339, 375, 379*
Adams, A., 254, *267, 334, 339*
Adamson, L., 141, *150*
Ainsworth, M. D. S., 254, *267, 336, 339*
Aitchison, R., 201, 219, *224*
Albin, S., 138, *152*
Aleksandrowicz, D., 141, *150*
Aleksandrowicz, M., 141, *150*
Allen, J. N., 160, 163, 163n, *190*
Allen, L., 229, *244*
Allison, T., 281, *313*
Als, H., 12, *16,* 137, 138, 139, 141, 142, 143, 144, 146, *150, 152,* 342, 349, 350, *358*
Ames, E. W., 195, 200, *221, 227*
Amiel-Tison, C., 138, *150*
Amlie, R., 286, 287, *318*
Anastasia, A., 4, 5, 6, *16*

Anderberg, M. R., 92, *107*
Anders, T. F., 118, 120, 125, 126, *132, 133,* 142, *154*
Anderson, B. J., 418, *429*
Anderson, D. R., 247, *267*
Anderson, L., 146, *150*
Anderson-Goetz, D., 149, *154*
Anderson-Huntington, R. B., 140, *150*
Andre-Thomas, C. Y., 138, *151*
Anthony, E., 139, *151*
Anthony, E. J., 9, *16*
Apgar, V., 137, 138, *151*
Applebaum, M. I., 77, 78, 83, 92, *107, 109,* 193, 199, 200, 212, *225*
Arabie, P., 98, 106, *107, 109*
Arakawa, K., 118, 120, *133*
Arnold, M. B., 394, *407*
Aron, M., 36, *42*
Asch, P. A. S., 150, *151*
Ashmead, D., 331, 332, *339*
Ashton, R., 114, *132*
Aslin, R., 272, 279, 280, 288, 292, 302, 306, 307, *311, 318*
Atwater, J. D., 214, *222*
Auerbach, S., 293, *311*
Auger, R., 293, *313*
Axelrod, S., 293, *314*
Aylward, G. P., 163, *185*

457

Subject Index

A

abstraction (*see also* categorization), 32–33
Academy of Otolaryngology, 273
Academy of Pediatrics, 273
Acetabularia, 27
achievement (school), 259
activity level, 12, 61–62, 114, 147–149, 169, 248, 338, 389, 411, 413, 419, 420, 421
adaptability, 169, 257, 391, 401, 414, 416, 417, 418, 419, 421
adoption studies, 48–50, 72
adrenocortical activity, 401–404, 405, 406
affect (*see* emotion/emotionality)
aggression, 261, 442
alpha
    internal consistencies (Cronbach's), 238, 415–416, 420
    levels, 80–82, 121
    values (*see also d*), 94–95, 101–104
American Speech and Hearing Association, 273
amygdala, 394, 396
analysis of variance (ANOVA), 80, 119, 104, 124–125, 128
anoxia (*see* hypoxia)
Apgar scale, 137, 145
apnea, 128, 176

approach-withdrawal, 169, 257, 259, 391–392, 395, 414
arousal, 141, 168, 241, 258, 388, 393, 394, 396, 397, 403
articulation errors, 290
asphyxia (*see* hypoxia)
assortative mating, 47, 66
attachment, 336, 338, 353
attention (infants; *see also* habituation, fixation), 62, 68, 72, 114, 169, 193, 194, 196, 200–212, 216, 232, 235, 252–254, 261, 262–266, 296, 298, 310, 338, 353, 411
    social interaction and, 216, 259, 261, 262–263, 265–266
    span, 140, 172, 250, 255–256, 266, 371, 414, 419, 421
    (as a) state, 247
    sustained, 220, 237, 239, 247–267, 397
    temperament and, 248, 256–259
    vagal tone/heart rate and, 396–397
attractor, 24–26, 32, 33, 36, 38
audiogram, 279
audiometry
    behavioral observation, 275–277
    visually reinforced, 277–281, 291, 309
auditory
    brainstem response, 281–288, 309
    categorization, 230, 304–308, 310